Cooperative Commonwealth

Cooperative Commonwealth

Co-ops in Rural Minnesota,
1859–1939

Steven J. Keillor

MINNESOTA HISTORICAL SOCIETY PRESS
ST. PAUL

FRONTISPIECE: Seated at tables adorned with Holstein and Guernsey cows and about to enjoy a twenty-one-and-a-half-pound birthday cake, two hundred women and men of the Askov Creamery Association celebrated its twenty-fifth anniversary at its annual meeting, February 4, 1936. Longtime members recounted its founding, and a play based on "the early minutes of the creamery . . . was presented by several of the patrons."

www.mnhs.org/mhspress

Manufactured in the United States of America

10 9 8 7 6 5 4 3 2 1

International Standard Book Number
0-87351-377-0

♾ The paper used in this publication meets the minimum requirements of the American National Standard for Information Sciences–Permanence for Printed Library Materials, ANSI Z39.48-1984.

Library of Congress Cataloging-in-Publication Data

Keillor, Steven J. (Steven James)
    Cooperative commonwealth : co-ops in rural Minnesota, 1859–1939 / Steven J. Keillor.
        p.   cm.
    Includes bibliographical references and index.
    ISBN 0-87351-377-0 (hc.)
    1. Agriculture, Cooperative—Minnesota–History.
    2. Cooperative societies—Minnesota—History.
    3. Cooperation—Minnesota–History. I. Title.
    HD1484.K45 2000
    334'.683'09776—dc21   99-40583
                                                                                            CIP

For Margaret,
My Fellow Cooperator

Cooperative Commonwealth

Acknowledgments

RESEARCHING AND WRITING the biography of the Danish-American politician and editor Hjalmar Petersen—who came from a cooperative-minded ethnic group, town (Askov), and state—first gave me the idea for a book on Minnesota's rural cooperatives. Living in Askov myself and doing some accounting work for the Midland cooperative there as it closed its books, I acquired some personal involvement, too. In a noon walk across the capitol mall, Jean A. Brookins, then director of the Minnesota Historical Society Press, encouraged me to pursue the idea. Deborah Miller and Jean generously provided me with MHS research grants to inventory cooperative records at county and regional historical repositories and to use these records to research the history of cooperation in Minnesota. The MHS grants were made from funds provided by the State of Minnesota. Deborah carefully watered and tended the project over the years. Tino Avaloz, the newspaper librarian at MHS's Cedar Street site, did heroic work in supplying my insatiable need for weekly newspapers. My thanks also to the other MHS library staff and to the late Timo Riipa of the Immigration History Research Center, Kathy Jensen of Clarks Grove, and cooperative activist Kris Olsen.

The staff at many county historical societies and regional research centers gave invaluable help. They are too numerous to name, but much of my work was done at the following county historical societies: Brown County (New Ulm), Freeborn County (Albert Lea), Otter Tail County (Fergus Falls), and Kandiyohi County (Willmar). Underpaid directors and unpaid volunteers at these societies do important but underappreciated work. I needed their help and am grateful for it. Terry Shoptaugh at the Northwest Minnesota History Center in Moorhead and the staff at the regional history centers in Morris, Marshall, and Mankato also guided me through their collections. Lois Hendrickson of the University of Minnesota Archives steered me to the right sources for information on the university's role in rural cooperation.

The American Scandinavian Foundation's Emil Lassen Fund provided funds for six weeks of research in Denmark. *Mange tak* to Kristian Krabbe of Roskilde and to Henning and Lise Krabbe of Brønderslev for their many kindnesses on that trip.

George Green, John R. Howe, and other members of the history department at the University of Minnesota helped to turn this research into a doctoral dissertation. Cooperative history was an exotic crop for a graduate student to be cultivating, but they allowed me to proceed. The underlying economic analysis owes much to George Green's thoughtful suggestions. Thanks to Claudia Parliament of the university's department of agricultural and applied economics for her input. The University of Minnesota History Department Endowed Fellowship, made possible by a gift from the Samuel Deinard family, enabled me to finish researching and writing the dissertation. Bob Clark of InterVarsity encouraged me as I completed my work at the university. Bob Osburn and Bill Monsma of the MacLaurin Institute provided me with an office on campus when I was making final revisions to several chapters.

This book is like the summer's third cutting of hay (the dissertation being the first)—less quantity but, in this case, better quality. My year teaching agricultural history at Iowa State University helped me to incorporate more of the recent writing on rural history. Colleagues R. Douglas Hurt, James Whittaker, George McJimsey, and Alan Marcus have my appreciation for that chance and for sharing bibliographic discoveries. The late Elaine Carte, Phil Freshman, and several anonymous reviewers gave helpful ideas. Ann Regan, managing editor at MHS Press, encouraged me to add the two final chapters on the 1920s and 1930s, and Deborah Miller offered me an office in the Knight research suite so that I could finish those two chapters. Alan Woolworth photocopied many newspaper articles on rural cooperatives around the state. Special thanks are due to editor Sally Rubinstein, who guided the project to completion. She could tell where the cutter bar was pulling up the roots and where it was leaving too much forage behind. Deborah Swanson painstakingly picked out the rocks from the alfalfa and that may be the most thankless task.

My daughter, Amanda, sat with me at the table under our maple tree and kept the cats off my thesis-in-the-making, and my sons, Jeremy and Will, accompanied me on several of the research trips. I cannot claim to have convinced them to go into cooperative studies themselves, but I have fond memories of their company along the cooperative trail. My wife, Margaret, patiently supported my research. I thank her, and I hope those who read and enjoy this book will quietly thank her, too. They should blame me for its deficiencies. I am responsible for translations from Dano-Norwegian newspapers and letters and for all matters of interpretation.

Finally, I wish to extend my sincere thanks to many friends in the Askov-Sandstone-Hinckley area of Pine County. For several years the work of research and revision was done away from campus. These friends provided a supportive environment for my work. Askov was a perfect place from which to envision Minnesota's rural past. The project became something of a local cooperative one, even if the other participants did not know that, did not vote on the interpretive issues, and never elected me — a nonfarmer — to interpret farmers' views for them. Now the reader must judge my views.

Cooperative Commonwealth

Introduction

Locating the History
of Rural Cooperatives

THE TOWN WHERE I LIVE—Askov, Minnesota—has a rich heritage of cooperative action. A cooperative feed mill on the east side of the railroad tracks still grinds and mixes feed. The 1920s and 1930s were the heyday of cooperation here, and the annual meeting was the democratic moment for each of the many cooperatives. One participant recalled how a large room full of farmers, dressed in barn clothes and smoking corncake tobacco, caused some in attendance to turn "rather green 'around the gills' [and] hurriedly get up and scurry from the room."[1]

I trust that no reader will have to discard this study of Minnesota's rural cooperatives hurriedly—overcome by the earthy smell of democracy with its motions, votes, calls for adjournment, and letters to the editor. This study is mainly about democracy, which is a time-consuming, untidy process. Today many Americans use the drive-through lane at Hardee's or KFC rather than taking the time to go inside. They would hardly be willing to purchase stock in their local fast-food restaurant, attend yearly meetings, vote on whom to hire, and keep informed about its employment practices or its insurance costs. They are convinced that the marketplace is inherently democratic; when they purchase goods or services, they vote for them, and the market respects their wishes.

A century ago, rural Americans did not see it that way. To them, the consumer lacked the voter's power, so they would and did buy shares and attend annual meetings to obtain democratic power in the marketplace. To them, living in rural areas, the goods and services of private firms were distant and difficult to access (firms had not yet brought products to

3

the mailbox, car window, or computer screen). Business was distant; democracy was as close as the nearest town hall or schoolhouse. By forming cooperatives, they used democracy to bring business to them, to control it, and to use it for their benefit.

In *Democracy in America*, Alexis de Tocqueville noted how readily nineteenth-century Americans formed voluntary associations to accomplish innumerable projects that government could not or would not undertake.[2] Cooperatives were voluntary associations for mainly economic purposes, formed apart from government but no less democratic for that. At many times and places in American history, the few cooperatives operated in a marginal way, but in rural Minnesota from 1870 to 1940, they played a significant role at the intersection of politics, economics, ethnicity, and religion. Mention of them now evokes a wistful nostalgia, like thoughts of a crossroads community bypassed by the interstate. But they were important to rural life a century ago, and centralized cooperatives are still vital to rural America. This book describes the history of rural cooperatives in one state where they were successful and influential, but Minnesota was not unique in that.

The intersectional location of rural cooperatives is important to this study. It is a major reason why this is the first study of a broad range of rural cooperatives, by type, over a lengthy period, and under a wide variety of conditions. Scholars have failed to examine them in their own right, rather than as parts of other movements. Historians of agrarian protest analyzed rural cooperatives as auxiliaries of Populism; labor historians treated workers' cooperatives as supporters of the trade unions. Business historians have neglected them, although they are business firms. It is hard to gauge a phenomenon accurately when it is seen only as an adjunct to other phenomena.

This study examines them, not to explain other movements but to shed light on how cooperatives influenced the politics, economics, social life, and ethnicity of rural Minnesota. Again, their intersectional location is an interpretive advantage that allows us to use insights from many disciplines to construct a fuller account of rural life and development in Minnesota.

Their location in Minnesota is clearly important as well. From 1860 to 1940, Minnesota underwent fundamental change in politics, economics, ethnicity, and economic geography. Its agriculture shifted to and then away from King Wheat, to alternative crops, and then to more efficient, scientific production of all crops. As its agriculture diversified and new forms of transportation increased regional specialization, its economic geography changed markedly. Its preautomobile network of towns and crossroads communities expanded and then declined when autos and trucks led to consolidation. Its politics was torn by struggles among farmers, Main Street merchants, and Twin Cities business interests over government policies. From the Grange to the Farmer-Labor Party, the political economy of agriculture often dominated the state's politics. Its politics was also fractured by clashes over ethnicity—first between Old Stock settlers and immigrants, then between most residents and the German Americans during World War I. Always the battle between ethnic preservation and assimilation affected Minnesota.

Into this complex, changing environment, rural Minnesotans introduced cooperatives to bring democracy to the marketplace. Yet these democratic assemblages could not escape the turmoil of change—indeed, they helped to shape it. Given this turbulence, it is not surprising that rural cooperation took many twists and turns and did not quickly find one stable, universal form in Minnesota. It is important to remember that from 1859 to 1939 the very meaning of the term "democracy" was taking twists and turns of its own.[3]

A rural cooperative was a business in a free-market economy, but it remained a democratic institution with its own internal politics. Though a business, it often shaped farmers' adaptations to new forms of agriculture. Committed to neutrality in partisan politics through its bylaws or customs, it often could not escape the politics of agrarian protest. Membership in any given cooperative was usually open to anyone, but members often belonged to the same ethnic group, and the cooperative preserved ethnicity as effectively as the reading society or mutual-aid association. Its membership was so large as to make it a community institution almost as important as the rural church in cementing social ties. (Business came first; a cooperative's minutes almost never included discussions of political, ethnic, or religious topics.)

Because of these social, ethnic, political, and economic roles, the term "cooperative" must be carefully defined. Economist Richard B. Heflebower defined a cooperative as "the means whereby members by-pass the market adjacent" to them—the market where "they would otherwise make individual arms-length transactions with investor-owned enterprises."[4] Instead, they make transactions with themselves—not arms-length ones.

Members deal with a company they own. The cooperative seeks not to accumulate profits but to maximize its members' income or to minimize their expenses. Such is the economists' definition of a cooperative's economic functions. A cooperative is also a polity governing its own affairs. Democratically, it conducts meetings, elects officers, and writes constitutions. In a social sense, it is characterized by mutual expectations: the cooperative will treat each customer-owner equally and fairly, and each will be loyal to the cooperative.

In this study cooperation is defined to include businesses lacking one or two technical characteristics. Where customers combined to own and manage a business through which they bypassed private firms, where this business was democratically operated and characterized by expectations of egalitarian solidarity, the business was accepted as being a cooperative. Nevertheless the importance of certain cooperative principles is not minimized. As early as the 1860s, some Americans felt that the cooperative principles developed in 1844 by the weavers of Rochdale, England, best preserved the democratic, cooperative character of a customer-owned business. Rochdale rules were seen as vital for Minnesota's rural cooperatives (though some cooperators criticized the Rochdale system). They can be summarized as:

1) One person, one vote
2) Membership open to anyone interested
3) Political and religious neutrality
4) Limits to returns based on stock ownership
5) Limited number of shares owned by one person
6) Emphasis on returning net margins to customers based on their patronage
7) Cash sales at market prices.

These principles were designed to ensure that the business would be run in customers', rather than investors', interests. To secure capital, Rochdale-style cooperatives sold shares, but they guarded against an investors' faction interested in maximizing its returns at customers' expense. Democracy was the means to keep customers in control; presumably customers would outnumber investors. The rule of one vote per member rather than one vote per share kept the cooperatives egalitarian and democratic.

Rural cooperatives varied in the degree to which they adopted Rochdale principles. Even without all the Rochdale rules, customers and not investors tended to control cooperatives, for few rural cooperatives were attractive investment opportunities. Rural cooperatives often performed an economic function that private investors had found unpromising; cooperatives might have to create a marketplace in rural areas that had none. Even where the Rochdale rules were ignored or unknown, the democratic ethos in many farm communities tended to preserve democracy and customers' control.

Occasionally the phrase "democratic coordination" appears in this study to describe the cooperative way of coordinating economic transactions. The phrase is an adaptation of a concept Alfred D. Chandler, Jr., used in *The Visible Hand: The Managerial Revolution in American Business*. Chandler argued that "an increase in volume of activity" during the nineteenth century highlighted the inefficiencies of purely "market mechanisms." Managers used an "administrative coordination" of transactions that "permitted greater productivity, lower costs, and higher profits than coordination by market mechanisms."[5] Chandler narrowly focused on the railroads and other high-volume, high-speed industries. Yet consumers and farmers also discovered the market's inefficiencies and organized democratically to coordinate transactions, decrease their expenses, and increase their incomes. Democratic coordination seemed as viable an option as administrative coordination in the rural United States in the mid-nineteenth century. Why the latter finally triumphed must be discovered in the historical record, not in some a priori assumption that it was destined to win out.

This study examines that historical record, the history of rural cooperatives in Minnesota from the Civil War to World War II. It is divided into chapters according to three criteria: the types of cooperatives, the different sponsoring agencies (Grange, Farmers' Alliance, and University of Minnesota), and the chronology of the origins of cooperative types. An added chronological theme is the move from local "grass-roots" cooperatives formed by farmers to regional "bureaucratized" cooperatives organized by state leaders.

This undertaking began as a project funded by the Minnesota Historical Society to inventory the records of cooperatives held by county historical societies and other repositories in Minnesota. That survey confirmed that sufficient primary source material existed to conduct a study of Minnesota's rural cooperatives. The availability of business records for a few cooperatives of each type, such as creameries, grain elevators, and stores, was vital. The economic role and viability of each type were examined before its political or social or ethnic functions were analyzed. It had to survive economically before it could perform in any other capacity. Access to the financial records and minutes was therefore necessary.

The rural weekly newspaper was also a major source. For each type of cooperative, significant decisions or events recorded in the minutes were traced in local newspapers to see if editors or correspondents or readers commented on them. Minnesota has long had a policy that a copy of each issue of each newspaper should be sent to the Minnesota Historical Society. The society's collections are unusually rich in this area. Rural weeklies from the period of this study contain firsthand reporting, editorials, and letters from readers that shed valuable light on the history of cooperatives.

Rural history is well served by careful use of "literary" sources like small-town newspapers and minutes of local meetings.[6] Here the supposedly inarticulate stated their views and participants defined the issues in rural cooperation before the historian framed issues in ways they would not recognize. Here democratic debate was expressed in the well-informed arguments made by rural people. Tocqueville stressed newspapers' role in voluntary associations: "Only a newspaper can put the same thought at the same time before a thousand readers."[7] Or present contradictory thoughts.

Minutes and newspaper accounts have their limitations as sources. We must depend on the candor or skill of the secretary who took the minutes and on the fairmindedness and integrity of the editor. Yet the democratic, public nature of rural cooperatives affords some assurance that biased or incomplete minutes probably would have led some faction to protest—and that biased news accounts would have provoked angry letters to the editor.

Throughout this study, the term "rural" refers to communities dependent on agriculture for their livelihood. Cooperatives organized by workers in the railroad or iron-mining industries of northern Minnesota were not studied. Differences between farmers' self-employed status and workers' employee status affected cooperation more than the similarity in community size.

That is why this study—like a crossroads community—is located at the intersection of several subdisciplines. Its conclusions will have to justify this choice of an unlikely academic "site." Analyzing cooperatives located at the real crossroads will shed light on the rural people who lived down the roads and who came to the intersection daily to buy and sell.

1

Cooperative Stores, 1859–72

*"Why have they not moved to the
Swedish settlement to enjoy the
advantages of the Union store?"*

BEFORE RAILROADS AND TELEGRAPH LINES were built in Minnesota in the 1860s–70s, any contest between cooperators and entrepreneurs had to occur at the country store. We must start there to find the history of rural cooperation in Minnesota. The country store was the link between farmers and markets and the first type of cooperation discussed in Minnesota. A store was the type of cooperation used by the Rochdale pioneers. New Englanders' Union stores were the first large-scale cooperatives in the United States—and early Minnesotans looked to New England for models.

The country store performed vital social and economic functions—in Minnesota and elsewhere. Historian Gerald Carson observed, "the country store ... tied the scattered farms into a community." It was a "window on the world"—with fellow farmers "to give it warmth and neighborliness, the candy agent from Milwaukee ... to add a touch of sophistication," the storekeeper as "a community leader ex officio," and, "the voluntarily unemployed, arranged around the store stove like a Greek chorus, ready to comment on each episode in the day's drama."[1]

Before Rural Free Delivery gradually expanded to all areas of Minnesota, the country store served as the post office. Daniel Boorstin noted, "the trip to town to get the mail was also a shopping trip to pick up supplies.[2] Before the advent of the country store, a rural neighborhood had no post office and only a "borrowing system" based on barter (250 pounds of bacon for twenty days' labor). The exchange of services and goods was recorded in dollars and cents, but little if any cash changed hands.[3]

11

A country store brought a rural area into a market economy, although only a step closer to a cash economy. Consumer goods entered an area from regional and national markets, and locally grown crops left for those markets. Goods were exchanged for crops at the country store. The storekeeper gave farmers credit and bought their produce—normally with store pay, a credit on each farmer's account. He carried over farmers until they settled up after the wheat harvest. Storekeepers "served as translators between the world of rural barter and the world of urban money," observed historian William Cronon. They bartered with farmers, sold produce to urban buyers, and paid cash to urban suppliers.[4]

Storekeepers charged for performing these services. To link national or regional with local markets, they had to know the changing values of many goods and commodities. One store clerk recalled that his employer "knew the value of everything in the market, from the highest down to wood ashes." Market prices could change rapidly. Another clerk told how his employers received "a great many hogs" that farmers had slaughtered and brought as pay, and "if a few warm days should come and find them on our hands, we would be sure to lose money."[5] Farm-made butter might be an inferior "make."[6] Rejecting such commodities was not a realistic option when that was all farmers had: if one merchant refused to trade, they would go elsewhere. Before the arrival of the railroad, there was no grain elevator, flour mill, or meat-packer to purchase farm produce, except in river towns. Country stores had to perform those functions. Storekeepers covered the risks of price changes, spoilage, and poor-quality goods by offering farmers less than the full market value for produce.[7]

In prerailroad days, Minnesota store owners needed an ample supply of capital. Business moved slowly due to the harsh climate and poor transportation. Produce had to be stored over the winter, and it might never find a buyer or a profitable price. Store owners "had to buy their stock months in advance," Cronon noted. Their money was tied up for months until goods finally sold—and they might not sell.[8] Selling brought more risk, for it had to be done on credit. Merchants hoped farmers would repay after wheat harvest, but some did not. A Madelia clerk recalled his bosses' outstanding accounts: "It seemed only a question of time when their little capital would be exhausted," but "to try to do business with the farmers on a strictly cash basis would be equivalent to closing up the store."[9] Store owners covered this risk by charging higher prices for goods sold on credit or for both cash and credit sales.[10] Or, they cheated customers by selling fraudulent goods. P. T. Barnum learned showmanship as a young clerk in a country store selling "ground coffee" made from "burned peas, beans, and corn."[11]

Wary of such chicanery, farmers were still happy to see a country store built, for it linked them to markets and enabled them to trade surplus crops. Once the novelty wore off, however, they often grew dissatisfied with the terms of trade offered there. Theoretically competition between stores should have reduced price gouging and cheating, but many farmers believed that merchants connived to set prices and to avoid true competition. In 1869 one writer complained "that all this community of tradesmen" had "a common understanding and agreement as to terms of sale, that is the very opposite of fair competition." So "there is virtually one invariable standard of prices, for similar goods, in all the stores."[12] That was not fully true. Competition forced merchants to sell partly on farmers' terms by offering credit and accepting farm produce of all kinds. Yet this complicated store-pay, credit-price system made it hard to compare one store's terms to another's, thereby hindering full and fair competition.

In this prerailroad world, the more merchants a town had, the worse off farmers seemed to be. Many merchants now supported their families

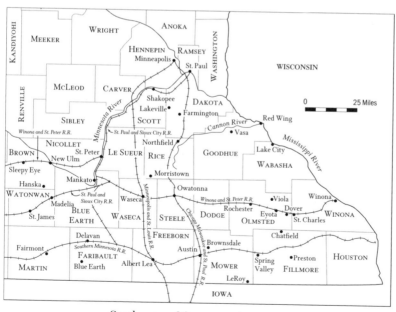

Southeastern Minnesota, about 1900

on a sales volume that had supported only one or two families before. "When competition" meant "that the dealer sells only from twenty-five to forty dollars' worth per day" instead of one hundred dollars, he had to increase prices "to make him his living, clerk hire, rents, interest on capital invested in stock[,] buildings, etc." That writer in 1873 saw "too much competition," for "every little town now has half a dozen stores." He believed that farmers should concentrate their trade by shopping in only a couple of stores so that they would have fewer middlemen to support.[13] Market mechanisms were not bringing efficiency.

Minnesota farmers discovered the inefficiencies of what Alfred Chandler termed the "coordination" of the distribution of consumer goods by "market mechanisms" in a seasonal, cash-crop, credit-dependent, pre-railroad economy.[14] Competition led to retailing practices that drove up retail prices—the acceptance of inferior farm produce as payment and the offering of credit to one and all. Also, the ease with which merchants could enter rural retailing encouraged a proliferation of stores, each operating with fixed expenses on low sales volume and charging higher prices.

To eliminate such inefficiencies and high prices, groups of Minnesotans tried to form cooperative or Union stores modeled on those of the New England Protective Union (NEPU), which operated in the late 1840s and 1850s. Transactions previously conducted between buyers and sellers in the open market were "internalized"—conducted between customers and their own NEPU stores and between those stores and their own wholesaler. Buying, selling, and pricing decisions were made through democratic mechanisms, which (the NEPU hoped) would put only one Union store in a town, not the "half a dozen stores" that market mechanisms placed there. Although the Union stores were a mainly non-Minnesota and nonrural phenomenon, the origins of Minnesota's cooperative stores lies in their development.

There is a larger point here about rural cooperation. Often studied as an auxiliary of agrarian protest, cooperation is assumed by many historians to have been a reaction to economic monopoly, to managers' and entrepreneurs' concentration of economic power. Yet the existence of the NEPU stores shows that ordinary Americans saw the inefficiencies of market mechanisms and sought to replace them with a cooperative concentration—at the same time as managers and entrepreneurs did. Cooperation was not initially merely a reaction to Big Business, as some believe, but a reaction to the old world of small merchant-owned businesses.[15]

The "Union Store" Idea Comes to Minnesota from New England

Minnesota's Yankee settlers referred to New England's experience with Union stores when debating the idea of creating their own. "I am committed to this new enterprise," one Union store supporter announced, "having helped to establish a store of this kind in an older State, and receiving its benefits extending back over twenty years."[16]

Urban workers—not farmers—originated the idea of cooperative stores. In October 1845 workers started the Protective Union Store in Boston as an outgrowth of a buying club linked to a local union. It became the first "division," or store, of the Working Men's Protective Union (WPU). Two years later the WPU had at least twenty-five divisions with a combined membership of almost two thousand members. By October 1852, there were 403 divisions of the New England Protective Union— renamed to include farmers and others who did not fit the workingmen's label.[17] Apparently the NEPU developed independently of and uninfluenced by the contemporaneous Rochdale movement in England. It adhered to several Rochdale rules, such as "cash sales, open membership, [and] equal voting by members irrespective of number of shares," but not others. (It sold at cost-plus prices instead of market prices, and it did not pay patronage dividends.)[18]

Like Rochdale's pioneers, however, New England consumers bypassed the market by buying from stores they themselves owned, rather than from privately owned stores.[19] Each store could also bypass private firms by purchasing from the NEPU wholesaler, called the Central Agency. These decisions were made democratically by the local division as well as by the Central Division, "a congress of delegates elected" by local divisions. Locally, members elected a board of directors "to supervise the trade and the conduct of the storekeeper." At the regional level, an elected Committee on Trade gathered market information and supervised the Central Agency. The storekeeper and Central agent had day-to-day control, but their decisions were subject to democratic review and reversal.[20]

Railroads made the NEPU possible. By the mid-1840s New England had an extensive railroad network centered in Boston, home of the Central Agency, which could ship goods by rail to member stores. Very likely, Yankee workers and consumers organized and expanded the NEPU to take advantage of the increased volume of transactions made possible by train service. They may have borrowed the term "division" from the Western Railroad, which separated its operations in Massachusetts and eastern New York into divisions. Chandler called the Western the first American firm to design a "modern, carefully defined, internal organizational structure." But the NEPU had a similar structure in place only a few years later.[21]

By facilitating increased business volumes and speeds of transactions, railroads reduced the amount of capital needed to do a fixed amount of business. They made it possible for NEPU stores to enjoy benefits that mass retailers, such as Sears, Roebuck, and Company, later reaped from internalizing market transactions and achieving remarkable sales volumes. By selling to nonmembers, many NEPU stores became the discount retailers in their towns. High sales volume cut per-unit costs and allowed prices to be discounted 25 to 50 percent. Robust cash-only sales enabled "a Union store [to] make a greater amount of sales on a small capital than an ordinary grocery could on a larger capital" and "the Divisions to turn over their capital again and again with astonishing rapidity," wrote historian Edwin Rozwenc.[22] Fast inventory turnover rates also cut per-unit costs.

Bypassing the market had its problems: inadequate working capital, members' apathy about democratic management, and strong merchant opposition. Democracy had its own inefficiencies. *New York Tribune* editor Horace Greeley criticized the factionalism, verbosity, and business incompetence of delegates to the Central Division. Disputes over Central agents' commissions meant that only one-third of NEPU stores purchased goods through the agency. The others used private wholesalers. By 1853 this split had created two rival Unions and two wholesale agencies "bidding against each other."[23] Six years later when the idea first appeared in Minnesota, NEPU Union stores had lost much of their idealism and had been battered by the Panic of 1857 and the ensuing depression.[24]

Knowledge of such losses and disunity caused skepticism among some rural Minnesotans, who also noted that the NEPU was a mostly urban phenomenon. New England's towns and cities might have enough customers to support a Union store, but that was unlikely in rural areas. Urban workers bought a larger percentage of their supplies and received paychecks at short, regular intervals. Their cash-only Union stores had a higher, more consistent cash flow than might stores selling to farmers who raised and made some of their food and clothing, who were paid at harvest, and who needed credit until then.[25] Farmers' purchasing was seasonal.[26] A Union store would have to survive the dry times when farmers were not buying.

Some Minnesotans wanted to try the Union store idea. Yet in pre-railroad days, only those living near navigable rivers could conceivably start such stores. Founded by Yankees and Yorkers after the 1851 Treaty of Mendota opened the west bank of the Mississippi River to white settlement, Red Wing had excellent steamboat service. Old Stock Americans (whites whose families had lived in America for several generations) considered "organizing a Union Store" there in February 1859. Resolving "to form a subdivision under the constitution" of the NEPU, they capitalized on its established legitimacy and avoided bickering over organizational details.[27] Adherence to NEPU rules was necessary. No Minnesota law authorized them to form a cooperative or specified how that might be done.

Red Wing's organizational meeting drew only twenty participants, some of them nonfarmers.[28] It produced a letter-to-the-editor exchange between a supporter named S. P. Snow, who argued for eliminating "intermediate, or middle-men," and a pseudonymous opponent, "Quien Sabe" (Spanish for "who knows?"), who attacked Union stores as a "panacea" that had "failed in nine out of every ten trials." There is no clear evidence that the Red Wing "division" ever operated a store.[29]

In the 1860s Minnesota's farmers were preoccupied with the Civil and Dakota Wars, railroad construction, and the rapid spread of commercial agriculture with King Wheat as the cash crop. New facilities for transporting, marketing, and milling spring wheat made wheat a very marketable crop. Price levels almost doubled during the Civil War—both the prices farmers received for crops and the prices they paid for consumer goods. During the postwar deflation, farmers thought crop prices fell faster than prices for store goods.[30] Writing in March 1870, one farmer asked merchants, "do you mark goods down accordingly—as you marked them up at the rise of gold? I think not." In 1869 a Norwegian-American farmer complained that "wheat, the farmer's most important source of income, stands at 45 to 50 cents per bushel, while we must pay the same high prices for labor, clothing, groceries, etc."[31]

Immigrants Attempt "Union Stores":
Vasa and New Sweden

If merchants were responsible for high consumer prices, as charged, then organizing cooperative stores seemed a likely solution. During the winter of 1868–69, Scandinavian-American farmers in Vasa, Goodhue County, and Marine on St. Croix, Washington County, formed what were probably the first cooperative stores in Minnesota. More is known about the Vasa store than about the one in Marine.[32] The *Goodhue County Republican* reported in December 1868 that a Farmers' Union Store would open that week in Vasa. It is unclear if Vasa's Swedish-American farmers used the term "union store" or if the editor turned to the familiar New England term.[33]

Begun in 1854, the Swedish-American settlement of Vasa was railroadless, but it was located only ten miles from Red Wing's steamboat service. Vasa's store was linked to a wheat-marketing cooperative, the Scandinavian Transportation Company (STC), located in Red Wing. Months earlier, recalled Vasa pioneer Trued G. Pearson, some one hundred Vasa-area farmers started the STC "because complaints were heard... about the manner in which Red Wing grain dealers treated them."[34] Here farmers attacked low wheat prices and high store prices by forming complementary cooperatives. Their store did not have to buy and market wheat. The STC did and paid them cash with which they paid store bills. Probably they saved on transportation costs by hauling wheat to Red Wing and store goods to Vasa on the return trip. Also, STC wheat shipments east may have helped the store pay wholesalers for store goods.

The Swedish Lutheran church dominated the skyline at Vasa (ca. 1900).

Within two years, Red Wing's grain dealers had derailed the STC by obtaining favorable freight rates from riverboat companies and by outbidding the STC for farmers' wheat. Merchants were less able to destroy a general store run by farmers in a rural township.[35] Vasa's farmers had to travel to Red Wing to market their wheat once a year (so Red Wing's grain dealers could compete for their wheat), but they were less inclined to travel to Red Wing once a week for groceries and supplies when they had a local store. It would have been foolhardy for a Red Wing merchant to start a store in Vasa to compete with one owned by farmers.[36] The Vasa store was insulated from competition. Likely the first store in Vasa, it added an economic function to a crossroads community formed by the religious, ethnic functions of the Swedish Lutheran church there.

In November 1868, some 150 Vasa farmers cooperatively purchased one year's worth of supplies—"clothing, groceries, &c."—on credit from Milwaukee jobbers. They sought "to save for themselves a part of the profits of retailers, by charging a uniform percentage above cost for goods ... sufficient only to cover freight and store expenses and the salary of their agent."[37] They also sought to bypass Red Wing retailers.

About sixty farmers purchased shares in the new store. Their reliance on jobbers for credit indicates a shortage of working capital, probably because little of the share price was paid in at the start. The agent, John Paulson, was the store's secretary and bookkeeper and the town's postmaster. The post office was part of the store, an arrangement that increased retail traffic. So did the store's location on the road from Red Wing to Cannon Falls, "at about the center of the town[ship]."[38]

So successful was the store that another one was started in southern Vasa Township at Belle Creek.[39] The first store built a solid reputation among Scandinavian Americans in a wide area. In 1870, when Nicollet County farmers were thinking of establishing a wheat-marketing and retailing cooperative, they told their organizing committee to examine farmer associations in Vasa, Goodhue County, and Lansing, Iowa.[40]

That first year, Vasa's Union store did not follow the Rochdale principle of cash-only sales. "On the abundant promise of large crops without expectation of a great decline in [the] price of wheat," the Vasa store, "as did most of [the] others engaged in mercantile business, gave too large credits," according to the *Red Wing Argus* editor in November 1869. Perhaps eight months' credit from Milwaukee jobbers encouraged the store to overextend credit to farmers. Like other country stores, it could not retain its customers unless it offered them credit. The editor called a rumor of its failure "an exaggeration," but the store owed between two and three thousand dollars in accounts payable, which it could not pay just at that time due to uncollectible accounts receivable.[41] Even after wheat harvest, farmers had not settled up. Still, largely because of Swedish-American ethnic solidarity, the Vasa store was a qualified success.

That same winter of 1869–70, those Nicollet County Scandinavian Americans who sent a committee to Vasa tried to start a similar store after area merchants took strong debt-collection measures. Credit problems could be a stimulus for farmers to create new cooperative stores as well as a setback that ruined old ones. Local farmers reacted angrily when a St. Peter merchant had the sheriff seize eight hundred bushels of wheat from a German-American farmer who owed three hundred dollars. The sheriff did not allow him to "drive his own wheat to market" and thus avoid the "high prices" the sheriff deducted to have others

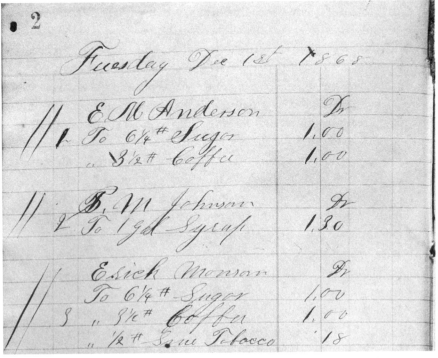

John Paulson entered his purchases as well as those of other customers. This page from the daybook shows the Union Store's first day of operation.

transport it.[42] In December 1869, the *St. Peter Tribune* reported a sheriff busy "serving summonses, executing Writs of Attachment, &c., &c. This is the harvest time for Attorneys and Court officers, but for those who are being pushed it is not quite so pleasant."[43] St. Peter merchants limited interest-free credit to thirty days and demanded that delinquent customers pay bills by December 20: "Unless the same are settled *by that time* we will enforce settlement and collection of the same."[44]

Two different, but overlapping, groups in Nicollet County reacted to these measures. The protests and organizational attempts of the Scandinavian-American farmers who had settled seven miles northwest of St. Peter contrasted sharply with those of that town's primarily Old Stock residents. St. Peter had been founded shortly after the 1851 treaty signed at nearby Traverse des Sioux. Its ties to leading politicians who promoted it (and their profit) as a future state capital caused it to surpass Traverse in size and ambition.[45]

In *Nordisk Folkeblad*, a Minneapolis Scandinavian-American newspaper, a correspondent reported "widespread discontent among farmers" over merchants' measures.[46] Hard times were not the right time to tighten credit. In response, Scandinavian-American farmers north of St. Peter formed an association to "search for a way to send our wheat to eastern markets and if possible to order our necessities, or seek to establish a Farmer-Union Store."[47] These men were organizational activists. Earlier that year, they formed a "skandinaviske Forening" (Scandinavian Society) and a farmers' mutual fire insurance company; the society considered creating "a business branch." Though railroadless, they might have duplicated the success of the Vasa farmers if their activism had not been overshadowed and co-opted by an Old Stock attempt at a Union store.[48]

Their common Lutheranism, class, language, and newcomers' status helped Scandinavian-American farmers unite in cooperative projects with limited and achievable goals. Events took a different turn when St. Peter's Old Stock Americans seized the initiative.[49]

Old Stock Americans Attempt "Union Stores": St. Peter

Located on the west bank of the Minnesota River about seventy miles southwest of the Twin Cities, St. Peter, the county seat of Nicollet County, was an excellent site for a Union store. The St. Paul and Sioux City Railroad already ran along the east bank and was accessible by ferry. St. Peter's postmaster boasted that soon "answers to St. Paul letters can be received the same day, a great convenience over the present slow plan." The Winona and St. Peter Railroad (W&SP) was to bridge the river by fall 1870, making St. Peter the western terminus of a line with connections to Chicago. From the start, St. Peter's Union store movement confusingly combined farmers' grievances over credit and promoters' dreams of new businesses using the telegraph's swift communications and the railroad's high-volume transportation.[50]

Stringent collection and credit policies also angered Old Stock settlers in Traverse Township and the village of Traverse des Sioux in Nicollet County. In mid-January 1870, they called a meeting to consider ways to eliminate or cut middlemen's profits. Misinterpreting the call so as to keep the meeting on a safe, partisan topic, the *Tribune* editor announced

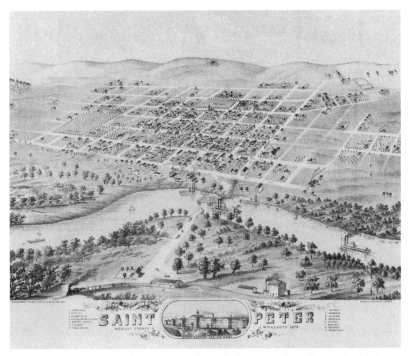

A step ahead of nearby Mankato in 1870, St. Peter used the St. Paul and Sioux City Railroad depot across the Minnesota River from downtown. By May 1871 the arrival of the Winona and St. Peter Railroad tracklayers brought train service to the city center and helped to end the steamboat era.

a meeting to protest high tariffs. Replying, a Traverse writer suggested that a farmer-owned wheat warehouse, independent political action, or "even . . . the plan of starting a Union store" were more likely topics. "Minnesota" suggested that the meeting consider joint marketing of wheat and cash-only purchasing of goods to avoid credit prices.[51]

Arguing that farmers should stop using credit, editor J. K. Moore turned to an editor's favorite remedy for farmer-merchant disputes: local ("home") manufacturing. This remedy would ensure that "the money . . . is kept at home" and show that "there need be no conflict of interests" in his town.[52] Starting new workshops or factories offended neither his advertisers nor his farmer-subscribers. That was better for him than a fight between private stores that advertised and a Union store that might not need to. He did not admit that a railroad would bring cheap, nationally made goods to St. Peter and thus undercut home manufacturing.

Scandinavian-American farmers could organize cooperatives better partly because Old Stock editors often did not know about, comment on, or attend their meetings. Word-of-mouth notice or notices in ethnic-language newspapers recruited participants who knew each other and had similar views. English-language newspaper publicity appealed to anyone with a grievance or an idea—and produced meetings too full of both. The difference should not be overstated. Scandinavian Americans could advertise in the press, and Old Stock Americans communicated orally, too. Yet the two groups tended to use different methods that brought different results.

Grievances and a grab bag of ideas reigned in St. Peter. About seventy-five people—not all farmers—attended the February 5 meeting and listened to impromptu talks on "the progress and condition of co-operative stores in the eastern States" and the possibility of milling wheat in St. Peter. Lawyer Charles S. Bryant gave a lengthy speech. A Swedish-American farmer and Civil War veteran, John P. Schoenback, reported that his home city in Sweden had "a union league" whose cash-only store thrived; "He would like to say much more, but had not sufficiently mastered

Republican editor and St. Peter booster J. K. Moore started the St. Peter Tribune *in 1860 after a fire destroyed his* St. Peter Free Press *office. Ten years later, the* Tribune *was "the oldest paper retaining its name and politics . . . in the Minnesota [River] Valley."*

the English language to do so." An Old Stock speaker replied, saying, "He had rather hear such men talk than one of your smooth-tongued Yankees who would talk half an hour and say nothing" (a none-too-subtle reference to Bryant). A former woolen manufacturer provided an estimate of the funds needed "to start a woolen factory" in town. They discussed political issues.[53]

The attendees took little action on a Union store but resolved to form a Farmers' and Laborers' Co-operative Society. Like promoters of grandiose railroad-aided projects, they agreed to "carry on merchandise [and] manufacturing, &c., for the benefit of the members and the better development of the country." The chair appointed a five-man committee to draw up a constitution and bylaws.

The committee's draft did not entirely conform to the law on cooperative associations that the Minnesota legislature had just passed.[54] It followed the NEPU model instead.[55] Calling their association the Minnesota Co-operative Union, the committee planned a statewide organization with its "capital" in St. Peter (which lost a chance at state-capital status in 1857). The St. Peter division would operate a retail store, a wheat warehouse, and other "branches [of] manufactures."[56] Proposing whatever the railroad might make possible meant that the committee lacked the necessary focus on a single goal.

At another mass meeting of seventy-five farmers in early March, a "snow-storm probably prevented as full an attendance" as expected. Inside the hall, a blizzard of ideas prevented a consensus. A former Indian trader, R. B. Pierce, protested the presence of nonproducers, namely lawyer Bryant, but a committee member overruled the protest, and Bryant had the floor. In court he had to focus on one charge, but here his talk wandered everywhere: New England's Union stores, the Massachusetts law for incorporating them, Chicago wholesale prices, merchants' profit margins, wheat marketing monopolies and freight rates, a former U.S. Senator's speech on railroad land grants, and statistics on the size of major railroad corporations. He was trying the railroad before it came to town. Former state representative and unrepentant Democrat Samuel ("Uncle Sammy") Coffin "launched forth into a regular anti-tariff speech" that annoyed the Republican editor. Coffin also "gave the farmers some good advice regarding the care of farm implements, &c." Finally they turned to the main topic but only to sign a pledge of association, reappoint most of the prior committee, and instruct it to recruit new members and report back at the next meeting.[57]

A few weeks later, a third meeting stuck to the agenda—approval of a constitution and bylaws—only to bog down in debate over their legality. A membership committee reported disappointing results, due partly to another snowstorm and bad roads. Old Stock Americans were slow to commit themselves; only fifty-eight people had signed up. One speaker insisted many "were favorably inclined" to the Co-operative Union, "but were waiting to [see] what its prospects" were, "and plenty will join when they see how it works."[58]

Lacking Scandinavian Americans' internal, ethnic unity, the Old Stock group sought external, legal guarantees to prop up its organization. Bryant read the new Minnesota law on cooperative associations and called for payment of the one-dollar membership fee so they could legally organize. That request sparked a lengthy debate over whether they were or were not legally and permanently organized. Four speakers offered their opinions. This supposedly antimerchant group then accepted the counsel of Alfred Wallin, an attorney who was "engaged in organizing" the merchants into a "Board of Trade in this town." (Similar laws governed cooperatives and boards of trade.) Eight men then signed the constitution, the merchants' attorney notarized it, and the group elected a committee to draw up bylaws to be discussed at the next meeting (although proposed bylaws had been printed in the *Tribune* two weeks earlier).[59]

Two weeks later they met to elect temporary officers. They narrowed their focus to operating a grocery store, but it took them four meetings to do so. With only one thousand dollars in capital stock, they did not control the grocery, but St. Peter merchant George W. Cryer would run it "and invest the money and do the required business for five per cent. on the amount invested." With an estimated inventory turnover rate of four times per year, Cryer would earn $150 per year on the deal. Editor Moore applauded a merchant-run Union store as "the most economical one possible." Cheaper goods, he predicted, would "make St. Peter a point where trade must concentrate." (He did not admit that even cheaper goods brought by rail might eventually end locally controlled retailing.)[60]

By late June 1870, the "St. Peter Workingmen's Co-operative Association" hoped to acquire five to ten thousand dollars in order to expand its operations. Cryer ran a weekly ad ("Union Store Going") in the *St. Peter Tribune* advertising coffee, sugar, and other goods—and 10 percent discounts for stockholders—for more than a year. Then he advertised a going-out-of-business sale, and the weekly ads ended in late November 1871, shortly after a Union store leader pleaded that "an institution of this character should not be abandoned" until its fate could be discussed at a promised general meeting that apparently was never held.[61]

St. Peter's would-be cooperators lacked experience, mutual trust, and consensus. The stressful process of organizing a business whose debts would be legally binding on them all was not an ideal time in which to forge solidarity from scratch.[62] Calling a meeting by newspaper notice brought together a varied group: Old Stock farmers and town residents, at least two Scandinavian-American farmers, two lawyers, a Democratic politician, and a Republican editor, who reported how the resulting cacophony of ideas distracted them all from the Union store idea. Old Stock Americans in a new railroad town could consider many possibilities: a woolen factory, other factories, flour mill, political action, or a statewide cooperative union. Small groups of Scandinavian-American farmers—belonging to the same church and living in railroadless townships and lacking political or financial clout in their adopted country—had fewer possibilities. They could focus on starting a cooperative store. The novelty of Union stores in Minnesota meant Old Stock organizers did not have the force of habit to keep them on task. Politics distracted them. Mostly Republican but not regarded as potential political candidates in 1870, Scandinavian-American farmers were spared partisan divisions and ambitions that paralyzed Old Stock candidates whose campaigns might be threatened if their rivals used cooperative ventures to impress voters. Suspicious of power and adversarial in debate, Old Stock republicans squabbled over molehills that a jealousy of power made into mountains.

The New Law on Cooperative Associations

Old Stock Americans were also eager to ascertain the exact legal status of cooperatives before they formed any. At the time when St. Peter's farmers were discussing cooperation, the legislature set up a legal framework for organizing cooperatives in Minnesota. On February 9, 1870,

State Senator Reuben J. Chewning of Dakota County, a Virginia-born Old Stock Democrat, introduced a bill authorizing cooperative associations, a word-for-word copy of the Massachusetts statute of 1866 on the same topic, except that the term "state" replaced the Bay State's venerable title of "commonwealth."[63] The *St. Paul Daily Pioneer* mildly praised this "somewhat important" bill.[64] Not a frontier innovation but a law from a New England state honored by Old Stock settlers, it easily passed both House and Senate after being amended to hold shareholders personally liable for an association's debts.

The *Pioneer* summarized its provisions. The maximum capital stock that could be sold was set at a high fifty thousand dollars. "It limit[ed] each shareholder to $1,000 value in stock" and to one vote, thus keeping "one or two capitalists" from ruling the business. Associations could pay patronage dividends to nonstockholders, too, "thus encouraging [them] to trade with the association." Cooperative stores therefore could become discount stores for the general public, just like NEPU stores. No dividends could be paid until 10 percent of the profits were deposited in a "contingent fund" and that fund equaled 30 percent of the issued stock. That rule forced an association to build up working capital.[65] A minimum of seven people could form a cooperative by filing articles of association with city or town clerks—not the secretary of state, with whom corporations had to file.[66]

The law failed to require adequate start-up capital: it set a maximum amount of capital stock but no *minimum*. As a result, the St. Peter association was undercapitalized from the start.[67] The law did not protect shareholders from being held liable for stores' debts. Many NEPU divisions had borrowed from their members, who thus opposed limited liability because it curtailed their debt-collection rights.[68] Very likely that explains legislators' refusal to give shareholders protection against liability.

Old Stock Americans Attempt "Union Stores": Northfield

In the same month that Chewning's bill moved through the legislature, some Northfield-area residents talked of starting a Union store. They, too, were reacting to the wave of foreclosures and "forced collections" that had hit rural Minnesota in late 1869.[69] Founded by Yankees of reformist bent, Northfield had train service; thus the ease of ordering and receiving goods from wholesalers by rail may have encouraged them to consider a Union store. They may also have acted upon hearing news of Senator Chewning's bill. He may have introduced it at their request; he lived in Castle Rock, just up the road from Northfield. The Northfield group met in late February to elect officers for a Union store. Before the election, a New Hampshire native and Grange Master, Ara Barton, "read a history of the Co-operative System of Massachusetts."[70]

Routine and uneventful, this meeting sparked a lively debate in Northfield's two newspapers, the *Standard* and the *Enterprise*. The exchange revealed some predictable antimerchant feelings—and some surprisingly sophisticated economic analyses by ordinary Americans who saw the inefficiencies of market mechanisms and proposed remedies as early as entrepreneurs and managers did.

"Merchant" opened the debate. Reacting to the call for a meeting, he warned of hidden expenses that might doom a Union store selling at cost: price fluctuations, "waste, short measure, rent, taxes, wages, loss on unsal[e]able stock," and other "leakages." Assuming—for argument's sake—it would survive anyway, he lamented the consequences: unable to sell at cost, merchants would leave town with their one hundred thousand dollars in capital, causing "rows of empty stores," falling property values, increased taxes, and fewer donations for public projects. "Newspapers," he warned the editor, "would receive their death blow."[71]

Such calamity-howling drew two replies the next week from "Farmer" and "Abraham Quipps." Both writers referred to New England's success with Union stores. "Quipps" stressed cheap goods as the great incentive for people to flock to Northfield—farm buyers, invalids, farmers with cash to spend, and craftsmen. Property values would rise for miles around, he predicted.

"Farmer" emphasized justice over prosperity. A Union store would allow farmers to buy with cash at low wholesale prices, "instead of paying merchants the old [Civil] war prices." High war prices supported "too many merchants . . . keeping fine horses, and carriages, building fine residences, stores &c." He disputed "Merchant" 's list of hidden expenses. A Union store would eliminate "waste"; it would not have "unsaleable goods" to write off; its labor costs would be lower, for one Union store clerk would sell as much as six private store clerks. It would not "sell at cost," but "at such a rate that it will be self-sustaining." Selling at low profit margins, it would be what American governments no longer were—"the great mercantile regulator, fixing the price of merchandise, and, as far as possible, the price of produce." It would drive out merchants who made excessive profits, but "farmers and mechanics" would increase their charitable donations and newspaper subscriptions to replace these merchants' share, added "Quipps."[72]

Responding, "Merchant" retreated to less cataclysmic prophecies. Only undercapitalized merchants would fail, thus "creating a monopoly, a thing which the farmers ought to dread." (Farmers did not oppose monopoly when they could gain it for their cooperative.) He ridiculed the idea that cheap prices would draw people to Northfield. "Is cheap living the controlling idea—as is asserted—which decides a person's location?" St. Paul residents did not flock to rural towns "where living is 50 per cent cheaper." Other factors were more important than low prices. He asked, "Why have not friends 'Farmer' and 'Quipps' moved to the Swedish settlement [Vasa], near Red Wing, to enjoy the advantages of the union store?"[73] He did not note that cheap goods brought by rail from distant factories would hurt local business. Railroads were not mentioned at all in the debate.[74]

"Farmer" insisted he would not move to Vasa "for we expect to have a more thoroughly managed union store nearer home." He appealed to antimerchant feelings: merchants were "holding on to the old war prices" and were issuing "threats of sueing [sic] all that join the union store, who chanced to be in debt to them." They had recruited a teacher to ask "school children to tell their father not to join the union store."[75]

The next week, "Merchant" denied that farmers had been pressured to reject the Union store. He sidestepped the charge of outdated Civil War prices, instead offering an economic analysis. First, NEPU stores were in "manufacturing towns," and their customers were "regularly paid at short intervals." Thus they had business year-round and customers who did not raise foodstuffs. How could a Union store survive in a farming area with an inventory "consist[ing] mainly of the *staples that farmers raise*"? Second, the projected 2 percent savings was a "ridiculously small sum." Just "providing a reaper with shelter" would save a farmer that much. Third, farmers would be wiser to invest their money in the editors' panacea, home manufacturing—a "beet sugar factory; cheese factory; . . . starch factory." He vowed to investigate these options on his next eastern buying trip. Fourth, he recommended that farmers form agricultural societies to improve livestock breeds and crop seeds and "attend to their legitimate business—something they understand, benefiting themselves and the State at large."[76]

"Merchant" urged farmers to trust market mechanisms and concentrate on their role as producers, not consumers. They should specialize, produce quality goods, and control the processing of their crops—then the market would reward them. Yet "Merchant" failed to acknowledge that farming had too many practitioners ever to be a specialized occupation, supply would always threaten to exceed demand, and better breeds and seeds would only increase overproduction. To a cash-poor farmer, even small savings from consumers' cooperation could be significant.

Two weeks later, "A Farmer," who was a Union store stockholder, brought the debate to an end. He noted that cheese, starch, and beet-sugar factories required more capital than a Union store—more than farmers had to invest. Farmers running factories would be "engaging in something we know less of than of the mercantile business." He was right. Many farmers had clerked in a country store and knew the potential profits. "There are," he concluded, "too many live Yankees" around Northfield with the "traits of character peculiar to their race, to allow a good thing, in which there is money to be made, to be monopolized by the few." Apparently there were not enough "live Yankees" near Northfield, for no Union store seems to have survived for long there.[77]

One result of the Northfield debate was a series of newspaper ads for a private general store, J. D. Blake and Company. The series cleverly capitalized on the concept of one cash-only price and on the merchant-versus-farmer rhetoric that marked the debate.

Here the discount store posed as "the great mercantile regulator, fixing the price of merchandize." It defended consumers' interests, incurred merchants' wrath, overthrew the credit system's dual cash and credit prices, and cut those high margins to cover bad debts. Of course, consumers had no voice in J. D. Blake & Co.'s decisions, but then they did not have to buy stock, attend annual meetings, or serve on committees either. Blake promised them the savings they sought without the work or risk of starting a Union store.

Merchants could adopt farmers' antimerchant rhetoric and ideas for ending the market's inefficiencies. An alert merchant could use high-volume, cash-only sales to achieve efficiencies, lower prices, drive out competitors, and obtain a near monopoly while sounding as democratic as the cooperators.

Except in ethnic enclaves like Vasa, few Union stores in Minnesota made it past the planning stage. Several factors led to failure. Union stores in the East were in serious trouble by the 1860s. Minnesotans had a less extensive rail network than the New England one that NEPU stores relied on, and they did not use it to organize regionally as the NEPU had. New rail links gave St. Peter's organizers visions of leading a statewide cooperative, but they needed a statewide group to help *them*, and none existed until the arrival of the Patrons of Husbandry (Grange). Consumers' cooperatives did not achieve such great savings as to expand solely on their economic merits without a sponsoring group to help them grow.

Forming a cooperative store meant creating a political unit, a polity, that could debate and decide economic questions in a democratic way, then secure its "citizens' " support for the decisions and for the elected officers. St. Peter's failed attempt revealed how difficult it could be to create such a polity. Vasa's success showed it was possible. Political geographer Richard Hartshorne listed four factors that helped make a polity stable and effective: (1) "contiguity of settled population"; (2) "homogeneity... of the population"; (3) "historical continuity of the political area"; and (4) "coherent unity of the area."[78] Translating from Hartshorne's purely political realm, we arrive at four factors helping to make a workable polity in the political-economic realm of rural cooperation: (1) members purchasing and selling in the same market; (2) members having similar racial, religious, political, occupational, and linguistic characteristics; (3) members sharing a tradition of jointly running an organization such as a church or a voluntary association; and (4) an absence of factions or contradictory economic interests among members.

Cooperatives were more likely to succeed if organized among a subset of the population with common characteristics, interests, and traditions. St. Peter's organizers were a heterogeneous group, a composite of the entire population of the town. Differences in interests, goals, and backgrounds abounded. Vasa's cooperators were a homogeneous subset: Lutheran, Swedish-American wheat farmers living in a single township and shipping wheat to the Red Wing market.

Ethnic solidarity, common economic interest as farmers, narrower choices as immigrants—these factors helped Scandinavian Americans start successful cooperative stores. Old Stock Americans had too many competing interests, too many economic options, too much hope in political solutions, and too great a reliance on legal guarantees to succeed for long with Union stores, despite the pride many of them took in the New England Protective Union.

2

Grangers as Consumers

*"No bonds of union except
that of buying cheap"*

IN HIS JANUARY 1873 ANNUAL MESSAGE delivered to the Minnesota legislature, Governor Horace Austin advised farmers "to find independence in their own resources." Do not look to the state, he implied. Noting that "the means of organization are theirs," he referred "this subject" to "our agricultural societies and farmers' clubs."[1] Old Stock farmers had discussed "means of organization," but their unruly public meetings with lawyers, editors, and manufacturers had accomplished little. They had to get off in a corner by themselves to discuss, organize, and act. Massive immigration posed another threat to unity, but it also presented an opportunity. They could unite with immigrant farmers on common economic concerns, or they might prefer their ethnic ties to Old Stock townsmen who had different economic interests.

Old Stock Governor Austin's advice was shaped by his politics and so was only partly useful to farmers, many of whom rejected the county agricultural societies that he found impolitic to spurn. *Minnesota Monthly*, a new farm journal, charged that "a few city farmers, business men and amateurs" ruled the societies, whose county fairs were a "temporary amusement." Fair visitors made an unpromising polity: "very few of them would contribute as much as one dollar towards the expenses, if not fenced out, and required to pay to get in."[2] Many farmers had not rejected farmers' clubs, which were neither temporary nor ruled by businessmen or amateurs.

33

Halfway Farmers' Clubs and All-out Organizing of Farmers

On November 4, 1869, Old Stock farmers in eastern Olmsted County met at "the Halfway school house" (halfway between Dover and St. Charles, which was in Winona County) to start a farmers' club—"to resist the exactions of the railroads, and the business community" and to plan a farmers' store. With many political options available, Old Stock farmers tried to expand their groups to county, state, and even national levels. Those at the Halfway meeting urged farmers in nearby townships to form clubs so that a two-county farmers' convention could "bring their combined influence to bear on the Legislature and railroads." Eight months later, farmers in nearby Viola and Eyota started a club.[3]

Eastern Olmsted farmers' anger over high railroad freight rates at Rochester was the engine driving this movement. Feeling empowered by their location between Rochester and the Mississippi River, they discussed shipping their wheat by wagon twenty-seven miles to Winona's landing rather than the fifteen miles to Rochester's depot. A boycott might force the Winona and St. Peter Railroad to cut its freight rates. Concerned about loss of trade for the town, the *Rochester Post* argued that progress was irreversible: "It is impossible for a community to go back from the use of steam to that of teams."[4] True, but farmers could use railroads' linkages to construct organizational networks reaching across county or state boundaries. Yet extensive networks could not be built on a localized solution like driving wagons of wheat to Winona. Nor could farmers west of Rochester make that threat. A local boycott was not likely to lead to a statewide organization.

Shortly after the Halfway meeting, editor C. H. Slocum of the *St. Charles Herald* called on farmers to go beyond "isolated" farmers' clubs and recommended joining the Patrons of Husbandry, or Grange. The *Minnesota Monthly* endorsed his idea. Grange founder Oliver H. Kelley had visited St. Charles less than two weeks after the Halfway meeting to form a Grange, with Slocum as secretary and the local undertaker as Master. Slocum invited "farmers and their wives, and all others interested" to join the Grange.[5] Kelley had a plan for a national farmers' organization.

Born and raised in Boston, Oliver Hudson Kelley arrived in the newly created Minnesota Territory in the summer of 1849. Although a Yankee, he was a Democrat and not an abolitionist. In his fine biography, Thomas A. Woods showed that Kelley lacked the moralistic, preaching, meddling traits that other Old Stock Americans detested in many Yankees. He belonged to the Masons and was a jack of many urban trades.[6] He knew many regions of the country. After the Civil War, he took a fact-finding trip through the South. He was "remarkably free from animosity toward Southern whites" (he had not fought in the war).[7] A "book farmer" who read farm journals and tried new ideas, Kelley felt farmers needed education, social interaction, and protection against monopolies.[8] He thought in agrarian-republican terms. Republicanism was part of the Old Stock heritage, a sort of ideological cement uniting Old Stock Grangers.[9]

Old Stock Americans in St. Charles and Viola liked this Grange republic with its state-level and national-level units. Politically experienced, Old Stock farmers preferred a "federal" farmers' organization whose hierarchical levels paralleled American governmental levels. American history had not been one long hand-holding toast to republicanism, but Kelley nicely bridged barriers among Yankees, Yorkers, southerners, midlanders, and Maineites. He took reforming, educating Yankeeism, stripped it of moralistic preachiness, and applied it to the less controversial task of uplifting American farmers. So broad was the Grange's Old Stock appeal that it helped unite North and South after the Civil War.[10]

For Minnesota, the Granger period began in 1868, when Kelley returned from Washington, D.C., to form the first Granges in Minnesota. Over the next ten years, the Grange became a strong movement with 538 local units in Minnesota before suffering a serious loss of members and entering an irreversible decline in the state. It peaked in Minnesota in 1872–74, when it greatly influenced politics by intimidating the Republicans into nominating Cushman K. Davis for governor, by starting the Anti-Monopoly Party, and by electing several farmers to the legislature. The Grange proved to be far more politically potent than the assorted farmers' clubs had ever been.[11] It was a unique farm group with strengths and weaknesses that left its mark on the cooperative activities it sponsored.

An Organization for (Mostly) Old Stock American Farmers

Describing a Grange picnic in 1873, a Rochester reporter wrote, "The clans gathered from Elmira, Dover, Quincy, Viola . . . ," and he listed many Old Stock towns. The clans, choral numbers, brass band, "poetic address," and speeches made this an ethnic festival as well as a protest "against the oppression of monopolies." Many townspeople attended. For Old Stock farmers concerned about increasing immigration and decreasing status of farmers, the Patrons created an ersatz ethnicity—a pride in Old Stock heritage and farming—to match that of the immigrants.[12]

Four Grange features appealed to Old Stock Americans: secrecy, ritual, exclusiveness, and the inclusion of female participants. Using his Masonic experience, "Kelley [pinned] Grange success to the influence of oaths of loyalty and brotherhood along with the spell cast by mystical and secret ritual," wrote historian Dennis Sven Nordin.[13] The first three features drew quasi-ethnic boundaries separating insiders and outsiders. Grangers pioneered in admitting women to full membership in a fraternal group, noted Donald B. Marti: "The Grange was domestic and so a legitimate part of women's sphere."[14] At one Grange gathering, a woman responded to the toast "Woman—her Sphere," not by denying separate spheres but by asserting that women had their own sphere.[15] Female participation did not specifically exclude immigrants, but it displayed

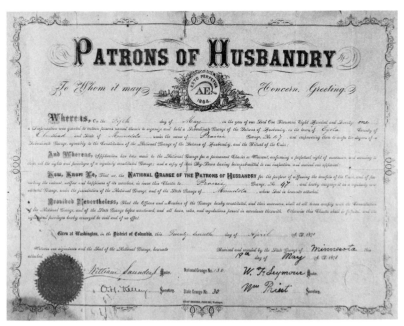

The certificate of Prairie Grange No. 47, an early Minnesota Grange, was signed by a hierarchy of federal, state, and local officers. Eyota was a railroad village west of St. Charles in Olmsted County's Old Stock area.

Old Stock Americans' condescending view that they were more en-lightened than immigrants in their treatment of women. Kelley noted, "Our foreign population seem to get ahead ... in the business" of farm-ing, "but a Yankee can't do it, and no man who had any regard for his wife and children would compel them to undergo the hardships required."[16]

Some Grangers went further. A Granger from Quincy Township advocated equal pay for women, especially schoolteachers.[17] Seeing farm wives subscribe for shares in a Grange warehouse, another Granger concluded in a letter to the newspaper, "It all goes to show, Mr. Editor, that the ladies should have the right of franchise."[18] Most Grangers stuck to a more conservative view of women's role, but even that view differed from the perspective of many immigrant groups. That gulf may have kept some immigrant farmers from joining the Grange.

Grange women seemingly did not participate in Grange discussions regarding economic action.[19] Nineteenth-century spheres for men and women were workplace and home; cooperatives were extensions of the workplace. Cooperative activities were debated mainly at county-level meetings of male delegates, not at the township Grange halls that wo-men entered.

Factors external to the Grange movement also attracted Old Stock farmers to the Patrons. Rural isolation and high rural mobility caused them to welcome Grange sociability. Commercial farming led to their concerns about farming's lowered status and dependence on distant mar-kets, concerns that the Grange addressed.[20] Old Stock Americans were first to become commercial wheat farmers, first to detect unfairness in the wheat marketing system, and, later, first to turn to more diversified agriculture.[21] Yet they ceased raising wheat after the Grange period. In the early 1870s, Old Stock farmers were tackling problems of wheat marketing and blaming these on middlemen and speculators. Grangers' antimonopoly goals still appealed to them.

In Minnesota, Patrons were mostly Old Stock Americans. The officers of newly created Granges almost invariably had Old Stock names — even in counties like Freeborn with many Norwegian, Danish, and Ger-man farmers.[22] The Grange first drew support among the Old Stock group in southeastern Minnesota, in such counties as Dakota, Rice, Olm-sted, and Dodge. Greater appeal to Old Stock than to immigrant farmers is one reason why in Minnesota, an immigrants' state, the Grange and its cooperatives were relatively weak.

The Grange's Relative Failure to Appeal to Immigrant Farmers

The first immigrant Grange was Vasa Grange #188, formed in March 1873 and likely motivated by Vasa's strong cooperative spirit. Other Scandinavian ones were: Linden Grange #265 (Brown County), First Scandinavian Grange #441 (Freeborn County), and Scandinavian Grange #452 (Renville County).[23] In December 1873, "a grange, composed entirely of Germans" began at Getty in Stearns County.[24] The existence of ethnically segregated Granges showed the difficulty of uniting Old Stock and immigrant farmers in the same farmers' group when they separated in different congregations. It was possible: Olof Charleson was a leader in Burnside Grange #148 (Goodhue County), which welcomed three Vasa Grangers on one visit.[25]

The traditional explanation is that immigrants' Catholic and Lutheran churches strongly discouraged members from joining secret societies. Historian O. Fritiof Ander claimed that "continued membership in the Grange after a warning meant excommunication" from the Lutheran church. Until research has unearthed evidence of excommunications in church minutes, this blanket statement must be questioned.[26] Lutheran pastors also objected to the "occupational civil religion" in Grange ritual.[27] Criticism began in the Lutheran newspapers as soon as the Grange gained a following: January 1871 (German Lutheran press), September 1872 (Swedish Lutheran press), and September 1873 (Norwegian Lutheran press).[28]

Vasa residents debated the issue in the spring and summer of 1873, right after the Vasa Grange was formed. The exchange showed what a local pastor (a distinguished one) faced when opposing the Grange. Pastor Eric Norelius criticized Grangers' secret ceremonies, signs, oaths, passwords, and pagan ritual, in which women played goddesses Pomona, Ceres, and Flora. He asked, "Can any Christian woman act as—and let herself be called—a goddess?" New members joined the Vasa Grange despite his warnings of excommunication. To counter his attack, Grangers used republican arguments about separation of church and state, instilled in immigrants a fear of clerical domination, and pointed to a class line between farmers and clergy. Immigrant farmers respected the church's religious authority but not necessarily its advice on this political and economic matter.[29]

More than pastoral admonitions kept immigrants away from the Grange hall. Old Stock Grangers misunderstood, stereotyped, and offended immigrants. In one instance Norwegian Americans were angered when a Granger-dominated, Anti-Monopoly state convention in September 1873 rejected a Norwegian-American candidate for state treasurer. It nominated only Old Stock Americans for its state ticket.[30] In Freeborn County, angry Norwegian Americans charged that Grangers held "secret meetings" to plan their strategy, "'packed' all the caucuses," and tried to "bind the hands of the foreign-born" to get Old Stock Grangers nominated.[31] Partly, Old Stock antipathy toward immigrants arose from their perception that the presence of too many low-status foreigners in farming was the cause of farming's declining prestige.[32] For some immigrants the class line ran between Old Stock and immigrant, not merchant and farmer. One Norwegian-American Granger expressed class-consciousness in terms of a Yankee "aristocracy" against immigrant "laborers."[33] Grange lecturers could not use class appeals to recruit immigrants who saw Yankees and immigrants as the two classes.[34] Also, immigrant farmers did not participate in an Old Stock group before they felt comfortable with English, with American culture, and with the American political process.[35] When the Farmers' Alliance appeared in the 1880s, they were better prepared to participate.

Finally the Grange goal of raising farming's status arose out of Old Stock anxieties, which immigrants did not share. Often dabbling in land speculation, journalism, and other pursuits, Kelley had to reevaluate farming in the light of alternatives. For a German or Norwegian immigrant who was delighted to own a 160-acre farm and prevented by a lack of English-language skills, training, or status from pursuing other occupations, a concern with improving farming's prestige in America likely seemed quixotic.[36]

Consequences of the Old Stock Character of the Grange

Thus, Grange cooperatives could not count on patronage from immigrants. They could not rally all farmers against middlemen and monopolists because ethnic differences divided farmers and ethnic ties bound Old Stock farmers to the middlemen they were supposed to be fighting. Old Stock townsmen would not have joined a group uniting farmers around common class interests, but they did join Granges uniting Old Stock Americans around common ethnic bonds. Granges often did not limit membership to farmers despite their national constitution's exclusion of those not "interested in agricultural pursuits." To gain support and publicity, Kelley allowed editors and other nonfarmers to join.[37] As a man who crossed rural/urban, farmer/nonfarmer boundaries, he had no qualms about admitting urban members.[38]

After the Grange's explosive growth, some Grangers questioned this policy.[39] In early 1873, State Grange Master George Parsons ruled that only farmers who worked their own land could join. James E. Child, Granger and *Waseca Weekly News* editor, objected.[40] When town Grangers were denied seats at a Waseca County Grange meeting, Child protested that he was an old settler, and Waseca's county council reversed itself and seated Child and two other townsmen.[41] Old Stock farmers could not eject the local Old Stock editor and president of the Old Settlers Association.[42] Editor W. A. Hotchkiss of Preston boasted that his Grange membership "dates at least two years further back than that of any other Patron in this county." He was the secretary of the Fillmore County Council.[43] "The business interest of" Albert Lea's Grange "caused it to be looked upon with distrust by Grangers in other towns," so it "was wisely abandoned"—but only for a time.[44]

Also, Old Stock merchants, editors, and politicians often aided Grangers' cooperatives, joined them in joint-stock companies, or made deals with the Grange, which thus could not discriminate between farmers and nonfarmers. Immigrant farmers were reluctant to join while Old Stock townsfolk were only too willing to help. The lines between town and country blurred. Merchants and farmers had a common interest in wheat. In 1868 a visitor to St. Charles reported that when farmers could not hire help to harvest wheat, "merchants, wheat-buyers, mechanics, persons of all interests and ranks... felt a call almost as strong as that of patriotism to go into the fields." "Every body knows nearly as much of farming and its appliances as if they were farmers themselves." Many were. Several townsmen owned small farms "which they partly work at intervals, and partly sub-let to others interested jointly with themselves in the crops."[45] The line between farmer and townsman was not clear. In a newly settled area, a farmer might hope to own a store some day; a merchant might fear he would return to farming.

Still most Minnesotans identified more closely with either farmers or merchants. To have both in one Old Stock polity encouraged factionalism. To have immigrant farmers organizing separately from Old Stock farmers meant having common economic interests in separate polities and competing cooperatives in one town. The Grange's Old Stock identity hindered its efforts no matter which strategy it used to advance farmers' interests. It could bypass markets in three ways: (1) by jointly purchasing supplies in the local or county Grange; (2) by negotiating deals with merchants, thus circumventing the normal individual-to-merchant bargaining; or (3) by incorporating Grange-sponsored cooperatives.

Joint Purchasing Activities of the Patrons of Husbandry

Joint purchasing meant buying supplies and farm implements in large quantities directly from wholesalers and manufacturers on cash terms at reduced prices. Minnesota's new rail connections to Milwaukee and Chicago made that endeavor possible. From the start Kelley and the State Grange planned for a state business agent to handle joint purchasing.[46] On April 2, 1869, they chose C. A. Prescott and gave him quasi-governmental duties as a virtual agricultural trade commissioner. (Nineteenth-century ideas of limited government and laissez-faire meant the state refused to regulate the price or quality of goods, so the Grange tried to.) Prescott was to receive sample machines from manufacturers, test the machines, issue "diplomas" to satisfactory models, recommend their purchase, and negotiate terms of sale. He was to obtain monthly crop reports from Granges and issue weekly crop price bulletins.[47] All this by an appointed, not elected, agent.

By spring 1873, Prescott had ordered groceries wholesale, sold produce, and rented a storage room in St. Paul. But his powers, his appointed status, and his compensation aroused controversy, as had those of the NEPU agent. Some Granges opposed paying him a commission, so the State Grange secretary recommended decentralization: each county could appoint an agent. Instead, the State Grange appointed seven agents—each assigned to a single county—to assist the state business agent.[48]

Another controversy erupted over whether Grange agents could sell to nonmembers (as Union stores had). In late September 1873, the state executive committee chose a new state agent, J. S. Denman of Winona, to contact manufacturers before they committed to deal only with non-Grange farm implement agents. Manufacturers needed contracts before the spring marketing season, so the committee acted before that winter's state convention. The committee and the agent made a suggestion: let non-Grangers buy through the state agent at wholesale rates.[49] That idea set off a letters-to-the-editor fight in the *Farmers' Union.* One correspondent who called himself "Bittersweet" opposed selling to non-Grangers: "Why are we Patrons, and what do we gain by it if every farmer outside the order enjoys the same advantages?"[50] Here was the classic "free rider" problem. Why should some farmers incur expenses to organize if nonmembers then received the same benefits? Denman replied that it was more democratic to let nonmembers participate: "We don't propose to make a monopoly of the institution but make it a blessing and a benefit to our brother farmers."[51] The Grange could hardly keep its democratic image while denying services to some farmers when markets were open to all. Markets would appear to be more democratic and egalitarian than Granges.

Denman's appointment raised anew the question of whether joint purchasing should be centralized or decentralized. Having great economic clout, the State Grange was too large to be readily controlled by members, but local Granges, although easily managed, were too small to have much power in the market. Grangers saw a need for an intermediate level. Kelley sought National Grange approval for "County Granges," but it was not granted until 1874, so local Granges formed county councils prior to national sanction. National officers tolerated them as a safety valve, a forum where Grangers could discuss "transportation and political questions" not allowed in local Grange halls.[52] As grass-roots innovations, county councils were begun and run by local Granges, not by the State Grange.[53]

A county council could deal as a unit with wholesalers and manufacturers outside the county but might split between different towns' boosters when bargaining with retailers within the county. So district councils could be formed in counties that had more than one trade center. Five Fillmore County and two Mower County Granges formed the Spring Valley [District] Council "to meet the local interests of the Granges tributary to that place"; a separate council met in Preston, the Fillmore County seat.[54] A polity worked best if its members traded at the same place.

A county council held about four meetings every year, normally at the county seat. Farmers did not yet have the intense anti-county-seat feelings that later prevailed in the Farmers' Alliance era of the 1880s and 1890s, feelings that would cause them to hold countywide meetings away from the county seat. A body of farmer-delegates meeting at the county seat to discuss grievances alarmed local editors and county officials. Agrarian republicanism, the Grange's aspirations to inclusivity, and its focus on political and economic issues made its county council a greater potential threat to elected officials than was any church conference or lodge meeting. In the county council, the Grange republic came the closest to paralleling and second-guessing the constitutional republic, in which the people were sovereign but which did not provide for their elected delegates to meet separately from (but in the same town as) their elected officials, the county board. The county board and the county council might maintain their separate spheres, but which would have greater legitimacy in case of conflict remained to be determined. Yet clearly where the official democracy limited its power to act in eco-

The State Grange met for an important social function during its two-day annual meeting in Northfield in 1878. Founder Oliver H. Kelley's portrait hangs above the Welcome banner.

nomic matters, it had to accept unofficial ones assuming the role in such matters.[55]

Old Stock politicking meant the county council did not stick to its economic sphere. The county council became a watchdog warily eying county government. In Freeborn County, it fought with county commissioners over the county attorney's pay raise, advocated cost-cutting measures, and considered calling a county convention to nominate independent candidates for county and legislative posts.[56] In the 1870s tradition and expensive courthouses had not yet given tenure to county seats; in Faribault County, the Grange secretary's campaign to move the county seat from Blue Earth to Delavan came close enough to success to alarm county-seat leaders.[57]

The county councils led the statewide drive toward a farmer-controlled third party in the 1873 state election. The Patrons were at the pinnacle of their popularity in Minnesota that year; political leaders like former Congressman Ignatius Donnelly used that popularity to create the Anti-Monopoly Party—primarily through the county councils, since rules forbade township Granges from discussing partisan politics. Republican Grangers protested, and "an acrimonious split developed in the Grange over the political activities of the Grange county councils," noted Woods.[58]

Thus editors of newspapers located in county seats had good reasons to try to influence county councils. They became council delegates and officers. They wrote editorials warning against radical moves, such as bypassing county boards and local merchants (prime advertisers in the newspapers) or relocating county seats. Two weeks after the formation of the Steele County Council, an Owatonna editor counseled against independent political action or ambitious economic measures, which he satirized as attempts "to dip the sea dry with a clam shell." Hotchkiss cautioned Patrons about "things . . . they should not do . . . acts calculated to embarrass home industry, home enterprise and business."[59] Some Grangers called these editorial nervous Nellies the Grange's "worst enemies," working to "build up the county seat." Given Old Stock ties to townsmen, however, farmers' anti-county-seat feelings were not yet strong enough to uphold that charge or to exclude editors.[60]

Despite editors' worries, the county council was not invariably radical or antimerchant. It was whatever local Grangers wanted it to be, and some did not want strong action. Freeborn's council rejected third-party politics and a proposed cooperative store. For its first three years, it elected a purchasing agent, but it declined to do so after 1875.[61] A Fillmore council motion to appoint a purchasing agent provoked "a spirited discussion" of its "propriety." Hotchkiss "moved to indefinitely postpone the whole subject, which was adopted." Eight months later, he changed his mind, and the council elected a Preston man as agent.[62] The Rice County Council, for its part, cooperated with the merchants' board of trade.[63]

A county council's joint purchasing was straightforward. Its agent was either paid a salary or received a commission—Fillmore's earned a one thousand dollar salary; Freeborn's, a 5 percent commission.[64] The agent ordered directly from wholesalers or manufacturers, often at considerable savings. Freeborn's Grangers saved 43 percent on thirteen Workman seeders and, indirectly, "a much greater Sum" by forcing local implement dealers "to moderate their prices."[65] Windom's Grangers claimed to get a 30 to 40 percent price reduction on goods their agent ordered from Chicago.[66]

Grangers lowered expenses by buying (1) directly from wholesalers or manufacturers—avoiding middlemen's commissions and margins, (2) in large quantities at a lower per-unit cost, and (3) with cash, thus eliminating credit fees.[67] NEPU Union Stores earned these same savings, but there wholesalers dealt with established stores. Here a purchasing agent had to convince wholesalers and manufacturers that a joint order from an informal farmers' organization was as credible as a store's order and that their savings on credit and commission costs and their higher sales volumes would guarantee them lower per-unit costs to pass on to Grangers in the form of lower prices.

Backward Integration Collides with Forward Integration

Some manufacturers already knew that bypassing middlemen and dealing with customers directly meant lower costs and higher profits. Economists call this forward integration—moving forward (closer to consumers) on the chain of production and exchange that carries products from raw materials to final use. Joint purchasing was consumers' effort at integrating backward to deal with wholesalers or manufacturers directly—instead of through retailers. Railroads and telegraph lines made both types of integration possible by enabling the consumer to order from the manufacturer directly and the wholesaler or manufacturer to ship goods right to the consumer—by enabling all of them to bypass the local merchant. With rail and telegraph service, the merchant's functions had been simplified so united consumers or determined manufacturers could act as their own merchants, if they would do the needed work. With rail service, for example, Grange agents needed little capital because long-term storage of large inventories to last the winter was no longer necessary.[68]

The Grangers' backward integration collided with one manufacturer's forward integration when the Grange tried to deal with C. H. McCormick & Bro., maker of farm implements. McCormick's reapers and other machines were too expensive for small capital-starved implement dealers to stock or for most farmers to purchase with cash. McCormick had to be its own wholesaler and retailer. It employed agents with exclusive territories to demonstrate, sell, and repair machines, set credit ratings, and collect on overdue accounts.[69] In March 1873, O. E. Rundell, a Grange purchasing agent, wrote to M. T. Grattan, a local McCormick agent, to ask if he wanted "to make any arrangements to sell machines to Patrons" and hinted at a boycott if Grattan refused.[70] Grattan sent the letter to McCormick; the company replied that its integration forward was a nonnegotiable item. Rundell's demand that it sell through Grange-approved agents was like ordering a store owner to hire only Grange-approved clerks. McCormick threatened to halt sales in areas where Grangers insisted it use their agents. The company had internalized market transactions by bypassing wholesalers and implement dealers, but it now preached market mechanisms: "Prices are things that regulate themselves and cannot be changed by all the societies in creation."[71] Forward integration gave it more control over retail prices than that disingenuous statement indicated. It reaped two of the three savings Grangers sought: no middlemen's commissions or margins and low per-unit costs stemming from high-volume sales.

After someone leaked the McCormick letter to the press, Editor Hotchkiss noted that the company showed "more testiness in their reply than comports with their reputation as discreet business men."[72] To quell the storm, Cyrus H. McCormick, in an open letter to the *Chicago Daily Tribune*, offered Grangers a chance to buy direct from the factory at a lower, cash-only price, which was available to non-Grangers, too. Insisting on one price for all enabled him to sound more democratic than the Grange.[73] The Patrons' decline ended the matter.

The Relative Failure of Grangers' Joint Purchasing

Even where manufacturers had not integrated forward, the drawbacks of the agency system hindered joint purchasing. The agent was a part-time, temporary salesman whose future did not hang on customer satisfaction and sales volume. The county council was a democracy, not a store that could be easily held accountable. A disgruntled customer had to work at political persuasion to win majority support for his complaint. It was easier to take his business elsewhere. For one thing, Grangers could not hold agents responsible for defective goods.[74] After the state Grange master sent the Freeborn council a letter praising the Warner harvester, which was manufactured by the Iowa state Grange, several Grangers ordered it, but four complained the Warner "failed to work as represented." So Freeborn's Grange leaders wrote to their state agent about "the said defective Harvesters, and request[ed] him to cause those machines to be put in good working order as soon as practicable." There is no evidence that he did. It is unlikely given the Warner's—and the agency system's—poor record.[75]

Thus joint purchasing had advantages and disadvantages. Because it required little capital, it brought few risks, being easily started, easily ended. Moreover it could be delegated to a self-seeking promoter. These features were a reflection of the Grangers' lack of solidarity, which brought disadvantages. Citing joint purchasing as "one of the main Objects of our Order," the Burnside Grange supported a boycott of recalcitrant implement dealers and manufacturers but only "as far as it is possible."[76] Lacking solidarity, the members became suspicious of agents. Furthermore, the fear of county councils' meddling in politics and the bond of Old Stock ethnic ties brought in editors who frowned on joint purchasing and deterred its supporters from the task of perfecting it.

Immigrant farmers showed that, with solidarity, joint purchasing could work. By spring 1874, Norwegian-American farmers in Renville County had used Granger joint-purchasing methods for several years in Normania *Farmerforening* (farmers' association). They chose an agent to negotiate purchases of farm implements and formed a township mutual. A few farmers bound by ethnic and denominational ties, a homogeneous polity living in a small area, could successfully organize in limited markets—the farm implement and fire insurance markets.[77]

Entrepreneurs also used Granger joint-purchasing methods. Their high returns on invested capital were greater incentives than consumers' small savings on purchases. When Grangers made a deal with Aaron Montgomery Ward to purchase his goods at wholesale prices, their backward integration aided a wholesaler's forward integration. Both bypassed local retailers, but Montgomery Ward went on to become a high-volume, discount, mail-order house while Grange agents mostly disappeared with the decline of the Patrons.[78]

Grangers Attempt to Organize Consumers' Cooperatives

Grangers needed established stores, not ad hoc agents. They knew of the Union store precedent and of the 1870 law authorizing cooperative associations. They had the Grange, an existing farm group that simplified the task of organizing a store; organizational costs had already been paid in forming it, and it lent its prestige to cooperative stores it sponsored.

Grangers had county councils to start stores. Yet the story of the councils' attempts at forming cooperative stores is a tale quickly told. None succeeded. The Freeborn council tried. In April 1874 it appointed a three-man committee to explore the possibility of organizing a Grange store, but it was probably just trying to wring concessions from local merchants.[79] It incorporated as an association and sold shares but dropped the project after three years.[80] Ethnic ties between Old Stock Grangers and merchants discouraged that ultimate threat to merchants, a competing store. Also, Old Stock farmers knew of the NEPU's failure, and their county councils were handicapped by geographical factions. Some delegates would want the store located in one town and some in another.

A local Grange could set up a store, for its members traded in the same town or lived near the same crossroads, which became the agreed-upon site for the Grange store. Several Freeborn County Granges did that, and opposition to a Grange store in Albert Lea likely came from these Granges, who had their own small cooperative stores and would not welcome the competition.[81] In 1873 Oak Hill Grange in northwestern Bancroft Township had twenty-four mostly Old Stock members living in the Frost neighborhood near the District 20 schoolhouse. They started a store a half mile from the school on the farm of Grange Master Henry R. Loomis, a Pennsylvanian.[82] Being near a school did not generate much retail traffic for the store. Having a post office nearby would have helped, but Bancroft's post office was at the other end of the township. The Frost neighborhood was an Old Stock island surrounded by Scandinavian Americans. The Grange's limited appeal to immigrants meant that the store could not rely on their patronage, nor could it count on having a future.

Granger agitation led to only one long-lived cooperative store—one created by a Norwegian-American group. In November 1873, the Fremad reading society of north-central Pope County heard member Michael A. Wollan make an offer. Wollan and his brother, Casper T., owned a dry-goods store in Glenwood, while another brother, Nels B., had a grocery store on his farm near town. Michael Wollan invited Fremad's members to form a joint-stock company to run the dry-goods store. With their ethnic homogeneity and common membership in a reading society, they were an ideal polity to manage it. Grangers were thinking of starting a Grange store in Glenwood, the county seat. Wollan warned of "how impossible it would be to come to such harmony" as they enjoyed in Fremad "if they organized a so-called 'Grange' [store], which besides is a terrible idea in and of itself."[83] They agreed. Ethnicity linked Norwegian-American merchants and farmers, who formed the Fremad Association, which was "not a Grange store," they noted. It began with the Rochdale rule of one vote per person, but after the Grange declined and the Wollans no longer feared a Grange store, this rule was changed to one vote per share. The Wollans then dominated the Fremad Association, which stayed in business for seven decades.[84]

Old Stock Grangers often chose individual merchants to run so-called Grange stores.[85] This method was even less cooperative than the Wollans' management had been. Grangers decided what terms to demand (prices at 8 to 10 percent above cost) but had no voice in day-to-day operations and no share in the profits. A county council offered Grangers' patronage to the merchant in exchange for discount prices. Merchants wanted high-volume, cash-only sales, but Grangers demanded that the savings be passed on in the form of discount prices. Negotiations were not always amicable. Few merchants wished to bargain with a group of customers who proposed to make pricing decisions. After threatening to boycott one merchant, the Grangers heard that his "faith in the grange had increased amazingly."[86] In other cases no deal could be negotiated.[87]

Most such agreements involved stores in county seats (see Table A in Appendix). Grangers near small villages could rarely find merchants willing to sell on their terms.[88] There one or two storeowners controlled a small neighborhood market and refused to bargain. Fewer benefits accrued to Grange stores in villages because size limited the potential sales volume. Grangers living near a county seat more often found a merchant eager for the high sales volume of a Grange store.[89] During the Grange's heyday, such stores existed in Owatonna, Medford, Faribault, and Benson, all of which had the daily rail service a high-volume store needed.[90] Like the national arrangement that launched Montgomery Ward, local pacts created local high-volume, discount retailers.[91]

Owatonna's Grange store was a good example that was fully reported in the *Owatonna Journal*. In summer 1873, the county council selected John A. Cansdell's store "as the headquarters of the Grangers of Steele county." Cansdell was then building a two-story addition to his shop. A native of Wisconsin, he had moved to Owatonna four years earlier, with only thirty dollars in capital. Owatonna's location at the intersection of two railroads made such capital-poor stores possible. He may have agreed to the Grangers' terms because he was a newcomer desperate for patronage and without established customers. Deal in hand, he headed to the East Coast on a buying trip and returned with "an immense stock of merchandise." His hopes were realized as his store prospered despite "the financial panic [of 1873] and the combined efforts of those who oppose [it]." Owatonna merchants applauded its drawing power: "Hundreds of families come here for supplies who have been in the habit of trading at other points." Soon they built stores and shops near the Grange Store, whose receipts hit close to a thousand dollars on some days and nearly ninety thousand dollars per year. Its location next to the two train depots allowed easy access to the "car loads of goods unloading every few days." However, the county council did not renew the agreement in December 1874. "His health unequal to the work and care of so large a business," he sold off his inventory.[92]

Like J. D. Blake and Company's Union store substitute, Cansdell's store was really a Grange store substitute, for Grangers had "delegated" cooperation to him. With his fame as a discounter established, he could have continued without a Grange deal, as Aaron Ward did, if his health had not failed. After the Grange faded from its peak, it had little members' patronage to offer a merchant.

Such deals used a merchant's self-interest to make up for Grangers' disinterest in anything but cheap prices. In order to form a truly cooperative store more was needed. The *Grange Illustrated* (1874) noted, "In the ordinary co-operative store societies there are no bonds of union except that of buying cheap." Such stores did not last. To succeed, a store society's members "must belong, for the most part, to the same class; must have many interests in common, and must be drawn to each other by such ties that they will feel a deep interest in each other."[93] Such solidarity formed within a class that saw itself opposed by another class, not within a class whose one grievance was that of buying dear. Old Stock Grangers complained of too many country stores charging too high prices and of price collusion by the "kid-gloved gentry," but they did not see merchants as a permanent, opposing class.[94]

Immigrant farmers often felt Old Stock merchants were an opposing class. In Pope County, they used ethnic solidarity (even ethnic ties to a Norwegian-American merchant) to start their own store rather than join the Grange, whose failure to recruit immigrants weakened its attempts to establish its own stores. When the Grange declined, these few Grange-sponsored stores shared its fate, as they disappeared or converted to private ownership.

Grangers Attempt to Organize Farmers' Mutual Fire Insurance

Farmers were also consumers purchasing fire insurance, which they considered to be too expensive. Here was a more promising field for co-operation: great savings were possible, although only on one farm expense. There was a narrower field, which concentrated Grangers' minds on fewer choices. They need not risk capital, buy inventory, construct buildings, or debate a site, for there was none. No rail service was needed. And they all bought in the same market and had the same interest in low-cost insurance.

Like Union stores, farmers' mutual fire insurance companies were eastern innovations. Owned by the policyholders, they insured only farm properties, hired no salaried agents, and usually charged no premium, but assessed the members a pro-rata portion of the loss after each fire. More than one hundred such mutuals existed in New England and the East by 1850.[95] The movement spread to the Old Northwest and to Minnesota, aided by Walter A. Nimocks, an editor who had assisted in organizing a farmers' mutual in Michigan. In July 1865 he helped create the Minnesota Farmers' Mutual Fire Insurance Association of Min-

neapolis (MFMFIAM), which he promoted in his monthly, the *Farmers'*
Union. He distributed thousands of free copies of this journal, very likely
with the MFMFIAM's help; one page of each issue was devoted to the
MFMFIAM.[96]

The MFMFIAM was a statewide mutual formed by Old Stock Americans and headquartered in Minneapolis. It appeased localism by allowing
one director for each county that had at least fifty members.[97] Minneapolis business leaders, including a banker who was Master of a Minneapolis Grange, and prosperous farmers dominated it in its early
years.[98] With "aggressive marketing," a promoter could succeed with a
mutual; policyholders, not he, invested the capital by paying fees and
dues.[99] The MFMFIAM was a promotional scheme designed to benefit
Minneapolis's future, Nimocks's journal, and a Minneapolis bank. It was
not much as a polity. Only fourteen members attended its 1871 annual
meeting.[100]

The company became a high-volume discount insurer by meeting
the farmers' wishes for "actual cost" insurance. Using a complicated system of member bank deposits, it assessed members for fire losses after
they occurred. It did not collect premiums to pay in advance for fire
losses that might not happen. Nominal membership fees plus minimal
annual dues covered administrative expenses.[101] The state insurance
commissioner questioned this system, but it worked.[102] For the first two
years, the annual cost of MFMFIAM insurance was only fourteen cents per
one hundred dollars of property insured. By December 1872, MFMFIAM's
share of all insured property in Minnesota was over 19 percent, close to
that of the state's other home company, St. Paul Fire and Marine Insurance Company, whose 1872 rate was $1.24 per one hundred dollars in-
sured.[103] The MFMFIAM had a risk-sharing pool of thousands of members, low administrative costs, no policies on urban high-risk properties,
no full-time commissioned agents, and no shareholders demanding
dividends.

Grangers were interested in this Old Stock statewide mutual, although they did not fully commit to it. To avoid high premiums, they
used two tactics: (1) democratizing the MFMFIAM and (2) obtaining legal
sanction for more democratic township mutuals. Grangers' advocacy of
farmers' mutuals worried the insurance industry, which tried to frus-
trate this strategy by using Grangers' legalistic uncertainties and state
officials' friendly help.

Who Stole House File 77, the Township Mutual Law?

Grangers first tried forming township mutual fire insurance companies, covering from one to several townships. Agitation for a law authorizing such mutuals came from Olmsted County's Old Stock farmers, who were familiar with similar mutuals in the East.[104] By January 1873, Viola Grangers had decided to organize a township mutual.[105] Probably at their request, State Representative Manley C. Fuller (Olmsted) introduced House File 77, "A bill to authorize the organization of town insurance companies." Under its provisions, township residents with combined property worth twenty-five thousand dollars could set up a company to insure "against loss by fire and lightning," using assessments only (no premiums), with the right to sue members who were delinquent in paying assessments.[106]

Rochester's newspapers expressed support for the idea. Less than 20 percent of the premiums paid by Rochester-area residents was returned as reimbursements for fire losses.[107] The *Minnesota Record*'s St. Paul correspondent noted, "No city property is insured," so "the losses will be comparatively light," and no "salaried agent" would siphon off farmers' hard-earned dollars. "The money will be kept at home until actually needed, and when paid out it will be to a friend or neighbor in the hour of need."[108] Editors could endorse home insuring as well as home manufacturing.

The House also approved, passing H.F. 77 by a vote of seventy-one to seventeen. Senate passage followed by a margin of twenty-four to fifteen votes, after its Senate foes (at the request of private insurers) had amended the bill to authorize township mutuals in only eight counties.[109] Shortly after passage, Viola's Grangers formed a mutual and began to sign up members.[110]

Just then, the Olmsted County Council debated the two options—joining a Granger-dominated MFMFIAM or forming township mutuals. A local MFMFIAM agent reported for the council's insurance committee; they recommended (no surprise) the MFMFIAM. The agent "did not wish to see too much haste in endorsing" township mutuals. Critics of the MFMFIAM spoke up. A Viola man found its membership fee too high. Yet any mutual's postfire assessments would be cheaper than the St. Paul Fire and Marine premiums that he now paid. "In Viola there had not been losses by fire to exceed $2,000 in the past 10,000 years, (laughter) and he was willing to stand his portion at that rate." He favored township mutuals. A Chatfield Granger noted the difficulty of democratically running a statewide mutual with offices in Minneapolis. With the MFMFIAM books kept in a distant city, "it was impossible to know exactly the company's standing." A township mutual's books "would be under the inspection of all." The council endorsed the township mutual.[111]

The decision was moot. Viola Grangers had obtained pledges from persons owning only fifteen thousand dollars in property, not the twenty-five thousand dollars required. Worse, what they thought was a law was not. "Uncle Henry," a critic of the Grange, chortled, "But the fun of the joke is there is no law for any such company."[112] Six weeks after passage of H.F. 77, Governor Austin had not signed it. Representative Fuller wrote to him: "Question? was the said bill presented to you, if so did it, or not, become a law[?] Farmers are inquiring—with a view of organizing under its provisions, if it became a law." On the back of the letter, Austin scribbled a note for his staff, "What has become of H.F. No. 77?" He did not get a clear answer, for he instructed his secretary, "Write that the bill never reached me. That I heard that such a bill had passed & was looking for it but it never came to hand."[113]

Fuller informed Viola's Grangers, who were enraged: "The 'insurance law' that was passed last winter" had been "strangled by the monopolizing rings and licensed thieves, so abundant in this State and especially in St. Paul." H.F. 77 was "stolen," and farmers had been "betrayed by dishonest men."[114] They dropped plans for a township mutual. "Uncle Henry" was right; Old Stock farmers needed legal authorization: "There are some of their members who would pay losses just as long as it was for their interest, and no longer, and there is no law to compel them to."[115] Without a law to compel payment of assessments, they would not create mutuals.

H.F. 77 may have been stolen by Austin's private secretary, Andrew R. McGill, the state's delegate to an earlier national insurance convention and soon to be appointed insurance commissioner by Austin.[116] McGill, a critic of township mutuals, later called H.F. 77 "a bill ... for an indiscriminate organization" of mutuals. It "only awaited the signature of the governor—which was prudently withheld—to become a law."[117] Lobbied by the insurance industry, McGill probably "prudently withheld" H.F. 77 from Austin, who winked at this maneuver since it enabled him to tell Grangers he had not vetoed their bill.[118] Fearing that Granger-backed township mutuals would be dangerous competitors, insurance companies apparently convinced their state regulator to stop the threat.

Grangers Seize Control of the MFMFIAM and Investigate It

Gaining control of the MFMFIAM then became the Grangers' tactic of choice. At the 1873 state Grange convention, State Secretary William Paist recommended support for the MFMFIAM ("unless we organize one of our own on a similar basis") but called for a committee "to examine as to its safety." After "searching scrutiny," it "cheerfully and heartily recommended" MFMFIAM as good "actual cost" insurance. At the January 1874 MFMFIAM annual meeting, 90 percent of the new officers and directors were Grangers. The *Farmers' Union* exulted, "It Passes into the Control of the Order of Patrons of Husbandry."[119]

Private insurers were also apprehensive over the popular Grange running a proven statewide company that had 150 agents. Industry leaders tried to prevent this competition by political means, which was fitting— the subject of statewide fire insurance for farmers drew ambitious politicians like a candle's flame draws moths. At a January 1874 meeting of the Grange state executive committee, an insurance industry lawyer from St. Paul and an agent proposed a Farmers' Stock Insurance Company.[120] The two men obtained a second probe of the MFMFIAM, with former Lieutenant-Governor Charles D. Sherwood chairing the investigating committee. An unfavorable verdict from Sherwood's group would likely shift the Grangers' support to the proposed joint-stock company.[121] Private insurers also tried to destroy the MFMFIAM by having a bill requiring it to possess one hundred thousand dollars in capital stock introduced in the legislature.[122] No one expected it could raise that amount.

Predictably the Sherwood committee's report strongly criticized the MFMFIAM. The president of St. Paul Fire and Marine, J. C. Burbank, paid to have the report printed in the *St. Paul Daily Press*, along with his letter attacking the leaders who aided this "fraud upon the farmers," this "rotten concern." In their reply, MFMFIAM officers ridiculed the report: "In due time, after the great labor of the mountain, the egg was successfully hatched, and the Old Cock [Burbank] who had been watching the nest all the time, was the first one to cackle over [it]."[123] Seeing a Minneapolis company threatened by a St. Paul one, the *Minneapolis Daily Tribune* defended the MFMFIAM, attacked the insurance companies, and called Sherwood their "tool."[124] He denied it and charged that Nimocks had offered him free insurance in order to secure a favorable report.[125] The debate occupied the Twin Cities press for days.

Although lengthy and technical, the report found no smoking gun.[126] Using McGill's reasoning, it claimed the MFMFIAM lacked sufficient assets to guarantee farmers payment of fire losses.[127] It ignored the mutual's main asset, farmers' support. McGill was now insurance commissioner, his salary paid by fees levied on the insurance companies, and the report echoed his view that a mutual could not succeed without the capital stock that a corporation needed.[128] That claim ignored differences between mutuals and corporations. The main MFMFIAM defense was that it was a farmers' mutual (after all, John Q. Farmer was its president).[129] Showing their support of MFMFIAM, Grangers' letters and resolutions filled the *Farmers' Union*, which added an editorial defense.[130]

Meanwhile the Grangers' legislative leader, State Senator Ignatius Donnelly, led the fight against the capital-stock bill. An MFMFIAM policyholder, he had paid twenty dollars to insure his library at one thousand dollars for sixteen years. He declared, "That was, as Senators would see, much cheaper than any other company would insure," and he "felt like speaking well of the bridge which had carried him safe over." He built a bridge to carry the MFMFIAM safe over by lowering the amount to seventy-five thousand dollars and by "offer[ing] an amendment that the $75,000 now on deposit, belonging to the company be recognized as such capital stock." It passed and the MFMFIAM was home free.[131]

The debate showed the problems a statewide cooperative faced. As a private entity, it should not have been subject to public debate, but it was publicly discussed when voters and newspaper letter writers who did business with it interested themselves in its affairs. Its competitors joined in, although they could not similarly interfere in a private competitor's decision-making process. Also involved were politicians like Donnelly and Sherwood who sought popularity by saving the cooperative for voters or rescuing voters from it. Given Grangers' involvement in politics, a cooperative with ties to the Patrons could not completely avoid a similar entanglement. Near the time when the capital-stock bill was debated, the Senate honored a Grange lobbying committee, including Sherwood, and "ordered chairs to be placed for them upon the floor of the Senate."[132] The MFMFIAM could hardly avoid being placed on the floor for debate as well.

Sherwood did not save the Grangers from the MFMFIAM, which became their preferred farmers' mutual. It was still there in 1886 when voters promoted McGill to the governorship and when the Minnesota Grange was a shadow of its former self. Partly, that decline was due to a partisan political split between Anti-Monopolists like Donnelly and Republicans like Sherwood—a split that underlay the dispute over the MFMFIAM's soundness.[133]

Whatever the differences over the MFMFIAM, the Grangers had now agreed to abandon the township mutual tactic. When a Norwegian-American legislator introduced a township mutual bill in 1874, the *Farmers' Union* cautioned, "This plan of insurance does very well in the wealthy and populous counties in the Eastern States" but would not work in Minnesota "where the population is so sparse and the people so poor." Here, one statewide mutual able to absorb large losses was "more satisfactory" than many small ones that could be crushed by losses.[134] New England's example was seen as irrelevant for Minnesota's Old Stock farmers.[135]

In insurance, Grangers sought safety in numbers by turning to a statewide mutual started by promoters. In retailing, they harnessed one merchant's self-interest and pooled their efforts, rather than relying on their own cooperative spirit. In both cases, they had "no bonds of union except that of buying cheap"—and partisan political squabbling weakened even that bond. Although a merchant like Cansdell or an editor-promoter like Nimocks used that bond to build a business, it was not strong enough to sustain a true cooperative. Immigrant farmers had an added ethnic bond; Old Stock ethnicity was weak, even in the Grange. Yet perhaps the fault lay with consumers' cooperation, which offered only small savings (or a large saving on one expense—insurance).[136] Possibly farmers could cooperate as producers of wheat, their main source of income. A small per-bushel increase in wheat prices would bring a greater financial gain than a small per-barrel decrease in the cost of store candy. A common interest in selling dear might prove to be a stronger bond than buying cheap.

3

Grangers as Producers

"Success, say we,
to the Grange warehouse"

LESS THAN A YEAR after showing their unity by defeating the Jesse James gang in 1876, Northfield citizens split over a lawsuit filed by Jesse Ames and Sons, flour millers, against a Grange flour mill one mile downstream on the Cannon River. The Ames firm alleged that the Grangers' mill dam caused water levels to rise, hampering their milling, and demanded that the dam be lowered by eighteen inches.[1] Angered at reports that Northfield merchants "urged on the plaintiffs to crush out the [Grange] company," local Grangers adopted resolutions threatening a long war against the merchants. The Grangers charged that, for Ames and Sons, "the extra price paid for wheat" due to the Grange mill caused "ten fold more damage than the back water" from the dam. The lawsuit was meant to lower wheat prices, not a dam.[2]

Stung by the Grangers' statements that the merchants gave "biased testimony" in the case, Mayor Solomon P. Stewart, a lumber dealer, noted in a letter to the editor that farmers had been "very well satisfied" with the Ames mill. Then, upon joining the Grange, "you made the astounding discovery that Messrs. Ames & Sons were making money" and turned against them. Using the small-town maxim about boosting not knocking local firms, he advised Grangers to "not try to build up your business by tearing down another's."[3]

Agreeing, a writer calling himself "Fair Play" declared that the Grange mill was "a benefit to the community," which did not justify its exemption from "the ordinary laws of justice and right." Grangers "are not satisfied with the aid of the Courts . . . but they must invoke the strength

of a powerful secret order to . . . bully their opponents into submission."
(Again, the Grange's characteristics were used to judge the cooperatives
it sponsored.) John T. Ames, the miller, also warned against "secret societies" and denied that the Grange mill was a poor underdog battling the
rich Ames family, stating that "the wealthy farmers" of "the Grange
Mill Co. represent as much or more wealth than any company in Southern Minnesota" and "many times the wealth of Jesse Ames' sons." He
charged that Grange mill officers had asked the Ames firm "to reduce
the price of wheat [that it paid to farmers], saying, wheat was too high
here." That move would have hurt farmers but would have raised the
Grange mill's profits.

 After pro-Ames statements by the judge and a pro-Ames decision by
the jury, the Rice County District Court ruled that the dam be lowered
three and three-quarter inches, instead of the requested eighteen inches,
and that the Grange mill pay Ames $530. When the Grangers appealed,
the Minnesota Supreme Court upheld the ruling.[4]

*The Grange mill at Waterford, one mile downstream from Northfield on the Can-
non River around 1900, after it had passed out of the Grangers' ownership. Presumably the mill dam had been lowered the court-ordered level.*

This conflict involved the same antagonisms between merchants and farmers that often erupted in county councils. The Grange's essential features, such as secrecy, affected people's opinions of its business ventures. In this case, Grangers ran a separate business. An "extra price paid for wheat" was a strong incentive to do so. Selling dear was a greater "bond of union" than buying cheap. United by common interests as wheat farmers, Grangers formed wheat storage, marketing, and processing cooperatives in southeastern Minnesota—the center of Grange strength, of the Old Stock population, and of 1870s wheat raising. Not all were true cooperatives controlled by farmers, not investors.

Wheat Industry Improvements as Grangers' Opportunities

An abiding myth in American history is that the Grange's growth was due to "the advent of hard times in the early 1870's."[5] When the Panic of 1873 hit in September, however, there were already more than five thousand Granges nationally and some 330 in Minnesota. The Grange's greatest expansion occurred from 1870 to 1873, years of rising wheat prices and "fairly favorable" wheat harvests.[6] Identifying farmers' motives for joining the Grange is crucial to comprehending where and when they formed cooperatives, how these operated, and why these failed. Grangers were not merely agrarian protesters with knee-jerk reactions to grievances and hard times but also agrarian opportunists, seizing the right time to integrate forward into the marketing and processing of wheat.

When they flocked to the Grange in 1870–73, Minnesota farmers had completed a successful decade in which spring wheat had become their main cash crop. By 1869, 60 percent of the tilled land in Minnesota was planted in wheat. Wheat always commanded a cash market (other crops could often only be bartered), had low weight and bulk relative to its value so it could be profitably hauled long distances, was easy to grow on newly tilled land, and was readily harvested by the new farm machinery. In 1862 a Cottage Grove pastor noted that men there "dream about wheat at night, and I fear go to meeting Sabbath Day to think about wheat." Four years later that same pastor commented, "Nothing interests the people of this community more than the price of wheat."[7]

Almost everything about wheat farming improved during the 1860s. The price of wheat in the Twin Cities market rose from $.50 per bushel in 1861 to $1.50 in 1866. In the postwar deflation, prices declined to around

$.80 by 1870 but then showed an upswing.[8] Expectations of price in-
creases caused more farmers to grow wheat. For decades, farm spokesmen had called for expanding exports to Europe. During the Civil War
and the 1870s, a sharp rise in exports seemed to fulfill their dreams.[9]
Mechanization made these higher exports possible by allowing farmers
to plant and harvest more acres of wheat. Riding plows, grain drills,
self-raking reapers, and horse-powered threshers greatly aided farmers.
The value of farm machinery owned by Minnesota farmers rose from
little over $1 million in 1860 to $6.7 million a decade later.[10]

Transportation also improved. Before 1862 there were no railroads in
Minnesota, forcing farmers to rely on water transport. Farmers far from
a navigable river hauled wagon loads of wheat long distances—often 80
to 150 miles—to a river town. River transportation was frozen out in
winter and hampered by low water during some summers. By 1870 more
than one thousand miles of track had been laid. A Danish American in
Freeborn County recalled in 1869, "Four or five years ago, we traveled
about one hundred miles with our crops to the Winona or La Crosse
markets; now however we have three good-sized towns and four railroad
stations at a distance of about ten to twenty miles." Minnesota farmers
could ship their wheat by rail to eastern markets by way of Milwaukee or
Chicago.[11]

Wheat marketing became more efficient. When wheat was shipped
via the Mississippi from Winona, for instance, storage, transportation,
commission, and transfer costs cut the local wheat price to only 62 percent of the New York price. With trains came efficiencies: railroad-
owned elevators at local stations meant no long haul to river ports, rail
shipments to eastern markets ended the need for winter storage, and
lower middleman costs resulted once a few wheat buyers specialized,
bargained with railroads to cut freight rates, and won economies of scale.
Winona prices rose to an average of 70 percent of New York prices for
1868–75.[12]

The local wheat market also improved. Minnesota's flour-milling
industry grew during the 1860s from 81 mills to 216 mills and from $1.3
million to $7.5 million worth of flour produced. By 1876 there were 23
mills in Goodhue County alone.[13] Country millers "generally paid well"
for wheat, and their demand for it drove up local wheat prices. In the
early 1870s, railroads hauling to Milwaukee and to Duluth competed
for wheat with a rate war at competing points where shippers had a

choice of railroads. In 1874–75, competition between different haulers helped push the Winona price to 80 percent of the New York price.[14]

But what was an improvement to the frontier farmer was a grievance to the established, commercial farmer, who expected even more. In December 1870, farmer "X" complained, "Since the railroad touched Albert Lea, it has been a poorer wheat market than any other place in southern Minnesota." He expected relief from unfair wheat prices when a grain elevator was built, "but no relief comes."[15] Access to trains and elevators ended the farmer's need to make the long haul to Winona, but they did not make Albert Lea's wheat price equal to nearby Austin's.

Towns competed for the wheat trade. Local merchants had a bonanza when farmers streamed into town to market wheat and a disaster when they went to a competing town's wheat buyers who offered more favorable pricing, grading, or weighing policies. Merchants, their board of trade, and the editor then pressured local buyers to alter the policies. Thus competition between towns tended to limit unfair trade practices in wheat buying.

In July 1873 in Albert Lea, for example, the *Freeborn County Standard* reported a Granger's complaint that local wheat buyers offered him eleven cents per bushel less than buyers in a nearby town. The editor investigated and was satisfied with the buyers' answer: the wheat was damaged. Someone "weighed himself upon a wheat buying scale," then on one he knew was accurate, and "found that he had gained 27 pounds." The editor urged an investigation. He soon faced another problem—closed wheat warehouses—which, he assured farmers, was only temporary, for bookkeeping purposes; buyers would probably "accommodate any who should chance to come in with wheat." A month later, in regard to the alleged false weights, he endorsed a wheat buyer's plan that a "disinterested" party do the weighing. Then, shortly after the onset in September of the Panic of 1873, matters became more serious when W. W. Cargill, a major buyer, stopped buying at Albert Lea because he could not obtain credit in the East. Local merchants offered him credit if he would pay farmers "the highest price the Chicago and Milwaukee markets would bear." Some months later, the editor crowed about the benefits wrought by high wheat prices: "Hundreds of persons have been here to market their produce and do their trading, who never put in an appearance before."[16] Merchants, editors, and their towns had a huge stake in wheat buyers' treatment of farmers.

Grangers seized the opportunity to start wheat-buying cooperatives that would raise wheat prices, increase a town's trade, and enjoy merchants' and editors' support. Rail service was essential to fostering such developments. As with country retailing, by lowering transportation and storage costs, trains made it possible for a wheat buyer to buy and sell wheat with much less capital than before. Trains "created a year-round market," ending the buyer's speculative risk of holding wheat over winter. The telegraph brought the buyer daily price data. The small risk in holding wheat for days or weeks he could pass on to speculators through futures contracts at the Chicago Board of Trade.[17]

Moreover, the timing was right for the Grangers. Entrepreneurs did not have much of a head start—W. W. Cargill only began to build grain elevators and warehouses along the tracks in 1867–69. They would make rapid progress: in a few years, Jason C. Easton of Chatfield "built warehouses at every station on the Southern Minnesota" Railroad (SMRR), signed a sweetheart, low-rate deal with the SMRR, and even dictated to the SMRR's telegraph operators what wheat prices they could send along the line, thus deceiving his competitors. Railroads needed the wheat buyers. Wheat was an important source of freight revenues, which dependable wheat buyers could capture for a friendly railroad. And railroads preferred not to invest capital in warehouses or elevators but to let wheat buyers do so.[18] Private ownership of railroads, so unlike Europe's government ownership, plagued Minnesota farmers for fifty years. To ensure stability, railroads preferred local wheat-buying monopolies like Easton's and opposed cooperatives, which disrupted stable freight patterns by unpredictably entering and then leaving the wheat industry.

Paradoxically, both improvements in the industry and farmers' grievances over remaining problems were opportunities for cooperative action. The main complaint was low local wheat prices.

Wheat-Marketing Grievances as Grangers' Opportunities, Too

Farmers cared more about local wheat prices than about how Winona prices compared to New York prices. Although Easton's SMRR deal brought local wheat prices "three to five cents nearer Milwaukee prices" and increased local farmers' income by fifty to eighty thousand dollars during one ten-month period, they disliked his monopoly. Minnesota's Grangers, while part of a national movement, acted according to local economic conditions. Their grievances cannot be dismissed because aggregate statistics reveal that the terms of trade "show a relative improvement for the farmer" between 1865 and 1900.[19] The farmer's sense of his situation did not come from aggregate statistics. Local terms of trade, local freight rates, and his personal expectations drove his response to the Grange lecturers' arguments for cooperation.[20] A cooperative "is the means whereby members by-pass the market *adjacent*, vertically, to them," noted Heflebower.[21] It was the adjacent market that mattered. Farmers complained when the benefits from improvements were not evenly distributed to each community in Minnesota's wheat-growing area. As historian Henrietta M. Larson pointed out, in the wheat trade "rate conditions in one locality do not necessarily affect the price in the determining market." One town's high costs do not force a higher national price; the town "finds the value of its products reduced" due to its higher costs. In 1874, she noted, the price of No. 1 wheat varied greatly from town to town:[22]

Minneapolis	$.85	Shakopee	$.75
St. James	.71	Willmar	.70
Melrose	.69	Breckenridge	.66

Wheat farmers blamed this spread on *local* market conditions, freight rates, flour millers, or wheat buyers.

Local grievances motivated Minnesota's wheat farmers to cooperate. In January 1873, editor E. H. Farnham of the *Wright County Eagle* complained of the "rascally private or corporate monopolist, who demand[ed] his toll" when the farmer came to town. Grain buyers and merchants were only agents of distant companies from whom it was useless to ask a fairer price. "They will listen only when compelled by interest, and *until we are able to pass them by* and obtain other purchasers for our goods we cannot appeal to their interest." Through bypassing the adjacent market, farmers could deposit their "produce in the market where it will command the highest price." Starting new organizations might seem to be "too great an undertaking," so Farnham recommended an "organization already in existence"—the Grange. If Granges were "really co-operative," then "by all means, let us have a Grange."[23]

That option avoided new organizational costs. Also the Grange's emphasis on farmers' common interests helped to hide the fact they competed against each other. At its meetings in Burnside Township near

Red Wing in Goodhue County, Burnside Grange #148 discussed "the
price of freights and the monopoly of R. Road and Steam Boat Co's,...
wheat culture, [and]...the diversified plan of farming." It invited officers
of the Vasa Grange to attend and, presumably, to discuss Vasa's attempts
at cooperation.[24]

Farnham was naïve to think that when organized farmers showed up
in terminal markets private firms would deal with them. A farmers' association with "25,000 bushels of wheat to dispose of" could more readily "demand the best market price" than could one farmer. Yet buyers at
local markets resisted farmers' attempts to bypass them, and dealers at
terminal markets sided with local buyers on that issue. Farnham correctly saw that farmers were motivated by local grievances—fraudulent scales, wheat buyers' deceitful down-grading of wheat, "exorbitant"
storage charges at warehouses, and wheat buyers' collusion to lower
wheat prices.[25]

The greatest complaint was of freight rate discrimination that favored one town over another. Each railroad tried to capture wheat shipments by using lower freight rates in towns (competing points) served by
a competing railroad and to restore its profits by charging higher rates in
towns (noncompeting points) where it faced no competition. To ship to
Chicago cost ten cents per bushel more from Faribault (a noncompeting
point) than from Farmington (a competing point), although the distance was less. Faribault's buyers could not pay farmers as high a price as
Farmington's. In 1870 the rate from Rochester (a noncompeting point) to
Winona (only forty-five miles) was fifteen cents per bushel; the rate
from Owatonna (a competing point) to Winona (ninety-two miles) was
only ten cents. Competition at Owatonna between the east-west Winona
and St. Peter Railroad (W&SP) and the north-south Milwaukee and St.
Paul Railway lowered freight rates and raised wheat prices there.[26] Some
wheat buyers also paid higher prices at competing points. To capture
more business, W. W. Cargill paid price rebates to farmers who lived between the SMRR and the W&SP and who sold wheat to his elevators on the
SMRR.[27]

Only at noncompeting points, such as Rochester, Faribault, and
Meriden, did Grangers form cooperative warehouses or flour mills (see
Table 1). At these locations the price gains from cooperation were worth
the risk of investing capital in warehouses or mills. Four warehouses—
at Albert Lea, Alden, Delavan, and Spring Valley—were built on the

SMRR, where Easton's near-monopoly meant little wheat-buying or railroad competition.

Local grievances caused Grangers to form wheat-marketing cooperatives; national or regional grievances did not justify starting a cooperative in all towns. The costs of forming a cooperative, buying stock, and building a warehouse or mill were too high relative to the probable financial benefits in towns where railroad competition already caused higher wheat prices. By cooperating at noncompeting points, farmers hoped to raise prices to the levels prevailing at competing points. By pooling the wheat from many farms at their own warehouse, they planned to bargain with the railroad over freight rates, as Easton had done.[28]

The primacy of local grievances and local opportunities doomed Grangers' national and regional wheat-marketing ideas. Kelley had proposed to market wheat through Grange agents in St. Louis or Chicago, and Grangers had formed the Mississippi Valley Trading Company, a national direct-marketing cooperative.[29] Another plan recommended that a state agent in Milwaukee market Grangers' wheat jointly.[30] That scheme

TABLE 1
The Effect of Railroad Competition on the Location of Granger Flour Mills and Warehouses—Southeast Minnesota[31]

Town	Mill or Warehouse	Competing or Noncompeting Point
Owatonna	Neither	Competing
Austin	Neither	Competing
Hastings	Neither	Competing
Mankato	Neither	Competing
Farmington	Neither	Competing
Winona	Neither	Competing
Northfield	Flour mill	Noncompeting*
Faribault	Flour mill	Noncompeting
Waseca	Warehouse	Noncompeting**
Le Roy	Warehouse	Noncompeting
Albert Lea	Warehouse	Noncompeting**
Alden	Warehouse	Noncompeting
Delavan	Warehouse	Noncompeting
Spring Valley	Warehouse	Noncompeting
Lake City	Warehouse	Noncompeting***
Dover	Warehouse	Noncompeting

Notes:
  * This mill was located one mile from Northfield, in Waterford, which had no railroad service.
 ** The north-south Minneapolis and St. Louis Railway reached Albert Lea in 1877 and Waseca in 1875–76, making them both competing points afterward.
*** Lake City had immediate access to competing water transportation along the Mississippi River.

required Granger supervision of a distant agent, working capital (unless he sold on consignment), and warehouses.[32] Joint marketing had the same defects as joint purchasing: an ad hoc agency was subject to democratic meddling, lacked the stability of an incorporated business, and suffered from frequent turnover of its agents. Because of its link to the Grange, it would not be patronized by non-Grangers.[33] Even at the local level, where Grangers could supervise an agent, joint marketing was not as effective as an incorporated warehouse or mill. The Blue Earth and Martin county councils tried using an agent, but it is unclear how long their ad hoc agencies lasted.[34]

A Debate: Cooperative Flour Mills or Cooperative Elevators?

Even at more promising noncompeting points and with the more profitable venture of wheat marketing, farmers still faced the question of whether to run a flour mill or a storage facility.[35] Should the Grangers store, weigh, grade, and market their wheat, or should they also integrate forward and control the milling? In March 1874, the townspeople of Austin, an Old Stock town at the junction of the SMRR and Chicago, Milwaukee, and St. Paul Railway (CM&SP), debated that issue after weeks of Grangers "agitating the question of erecting an elevator." (They debated even though Austin was a competing point where neither a Grange mill nor elevator was constructed.) The *Mower County Transcript* editor advised Grangers to build a mill to cut out middlemen's profits, end grading frauds, guarantee a good local wheat market, and keep milling profits in Austin.[36] The *Transcript* editor preferred home manufacturing.

The following week "X" (presumably a farmer) responded in the *Austin Register.* He argued that since there were already four flour mills in the area and none was making a large profit, why should Grangers start a mill? Farmers were not "itching to get into" another business— "they *believe* that *their* lemon is getting squeezed too often." A farmers' elevator would give them adequate "cheap storage" and freedom to bring wheat "on any day that the market price happens to suit." They could borrow money with stored wheat as collateral and ship to the terminal market offering the best price. A farmers' elevator would operate in their interest.[37] A week later the *Transcript* editor stressed a flour mill's benefits for farmers, not just for Austin. The farmer's interest "requires

him to put his product into the *best possible condition for market.*" The editor stretched the point; the farmer "might, just as properly sell his crop
before harvest, or before threshing, as before milling." More profits were
available from "the application of SKILL to the work of *manufacturing*"
than from the mere application of labor to farmers' fields. (W. W. Cargill
would have seconded this point after his unsuccessful integration backward from storing grain to also running a 5,760-acre farm ninety miles
west of Austin.) In addition, a mill gave the same benefits as an elevator:
cheap storage, convenience, "certificates of storage . . . as collateral," and
independence from local buyers.[38]

"X" would have none of it. If forward integration was needed, then
the farmer must "first turn miller and grind his grain, next baker and
make his flour into crackers, and finally, start an oyster saloon to get the
crackers eaten up." No, "wheat in the grain continues to bring more
money to the farmer than after it is manufactured into flour." More storage capacity was needed. Without it, farmers had to sell at harvest when
prices were low. The previous fall, lack of storage capacity and credit
forced them to sell wheat at thirty-five to forty-five cents per bushel
less than "if they could have held it 90 days longer." An elevator would
benefit the town: "Thousands upon thousands of bushels of wheat will
reach this market that otherwise would have gone elsewhere."[39]

There the Austin debate ended. No Granger mill or warehouse was
built in Austin, a competing point, but the same debate occurred in
other towns where other editors favored Grange mills without admitting that railroads would bring in distant flour that was cheaper than
"home" flour. A Faribault editor hailed a Grange mill and summarized
its benefits: it raised the local price of wheat by ten cents per bushel, it
paid out $180,000 annually to farmers, it raised land values within
twenty-five miles, it increased farmers' demand for banking services,
and it bought from local suppliers.[40] In Northfield, despite the presence
of the Ames and nearby Archibald mills, the *Northfield Standard* welcomed the Grange mill: "We cannot have too many good mills in this
wheat growing country." Yet the *Standard* editor (perhaps deliberately)
misinterpreted Grangers' aim to do grist milling that would complement, not compete against, the Ames and Archibald's merchant milling.
He sought to avoid conflict, but conflict there would be. (Grist millers
made flour for farmers who paid a "toll" in flour. Merchant millers made
flour for cash sale beyond local markets.)[41]

Certainly projected increases in local wheat prices weighed most heavily with the Grangers, more than side benefits to the community.[42] As noncompeting points on the CM&SP, the towns of Faribault and Northfield complained of discriminatory freight rates, which meant lower wheat prices.[43] Farmers sought to increase local demand for wheat by constructing another flour mill, but the "home town" argument was not lost on them.[44] Merchants in Faribault cooperated with Grangers in organizing a flour-milling company.[45]

Probably the availability of flour-milling expertise helped persuade Grangers in Faribault and Northfield to choose mills over elevators. (The two were not mutually exclusive options; both mill companies built elevators on their properties.) Flour made at the Ames and Archibald mills already had a good reputation in eastern markets.[46] Faribault had several mills, representing much milling experience. Grangers needed to know such expertise was available before they invested in a mill. In the early 1870s, the capital (thirty to fifty thousand dollars) needed to build a flour mill to compete with the Ames and Archibald mills was three to ten times the capital (five to ten thousand dollars) needed to build a warehouse and buy wheat.

The presence of railroads lowered the capital required for warehousing and wheat buying but tended to raise it for flour milling as train service expanded the flour market beyond the small rural neighborhood that the township grist mill served. This access to regional and national markets provided firms with incentives for large-scale milling using costly new technologies. That upped the ante for a local mill, which had to buy the technology to compete with the lower-cost flour that the railroads hauled into town.

Once they opted for milling, Grangers faced a choice between large-scale and small-scale milling. Smaller, less-costly mills already dotted the countryside. The 1870 U.S. census showed the average capital invested in Minnesota per grist or flour mill was $13,430.[47] One milling expert warned Grangers against "large and expensive mills" requiring twenty-five to fifty thousand dollars in capital. He recommended small, four-run mills with the essential middling separators and construction costs under twelve thousand dollars.[48] Few Grangers took his advice.[49] A country mill's small demand for wheat would not raise wheat prices the way a large mill's high demand could.

Even small mills required more capital than farmers put into township mutuals (none) or Union stores (such as St. Peter's one thousand dollars).[50] That need for an initial investment meant the cooperative tended to be a joint-stock company dominated by large shareholders, often merchants whose advice and consent Grangers had to obtain. The mill was caught between conflicting goals: profits for investors and higher wheat prices for farmers. In deciding on mill size, Rice County Grangers stressed the latter objective and built larger mills. The aim of higher prices strongly motivated them to start a mill but not to improve one or add new technologies. Higher milling profits were stronger incentives to innovate; investors' capital could multiply without limit, whereas the finite size of a family farm restricted its potential gains from higher wheat prices. Entrepreneurs' motive of higher profits proved to be a stronger engine than Grangers' goal of higher wheat prices.

Granger Flour Mills: Faribault and Northfield

Yet some Grange mills mainly sought higher milling profits. The Grangers' milling strategy succeeded at first as their mill near

In 1874 farmers waited to have their wagonloads of sacked grain weighed, processed, and marketed by a merchant miller. Located in Meeker County on the North Fork of the Crow River, Forest City was bypassed by the railroad and lost its county-seat status to Litchfield in 1869.

Northfield flourished. In 1875, "the reputation of their flour [was] steadily growing in the Eastern markets."[51] Their company added a large forty to sixty thousand bushel elevator, purchased the mill in Goodhue County, and started a cooperage.[52] It could expand since it was an investor-controlled, profit-driven enterprise.

A farmer-owned mill chose one of two definitions of success: (1) large profits from large-scale, merchant milling, paying the minimum price for wheat, or (2) a break-even mill that raised wheat prices and did grist work to serve farmers. Gristing became less important and wheat prices more so as farmers moved from semisubsistence to commercial farming.[53] A true cooperative would use the second definition, but as joint-stock companies Grange mills often chose the first.

Thus Northfield Grangers claimed their mill raised wheat prices five cents, but John Ames declared that its managers asked him to help lower wheat prices. He also charged that it had "done a merchant and exchange *business*—refusing to grist."[54] He was probably right. Asking "Do you do custom [grist] work or make only for a market?" the 1880 census taker recorded the answer, "Make for Market."[55] The Grangers' substantial investment in a large-scale mill forced them to focus on merchant milling and to pay no more than market wheat prices.

The Grangers prospered at merchant milling for years. In 1882 the Grange mill was still owned by the same company. It was placed in receivership in May 1896. No reason was noted, but the Grange mill was probably unable to keep pace with changing flour-milling technology. In 1880 it used stones to grind wheat and milled only six hundred bushels per day. The Ames mill had switched to the new rollers and milled fifteen hundred bushels per day.[56] After 1880 economies of scale, favorable freight rates, specialization of milling skills, the world market for flour, and other factors gave a decided advantage to larger flour mills.[57] Minneapolis millers converted to "continuous-process" mills with rollers set up in sequential order "to assure continuing high-speed throughput." By 1890 their flour mills produced an average of 1,837 barrels of flour per mill per day.[58]

The two-year career of Faribault's Grange mill makes any judgment speculative. In its early successful days, it produced "about two hundred barrels of very superior flour per day, which ranked as such in the eastern market."[59] Unlike the Northfield Grange mill, it catered to farmers more than investors. The *Northwestern Miller* reported that the mill "is

grinding feed for the [P]atrons free of charge" and added, "That's where
the fun comes in of being a granger." A year later, the *Miller* commented
that the mill had not been "a profitable investment," but it had improved
the local wheat market.[60] By paying high prices at a break-even mill,
Grangers could not earn sufficient capital to purchase the new technologies that were needed to remain competitive.

On election night, November 7, 1876, with "a large crowd in town,"
the president of the Faribault Grange mill took the "extra precaution" of
inspecting it several hours after midnight, but fire broke out shortly after he left. It was destroyed. Arson was suspected but never proved. A
month later, local wheat prices had "fallen from five to seven cents a
bushel."[61]

Grange mills were important attempts by wheat farmers to capture
control of wheat processing and its profits. Forward integration would
have given them control of milling, eliminated middlemen, probably prevented Minneapolis millers' later near-monopoly over wheat purchasing
in western Minnesota, and greatly reduced their risks. Farmers would
have sold wheat in improved local markets while their flour mill cooperatives took the risks of selling flour in regional, national, or international markets.[62]

It was a worthwhile attempt, but it failed. First, they entered a milling
industry that was at the start of a technological revolution: adoption of
the middlings purifier, of rollers that replaced stones, and of continuous-
process milling. These capital-intensive technologies brought economies
of scale and speed and a higher-quality product. Entrepreneurs used
capital earned in lumbering to purchase these technologies whereas
Grangers lacked personal capital, and Grange mills did not earn the
needed capital through high-profit operations. The best time for forward integration was the prerailroad 1850s and 1860s when small, three-
run country mills dominated milling in Minnesota. Grangers could have
raised the five to ten thousand dollars it cost to build a small mill. Once
they controlled small-scale milling, they could have mastered the transition to new technologies. But the Grange had not yet been founded,
and cooperatives were not widely known in Minnesota. By the time the
Grangers entered milling, it was too late. Minneapolis millers were on
the verge of dominating the industry.[63]

Second, railroads and a marketing system with specialized buyers
and grain elevators created a regional, then national, market for wheat

and flour. Trains had a different impact on wheat from on flour. They carried wheat out of town toward terminal markets like Chicago. They carried flour into or out of town, and incoming flour from more efficient mills in Minneapolis threatened local mills by the mid-1870s. A processing cooperative often needed a local monopoly—something Grange mills could not capture.

Grange-Sponsored Cooperative Grain Elevators and Warehouses

Stymied by the challenges of operating a mill, Grangers turned to the alternative of running elevators or warehouses, which would have several advantages over milling.[64] Labor and construction costs were lower. Buying and storing wheat demanded less expertise than milling wheat, and controlling these steps still addressed the farmers' grievances: false weights, improper grading, fraudulent docking, mixing different grades, and low prices. Entrepreneurs had few advantages here. The low-capital simplicity of buying, storing, and selling wheat made it easy to enter the business, increased the competition, and reduced capitalists' ability to buy technological efficiencies or economies of scale. Trains aided cooperatives by hauling their wheat out, not their competitors' goods into town.

The Patrons Warehouse Company of Delavan (Faribault County) offers a good example. It resulted from farmers' dissatisfaction with local wheat buyers. In December 1870, W. W. Cargill built a warehouse at the time the SMRR arrived in town. Three other buyers also showed up to profit from this new wheat market. When they did not pass on freight rate reductions by raising wheat prices, farmers complained to the SMRR, whose agent threatened to raise rates to compel a price increase, albeit temporary.[65]

In June 1872, Delavan farmers created a Farmer's Association but failed to build a warehouse because they lacked the needed capital, solidarity, and stability.[66] Common grievances spurred farmers to attend meetings, but more was needed. In 1873–74 local Granges brought the necessary cohesion and organization. The Faribault County Council took the initiative, although its meetings were limited to electing delegates, not to organizing a warehouse. Furthermore, only elected delegates could attend its meetings. Farmers trusted their elected officers to run an existing cooperative, not to launch a new one. Direct democracy alone could create the needed consensus for that task, so the council called a Patrons' mass meeting.[67]

In the 1870s Grangers had fewer scruples about working with capitalists than did members of the later Farmers' Alliance. Before the meeting, "a gentleman representing eastern capital" promised that if they built a warehouse, "he would advance from eighty to ninety cents of the value of the wheat" in storage. This proposal would have supplied working capital, but it was not adopted apparently.[68] By late July 1874, they had incorporated. Making it easy to join, they required that farmers pay only one dollar down on a ten-dollar share.[69] By mid-October 1874 the Grange warehouse was in business.

To defeat the new competition, local wheat buyers first spread rumors that the manager, H. E. Mayhew, was guilty of improper or sloppy bookkeeping. To counter the rumors, the directors "examined the books" and proclaimed their "entire satisfaction" with Mayhew's management. They showed the books to a leading merchant and two other men, who expressed confidence in him, too. Advertisements in the county-seat newspaper elicited an endorsement from its editor: "Success, say we to the Grange warehouse," which did as much business as all other buyers combined and should be supported, although "other buyers are paying one or two cents higher." Its profits went "back to the farmers again in dividends," but others' profits "strengthen the gigantic ring that has so long oppressed the farming community." In three months it bought more than twenty thousand bushels of wheat and earned a profit of $234 on receipts of $20,311.[70] Raising wheat prices, not profits, was the goal.

Wheat buyers could not use technology or economies of scale to defeat it, and common rumor had failed. They resorted to another tactic, which the editor described: "A combination of all the others was formed to prevent any wheat from going to the Granger's warehouse." One buyer, G. G. Young, ran "from load to load as it come [sic] into town and offered the highest price." Still, "many farmers disregarded his offer and drove straight to the Grange warehouse" although "Young is shrewd and active, and it was as good as a circus to see him manoeuvre." Buyers paid less for wheat at other towns in order to afford the higher prices offered at Delavan. But farmers knew that if they abandoned the Grange warehouse, the price would eventually fall in Delavan, too.[71]

The Grange warehouse survived this second attack. In August 1875 Grangers began to build a ten-thousand-bushel elevator. By 1877 their warehouse and elevator were "shipping several carloads of wheat each day to Milwaukee" despite the presence of five wheat buyers in Delavan. A final threat was a controversy over Mayhew's leadership of a drive to move the county seat from Blue Earth to Delavan.[72] Grangers were tempted to use the popularity of a farmer-owned business for their political goals. In Delavan, they fell to temptation, and that strategy cost them local support. The county-seat newspaper never again praised the warehouse.

No trace remained of the warehouse after 1878. It may have fallen victim to the disastrous six-to-seven-bushel per acre yields of 1878, or stiff competition from private buyers may have killed it. Young was still buying wheat in 1879 at a low margin (sometimes at a loss), which meant "no profit to the other buyers." The Grange's decline in the late 1870s weakened farmers' loyalty and undermined their ability to resist buyers' higher prices. Tenuous Norwegian-American ties to the Grange probably hurt this Grange enterprise located amidst Norwegian settlements.[73] Delavan's warehouse was fairly typical of Grange warehouses and elevators in its size, its effect on wheat prices, and its short life (see Table 2).

Granges became catalysts for organizing warehouse or elevator cooperatives, which in turn brought members into Granges. Forming a cooperative that raised local wheat prices five to nine cents per bushel helped Granges near Alden. Farmers saw "something in the Grange movement that they had never before discovered" and joined.[74] Starting a cooperative had few "entrepreneurial rewards," Heflebower noted, for the organizers did not receive the profits.[75] A member-recruiting reward went to local Granges, yet this was a weaker incentive than the profit motive driving a Cargill or an Easton to expand a line of elevators.

TABLE 2
Granger Warehouses and Elevators — Southeast Minnesota[76]

Town	Impact on Wheat Price	Capacity (Bushels)	Volume(bu) Handled	Profit(P) or Loss	Years in Operation
Albert Lea	+$.05/bu.			P(1875)	1873–76
Alden	+.05 to .09/bu.				1873–74
Delavan		10,000	3,400/mo.	P(1875)	1874–78
Lake City					1874–77
Le Roy		25,000			1874–?
Oakdale		35,000			1874–?
(Mower County)					
Spring Valley		24,000	80,000/season	P(1875)	1874–78
Waseca	+.07 to .09/bu.		6,200/mo.	P(1875)	1874–75

Entrepreneurs needed capital to expand; Grangers needed capital and democratic consensus. It was hard to gain a consensus in one county for one warehouse; building consensus for a state network of warehouses was like trying to make peanut brittle by the square mile. Cracks were sure to appear somewhere.

Choosing a site was difficult. County councils sought a centrally located site. Freeborn's county council most likely took no part in Alden's warehouse decision because Alden was not centrally located. In the southeast corner of Mower County, Le Roy's Grange elevator resulted from local, not county, leadership.[77] At Albert Lea, Delavan, Lake City, Waseca, and probably Spring Valley, county councils took the initiative.[78] Such coordinated efforts stopped at the county line. No state network of Grange warehouses formed similar to Cargill's line of elevators so Grange warehouses lacked the clout to demand lower rates from railroads.

Grangers' failure to recruit immigrant farmers hampered their warehouse operations. Freeborn's Grangers sold shares to Scandinavian-American Lutherans and Baptists, but these non-Grangers protested when a newspaper characterized the business as a Grange warehouse. They saw it "not as a Grange, but as a farmers' movement." "Their religious training forbids encouragement of secret organizations," so most of its shareholders had "no contact or sympathy with" the Grange. It was incorporated as the "'Farmers Association' of Freeborn County." The county council did not discuss its affairs, nor did its members flock to join the Grange.[79]

Old Stock merchants and editors welcomed farmer-owned warehouses. The *Freeborn County Standard* noted, "Many parties who have heretofore carried their grain and done their trading at Wells, Waseca, Owatonna, Austin, and Northwood [Iowa] . . . are now coming here under the comfortable assurance that their local agents will keep the market up as high as the times will warrant."[80] Merchants and editors supported Grange warehouses more than Grange agencies or stores because the warehouses paid high wheat prices, earned low profits, and brought farmers to town.[81]

Many Grange warehouses enjoyed modest success in their first years: Albert Lea ("a respectable balance on the credit side"), Delavan, Lake City ("all seemed very well pleased with the manner in which the business has been conducted"), Spring Valley ("declaring a dividend to stock holders"), and Waseca.[82] Yet high-volume success also attracted wheat buyers to town to compete against them. Several may have failed as a result of such competition.[83]

Identifying causes of failure of Grange warehouses or elevators is difficult. Introduced with fanfare in newspapers, they quietly struck their tents and departed without public notice or finger-pointing. Success has many press agents, but failure few. An exception was the Waseca warehouse. Soon after a positive financial report, Waseca Grangers discovered their agent had embezzled thirteen hundred dollars. They ceased operations and rented out the warehouse. Charging the agent was "addicted to the use of intoxicating liquors," temperance-minded editor Child called it "humiliating in the extreme…what a commentary upon us as Grangers!"[84] Most failures were less spectacular. The last Grange elevator or warehouse "appears to have been discontinued in 1878," according to historian Henrietta Larson.[85]

Causes of Failure of Grange Flour Mills and Warehouses

Historians attribute the failure of Grange flour mills, warehouses, and elevators to a variety of internal causes: lack of capital and managerial expertise, inexperienced boards, dishonest managers, and internal dissension.[86] That is an easy catch list of causes, many of which characterize a cooperative by definition. It lacks adequate capital because members "do not effectively own a residual interest in its assets"; should it cease operations their invested capital would be refunded to them but not a share of the added capital earned through its operations. So members "minimize their contributions" to it and expect it to distribute cash returns rather than accumulate reserves or working capital.[87] Lake City's warehouse was incorporated at fifty thousand dollars in capital stock but sold only four thousand dollars of that to farmers, and only a little more than one thousand dollars of that was actually paid in. It financed operations by delaying shipments of wheat to buyers who had paid for the wheat.[88] Often paying lower wages than private firms do, cooperatives frequently cannot recruit and retain competent managers.[89] Farmer-directors lack experience in running a business; they learn while serving on the board.[90] Employee dishonesty occurs as in many businesses. Internal dissension is more likely in a cooperative where factions freely fight than in a top-down, hierarchical firm where disagreement with managers is a sure ticket to unemployment. This catch list of causes reflects historians' tendency to judge cooperatives by standards appropriate to private firms and to ignore their strengths, which can offset weaknesses.

Grange mills and warehouses were not inordinately plagued with these weaknesses-by-definition. Inexperience and a lack of capital or expertise ordinarily affect a cooperative in its first two years. Almost all Grange mills and warehouses were successful early on. More often, they failed during their third through sixth years, when they did not develop a cooperative's strengths. As a customer-owned business with favorable prices and members' loyalty, it should achieve high volume, cut per-unit costs, and offer high crop prices. Members' loyalty and high prices help offset managers' incompetence, directors' inexperience, and everyone's quarrelling at annual meetings. High volume means greater turnover of capital, which partially compensates for inadequate working capital.

Grange flour mills and warehouses did not sustain high volumes, member loyalty, or higher wheat prices. Grangers lacked solidarity and stopped patronizing Grange cooperatives, especially after the Grange's rapid decline. Immigrants never had patronized them faithfully. Ethnic and family ties between Old Stock millers and wheat buyers and Old Stock Grangers further weakened loyalty to them. As wheat raising moved to western and northern Minnesota, it declined in the southeastern counties where they were located. That threatened their supply of wheat and members' interest in them. Finally, Minneapolis millers like Pillsbury and line elevator companies like Cargill increasingly ruled the industry.[91]

The early 1870s was not the optimum time, but it was a window of opportunity, a decent chance for Minnesota's wheat farmers to gain control of marketing and processing their cash crop. Conditions were favorable for wheat-marketing and milling cooperatives: an embryonic rail-based marketing system, no monopoly of grain storage facilities, a milling industry of small country mills, and cheap technology. By 1880 these conditions vanished. An opportunity was lost, despite the Grange's efforts. As an Old Stock secret society, it failed to mobilize broad support for cooperation. Having social, political, and educational as well as economic goals, it never devoted adequate resources to cooperation. Long-term trends in the industry doomed its few cooperatives.

A broader point could be made. Democratic coordinators were slower to expand or to adapt to change than were administrative coordinators in large firms. Both began in the late 1860s or early 1870s. But by 1878 the Grange's democratic coordinators had failed to capture a toehold while entrepreneurs like Pillsbury, Cargill, and Easton built empires on "high-volume year-round operation."[92] A cooperative's way to secure high volumes (recruiting many members to a democratic polity offering higher prices) was harder to spread across wide areas. After initial success, it could recruit few additional members from within its limited locale. Entrepreneurs easily expanded to new regions by offering cash to smaller operators who cared little how the merged mill or elevator was run after the money changed hands. Although they were at first competitors, Easton "seemed quite taken with Cargill," became his mentor, and helped him to expand along the SMRR.[93] Personal ties did not so readily connect cooperatives—one could acquire another, but it had to convince a majority of the latter's customer-owners that services and prices would remain satisfactory and that they would retain democratic control.[94] Cash flowed across geographical spaces that tended to hinder democratic consensus. Investors' profits made a stronger engine of expansion than cooperators' desire for good services and higher wheat prices. Capital multiplied indefinitely; a farm's finite size limited the benefits a farmer could receive from a cooperative.

Corporations had the capital to buy new technologies to handle increased volumes at higher speeds. And it was in industries where technological innovation increased volumes and speeds that administrative coordination first developed. Northfield Grangers saw that "Messrs. Ames & Sons were making money" and "spending it making improvements." Lack of capital curtailed cooperatives' ability to do likewise. Members' desire for high wheat prices limited the capital a cooperative could accumulate through operations. Grangers had other priorities besides business efficiency. Entrepreneurs were not distracted by other matters but were able to follow what Cronon called "the logic of capital" with a single-minded zeal that democratic coordinators could not match. That abstracting logic used the language of prices and a focus on profits in a reductionist way to simplify and rationalize decision making. In this abstracting logic, "places lost their particularity" and became interchangeable, and futures trading could be done with no grain traded.[95] Democracy dealt with real people, places, and products, and it could not fully follow an abstracting logic that ignored their particularities. That hindered cooperatives' efforts to expand to new groups, places, or products.

When Minnesota's wheat farmers again formed cooperatives in the 1880s and 1890s, the debate over whether to build mills or elevators was over. Wheat raising had moved to northern and western Minnesota. It was too late to try cooperative flour milling, and new barriers to cooperative elevators had arisen. Nor could farmers look to cooperative mills or elevators as models on which to base cooperation in other fields. For models of successful cooperation, they would have to look elsewhere.

4

Fire Insurance

"There is no fathoming
the possibilities of novices
in the insurance business"

THE SWEDISH-AMERICAN FARMERS OF VASA had formed a Union store and a wheat-marketing cooperative before Old Stock farmers succeeded in doing either. Similarly they were the first to form a local fire insurance mutual. (In insurance, "mutual" and "cooperative" have the same meaning.)[1] On February 1, 1867, they met to organize a "mutual protection association of Vasa against losses by fire and lightning." They were undeterred by the fact that the state had not authorized insurance mutuals or cooperative associations. The Vasa association remained unincorporated for its first ten years. Lacking any capital, it assessed members pro rata for fire losses. The mutual's operations were simplicity itself: quarterly, the chairman and secretary met to enroll new members and conduct business "in the Swedish language, to which nationality the members belong, with very few exceptions."[2]

Cooperation and insurance were logically related within a local ethnic group. Insurance spread the financial burden of loss among many policyholders, each of whom became a passive cooperator sharing neighbors' risks as well as his or her own. The resulting payments resembled mutual aid, and in closely knit ethnic communities, they became exactly that. The members chose to be active cooperators who formed ethnic insurance societies or mutuals out of a strong sense of solidarity. Nineteenth-century entrepreneurs perceived insurance as a for-profit business in the broad national market, but its risk-sharing character led to the formation of many mutuals in small rural and ethnic markets.[3]

Apparently the first local farmers' mutual fire insurance company in

81

Minnesota, the Vasa association was organized more than a year before
the town's Union store and wheat-marketing cooperative. Farmers often
found it easier to put together an insurance mutual than an enterprise
requiring capital and inventory. Still Viola Grangers' failure to start a
township mutual showed success was not automatic. Ethnic solidarity
and a lack of concern over legalization helped Vasa's Swedish-American
farmers succeed where Viola's Old Stock farmers failed. As a nearly ideal
polity, Vasa's farmers—and similar rural ethnic groups—shared the tradition of jointly operating churches and ethnic societies. That experience
proved to be vital to the task of jointly running an insurance mutual.

  Minnesota's Scandinavian-American farmers did not totally divorce
themselves from Old Stock mutuals or completely rely on local ethnic
mutuals. Although Old Stock Americans formed and dominated the
MFMFIAM, they recruited immigrant farmers, too. In 1869 the editor of
Nordisk Folkeblad praised it: "We hope that our farmers will insure in
this their own company."[4] Support for the MFMFIAM, however, may have
been strongest among editors of Scandinavian-language newspapers
who hoped the MFMFIAM would advertise in their journals. Still the local
farmers' mutual was a popular alternative to the MFMFIAM in places
other than Vasa: early ethnic fire insurance mutuals were formed in
Washington County (March 1867), Nicollet County (March 1869), and
Goodhue County (February 1869).[5] All these mutuals may have had an
exclusive ethnic membership and conducted meetings in Old World
languages. However, Scandinavian-American farmers probably did not
base their first mutuals on European models, but rather on Old Stock
ones derived from New England and the Old Northwest. The Nicollet
and Goodhue County mutuals were established after former Michigan
resident Nimocks began to promote mutuals in his *Farmers' Union* and
were likely based on his model.

  The Scandinavian Fire Insurance Company *(Skandinavisk Bran-
dassurancekompagni)* of Nicollet County was characteristic of early,
unincorporated, ethnic mutuals. In February 1868, some twenty-five
Scandinavian-American farmers in Lake Prairie Township formed the
Scandinavian Society, whose members had to be Scandinavian Americans over fifteen years of age and of good character. A local pastor thought
it was "too much aimed at the devout Christian" to succeed there. It had
too many goals also: Scandinavian-American political success, mutual aid
in times of need, ethnic unity, and "Christian conduct and trade practices."[6]

Yet the shared experience of cooperating in this broad society helped farmers when they formed specialized associations for specific goals. They had already set up a joint-stock company that funded a wind-powered flour mill, and in March 1869, they organized a fire insurance mutual. The Scandinavian Society's requirement of good character would prove to be essential for a mutual seeking to avoid arson, delinquency in paying assessments, and carelessness in fire prevention. Later that year they sent a committee to Vasa to investigate its Union store and joint wheat-marketing operation. One Lake Prairie leader helped in St. Peter's attempts at a Union store. These forms of cooperation reinforced each other even when conducted by separate associations.[7]

The Scandinavian Fire Insurance Company was not some "business speculation," one correspondent assured *Nordisk Folkeblad*'s readers. Its purpose, another writer added, was "to prevent our countrymen from being robbed by the many unsound insurance companies whose agents swarm over the countryside." Clearly these farmers considered it robbery for companies to collect premiums to pay for fires that might never occur. With the farmers' mutual, "the money will remain in our own county" where it would pay for actual fire losses.[8] It was a mutual-aid society that depended on the ethnic solidarity already forged in area churches and organizations like its predecessor, the Scandinavian Society.

Ethnic farmers' mutuals had all four factors for successful cooperation: a homogeneous membership, buying in the same market, sharing common economic interests, and possessing a tradition of joint action in churches and other societies. Each served a homogeneous subset of the population. Rural fire insurance was an economic niche that narrowed the cooperators' task and precluded endless debate over numerous options. Farmer-members bought fire insurance and wanted it cheap. Few farmers were insurance agents or owned stock in for-profit insurance companies. They shared a desire for low-cost, actual-cost fire insurance. Ethnic solidarity meant that community pressure could enforce rules apart from legal sanctions or court decrees. Norwegian Americans had a precedent for dividing a large expense among members and collecting assessments; for instance, some Lutheran churches assessed members for their share of the minister's salary.[9]

With these four factors present, ethnic farmers' mutuals had less need for state legal sanction. Unlike Viola's Old Stock Grangers, immigrant farmers could proceed without incorporating (although many did incorporate) and without legal authority for compelling payment of assessments.

Vasa's association and other early ethnic mutuals were simple affairs that charged nominal membership fees, if any. Rather than collecting premiums or deposits, they waited for the first fire and then assessed members on a pro rata basis. The German Farmers' Mutual (Washington County) waited six years for its first fire.[10] In February 1869 the Vasa mutual insured eighty-five thousand dollars worth of property with no capital at all.[11] These companies escaped the eye of Insurance Commissioner Andrew McGill, who in 1874 attacked a bill legalizing township mutuals and called them "a failure" when several had been operating in the state for more than five years.[12] Immigrants' scattered efforts did not draw the attention of the state's Old Stock political or business leaders.

Immigrant Farmers Succeed in Legalizing Township Mutuals

Immigrant farmers acted without state authorization, but they were aware of its advantages. After the theft of H.F. 77, two Norwegian-American legislators took up the fight to enact a law authorizing township mutuals. Senator Anders K. Finseth and Representative N. J. Ottun were Republicans from Goodhue County, where farmers in Holden and Wanamingo Townships sought to form township mutuals like the nearby Vasa mutual. They probably asked Ottun and Finseth to introduce township mutual bills.[13] Ottun's 1874 bill passed the House by a five-to-one margin but died in the Senate judiciary committee.[14] It attracted little attention. The Twin Cities' newspapers did not comment on it, and the *Farmers' Union* summarily dismissed it.[15] Possibly the MFMFIAM-Sherwood brouhaha obscured Ottun's bill.

The failure of Ottun's bill (and a similar one that died that same session) emboldened Commissioner McGill to ridicule the idea, calling one bill "perhaps the crudest one on the subject of insurance ever introduced before a legislative body." For an expert like McGill, "there is no fathoming the possibilities of novices in the insurance business." Township mutuals concentrated their risks in one locality and lacked capital or assets to assure security to policyholders. Minnesota, McGill urged, "should steadfastly refuse all legislation looking to their propagation in this State."[16]

From his Old Stock perspective, McGill failed to see that local ethnic solidarity was the policyholder's security, the guarantee that neighbors would pay assessments so the company could reimburse him for his fire loss. Any assessment-based mutual faced a "collection problem" of delinquent payments and a "moral hazard" of arson by policyholders.[17] In a rural, ethnic community of face-to-face relationships, these two problems were less likely to occur than in a statewide mutual. Furthermore, township mutuals carried insurance in several townships. Their coverage area was not so small, and fires—except prairie fires—rarely spread from farm to farm.

In mid-January 1875, with his Holden neighbors "united about the necessity" of a township mutual, Finseth introduced Senate File 18, "a bill authorizing the formation of town insurance companies." Although the Senate Committee on Corporations recommended "that it be indefinitely postponed," the Senate passed it overwhelmingly.[18]

House action came slower. There was not unanimous support, even from the Norwegian-American press. *Nordisk Folkeblad* commented that "the various attempts that have been made to organize town insurance companies have failed, because the people have so often been fooled by worthless insurance companies that there has arisen a common aversion to them all—with the exception of old, known, solid companies."[19] Yet a township mutual was least likely to operate fraudulently, for farmers knew the organizers, and tempting chances for large profits were hardly present in such a miniscule company. The Norwegian-American newspaper *Budstikken* supported Finseth's bill but reported that there was much opposition from established insurance companies.[20]

Finally, on March 4, due, according to McGill, "to the persistent appeals of certain petitioners," the House passed s.f. 18, and Governor Cushman Davis signed it. The votes against the bill came largely from legislators from Old Stock towns such as Northfield, Anoka, and Owatonna and from Grange strongholds like Rice, Dodge, Steele, and Wabasha Counties.[21]

Despite Old Stock farmers' abandonment of the idea, Minnesota now had legalized township mutuals. Presumably due to pressure from the insurance industry, the new law authorized township mutuals in only thirteen counties (by 1878 that number had been increased to twenty-two). To that extent, it was local legislation, a dubious experiment authorized only in a limited area. Local efforts to organize township mutuals began shortly thereafter in Goodhue and Freeborn Counties. Old Stock Americans tried to form a company in Featherstone Township (Goodhue County) but apparently failed.[22] Scandinavian Americans were soon successful in forming long-lived companies under the 1875 law, which is hardly surprising, given that some Scandinavian-American mutuals were functioning long before the law was entered on the books.[23]

Rural Fire Insurance Was Well Suited to Cooperative Action

Ethnicity was not the only important factor. The economic characteristics of fire insurance in rural areas also helped to account for early successes. Risk sharing is a quasi-cooperative principle that an ethnic community could successfully practice in a township mutual fire insurance company. Also, Minnesota farmers in the Civil War era were dissatisfied with the private insurance industry. Very practical, they disliked paying premiums without receiving something tangible in return. They recognized their need for fire insurance: prairie fires, lightning strikes, and house and barn fires were clear risks. However, protection from risk was an intangible service. To farmers, it appeared that, for all the premiums they collected, companies made few payments for losses.

In 1872 private fire insurance companies operating in Minnesota collected about $725,000 in premiums and paid out less than $292,000 for losses.[24] This money left the state as well as the farmer's pocket. Only two of forty-five companies operating in Minnesota in 1872 were based in the state. In his 1872 annual message, Governor Austin complained that "our State is perpetually drained of money by these non-resident fire and life insurance companies which carry the funds to the eastern cities" and "not a dollar of the surplus" went to help capital-poor Minnesota.[25] Austin proposed legislation forcing the companies to invest in Minnesota. He and his insurance commissioner accepted the companies' reason for high premiums: covering the staggering losses incurred in the Chicago fire of 1871 and the Boston fire of 1872.[26] Like a regulator taken captive by the industry he regulates, the commissioner called for an end to Minnesota's 2 percent tax on premium receipts: "premium rates have been so nicely adjusted to the principle of averages, as to leave little profit for insurance capital."[27]

Many farmers did not see premiums as "nicely adjusted," nor did they see an eastward drain of capital as the key problem. Fire insurance premiums ran as high as $4.75 on property insured for $200.[28] High premiums meant that "more than two-thirds of the destructible property of the State was uncovered by insurance at the close of 1872."[29] Farmers suspected that high profits and high commissions to insurance agents caused high premiums. The *Farmers' Union* charged that 25 percent of premium receipts went to agents, 25 percent for company expenses, 25 percent for profits, and only the remaining 25 percent to pay losses.[30] In his report for 1874, McGill confirmed that charge. Only 26 percent of premium receipts was paid in losses, 30 percent was allocated to "management expenses," and 2 percent was paid in state taxes, "leaving the generous margin of 41.66 [percent]."[31]

Isolated, lower-risk farm buildings were made to pay part of the cost of insuring higher-risk, closely concentrated buildings in urban areas.[32] Surely savings could be made by forming companies to insure only rural properties, where fire was unlikely to spread from one property to another. Farmers constituted a specific, identifiable risk category that was overcharged due to "insurers' failure to take account of various risk-reducing aspects of [farmers'] facilities and operations."[33] Farmers had incentives to organize a polity of the overcharged, bypass the private insurance market, and purchase insurance from themselves in a mutual.

Mutuals were, simply, insurance companies owned and controlled by their policyholders. Some mutuals evolved into profit-maximizing companies and ceased being true, low-cost, policyholder-controlled companies.[34] A farmers' mutual, however, retained its cooperative, low-cost character. Rural policyholders, not investor-shareholders, controlled it, for it insured only rural properties, issued no shares, and gave each policyholder only one vote at its annual meeting. It kept costs low by limiting officers' and agents' compensation and by insuring properties for only two-thirds or three-fourths of their value. It earned no profit but operated on a break-even basis. Rochdale rules on share ownership, profit distribution, and market prices did not apply to the mutual that had no shares or profits and a goal of below-market premiums.[35] This simplified form facilitated democratic coordination. The possibility of factional disputes was minimized (although not eliminated). There were no arguments over the size of the patronage dividend or the interest paid on shares and, in assessment-based mutuals, no disagreement over prices. Few farmers could dispute the fairness of paying their proportionate share of a fire loss. A farmers' mutual insured only farm properties, which did not vary in value as much as urban properties. Its members were unlikely to divide into rival groups owning high-value and low-

value property.[36] Its simplicity enabled farmers to understand its operations and encouraged them to participate in its annual meetings.

A cooperative's members have two ways to exert control over it: external control (threatening to "take their business elsewhere") and internal control (participating in annual meetings and board meetings).[37]
Farmers' mutuals achieved such significant cost reductions that members could not realistically threaten to take their business elsewhere.
That lessened the risk of defection and encouraged members to engage
in democratic internal control.

This new idea was sarcastically attacked by Minnesota's first two insurance commissioners, committed to the opposing idea that market
mechanisms alone could supply insurance services. Even the statewide
MFMFIAM was a "peculiar mode of business" that was "difficult to classify... according to any grade known to the principles of valid insurance."[38] A small township mutual providing insurance "at its actual cost"
was stranger still. If cost cutting was the goal "then perfection will be
reached when every man insures his own property." But if farmers wanted
"security against loss ... then, indeed, are 'township mutuals' a failure."[39]

Township Mutual Insurance Companies: The Case of Manchester

It is helpful to examine one township mutual in detail in terms of Commissioner McGill's criticisms. He made several points. Concentrating a
company's coverage in one locality risked having one fire affect many
policyholders and ruin the company. A township mutual had too few
policyholders to share the costs of even one fire. Without capital or assets,
it offered no guarantee of payment to fire victims. It could not collect assessments from members who gave no security to guarantee they would
pay them. It provided low-cost insurance that was therefore "of doubtful
value."[40] Such was the common wisdom among private insurers, who
pooled risks among many prepaid customers whose security rested on
the company's capital. (The common wisdom may have feared that township mutuals might succeed as much as it reasoned that they would
surely fail.) The early history of the Farmers' Mutual Insurance Company of Manchester demonstrated that McGill and private insurers mis-
judged the possibilities of novices offering localized fire insurance.

In the summer of 1875, Norwegian-American farmers in Freeborn
County discussed the idea of organizing a farmers' mutual. Their com-

mittee drew up a constitution and bylaws that were modeled after a (possibly Norwegian-American) farmers' mutual in Iowa. Two Albert Lea attorneys helped them amend the constitution to conform with the 1875 Minnesota law.[41] Members began holding meetings, conducted in Norwegian, at a Norwegian Lutheran church in the summer of 1876 and formally incorporated as the *Farmers Gjensidige Assurance Selskab* (Farmers' Mutual Insurance Company) in December 1876. The bylaws stated that it was established for Scandinavians residing in several Freeborn townships. Their drive may have been aided by the MFMFIAM's suits "against nearly one hundred farmers in this county, on their notes given for insurance."[42] The MFMFIAM was vulnerable to such low-cost competition from a township mutual.

Apparently the intent of the 1875 law was that farmers of all ethnic groups in a few contiguous townships would form one mutual. That did not happen initially. Ethnicity prevailed over proximity. In late nineteenth-century Minnesota, the ideal polity shared a common ethnicity. The Manchester company primarily recruited Norwegian-American farmers in nine townships spread across north-central and northwestern Freeborn County. By January 1878 Danish Americans had formed the Farmers' Mutual Insurance Company of Bath [Township], whose business territory encroached on the Manchester company's. Instead of different mutuals for different localities, Freeborn had different mutuals for different ethnic groups.[43]

As Manchester's mutual prospered, it added noncontiguous townships despite the provisions of the 1875 law.[44] Thus it did not have "such circumscribed limits" as McGill feared but resembled the "county mutuals," which he granted "would be better than township mutuals."[45] Its risks were dispersed to the degree that Norwegian-American farmers were dispersed in Freeborn County.

A township mutual incurred little added cost when it expanded its business territory. No offices had to be built or rented, for the secretary conducted its business out of his home. Manchester's mutual had nine directors, one from each of the original nine townships. An agent was assigned to each added township, but they were not highly paid. Officers earned $1.50 per day when conducting company business. The officers and agents were farmers for whom insurance was a minor sideline, and both were paid only a nominal fee for each insurance application they collected.[46] To cut travel costs to townships far from Manchester, local directors inspected fire damages, determined reimbursements, and appraised newly insured properties.[47]

Expanding territory meant more policyholders, which increased each member's security. The more members, the faster fire losses could be paid. A township mutual succeeded by cheaply recruiting a large number of policyholders within a relatively small area so that sales, information, and administrative costs were minimized. Often a higher percentage of area farmers belonged to the mutual than to any other farmers' cooperative.[48]

The Manchester mutual steadily increased its membership, from 102 in 1877 to 211 in 1881 and to 422 in 1886. The growth slowed dramatically when it had to levy high assessments after suffering huge fire losses in 1888, 1889, and 1891, amounting to 16.9 cents, 24.4 cents, and 23.4 cents respectively per one hundred dollars of insurance in force. Thus 1888–89 and 1891–92 were years of small additions in membership, and 1891–92 saw a decrease in the amount of insurance in force. Yet in no year did total membership decline.[49]

The Manchester mutual had a large pool of potential members — the Norwegian-American farmers of Freeborn County who could be easily recruited by its agents or directors through personal contacts in Norwegian-American churches and societies and through publicity in the Norwegian-American press.[50] As churches and societies grew, so did the farmers' mutual. The low cost induced many farmers to join; a farmer paid only a two-dollar application fee, which in 1877 amounted to about fifteen cents for each one hundred dollars of insurance coverage.[51]

McGill was correct. Farmers' mutuals lacked capital, reserves, or other assets to guarantee farmers reimbursement for future losses. Their insurance was only as good as their fellow members' willingness to pay assessments. The Manchester mutual began business with no initial capital. In 1877, its first year, it earned only the two-dollar application fee from its first 102 members, plus one dollar for each policy amendment. This income was enough to cover the first year's losses, which totaled ten dollars, plus expenses, and still leave a fifty-dollar cash balance at the year's end.[52] The first year's losses were unusually light, however.

In 1878 reality struck. Lightning hit Christen Petersen's farm on July 11, starting a fire that killed four horses and caused $370 worth of damage. One week later the Manchester board assessed members two and a half mills per dollar of insured property to cover the loss. Members were slow to pay. Petersen did not receive his first installment until September 21, nor the final payment until November 30—more than four months after the fire. That September, Rollef Thykeson's stack of wheat burned; he did not receive his final reimbursement until well into 1879. The board ordered the secretary to send all delinquent members a "new notice with a strong order to fulfill their responsibilities." A month later it "hand[ed] over all delinquent accounts to G. Gulbrandson," an attorney in Albert Lea, for collection.[53] The board discussed filing lawsuits but was advised that court costs were too high and that the recalcitrant members lacked property that could be seized. Using its one recourse, it expelled three members in January 1881.[54]

McGill charged that township mutuals could not collect assessments without some guarantee that members would pay. Manchester's members were "slow pay," which delayed payments to victims and worried the board. Yet in December of most years, only a small percentage of that year's assessment was unpaid: 5.4 percent (1878), 6.5 percent (1879), 3.2 percent (1881), and 2.2 percent (1884).[55] The board's anger over the few delinquencies was testimony more to a strong mutual-aid spirit than to

Manchester's township mutual did not operate or manage the local fire department, shown here in 1903. Yet even volunteer firemen with primitive equipment helped a mutual cut its fire losses on properties close enough to town to be reached by their horse-drawn wagon.

a high rate of nonpayment. In 1882 officers stressed that it was a mutual-aid society for "brotherly assistance between men built upon the state's laws.... People who don't feel the urge to help members who suffer loss or damage ought not to belong to our society."[56]

Several early losses, such as Thykeson's, were paid with revenues from the two-dollar membership fee. In January 1879 the board urged directors and agents to sign up new members "so we thereby could collect the money we have to pay" fire victims. In its first five years of operation, almost 35 percent of its cash revenues came from fees for new policies and policy amendments.[57]

In the hazardous early years of a township mutual, when a large loss could threaten ruin, many new members paying entrance fees kept assessments low and bearable. Critics called a similar MFMFIAM practice "drawing on the *future* for the *past* ... by using the premiums received for new business to pay losses on the old business."[58] That it was. If a corporation did the same, it would appear as if investors were duping policyholders. In a mutual, where the insured was also the insurer, there could be no question of farmers duping themselves.[59] Low and infrequent assessments were in the members' own interests.

However, old members might be duping new members. Old members gained when new members' fees made for lower assessments. New members suffered when their initial fee covered actual fire losses of old members and was not available to cover their own risk of future fire losses.[60] Yet this practice was not perceived as being unjust if the mutual retained the key principle of low-cost, actual-cost insurance. No one pocketed the money. Could a new member accept the fairness of a fee and then complain about how the mutual spent it? Perhaps ethnic solidarity was too great or the entrance fee too low, but no one is recorded to have objected.

McGill predicted that township mutuals would have no assets, yet many dropped the actual-cost, assessment-only principle and accumulated a large cash balance. In its first six years, the Manchester mutual kept the principle; on December 31, 1879, it had a cash balance of $51.30, less than two and a half cents for every one hundred dollars of insurance in force. That seemed inadequate. By the mid-1880s, board members felt an annual assessment was needed to "cover existing losses and to have a reserve for possible future small losses."[61] Annual assessments were really prepayments, or premiums, that reduced the mutual's risk that delinquencies on postfire assessments would delay the payment of claims.[62] By December 1896, the cash balance exceeded fifteen cents per one hundred dollars of insurance in force.[63]

Actual-cost, assessment-only insurance was in members' interest, but operating on a small cash balance and relying on the next assessment placed a strain on the secretary and treasurer, the mutual's managers, a situation they communicated to the board. With experience (the company had only two presidents, one secretary, and one treasurer in its first twenty years), they acquired enough authority to convince the board to accumulate a large balance.[64] Their perspective became the board's perspective, and the mutual's interests overrode members' interests: "We certainly all find these to be hard times, but the board also finds it to be hard times to have to keep on current accounts with so many people."[65]

This change illustrated how board members, in one economist's words, became "socialized into favorable attitudes toward management's view of the cooperative's problems and of appropriate responses."[66] An ad hoc device to supply low-cost insurance took on a separate institutional existence, with its own traditions and interests. This change provoked no serious protests from members, although the officers' expertise and experience threatened to limit members' effective democratic control.

True, members suffering fire losses benefited from annual assessments because that eliminated long delays in receiving payments. By the mid-1880s the mutual was paying off even its largest damage claims within four to six weeks.[67] Claimants were a small minority, however. The majority probably preferred minimal costs for all members over improved claim service for a few.

The board's prepayment policy also reduced the level of uncertainty about what insurance costs would be from year to year. Members had not paid a premium in order to transfer fire risks entirely to the mutual but to exchange "a small chance of a large loss" to their property for "larger chances of smaller losses" to others' properties—losses that caused assessments.[68] By the 1890s, Manchester's members could rely on an annual two-mill assessment. The benefits of predictability may have eased the way for the company to abandon the actual-cost principle.

McGill predicted that low-cost mutual insurance would be low-value insurance. What McGill (who was from St. Peter) or other urbanites thought essential was not so regarded by farmers. Urbanites saw a loss of "value" in lacking an agent to handle claims and in suffering the indignity of having a committee of neighbors prying into the worth of one's horses or one's arson risk or the adequacy of one's fire prevention meas-

ures. To farmers used to neighbors knowing their doings, that did not reduce "value."

To farmers, the low cost made the insurance highly valued. In most
years, the Manchester mutual kept costs (including loss reimbursements)
remarkably low. From 1877 to 1885, expenses per one hundred dollars of
insurance averaged less than thirteen cents. By contrast, reimbursements alone at St. Paul Fire and Marine averaged 57.5 cents for four selected years between 1872 and 1885.[69] A township mutual cut costs by
keeping payments for personal services to a minimum: no full-time
salaried agents; officers paid $1.50 per day while on company business; a
secretary paid a piece rate of ten cents per letter and five cents per assessment notice.[70] These costs were extremely low. In 1877, Manchester
paid 5.2 cents per one hundred dollars of insurance for personal services.
In 1887 they paid 2.7 cents, much less than was paid by joint-stock companies or statewide farmers' mutuals. St. Paul Fire and Marine paid
thirty-three cents per one hundred dollars in 1872, and MFMFIAM paid
fifteen cents that same year for salaries and commissions.[71] Farmers did
not see any loss of "value" if officers and agents were underpaid.

Manchester's mutual also had far fewer losses per hundred dollars insured than did joint-stock companies or state mutuals in 1877–85. While
St. Paul Fire and Marine averaged losses of 57.5 cents per one hundred
dollars insured and the MFMFIAM averaged 45 cents, Manchester averaged 8.6 cents per one hundred dollars insured.[72] Other township mutuals in Minnesota had similar results.

Lower losses resulted from several factors. First, rural fires did not
normally spread from one property to another. Second, the Manchester
mutual limited its potential liability by insuring up to 67 percent of the
value of the farm buildings and contents; the member absorbed at least
one-third of the loss. This rule reduced the "moral hazard"—the temptation to arson. Manchester also initially refused to insure schoolhouses,
creameries, or churches or to pay for fires started by sparks from passing
trains or by steam-powered threshing machines (a decision later reversed).[73] In 1894 the board announced that the owner of a temporarily
unoccupied house would "stand at his own risk if the same were to burn."[74]
These rules lowered a policy's "value," although members probably
counted on never being hit by a fire under these conditions.

Finally, the township mutual exercised strong local oversight to limit
loss awards. A committee of its officers and local residents visited each

fire site and conducted a thorough investigation to check for negligence or arson. When a prairie fire burned Ole Rodahl's stall and some wheat, oats, and hay in October 1883, a three-man committee determined that it had been set by a neighbor's hired man and took the case to the justice of the peace. The mutual paid Rodahl's loss only when the board became convinced that suing the nearly bankrupt neighbor would be pointless and that they would lose a criminal case.[75] A two-man committee recommended no payment to Jorgen P. Skov, who had worked to save his neighbor's property instead of his own haystack during a fire.[76]

President Rollef Thykeson and Secretary Iver A. Rodsaeter investigated a fire at Henry Tunnell's farm on May 21–22, 1889, after "talk that it might have been set." They found no "proof for such an allegation" after "a very careful ex[amination]." By questioning, they determined that Tunnell "lived in a good relationship with his neighbors with one exception." They recommended a modest payment: "Mr. Tunnell thought that it [the award] was much too low and that he had suffered far more damage, but we didn't think that we could grant any more."[77]

In a township mutual, the insured was closely inspected by his neighbors, his fellow members, who knew his character.[78] The majority of members favored these stringent claims investigations. It was in their interest to see that loss awards were limited.[79] Fire victims were a tiny minority within the polity. In rare instances, however, disgruntled fire victims formed a troublesome faction. Manchester's most bitter claim dispute began in 1889 when the board refused to pay damages to seven members whose haystacks, located some distance from their homesteads, burned in a prairie fire. A three-man committee reported that not all of the seven had plowed protective furrows around all of their haystacks as required in the bylaws, but it recommended payment. After "animated" and "bitter discussion," the board rejected the claims due to the lack of furrows and the haystacks' distant location. "A quite spirited debate" hit the 1890 annual meeting. The claimants appealed to the district court, and in 1892 the board finally agreed to pay them.[80]

The case showed that even part-time, underpaid officers took seriously their duty to keep costs down.[81] In a mutual, however, cost cutting could bring dissension when the practice hurt numerous claimants. Also some members' use of their right to pursue redress in the courts limited the majority's democratic control.[82]

To keep such factional disputes minimal, the collection problem manageable, and the membership steadily increasing, the board had to maintain the appearance of equal treatment for all members. A democratic entity like a cooperative is more vulnerable to charges of favoritism than is a private business. Manchester's officers saw equity as their duty: "it requires the greatest care to lead this business in the right track, so that the whole company and each individual person in it can receive equal rights."[83] Inequities led to delinquencies on assessments, to lost members, or to expensive court cases.

As long as there was fairness, most Norwegian-American farmers in Freeborn County did not think cost-cutting features meant "low value" insurance, an opinion expressed by McGill. Dealing directly with a local mutual's officer did not seem inferior to dealing indirectly with a distant insurance company through its agent. Most members appreciated the cost controls. In 1881 Manchester's officers told members how good they had it: a two thousand dollar policy cost only $9.50 for the company's first four years. In January 1888 the message was similar: members had saved five thousand dollars on insurance in the past five years.[84]

The Problem of Ethnic Exclusivity: "Lige Børn Lege Bedst"

Over time the Manchester mutual became less exclusively Norwegian or even Scandinavian. As its territory expanded into townships with more German, Old Stock, and Irish farmers, more non-Scandinavians joined. Ethnic homogeneity gave a mutual a united polity during its potentially contentious early years. Yet few businesses will for long limit their pool of customers. Expanding the risk-sharing pool had clear advantages. Also directors were paid for new applications regardless of the applicant's ethnicity.

By 1893 some fire inspection reports were written in English. "After some talking about what language should be used" in 1894, the board instructed the officers to use English, but "both the Norwegian & english language may be used by speakers at the annual meeting."[85] Older Norwegian-American farmers hesitated to speak halting English at a public gathering.

Transforming an ethnic mutual into one for all ethnic groups was not so easily done elsewhere. In 1888 members of the Acton & Gennessee Farmers' Mutual of Kandiyohi County voted against an amendment ending its Scandinavians-only restriction. Excluded farmers then took their business elsewhere by forming the Willmar Farmers' Company. Members later reversed the decision and approved the nonexclusive amendment by a sixty-to-five vote.[86]

Exclusivism damaged a mutual's public image. In 1891 the *Ashby Farmer* criticized an Otter Tail County mutual for excluding non-Scandinavians: "If such be the case, the company should be squelched, and no company should be allowed to do a general business in this country simply on nationality. When foreigners become American citizens the question of their nationality, in business transactions at least, should be forever buried."[87] The mutual's officers could respond by saying that it was a voluntary association with the right to limit its membership. Yet in rural areas with their democratic, egalitarian ethos, editors' arguments against exclusivism were damaging. The irony was that market mechanisms seemed to be more democratic than cooperation—the market was open to all while the mutual was not—but admitting the excluded might lead to factionalism, less solidarity, and less democracy in the long run as members used threats to take their business elsewhere rather than use a mutual's internal democratic processes.

Ashby's editor may have been referring to the Sverdrup Scandinavian Mutual Insurance Company, formed by Scandinavian-American farm-

Not the farmers' mutual but a cooperative creamery, begun in 1891, built the railroad town of Manchester. A creamery patron has parked his wagon loaded with cream cans in front of a retail establishment.

ers in central Otter Tail County. Its bylaws limited membership to "each Scandinavian residing" in its territory and required that notices of meetings appear "in the most widely circulated Norwegian newspaper in the county."[88] (The Norwegian Mutual of Lyon County even held its annual meetings on the Norwegian holiday, Syttende Mai.)[89] In January 1887, "the question of admitting other nationalities to the company arose, but was voted down." It came up again at the 1889 and 1890 annual meetings with the same result.[90] Most likely, it kept coming up because the new Farmers' Alliance movement supplied a standard of open democracy that the mutual was failing to meet.[91]

One of the mutual's founders, O. T. Bjørnaas, wrote an angry letter to the editor three days after the 1890 vote. An exclusivist, he stressed that it was the "greedy monopolists," "these American companies," who were undemocratic, not the mutual, which he called "persuasive proof of what unity can accomplish," a hint to "American corporations and monopolies that we have managed to take a step on to their own bailiwick." Supporters of change were "a few persons [who] seek to build up a faction as a tool to open the door for non-Scandinavians." A "divisive spirit" from "a few leaders' self-interest" would ruin "the good morale and contentment which up to now has prevailed within the company."

He denied that exclusivism had irremediable, undemocratic consequences for those excluded. Supporters of change argued that the law allowed only one mutual in a given area; local non-Scandinavians could have no mutual if they were excluded from the Sverdrup company. He replied, "The insurance companies which were so against us earlier are still ready to serve these excluded people, so let them go there" and added a Scandinavian proverb—"*lige børn lege bedst*" (like children play together best). Market-minded Old Stock Americans could buy insurance in the market. Cooperative Scandinavian Americans would jointly insure themselves. Mixing ethnic groups might end the unity in their farmers' mutual.[92]

The proposed change was again defeated in January 1891. Finally at the 1896 annual meeting, members voted by a thirty-eight-to-one margin to admit non-Scandinavians, twenty-eight of whom joined the first year.[93] Similar changes occurred in other farmers' mutuals, but some evidence supports Bjørnaas's point that multiethnic companies experienced more factionalism and dissension.

Consequences of Successful Cooperation in Fire Insurance

Low-cost, reliable mutual fire insurance convinced many Minnesota farmers to cooperate in this field. The number of township mutuals increased from nine in 1878, to eighty in 1889, and to 119 in 1897.[94] By 1898 the state's insurance commissioner, Elmer Dearth, admitted that the township mutual law "has, beyond question, saved to the farmers of Minnesota vast sums of money." He reported a cost of only fifteen cents per one hundred dollars of insurance for all township mutuals for 1878–97. By 1898 they had underwritten more than eighty-six million dollars of insurance—a little more than one-third the amount of fire insurance carried by the joint-stock and state mutual companies that year.[95] They were a significant part of the fire insurance business in Minnesota.

Norwegian-American farmers were more likely to read the newspapers' praise. In 1889 the *Fergus Falls Ugeblad* commented that "these companies must be extremely beneficial, as the expenses of keeping buildings insured against fire are so very small."[96]

This success was extremely important for the cooperative movement in rural Minnesota. By 1889 no other form of cooperation had yet succeeded in so many areas over such a long period. Stores and warehouses, joint purchasing and marketing—all had proved to be short-lived. Township mutuals became models for later cooperation—although their simplicity could not be transferred to cooperatives needing buildings, salaried managers, inventories, shares, and patronage refunds. Their annual meetings became forums at which other cooperative efforts were discussed. They trained farmers to organize cooperatives, serve as board members, trust each other in a joint venture, and ignore prophecies of failure. Using ethnic solidarity, a mutual's simplicity, and the quasi-cooperative nature of insurance, immigrant farmers created this model from New England, not Old World, precedents.

5

Cooperative Creameries I

*"Men and boys flock to the
Clarks Grove creamery to see
how the business is managed"*

IN LATE NINETEENTH-CENTURY COOPERATION, township mutuals
provided the necessary model of success, and ethnicity furnished the essential ingredient of solidarity. But neither was sufficient alone to induce
farmers to cooperate as producers. The mutuals' existence did not prove
farmers could control crop processing or marketing—or show them
how. Ethnic communities supplied a cooperative with members but did
not give farmers a market for crops. Producers' cooperatives, for whom
spending money was a reality and not a risk, needed capital, not just
membership fees. Construction costs, supplies, labor, and managerial
expertise had to be paid for, as managers of Grange mills and elevators
learned.

Southeastern Minnesota Farmers' Need for a New Cash Crop

Farmers needed to abandon their reliance on wheat not only to replace
past cooperative failures with successes but also for other reasons. In the
late 1870s and early 1880s, after twenty years of single-cropping wheat
on the same land, farmers in southeastern Minnesota sought an alternative to wheat. "The one-crop system had already begun to exhaust the
soil." Yields in the region had fallen 50 percent, from twenty-two bushels
per acre in 1860 to eleven in 1879. Grasshoppers infested fields in the
mid-1870s, and diseases like wheat blight and stem rust cut yields. A
poor crop in 1878 pushed farmers to innovate. Moreover, wheat was a
frontier crop. With abundant cheap land, the farmer just expanded the

area planted in wheat if yields declined. Once land values rose with settlement, he could not easily add more acres, and each acre he owned
now had to earn more to pay for itself. He could not compete against
frontier farmers who had access to cheap land. He could move west to
join them, but if he stayed in southeastern Minnesota, he had to diversify
to other crops.[1]

Minnesota farmers followed a pattern repeated many times as the
frontier moved west. New England, New York, Ohio, Illinois, and Iowa
farmers had switched from wheat as frontier competitors outproduced
them. First, Illinois and Iowa farmers had changed from winter to spring
wheat, but Minnesota farmers in the 1870s already grew spring wheat so
that solution would not do.[2] Learning from eastern farmers, they would
have to choose a specialty: horticulture, sheep raising, corn-livestock
farming, or dairying.

Any alternative crops had to possess some of wheat's advantages.
Since farmers could rely on getting cash for wheat in order to make debt
payments or meet emergency needs, they needed a substitute crop earning cash at prices comparable to wheat prices. Large millers and owners
of line elevator systems were not seeking an alternative to wheat; they
just expanded to new wheat-growing areas and reduced investments in
old ones. That left farmers free to experiment with cooperation as well as
new crops. They could get in at the start of a new industry, before entrepreneurs dominated it. Selling dear had been a stronger motive for cooperation than buying cheap, but shifting to a desperately needed new
cash crop proved to be an even stronger motive. For farmers in southeastern Minnesota, it was a matter of survival.

Culture, climate, and timing influenced the choice of an alternative
to wheat, but the story behind this decision is peripheral to a discussion
of rural cooperatives. To summarize, Minnesota's comparatively short
growing season and severe winters made horticulture problematic and
made corn-livestock farming risky until after 1897 when the Minnesota
Agricultural Experiment Station developed Minnesota 13, a corn variety
suited to the climate. Corn-livestock farming was developed by former
southerners in southern Ohio and Indiana, few of whom moved to Minnesota. Yankees and Scandinavians were more inclined to dairying, and
in the late 1880s, the butter market had not yet been captured by another
region. In another ten years, it would have been, and they might have
turned to Minnesota 13 without ever trying dairying, but that is hypo-

thetical. Culture, climate, and timing—and cooperation—led many southeastern Minnesota farmers to choose dairying.[3]

Newspaper editors called the move away from wheat "diversification," and some farmers changed from raising one cash crop to growing many cash crops on one farm—true diversified farming. But many farmers sought one crop to replace wheat. They chose several different replacements so the regional effect was crop diversity, but individual farmers were often specialists. Dairying could be a specialty or one of many activities on a diversified farm.[4] Dairy specialists called for the former; editors, the latter. Arguing that "dependence on specialties sooner or later proves a broken reed," the *Canby News* advised farmers to "grow a sufficient variety of crops to have something to sell at all seasons." Replying to the call to specialize, the *Freeborn County Standard* agreed, "That dairying should be encouraged" but the farmer's "salvation ... is in diversified farming." With "ten good cows," he might see "no great profit" from butter sales, but the benefits "from the use of the manure will be large."[5]

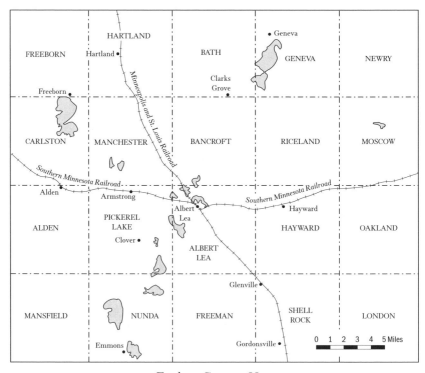

Freeborn County, 1880s

To diversify fully on the individual farm was to return to pioneer farming a generation earlier, before wheat became Minnesota's cash crop. That alternative was unrealistic. Railroads were slowly eliminating the local markets to which pioneer farmers brought "odds and ends to sell at different seasons." Regions were specializing in products to sell in a national market. Farmers could not reverse that process even if they had wanted to. Neither did merchants wish to return to a prerailroad economy where they bought "odds and ends" they then had to market. Nor did specialized buyers want to abandon wheat and set up marketing networks for "odds and ends" because each town's buyer of each product would handle too small a volume to be profitable. It made no sense to return to smaller volumes after railroads had made the marketing of higher volumes possible.[6]

Farmers had to switch to a new specialty, and it would not be easy or painless. It might mean substantial capital investments in livestock, larger barns, or new machinery. A move to dairying entailed a new gender-based division of labor on farms where women had milked cows, made butter, and marketed it. Unsure that farmers would stick with a new crop, entrepreneurs would be reluctant to invest in processing or marketing a new crop, but if farmers formed cooperatives, the risks of shifting to a new crop would fall on them and on the marketing or processing cooperatives they owned.

For merchants and, by extension, the towns, a new specialty meant retaining a cash economy and not returning to a pioneer barter system. It meant economic opportunity for those willing to take the risk that farmers would persist at a new crop. Yet change threatened wheat buyers, elevator owners, and implement dealers selling wheat-harvesting machinery. An economic geography had been built on the yearly wheat harvest, the demand for credit until then, and the need for just a few wheat-marketing towns, which farmers would visit only infrequently. A new specialty threatened to create a new economic geography and a new county politics.

This transition endangered wheat towns' county-seat status, not secure in the late 1870s. From 1867 to 1886, twelve towns in southern and central Minnesota lost county-seat status; others had to fight to retain it.[7] Politics was not divorced from economics. By 1879 most county seats were rail towns, but those that were not, like Blue Earth, felt imperiled. In 1875 Blue Earth fought off a challenge from Delavan, a wheat-buying rail town and Grange center. That year, Blue Earth leaders began a cheese factory—as the center of a hoped-for countywide "system of cheese factories." Cheesemaking would make up for Blue Earth's weakness in wheat marketing and thus help preserve its county-seat status.[8] Wheat-buying county seats feared the opposite—that a new agricultural specialty would lead to a new marketing network and consequently a new county seat.

From Farm-made to Factory-made Butter and Cheese

In the mid-nineteenth century, the American dairy industry was developing a national market for butter and cheese. The move to dairying in southeastern Minnesota followed the pattern established in New York, Wisconsin, and Illinois. "As late as 1877 butter factories in Minnesota were considered something new," noted historian Merrill E. Jarchow.[9] When Minnesotans turned to dairying in the 1880s, they benefited from the fact that many difficulties had already been solved. As with Union stores and township mutuals, Minnesotans used models developed by others.

Farmers had always raised milk cows, made butter on the farm, and sold or bartered it at the country store. Some farms had skilled buttermakers, but many farmers and farmwives knew little about the task. An Owatonna buttermaker charged, "The class of dairymen who make the poorest butter, think they know the most." They "half starve their cows, and what little milk they do get, they will set in open pans behind the cook stove, and hang a sheet off a bed in front of it to keep the smell of turnips, potatoes, cabbages, onions, or the smell of home-grown tobacco out of it."[10] Their butter sold for little where they could get cash. They bartered the rest for store goods. The storekeeper dared not refuse it lest he lose customers to competitors who would accept it. It sometimes "had to be sold to soap-makers for from 1½ to 3 cents per pound," according to one economist.[11]

Many jokes were told about farm butter. In McLeod County, so the story goes, grocers could determine buttermakers' ethnicity by the butter's smell: a kolacky odor (Bohemian), a sauerkraut smell (German), or "a fishy odor" (Scandinavian).[12] To merchants and editors, this was no laughing matter. Low butter prices hurt the local economy. Reduced farm income meant fewer retail sales or more credit sales and overdue accounts. In 1873 one editor complained that carelessness in handling milk cut the price from twenty cents down to ten cents a pound. "One day last week we went through this village [Albert Lea] inquiring for butter, and at every store the answer received was, 'We have none that you want.'" What they had was sold "for soap grease or some coarse use of that sort."[13]

Not all these criticisms can be taken at face value. Farm women made much of the butter, and they endured "disparaging remarks about the products of women's work on the farms being 'unscientific' and 'unable to compete.'"[14] Editors undoubtedly underestimated butter's role in the market because it was "women's work." Replacing farm with factory butter meant separating women's sphere (home) from men's sphere (work). One male advocated it because it would relieve "farmers' wives and daughters of the endless round of washing pans, churning and working butter" so they could engage in "those little beautifications of person and home which give cheerfulness and comfort to domestic life." Limiting women to indoor tasks was a sign of social advancement. Some farm women probably welcomed the change while others regretted the loss of their separate source of income.[15]

New York dairymen first introduced this farm-to-factory transfer: for cheesemaking in 1851, for buttermaking in 1861.[16] Dairy specialists focused on raising milk cows, then on making butter and cheese from their own cows' milk, and finally on processing milk from their neighbors' cows. Two innovations were at work here: the *cooperative* pooling of milk from several farms and the *specialization* of using expert makers. The "economy of skill" from specialization "did more to elevate dairy standards and improve products than" did pooling.[17] It brought efficiencies, a higher quality product, and better prices. Pooling milk saved money; one set of buttermaking equipment was needed rather than one set for each farm. But if farmers hired an unskilled farmer or farmwife as maker, their factory butter or cheese earned them no higher price than before. The "economy of skill" was vital.

Of course, the farm-to-factory move changed the farm's sexual division of labor. One historian has argued that this was a major reason for making the move and has downplayed the role of higher prices and profits in motivating farmers to make the move. That argument is not fully persuasive. Relieving farm women of buttermaking or cheesemaking tasks was only one in a grab-bag of arguments factory proponents used, but not the decisive one. Quoting some complaints about factories' deficiencies does not prove that factories were less profitable than proponents claimed or historians later said.[18] Only the financial records or reports of butter factories can indicate how profitable they were.

The economic advantages of factory-made over farm-made dairy products does not add up to the benefits of cooperation over private enterprise. In New York, the factory system grew "independently of other organized efforts" like the New England Protective Union. "There was no reference to the Rochdale system, nor to . . . the Grange," according to one historian. The word "cooperation" was not used to describe New York's "associated dairies" until the late 1860s.[19] Pooling milk and hiring a cheesemaker were not attempts to bypass existing factories but farmers' attempts to "bypass" their own inexpert cheesemaking. In the absence of competing entrepreneurs, they had time to try several options: selling milk to a cheesemaker or jointly marketing cheese that he made or incorporating a cooperative cheese factory to control both making and marketing.

Jesse Williams was an Oneida County, New York, farmer who specialized in making cheese. At first he purchased milk from neighbors and sold his cheese at his own risk and for his own profit. He paid for milk according to estimated cheese prices in the coming fall markets. But milkers and maker had rival interests; "farmers were inclined to be optimistic as to fall prices," and Williams, "conservative." Farmers grumbled about his prices so they began paying him a set fee for making and marketing cheese. They then received the sales proceeds, took the marketing risks, and divided the profit—or loss. Joint marketing of the cheese they delegated to "a salesman or a sales committee." But cheese buyers objected to working with a committee as "too awkward and time-consuming" so farmers incorporated joint-stock companies to market cheese. Finally they formed such companies to run their own cheese factory and to control both making and marketing. These companies were quasi cooperative, for shares were cheap and widely owned, thus "creating a general desire for the success of the institution" and helping "to secure patronage."

Farmers who reached this final stage controlled the entire process and kept makers' or marketers' interests from competing with their own. With assurance that the profits would be theirs, they could shift to dairying and stick with it.

Minnesota's dairy industry copied the methods prevalent in New York and hired Yorker cheesemakers after the Civil War. At Owatonna (1869), Brownsdale (1872), and Blue Earth (1875), entrepreneurs built cheese factories, hired New York cheesemakers, and convinced farmers to pool their milk and deliver it to the factory.[20] In all these cases farmers had the final risk of profit or loss, yet they lacked control of the process. Factory production was possible only with an adequate, assured supply of milk from farmers who had definitely shifted to dairying. Uncertainty about a milk supply limited entrepreneurs' willingness to invest in cheese factories or creameries. One writer to a Glenwood newspaper urged "every man who owns two or more cows to patronize" the local creamery.[21] Still failure was certain if farmers did not expand their herds to far more than two or three cows.

Farmers hesitated to make the move to dairying or to persist in it. Besides dealing with an altered sexual division of labor and increasing their investments in barns and equipment, farmers faced problems arising from milk's highly perishable nature. Dairying's daily harvest imposed an onerous diurnal regimen of hard work on farmers used to annual harvests and slack times. They must haul milk each day to factories over poor roads in all kinds of weather. A factory manager might reject the milk as spoiled, although he lacked testing technologies to reward superior or penalize inferior milk. Collectivized, regimented, industrialized (the factory)—dairying seemed like "socialized farming" when compared to wheat's free, individualistic ways.[22] Some farmers would not put up with it.

Still those who switched to dairying found that the specialized skill of the butter- or cheesemaker did more than cooperation to cause milk prices to rise. And higher milk prices were the key to convincing farmers of the lasting benefits of dairying. Entrepreneurs owned the Blue Earth, Brownsdale, and Owatonna factories, but a farmer patronizing them received higher prices for his milk than he could get when he made his own butter or cheese. In Blue Earth, farm-made butter brought farmers fifteen cents for thirty pounds of milk. Sending it to the cheese factory earned them about thirty-two cents per thirty pounds—after deducting the fee for making. But Blue Earth's factory failed due to a 50 percent decline in cheese prices in 1878.[23] That drop lowered farmers' income to about fourteen cents per thirty pounds—less than could be earned from farm-made butter. That price collapse gave them no reason to haul milk to a factory and tempted them to return to raising wheat.

New York dairymen had developed markets for butter and cheese, but these were unstable and subject to the same demand and price fluctuations as all markets. Some high-quality cheese was exported. Urbanization expanded eastern markets, but urban demand was susceptible to economic depressions, such as that of 1873–79, which doomed Blue Earth's factory.[24] And New York and Wisconsin dairymen's success in capturing much of the cheese market posed problems for Minnesotans, who were forced to seek their niche in the butter industry, which was more promising for latecomers.

A butter-factory system developed slowly. Buttermaking took less skill and equipment than cheesemaking. Farm makers could better compete with factory experts, and "butter remained a branch of household economy for several decades after cheese had been concentrated in the factory." The first creamery was in Orange County, New York (1861), and the idea spread to Elgin, Illinois (1870), to Iowa (1872), to Wisconsin (mid-1870s), and to Minnesota (about 1876). By 1872, Elgin dairymen had organized a board of trade to market their Western Creamery Butter, "the most highly priced butter in the American market." Still no region had captured the national butter market, and "Americans were greater consumers of butter than of cheese."[25] The 1880s butter market offered a good niche for Minnesotans if they shifted to factory buttermaking.

Technological change made the 1880s a good time to shift, too. The first innovation was the formation of "gathered cream" factories. Farmers separated cream from milk by a gravity method and hauled it to a creamery. The advantages were several. Cream had a much higher butterfat content per pound than did milk and so could be profitably transported longer distances, a huge advantage in newly settled, sparsely populated Minnesota. Skim milk stayed on the farm to be fed to livestock. Payment per inch of cream was more equitable than payment per pound of milk, given the varying butterfat content of milk.[26] By 1883 more than seventy creameries were operating in Minnesota. Azro P. McKinstry of Winnebago City sent cream-gathering wagons up to eighteen miles from his factory.[27]

Dairy experts criticized this system. One cited "an enormous loss of butterfat . . . about 20 percent of the cream is left in the milk"; farmers let milk and cream stand in areas where they absorbed room odors, and the result was poor-quality butter.[28] Yet it introduced the key element — a trained buttermaker.

Soon the centrifugal separator confronted the gathered-cream system's gravity method. A centrifuge separated cream from skim milk by spinning a container of milk at high speeds. In 1879 the first commercially successful centrifugal separators were introduced in Denmark and Sweden. Throughout the 1880s and 1890s the battle raged among promoters, operators, and patrons of each system.[29] The centrifuge had several advantages: it separated more rapidly, thoroughly, and efficiently; it was run by an expert while on-farm, gravity separation by amateurs brought quality-control problems; and it separated cream right before buttermaking whereas gravity-separated cream might sit for days before delivery to the creamery. But it meant returning to the difficult, inefficient practice of delivering whole milk to the factory.[30]

These technological changes were essential to the move to dairying. The centrifugal separator, not the cooperative form of organization, was the key innovation. Yet cooperation facilitated use of the centrifugal separator, as both were brought to Minnesota from other states. A series of increasingly cooperative enterprises began in Minnesota in the early 1870s and led to the completely cooperative creameries of 1889–90.[31] Both the technological and the organizational changes are exemplified in the history of Freeborn County, which became Minnesota's model dairying county.

Dairying in Freeborn County before 1889

As elsewhere, Freeborn's dairying began with farm-made butter, some of which was sold or bartered in the local market. In 1879 Freeborn had no creameries, although a cheese factory operated across the Mower County line, and its 6,601 milk cows produced 532,657 pounds of farm butter.[32] Farmers in eastern Freeborn and western Mower Counties organized the Turtle Creek Cheese Company in 1874. Leading the drive were two farmers from New York who "were enthusiastic over the cheese question." It was not a cooperative, but a joint-stock company. It did not control making or marketing but rented its plant to an independent cheesemaker while individual farmers did their own marketing. Only building and equipping the factory were done jointly.[33] The economy of skill was mostly wasted when the cheesemaker's product was sold only in local markets.

In 1886 a different group began to use the same system and cheesemaker nine miles to the south, at London. Meeting as a farmers' club in the local schoolhouse, these Old Stock farmers showed an ethnic preference for cheesemaking: "The residents of that district had come themselves, or were descendants of families in the cheese making districts of New York, Ohio and Wisconsin." They built a cheese factory near the schoolhouse but neglected to market their product jointly and earned meager returns from bartering it for store goods "in neighboring towns… [with] very little sold for cash."[34] They failed to bypass local merchants or to control making or marketing. Yorker and Badger dominance in the national market limited them to local ones, thereby defeating the factory idea. There was little point to making cheese in large volumes if they could not sell it in large volumes.

By 1889 Freeborn's farmers were patronizing three cheese factories and seven gathered-cream factories or creameries.[35] Farmers organized some as cooperatives while entrepreneurs or joint-stock companies owned the others. In the spring of 1881, for example, prominent businessmen of Albert Lea formed a joint-stock company to build and operate a gathered-cream plant modeled after ones in northern Iowa.[36] These factories inaugurated the cash-basis dairy industry in Freeborn County, but farm butter continued to be sold and bartered in local markets. Under this mixed farm-factory regimen, the number of milk cows almost doubled between 1879 and 1890.[37] Despite the progress made, these factories, whether entrepreneurial or cooperative, failed to convince Freeborn's farmers to switch decisively to dairying.

The Albert Lea plant was a financial failure for its Main Street investors.[38] At an October 1884 meeting of the Farmers Club, farmers complained that the creamery was not paying enough for their cream. With long, cream-gathering routes and few farmer-patrons, the manager explained, "the gathering of cream is very expensive and with more cows better rates per inch could be paid." Entrepreneurs could not persuade enough farmers to milk cows so the creamery had to gather cream from a larger territory and had to pass these higher per-unit costs on to farmers in the form of lower cream prices. Then even fewer farmers found it profitable to sell cream, and per-unit costs went even higher. The creamery had to close during the winter for lack of milk.[39] Local editors who advocated diversified farming with ten cows per farm as an adequate number were no help in convincing farmers to milk more cows.[40]

Cooperatives fared no better than entrepreneurs in using the gathered-cream system. Cooperation by itself was not the answer. Early in 1889, "the farmers and business men around Gordonsville were desirous of making a trial of the creamery business." They accepted a

Chicago firm's offer to build a gathered-cream plant for five thousand dollars, "a very exorbitant price." Their aptly named Gilt Edge creamery was not a Rochdale-style cooperative but may have been quasi cooperative in spirit. The plant was overbuilt and probably undersupplied with cream. After a few months and the loss of about two thousand dollars, it burned, which ended local dairying "for several years."[41] The Alden Farmers' Cooperative Creamery was "controlled and officered by farmers." Yet its "attempt at buttermaking on the gathered cream plan . . . proved about as unprofitable for the co-operative company as it had everywhere else in Freeborn county."[42]

By late 1889 both entrepreneurs and cooperators had failed to develop a factory system that paid high enough prices for milk or cream to ensure an adequate volume. Neither made butter at a per-unit cost low enough to afford high prices. There was a benefit from this failure because there were so few successful creameries creating barriers that farmers must bypass. If farmers could develop a workable factory system, they would have the creamery field largely to themselves. They

The belt-driven inner workings of Geneva's creamery, with the centrifugal separators on the right, about 1910.

first did so at Clarks Grove, which became a model for Minnesota's
cooperative creameries.

The Limits of Ethnicity:
Clarks Grove, Tyler, and West Denmark

In December 1889, Søren Nelson, a Danish-American farmer from
Meeker County, stopped in southeastern Bath Township—a heavily
Danish-American area of Freeborn County—to visit his brother-in-law,
Hans Peter (H. P.) Jensen. Nelson was returning from northern Iowa
where he had inspected centrifugal-separator creameries (some of them
cooperatives) in Bremer and Fayette Counties. Inspired by this report,
Jensen recalled observing cooperative creameries in Denmark during an
1884 trip. A few days later, at the end of the Bath township mutual's annual meeting, he "brought up the question of organizing a co-operative
separator creamery." The farmers called a meeting for January 28, 1890,
to discuss the matter.[43]

Danish Americans organized the Clarks Grove creamery. Similar
creameries began in Denmark in 1882 so historians have linked the two
events and have assumed the Clarks Grove creamery was modeled after
Danish creameries: "a direct line of influence ran from Denmark to
Clark's Grove"; Clarks Grove's success "grew from practices and theories
imported from Denmark"; the Clarks Grove creamery "was fashioned
after successful operations in Denmark and Iowa."[44] This creamery
is cited to prove what historian Eric E. Lampard called "the popular
notion . . . that co-operative farming generally, and dairying in particular,
represent[s] 'immigrant contributions' to American agriculture."[45] That
notion does not stand up under close scrutiny. An analysis of the Clarks
Grove creamery and the reasons for its success must begin with a close
look at its supposed ethnic origins. If the Danish model does not account
for success, as alleged, then some other explanation must be sought.

The most extravagant claims for the creamery's Danish origins come
from Danish Americans as well as Danes. Some rest on the testimony of
Lars Jørgensen Hauge (also called Lars Jørgensen), a onetime Danish
Baptist missionary who briefly served as pastor of the Clarks Grove
Baptist church. According to Hauge, he sought to improve dairying in
the area after seeing a Danish-American farmwife cry when a merchant
offered her only five cents per pound for her butter—not in cash but in

trade for store goods. He claimed to have invented a crude milk refrigeration process that produced better cream. After an 1887 convalescence in Denmark where he visited the new cooperative creameries, he returned to Clarks Grove and supposedly preached "what he calls his 'butter sermons,'" which led to the start of the famous creamery.[46]

Hauge's story is suspect. A missionary to the Dakota Indians in Dakota Territory, he lived in Clarks Grove only briefly and sporadically. In 1871 he preached Seventh-Day Adventism, which caused Clarks Grove Baptists to withdraw their fellowship from him. After that, it is unlikely he could have influenced these Baptists or have preached to them.[47] By 1890 when the creamery was started, he had left the area.[48] A Danish Baptist history called him "one of these half-learned men, who never lacks the boldness to let his own deeds shine forth."[49] Hauge is the main testifier to his own role, so this description speaks loudly.

Several Clarks Grove Baptist leaders visited Denmark in the 1880s, and some writers claim that their reports of the Danes' success with cooperative creameries led to the creation of the one at Clarks Grove. One of the travelers, H. P. Jensen, noted this success in 1884 and reported it to friends and neighbors, but his report was not publicized at the time. Nor did it lead to any attempts at creamery organization.[50] Baptist leader N. P. Jensen (no relation), a Clarks Grove native, visited Denmark in the summer of 1884 on a mission to aid the Danish Baptist church. His travel letters mentioned Danish politics and religion but not cooperative creameries.[51] In 1889, J. S. Lunn, a former Clarks Grove pastor, visited the Danish province of Jutland, where the cooperative creameries originated, but there is no evidence he reported on them at the time of his return or before the January 1890 meeting.[52]

Clarks Grove Baptists maintained contact with Baptists in Denmark, an often-impoverished minority then denied true religious freedom in an overwhelmingly Lutheran land. Twice a year, they sent monetary support "for needy fellow believers in Denmark."[53] It seems unlikely that these ties connected them to the Danish cooperative movement in which Denmark's Baptists were not prominent. Such bonds possibly made them skeptical of reports of Denmark's newfound dairy prosperity and reluctant to adopt Danish innovations on the basis of hearsay evidence from returning visitors. After all, they were the beneficent donors and the Danes the poor recipients. That may be why, when H. P. Jensen told his story, he reportedly "was not widely understood."[54]

Clarks Grove did not strive to save its Danish heritage. Like many pietist Danish-American communities, it lacked a school to teach children Danish and did not conduct its Sunday school in Danish. Even older residents often spoke English. Few traveled back to Denmark to visit. Its Baptist heritage took precedence over its Danish one.[55] Its farmers would not have risked their futures on cooperative buttermaking just because it was done in Denmark.

At the meeting on January 28, 1890, J. P. Larson "gave some information about the creameries in Denmark and here in this country... different things were said by others on the matter."[56] H. P. Jensen, J. S. Lunn, and "other old settlers spoke at length on the benefits of dairying in the old country."[57] But Iowa's cooperative creameries, not Denmark's, were the main model. It was Søren Nelson's story of Iowa's success that led H. P. Jensen to ask for this meeting at which it was decided to send a committee to Iowa to "investigate the creameries there"—not to get building plans or machinery specifications but to verify Nelson's report. Despite news from Denmark, they were doubtful until the committee saw a successful creamery in Oran Township (Fayette County) and one in what was probably Fremont Township (Bremer County), Iowa.[58] Only then were they "convinced" that cooperative creameries were "practical and profitable."[59] When they met to start one, they read aloud Oran's constitution and bylaws, translated these into Danish, and used them as a rough draft in drawing up their own. They altered some articles but not to conform to Danish models.[60] For the new creamery's buttermaker, they chose "an experienced dairyman from Iowa."[61]

Although conducting meetings in Danish, the members did not transplant Danish practices to American soil. As practical farmers seeking profits in U.S. markets, they did not act on reports of Danish cooperative creameries until they saw a successful American model. In his study of Swedish-American farmers in Isanti County, Robert C. Ostergren noted that they belonged "to a social community," retaining Swedish culture and language, and "to a much larger economic community... the world of business and markets... dominated by the English-speaking host culture." In the economic community they quickly adopted American crops, machinery, and marketing and abandoned Swedish farm practices for American ones.[62] Sentiment and tradition counted for little in farming—and that was true of Danish-American farmers in Bath Township also. They did not adopt cooperative dairying to mimic Danish practices, even innovative ones actually superior to American methods. Accustomed to replacing Danish practices with American ones that they assumed were superior in the U.S. market, they primarily adopted Iowa's methods of cooperative dairying.

If any Danish-American farmers were to use Danish models, it would more likely be those of Lutheran colonies like Tyler in Lincoln County rather than Clarks Grove. Tyler had closer ties to Denmark and a greater stress on cultural preservation, yet its farmers did not rush to adopt Danish dairy ideas. A Tyler resident wrote to a correspondent in Denmark in 1889, "What we most desire is a *Danish creamery*—that we must finally have in operation for the spring." Yet they did not start one then. Another Tylerite reported to a Danish friend, "Here no special importance is given to a creamery, for butter costs very little." Churches, folk and parochial schools, and other social institutions were higher priorities for Tyler's leaders than an economic institution such as a creamery. The leaders were ministers and teachers who maintained close ties to Denmark, but the Danish news they desired to receive and their Danish correspondents wished to send them was of exciting cultural and political events in 1880s Denmark, not of farmers' forming dairy cooperatives. Their ears were tuned to Danish traditions, not Danish innovations like cooperative creameries.[63]

In 1887 the colony's land agent planned a creamery for Tyler, but it is unclear if this was to be privately owned or cooperative. He never carried out his plan. A cooperative creamery started in Tyler in 1894, but by then the many Minnesota cooperative creameries were likely the model more than Danish ones. In addition Danish-American Lutheran leaders saw that cooperation could aid their goal of cultural preservation, but American events may have sparked that idea as much as Danish ones.[64]

Actually, by sponsoring Danish-American colonies like Tyler, the leaders engaged in a form of cooperation—cooperative land settlement. To concentrate the Danish population, they bypassed the usual land markets in which individual buyers dispersed to cheaper frontier lands. Instead, they jointly negotiated terms of sale for a block of land through a land agent, in what resembled joint purchasing. In the Tyler colony, thirty-five thousand acres were to be sold to Danish Americans only for three years, with the maximum initial price, maximum price increases thereafter, the interest rate, and other terms negotiated in advance. This deal was economically advantageous to settlers, but the main goal was to concentrate the Danish-American population in order to facilitate cultural preservation. It was only later that the leaders realized that concentration would aid cooperation—and vice versa.[65]

In Clarks Grove, also, cooperative dairying helped to support a more concentrated Danish-American, Baptist population, and that aided the church. But Clarks Grove's leaders were not distracted by the goal of preserving Danish culture, and they moved more quickly to start an American-style cooperative creamery.

Even if Tyler's or Clarks Grove's Danish Americans had followed Danish models, that would not have guaranteed success. In March 1885, farmers in West Denmark, Wisconsin, started the Luck Creamery Company in a strong Danish Lutheran colony. It hired a Danish buttermaker, a woman trained by one of Denmark's best-known dairy instructors. It later advertised for "an experienced Danish buttermaker to manage a cooperative creamery... in a large Danish settlement." Danish dairying was its model.[66]

Clarks Grove was well advised to wait for an American model. Dissension and dissatisfaction began early at Luck. At the first annual meeting, members instructed the directors "to rent the creamery to some responsible persons"—quickly! Patrons expressed displeasure by withholding cream. The board was confused over how and where to market butter. A board member went to Duluth to find a market; another wrote to towns in western Wisconsin to find one nearby. Shareholders were asked their opinion at a special meeting. The board followed their advice to ship to commission houses in New York, but one firm could not sell October's shipment and refused to pay for it.[67] After two and a half years of cooperative management, the creamery was rented to the buttermaker and her husband.[68]

The gathered-cream system it used was part of the problem. Still as a Danish-style cooperative in action, it was a poor "immigrant contribution" to U.S. agriculture. Using Iowa models and an Iowa buttermaker who knew where to market butter and which commission firms could be trusted, Clarks Grove's farmers adapted to the American market. The Luck creamery tried to reinvent the wheel, to tackle problems already solved by Iowa's creameries.[69]

Minnesota's early cooperative creameries traced their origins to antebellum "associated" cheese factories of New York, not to Scandinavia or Germany. Ethnicity played a role in their success, but that role was to sustain and support, not to innovate. Ethnic solidarity helped to sustain loyalty to the cooperative when entrepreneurs offered higher milk prices to lure farmers away. Danes played a key technical role in the growth of America's (especially Minnesota's) butter industry. Danish *mejerister* (buttermakers) emigrated to the United States in the early 1890s and managed cooperative creameries. Danish Americans trained in this country had similar success.[70] In 1904 Danish-American dairy expert J. H. Monrad proudly noted "the scores of prizewinning Danish-American buttermakers" with "names ending in -sen, -son, -dahl, -gaard, and the like."[71] But this later role of the Danish buttermaker cannot be read back to 1885–90 as proof Minnesota's cooperative creameries were a Danish innovation. The *mejerister* arrived too late to start the cooperative creamery movement. They came after its success ensured a market for their services.

Economic Efficiency:
Centrifuge versus Gathered-Cream Methods

Clarks Grove's creamery thrived and Luck's failed for specific economic reasons. A creamery is a business. No farmer accepted Danish flags or Bibles in payment for milk. The economic efficiencies of a centrifugal separator compared to the gathered-cream system's gravity method were key factors convincing farmers to shift to dairying, for they meant higher milk prices (see Tables B and C in Appendix).

The principal reason for Clarks Grove's success was not the high price it received for its butter. Freeborn County's farm-made butter averaged ten cents per pound in 1890, while Clarks Grove butter brought more than eighteen cents.[72] But that benefit of the economy of skill accrued to most creameries: the Luck gathered-cream cooperative sold butter at 76 percent of the prevailing New York price during its first year (1886) while Clarks Grove sold at 77 percent its first year (1890).[73] The Clover Valley Creamery Association's cooperative separator creamery at Clover in Freeborn County sold at 78 percent its first year (1891). All three cooperatives received similar prices when they shipped butter to New York, their primary market.[74]

Where Clarks Grove and Clover Valley outperformed Luck was in their low operating expense per pound of butter made.[75] Clarks Grove's operating costs averaged less than two cents per pound during its first three years (1890–92) while Clover Valley averaged three cents per pound, which was much less than Luck's average of eight cents in its first year. Lower per-unit costs of making butter enabled each separator creamery to pay farmers 50 percent more for their milk than did the gathered-cream plant. In their first year, Clarks Grove paid sixty-six cents (per one hundred pounds of milk), and Clover Valley paid sixty-seven and one-half cents while Luck paid only forty-one cents.

This difference derived from two advantages of the centrifuge. First, the centrifugal separator separated cream much more rapidly than did the gravity method. Even creameries' smallest centrifuges separated twelve hundred pounds of milk per hour.[76] That produced "economies of speed." In its first six months, Clarks Grove made more than eight times as much butter as did Luck. More butter meant lower fixed expenses per pound of butter. For example, buttermakers' wages were about the same under both systems, but wage costs per pound of butter were much lower with the centrifuge because of its greater output. Second, the centrifuge left less butterfat in skim milk so the creamery made more butter per hundred pounds of milk.[77] The creameries at Clarks Grove and Clover Valley made about one-fourth pound more butter per hundred-

Danish dairying expert Professor Bernhard Bøggild and the University of Minnesota's Dean Albert F. Woods addressed the crowd at the twentieth anniversary of Clarks Grove creamery. The schoolhouse was a more neutral site to celebrate an economic entity than the Baptist church where the organizing meetings were held.

weight of milk than did the one at Luck. A greater output lowered per-unit costs.[78] Consistently high milk prices were the key factor in con-vincing farmers to stick with dairying. Centrifugal-separator creameries' high milk prices depended not so much on unstable factors like one but-termaker's skill but a great deal on the unchangeable efficiency of the centrifuge.

Timing was also important. Improved technologies like the cen-trifuge usually invite entry of new firms into an industry. They enable these firms to pay suppliers higher prices, charge customers lower prices, and still make a profit because efficient technologies have lower per-unit costs. In markets with stagnant demand, the resulting increase in supply will lower retail prices, thus threatening both existing and new firms. But where "the market is growing, actual entry" of new compa-nies "need not affect prices."[79] Clarks Grove, Clover Valley, and other creameries begun in the early 1890s entered a butter market growing due to immigration and urbanization so their greater volume of butter did not (immediately) swamp the market and depress butter prices.

The cooperative creameries returned to farmer-patrons almost all the profits resulting from the centrifuge's efficiency and from the grow-ing market. At Clarks Grove, farmers' milk checks went from $.415 per hundredweight in June 1890, the first full month of operation, to $1.05 in November 1890.[80] Part of the profits went to pay debts incurred in build-ing the creamery. That was good news for farmers who had co-signed notes of indebtedness. With high milk volumes, a $.05-per-hundred-weight deduction from milk checks rapidly paid the debts. Similar charges only slowly paid off debts of gathered-cream plants with lower volumes. Farmers co-signing notes or creditors lending money to build separator creameries faced less risk than did those financing gathered-cream factories.

The Role of Religion and Ethnicity:
Clarks Grove Creamery

The importance of economic factors does not negate the role played by religious and ethnic solidarity, which aided farmers in implementing the Iowa model at Clarks Grove. Danish and Baptist homogeneity helped create the mutual trust needed for a group of farmers to take personal responsibility for three thousand dollars in loans. In other towns, directors had to co-sign for notes; members would not do so.[81] Clarks Grove farmers made an ideal polity: ethnically, linguistically, religiously homogeneous with common economic interests, a shared desire for a local trade center, and a history of jointly running their church.

The fact that four or five miles was about as far as milk could profitably be hauled contributed to creating a homogeneous membership. Distance excluded most Irish farmers living in Bath's northwest corner, though some Irish lived as close to the creamery as some Danish-American members did. Its meetings being conducted in Danish for the first three years also discouraged Irish membership. Several Norwegian-American farmers from Bath joined it. Bancroft Township's Norwegian Americans stayed out, though many lived closer to it than did some Danish-American members in Bancroft.[82] The Baptist faith of its farmers caused Norwegian-American Lutherans and Irish Catholics to form their own creameries rather than to join Clarks Grove's.

The bonds of ethnic solidarity induced the cooperative's members to donate in-kind services, which reduced the creamery's cash outlays. Farmers carted lumber to the building site instead of hiring someone else to do it. Neighbors took turns hauling milk to the creamery, rather than paying an outsider.[83]

Religion and ethnicity also helped Clarks Grove farmers shift to dairying—to hard, intensive, regimented farming. One Danish-American farmer from another area reported, "We milked from 28 to 32 cows and never have I tried any work that seemed more like slavery."[84] An observer reported that religious life in Clarks Grove was disciplined: no traveling or working on Sunday, no alcohol, no dancing. Church members could be expelled for marrying unbelievers. That collective discipline was invaluable in dairying.[85] A creamery member must accept a creamery's dictates in his farming practices, such as what to feed cows, just as a church member had to accept a church's mandates in his or her private life.

Here, the line between economic and social communities became blurred. The economic cooperative was formed in the church's social community. Led by the church's leaders who became its early officers, its organizational meetings were held at the church.[86] The same men oversaw both the Sunday schedule and the cow-feeding schedule. Mutual accountability aided both church and creamery.

Intensive dairy farming aided the church, too, for it reduced the dispersal of church members to distant places. Already in the 1870s, in the chain migration common to many immigrant groups, Baptists had left crowded Bath Township to move to Brown and Martin Counties in Minnesota, Gilmore City in Iowa, and Oldham in South Dakota.[87] Dairying could not end that process, but its more intensive farming could support more Baptists per square mile than could extensive wheat farming. Dairying demanded fewer acres. Bath's Baptist corner already had smaller farms and more intensive farming than nearby areas. In 1878 there were thirty-five farms of eighty acres or fewer in the eleven sections nearest the Baptist church; in the eleven sections nearest Bancroft's Norwegian Lutheran church there were only ten.[88] A creamery preserved this pattern. The Baptist church was the de facto sponsor of the creamery, and to this unofficial sponsor went many of the benefits.

A year after the first meetings, the *Freeborn County Standard* reported, "Men and boys from all directions flock to the Clark's Grove creamery this warm weather to get a drink of buttermilk, and to see how the business is managed."[89] Cooperative creameries began organizing throughout Freeborn County.

Freeborn's farmers had created a successful form of rural cooperation to add to township mutuals. As a producers' cooperative, it promised

The Hartland Band helped H. P. Jensen and company celebrate the twenty-fifth anniversary of the Clarks Grove creamery in 1915.

greater monetary rewards than a consumers' cooperative. Cooperative commitment helped, but the new technology of the centrifuge proved to be more beneficial. The timing was excellent. The centrifuge was coming into widespread use, and entrepreneurs had not yet dominated this new technology. Unlike Granger flour mills, cooperative creameries never lacked high volumes to benefit from efficient technologies. The high milk prices they paid ensured the availability of large quantities of milk and provided the incentive for farmers to move to dairying. Finally cooperative creameries were not tied to any farmers' group, such as the Grange. No matter how farmers fared in politics, the creameries' efficiencies and high milk prices saved them. Now the challenge for farmers was to try to extend this new form of rural cooperation across the Minnesota countryside.

6

Cooperative Creameries II

*"People would rush around
among their neighbors and want
a creamery on every cross road"*

BY THE FIRST WEEK OF APRIL 1890, residents of the Irish Catholic
community in northwest Bath Township could hear the whistle from
the Clarks Grove creamery seven miles away: "It makes us think we
live near a station."[1] No railroad tracks passed through Bath, however.
The Irish, Danes, and Norwegians lived in their separate communities
surrounding their churches. No villages interrupted the pattern of small
farms spread across the gently rolling countryside. To buy supplies, the
Irish and Norwegians in western Bath Township journeyed six miles
west to the village of Hartland. Danes drove their wagons four to five
miles northeast to Geneva by picturesque Geneva Lake. To market grain,
all these groups went west to railroad depots at Hartland or Manchester.

At the organizational meeting in January 1890, farmers called the
southeast corner of Bath Township "Clarks Grove," but the Clarks Grove
post office was not in Bath but in northeast Bancroft Township, and it
was certainly not a town. Besides Albert Lea, Freeborn County had only
two towns of any size—Alden and Freeborn. Albert Lea was almost ten
times larger than these two villages combined. Wheat farming did not
raise a good crop of towns, nor had Manchester's mutual insurance company produced one there.[2]

Cooperative dairying would be different, and farmers knew it; that
was why selection of a creamery site was so important. The four-to-five
mile limit for hauling milk by wagon was another reason. Farmers from
Bancroft and Riceland Townships attended the creamery meetings at
Bath's Danish Baptist church, but some would be too far from the cream-

ery site to participate. Before the final vote, farmers decided to allow those living more than four miles from the winning site to withdraw from the association.[3] Choosing a site could be contentious in townships that lacked a village. (Where there was a village, it was usually picked as the site.) A founder of Union Creamery in Steele County recalled a heated debate among farmers over the location: "They were ready to pull one another's whiskers."[4]

Farmers knew they were selecting the site for a crossroads community. Before choosing, Clarks Grove farmers approved a motion: "No one is permitted to set up any store near the creamery unless he is a member of it."[5] They showed foresight. Two weeks after the whistle first blew, a store and a blacksmith shop were selling and shoeing nearby.[6] Eighty-one farmers signed up to deliver milk. Some shared hauling duties with neighbors, but fifty farmers came daily to one spot and waited while their milk was separated.[7] The creamery later "built sheds to accommodate 25 teams" of horses for "shelter on a rainy day."[8] The retailing opportunities were obvious.

In May 1891 farmers talked of adding a cooperative store, which opened in January 1892. The Clarks Grove post office was relocated from Bancroft to Bath Township, to a site across the road from the creamery. The Clarks Grove creamery built a buttermaker's house, and the Baptist church erected a parsonage. By 1896 a windmill and a hardware store also graced the new crossroads town of Clarks Grove. Nine men (non-farmers) with some twenty dependents lived there by 1895. This hamlet was no threat to Albert Lea, which had a population of 4,158. Dairying made for daily, short trips; wheat farming, for long infrequent ones. Railroadless crossroads towns drawing trade from a few townships could not compete with a county seat, whose elites were not opposed to crossroads creameries that still hauled supplies from and butter to Albert Lea.[9]

Clarks Grove's whistle signaled other Freeborn farmers to form their own creameries, their own crossroads villages. Unlike Grangers who were slow to start mills or elevators, Freeborn's farmers rapidly formed a multitude of dairy cooperatives. By December 1892 they had fifteen cooperative separator creameries; by 1900 the number reached twenty-eight. This rapid diffusion was not limited to Freeborn County; Minnesota had 149 cooperative creameries by December 1894.[10]

Farmers quickly multiplied the number of cooperative creameries for many reasons, but the main one was the ability of centrifugal-separator creameries to pay a high price for milk. The report of the state

dairy and food commissioner to the 1893 legislature confirmed the contrast between Clarks Grove and Luck. At the end of 1892, only 38 percent
of the state's 235 creameries were centrifugal-separator plants; 60 percent were the less-efficient gathered-cream plants. In the more advanced
Freeborn County, twenty-one were centrifugal-separator plants and only
one a gathered-cream plant; one used both systems. Freeborn's farmers
had recognized the centrifuge's superiority; the county averaged fifty-
four farmer-patrons per creamery while creameries elsewhere averaged
only thirty-four patrons. Once the centrifugal separator was purchased
and operated by cooperating farmers, more farmers were persuaded to
shift to dairying, thus assuring Freeborn's creameries an ample, reliable
milk supply.[11] Farmers in other counties soon followed the example set in
Freeborn.

Intrinsic Reasons for the Diffusion of Cooperative Creameries

The proliferation of cooperative separator creameries hinged on a number of factors—some intrinsic to 1890s dairying and some extrinsic, dependent on local circumstances. Although the Clarks Grove creamery
had more patrons (113) than any other plant in 1892, as an entity it was
not indispensable to this diffusion. Probably unaware of the Danish Baptists' plans, farmers in Nunda and Pickerel Lake Townships began the
Clover Valley creamery by early April 1890.[12] The Clover Valley operation also showed the centrifuge's superiority. Nor was cooperation the
key factor in diffusion; at gathered-cream factories in Alden and Hayward cooperation failed.[13] In June 1890 Hayward farmers held "a rousing
meeting" due to the "depressed condition of the butter market" for "cream
at only 7 cents per inch scarcely pays for milking the cows."[14] Yet the
Clarks Grove creamery was beginning to flourish that same summer.
High New York butter prices were not needed for diffusion; despite a 14
percent decline in New York butter prices in 1888–90, efficient separator
creameries survived. Nor did a three-year price rise in 1891–93 save the
inefficient gathered-cream plants; they were either converted to separator plants or abandoned.[15] Rising butter prices aided farmers in financing their cooperatives, but they were not necessary to or a sufficient
cause of the diffusion.

More intrinsic factors led farmers to cooperate in dairying. They
needed less capital (three to five thousand dollars) to build and equip
creameries than flour mills (five to thirty thousand dollars) or wheat

warehouses (five to ten thousand dollars). The best technology, the centrifugal separator, required less capital than the latest milling technologies. Also milk was bulkier, highly perishable, and harder to ship in raw form than wheat. Before refrigerated cars became available, they could not ship milk to Twin Cities dairies as they could wheat to Minneapolis mills. Local processing was both affordable and necessary.

Financing the smaller start-up costs was easier. Clarks Grove's eighty-one charter members signed on to borrow up to three thousand dollars: "We pledge ourselves, individually and as a group, to become personally responsible for the above-named sum." The best security for the loan was their promise "to deliver milk from so many cows (or more) as are set opposite our names." Each gave a personal note guaranteeing repayment of four dollars for each cow pledged. Five cents per hundredweight of milk was deducted from the milk check, placed in a sinking fund, and used to repay loans.[16] Only the personal note guaranteeing repayment was a legally binding document, not the promise to deliver milk. Unlike Denmark's cooperative creameries, Minnesota's did not normally sign members to a binding milk-delivery contract.[17]

The ability to repay a loan depended on an adequate milk supply. A cooperative could best secure that volume even without binding contracts. Community solidarity motivated farmers to deliver milk, and it was in members' interest to deliver milk to secure their investment in the creamery and to repay the loans. High milk prices paid by centrifugal-separator cooperatives almost guaranteed that milk supply. A private investor could not know whether farmers would find it in their interest to deliver milk to his creamery over the long term. He would not buy a high-volume separator if he were unsure of a long-term, high volume of milk. A cooperative that used the efficient centrifuge and paid high milk prices ensured that it would receive the high volumes it needed.

The Clarks Grove creamery was financed through $1,850 in loans from individual farmers, plus $943 in an advance draft from a Freeborn County bank. It paid the remaining start-up costs with butter-sales receipts. It repaid the advance draft in 1891 and the loans by March 21, 1892, two years after it started.[18] This speedy repayment encouraged others in their creamery ventures.

The driving force in spreading cooperative creameries in Freeborn County was their high milk prices, publicized in weekly newspapers.[19] Press reports of the high prices paid at Clarks Grove caused Freeborn's

farmers to get excited about separator creameries and to be critical of
other methods. By October 1890, the farmers of northeastern Bath were
hauling milk to Clarks Grove, not to "the Geneva cheese factory," reported the local correspondent for the *Albert Lea Enterprise*, because
"They think it pays better." Clarks Grove "netted its patrons 92 cents per
100 pounds of milk for October." This was "better than raising wheat at
70 cents a bushel."[20] In mid-January 1891, a local buttermaker began "to
send her milk to the creamery. Where will her patrons buy good butter
now?" the *Freeborn County Standard's* correspondent inquired.[21] High
milk prices were the key factor in farmers' move to cooperative creameries and dairying.

In February and March 1891, persons planning to start creameries
flocked to Clarks Grove; Lars O. Esse of Hayward, the directors of the
Armstrong creamery association, and Jay Jones and Albert Schutt of
Geneva all visited the creamery to investigate its operations.[22] Creamery
fever drew cautionary criticism in the *Standard*. Disputing a report that
Clarks Grove butter averaged thirty cents per pound, one critic warned,
"Lots of people would read the statement . . . and rush around among
their neighbors and want a creamery on every cross road."[23] A Clarks
Grove patron admitted eighteen cents was the correct figure, but that
was a gain of eight and a half cents over the average price for farm-made
butter. He was making a profit of almost twenty-seven dollars per cow;
that should dispel the fear that "lingers in the minds of many farmers
[—] the fear that the business will not permanently be profitable." Anxieties vanished as Freeborn farmers heard Clarks Grove paid $1.05 per
hundredweight for milk. Farm-made butter earned thirty to forty cents
per hundredweight for milk.[24]

Local, Extrinsic Factors in the Spread of Cooperative Creameries

The distance limit on hauling milk by wagon made it necessary to have
many crossroads creameries. Lacking adventuresome entrepreneurs,
farmers would have to finance and run them. Unlike Wisconsin, Minnesota lacked dairy specialists with the capital to establish creameries.[25]
Merchants started and financed creameries in villages, but they did not
consider crossroads sites as promising places to invest up to five thousand dollars. Farmer-patrons might respond to price changes, drop
dairying, and shift to hogs or sheep or back to wheat. They could haul

milk to another creamery offering a higher price. A merchant's choice of a site might prove to be unpopular with farmers, who would then haul to a village where other services were available or start a cooperative to compete with the merchant's creamery. Making a three to five thousand dollar investment in an unproven industry at an unproven crossroads location was not attractive to investors.

Cooperators could do what entrepreneurs could not. Democratic decisions about the site and the sharing of investment risks secured consent from farmer-members, conferred legitimacy on the new enterprise, and gave farmers a stake in it. Pooling resources, committing farmers (at least through community pressure) to deliver milk, picking sites democratically, and assuring that the farmers as a group gained by their success and lost by their failure—these factors intrinsic to cooperation eliminated many risks that discouraged investors and enabled cooperatives to run a vast majority of Freeborn County's twenty-eight creameries by 1900.

Various local means and motives that were extrinsic to dairying and cooperation also contributed to the formation of cooperative creameries—when joined to the overriding motive of high milk prices. First, distance from an existing creamery motivated farmers to establish their own. Having lost the vote on the Bath site, farmers in western Riceland and eastern Bancroft Townships organized one for themselves less than a month later.[26] Three years afterward, patrons of the Riceland and Hayward creameries who "had a considerable distance to haul their milk" began the Sumner Valley creamery.[27]

A second cause was a dispute over a site. Farmers in Pickerel Lake and northern Nunda Townships held a joint meeting in March 1890. They considered building a creamery at a compromise site in the middle of Pickerel Lake Township. When a site at the township's southern edge was chosen instead, farmers from its northern section withdrew and formed their own creamery.[28] Democracy conferred legitimacy on a site only if the selection process seemed fair. In February and March 1891, farmers in Mansfield Township formed two associations and planned for creameries three miles apart. "Convinced that two creameries could not succeed so close together...the Kiester association agreed to give in two miles if the Niebuhr [association] would give in one mile." Diplomatic negotiations between the two broke down, and farmers started a third association. There was talk that "the southern part of the township" would secede and start its own creamery, but that plan failed. Many farmers refused to haul milk to the new Mansfield creamery due to "dissatisfaction on account of [its] location." Mansfield's high milk prices ultimately healed the sore feelings over the site.[29]

Third, politically prominent farmers played key roles in establishing creameries. Erick Johnsrud, a Norwegian American from Riceland Township, was a leader at the meetings in Bath and later organized the Riceland and Manchester associations, both of them Scandinavian-American ones.[30] Erick Johnsrud and C. G. Johnsrud were political leaders among the county's Scandinavian-American farmers, who entrusted Erick with the task of organizing creamery associations.[31] Few financial rewards accrued to creamery organizers, but the farmers' gratitude aided aspiring politicians. L. P. Lawson of Clarks Grove and John L. Gibbs of Geneva used their dairying prominence in political campaigns. Gibbs won brief terms as lieutenant-governor and railroad and warehouse commissioner, served as speaker of the House, and sought the Republican nomination for governor after being elected president of the Minnesota State Dairymen's Association.[32]

In Hartland, a strong Farmers' Alliance town, the members of the Alliance and the merchants took a leading role in starting a creamery.[33] The Alliance was an agrarian group that sought to improve farmers' lives and focused on economic and political action more singlemindedly than had the Grange. It began to recruit farmers in Minnesota in the early 1880s. In Hartland the Alliance and the creamery held meetings on the same Saturday afternoons and had the same secretary and vice-president.[34] The sign-up list for creamery membership was kept at the hardware store of James Donovan, the dual secretary. Hartland merchants were officers in both groups. They closed their stores for an hour and a half so creamery men could hold an organizational meeting. They had their reasons: "A regular boom in business may be expected as soon as the creamery is started."[35]

Lieutenant governor and dairy farmer John L. Gibbs was a good man to nominate for governor in a dairy state, but the Republicans never did. "If Gibbs can milk a cow without squirting milk up his coat sleeve, it is an accomplishment," noted the Canby News, "but this alone will not qualify him for the position."

Even before the creamery began receiving milk, business boomed. One merchant filled the lumber order for the new creamery building. The hardware store supplied the paint and hired a tinner to make creamery cans, which sold "like hot cakes." When the creamery opened in mid-June, the town filled with farmers' wagons. The *Hartland Vidette* exulted, "At last Hartland has blossomed into a full fledged manufacturing town," and a week later it stated, "already business is more lively and the merchants wear a smiling face."[36] The town now had the home manufacturing that many small-town newspaper editors had advocated since the Granger heyday.

A fourth local motive for starting a creamery hinged on the merchants' economic interest in the creamery's success. A village creamery daily brought farmers to town, where they were likely to patronize the stores. Even if located at a crossroads site, a creamery benefited merchants. They filled lumber orders or made creamery cans or sold goods and services to it. Creamery supply businesses sprouted in the Freeborn County seat, two of them being the Albert Lea Butter Tub Factory and a creamery supply house that sold and repaired creamery machinery. The *Enterprise's* editor became an agent for New York commission firms buying Freeborn County butter. The *Standard* sold "creamery record books."[37] With its rail links to eastern suppliers and commission firms, Albert Lea was helped, not hurt, by crossroads creameries.

Even better, creameries helped to move Freeborn County from a barter-and-credit economy to a cash one. Merchants no longer had to take poor-quality, farm-made butter on trade or extend long-term credit to farmers until the wheat harvest.[38] By 1897 Freeborn merchants reported "that while their sales are much greater their book [credit] accounts are less than 20 per cent of what they were ten years ago" before cooperative creameries arrived. From 1886 to 1896, farmers' deposits in Albert Lea banks grew from $56,000 to $320,000—an increase of 470 percent in ten years.[39]

Few Minnesotans anticipated this change in 1890. Yet the early success of the Clarks Grove and Clover Valley creameries in paying cash monthly to farmers showed the likely results if a creamery stood at every crossroads. Freeborn's creameries did not face the Main Street opposition encountered by cooperative stores and elevators competing with private firms. Creameries did not radicalize farmers as stores and elevators often did, for they competed with gathered-cream plants whose inefficiencies were obvious to merchants. In the summer of 1890, the village of Emmons boasted that "nowhere do the merchants and farmers work together more harmoniously than here . . . and the results both to the creamery and the mercantile business have been most gratifying."[40]

Once crossroads stores sprang up next to creameries, merchants feared a disastrous eroding of business if their village lacked a creamery. In January 1891, James F. Jones, a businessman in Geneva, stated, "if we don't get a co-operative creamery we will have an individual one."[41] After farmers started a creamery three miles east of Geneva, the merchants apparently tried to persuade them to move it to town.[42] By the winter of 1893–94, creameries lay to the north, west, east, and southeast of Geneva: "The creamery territory around the village became so contracted that it was evident that all differences of opinion must be laid aside if we were to have a creamery." One was soon organized with Jones as its treasurer.[43]

A fifth cause of creamery diffusion was the promotional efforts of companies that sold machinery and equipment for separator creameries. The creamery movement promised to multiply their number of

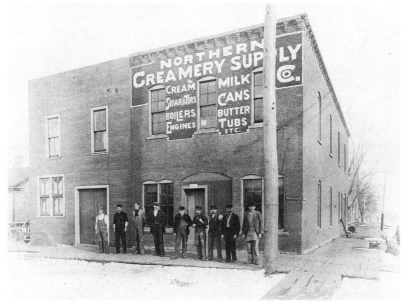

Edward Knatvold's Northern Creamery Supply Company created several jobs for Albert Lea's workmen in the 1890s. The county seat thrived despite a loss of some retail traffic to the new crossroads communities.

customers. Often they waited until an association was formed and then sent agents to make the sales pitch or to submit bids.[44] Sometimes the agent took the initiative. Going around Oakland Township for several weeks, a Davis and Rankin agent "aroused considerable interest in the creamery movement." A site dispute seemed to doom his efforts, but he took the farmers' subscription list, "secured more signers in the district further west," and had a creamery built there, "a considerable distance from where it was first intended."[45] Davis and Rankin won the contract to construct and equip the creamery.[46] By starting a creamery, a creamery supply firm secured for itself a dependent board ignorant of other options for buying equipment, and it thereby excluded its rivals.

These so-called "creamery sharks" were even more successful elsewhere. While on an 1892 inspection trip around the state, dairy expert Theophilus Levi Haecker visited Browns Valley (Traverse County) and "found a Davis & Rankin creamery on the east side foothills." A Davis and Rankin agent had painted "the creamery business . . . in glowing terms, big money in it; but all that has ever been realized out of this was the profit on the construction and equipment of the creamery which D & R pocketed." The creamery lasted only two months.[47]

Such creameries were frequently overcapitalized, equipped with too-expensive machinery, located in areas with too few milk cows, and crippled by an inadequate volume of milk.[48] Farmers on creamery boards starting an unfamiliar business lacked good information about how much was enough when ordering machinery and buildings. In fire insurance, facts about policyholders were vital, and township mutual boards had better information than did the industry experts. The reverse was true in the dairy industry, where facts about the buttermaking process were vital.

A sixth cause was the promotional efforts of dairy specialists, such as unemployed buttermakers who wanted more creameries started. In October 1890, D. U. Richards, a buttermaker from Northwood, Iowa, came to Glenville and became one of the "principal agitators" for a creamery. Despite farmers' reluctance, he succeeded, invested in creamery stock, and became "the No. 1 butter maker." Two years later, he was in Freeborn village "working up a stock company to build a creamery." He was its secretary, construction supervisor, general manager, largest shareholder, and buttermaker. He persuaded farmers to allow one vote per share. Owning 40 percent of the shares, he kept "the management of the affairs of the association in his own hands" until farmers' discontent ended this unusual voting rule and his control.[49]

Farmers had to be wary of self-interested promoters like Richards. They had to organize, make the plans, and do the purchasing themselves. Otherwise, the cooperative form became a façade barely concealing control by a dairy specialist, a Davis and Rankin agent, or a few Main Street merchants.

A seventh motive worked behind the scenes, unlike a promoter. Ethnic, church-centered communities sought to add the economic functions of a crossroads store and creamery to the church's social and religious functions in order to meet their members' needs more completely and thereby reduce the number of occasions when members had to obtain goods or services in other communities. Sociologist Raymond Breton noted that "institutional completeness" enabled an ethnic group to retain the loyalty of its members.[50] The Irish Catholic community in northwest Bath Township, for example, could better preserve its identity among neighboring Protestant Scandinavian Americans after a crossroads town sprang up near the Poplar Grove creamery.[51] That rationale for a creamery was not openly stated in the minutes of the associations—economic motives had to be stressed—but it must be assumed that where the ethnic benefits were so clear some local ethnic leaders recognized them.

The University Promotes the Spread of Cooperative Creameries

Aided by these seven local motives, the movement to organize cooperative separator creameries quickly succeeded in Freeborn County. By January 1, 1893, Freeborn's twenty-one separator creameries constituted nearly one-quarter of those in Minnesota. Averaging twenty patrons more than the others, Freeborn's creameries had the high milk volumes needed to capitalize on the centrifuge's efficiencies.[52] Freeborn's and Clarks Grove's successes were major factors in the statewide diffusion of cooperative separator creameries.

On August 2, 1892, Haecker, dairy instructor at the University of Minnesota's School of Agriculture, visited the Geneva Township creamery. He noted in his travel diary, "creamery not as clean and sweet as it ought to be." What was worse, he had to sleep that night in the attic of Geneva's hotel, which had no vacant rooms. At Geneva, he met dairy leader and politician John Gibbs, who invited him to visit Clarks Grove the next morning. Haecker was "well pleased" with it. He recalled telling himself, "This is what I must establish in this state."[53] Haecker and the university played a key role in publicizing the Clarks Grove model around the state, but there is more to the story than this single visit suggests. Dairy professionals do not wander into small villages by chance.

Under the provisions of the Morrill Act of 1862, the university had to teach agriculture, but the school struggled for years to find a way to do so. Farmers' sons sought a university education in order to escape the farm, not to return to it. Attacked by the Alliance for its failures in agricultural education, the university started the Minnesota Farmers' Institute, a traveling lecture series, in 1886. Led by dairy farmer and advocate Oren C. Gregg, institutes were held in thirty-one locations that year.[54] Gregg and his lecturers preached diversification—specifically, dairying and raising hogs or poultry. Their lectures dealt with breeding, feeding, and other technical matters, not cooperation, which was too controversial among the local merchants who often sponsored institutes. Yet better breeds or feeds could not convince farmers to shift to dairying in the absence of an efficient creamery that paid high milk prices.

The Alliance criticized Gregg's focus on diversification and neglect of cooperation. He held institutes mostly in southern Minnesota, not in the Alliance stronghold, the wheat-growing northwest.[55] One writer noted, "we farmers are wearied" with Gregg's lectures on "what kind of stock to raise or how to diversify our crops." Let him tell "merchants, bankers and railroad corporations . . . how to WATER their stock when it gets too dry. . . . What the farmers want to know, about this time, is how to find a market for their produce when they raise it."[56]

The strong Alliance vote in 1890 persuaded Minnesota's Republican politicians that a move from wheat to dairying was in their interest. Gregg's institutes were not producing it. In 1890 university regents and fellow Republicans John S. Pillsbury and Knute Nelson—Pillsbury, a former governor and Nelson a future one—visited the University of Wisconsin's dairy school, the nation's first. In January 1891, the University of Minnesota asked Haecker, assistant dairy instructor at Wisconsin, to start a similar school at Minnesota. He arrived in September 1891.[57] Again Minnesota borrowed an innovation from an older state and used its expert.

Haecker had more to offer than dairying expertise. He had worked for fifteen years for Republican governors in Wisconsin, and this political experience served him well in Minnesota. He had experimented with cooperation, specifically joint purchasing and marketing, as a member of Cottage Grove Grange, near Madison, in the 1870s and had researched the English Rochdale cooperatives. "We organized a co-operative creamery three-fourths of a mile from my place," he recalled, and the Cottage Grove cooperative fire insurance company, which he termed "an outstanding success."[58] His experiences as a Granger predisposed him to favor cooperatives.

The university had institutional reasons to support the diffusion of cooperative creameries. It needed students for its year-old dairy school, especially for Haecker's winter course in buttermaking. He did not yet have much scientific advice to give students; his experiments in feeding dairy cattle were just beginning.[59] As he noted, the university asked him "to make a general survey of the dairy industry," travel around the state, meet the "leading men in each locality," and "study the best course to pursue to advance the industry." He began on June 11, 1892, traveling by train as far as he could and walking to "localities inland" where creameries were located off the railroad track.[60]

He found conditions "very discouraging" until he came to Clarks Grove and saw its high milk prices, large volumes, many patrons, true cooperation, and clean operation.[61] On his trip he had already seen cooperative creameries and had criticized some on technical grounds, but Clarks Grove was different. He began to urge farmers to start creameries modeled after that one. He limited his role, believing that "the more you helped them, the more they would lean on you."[62] Private creamery owners complained to the university about his promotional work, so he traveled each spring and summer for four years quietly advising farmers to start cooperative creameries. In the 1893 Farmers' Institute *Annual*, he wrote a brief public endorsement: "Do you believe in co-operative creameries? A[nswer]. I do, most emphatically."[63]

His political experience helped him to win support for his activities. He wrote to Governor-elect Knute Nelson in December 1892 regarding the inept, patronage-ridden Minnesota State Dairy and Food Commission. He formed a good working relationship with Nelson, who took his (and others') advice, removed fellow Norwegian-American Anders Finseth, and made a Swedish-American editor the new commissioner.[64] Likely with Nelson's help, he strengthened his position at the university. In May 1893, the board of regents promoted him to professor, in July his chief campus rival resigned, and in September the board followed his advice in hiring dairy instructors.[65]

By March 1894, he was politically secure enough to make a public declaration of his support for cooperative creameries. He issued "Press Bulletin No. 2," entitled *Organizing Co-operative Creameries*, the university's first recognition of cooperatives. Haecker used the technical style of most farm school bulletins to advise farmers on how many cows and what size creamery they needed and to present Rochdale principles as scientific facts, not as a debatable ideology. Sensitive to anti-cooperative attitudes among merchants, he urged farmers to allow "local business men [to] assist in the enterprise" and to buy supplies from "creamery supply houses in the state"—as if only out-of-state companies were "charging exorbitant prices."[66]

This bulletin also publicized the fledgling dairy school and helped to increase its enrollment. As the school tried "to build the industry upon a purely co-operative plan," farmers looked to it for advice. Private creamery owners were less dependent on it, for they sought counsel from industry sources, too. Cooperative creameries and the dairy school formed a symbiotic relationship. They grew up together and needed each other: "By a system of judicious, paternal supervision all the milk producers are brought in close touch with the school and look to it for counsel and advice." With its help, the number of cooperative creameries increased to 560 by 1898.[67] Yet Haecker and the dairy school only communicated information on cooperation. They did not take the initiative in forming cooperatives as university experts later did. Initiative and decision making still rested with farmers.

Political motives played a role in the diffusion of the cooperative creamery. Haecker had personal and professional motives, not political ones, but Republican Governor Nelson acted to dampen the political protest in western Minnesota caused by declining wheat prices. In January 1893, he came into office committed to retaining long-time Republican state jobholders, but he would not keep a do-nothing patronage appointee in a Dairy and Food Commission that was necessary to his campaign to promote the switch to dairying that could reduce agrarian protest.[68]

The Farmers' Alliance and Cooperative Separator Creameries

The Farmers' Alliance also had political reasons to use the creamery movement, as the Grange had used wheat marketing cooperatives to increase its popularity among farmers. Alliancemen were slow to react as Republicans seized the initiative. The Hartland case showed a suballiance, the local unit, could take the initiative to start creameries. If these cooperatives were coming anyway in areas where dairying was feasible, then the Alliance's best tactic was to form them in its suballiances so that the creamery's popularity would be transferred to the Alliance.

Attempts by two suballiances in southern Brown County to form a cooperative creamery revealed the obstacles the Alliance faced in this field. The neighboring townships of Lake Hanska and Linden were in the area swept by the creamery movement in 1890–92. A newly elected Alliance state representative, Christian Ahlness of Lake Hanska, first heard of cooperative creameries from fellow legislators at the 1891 session. Coming home during a legislative recess, he promoted the idea among his neighbors, who asked him to go to the do-nothing dairy and food commissioner for advice. Ahlness recalled, "I found him in his office, sitting in a swivel-chair, with his legs resting on top of his desk." Ahlness's curiosity about creameries "seemed to awaken him to the responsibility and dignity of his" office—to the extent of "taking first one leg and then the other down from its elevated position." The commissioner then laconically told Ahlness, "in order to start a creamery you must have cows."[69]

In January 1891 the Lake Hanska suballiance voted to start a creamery and chose a five-man committee "to go around and find how many were willing to join and [how] many cows each had." Cows were not the problem. To start a creamery you must have a site. This suballiance could not settle on one meeting place, let alone a creamery site. In early February, they chose two possible sites and sent the committee to see how many members and cows could be secured for each one. In March, a trial vote favored the north site (twenty-four to two), but they hesitated to select it, although it was at the township's exact center. Eleven farmers vowed not to "take part in the creamery unless" the south site was chosen. So the suballiance sent two committees, a northern and a southern one, to poll farmers again. At their next meeting the members voted to "drop the creamery question."[70]

In a self-deprecating comment, Christian Ahlness recalled that he sometimes did not know the Alliance's position on legislative bills. As an "A" who voted early, he said, "my vote led the less attentive members to vote 'No' on their own party's measures."

During those months, the Linden suballiance also tried to start a creamery. Neither suballiance approached the other about jointly building one on the border between them. By mid-March, Linden also admitted failure.[71] A year later, a creamery was built near the township border, but leaders in the Nora Unitarian church (located near the border) took the initiative, not the suballiances. A consensus to start a creamery with all its risks had to be stronger than even a twenty-four-to-two trial vote. A ten-year-old church proved to be better at securing consensus than a ten-month-old suballiance whose votes could commit members to send a delegate to a convention hall but not to deliver milk daily, indefinitely, to a creamery.[72]

Site selection was contentious in ad hoc organizational meetings such as the one at Clarks Grove, but then the disputants could separate without splitting an existing organization. A suballiance existed for other purposes than forming cooperatives, and members would not risk its survival to accomplish that purpose. If suballiances could not organize creameries in an area like Lake Hanska where the creamery movement was strong, they could not hope to do so in western and northwestern Minnesota where farmers still had competitive advantages in wheat growing: fertile soil, newly cultivated lands, and plentiful cheap land for extensive farming. By 1896 some creameries were started here, but in established railroad towns and by merchants, not by suballiances.[73] Here wheat was too profitable for farmers distant from a depot to switch to dairying and start a crossroads creamery. In the early 1890s suballiances and creameries multiplied rapidly, but, like ships passing in the night, the two movements had surprisingly few connections to each other.

Apart from Republicans' and university dairy experts' political and professional motives, most cooperative creameries were begun for local reasons, not to advance some statewide cause. Local initiative meant that creamery operations varied from one locality to another.

Cooperative Creameries in Operation: Freeborn County

At the 1893 Minnesota State Dairymen's Association convention, President John Gibbs of Geneva succinctly described the operation of a Freeborn County cooperative separator creamery:

> Work begins. Each patron takes his milk to the factory, receives credit
> for the amount and takes home ... skimmed milk and his share of the
> buttermilk.... Each week the butter is shipped to a commission house

in New York with instructions to sell and remit promptly.....On a certain day, usually from the 20th to the 25th of the month, the officers
meet, figure up the amount of milk received, the butter made, and the
money received and expended, all for the previous month. Each patron
receives a check in proportion to the amount of milk furnished.[74]

There were a few complications: a sinking fund deduction from the
milk check to repay loans, hauling milk to the creamery, carting supplies
to a crossroads site, occasional problems with the centrifugal separator,
and disputes with buttermakers about their wages. But basically, a cooperative separator creamery operated in the straightforward, simple way
Gibbs described.

During the 1890s, this simple procedure was significantly affected by
ethnicity and the competition between creameries. Many Freeborn
County creamery associations were dominated by one ethnic group.[75]
Clarks Grove had mostly Danish Americans and Norwegian Americans as members.[76] Norwegian Americans predominated in Manchester's
association; four German Americans and one Old Stock American
signed its initial "Article of Agreement," but many more living within
the four-to-five-mile range did not sign. Manchester's meetings were
probably conducted in English, so language did not exclude other groups.[77]
German Americans and a few Old Stock Americans organized the
Clover Valley creamery. An 1896 membership list had no Scandinavian-
American names, although ten Scandinavian Americans lived close
enough to haul milk to the Clover Valley creamery. Clover Valley's minutes
are in English, so language did not keep them out—assuming that they
knew English in the 1890s.[78]

This ethnically based membership is not surprising. Members needed
to have mutual trust and solidarity to co-sign notes, keep promises to deliver milk, and democratically run a cooperative. Ethnic loyalties were
the strongest sources of that trust and solidarity in the 1890s. Much of
Freeborn County was divided into identifiable ethnic enclaves surrounding ethnic churches, and each enclave could have its own creamery.[79]

Ethnicity affected operations (see Table D in Appendix). Six
Scandinavian-American creamery associations took an average of 3.67
years to repay initial construction loans. Five associations dominated by
German Americans or Old Stock Americans or both took an average of
6.25 years; one dissolved before paying off its debts.[80] Old Stock and German-American associations suffered from greater dissension. At Clover

Valley, a proposed new fine for feeding turnips, rutabagas, and other root crops to cattle and an added milk check deduction caused "a stormy & almost bloody meeting" that "adjourned Sine Die." Complaints surfaced about members hauling milk to other creameries, and the board was replaced due to discontent with milk prices. Geneva's Old Stock Americans wrangled over threats to move the creamery from the crossroads site to the village. Organizing efforts by Old Stock and German Americans at Moscow "fell through for want of harmony and cash."[81]

Scandinavian Americans showed a greater solidarity and more efficient operation of their creameries, whose history shows nearly universal adherence to the one-man, one-vote rule, no recorded failures, speedier repayment of initial loans, and a lack of serious disputes.[82] Most important was their greater reliance on their members' labor in organizing associations (not using outside organizers), deciding on building plans and machinery models (not relying on sales agents' advice), constructing the creamery (not hiring workers), and taking turns hauling milk and supplies (not paying cash for such services).

The Bancroft creamery's secretary described how its Norwegian-American members "avoided the creamery sharks and also did most of the [construction] work ourselves thus saving expense." That was a shrewd use of farmers' free time, for "the average farmer's time in winter is not very valuable." They hired a carpenter to supervise the winter's construction, "the rest of the work being contributed by the shareholders free of charge," which lowered construction costs "to about $2,500." The secretary noted, "We did not buy any more machinery than was absolutely necessary to start, nor pay out money for labor that shareholders could do themselves."[83] At Manchester each member helped to haul lumber to the site, to "bring in a few stones for the creamery foundation," and to lay the foundation. "Shareholders and others interested in the creamery" transported ice from a lake to the creamery.[84]

Hauling whole milk and disposing of skim milk were often done on a cash basis at German and Old Stock creameries while Scandinavians "took turns," although that, too, had its problems. Clarks Grove's records show no cash outlays for transporting milk in the creamery's first three years. Each farmer took turns hauling his and his neighbors' milk.[85]

Manchester did not ask for bids on skim milk, which was valuable as feed for hogs and which some creameries sold to the highest bidder. The board "agreed to let those that wants the milk . . . to come and take it by turns, as soon as they hear the whistle, and any-one failing to take the milk when his turn comes, he misses the right to git any more milk." When the buttermaker complained of patrons abusing the system, the board told him to "watch the patrons" and did not change the plan.[86]

Crossroads creameries had to haul coal and supplies from the depot to the creamery site. Scandinavian-American creameries had patrons take turns and fined any shirkers. Other creameries paid the buttermaker, secretary, or patrons to do this work.[87]

Scandinavian Americans stressed cooperation and avoided cash outlays. Perhaps this trait came from the Scandinavian village tradition of joint decision making in agriculture, although that existed elsewhere in Europe. If so, then Scandinavian Americans combined ethnic strengths with a willingness to disregard ethnicity if needed, for they often hired buttermakers from Iowa or Elgin, Illinois, until they could train members of their own group.[88]

Scandinavian Americans reaped immediate benefits by minimizing cash outlays. County newspapers regularly published the milk prices paid by Freeborn creameries (see Table E in Appendix). Scandinavian-

A cooperative creamery often built a house for its buttermaker. Armstrong's maker, Frank C. Lindeman (left), Mrs. Lindeman (far right) holding daughter Agnes, her sister Mrs. C. A. Lawler, and an unknown creamery helper (center) stood in front of the Lindemans' four-year-old house and the creamery in 1899.

American creameries often were among those paying the highest prices (members' costs for hauling were not reflected in the figures). The high milk prices were a major reason these creameries experienced less dissension. For October 1893, the newspapers reported that Clarks Grove paid $1.05, Riceland $1.09, and Bancroft $1.02 per hundredweight—all Scandinavian-American creameries. By contrast, Armstrong paid only $.97 cents per hundredweight.[89] Armstrong's German-American and Old Stock members protested when "the creamery failed to pay up with" other Freeborn County creameries. They "blamed" their association's directors and officers and "suspected them of [mis]appropriating funds." The officers "blamed the buttermaker." The real cause of the lower milk price was that Armstrong's centrifugal separator was less efficient and left butterfat in the milk.[90]

Freeborn County creameries operated in a competitive environment. Frequently published milk prices put pressure on a creamery to change its practices, forced gathered-cream plants to shift to a centrifuge, and induced creameries using the Danish Weston to switch to the more efficient De Laval Standard or Alpha separators. Otherwise some patrons might use external control and deliver milk to a higher-paying creamery. Paying $1.20 for milk, Manchester creamery seemed "to be gaining ground all the time of late; two loads from Carlston are bringing their milk here," although they were much closer to the Carlston creamery. Carlston was soon out of business.[91] If distance prevented a switch, patrons used internal control to pressure the board or the buttermaker to adopt new methods or machines, as at Armstrong, Gordonsville, and Clover Valley.[92]

This competition was unusual, for American cooperatives did not normally compete against each other. Each often had a local monopoly. Competition was helpful in forcing cooperative creameries to be efficient. The same higher milk prices that enabled separator creameries to defeat gathered-cream plants pushed the former to greater efficiency. Yet efficiency could create conflict with other goals, such as democratic decision making. For instance, if milk price variances dictated that a creamery replace a Weston with an Alpha separator, the democratic process of debating and voting became a moot point. When selling butter, Freeborn County's creameries also operated in a competitive environment. Many buyers were competing for their product. After Freeborn creamery butter earned a good reputation and before the butter market was glutted in 1896–97, commission houses in New York, Chicago, and the Twin Cities vied for it. In October 1893, the *Albert Lea Enterprise* reported, "R. Duke Barnum, a member of the butter firm of Pitt, Barnum & Gidden, New York City, was here last week looking up business for his firm." Barnum praised Freeborn butter "and talked hopefully of continuing business with Freeborn county creameries."[93] Most New York firms used local agents such as editor Marcellus Halvorsen of the *Albert Lea Enterprise* to buy Freeborn butter. That October, 86 percent of the butter shipped from Albert Lea went to New York and only 14 percent to Chicago.[94]

Chicago and Minneapolis fought New York's dominance of Freeborn butter. A year earlier, an agent from a Chicago commission firm also praised Freeborn butter, criticized weighing and payment policies of New York firms, and recommended a board of trade be formed at Albert Lea "for the competitive sale of butter in the open market."[95] In September 1893, "an oily tongued solicitor for a Chicago commission house" tried to persuade Moscow's patrons to switch to Chicago.[96] A daily produce bulletin published in Minneapolis criticized Freeborn County creameries for paying high freight costs when they could easily market butter in Minneapolis or Duluth.[97]

Halvorsen rejected the bulletin's implicit appeal to state loyalty (sell Minnesota butter in Minnesota markets) by arguing, "money talks every time and the farmers have joined the creameries for what there is in the business and they don't believe in sending butter to a market that is unreliable and receive[ing] slow returns for goods." With the fierce competition among creameries, "managers dare not run any risks of losing money." A New York agent himself, Halvorsen asserted, "New York has been found to be the most reliable market."[98] Editor Harwood G. Day of the *Freeborn County Standard* claimed that Twin Cities and Duluth firms "have been charged with dishonest dockages, short weights, slow remittances and even in some cases an embezzlement of all or a portion of the returns."[99] It was unthinkable to chance doing business with them.

During this period, wheat farmers also complained about dishonest dockages, short weights, and fraudulent grading. Yet Chicago and Minneapolis buyers did not visit them, praise their wheat, and plead for their business. Not having integrated forward, they had no finished product to sell, just a fungible, easily transportable, oversupplied raw commodity. Because of their forward integration and the strong demand for good-quality creamery butter, Freeborn's dairy farmers could combat marketing abuses and wait for dealers to come to them.

It is not surprising that they were less radical than wheat farmers.

Agrarian protest was partly due to local conditions: farmers' isolation, their cash-poor status until the annual wheat harvest, the distance they traveled to buy (or charge) supplies, and their lack of control over wheat processing. Creameries partly alleviated these conditions in Freeborn County. They increased the number of crossroads communities, each with a post office, a blacksmith's shop, a store, and a creamery. They reduced rural isolation and anti-county-seat resentments because farmers no longer had to travel to the county seat. They provided a monthly cash income that enabled farmers to escape barter and credit: "It is no longer necessary to run up store bills and other accounts and depend upon the uncertainties of a grain crop with which to meet them in the fall."[100] Daily trips to the creamery where other farmers met reduced rural isolation for males, at least. In June 1893 the *Standard* noted, "Wheat prices are now the lowest ever known, and . . . there does not seem to be any immediate prospect of a rise. Fortunately Freeborn county is no longer dependent on the rise or fall in the price of wheat for its prosperity."[101]

These changes were welcomed, not opposed, by Freeborn's merchants and bankers. There is no evidence of what historian Lawrence Goodwyn noted among southern farmers: "The resulting cooperative experience radicalized enough of them to make independent political action a potential reality."[102] Creameries did not radicalize Freeborn farmers. Both the Farmers' Alliance and the cooperative-creamery movement flourished in Minnesota in the early 1890s. There was interaction between them but only tangentially. The role of creameries in partially resolving farmers' local grievances helped to undercut the Alliance. To be successful, cooperative creameries depended on a new technology in a new industry—not on political unity or radical ideology—so they tended to undermine those rationales for cooperation. They used higher milk prices, not radical platforms or eloquent lecturers, to recruit members. A competitive environment encouraged them to make decisions for economic efficiency, not for political reasons.

Republicans Use Cooperative Dairying against the Alliance

By the fall of 1893, the Republicans took notice of Freeborn creameries' success and sensed the political implications. Illness prevented Knute Nelson from attending the 1892 Freeborn County Fair, but he came as governor in 1893. On Tuesday, September 5, he gave "a glowing tribute to the husbandmen" before some ten thousand people. The elite in county-seat society hosted a reception for him at Dr. Albert C. Wedge's house in Albert Lea.[103] Also at the fair were two officials from Nelson's rejuvenated Dairy and Food Commission. The next week, they hailed Freeborn's dairying in the state's press: "The farmers in the wheat growing sections, [commission secretary Andrew H.] Bertram thinks, may learn a lesson from the farmers of Freeborn county." The assistant commissioner assured farmers, "Don't be afraid of an over-production of this fine butter for it will not occur . . . in this generation at least."[104]

A week later, at Redwood Falls, Nelson reported that "he had visited Freeborn county two weeks since, and he found the farmers of that county more than prosperous; the financial question of the present not affecting them in the least, and their prosperity was all due to diversified farming." (Alliance lecturers were raising "the financial question" of unlimited coinage of silver dollars to create inflation and raise wheat prices.)[105]

During the next campaign year, Republicans threw Freeborn's success into the teeth of the Alliance's "calamity howlers." In his 1894 keynote speech, Nelson pointed to Freeborn with its "24 creameries and a great amount of dairy products"; there, "money is not scarce, and the times are far from hard and depressed." By contrast "money is quite scarce and times are very hard and trying" in Polk County with "only two creameries," few dairy products, "and a system of farming mainly devoted to wheat culture." Republicans regarded this speech as the definitive answer to the Alliancemen, and the New York *Evening Post* quoted it at length. Nelson did not mention the role of cooperation in Freeborn's dairy industry; cooperatives were still too controversial among his Republican backers. It would take another twenty-five years before a Republican, a Nelson protégé, would campaign openly for more rural cooperatives.[106]

Nelson was back at the Freeborn County Fair in September 1894, but he was quietly angling for election to the U.S. Senate and said nothing about dairying. Speaking ahead of him, Haecker praised Freeborn as "the banner county of the northwest" whose "fame extended . . . throughout the civilized world."[107] Not that far perhaps, but surely up to Republican party headquarters. Freeborn seemed to prove the Republicans' point that farmers' problems required not government action but diversified farming.

Thus some farmers' success with cooperative creameries undercut other farmers' political and cooperative efforts. Nondairy farmers found it hard to duplicate the creameries' success, which was based on unique technological and economic factors and on the cost-cutting practices of some ethnic groups. Cooperative creameries paying high milk prices convinced many farmers in southern Minnesota to shift to dairying and gradually away from agrarian protest. Yet western and northwestern Minnesota were still fertile ground for the Farmers' Alliance, which picked up where the Grange had left off—trying to use cooperation to recruit members and to prove its usefulness to them. The Alliance altered Minnesota's cooperative movement, which was shaped partly by the interplay between radical and conservative types of cooperation, but the movement would be permanently affected by the dramatic success of the cooperative creamery with its conservative political implications.

7

Farmers' Alliance

"We ask merchants to submit to this Alliance
a schedule of discounts"

THE FOURTH OF JULY CELEBRATION at Henning in Otter Tail County in 1891 seemed typical: parade, band music, reading of the Declaration of Independence, a "patriotic address," baseball games, horse races, and a foot race.[1] But this observance was not the usual small-town Fourth. Earlier, residents of nearby Battle Lake complained "that the celebration was going to be nothing more than a big alliance picnic," and they would not dignify it with their presence. When the Henning *Alliance Advocate* gave the Farmers' Alliance equal billing with the nation's Independence Day, patriots went to the editor's office to protest.[2] During the night of July 2, two anti-Alliance men hung an effigy on Henning's "liberty pole" to disfigure it.[3] In Minnesota's small towns, deeply divided over the Alliance, a liberty pole was too strong a reminder for some citizens of the revolutionary implications of the Fourth of July.

The residents of Otter Tail County split sharply on the subject of the Alliance. Henning was an Alliance center, battling the Republican elite of Fergus Falls, the county seat. Earlier in 1891, Alliancemen founded the *Advocate*, which became a thorn in the side of the *Fergus Falls Weekly Journal* and other county papers.[4] The Alliance elevator in Henning competed briskly with elevators owned by the Northern Pacific Railroad and the North Dakota Elevator Company.[5] The county Alliance president and elevator manager, Charles W. Brandborg, lived near Henning.

Organizers of the Fourth's events separated the morning's patriotic doings from the afternoon's Alliance picnic, but past and present revolutions were not easily parted. When the morning speaker, lawyer

147

W. W. Erwin, "commenced to talk 'monopoly' 'wheat stealing' and 'robbing the farmer,' it seemed to start the ball [of dissension] a rolling again." Angered by Erwin's words and intoxicated, a onetime wheat buyer from a nearby town "got upon the stage" to abuse and mimic Erwin.[6] Alliance leaders on stage had him arrested and jailed. Furious (and likely drunk on "free beer furnished" by the North Dakota Elevator Company), his friends went after Brandborg, whom they blamed for the arrest. Brandborg knocked one down, then started for home. They followed, yelling "string him" and "lynch him." He grabbed a stick and hit a Swedish immigrant, Ole Anderson, on the head. The victim died several days later.[7]

This sensational event deepened the divisions. An Old Stock Allianceman noted that Anderson "was a Swede, just six months from the old country—perfectly fit material to help make up an American mob." (Brandborg was Swedish American, too.) The anti-Alliance *Battle Lake Review* rushed to defend Swedes, whom it "classed among our best inhabitants."[8] The *Advocate's* editor saw a conspiracy; *Journal* editor Elmer E. Adams and the elevator companies were punishing Brandborg, whom they hated for "making Henning an open wheat market." Adams posed as justice's friend; Brandborg should be tried "as if he was a friendless laboring man instead of the domineering chief of a large political party."[9] Brandborg was tried and acquitted on grounds of self-defense.[10]

As it was in Granger days, so was it also from 1886 to 1896 when rural Minnesota split over rival papers, rival elevators, and rival candidates, but there were differences. Brandborg's ethnicity is an example of how the Alliance recruited more immigrant farmers. The existence of more Alliance-affiliated newspapers and third-party politicking showed that Alliancemen were come-outers, who avoided entangling alliances with Main Street merchants and Republican county-seat elites. No Granger rules against discussing politics hemmed in suballiances. Fewer Old Stock ties linked merchants with Alliancemen.

Minnesota's economic geography had changed. Nonexistent in the early 1870s, Henning was one of many new towns created by railroad construction in the 1870s and 1880s. More of Minnesota was in the post-railroad economy of elevators owned by "line" companies or Minneapolis millers, of small-town retailers tied to Minneapolis or Chicago wholesalers, of quick ordering by telegraph, in short, of more economic centralization, faster transactions, and more regional specialization. Alliancemen faced greater obstacles in trying to control crop processing and marketing now that entrepreneurs and their managers had a head start. Technology seemed to be a means to catch up: "Farmers could read the telegraphic reports," too, so "why not bargain collectively with the purchasing agents or bypass them altogether?"[11]

Technology appeared to be democratic, open to all, but entrepreneurs laid track and strung wires to maximize profit, not to give farmers the means to bypass them. Henning's farmers specialized in wheat. Centralizing entrepreneurs had the greatest advantage in that industry. In 1892 Otter Tail had two creameries (both gathered-cream ones) and three cheese factories (none in Henning). The creamery movement had yet to reach the county. Still, Alliancemen had the benefit of an estab-

Minnesota, 1922

lished cooperative movement, which 1870s Grangers lacked. Brandborg was also president of a township mutual.[12] Township mutuals, ethnic cooperative stores, and a few cooperative creameries were in place. How would the new agrarian protest movement affect them, or they affect it?

Lawrence Goodwyn argued that the "cooperative crusade" was the "source" of the Alliance's "agrarian revolt."[13] Cooperation explained the Alliance and the People's Party: "The cooperative movement recruited the farmers to the Alliance in the period 1887–91, and the resulting cooperative experience radicalized enough of them to make independent political action a potential reality."[14]

His analysis has been strongly criticized. He emphasized cooperatives as separate businesses, although he also discussed "bulking" (joint marketing of cotton) and joint purchasing of farm implements and supplies.[15] Yet only joint purchasing and marketing were so widespread as to (potentially) "radicalize" farmers. Historian Stanley B. Parsons and his coauthors argued that "co-ops were neither numerous nor economically viable" enough to radicalize farmers into Populism. In Minnesota by 1896, cooperative creameries were both numerous and viable, but they did not radicalize farmers. Parsons looked too singlemindedly for cooperative businesses and too little for suballiances' joint activities.[16] Farmers radicalized by opposition to incorporated ventures would probably also be radicalized by opposition to informal ventures in the suballiance. Like the Grangers, the Alliance's small producers tried joint purchasing and marketing.

That was one of the Alliance's problems. It revisited twenty-year-old, failed Granger tactics, less likely to succeed now that a postrailroad economy had solidified entrepreneurial links among retailers, wholesalers, and manufacturers. A weakness of democracy was that old tactics could still command a majority while cooperative innovations often failed to win majority approval. An agrarian protest group moved down the same well-worn grooves made by its predecessor. Suballiances were quick to purchase jointly and slow to form cooperative creameries or farmers' elevators, although some did.

Basic Character of the Alliance and of Its Suballiances

Alliance democracy had other strengths and weaknesses, which affected joint activities or cooperative businesses that suballiances sponsored.

Such attributes are apparent in the basic character of the suballiance as compared to Granges and farmers' clubs.

Minnesota's suballiances were part of the Northwestern Alliance, started in 1880 by Milton George, editor of the *Western Rural*. He organized a Farmers' Alliance in Cook County, Illinois, "apparently basing it on" a Farmers' Alliance formed in New York in 1877.[17] As with township mutuals, Union stores, and cooperative dairying, an innovation that began in New York or New England migrated to the Old Northwest and then to Minnesota. George created the Alliance partly to increase the *Western Rural's* circulation, as editor Walter Nimocks had devised the MFMFIAM in Granger days.[18] Unlike the Grange, the Alliance was not tightly bound by its founder's rules and rituals. It was shaped by farmers of various ethnic groups, religious denominations, political views, and crop specialties. Unlike the farmers' clubs, it had a federal, hierarchical structure of county, state, and national units.

The basic character and local variations of the Alliance are apparent in five suballiances whose minutes have survived. These five local units vary, in terms of ethnicity, religion, politics, year of founding, and activities. Formed by Old Stock farmers, the Washington Alliance #110 of Dewald Township in Nobles County represented the early 1880s Alliance. Of mid-1880s origins, the Blooming Grove Alliance #370 (Waseca County) was led by prosperous, Protestant, German-speaking farmers. The Lake Hanska Alliance #1014 (Brown County) and the Lisbon Alliance #777 (Yellow Medicine County) were both Norwegian-American groups and formed later, when the Alliance was decidedly political, but Lake Hanska's was divided between contesting Unitarians and Lutherans. Also begun in the late 1880s, the Moorhead Alliance #148 (Clay County) was only political and did not take economic actions.[19]

Three of these groups were organized by local politicians who had an eye on their own advancement. A campaign visit by an "Alliance candidate for Congress" very likely precipitated the organization of the Washington Alliance.[20] In Lisbon Township, the initiator was John J. Mooney, a sometime county commissioner and a frequent Prohibition and Alliance candidate for elective office.[21] In Blooming Grove, former County Commissioner George W. Soule took the lead.[22] Editors of Alliance newspapers also encouraged farmers to form suballiances, thereby adding to their list of subscribers. Alliance lecturers traveled around organizing suballiances and earned fifty cents from the fee paid by each new member.[23] Lecturer L. C. Long reported on a "pretty warm" meeting in Ellsworth (Nobles County), where opponents "put up a job on me" by picking a "railroad stockholder for chairman, a wheat-buyer for secretary, and a lawyer and a banker to answer me." He set up the suballiance anyway.[24] Wheat buyers, lawyers, and bankers were ineligible for membership in the Alliance. More than the Granges, suballiances enforced their constitution's exclusion of anyone "not a practical and operative farmer."[25]

Alliancemen's wives and daughters were also entitled to be elected members, but Minnesota's Alliance did not emphasize women's role as the Grange had. It stressed political and economic action, not the social and educational functions that Grangers assigned to women. With women still lacking the right to vote, their active participation in what was often an on-going partisan political convention may have seemed awkward to Alliance leaders. In states where suballiances were also social lodges like the old Granges, women were more active.[26]

Antimonopoly protest led farmers to form suballiances. As in the Grange, local grievances often provided the strongest motivation. On March 5, 1886, the *Waseca County Herald* reported, "The wheat market has been the all-absorbing topic in Waseca during the past week or ten

The Torgrimson threshing crew from Lake Hanska Township in the 1890s. Two members of the family belonged to the Lake Hanska suballiance, and others in their crew probably did also.

days." Waseca's wheat buyers offered lower prices for wheat than did buyers in nearby towns. (Were local wheat buyers or the railroads to blame?) Farmers responded by holding a mass meeting, listened to lawyer Lewis Brownell accuse a local flour mill of earning exorbitant profits, talked of boycotting the mill, and began to organize a suballiance.[27] In this case the largest wheat growers had the most pressing reason to join the Alliance. In nearby Blooming Grove Township, suballiance members averaged 53.76 acres each planted in wheat, and nonmembers, 32.25 acres.[28] This suballiance was dominated by prosperous farmers recruited by means of a local grievance and unlikely to be radicalized by cooperation.[29]

   Blooming Grove was a township of mixed ethnicity: Swiss and German American (both German speaking), Irish, Norwegian American, Old Stock, and others. The ethnic composition of its farmers did not match that of the suballiance's members:

Irish were 10% of the farmers and 16% of the members;
Old Stock, 12% of the farmers, 26% of the members;
Norwegians, 16% of the farmers, 3% of the members;
Swiss or Germans, 18% of farmers, 55% of members.[30]

German and Swiss Americans were overrepresented; Norwegian Americans, underrepresented. Distance to the meeting site may have discouraged the latter from joining.[31] Meetings were conducted in English, not German, so language was not a barrier. Religious differences were; German Methodist and United Evangelical churches were near the meeting site, and many Alliancemen were members.[32] Norwegian Americans likely joined the suballiance in adjacent Iosco Township instead.

   In forming suballiances, farmers often ignored political boundaries and welcomed as members those whom they knew and trusted. Suballiances often spilled across county and township lines. Trading at Morristown (Rice County) more than at Waseca, the farmers of northern Blooming Grove Township welcomed neighboring Rice County farmers into their suballiance.[33] Worshiping at a Norwegian Lutheran church located on the border between Lisbon and Stony Run Townships, farmers organizing the Lisbon suballiance ignored this line and welcomed fellow parishioners from Stony Run as members.[34] Solidarity and mutual trust helped suballiances fulfill social, educational, and economic functions. Those with self-selected boundaries functioned more smoothly than those following political lines. (The convenient fiction of township-

specific suballiances was retained in determining representation at conventions.)[35] Ethnic and religious boundaries produced a homogeneous
polity that possessed the common experience of governing a church
congregation.

Thus the Blooming Grove suballiance had four factors that facilitated
cooperation. Its members traded in the same market—Morristown.
They shared ethnic, economic, religious, and linguistic bonds, and they
had a history of running two congregations, a farmers' club, and a Grange
ten to fifteen years earlier. They had been among the first in Waseca
County to start a farmers' club and to call for both a county agricultural
society and a county fair.[36] In 1870 they ran a primitive cooperative cheese
factory.[37] The leaders in these efforts, the Remund and Schutte families,
guided the suballiance, too.[38] Strong continuities linked the suballiance
with earlier activities.

Continuity may have played a role in making farmers more radical or
more conservative. Historian Robert C. McMath, Jr., argued that the Alliance sprang from rural "cultures of protest"—voluntary associations
like the Grange, antifencing campaigns, vigilantism, the Knights of
Labor—although Milton George's Alliance "drew on only some of the
traditions of protest." Goodwyn minimized the links to the Grange and
stressed the novelty of Alliance radicalism. Grange historian Woods saw
a great similarity between the Grange and the Alliance as two radical
groups.[39] Yet continuity had both conservative and radical effects. Woods
missed the conservative, Old Stock, ethnic side of the Grange; McMath,
the conservative effect of rural bodies like school districts and literary societies. Arguably radicalization was greater where there was less continuity. In the Red River Valley and Otter Tail County, where Granges and
farmers' clubs had been rare, suballiances were provocative liberty poles,
suddenly and unexpectedly erected.

Continuity between the Suballiances and Local Public Boards

Rural life was characterized by continuity and similarity. Suballiance
meetings resembled school district or town board meetings, not Jacobin
club conclaves. Suballiances met at the local schoolhouse, even if a church
was more centrally located: Blooming Grove met at the District #3
schoolhouse, not the Methodist church; Lisbon, at the Districts #26 and
#14 schoolhouses, not the Norwegian Lutheran church midway between

them; Lake Hanska, at the schoolhouses, not the Unitarian or Lutheran churches.[40] Washington met at the Districts #42 and #72 schools until its stock-company project led it to select the Nobles County courthouse in Worthington, a site better suited to seeking support from farmers in other townships.[41]

Historian Wayne E. Fuller noted that "the one-room country schoolhouse was more than a school.... [It was often] the only public building in the neighborhood, it gave the community its identity" and "served as a social center." Debates, plays, political meetings, and church services were held at the school. Suballiance members might belong to one ethnic church, but it seemed inappropriate to hold Alliance meetings in a church or in ethnic languages. Political acts—electing delegates and nominating candidates—should be done at a site accessible to all. Moreover school districts were "invaluable laboratories of democracy" where "many Americans learned parliamentary procedures" and "wrestled with such intricacies as bond issues, taxes, and contingency funds." The suballiance applied these lessons to its activities. In Lisbon, members of the District #26 school board became officers in the suballiance. The top school official, treasurer Jacob Anderson, chaired the suballiance's organizational meeting and was its first president. District Clerk Ole K. Rollefson became its vice-president while district board member N. J. Nelson convened the organizational meeting. Other suballiance members had performed paid services for the school and had been found trustworthy by the school board.[42]

Township and county boards provided similar lessons, legacies of joint action, or a site for political conversation. In Hartland, while farmers voted in the township election, "several prominent farmers met in one corner of the house and talked up a farmers' union or alliance."[43] In Blooming Grove and Lisbon, former county commissioners served as suballiance organizers and officers. Historian Parsons noted that Alliancemen were "a people with a long tradition of political participation." Far from being recently radicalized into politics, they had always been active in it.[44] In economic matters, suballiances used the same tools as did the public boards. They appointed committees to negotiate favorable prices, heard committee reports, approved or disapproved committee actions, and called for bids. In June 1891 the Granite Falls suballiance purchased twine much as any school district purchased wood. It published a notice calling for dealers to submit bids to a committee, with "full ball samples of different grades offered, and both cash and time price stated."[45] Such tools were often more useful to school boards than to suballiances, where amounts bought or sold were much greater, the need to sell or buy more urgent, and merchants less accepting of their right to act like public boards.

The issue of secrecy differentiated a suballiance from a public board. The members had to decide if meetings should be open to the public or to editors and if the minutes should be printed in local newspapers. The Grange's secrecy rule (often ignored) drew charges that it was unrepublican. In the South and parts of the Great Plains, the Alliance, too, was "a secret, oath-bound society," for secrecy might be needed in economic bargaining. Immigrant churches' attacks on Grange secrecy possibly led Minnesota's Alliance to hedge on the issue. Its constitution stated it was "not a secret society, and its meetings should be public" but added, "Secret sessions may be held" and business "transacted with closed doors."[46] As a political group, it risked a loss of legitimacy if it closed the doors, so most often they stayed open.

Openness was often dropped when discussing business deals or negotiating positions. After Washington's secretary was instructed to publish minutes in Worthington's newspapers, "a protest was made by some members against" that policy. Others objected "that this was not a secret organization, that we were working for the benefit of humanity and that we were not only willing but wished the world to know what we were doing." Due to the late hour and the clashing views, they postponed action for two months. Then they passed a resolution "that all private business be kept secret and nothing be published that would have a tendency to give nonproducers any advantage over the Alliance." They also agreed to pass and publish a few minor resolutions at each meeting as a smokescreen to hide their important business, to consider an initiation oath of secrecy, and to adjourn the next courthouse meeting "to some better place for a private meeting."[47]

Here was a choice between democratic image and economic effectiveness. Trying to be effective bargainers, they risked being seen as undemocratic. If they were open and democratic, they risked being ineffective bargainers. The Alliance compromised between secrecy and openness. Just as it did with Grange county councils, the press often reported the names of candidates nominated at county Alliance conventions but seldom noted suballiance meetings on joint purchasing and marketing.

The Alliance and Antagonism against the County Seat

As a democracy within a democracy, the suballiance was immersed in lo-cal politics. Frequently this was anti-county-seat politics that affected its economic activities. In Nobles, Yellow Medicine, Brown, and Otter Tail Counties, farm protest was linked to resentments of the county seat. More come-outers and outsiders than the Grangers, Alliancemen were also more antagonistic to the county seat than had been the Patrons, who allowed county-seat editors to participate in their county councils. In Alliance years, that was highly unlikely. What Goodwyn called a "movement culture" often developed in areas far from and antagonistic to the county seat.

Meeting in Worthington, the Washington suballiance failed to start an Alliance newspaper or elevator or many new suballiances in eastern Nobles County. In Adrian, Worthington's western rival, Alliancemen founded *The Citizen* and the Alliance Mercantile and Elevator Com-pany, whose directors were from western Nobles County.[48] *The Citizen* began in spring 1891, when Adrian citizens hastened to the legislature to prevent construction of a courthouse at Worthington and to propose Adrian as the new county seat.[49] By February-March 1890, the Adrian suballiance had ninety-one members; by October, the *Great West* reported, "Adrian is astir."[50] Anti-county-seat feelings helped stir up pro-Alliance activity in western Nobles County.

Yellow Medicine County is a narrow fifty-four-mile sliver, running from the Minnesota River west to the South Dakota border. Granite Falls, the county seat, is located at its extreme eastern end. Since 1884 farmers had campaigned for an election to move the county seat to Clarkfield, more centrally located and linked by rail to the rest of the county. The county commissioners' refusal to call an election "caused a division politically between the east and west ends of the county." In 1886 a proposed new courthouse in Granite Falls aroused western oppo-sition and "talk of a division of the county."[51] After farmers organized suballiances in 1890, Clarkfield became the Alliance center where county conventions were held and an Alliance newspaper published.[52] Granite Falls merchants' hostile reaction to Alliance joint purchasing and marketing helped to make Clarkfield the Alliance center.

Farmers in southern and western Brown County resented New Ulm's predominance and the county commissioners' plan to build a new

courthouse there. The first county Alliance convention strongly opposed financing a new courthouse without a popular referendum.[53]
That, and future ones, were not held in New Ulm but in the central
hamlet of Iberia, where an Alliance "movement culture" developed.
The Alliance's Farmers Warehouse and Elevator Company built its facilities in centrally located Sleepy Eye, also home to the county's pro-
Alliance newspaper.[54]

    In all three counties, hostility to the county seat caused Alliance-
men to put their institutions in smaller towns, often ones with county-
seat aspirations. Henning is another example. Anger at Republican
"courthouse rings" ruling Otter Tail County politics caused grumblers to
aid Alliancemen there.[55] Editors and merchants in smaller towns had
ulterior motives for supporting the Alliance: they looked to pro-Alliance
county officers for more county printing, county purchase orders, and
the chance to become the new county seat. They tolerated the Alliance's
economic activities. Farmers far from the county seat resented its merchants and wheat buyers more as they incurred greater transportation
costs to use its high-priced services. A county seat was a spatial monopoly, of sorts, and Alliancemen attacked monopoly. Political isolation due
to distance from the seat of government also bred reform attitudes.[56]

*In 1892 the Main Street stores of Granite Falls followed the west bank of the Min-
nesota River, the eastern edge of Yellow Medicine County. The county's prairie
farmland stretched nearly forty-five miles west to the South Dakota border.*

Alliance Efforts at Statewide Joint Purchasing and Marketing

These characteristics of suballiances affected their ability to market and purchase jointly. Understanding these suballiance activities requires examining similar projects of the state Alliance, which could best conduct joint marketing and purchasing and whose bargaining clout was greater than that of the suballiances. In Texas and Georgia, for instance, state Exchanges handled joint purchasing and marketing.[57] Goodwyn incorrectly claimed that Ignatius Donnelly (and, by implication, other Minnesota leaders) "did not believe in the cooperative movement" and based Minnesota's Alliance totally on "stump speeches and ... parliamentary dexterity."[58] As early as October 1889, Donnelly had a long, enthusiastic letter published in the *Great West* describing his visit to the Dakota Farmers' Alliance Company in Aberdeen, Dakota Territory. He hailed its harness-making venture, its bulk purchasing of buggies and wagons and farm implements, and its low-interest financing of farm mortgages. He called on Minnesotans to use the Dakota model, and the state executive committee sought to organize a state purchasing agency like the one in Aberdeen.[59]

The state committee soon became entangled in conflicts over methods of controlling an agency. Using organizational precedents from the Grange, it chose one person—Austin promoter and implement dealer Joseph Keenan—to find out how to start an agency or to be the agent (exactly which was unclear at the time). Less familiar with precedent, Alliancemen in western Minnesota favored using cooperatives, not one agent. So the state committee selected the Alliance Elevator Company as the permanent agency or as a temporary one until Keenan began acting as agent (this, too, was unclear). For wheat farmers, picking Alliance Elevator had the added benefit of combining joint purchasing and wheat marketing.[60] Here was a conflict between the diversifying southeastern region and the wheat-growing western area of Minnesota. Longtime state Alliance president George W. Sprague, a southeasterner, took the Granger view that choosing one business promotor as agent fit with the goal of overall cooperative action. Westerners, newer to the Alliance, disagreed and called Sprague's Alliance "a barnacle attached to the political boodlers." Members "residing west of the 'big woods'" should teach the older leaders "a lesson." They objected to Keenan's promotional use of the agency, which Sprague found inoffensive.[61]

This internal political conflict was resolved in favor of Alliance Elevator, but this newly confirmed agency faced a tough external economic conflict with entrepreneurs who denied its legitimacy or insisted on secrecy if they dealt with it. Its president, Henry L. Loucks, found that local dealers did not "hesitate to use their influence on wholesale dealers and manufacturers to prevent them selling to us direct." Dealers did not submit to being bypassed, and wholesalers hesitated to bypass them in order to sell to an unreliable agency. Loucks reported, "The first thing they [the wholesalers] want to know is: What is our financial standing? Can they compel us to keep contracts we make? How large a trade can we guarantee them?" To reassure them and to gain discounts on cash purchases, an agency needed sufficient capital. Loucks, too, wanted "the cash system for both buying and selling."[62] Yet a democratic decision to terminate credit would not end wheat growers' need for it.

Wholesalers and manufacturers wanted the Alliance not to reveal the price lists they gave to Loucks. Bypassing retailers required secrecy about the "bypass" prices. Loucks noted that local dealers "object to trading with manufacturers who sell to farmers direct" so Alliancemen must show manufacturers that they could keep "business affairs" secret "as well as business men do."[63] Once again a farmers' group operating on avowed democratice principles faced the issue of secrecy, which seemed incompatible with democracy. Openly talking politics seemed to be inconsistent with secretly making business deals. Markets open to all at stated prices appeared to be more democratic than an agency with secret prices and secret deals to bypass markets.

Having a company with paid-in capital of fifteen thousand dollars do the purchasing looked like the best way to meet these concerns. A business like Alliance Elevator could better justify secrecy. Seasonal capital requirements of joint purchasing (peaking in May-June) and wheat marketing (heavy in August-September) complemented each other. Yet Alliance Elevator needed more capital to add joint purchasing to its wheat-marketing task. Loucks argued, "The handling of our grain, particularly our wheat crop, is of very much greater importance to the majority of our members than all other things combined."[64] Alliancemen in southeastern areas rejected Loucks's stress on wheat marketing over joint purchasing. By including both wheat and dairy farmers (and others), the state Alliance was more divergent in its aims than was the state Grange, whose members had been overwhelmingly wheat growers.

Democracy could not create a consensus on priorities. The Alliance failed to combine joint purchasing and wheat marketing. In December

1890, the *Great West* reported, the "Alliance Purchasing Agency and the Alliance Elevator Company… are wholly distinct institutions.…There is no official or financial connection between the two." The agency rented a store and a warehouse and made bulk purchases of wagons, plows, binding twine, and other items, but it never worked to the Alliancemen's satisfaction.[65] Furthermore Alliance Elevator failed to gain access to the terminal wheat markets.

The state Alliance bypassed eastern manufacturers and wholesalers in one product: binding twine. For years, farmers had demanded that the state open a twine factory at the Minnesota State Prison in Stillwater. They felt that the manufacturers' twine trust kept prices artificially high. To lower twine prices and meet farmers' demands, the Minnesota legislature in 1891 appropriated the funds, and the prison was producing twine by the summer of 1892.[66] If manufacturers responded by lowering prices in order to drive the state out of the business, then that would be fine, wrote one Allianceman, "and we could afford to allow our [twine] mills to lie idle."[67] (Some cooperatives shut down during price wars.) It was hardly surprising that the state agreed to turn its prison into a device to lower twine prices. This was home manufacturing, which most editors favored. No Minnesota companies made twine so none would be hurt by prison competition. Twine making was simple, inexpensive, and required little capital. Product defects and customer complaints were expected to be minimal. And the product was necessary for the operation of most farms so demand for it was high.

Achieved through Alliance clout in the 1891 session, the twine victory showed that the state Alliance was better at electing and lobbying legislators than at bypassing local dealers. Yet nineteenth-century laissez-faire ideology limited the usefulness of its politicking because state aid for cooperatives was an alien concept—even to Alliancemen, who did not think of asking the state to assist cooperatives. They had to sink or swim on their own.

Suballiances' Joint Activities: Marketing Wheat

The state Alliance's failures placed the burden of joint economic action on local suballiances and county Alliances, which lacked the state Alliance's bargaining power. Conversely they were often not plagued by disunity. Suballiances, such as the one in Blooming Grove, jointly marketed wheat, their members' main cash crop. The Waseca County Alliance sought a better market at Waseca, the county seat.[68] Closer to Morristown than Waseca, farmers in Blooming Grove negotiated with wheat buyers to the north in Rice County.

A month after forming a suballiance in Blooming Grove, the members had already "voted to sell the wheat in one lot." Details of the negotiations were left to a three-man committee, which was to report in four days (see Table F in Appendix). Only one committee member showed up at the meeting to give the report so the members tried to appoint a man to examine the "wheat market here and [in] Minneapolis," but two men declined, and the one who accepted did not do it properly ("he ought to have declined"). Next month, they decided "after a long debate on the wheat question" to sell to Bean Brothers at Warsaw in Rice County. They had not obtained price quotes from beyond their trading area to use against local wheat buyers, however. By September, after the wheat harvest, members were still content with the Bean Brothers deal, but the president appointed another three-man committee, which failed to contact Bean and was replaced by a new five-man committee. Armed with a "list of the amt. of wheat" each farmer had to sell, the new team sought a better deal but once again contracted with Bean. By mid-January, the sale and delivery were made and the proceeds divided among farmers on the list.[69] After all this coming-and-going, they dealt with the same local buyer as in June.

Problems plagued ad hoc committees handling joint wheat marketing. A high turnover on such committees meant a high degree of democracy—many farmers could participate in the negotiating and decision making and no ruling oligarchy could develop—but that reduced their efficiency. New committee members had to learn the process from scratch, and long delays occurred.[70] Unlike agents, committees did not abscond with the funds, but they might do nothing. In addition there was the free-rider problem. Committee members who volunteered valuable time for bargaining during busy summer months earned no more extra profit than Alliancemen who spent no time at it. Also wheat buyers questioned their authority to transact business for the suballiance.[71] Or buyers claimed to question it but really objected to bargaining with farmers as a group. Suballiances had to insist on that solidarity if they were to retain their collective purpose and protect their members.[72]

Such problems led many suballiances to build or rent their own warehouses or elevators. Nine months after naming its first wheat commit-

tee, the Blooming Grove group considered starting an Alliance warehouse in Morristown. The project was unanimously approved, building
committees began work, and no wheat committees were chosen.[73] The
Adrian Alliance #555, too, met "to organize some kind of a company to
ship grain" because Adrian "had from 7 to 11 wheat buyers that loaf around
smoking imported cigars, while we smoke a pipe and tobacco that is half
cabbage leaves. We propose to try and reverse matters."[74] Wheat-growing
Alliancemen in many regions were often more eager to invest in a warehouse to capture imported-cigar profits than in a store to lower the price
of cabbage leaves.[75]

Suballiances' Joint Activities:
Purchasing Supplies

Joint purchasing paralleled joint marketing in many aspects. Farmers
purchased jointly in bulk quantities for cash to increase their bargaining
power and secure lower prices. Appointed or elected committees obtained lists showing which suballiance members wanted what quantities of a wide variety of farm supplies, such as binding twine or plows or
corn planters. Then they went to merchants, mostly in nearby towns, to
negotiate prices for bulk purchases. Since merchants offered cash-only
terms, poor farmers could not participate, for a suballiance could not
carry them until harvest. Before the availability of prison-made twine,
the earliest, most persistent, and most time-consuming efforts went
into buying twine. Blooming Grove had a twine committee in place two
months after organizing. By spring 1887, it chose another committee "to
look up the twine market," and others followed in 1888 and 1891. Supplied with members' names and amounts of twine desired, they negotiated with twine dealers.[76] Which dealers, how many, and how far away
depended on the committee's resources and competence. Washington's
committee reported quotes from Chicago and Champaign, Illinois, and
Milwaukee, Wisconsin; Lake Hanska's, from Austin, Minnesota.[77] Some
did not go beyond the nearest town. All brought price quotes to the suballiance for discussion and decision. Farmers did not give committees the
final say. They preferred direct rather than representative democracy
when their money was involved.

The democratic method had its difficulties. As with wheat buyers,
twine dealers might not recognize the legitimacy of this polity of twine
buyers. One Waseca dealer refused to accept the Blooming Grove com-

mittee's list: "He wanted an order from every man instead of a list of names."[78] Committees sometimes delayed. Lisbon's was too busy with spring farm work to get quotes so the suballiance gave it a deadline.[79] By late July 1890, when Lake Hanska's committee was still gathering quotes from Austin and elsewhere, farmers "concluded that Harvest was to[o] close at hand to admit of any further delay in this matter." They dealt with a nearby merchant.[80] Suballiances also took their time discussing and deciding. At a Washington suballiance meeting, after quotes were reported, "Mr. Mattson moved that pure manilla only be ordered." The motion carried, but a minority objected to buying the majority's type of twine so the choice of the "kind of twine wanted" was left to each individual.[81] Majority rule could not force those who did not want pure manilla twine to order it and pay for it.

Majority decisions were harder to enforce in the county Alliance, where several trading areas were represented and factionalism was more likely. When a county "committee on twine reported" to Waseca's county Alliance, Blooming Grove delegates argued for accepting a Waseca dealer's offer. Others favored distant manufacturers' cheaper twine. Blooming Grove's prosperous farmer-delegates "advised dealing with home dealers if favorable prices could be obtained in preference to foreign dealers" and threatened to "close the contract with this" dealer: "We should like to have all the other alliances join in this order, but we can't wait." Faced with this ultimatum, the county group accepted the local offer without considering any other.[82] Alliance threats to bypass local dealers and buy direct from manufacturers were often all bark and little bite.

Slow to learn that fact, local editors admonished farmers to support hometown businesses. The *New Ulm Weekly Review* warned that eastern mail-order firms advertised "the apparently best grades of twine for less than our home dealers say it is possible to buy them." These were really "inferior grades," according to the newspaper, and the farmer should "buy his twine of the home dealer." The *Madelia Times* agreed: "It is much the safest in the end to order of home dealers who are responsible."[83] Local twine dealers could not reproach farmers but had to show up at suballiance meetings with price quotes and samples in hand.[84] In most cases, the suballiance quickly closed a deal with the local man even if his offer was higher. Lake Hanska bought pure manilla twine from a Mr. Foss of Madelia at fifteen cents per pound although an Austin dealer offered it for thirteen and a half cents.[85] The local dealer provided both convenience and a known quality. Farmers would not bother with rail shipments from Chicago unless the savings were substantial. Suballiances were often not means to bypass the local market but ways to negotiate with it.

Some merchants still saw joint purchasing as a threat. At best, it forced them to make cuts in their profit margins. At worst, it led to the formation of Alliance stores.[86] Adrian's merchants did "not take kindly to the Alliance" when joint coal purchasing forced local dealers to reduce prices by two dollars a ton.[87] Merchants' fears of competition worried the editor of the *Sleepy Eye Herald*, an Alliance organ that was dependent on merchants' advertisements. (Plans for an Alliance elevator in town caused the anxieties.) The editor noted "a feeling of uneasiness among a few of our business men for fear the Alliance will put in a store which will retail goods of all kinds to farmers." Fortunately he had "interviewed a number of our leading Alliance men and without any exception, they have expressed themselves as opposed to going into the mercantile business." Quite the contrary. "They believe in patronizing the home merchants as long as they are treated with fairness."[88]

The strongest reaction to joint purchasing came in Granite Falls. In March 1890, a committee of the Lisbon suballiance went to "the several villages of the surrounding country" to bargain with merchants. Members of the suballiance would trade "with the merchant or merchants of any place where said committee can obtain the best figures on goods in general."[89] Other suballiances did likewise, prompting one C. S. Tredway to write a letter to the editor in which he publicly attacked buying from "wholesale merchants" as a "penny wise and pound foolish policy." Farmers should be "very loyal to their home merchants." To prove town and country had the same interests, he cited merchants' taxpaying, investing, charitable, and creditor roles: "Our merchants have been a friend indeed to the farmers." Editors sounded this note. The *Granite Falls Tribune* and *Canby News* seconded Tredway's point.[90]

Granite Falls merchants went beyond this appeal and organized a "Retail Commercial Agency," a debt-collection agency that promised to publish in local newspapers the names of delinquent customers. Because of its timing, Alliancemen saw it as a threat aimed at joint purchasing. A suballiance replied by ordering merchants to "submit to this alliance a schedule of discounts from their present established price, that cash or secured notes will secure." If their prices were still too high, "we shall consider ourselves at liberty to buy goods where the dollar will buy the most."[91] The Hammer suballiance pledged to boycott any merchant using these debt-collection tactics.[92] One or both sides must have backed down, for local newspapers ran no further stories on the issue.

Unlikely to be bypassed, Chicago wholesalers were less frightened by Alliance joint purchasing, but many refused to deal with Alliances that bullied their retailer-customers. "We stand for the regular retailer first, last and all the time," stated a spokesman for the W. M. Hoyt Company. The firm of Carson, Pirie, Scott and Company predicted the Alliance "would ultimately fail"—especially "if regular merchants brought out [loss] leaders." Another wholesaler agreed; an Alliance agent had a very small profit margin and could not offer loss leaders "as he will be unable to make up the loss on other articles as the regular merchant can do."[93] Wholesalers seemed unaware that most suballiances used committees, not agents, and these had no margins to worry about because they did not buy and resell goods but only negotiated on behalf of farmers. Closer to farmers and more familiar with their methods, Main Street retailers were less sanguine about the Alliance's fate or the ability of loss leaders to undercut bulk purchases.

Like the Granger-store merchants before them, some small-town merchants saw in the Alliance an opportunity for high sales volume even if at a lower profit margin. A new storekeeper in Canby advertised "a special invitation to the farmers and members of the Farmers' Alliance to come and see my goods and prices." He denied any ties "to the Merchants' Retail Commercial Agency."[94] The *Granite Falls Tribune* reported, "Sam Mather came over last Thursday to deliver his contract of [grain] drills to the Alliance. Every team ... had a drill for a load and the men ... seemed well satisfied with their bargain. Verily Sam is a hustler."[95]

Not all merchants were hostile to the Alliance, nor was the reverse true. Some suballiances accepted local price quotes while others refused to pressure merchants by even asking for quotes. Lisbon's members found joint purchasing of grain drills too controversial and dropped all discussion of it.[96] The Washington suballiance talked about joint purchasing but never followed through with it; neither did the Moorhead #148.[97] Even in Granite Falls, it was unlikely that the merchants' hostility radicalized farmers. One local suballiance supported a third-party ticket at the same meeting that it condemned the debt-collection agency, but it would likely have taken that step anyway.[98] Lisbon rejected a state executive committee's call for a formation of a third party, despite the agency issue. After the 1890 election, it had to vote on whether even to hear a letter from Ignatius Donnelly or to send delegates to the county Alliance meeting.[99]

Joint Purchasing and Marketing Did Not Radicalize Farmers

At its most basic level, the Alliance joint purchasing and marketing was a democratic process, including such features as elected committees, high turnover on committees, a suballiance veto over committee decisions, and extensive discussion by all members. Democracy, however, was inefficient. Committees failed to do the job, lacked expertise due to high turnover, needed to secure suballiance approval of their decisions, and faced merchants who felt they lacked legitimacy or posed a threat. If Alliancemen had recalled Grangers' joint purchasing and marketing, they might have seen these problems coming. Perhaps some did. But joint action suited farmers' practical desire to take economic action here and now. The momentum of organizing suballiances carried them straight into joint purchasing and marketing with little thought for past failures or future problems. Joint action squared with a suballiance's character as a direct democracy. It recruited new members for the suballiance through its promise of immediate, practical results. It required no risky investments, no buildings, no inventory, no overhead. It was quickly organized and quickly abandoned.

Its democratic nature meant potential radicalization. Merchants' refusal to deal with this direct democracy could be seen as a slap in the farmer's face. Moreover the suballiance did not have to petition the state for redress of grievances or take merchants to court, as a cooperative business would. It could take revenge by boycotting the county-seat merchants or using the county Alliance to overturn county politics. However, there is little evidence of radicalization. Merchants routinely dealt with suballiances, which often hesitated to press joint purchasing to the point of a complete break with merchants.

These problems spurred farmers to incorporate separate businesses. Reporting on the Dakota agency, Donnelly noted, "The Farmers' Alliance proper, being only a social unincorporated Society, could not transact such business. It was deemed necessary, therefore, to form a separate association, which could be incorporated."[100] Suballiances spawned many such associations. In Lake Hanska, a cooperative store and creamery grew out of the suballiance, although not organized at its meetings. Meeting outside the suballiance for economic ends, Alliancemen started cooperative elevators or warehouses in Sleepy Eye, Adrian, Herman, and Waseca.[101]

Cooperative stores and creameries formed in the 1890s often created crossroads communities, such as the ones at Hanska and Clarks Grove. Committees—too temporary and unstable—had no similar lasting results. No merchant would start a store near the schoolhouse where the suballiance met to hear committee reports. But when farmers formed separate cooperative businesses, they created farmer-controlled crossroads towns. Farmers who joined the Alliance tended to suffer from "geographic isolation from towns and villages." Cooperation helped them to overcome isolation by establishing new towns and villages closer to their farms.[102]

Cooperatives actually reduced the potential for radicalization because they had to appeal for patronage to farmers outside the Alliance. For economic survival, most cooperatives followed the Rochdale rule of political neutrality. They were more cautious than suballiances because they had to consider their balance sheets. A cooperative whose members attended annual meetings run by its officers was less democratic than a suballiance meeting weekly or monthly. Suballiances were direct democracies; cooperatives, representative democracies in which authority was delegated to the board of directors. As years passed, they often became board oligarchies: elections were pro forma; candidates ran unopposed; the unanimous ballot ruled. Such cooperatives were not seedbeds of radicalism, and merchants were more willing to deal with them. If merchants refused, it was a quarrel among businesses, not a slap in the face to a democratic assembly of farmers. Still the suballiances were seedbeds for such cooperatives, and that made them important in the history of rural cooperation.

8

Cooperative Stores, 1890–1905

*"Working for a Farmers' Store
in connection with the creamery"*

THE JOINT PURCHASING carried out by suballiances could provide the seedbed for a cooperative store. Farmers purchased jointly to protest merchants' high profit margins, then they incorporated separate businesses, which had enough year-to-year stability to command wholesalers' respect. That series of events occurred in central Otter Tail County where the debate between farmers and merchants was more articulate and more lively than the one at Granite Falls and, thus, worth listening to at length.

In the summer of 1889, Battle Lake merchants denied credit to several apparently reputable and creditworthy farmers, who were used to obtaining "credit from just before harvest until after threshing." Farmers saw the denials as part of the merchants' plan to "make farmers pay cash," thereby forcing them to borrow from banks "at a high rate of interest." Angry farmers responded by ordering "a car load of groceries" and other supplies from a Minneapolis firm at cash-only prices up to 50 percent less than Battle Lake prices.[1]

That order was made possible because of the completion of the Northern Pacific line through southern Otter Tail County in 1881–82, which may have been a factor in the merchants' denial of credit.[2] With access to a railroad, merchants hoped to escape their role of accepting farm produce as payment for store goods. Merchants could point to the tracks and tell farmers to get their own produce to market and pay cash for goods.

When the carload of goods arrived in late November, a controversy erupted in the county's English-language press. Pleased at the farmers' triumph over the merchants, Old Stock farmer Anson Sherman exulted, "Now, I think the tables are the other side up." Old Stock editor Bronson Strain of the *Battle Lake Review* defended local merchants and claimed the Minneapolis firm had swindled the farmers. He reprinted a recent editorial attacking a similar move by farmers near Hallock in Kittson County: "The local merchants have carried these same persons along, year after year, and when the farmer has cash in the fall, to send away for goods is not right and should be stopped." Hallock's "incensed" merchants filed suit and foreclosed on delinquent farmers to stop the practice. Strain praised Battle Lake merchants for not doing this but disapproved of farmers' carload orders. With a polite aside ("Now Anson, this discussion is settled"), this short Old Stock debate ended.[3]

A longer, wider-ranging debate began among Norwegian Americans in Otter Tail County. Showing more antimerchant feeling, the dispute went beyond discussing credit terms to examining profit margins, town-country antagonisms, and links between wholesalers and retailers. Concerned about losses to local merchants, Anfin Solem of the *Fergus Falls Ugeblad*, a Norwegian-language newspaper published in the county seat, titled his editorial "Over Vækken efter Vand" (Crossing the Creek to Find Water)—buying from distant suppliers goods readily available locally. He reminded his readers that town and country were interdependent, and farmers should not begrudge merchants a livelihood. He cited a battle between coopers and tinsmiths in Bergen, Norway: "The coopers have begun to make tin kegs and in retaliation the tinsmiths have set up a cooperage."[4] In Otter Tail, where might it end—with farmers printing their own newspaper and editors growing their own food?

The farmers replied in letters to the editor: (1) retail trade was a mutual protection scheme of wholesalers and retailers that farmers had to bypass; (2) few farmers had the cash to buy from distant wholesalers so merchants need not worry; and (3) Fergus Falls merchants' profit margins ranged from 25 to 300 percent.[5] Alliance leader Charles Brandborg attacked a "protection" scheme to keep farmers from bypassing retailers. A "huge tariff" meant "the protection of our manufacturers, coal mine owners and iron mine owners" who then sell "their products only to 'jobbers' or 'wholesalers' in order to protect them." These " 'wholesalers' sell only to regular 'storekeepers' in order to protect them." Railroads added "indirect protection," for "the freight rate for smaller quantities is nearly three times higher than that for whole car loads. Everything is to help the big against the small."[6]

This was hardly the conspiracy Brandborg suspected. Large investments had to be protected so entrepreneurs moved from unpredictable free markets to managed relationships. With high fixed costs, railroads had to capture freight even if that meant below-cost rates for large shippers who could guarantee them reliable, sizable shipments. Needing to pay traveling salesmen and to turn inventory over rapidly, wholesalers had to maintain ties to reliable retailers. Brandborg described a post-railroad economy that Alliancemen would find harder to crack. Yet railroads made their carload orders possible, too.[7]

Sidestepping Brandborg's analysis, Solem replied that towns competed. (But few farmers could travel far by wagon to benefit from this competition.) He listed grocery items sold in Fergus Falls, merchants' costs for each, prices charged, and percent markup. The markups ranged from 3 percent for plain rice to 14 percent for syrup—not 25 to 300 percent as critics claimed.[8] He and others argued that merchants earned the markup by giving credit and taking farm produce as payment. Just having nearby stores was invaluable compared to pioneer days when they traveled eighty miles to St. Cloud for supplies.[9] He called for compromise and proposed the editor's solution: home manufacturing or processing. Nervous about cancelled subscriptions, he tried to exit from the debate, but it took three more weeks to fizzle out.[10]

Another cause of farmer-merchant antagonism was haggling over prices. Coming into a store, the farmer seemed "under the impression that the merchants... are making much more profit than they ought to," reported the *Canby News*. So "nine times out of ten," he "begins to beat the merchant down" on the price.

Six years after the local brouhaha, Bronson Strain (left) proudly advertised his newspaper's Republican principles and prepared to fight the Democratic-People's Party in the 1896 campaign.

"Then begins a series of arguments on both sides that is simply ridiculous" and antagonizes both sides.[11] Led by department stores, merchants were dropping this system and adopting a "fixed-price, one-price policy" that made the market appear democratic and fair. "One price for everybody! Regardless of age, sex, wealth, poverty, or bargaining power."[12] That may have reduced suspicion.

One month into the debate, a notice of a meeting in Underwood appeared in the Ugeblad: "Farmers will seek to 'agree to order from one or another wholesale house such goods as are commonly required by households, in order that we may in this way save ourselves the profit margins which middlemen demand.'" Coming after he had attacked the idea, this notice struck Anfin Solem as "bitter sarcasm against the Ugeblad." The meeting led to a decision by the farmers to drop joint purchasing and to start the Farmers' Store.[13]

That store, Underwood Handelsforening, later called the Farmers Mercantile Corporation (FMC), was formally organized in February 1892, but it was already running by October 15, 1891. Several factors led to its formation: the newspaper debate, farmers' success with the eight-year-old Sverdrup Scandinavian Mutual Insurance Company, and the Alliance's strength in the grain-growing Underwood area. Two local men, State Representative Hans P. Bjørge and County Commissioner Knud Pederson, were leaders in the county Alliance, and the latter attended the first meeting to consider a store.[14] Local suballiances played indirect roles in starting the Farmers' Store.[15] Though farmers met apart from the suballiance, its members probably participated in that first meeting. Blocking direct Alliance sponsorship of the store was Bjørge's coownership of the rival Bjørge and Sjordal store in Underwood.[16]

A final factor was an 1889 split in the Sverdrup Lutheran Church, which led to the founding of a Unitarian church in Underwood. Several Alliance leaders or store organizers were Unitarians, including Bjørge and store leader Even Sæther.[17] Several were prominent Lutherans, including the first FMC president, Ole Bjørnaas, and Knud Pederson.[18] Instead of creating a fatal factionalism, this split seemed to help the FMC. (Religious neutrality was one Rochdale principle, but principles were sometimes ignored.) The churches competed, each trying to appear more farmer friendly than the other. Unitarian minister Kristofer Janson spoke at the county Alliance convention, declaring, "I have been a friend of the farmer all my life."[19] His speech followed that of another friend of the farmer, Sverdrup Lutheran pastor B. B. Haugan.[20]

In general, Norwegian Americans leaving Lutheranism to start a Unitarian church had to have initiative, a bold cooperative spirit, and a disregard for neighbors' opinions. The act strengthened those qualities.[21] Organizing an unpopular, solitary church among locally dominant Lutheranism was like starting a lone cooperative store amid prevalent private stores. Unlike the Lutherans, these Unitarians were not linked to merchant-controlled churches in Fergus Falls. Already unpopular for their doctrine, they had little to lose by supporting the Alliance or the FMC store.[22]

All these factors motivated farmers to start the FMC. Yet, perhaps from necessity, they settled for a halfway measure similar to the merchant-run "Granger stores." They leased a building from Ole Sivertson, who had started the town's first store when the Northern Pacific arrived in 1881. Ten years later he managed the Farmers' Store and served on its board.[23]

Changes between the Granger Era (1870s)
and Alliance Era (1890s)

Despite this compromise, many cooperative stores of the 1890s were long-term successes, for much had changed since the early 1870s when residents of St. Peter tried to start a Union store. Old Stock, immigrant, and Granger cooperative stores had achieved only brief and occasional success. Twenty years later, they were gone. Only a few ethnic stores like Fremad lasted more than a few years. In the 1890s, the main change agents—suballiances and cooperative creameries—helped produce the first long-lived stores.

These stores were not the beneficiaries of aid from state government. It did not aid cooperative stores or significantly change the laws authorizing them. In 1894 the state law on cooperative associations was still basically the 1870 one that had been written for Union stores. In 1876 and 1881, the legislature had amended it to give more latitude to cooperatives. The maximum capital stock was raised to one hundred thousand dollars (there was still no minimum). Rules for filing annual financial reports were loosened, and the ban on paying dividends before accumulating a 30 percent reserve was lifted. These issues were left up to each cooperative to decide.[24] The legislature failed to write into law any lessons that farmers had learned from the early failures of consumers' cooperation. The only Rochdale principle it mandated was that each shareholder have one vote, a provision of the 1870 law. Cooperatives were free to experiment and to innovate—and to fail.

Farmers had learned even if the state had not. Both township mutuals and creameries had become models of cooperation, their meetings forums for discussing consumers' cooperation, and their members a core group ready to support a store. The creamery, by having its own building, resolved locational disputes better than did a majority vote; daily, it brought customers to one crossroads site. By paying monthly milk checks, it provided a store with customers who could purchase more store goods and pay up more regularly than could 1870s wheat farmers. Finally suballiances' joint purchasing provoked farmer-merchant debates, like that in the *Ugeblad*, which motivated farmers to start cooperative stores. The Alliance provided ideological support for such stores.

Township mutuals, creameries, and suballiances created a vital cooperative context. Cooperative efforts in the same community in different economic realms reinforced each other: the "idea of co-operation, separate and apart from any specific instance of co-operative activity, . . . permeated the community."[25] The sum was more than the parts, as exemplified in both Underwood and in a community in a different region—Lake Hanska and Linden Townships in Brown County. By the early 1890s, this was becoming a dairying area. The creamery more than the suballiance led to the start of a cooperative store on the border between the two townships. Dairying made the Hanska-Linden Store different from the Farmers' Store in grain-growing Sverdrup Township, yet there were similarities: both were successful ethnic cooperatives run by Scandinavian Americans (mostly Norwegian Americans). An in-depth analysis of both stores reveals contrasts and similarities.

The Origins of the Hanska-Linden Handelsforening

Lake Hanska and Linden also had strong suballiances and a Lutheran-Unitarian split. However, the origins of the Hanska-Linden Handelsforening (HLHF, also known as the Hanska-Linden Store) differed from the FMC's. A key difference was that no town existed at Hanska before the store. The farmers' main grievance was the lack of one, requiring them to travel ten miles to Madelia or New Ulm to purchase goods. Farmer-merchant debates also occurred in Brown County, and the Lake Hanska suballiance tried to purchase coal, wood, twine, and seed wheat

from distant suppliers. Yet, it did not start a store.[26] The chief obstacle
was lack of an acceptable site. Any choice it made, however democratic
its decision-making process, would inconvenience some members. It
tried to start a cooperative creamery, but its members could not agree on
a site.[27] And a Lake Hanska consensus would not have secured the Linden suballiance's approval of a creamery site in the middle of Lake Hanska Township. Interestingly, disagreement over a site on which to build
a church was a major cause of the Lutheran-Unitarian split. The Unitarians built a church near the border between the two townships, probably to maximize the number of settlers who could attend it.[28]

A year after the suballiance failed to choose a site, a "well attended"
Norwegian-language meeting likely dominated by the Unitarian leaders
was held at their Nora Free Christian Church. Seventy-five farmers
were set to join. They built on a site just across the line in Lake Hanska
but close enough for farmers in western Linden to haul milk there.[29]
The Nora church's central location and its members' organizational
skills meant the Unitarians led the way in starting the creamery that began in the summer of 1892.[30]

Before the creamery turned out its first butter, Anton O. Ouren, a
prominent Unitarian, was "working for the erection of a Farmers' store

*Ellef Asleson and a helper prepared to haul 3,273 pounds of butter in tubs from the
Hanska-Linden Creamery to Madelia sometime in the 1890s.*

in connection with the Creamery."[31] A creamery site was a natural location for a cooperative store, and no private store stood there to offer competition. One creamery activist, Christian Ahlness (a Lutheran), may have threatened to start his own store if a cooperative one was not begun.[32] Even if he did not, farmers knew some merchant would.[33]

Here was the farmers' chance to escape the merchants' high profit margins by establishing their own store.[34] Providing institutional support, the creamery hosted the first organizational meeting, and its members were the store's core group of shareholders and customers. With the store still only an idea, the *Madelia Times* correspondent understandably conflated the two projects: "The Hanska & Linden Creamery company have organized to build a general merchandise store near Linden Lake in the spring."[35] Although separate businesses, the store and creamery cooperated. They cut costs by sharing a driver, Ellef Asleson: "[Going to Madelia,] Ellef loaded up with butter from the creamery, and eggs from the Farmers Store and returning from Madelia, he generally took empty butter tubs and salt for the creamery, and diverse merchandise for the Store."[36] The producers' cooperative had top priority; farmers saved only small amounts of money buying at a cooperative store.[37]

Characteristics of the Hanska and Underwood Stores in Operation

A greater bond was needed than that of buying cheap. Solidarity had to overcome the inevitable clashes. An Underwood woman recalled that the FMC was truly cooperative; members "knew how to work together, and the articles for sale learned to cooperate," too. She marveled that "hand-painted china, lamp wicks, pencils and postcards could live together on the same shelf under adverse conditions." Like Swedes and Norwegians, "Could the kerosene pump and the cookie boxes live happily so close together if they were the least antagonistic?"[38]

The Hanska-Linden and FMC stores were ethnic cooperatives whose meetings were conducted in Norwegian. The FMC rules required that notices of meetings must be "advertised in the county's most widely-circulated Scandinavian-language newspaper."[39] Neither store excluded non-Scandinavians from membership, although Norwegian speech and writing discouraged them from joining. The Sverdrup mutual excluded non-Scandinavians, but mutuals' members needed more trust (due to the risk of arson) than did store members. A store could not be so selective about its customers. Still Norwegian-American solidarity reduced the threat of secession and gave store members what Grangers lacked: common interests besides that of buying cheap. Also the FMC sold ethnic foods like herring and lutefisk (at Christmas), but the private stores in Underwood undoubtedly did likewise.[40]

The two stores varied in their use of Rochdale principles (see Table 3). State law left cooperative stores wide latitude, and no experts traveled around preaching the Rochdale doctrine. Though the FMC had radical antimerchant origins, it followed Rochdale principles less than Hanska did. Later its members tried unsuccessfully to amend the rules to adhere more closely to the principles.[41]

Both stores' rules reflected the economic conditions of their members. Located in a dairying area, Hanska limited credit more stringently. Farmers receiving monthly milk checks were expected to pay their store accounts monthly. The store accepted "commodities which are produced by the farmers (except livestock and vegetables) as a medium of exchange worth the same as at the stores in the nearest towns."[42] Membership was limited to "residents of the country (Farmers and Workers). Townspeople are excluded."[43]

Because it was located in a wheat-growing area, the FMC formulated goals that included meeting local needs and "seek[ing] the best market for our farm products"—a feasible goal given Underwood's rail service.[44] Its board considered starting a livestock-marketing system at the store. To create a local wheat market, members voted a four-hundred-dollar donation toward a proposed flour mill in town (the project failed). They inconclusively discussed building a creamery (built later).[45] No impenetrable wall separated farmers' consuming and producing roles. The FMC

TABLE 3
Adherence to Rochdale Principles — Hanska and Underwood

Rochdale Principle	Hanska	Underwood
One vote per shareholder	Yes	Yes
Limit on interest on shares	Yes (7% limit)	No
Dividends paid per patronage	Yes (but forgone)	No
Goods sold at market prices	Yes	No
Membership open to all	No (no townsmen)	Yes
Limit on one person's shareholding	Yes (1 – after 1900)	Yes (4)
Cash sales only	No (30-day credit)*	No

Note:
* After 1900 the Hanska store allowed 60-day credit.

tried both to assist in wheat marketing and to help farmers wean themselves from a reliance on wheat.[46]

Credit Sales and Overdue Accounts at Hanska and Underwood

Both stores adjusted to farmers' circumstances by selling on credit, thus
violating one Rochdale principle. The problem of credit had plagued
Vasa's Union Store, as well as most other cooperative stores. Farmers received credit at private stores, so cooperatives often granted it but tried to
limit it. One HLHF goal was "to seek as much as possible to prevent the
misuse of credit." At the HLHF, credit was limited to thirty days.[47] The
FMC tried to limit credit to reliable customers. In its constitution, paragraph nine called for debtors to settle up by the next quarterly board
meeting to avoid being charged 8 percent interest on unpaid balances.
No account was to be outstanding more than six months.[48]

Enforcing these rules was nearly impossible in a wheat-growing
area. After the grain harvest in late August or September, the board
usually ordered the store manager to start collecting debts. He sent letters asking for payment and threatening to impose interest on unpaid
balances, but this tactic often failed.[49] Then, at the January annual meeting, the members would hotly debate the issue.[50] Already, in the first
year, the board complained that paragraph nine "was felt to be difficult to
carry out." They decided not to enforce it, pending discussion at their
next meeting, at which time they "found that they still could not carry
out this paragraph's provision," so "they decided to continue as before,
presumably until the next annual meeting, then to implement this paragraph if that is agreed on then."[51]

But "the ongoing question regarding paragraph 9" was not resolved at
the January 1893 annual meeting either. Democracies often avoid divisive subjects in order to keep support and prevent secession; that was
what the FMC members did. By the January 1895 meeting, some accounts
were eighteen months past due. At the next annual meeting, the board
publicly disgraced debtors by reading their accounts aloud.[52] By January
1899, the store manager threatened to quit unless "the association takes
steps as soon as possible to collect 50 per cent of all debt owed to the
store."[53]

This was no legalistic quibble. Overdue accounts caused real problems. As farmers charged items in spring and early summer, the store's

accounts receivable increased, and its working capital decreased. In 1899 FMC's accounts receivable more than doubled from $2,207.99 (April 3) to $4,872.47 (July 3). In 1893 and 1898, the board had to borrow to get through the summer.[54] Unpaid accounts jeopardized the store's ability to earn wholesalers' discounts for paying cash. In 1904 directors debated if "we should borrow money... to pay for goods in order to earn the customary cash discount, or if we should borrow from the 'wholesale houses.'" For a low-cost, low-price farmers' store, cash discounts mattered.[55]

By being located next to a creamery that issued monthly milk checks, the HLHF store suffered less from overdue accounts. Yet the accounts receivable exceeded nine thousand dollars in October 1900 (a constitutional change had liberalized credit terms in 1899). From 1901 to 1905, prolonged, worried discussions about the problem occupied the HLHF board. Remonstrating letters were mailed, deadlines stated, dunning visits recommended, interest charges ordered, and the services of a bill collector threatened.[56] The HLHF escaped summer cash shortages and fall collection efforts only to have overdue accounts become a year-round problem.[57]

Democratic control of credit was difficult. A majority of members depended on it and did not want policies to be too stringent. Chronically delinquent members may have been less willing to pay off their cooperative creditor than their private creditors and may have cited their disagreement with the former's policies to excuse their delinquency. They were both its voting members and its debtors. Both the cooperative and its debtor-members must have struggled to keep those two roles separate.

Offering credit caused other problems. Borrowing brought interest charges, which forced both stores to sell at a higher profit margin, to keep profits in the business, and, thus, to refuse to pay a patronage or stock dividend. They tried to accumulate cash reserves to carry them through periods of cash shortage.[58] From the start, FMC shareholders decided to forgo cash distributions of annual profits. Instead, half went to a *Grundfund* (basic capital fund), and half was added to the book value of members' shares.[59] Apparently no shareholders pressed for a cash dividend.[60] Two years later, some grumbled about the *Grundfund* (calling it "exorbitantly large") and pressed for smaller margins and lower store prices—but not for a patronage dividend in cash.[61]

In the Rochdale system, regular patronage dividends aided in the recruitment of new members. Lack of cash dividends plus higher margins and higher prices reduced the incentives for prospective members to join. Only five persons joined the FMC (by purchasing shares) after 1892–93 (two were probably close relatives of FMC shareholders).[62] A small, select group, the FMC was finally challenged by a more open cooperative store in 1908.

Similarly HLHF shareholders voted to forgo cash dividends from 1893 profits and to put them into the business. In January 1896, they voted to retain 25 percent of the past three years' dividends in the store; in 1898 and 1900, to retain 100 percent of the profit in the business. Because of its leadership role in the new town of Hanska, however, the HLHF did not become a small ingrown group seeking only its own interests.[63]

Supervising Managers and Clerks at Hanska and Underwoood

The HLHF encountered more serious problems with store clerks than with delinquent customers. Overseeing the store's manager was a difficult task for a board of toiling farmers with little retail experience. Hiring a manager was not the board's prerogative. Members voted on a manager, who thus gained political leverage that could be used against the board. The first two managers, Peter Ahlness and Nels J. Ouren, were elected at general meetings of shareholders.[64] They became more than mere employees. The board hired clerks and set salaries, but shareholders' support gave the manager a strong voice in both matters.

Cooperatives had trouble supervising clerks and creamery workers living at a creamery-and-store crossroads. In 1894 or 1895, the Hanska-Linden creamery built a house for these bachelor employees. No board member would oversee it, so they hired buttermaker Ephraim Brubaker to be the boardinghouse manager, too, for an extra twenty-five dollars a month. The bachelors hired him as their cook. "Mr. Brubaker being now invested with the toga of three different, official and culinary, positions" had "reached the limits of his variegated capabilities, as reports began to leak out of deficiencies in the creamery work." The boardinghouse, one creamery leader recalled, "became notorious for its gambling and ribaldry which threatened to demoralize the whole neighborhood."[65] The farmers had to act. First the creamery board forced Brubaker to resign as buttermaker. Then the store board hired its president as a clerk to replace one bachelor. The other left in six months.[66]

Being both president and store clerk created a conflict of interest, for the president now helped to set his own salary as clerk and became both the manager's employee (as clerk) and employer (as board president). Furthermore, the manager now had difficulty controlling the clerks' behavior. They began to leave for lunch before noon and to lock up the store instead of keeping one clerk on duty over the lunch hour. They gave out free tobacco and probably themselves smoked in the clothing department. By March 1897 the store had to sell at cost almost a thousand dollars worth of ready-to-wear clothes saturated with tobacco fumes. In January 1897 the store had two new clerks. The (now former) president was not rehired as a clerk.[67] Members at the annual meeting also ended his term as director in order to restore managerial control.

A democratically elected board had problems restraining labor costs. Hiring clerks and setting their salaries was hard for the boards at Hanska and Underwood to do. At a start-of-the-year board meeting (January for HLHF and April for FMC), the boards hired clerks for the next year and set monthly salaries. If the clerks were rehired, their salaries were usually increased for the new year.[68] To curb these rising labor costs, the HLHF board voted in 1902 to advertise clerk positions at a set salary instead of automatically rehiring clerks at higher salaries.[69] Perhaps they hoped the labor market could nominate clerk candidates and limit clerks' salaries better than democratic processes subject to the political pull of clerks and their relatives.

The challenge for a cooperative store was to maintain an arm's-length relationship with its employees when it could not with its customers, who were also its owners. By hiring clerks from among its members or their teen-age children, the Hanska-Linden Store acquired employees with conflicting roles in the cooperative. Members might later run for election to the board and lead a faction to seize control of it. Members' relatives might rally a faction to support higher pay, more vacation time, or a promotion. While the employee clerked, he or she talked to members more often than did the directors and could thus recruit supporters. Factions favoring or opposing an employee threatened the store's unity.[70]

In 1899–1900, as both stores began to sell more ready-to-wear clothing, they hired their first female clerks. The FMC board acted over the objections of the manager, a storekeeper of the old school, who complained that "it would take a long time to teach one, and the result would be that we would lose more than we gained."[71] The board hired one anyway. Female clerks were needed to wait on female customers purchasing clothing.

Clerking in a cooperative store was a promising job for farmers' sons and daughters living near a crossroads community that lacked private businesses. Once known by customers, they could start their own businesses. By 1901 one former HLHF clerk was part owner of a restaurant and meat market; another, of a furniture and implement dealership. A third operated a blacksmith shop.[72]

The Hanska and Underwood stores were similar in most respects, but when the FMC was formed, Underwood had already been a town, and its first manager had been a storeowner there so its board had more trouble dealing with him than with its clerks. When the Farmers' Store began, Sivertson sold it his inventory (for an interest-bearing note), rented his store to the FMC, and served as its treasurer and manager. At each annual meeting, shareholders voted on whether to continue the business for the coming year. If the ayes won, a three-man committee negotiated a new rental agreement with him. His salary as manager was also set then.[73] As manager, landlord, and treasurer, Sivertson had clout. The farmers' retail inexperience and inability to finance construction of their own building limited their leverage over him. When he threatened to quit if the board did not collect 50 percent of the accounts receivable, they had little choice but to comply.[74] Later he persuaded them to hire extra help for the spring and temporarily prevented them from employing a female clerk.[75]

When they tried to escape their dependence on him by purchasing or building their own store, he was one potential seller with whom they negotiated. In January 1899 they tried but failed to get him to name a price for his store. A year later, they went ahead anyway and voted to purchase a lot and a building. The board discussed buying Bjørge & Sjordal's store. Then, at the last moment, it gave him another chance to name a price, and he demanded eighteen hundred dollars—three hundred dollars more than either of the other two offers. Still "the board found it wisest to buy from Ole Sivertson and made a deal with him to pay $1800."[76] The deal fell through. They "could not give a satisfactory guarantee"— satisfactory to him, evidently.[77]

That same year he fell ill and had to resign his posts as manager and treasurer. The store earned its smallest surplus ever. Members were evenly divided on whether to continue the store without him so it kept running, but the tie vote was not a vote of confidence in its future. The man elected to replace him refused the job. Only "after a great deal of persuading" did a second man agree to try it.[78] Sivertson's resignation led to more negotiations about purchasing the store. He strengthened his bargaining position by giving one month's (not the required six months') notice to end the annual lease.[79] The farmers had to act. They thought of building a store but were too busy with summer field work to construct one. By haggling, they got him to come down $250 from his asking price (now nineteen hundred dollars), and they struck a deal.[80]

It was dangerous to become dependent on one manager-cum-landlord. Cooperatives with their egalitarian ethos (all members are equal) had problems hiring skilled labor in a labor market that was inegalitarian (all labor skills are not equal). Their problems worsened as they moved up the hierarchy of skills. Stores needed skilled managers, yet farmers balked at paying competitive salaries to get them because the market set those salaries higher than farmers thought justified. Yet a

The manager, the first female clerk, and three male clerks displayed their small-town public prominence outside the Hanska-Linden Store around 1900.

democratic vote to operate a cooperative store at Underwood was useless without an experienced storekeeper to run it. In the end, they had to accept his terms both for running and selling it.[81]

Internal Unity or Disunity in a Cooperative Store

Two other problems troubled the 1901 FMC annual meeting. The 1900 surplus had been its lowest ever: "small disagreement [arose] within the association" due to the small surplus and the members' failure at the past two annual meetings to adopt the Rochdale principles of low share prices and patronage dividends.[82]

Dissension often surfaced at the annual meeting, the democratic moment for a cooperative. The election of officers at the annual meeting conferred legitimacy on the board. Yet the event offered a stage and a moment for factions to disrupt a cooperative. It was election, constitutional convention, and legislative session all rolled into one. Almost any motion was in order and could be acted upon. Prices could be set, store goods marked down, credit terms altered, clerks hired or fired, or constitutions amended. The cooperative briefly became a direct democracy. After the meeting adjourned, it reverted to a representative democracy run by a board. Members' participation at annual meetings was a cooperative's great strength but, potentially, its great weakness, too. Unanimous reelection of incumbent directors year after year with few motions marked the death of its democratic spirit. Yet high board turnover or controversial resolutions meant factionalism and dissension.

In both Hanska and Underwood, dissatisfaction with boards and their policies sometimes produced high turnover. In 1899 the FMC members defeated a motion to lower the share price and began an effort to persuade Sivertson to sell his building; it was also the one year when more than two new members were elected to the FMC's board.[83] Four HLHF annual meetings elected more than two new members (see Table 4).[84]

At the January 1902 meeting, dissatisfaction erupted over some members (probably directors) who did not patronize the store.[85]

One device to soften disunity was the trial ballot, a nonbinding poll of members' opinions that was taken at a shareholders meeting before voting on a major issue. At a special meeting in February 1900, for example, the FMC held a trial ballot on whether to buy a store building. After a twenty-three-to-eighteen majority favored the step, many opponents did not vote on the official ballot (twenty-three in favor and eleven opposed). They did not have to support the losing side publicly.[86] At yet another special meeting in February 1903, a trial ballot on building an addition found a majority (sixteen-to-eleven) favored the plan so they voted unanimously to make the trial ballot official.[87] A trial ballot allowed members to express their views informally before a highly charged, divisive vote was taken.

The Cooperative Store Helps Create a New Trade Center

Like many cooperatives in Minnesota, the Hanska-Linden Store played a pathbreaking role in its community. The FMC did not; in 1881–82, Underwood already existed as a railroad town, ten years before the FMC began. In 1892–93 the Hanska-Linden creamery and store created a crossroads community (Blessum), and they led the way in 1899–1901 when the Minneapolis and St. Louis Railroad (M&SL) laid track through the community, put a station there, and birthed the town of Hanska.[88] The M&SL would not have chosen that route had it not been for the high-volume creamery and store located there.

In the summer or fall of 1898, an M&SL representative visited the creamery manager, Christian Ahlness. "Sitting down on a drygoods box in [the] shade of the Icehouse," the two "had a long confidential talk." Ahlness gave him "all the information he wanted as to the volume of business at the Creamery and many other matters." They parted with these words: "you do what you can for us and we will do what we can for you."[89] In January 1899 a Linden observer reported that rail surveyors were "locating a line close to the Hanska-Linden store. They seemed to be heading toward St. James." The *Madelia Times* editor agreed that rival St. James might be their destination but noted "a rumor they will come to this place."[90]

TABLE 4
Causes of Large-scale Turnover on the HLHF Board

Year	Number of New Members	Likely Cause of the Turnover
1894	3	Need to raise working capital
1897	4	Crisis over clerks' behavior
1901	3	Large outstanding accounts
1902	4	Directors not patronizing store and low dividend the previous year

In February, M&SL General Manager L. F. Day traveled to both towns and sparked a competitive frenzy by telling them "what the company would need in the way of yards, station sites, etc., thus putting the citizens in a condition to make intelligent offers of assistance to the company." Needless to say, "very anxious" towns "seemed to be willing to be generous."[91] Hanska area citizens met in late March "for the purpose of offering inducements" to the M&SL "to locate their road by that place."[92] A late April article ("Our Plum") in the *St. James Journal* reported the M&SL announcement that the line would pass through St. James and right by the HLHF store.[93]

The prospect electrified Hanska. In April the observer from Linden reported, "Many of our farmers have expectation of business opportunities and contemplate abandoning farming in case the 'new road' is properly located." The *New Ulm News* predicted "that an important business village will be built this year at Lake Hanska."[94] Prospects of a village on (then) cheap farmland excited the land speculators. Earlier, Hans Blessum, who owned land by the creamery and store, had profited from their success. After waiting several years to see if they lasted, he platted the townsite of Blessum in June 1898. Encompassing only three blocks and twenty-two lots, Blessum was modestly sized for the minimal growth expected of a railroadless hamlet.[95]

In anticipation of a railroad's arrival, expectations grew exponentially. M&SL agents bought land from three owners in late July 1899. The townsite of Hanska was platted in October 1899 with sixteen blocks.[96] Although the new site competed with his hamlet a quarter-mile away, Blessum also profited from the new one: a parcel of land he bought for four hundred dollars in 1882 he sold to M&SL agents for over eighteen hundred dollars. They paid between sixty-five hundred and eight thousand dollars for the townsite, but "a business lot in the newly laid out town of Hanska sold for $600, at the [later] auction." Landowners anticipated sizable profits as would-be merchants and craftsmen flocked to the new railroad town.[97] There were charges of profiteering; Mr. Blessum was reserving the best lots near the depot for himself; six hundred dollars was "too much money" for a lot in such a new town.[98]

Excited speculators and promoters pressured the HLHF to disband or to move the store the quarter mile from Blessum to Hanska. Slow-moving cooperatives in Blessum were blocking fast-moving entrepreneurs' boom town of Hanska. The HLHF store "was claimed by many outsiders to be a scare-crow to the proper influx of other retail dealers; and it had purposely been left to one side of the Village proper by the Townsite promoters," who "suggested that if the farmers wanted to see a thriving Village grow up in their midst, we must discontinue the 'Farmers Store.'"[99] The store and creamery drew so much customer traffic that their separate location endangered a new town's success. A "rivalry" between cooperative Blessum and entrepreneurial Hanska was feared to "be detrimental to the new town in the future."[100]

The townsite company tried to persuade farmers to move the store to the new town. Its representative came to the HLHF's November 1899 board meeting and offered to move the store at the company's expense to any lot they chose. Unaware he was violating their democratic ethos, he proposed that one board member accompany him as he visited HLHF shareholders—to help him obtain signatures supporting the move. The board refused to be used by the company.[101]

No attempt was made at the January annual meeting to pass a motion to move the store. No company agent was present, "probably due to the great opposition to the measure that has developed."[102] Negotiating with a cooperative was not like exchanging handshakes and making deals with storeowners. A democratic polity, the HLHF could refuse to negotiate, and no amount of pressure would change its policy.

Supporters of the new townsite then circulated a petition "asking for the removal of the post office from the Farmer's Co-operative store to" a hardware store "in the townsite." That would have dealt a severe blow to the HLHF, whose board circulated a "counter-petition," which garnered five times as many signatures as the first.[103] The post office stayed at HLHF for the time being.[104]

Farmers welcomed the many services available in the new town. They were "delighted over the prospects of having a near market for their grain." The elevator "seem[ed] to say, Here is Hanska." They "smil[ed] to think they don't have to go to Madelia after their fuel this winter."[105] By January 1900 many businesses were saying, "Here is Hanska": hardware store, furniture store, bank, three lumberyards, blacksmith shop, icehouse, saloon, and privately owned general store. Blessum had a harness shop, meat market, blacksmith shop, drugstore, and boardinghouse. Together, they boasted of six residences.[106]

Yet new stores brought storeowners determined to protect their financial stakes and to control the new town. Farmers disliked surrendering control of what their cooperatives had built, but the alternative was even less attractive—economic stagnation. Also built by a creamery and a (private) store, the crossroads community of Linden (four miles east of Hanska) disappeared after the railroad bypassed it. By 1911 its creamery, store, and post office were gone.[107]

Cooperation Adding to (not Competing with) a Private Retail Network

Cooperatives had also produced new rural trade centers ten to twenty years earlier in Denmark and Norway. An interesting comparison, with similarities and differences, can be made between those countries and Minnesota. In 1892 much of Minnesota was only twenty years removed from its frontier days. Its railroad grid was unfinished. Merchants had not yet built a network of smaller trade centers, more of which were needed as farmers switched to the cash economy. Ten miles was too far to travel by wagon for the groceries and clothes that more families no longer grew or made. Danish and Norwegian farmers also switched to a cash economy around the same time, but their lack of small trade centers was due to laws giving each *købstad* (market town) a local trade monopoly. Starting in the 1840s (Norway) and in 1857 (Denmark), these laws were repealed.[108]

Lifting the *købstad* monopoly did not magically create the capital needed to start all the country stores that cash-carrying farmers wanted

The Minneapolis and St. Louis train arrived at the new depot in Hanska, thereby creating a new town and ending the old crossroads community of Blessum.

or magically persuade investors that these stores were good investments. Inge Debes, a Norwegian, observed that "the direct precondition" for so many cooperative stores was "that the end of the trading monopolies came so abruptly that there had not yet been enough time for the ordinary merchants to start stores everywhere there was a need." So farmers started cooperative stores, which "appeared first in many places" and thus "had to a great extent no nearby merchants to compete against."[109]

Southwestern Jutland had cooperative stores that were more like Hanska's than Norway's. Due to new cultivation of large areas of heath land, it resembled a frontier area: large in-migration, many new farms, greater social mobility, a younger population, fewer market towns. Its many cooperatives did not compete with merchants but met a need for retail outlets on this "frontier."[110] That also occurred in rural Minnesota in the 1890s. Following the creameries, cooperative stores met the need for new stores and helped create the crossroads communities that completed the network of trading centers. Hanska—and Clarks Grove, Manchester, and Bath in Freeborn County—followed the same pattern: first a creamery, then a cooperative store, then likely a blacksmith shop, and a post office, and soon a town where none had been before.[111] Such towns reduced farmers' isolation and ended farmer-merchant debates like that in the *Ugeblad*. Such stores "had to a great extent no nearby merchants to compete against."

Merchants' fears that more stores meant lower sales volume, prices, and profit margins were unfounded. Distance to the nearest store had limited farmers' demand for store-bought goods and encouraged homemade substitutes. New and nearby cooperative stores expanded demand and did not divide a fixed demand among more stores—there often were no others.[112] Like cooperative creameries entering an expanding dairy industry without many private competitors, cooperative stores entered an expanding retail market. Their entry did not cause devastating cooperative-merchant price wars. At crossroads sites, they often had a monopoly.

Entry at the 1890s crossroads was entry at a marginal niche in a national market. Timing was important. Railroads and telegraphs created tighter links between wholesalers and retailers, but some wholesalers would sell to a cooperative store. The FMC bought goods from Duluth wholesalers, also on the Northern Pacific. Railroads brought competition from mail-order firms like Sears, but Rural Free Delivery did not yet bring catalogs or packages directly to the farm. Automobile trips to the county seat were still a few years in the future, too.

The 1890s were helpfully early for cooperative stores but also regrettably late. Gone was the NEPU's 1840s hope that the inefficiencies of market mechanisms (too many country stores) would be replaced by the efficiencies of democratic coordination (high-volume, cash-discount stores with local monopolies buying from their own wholesale agency). By the early 1890s, mass retailers—Sears, Montgomery Ward, and Woolworth's—captured these efficiencies with internal, administrative coordination.[113] They were no longer unique to cooperatives, and private firms could best run large, multiunit retail chains.

By the late 1880s, local firms had grabbed these efficiencies, too. In December 1889 one Battle Lake merchant announced he was now buying and selling for cash only. Sounding democratic, he advertised this policy as "advantageous for both parties: for me, because I lose nothing [from delinquent customers], and for my customers, because they buy goods cheaper than otherwise." Wholesalers' cash discounts he promised "to share with my customers."[114] Calling itself the "Bee Hive" to suggest high volume, another store advertised that the benefits of its low costs would go "to our customers just as much as to ourselves."[115] Cooperatives facing such competitors could no longer offer greater discounts or obtain higher sales volumes than private discount cash-only stores.

9

Farmers' Elevators

*"Not a great many left of the old
pioneer farmers' elevators,
and they did not die of old age, either"*

IN 1899 the Chicago and North Western Railway (C&NW) took drastic action against an independent elevator along its branch line in Vesta in Redwood County. The facility was

> half constructed when a locomotive and a caboose full of men suddenly appeared alongside, with designs on the would-be elevator. Cables were hastily attached to the timbers, the locomotive began panting, and onlookers thought they were about to witness a novel proceeding, that of capturing a country elevator and scooting off up the track for the round house where it could be safely corralled. But the object of the train crew was to destroy, and destroy they did. The building was soon a wreck, and with the ruins before them the prospect of independent buying was not very bright.[1]

Like Hanska, Vesta was a new railroad village on a new rail line, but its independent elevator, unlike the HLHF store, was not politely invited to relocate. In a grain-growing region, elevators were vital to a successful railroad, which could show as much hostility to cooperative elevators as to this independent one. For instance, the Northern Pacific brought Duluth wholesalers' goods to the FMC, and the M&SL welcomed the Hanska creamery's outgoing freight, but a grain elevator offered a railroad more revenues than did a store or creamery.

Thus farmers seeking to establish cooperative elevators met more obstacles and constraints than they did when starting cooperative stores, creameries, or fire insurance companies. In the latter cases, they often faced little or no private competition—or the private competitor received little or no support from other businesses when confronted by a cooperative. Then farmers could design the store, creamery, or mutual according to their own ideas or experts' advice. In establishing farmers' elevators, however, they encountered the vital stake that merchants, railroads, grain exchanges, millers, and commission firms had in grain marketing. That complicated their organizational work, which tended to be squeezed into molds that the other stakeholders could tolerate.

When competing with farmers' elevators, line elevators could often count on support from the railroads. Line elevators' bulk handling of grain was impossible without railroads, and profitable railroads could not exist in western Minnesota without carloads of wheat. More money was invested in tracks, elevators, and flour mills than in stores or creameries. Farmers' elevators threatened those investments.[2]

Railroads and line elevator companies did not fully agree with each other, much less with farmers. A railroad preferred "to deal with just a few line elevator companies"; each elevator company would have "a lease in every town" but no competing railroad from which to obtain lower freight rates. Some such leases were restrictive: the elevator's capacity, additions, shipments, and future were subject to the railroad's approval. Line companies, for their part, preferred to have competing railroads but few competing elevators for farmers to go to for better grain prices. Farmers preferred to have more competing railroads *and* elevators. All these wishes could not be met. A railroad did not lay more track to satisfy farmers—it "did not care how far a farmer had to travel to market his grain"—but to meet or beat competition from other railroads. More track, leading to more elevators and more competition for farmers' grain, had to await the rail network's completion.[3]

In the 1880s and 1890s, farmers faced an incomplete network and insufficient competition. They sought to bypass private buyers and to sell to an elevator they owned. However, they confronted a harder task than in the 1870s. The Grangers' failures with flour mills and warehouses, plus the greater dominance by the 1880s of Minneapolis millers and line elevators, left them isolated at the local end of a highly organized marketing system.

The Wheat Marketing System
in Late Nineteenth-century Minnesota

Having achieved dominance of the flour industry with new milling technologies, Minneapolis millers tried also to control wheat supplies and prices. The Millers' Association set prices, especially on the St. Paul, Minneapolis and Manitoba Railway line through wheat-growing western Minnesota. They attempted "to retain for themselves the increase in value resulting from new milling methods" and to keep farmers from capturing part of that increase.[4] Line elevator companies, such as Cargill or Northwestern Elevator Company, controlled local wheat buying and storage; each owned a chain of country elevators from which it shipped wheat to Minneapolis, Chicago, or Duluth to be sold on the floor of the Minneapolis Chamber of Commerce, Chicago Board of Trade, or Duluth Board of Trade. Ironically, Minnesota's 1885 railroad and warehouse law regulating these terminal markets and setting up standard "Minnesota Grades" for grain aided this consolidation of the grain trade and speculation in grain futures on the exchanges. Price competition occurred between line elevators selling in different terminal markets (for instance, Minneapolis versus Chicago) or operating along different railroads. But elevators shipping to the same market along the same road might not compete. By the 1890s, they often united in "pools," which divided the wheat crop among member firms, held meetings to set prices, hired an agent to monitor prices members paid for wheat, and levied a fine of two-and-a-half cents a bushel on a firm buying more than its share. Forty companies owning 950 elevators joined in the Minneapolis pool. Yet such pools were unstable. And railroads and telegraph lines eliminated some "intermediaries" with their fees and charges, and the rationalization they fostered had lowered line elevators' profit margins by the 1890s.[5]

Thus it is hard to assess farmers' complaints that line elevators did not compete, earned exorbitant profits, and cut wheat prices paid to farmers. Wheat farmers received a net price after many deductions for marketing and processing (see Table 5). Elevator companies and flour millers administratively coordinated the wheat market. Farmers were not invited to help with the administering.

Dairy farmers' cooperative creameries greatly reduced deductions to their milk price. Processing milk locally, they cut freight charges (shipping only finished products), seized processing profits, and ended or cut storage fees. Wheat was a fungible commodity, easily stored and preserved, and easily transported. That characteristic worked against local processing and local control. Of all grains, wheat was the one most likely to be shipped out of the county in which it was grown.[6] Local farmers' elevators could lower only the last two deductions: local elevator profits and storage fees. Due to Grangers' milling failures and Minneapolis millers' successes, capturing processing profits was now impossible. To reduce terminal elevator fees and commission fees, farmers had to form cooperative elevators in Minneapolis, Chicago, and Duluth—to sell wheat in terminal markets themselves.

Alliance-sponsored Attempts to Cooperate in Terminal Markets

The mobilization of farmers in hundreds of suballiances and the Alliance's political clout encouraged them to try. In April 1888, they formed the Scandinavian Farmers' Elevator Syndicate "to get wheat from the farmers to the millers at the lowest cost of handling and in its purity as grown." Its president and vice-president were officers in the Dakota and Minnesota Alliances. Some two to three hundred independent elevators would join the syndicate to gain a guaranteed market. The wheat they bought from farmers would be shipped to syndicate elevators in Duluth and Minneapolis, then east to England.[7] The syndicate would bypass the Minneapolis and Duluth grain exchanges. It would eliminate fees and profit margins charged by commission houses, grain exchanges, and terminal elevators (the syndicate would charge farmers to provide these services). It would not mix lower quality with higher quality wheat, so that Minnesota and Dakota farmers could be financially rewarded for growing high-quality wheat. Those were the hopes.

The scheme failed. The syndicate could not obtain "the co-operation of the British millers."[8] Very likely, they were uncertain of the organiza-

---

TABLE 5
Hypothetical Calculation of Net Wheat Price

Wholesale price of flour*	$2.50
Less: Processing costs	-1.00
Processing profits	-.35
Price of wheat on terminal grain exchange	1.15
Less: Commission fees	-.07
Terminal elevator storage fees	-.08
Price on arrival at terminal market	1.00
Less: Railroad freight charges	-.05
Price on track leaving local market	.95
Less: Local elevator storage fees	-.01
Local elevator profits	-.04
Net price paid to farmer	$0.90

Note:
* The price is expressed per bushel of wheat milled. The figures are hypothetical — fees, prices, and costs fluctuated constantly.

tion's long-term viability and afraid to antagonize established commission firms and grain exchanges.[9] Established trading networks resisted being bypassed.

The syndicate's successor was the Alliance Elevator Company.[10] (The national Alliance asked that the exclusive "Scandinavian" be changed to the inclusive "Alliance," which was done in 1889.)[11] Alliance Elevator also tried to ship wheat to English millers but failed. When it sought membership in the Minneapolis Chamber of Commerce to sell wheat on the Minneapolis exchange, its application was rejected.[12] It could not market farmers' grain: no buyers, no bypassing. And there were few farmers' elevators in 1889–90 to sell it grain.[13] By October 1889 it was soliciting the business of lone farmers shipping single carloads of wheat.[14]

Alliance leaders from western Minnesota and Dakota Territory showed more persistence than the Grangers had in trying to penetrate terminal markets. Two new attempts followed: the Northwestern Farmers' Protective Association (NWFPA) and the Minnesota Grain Growers Association (MGGA). The two absorbed different lessons from earlier failures. The NWFPA learned to get along with corporate interests. It cooperated with leading grain merchants such as Charles A. Pillsbury, purchased a seat on the Duluth Board of Trade, and secured terminal elevators in Duluth.[15] To gain a competitive advantage over Minneapolis, the Duluth board allowed a farmer-controlled group to sell on its grain exchange. However, farmers were still shut out of the premier wheat market—Minneapolis.

The MGGA learned to be more aggressive and to seek government support. Formed by Alliance leaders to influence the legislature's 1891 investigation of the wheat trade, the MGGA sought to unite farmers' elevators and to persuade the legislature to pass laws to regulate the industry.[16] In regard to terminal marketing, it took a more radical stance than the NWFPA, which its leaders felt was "tied to Pillsbury's office in Duluth." It viewed with suspicion the NWFPA's success in securing a seat on the board of trade. Yet it failed like its predecessors.[17] Though failures, the NWFPA and MGGA paved the way for post-1900 attempts at organizing farmers' elevators, both statewide and in the terminal markets.

Alliance-sponsored Local Cooperative Grain Elevators

More farmers' elevators were needed before such attempts could succeed. Some suballiances started cooperative elevators when joint marketing failed.[18] An elevator had officers and managers who, unlike committee members, acquired long-term experience. Private firms were more willing to do business with it, and it could borrow money—if it found willing lenders. It bought grain from farmers who were not Alliance members. The president of Sleepy Eye Farmers Warehouse Association assured the public that "the company is not an Alliance concern. We have stockholders who are adherents to all political parties."[19] It assumed marketing risks that committees, as mere conduits, left to farmers.

Yet it might pay farmers less for wheat than did private buyers. It had a profit-and-loss statement to consider. Sleepy Eye's president admitted that "we do not want to run at a loss and if the fellows in the [wheat] ring have paid more for wheat than we could[,] so much better for the farmers." He tried to claim this outcome as a victory: "If we do nothing more than keep-up prices we have accomplished what we started out to do."[20] Farmers' elevators were stronger tools for forcing up prices than were ad hoc committees asking for price quotes. Hidden in his cheery optimism, though, was an admission of weakness. Cooperatives were marginal in the wheat-marketing system.

Just how marginal was seen in Waseca. W. D. Armstrong, the county Alliance secretary, tried to start an Alliance warehouse there in 1886. When he asked both railroads serving Waseca for a sidetrack and a warehouse site, they refused; the C&NW and M&SL had "an agreement not to allow independent buyers on their sidetracks at Waseca."[21] But Waseca was a competing point. A need to capture more freight tempted the M&SL to renege on that deal. It made an offer: if wheat buyer Charles C. Wolcott "would go there [Waseca] and work with the Farmers' Alliance, buy their grain and ship over their road," the M&SL would give him preferential rates.[22] Wolcott agreed, and a warehouse was built. But when he pressured the M&SL to grant him favors at other towns, it refused. So he (and his Alliance partners) began shipping over the C&NW. They expected the M&SL to switch C&NW railcars over to their warehouse. Instead the M&SL tore up the sidetrack to his warehouse in the dead of night.[23]

Outraged farmers and townsmen held a mass meeting. Alliance leaders seemingly had a perfect issue with which to radicalize farmers, but their connection of convenience with Wolcott compromised their position. The M&SL argued that it "was not fighting farmers but Wolcott."[24]

When Armstrong took the case to the state Railroad and Warehouse Commission, a technicality emerged: the sidetrack was on a platted (though unconstructed) "street." The Waseca city council asked the M&SL to vacate the premises. Glad to comply, the M&SL now had legal justification for removing the sidetrack.[25] Tied to Wolcott as it was, the Alliance warehouse was too weak even to qualify as a victim. (The city council could claim to be acting only against the railroad.) It was nearly a non-entity. Two railroads, the established wheat buyers, and Wolcott were the important actors.

Merchants and Farmers Start Local Cooperative Elevators

Perhaps the Alliance warehouse failed by not getting the support of Waseca's city council, probably dominated by merchants. In many towns, farmers' elevators depended on support from the merchants. As in Granger days, farmers were mostly angry at local wheat buyers, who, by the early 1890s, were increasingly employees of line companies. Merchants feared losing business to towns paying higher wheat prices.[26] Both farmers and merchants saw low wheat prices as injustices perpetrated by outsiders against their town.

Merchants in the 1890s reacted as Albert Lea's had in the 1870s when a poor local wheat market caused farmers to haul wheat to nearby towns and buy goods there. In 1892 farmers near McIntosh (Polk County) were "hauling their wheat to Fosston and doing a large part of trading in that city." One admitted, "McIntosh merchants are more reasonable on prices than their Fosston brethren," but "the same elevator companies are giving better grades and more money for the same wheat at Fosston than they are at McIntosh." Both of McIntosh's newspapers favored a farmers' elevator to remedy this intolerable situation.[27]

The line elevator companies resented editors' localistic biases. An Ada (Norman County) editor criticized line elevators for "an unprincipled spread between the local price paid by the elevators and the Minneapolis price." Cargill head John H. MacMillan, Sr., complained to the local Cargill buyer that "his statement is so utterly at variance with the truth." MacMillan guessed "that the [Ada] *Herald* makes more money out of one 'ad' that takes perhaps two minutes to set up than we could make on handling a carload of grain." He warned, "It certainly does not do your town any good, and it does a great deal of harm for the newspaper, to single out the various industries of the town and abuse them."[28] The implied threat was probably relayed to the editor.

Editors did not oppose middlemen as a class but joined with merchants and farmers to bypass objectionable local buyers. Such cooperation came easier if farmers acted outside the Alliance, which often irritated editors and merchants by its meddling in county politics.

Merchants often helped organize farmers' elevators. Windom merchants offered farmers the use of an elevator rent free for a year, "the business men already having subscribed the necessary amount for the rent." A Windom newspaper hailed this "splendid proposition" that would "quiet any talk about other towns paying higher prices" for wheat. Although they had a farmers' elevator at nearby Delft, farmers accepted the offer and repaid merchants' generosity. Rather than start a farmers' store at Delft, "they preferred to haul their grain to the town in which they did their trading," which was Windom.[29] In areas where grain elevators were customers' main source of income, merchants aiding a farmers' elevator were rewarded for such assistance.

Entrepreneurial Railroads Oppose Cooperative Elevators

The American tradition of many competing, privately owned railroads hindered the formation and operation of farmers' elevators. By contrast, each European nation normally had one government-owned railroad, which did not discriminate against cooperatives. To U.S. railroads, the existence of farmers' elevators threatened to upset a stable wheat-marketing process by routing wheat shipments along a competitor's road. In Pope and southern Douglas Counties, for instance, when farmers switched to the Lowry farmers' elevator, wheat shipments increased on the Minneapolis, St. Paul and Sault Ste. Marie Railroad (Soo Line) from Lowry but dropped sharply from Alexandria on the Great Northern Railway (GN) and from Starbuck and Glenwood on the Northern Pacific Railroad (NP). The start of a farmers' elevator disrupted railroads' plans for handling busy harvesttime freight traffic and left large grain elevators standing nearly empty in some towns.[30]

To a railroad an empty line elevator was alarming. The line elevator company was its best long-term wheat-marketing partner, with a centralized management and stability matching that of the railroad. Both sought the efficiencies of administrative coordination of wheat marketing and shipping. Neither desired a return to chaotic market mechanisms, such as those unleashed at Lowry. In this symbiotic relationship, a line elevator's goal of a local monopoly on grain storage complemented a railroad's similar goal in regard to transporting grain.[31] An elevator provided the storage service that the railroad's depot offered for other items.[32]

Even where both partners had to settle for competition instead of monopoly, the line elevator could help draw wheat toward one railroad and away from its competitor by aggressively buying wheat at favorable prices. Writing to James J. Hill of the Great Northern, the general manager of the Northwestern Elevator Company claimed, "We have always made it a special point to guard your interests at this station [Fisher in Polk County]." Northwestern had assigned to Fisher a skilled wheat buyer, "one who is active and ambitious." The general manager complained that Hill's agent encouraged track-side buying and loading to draw wheat to the GN "instead of calling upon us to protect your interests." Hill denied the charge but not the close ties between elevator and railroad. Indeed, at one point Hill loaned five hundred thousand dollars to a Duluth grain-buying firm so it could make short-term loans to line elevator companies.[33] The Northwestern manager's objection was unusual—more often, the line elevators' competitors complained that railroads discriminated against them, not because they were cooperative or "socialistic" but because they threatened the preferred partner. Railroads discriminated against small independent elevators like Vesta's or against "scoopers" loading directly from wagons to railcars. Nor did farmers always favor cooperatives over independents or scoopers, which demanded no investment on their part. They wanted buyers competing for their wheat,

One of a string of Equity elevators feeding grain to the Equity Cooperative Exchange in St. Paul, the Chokio Equity Exchange battled its many competitors around 1914. The elevators flanked the Great Northern sidetrack and main track.

not conniving to set prices in a pool. Railroads did not gain from lower pool prices, but antipool competition produced unpredictability, which threw a wrench into their administrative coordination.

One tactic railroads used against farmers' elevators was to deny them railcars during harvest on the pretext that there were no extra cars. In one such instance, the manager of the Balaton farmers' elevator in Lyon County reported at harvesttime that his elevator was "full to the top, and although he has made repeated requests for cars he is unable to get them." Since "other elevators" were "able to get cars," it seemed the railroad was "discriminating against the farmers."[34] In 1889, Brandborg of Henning's Alliance elevator had to ask Governor William R. Merriam to intervene to secure cars.[35]

Railroads often tried to prevent construction of farmers' elevators by denying them building sites or refusing to build sidetracks to serve them. In 1889 Grant County farmers grumbled that the Elbow Lake line elevators docked their wheat for alleged impurities and offered a price "below that being paid at other places." Some farmers retaliated by loading wheat directly from wagon to railcar along the Soo Line sidetracks. Others enviously complained that sidetrack loaders "averaged from three to five cents net per bushel more than the price paid by the local wheat buyers on corresponding days."[36]

Wheat buyers protested to the Soo Line general manager, who issued a "Special Circular" severely restricting sidetrack loading. Farmers had to pay a five dollar fee (in advance) for cars held more than twenty-four hours, and only one car per farmer was allowed. The Soo Line agent was to inform local elevators of all requests for sidetrack loading so "they may be given an opportunity to satisfy the shipper [the farmer] that the prices and grades offered by them are fair and reasonable." The new rules were meant to convince farmers that marketing through elevators was "reasonable": "It is the wish of the company that the elevators along its line should receive . . . the wheat for shipment."[37]

Elbow Lake merchants and area farmers decided to circumvent the orders in the circular by building a warehouse, which was not sidetrack loading. When pressed for a site, the Soo Line officials "very resolutely stated in effect that the elevator companies along that line had about $100,000 invested in the wheat business and it was the duty of the company to protect them in making a legitimate(?) profit on their investment." (They did not mention the Soo Line's own investment.) With too many elevators at Elbow Lake, all "would lose money." They denied that the Railroad and Warehouse Commission could require them to lay a sidetrack for a farmers' elevator.[38]

Strengthened by its partner's support, the line elevator company issued an ultimatum: it would buy "the present wheat crop on a margin of four cents a bushel, or not at all." Angered, a local editor criticized the commission's failure to enforce an 1885 law requiring railroads to grant such sites. The law had "fallen into 'in[n]ocuous desuetude,' except in the matter of drawing salaries." The commission did not work in this case, but its "monthly payroll works with increasing vigor year by year."[39]

In an earlier report, the commissioner admitted farmers' or independent elevators might cause "an inconvenience to the roads." Yet railroads were well paid for serving "the public as common carriers, with such inconveniences" as that.[40] The "vital principle" was "that railways are public highways, constructed for the benefit of the people." That was a noble thought from a public servant. Yet these public highways earned private profits, and their profit-seeking owners preferred line elevators regardless of farmers' right to use a common carrier.[41] The owners preferred the efficient administrative coordination facilitated by line elevators over the chaotic market mechanisms brought by farmers' elevators. Naïvely, the commissioner saw railroads as friendly to market mechanisms and willing to be coordinated by him for the public good. Yet they were avoiding open wheat markets and his authority.

A farmer-built cooperative railroad could end the paradox of a private public carrier. Farmers tried. In 1893 Alliance leaders promoted a "grandiose" railroad from Minnesota and the Dakotas to the Gulf of Mexico. It was never built. North Dakota and northern Minnesota farmers angry at high freight rates and lack of tracks started the Duluth and North Dakota Railroad Company in 1894. With "minimal construction standards" and farmers' track-laying work exchanged for stock, the railroad tried to get by without much capital but failed. The Farmers' Grain and Shipping Company (FG&S) railroad was built in 1900–1905 over fifty-four miles of North Dakota farmland. True to its name, it favored "independent grain buyers," but James Hill soon made it his nonunion, low-cost feeder road. It occupied a small niche because Hill allowed it to, but farmers lacked the capital to build truly independent lines.[42]

Pushing on a Rope: Laws to Protect Farmers' Elevators

Knowing they could never compete with tycoons in track laying, farmers asked the legislature to regulate railroads. Yet the Minnesota Supreme Court allowed railroads to avoid an 1874 law requiring them to provide warehouse sites and an 1885 law forbidding them to discriminate when leasing elevator sites or assigning railcars.[43] The court ruled the first 1885 ban unconstitutional, and heavy harvest demand for cars made the second one hard to enforce.

Railroads straddled the line between public functions and private ownership. When acquiring land for tracks, they had public functions and eminent domain; when asked to lease that land to farmers' elevators, they were private companies who did not have to. In 1887 the court declared that their property was "held for a public purpose," but it was, "so far as the right of property is concerned, private property." When the Soo Line denied a site and sidetrack to a farmers' warehouse, the court ruled in 1893 that the Soo Line was a private entity "not obliged to grant such concessions." Yet it forbade the railroad to grant to one shipper what it denied to others. Apparently the Soo Line could refuse to accommodate *all* grain shippers and thus evade its duty as a common carrier.[44]

The Alliance campaigned for laws to end this type of evasion. At the 1891 legislative session, State Senator John B. Hompe secured passage of a bill requiring railroads to grant elevator sites, but Governor Merriam refused to sign it.[45] Alliancemen sought "free and unlimited competition in wheat buying, selling and shipping at every railroad station in the state."[46] They believed in market mechanisms and wanted the government to guarantee open markets and prohibit discrimination against farmers' elevators. They did not ask government to aid farmers' elevators. Like the commissioner, they naïvely assumed local free markets would work even after line elevators and railroads had discovered the efficiencies of administrative coordination.

At the 1893 session, politicians turned their attention to farmers' grievances against line elevators. Governor Knute Nelson recommended state regulation of country elevators. Responding to what he heard on the 1892 campaign trail, he hoped to take this issue away from future Alliance candidates. Republican State Representative Jacob F. Jacobson argued that "an open and free market can't be had" for ten years, "and meanwhile this bill will help many."[47] The Republicans did not oppose farmers' elevators, which were often merchant-led and rarely radical. Indeed the Republican *Minneapolis Tribune* praised the "independent elevator controlled by the producers."[48]

Alliance legislators still believed an open, free market could be had, so they opposed the bill. They wanted state regulation, even state ownership, at terminal points, but at the local level that measure violated the principle of local control.[49] They supported scoopers and warehouses that might not meet state guidelines and distrusted the commissioner's Republican appointees who would do the regulating. Alliance State Represpresentative John J. Furlong felt state regulation "would result in shutting out the small, independent buyers" and jeopardize the goal of "a free and untrammeled market." Representative Hans Bjørge doubted the commission could act independently of railroads' influence.[50] Senator Hompe gave an "inflammatory speech" against this "Jim Hill measure," which wheat farmers would "resist, even to the extremity of civil war."[51] State Senator Ignatius Donnelly tried to avoid the extremity by offering an Alliance plan for public aid to farmers' elevators, a resolution authorizing counties to issue bonds for building (in effect) farmers' elevators. It was not adopted.[52]

Alliance legislators were reliving the antebellum, prerailroad past if they thought a local free market was still possible. Capital invested in line elevators and railroads worked against it; the scoopers' day was over. They were right to distrust a patronage-ridden state government's ability to regulate impartially, but they failed to secure legislation helpful to farmers' elevators, even at the peak of their political influence.[53] They stressed winning elections and penetrating terminal markets, not aiding farmers' elevators, which they thought could survive in a free market. Line companies challenged farmers' elevators to try.

Line Elevator Companies Fight Cooperative Elevators

By the mid-1890s farmers blamed the line elevators more than the railroads for inequities in wheat marketing.[54] Nelson's bill (which passed) only regulated grading and dockage and banned fraud or cheating. Prices were left to the market. A line company could run at a loss in one town to defeat a farmers' elevator, while recouping it at other towns. No law prohibited that practice.[55]

The most dramatic and amusing case occurred in Lowry in Pope

County. Farmers protested that Lowry's line elevators did not compete for the 1904 crop but instead set a low price. Merchants complained "that a large volume of business from Lowry territory was diverted to other towns."[56] The next year merchants and farmers formed a cooperative, bought an elevator, and began buying wheat by September.[57]

Representatives of two line elevator companies—Atlantic and Osborne-McMillan—visited the merchants and "threatened them with the establishment of a store in Lowry" to sell "merchandise ... at cost if the farmers' elevator did not cease doing business." The elevator's board decided to continue anyway. The threat was "not generally credited" but was thought to be "only a bluff to scare" merchants, whom one local editor defended for assisting farmers.[58]

It was not a bluff. Rather than submit to being bypassed, the elevator companies would induce consumers to bypass Lowry's merchants. Warning "We will teach the town a lesson," the elevator men signed a three-year lease on a store building and stocked it with "general merchandise, hardware and drugs." They "made the statement that everything will be sold at cost, they standing the freight." On October 6, the Elevator Store advertised "Big Bargains in All Lines of General Merchandise." Hinting that they were outsiders, the *Glenwood Herald* noted the doubts as to "how well the itinerant grain merchants will succeed in this enterprise." The store opened in mid-October.[59]

Meanwhile the farmers' elevator did "an excellent business" and received "the bulk of the grain at that point."[60] Grain from a wide area flowed into it, for it paid three to five cents more per bushel than nearby towns' elevators. It was "a great drawing card" for Lowry, whose merchants were not much hurt by the Elevator Store. The *Herald* reported that Lowry's farmers "do not patronize the store but buy their goods from the old established and reliable merchants who have been instrumental in giving them such a good [wheat] market."[61] But those coming from a distance seized the chance to win both ways: selling high at the farmers' elevator while buying low at the Elevator Store.[62] The battle upset trading patterns in Pope County and disrupted the dominance of Glenwood, the county seat. A Glenwood newspaper ran a front-page article claiming the town's wheat market to be "equally good as at other competitive points," a reference aimed at Lowry.[63]

The line elevator men retaliated against two Glenwood newspapers that opposed their store. In early November, they started Lowry's first newspaper, the *Lowry Post*, edited by Ralph Pennar of the Elevator Store and printed in Ashby, thirty miles away.[64] If push came to shove, newspapers could be bypassed, too.

Such maneuvering was short-lived. In late November, "the business men of Lowry" took "the war into the Elevator companies' territory with a vengeance."[65] The scene of battle shifted to the Twin Cities, where Lowry merchants went to complain to Attorney General Edward T. Young. Evidently supported by Governor John A. Johnson (also a Progressive), he filed suit; their corporate charters did not authorize them to operate a general store, and their actions violated a state antitrust law.[66]

Progressives gladly seized on this issue, for many were small-town leaders who feared big business as a threat to their independent enterprises.[67] Young could not sue the real threats, mail-order giants Sears, Roebuck and Montgomery Ward, which were interstate companies operating within their field of retailing and winning consumers' approval with their low prices. The Lowry case was tailor-made for him. Giant line elevator firms that operated outside their field for the express purpose of intimidating small-town merchants angered both the merchants and their customers. Unlike private merchants mimicking Granger stores' policies, the Elevator Store's low prices could not appear democratic, for its punitive, raiding tactics seemed unsavory. Knowing this, Young rebuked its line elevator sponsors for "Standard Oil practices" and "coercive methods."[68] Progressives feared a class conflict between farmers and merchants; the Lowry case united the two groups in a way that few progressives could resist.[69] Editors could editorialize without risk: "Hardly a paper in the state but what has had something to say about this little burg [Lowry] in the past ten days."[70]

The lawsuit's filing persuaded Atlantic and Osborne-McMillan to cease and desist, in part because Young called for the revocation of one company's charter. Little more than a week later, the Elevator Store's managers were no longer selling, "their principal work being that of keeping warm the stove and going to their meals." By mid-December, the store was no more. Its goods were sold to local merchants at wholesale prices.[71]

Of course, the Lowry case was unusual. Wheat prices, not store prices, were the usual battleground, and the key test was whether farmers would bypass a line elevator paying higher prices. A new farmers' elevator often set off a local price war, with prices rising about five cents a bushel. Line companies could run one elevator at a loss while recouping the loss with low prices at noncompeting points. Such price wars were numerous.[72] In Audubon (Becker County) a "merry grain war" raged in September 1907 between the farmers' elevator and Frank Hutchinson Peavey's line elevator. The Peavey buyer offered two to four cents more per bushel of wheat, but farmers stayed loyal.[73] Farmers' elevators did not have to out-bid their foe. They could bid up the price and then let the line elevator buy at a loss.[74] Or they could close until prices fell.

"The storm center of the wheat fight" of 1904 was the town of Redwood Falls (Redwood County). The clash revealed a price war's disruptive impact on elevators, railroads, and merchants. To destroy the farmers' elevator there, the line elevator companies raised prices three to five cents above prices paid "within a radius of 30 miles." Farmers within a ten-mile radius sold wheat there, not at their usual markets. Fifteen towns suffered from a loss of trade—several were on the M&SL, whose freight business dropped. Even the C&NW serving Redwood Falls was inconvenienced by having to shift resources there. Many disloyal members of the farmers' elevator "sold to the line elevators," but it survived. Indeed, when a price-stabilizing deal was negotiated, it was ready not to "enter the compact" if it received "encouragement from local business houses" who would benefit from the increased retail traffic that a renewed price war would bring to Redwood Falls.[75] The effects of the price war and the ratified compact were clearly seen on its profit-and-loss statement: a $464 loss for the 1904–05 price-war year; a $1,258 profit for the 1905–06 truce year.[76] Merchants' statements probably showed the opposite trend.

Before the war ended, members of the farmers' elevator board considered a "penalty clause," used by Iowa farmers against price-warring line elevators.[77] The report of a $464 loss "caused something of a sensation" at the June 1905 annual meeting. A board member offered a resolution: "That when a stockholder sells his produce to other than the Farmers' elevator he shall be required to pay" a penalty of "½ cent a bushel on wheat, ½ cent a bushel on flax, ⅕ cent a bushel on barley and oats."[78] He argued "that the old line elevator men would get sick of fighting the farmers when they saw a percentage of the money they pay for wheat turned into the treasury of the Farmers' Elevator to provide a fund with which to fight back." The resolution was tabled until a later meeting could draw a larger attendance.[79]

In Iowa and Illinois, the penalty clause was a valued tool to save farmers' elevators, and line companies attacked its legality.[80] In Minnesota, the University of Minnesota later reported, only 1 to 2 percent of farmers' elevators enforced a penalty clause, which was "of minor importance in Minnesota."[81]

Line companies increasingly found price wars to be ineffective as the number of farmers' elevators multiplied. By 1906 Minnesota had 151 farmers' elevators; by 1912, about 300 (depending on the definition).[82] Raising prices might work against a few farmers' elevators but not against many. With fewer noncompeting points where losses could be recouped, it became a prohibitively expensive tactic. Farmers' loyalty to their elevator often defeated this tactic, for net losses rarely caused farmers to terminate their cooperatives. Finally farmers' elevators' higher volumes meant economies of scale and lower per-unit costs that helped them win price wars (see Table G in Appendix).[83]

New Farmers' Elevator Movement Copies Illinois and Iowa's

As in other cooperative fields, the leaders of Minnesota's new farmers' elevator movement copied innovations made and victories won in older states—namely Illinois and Iowa. By 1905–06 the farmers in those states formed Farmers' Grain Dealers' Associations (FGDA) to coordinate the fight against line elevators and to help start new cooperatives. Their *American Co-operative Journal*, according to one observer, was "a very powerful agent in the advancement of the movement." They were aided by several grain commission firms, boycotted by line companies for dealing with them, and now dependent on them for commissions on grain sales.[84] By 1910 farmers' elevators were fairly secure in Iowa and Illinois. At the first convention of the Minnesota Farmers' Elevator Association, President Burr D. Alton praised Iowa: "She has outstripped us in many matters pertaining to the handling of" farmers' elevators—"let us profit by her example."[85]

Solidarity was important in Iowa farmers' victory, and the penalty clause enforced solidarity. Iowa's FGDA provided organizing resources, expert advice, and legislative lobbying. The FGDA was not linked to third-party politics—unlike the MGGA and the Syndicate. It argued for procedural fairness, not for producers to battle nonproducers, and used the language of Progressivism to urge farmers' elevators to combine into associations. Alton quoted a speech by Theodore Roosevelt on farmers' need for "combination" to compete with "highly organized interests which now surround them on every side."[86] This softer Progressive appeal facilitated negotiations between commission firms and farmers' elevators.

Minnesota's farmers' elevators could defeat line elevators, too, but without cooperative allies in terminal markets, they could not bypass middlemen to sell directly to grain processors. They just pooled farmers' grain to gain more bargaining clout with middlemen, the commission brokers.[87]

The new farmers' elevators of 1900–1914 seemed to be content with their small niche in the marketing system. Promoters of this new movement saw it as very different from the old one, which, they thought, had "too much sentiment and too little business": elevators too small, working capital too limited, managers too inexperienced, paying too high prices for grain, and failing to hedge on the market. Henry Feig, the supervising inspector of local warehouses for the Grain and Weighing Department of the State of Minnesota, noted, "There are not a great many left of the old pioneer farmers' elevators, and they did not die of old age, either." By contrast, "In numbers, in business talent, in capital invested, and in credit at local and terminal banks the new farmers' elevators can be classified as first-class business enterprises."[88]

The New Farmers' Elevators
and the Private Grain Trade Coexist

Commission firms helped make the new farmers' elevators more acceptable to the terminal exchanges. The farmers' elevators depended on these firms to sell their grain on the exchanges and, often, to finance their operations. Banks frequently refused to lend to them. Lenders and investors preferred to deal with established businesses or trusted individuals and felt no obligation to conduct business with democracies, whose factionalism seemed to be dangerous. Farmers valued democracy, but they could not provide the working capital their elevators needed for grain buying at harvest. A commission firm could secure credit from Minneapolis banks or a parent company and extend it to farmers' elevators. The firm stood to gain, for it obtained the farmers' business. By 1915, 51 percent of Minnesota's farmers' elevators were partly financed by such firms.[89]

Not surprisingly, such financing came with strings attached. As creditors, commission firms insisted on annual financial statements and standard business methods.[90] That these sensible requirements were demanded by outsiders, not by members, represented a partial loss of democratic control. The farmers' elevator normally had to agree in writing to "ship all or a certain proportion of its grain to the commission house that makes the loan."[91] That meant it could not get commission firms to compete for its trade nor could it help organize a terminal marketing cooperative—it could not ship grain to one.[92] A writer for *Farm, Stock and Home* compared this financing to "the co-operation of lion and lamb, which results in the incorporation of the last in the stomach of the first."[93]

Financing by commission firms was the movement's Achilles' heel. Interest owed to the firm was often a sizable part of an elevator's total expenses.[94] A firm might come to a rural area, start a farmers' elevator, sell shares to farmers and merchants, and get all the elevator's trade and most of its profits. "Such companies take on the appearance of line-house country elevators," warned the *American Co-operative Journal*, "when a concern steps in and demands stock or offers to furnish working capital with the specific purpose of holding the reins, it is then all wrong and a graft proposition."[95]

The Cokato Elevator Company was one organization that did not hold its own reins. Formed in September 1889 by the farmers and merchants of Cokato (Wright County), it did not use the one-person, one-vote rule but was governed by a few shareholders. Its officers and directors were mostly businessmen.[96] In September 1902 two commission firms competed to handle its grain for the crop year 1902–03 (the selling of one year's crop continued into the following year). The winner was Woodward and Company, which guaranteed it "a profit of at least 12% over Running Expenses" but required the elevator to buy grain on the "same margin as at present viz ½ cent over list."[97] The Cokato company tied its hands by agreeing to a set margin. The guaranteed 12 percent profit reduced its manager's incentive to buy grain aggressively. So the commission firm insisted on a clause stating the profit percentage would be cut to the extent that the elevator trimmed its total grain purchases.[98] In exchange for security, the Cokato operation surrendered its independence and became a purchasing agency and storage depot for Woodward, while guaranteeing the investments of its own large shareholders.

No doubt this surrender was recommended by the local merchants who helped organize the company. They wanted a secure elevator, for a failed one endangered their town. They lacked commitment to cooperation. Financial needs often led a farmers' elevator to sell shares to local merchants, who then ran it as a profit-maximizing enterprise, paying farmers as low a price and shareholders as high a dividend as possible. Such a "farmers'" elevator cooperated quite well with the private grain trade since it was essentially a privately owned, for-profit company itself.[99]

The New Farmers' Elevator Movement in Minnesota in 1914

By 1914 Minnesota had 270 farmers' elevators with a combined membership of 34,500 farmers, some 20 percent of Minnesota's farmers. They marketed about 30 percent of Minnesota's grain, a percentage that was steadily increasing. Adherence to Rochdale principles varied greatly. Most followed two principles: one-person, one-vote and a limit on shares owned by each member. Most did not pay patronage dividends or limit stock dividends to the current interest rates—thus not rewarding their farmer-members above their investors.[100] They achieved economies of scale, since "on the average each coöperative elevator [did] at least twice as much business as each proprietary concern." For 1914–15 they averaged 148,000 bushels; private ones (including the line elevators) averaged 60,000 bushels per elevator.[101]

The farmers' elevators were strongest in the southwestern counties, from Nobles, Jackson, and Martin on the Iowa border north to Swift and Kandiyohi. Here they handled more than 40 percent of the grain marketed. Here most were organized early, from 1890 to 1910. Elsewhere the movement peaked after 1910.[102] Two university experts attributed this regional strength to "the nationality of the farming population,... the degree of mixture of different nationalities,...the policies of the noncooperative elevators in their dealings with grain-growers," and "numerous other factors."[103] Yet those counties did not differ from others in ethnicity. It is unlikely that line elevators' policies varied from region to region. Railroads' policies did vary. Though cooperative-minded Scandinavian Americans were numerous in the Red River Valley, the Great Northern serving that area was hostile to farmers' elevators in the 1890s. In the southwest, except at Vesta, the C&NW showed less hostility.[104]

Thus railroads' opposition hindered the movement. Railroads' heavy investment in rolling stock and trackage and their dependence on wheat shipments meant they could not be indifferent about who stored and shipped wheat on their lines. Well suited to rapid track laying into frontier areas, the U.S. system of privately owned railroads posed a public-private paradox that hurt farmers' elevators. Railroads preferred line elevators and resisted government efforts to make them accept farmers' elevators. Farmers' railroads were impractical. Farmers' governments were a fantasy, too—given Republican patronage politics.

Thus the capitalist economy in the Age of Railroads first slowed then coopted the farmers' elevator movement. The "logic of capital," wrote historian William Cronon, sought the highest return and protected past investments. Like grain it "flowed" with the mobility granted by railroads and telegraph wires. The grain farmer's problem was that his crop was fungible, easily transported, durable, too much like capital, and, like the prices that were capitalism's abstract language, spoken in tiny Vesta and giant Chicago. The similarity showed in the futures market, where grain was abstracted into elevator receipts, bought and sold like stock, but often never delivered. By 1885 trade in fictitious, never-delivered grain "was probably fifteen to twenty times greater than [Chicago's] trade in physical grain."[105] In capital's (and grain's) abstractions, "places lost their particularity," and farmers' localism lost some power. Milk's perishable nature empowered dairy farmers' localism; grain's durability did the opposite.

Capital flowed to line elevators as the safest bets, but the system accommodated farmers' preference for farmers' elevators. Commission firms' capital hooked these into systemwide flows of grain and capital and used their higher volumes and lower costs just as the Great Northern used the low-cost FG&S railroad. Both farmers' elevators and the farmers' railroad were "feeder" lines for profit-driven systems. Locally they lowered freight rates or raised grain prices, but they had little impact on national networks or terminal markets. Completion of the rail network may have done more to lower freight rates and elevators' profit margins than did farmers' elevators. Shorter distances to depots and elevators brought nearly as much competition for the farmers' grain as did more farmers' elevators. For the more radical grain farmers, that kind of limited success was failure.

10

Problems of Success

*"The officers have made an
exceptional record for themselves"*

BY 1895–1905 MINNESOTA FARMERS had created four successful cooperative types: township mutuals, cooperative creameries, farmers' stores,
and farmers' elevators. Yet this was not the entrepreneur's success that
accumulated capital with which to start more profit-making enterprises
to add more capital. It was democratic success that spread cost savings
and higher crop prices among thousands of farm households—the added
dollars often to be spent on necessities, not invested in new cooperatives.
Lacking was the "logic of capital" where success breeds success. By their
very nature cooperatives limited the returns on capital invested and
thus attracted little of farmers' added income. Farmers had scant incentive to expand cooperation beyond their immediate cost-saving and
price-raising needs.

The fact of the success of their cooperatives could be dangerous.
From the economists' perspective, rural cooperatives are a special type of
small business, prone to the same risks as the other types. Growth and
unexpected success threaten small firms. They can grow too rapidly,
beyond their owners' capacity to manage them, into new localities or regions or new products or services. Their success can attract new competitors into the field. Their or their competitors' expansion can glut
the market with more products or services than customers want to buy.
New technologies can destroy a business built on an old technology.

Rural cooperatives encountered special problems of success. Usually
undercapitalized, they lacked the money to buy new technologies. They
were less likely than private firms to move into new fields that did not

promise to cut their farmer-members' costs or to raise crop prices. Yet within the old, promising fields, they were as likely as private firms to expand even though they tended to have less capital with which to do so. Willing members could democratically carry them from storage into processing, from local to terminal markets, or from one service to a related service. An entrepreneur's experience might temper his enthusiasm, but members at annual meetings lacked experience. Their enthusiasm could carry the cooperative too far. Once they became profitable, some farmers' elevators were susceptible to a takeover by large shareholders who ran the enterprise more for investors than for farmers. Cooperative stores that sold goods at higher profit margins for safety's sake found that their success encouraged the entry of new cooperatives offering consumer-members better terms. Minnesota's creameries discovered that falling prices caused by oversupply posed a threat to cooperatives; private firms could simply refuse to market the excess supply, but members pressured a cooperative to market it at the previous higher price and resented any failure to do so.[1] Around the turn of the century, these three cooperative types (but not the township mutuals) confronted challenges brought by their achievements.

Creameries and the Crisis of Declining Butter Prices, 1896–97

The success of cooperative creameries in Freeborn County specifically and in Minnesota generally helped to cause an oversupply in national butter markets in 1896–97. Dairy farmers confronted the crisis wheat farmers had faced earlier: a sharp decline in prices. In late April 1896, the editor of the *Freeborn County Standard* moaned, "'Oh, what a fall was there, my countrymen!' in the price of creamery butter; only 14 cents in New York."[2] Editor Marcellus Halvorsen of the *Albert Lea Enterprise* urged New York commission men to "brace up, which they can afford to do," and end the "general demoralization... of the New York market." They failed to brace up. The wholesale price of many goods fell in the 1893–96 depression, but an oversupply deepened butter's decline. In 1896 butter shipments to New York increased by almost 13 percent, and average New York butter prices hit their lowest level since 1851—down almost 32 percent from their 1893 peak.[3] The gains in productivity caused by the move from farm to factory butter, from part-time to specialized dairying, and from the gravity method to the centrifuge had glutted the market. Freeborn County farmers learned "that one can be imprisoned by the market he captures," as historian Morton Rothstein noted.[4]

A farmers' processing and marketing cooperative is prone to over-supply, noted economist John A. C. Hetherington: "The more the co-op gets for its members this year, the more the members are likely to try to produce next year." Members want it to process all their increased production even if falling prices cause it to lose money marketing their (over)supply. They demand that it—not they—assume the risks of over-production. Because it is member owned, it will tend to comply—"to cut prices and maintain production when" good business sense suggests the opposite strategy of cutting production to increase prices.[5] A cooperative creamery could hardly reduce members' milk deliveries or its own butter output. Limiting membership was difficult; open membership was a Rochdale principle and excluding neighbors was hard in a community of face-to-face relationships. In late nineteenth-century America, production quotas were an unthinkable violation of farmers' traditional independence.

Freeborn's dairy specialists initially tried to whistle their way past the dark crisis by boasting that low prices would enable more consumers to buy creamery butter. But demand for butter was fairly inelastic—it did not greatly increase with lower prices. They then reacted with alarm. Halvorsen worried that milk prices of thirty to forty cents per hundred-weight would come as "a rude shock" to farmers who had received one dollar three years earlier: "They will feel anything but in a friendly mood to the 'promoters' of creameries and the apostles of dairying."[6] One creamery leader "found it unprofitable to take his milk to the creamery and made butter at home instead."[7] Farmers moved to sheep raising and planting more wheat. Albert Lea's commercial club suggested that locals start a sugar beet factory. In July 1897 milk checks were half the October 1893 level.[8] Trying to save six years of work, the "apostles" urged farmers not to be "discouraged" but to "learn how to produce milk cheaper."[9] Cost cutting was the watchword.

Dairy specialists organized to cut costs. In late January 1896 about thirty creamery officers and dairymen of Freeborn County formed a county association of cooperative creameries. The *Freeborn County Standard*'s story was mistakenly (but revealingly) headlined "Corporation the Watchword." The editor meant "Cooperation," but the new Freeborn County Creamery and Dairy Association limited its membership to creameries. It rejected individual farmers and buttermakers as members.[10] Cutting the creamery's costs was first on the agenda. That fit with its member-creameries' duty to maximize returns to farmer-patrons, but it stressed creameries' profit statements more than farmers'. Priorities had changed now that creamery officers, not farmers, gathered to discuss mutual problems. Institutional maturation produced creameries that were now institutional "persons" capable of jointly acting for their goals apart from those of their members.

What farmers jointly tried, creameries could do also: bypass middlemen. The officers talked of reducing "extortionate commissions charged by commission merchants," cutting the "excessive" cost of creamery insurance by forming a creamery insurance mutual, lowering freight costs by jointly ordering coal in carload lots, and getting better freight rates and "facilities for handling and loading our butter."[11] One measure they rejected was joint purchasing of supplies, which would threaten a local creamery supply house, whose owner belonged to their association.[12]

They preached cost cutting to area farmers also. They arranged for University of Minnesota dairy expert Theophilus Haecker "to hold meetings at school houses near the creameries of this county when he would deliver lectures on feeding, breeding and the handling of dairy cows." Haecker tried to raise farmers' morale during the price decline and to teach them how to increase milk output and reduce per-unit costs.[13] Of course, greater output of milk would only worsen the national oversupply of butter, but local dairy leaders hoped that the immediate hike in farmers' monthly milk checks would dissuade them from turning to sheep raising or from going back to growing wheat.

The county association almost broke apart during the bitter 1896 presidential campaign. Halvorsen, its secretary, supported the Republicans and William McKinley. Its president, L. P. Lawson, was a Populist candidate for the state legislature. He used his presidency to win support for his candidacy, stating that one of the two issues "that I especially wish to work for" is "the interests of the creamery in regard to mutual insurance and civil action suits."[14] Dairy leader John Gibbs of Geneva ran for lieutenant-governor as a Republican (and won). Although its rules mandated meetings for July, October, and January, it failed to meet from March 1896 to February 1897.[15] The county creamery association was not a homogeneous, harmonious polity in that contentious year.

When it resumed its meetings in 1897, the institutional maturation of cooperative creameries became evident.[16] They had common interests that differed from patrons' interests. Creamery officers tried to limit their creameries' competition for patrons. They criticized the creamery that took milk "that has been previously rejected" by another "to lure [farmers] away from [other] creameries."[17] Managers complained of members "satisfied" with milk prices "until they see the published monthly report of [how] the neighboring creameries have in reality paid so much more than their own." The value placed on democratic openness made it impossible to refuse to publish these reports, so they recommended a standard reporting form to ensure that all published prices were calculated on the same basis. That would end unfair or misinformed competition between creameries over milk prices.[18]

Minnesota's dairy specialists felt that middlemen's commissions and fees greatly lowered creameries' profits. Supported by the Freeborn association, they formed a Minnesota Dairy Board of Trade (MDBT) in St. Paul as their own terminal butter market. The MDBT began selling butter directly to wholesalers and retailers on May 25, 1897, with the goal of "establish[ing] a high grade of a uniform quality of butter to be known as a Minnesota product" and thereby to command a higher price. By using the board's services, individual creameries would "stop consigning butter to New York and force the New York or other buyers to come here and buy it by openly bidding for it." That would end "commission men's profits which takes [sic] at least $500,000 out of the dairymen of the state annually."[19] Many wholesalers and jobbers refused to come to producer-dominated boards of trade with open bids. The MDBT died in the late 1890s, and cooperative creameries had to seek other means to achieve the MDBT's goal.[20]

During the price slump, Freeborn's dairy specialists briefly indulged hopes that export markets would eliminate the butter surplus. In this way, they copied American wheat farmers, who had long cherished "the idea of the West as the granary of the world."[21] The association heard two talks on export markets and "the requirements for the English market, which wanted butter with a mild flavor, and less salt and coloring."[22] The MDBT tried to interest Montreal butter exporters in buying Minnesota creamery butter for sale overseas.[23] But by October 1897, many knew "it would not pay at present to ship abroad." Exporting was not the answer.[24]

Nor did Freeborn farmers and creamery officers ask government to change market conditions. The Populist L. P. Lawson sought only lower creamery insurance rates and protection against civil suits, not state action to fight a butter trust or to raise prices. Creamery men were confident they could help themselves. As in 1890, so in 1896–97 they organized cooperatively, not politically—this time to cut costs, inform farmers of good dairying practices, and control marketing through a board of trade.

Success and New Technology Bring New Competitors — Centralizers

Cooperative creameries' success in converting many farmers to dairying and the new technology of small hand-powered centrifugal separators created a changed environment for those creameries after 1900. Despite their convenience for many patrons, Lawson criticized farmers' use of them because they could "materially cripple every co-operative creamery in the county."[25] Despite such warnings, many farmers heeded salesmen's pitches, bought the new tool, and separated cream at home. Farmers benefited from having a less bulky product—cream—to haul to the creamery and freshly skimmed milk to use on the farm. But the creamery lost control of production and quality. It could not dictate or determine how long cream was stored on the farm, nor could it refuse members' poor-quality cream. It was member-owned; other buyers might accept what it rejected.[26]

Minnesota farmers were slow to adopt the hand separator—otherwise there would have been fewer cooperative creameries. The hand separator was introduced by De Laval in 1885–86 but was not commonly used in Minnesota until after 1900.[27] Its widespread use, the return to hauling cream, the greater distances that cream could profitably be transported—these made a creamery in every township unnecessary. By 1900, however, nearly every Freeborn township had a cooperative creamery. Once set up, it was maintained by loyalty, inertia, and crossroads communities' desire to survive. The 1890s were a brief window of opportunity for the crossroads creamery.

In the early 1900s, it faced a new threat. Farm separation and long-distance hauling of cream encouraged private firms, called centralizers, to compete for farmers' cream. With completion of the rail network, more railroads were there to do the transporting. Whereas in the 1880s investors had balked at financing a fledgling dairy industry to which farmers were still uncommitted, now farmers were committed, thanks to cooperative creameries, and a large supply of milk or cream was ensured. Prospects for private investment had greatly improved. The conditions that had insulated cooperative creameries from private competition no longer existed.

In 1908 the editor of the *Todd County Independent* complained that "after local creameries have put the dairy industry on a firm footing, in come the centralizers to reap the benefit and undo what the creameries have built up." He recalled, "These city fellows would have treated the suggestion to come here and buy cream, six years ago, with contempt" and asked, "Now is there any valid reason why they should receive patronage at this stage of the game[?]"[28] The centralizers cited efficiency as the valid reason. In the early 1890s, the centrifuge's efficiencies aided the spread of cooperative creameries, but the credit mistakenly went to cooperative principles. After 1900 investors erroneously called their system the efficient one when credit was actually due to the new technology of hand-powered, on-farm separation. "They described the centralized system, the making of butter on a large scale where everything would be bought and sold on a carload basis, as a logical step in progressive dairying," noted writer Kenneth D. Ruble.[29] Here was an ironic reversal of roles.

Cooperative creameries had become vulnerable to centralizers because in resisting innovations many relied on their local milk monopoly that was based on the distance limit for hauling milk.[30] To use their centrifuges efficiently, they needed large volumes of milk. They could ill afford to lose patrons to centralizers. They had no binding contracts compelling their members to deliver milk or cream to the cooperative. Refusing to adapt to the hand separator or to acknowledge its convenience for their members, they placed their interests above members' interests. Engine-driven centrifuges improved speed and quality, but they were efficient for the creamery, not the farmer. Salesmen hawking hand separators made themselves and centralizers look more democratic than cooperatives by offering the centrifuge's efficiency to each farmer.

By 1915 about forty centralizer companies running some two thousand cream-collecting stations threatened the existence of the smaller cooperative creameries. A 1912 survey of Northfield Township (Rice

County) revealed that 37 percent of its milk supply went to centralizers who had built nearby cooling plants and local depots for farmers' convenience. Cooperatives received 48 percent of the milk. Farmers shrewdly took advantage of the competition. In the fall and winter, when centralizers paid more, farmers sold to them. In spring and summer, they accepted the cooperative's higher payments. Owners of the largest dairy farms negotiated contracts with centralizers and never shipped to the cooperative, which failed to enforce a penalty fee on members who refused to deliver milk. They gave up their shares rather than pay the fee.[31]

Fortunately cooperative creameries won the support of University of Minnesota dairy experts and state politicians. In 1907 Haecker backed an attempt to unite them in a Minnesota Co-operative Dairies' Association (MCDA) to counter lower prices and centralizers. The association had many purposes. Creamery managers knew the failure of small creameries eliminated managerial jobs. The MCDA's joint purchasing of supplies and bargaining to cut freight rates could save some small creameries. Its joint marketing of butter could end marketing competition among creameries and cut out commission men "interested in their own rake off only."[32] In actual operation, the MCDA sold butter that creameries consigned to it—not all they produced—and it failed to convince them to adopt uniform quality standards and a common Minnesota brand. Joint marketing of a Minnesota brand of butter was yet to come.[33]

Creamery leaders also called on their political allies, who prevailed on the 1913 legislature to pass a law "that cream shall not be carried more than sixty-five miles on railroads unless it is pasteurized or shipped in refrigerator cars." It was almost "a prohibition on the shipment of cream beyond" sixty-five miles, due to costs of pasteurizing and refrigerating.[34] Supporters "openly declared the bill is a co-operative creamery bill, and will work in favor of the country creameries."[35] The legislation was an attempt to preserve their local monopolies.

Cooperative creameries weathered the storm. Yet the centralizers' challenge showed how cooperatives born in technological innovation could be shaken by further innovation. Their success in proving dairying's profitability attracted competitors and created an oversupply. They built crossroads communities, but better means of transportation rendered these obsolete. They began with no government aid but needed a state law to survive competition.

The Success of Farmers' Stores Brings Them Competition

Similarly the FMC's partial success helped to bring competition in the form of a new cooperative store in Underwood. The FMC proved a cooperative store could succeed in Otter Tail County, while its failure to attract new members temptingly left many farmers available for a new cooperative to recruit. A major crisis hit the FMC in the summer of 1908 when two organizers from the Right Relationship League (RRL) visited the Underwood area for "a few days work." They persuaded seventy-three farmers to sign up to purchase shares in an Underwood branch or "department" of the new Otter Tail County Co-operative Company (OTCCC).[36] This department bought the O. F. Loseth and Son store and hired Odin Loseth as the manager.[37] It was the third branch in the county—RRL stores had started at Wall Lake and Weggeland that spring—and more were to come—at Phelps in July and at Fergus Falls in May 1909. All were departments in the OTCCC, which was a countywide company.[38]

The Underwood Department of the Otter Tail County Co-operative Company (right) was in helpful proximity to a drugstore. Cooperatives marketed daily necessities better than they did occasional needs like drugs.

This tree had so many branches that Main Street merchants could perch in its shade and use cooperation to shelter them from Wards and Sears. The RRL was organized in 1900 by midwestern merchants concerned about competition from department stores and mail-order houses. The RRL plan was to have a merchant sell his store to a group of customers, who each paid one hundred dollars per share and had one vote in the new cooperative store. The merchant often became the store manager, making cash-only sales, selling at local market prices, but paying members an annual patronage dividend. The RRL earned a commission for arranging this reorganization. By 1907 the RRL was independent of its original sponsor, the Cooperating Merchants Company, and was headquartered in Minneapolis. By January 1908 it had forty-seven stores, all located in western Wisconsin and Minnesota.[39]

This regional operation was similar to a chain-store system. All stores were to follow standard bookkeeping and accounting practices, overseen by an RRL auditor. The RRL promoted "united buying" from wholesalers to cut its costs, internalized market transactions, and coordinated them democratically. Each county company had a president, a board, and branch stores in several towns.[40] Each had a democratic voice in the regional RRL's affairs.

Begun in the Progressive era, when Americans found the "advantages of organization, consolidation, and integration," the RRL was a new form of county-level, merchant-led consumers' cooperation.[41] But there were precedents. The Grange and Alliance had used county units to gain bargaining clout; creameries had formed county associations. Like the NEPU, the RRL was a regional plan to replace many small-volume country retailers with a few high-volume cooperative ones. Using merchants' fears of giant retailers to create a cooperative mass retailer, the RRL mixed cooperative idealism and entrepreneurial self-interest.

The RRL stores sometimes failed to rescue merchants as intended. In payment for his store, the merchant received shares, which he redeemed for cash if the cooperative could raise cash by selling shares to customers. If few shares sold, he owned tens or hundreds of shares in a company headed for failure. If many sold, he became both the manager and the largest shareholder. That violated democratic ideals. Like Ole Sivertson manipulating the FMC, he might rule over a compliant board.[42] Cooperation might be advanced by harnessing his interests, or it might suffer by being used to bail him out.

Nevertheless, stores like the FMC had to fear even this cooperative-entrepreneurial mixture, for it might prove to be more attractive to farmer-consumers than their cooperative ideals and small savings. News of the arrival of an RRL store in Underwood caused the FMC to hold an "extraordinary" shareholders meeting on July 25, 1908, to discuss "matters of the greatest importance."[43] Opening the meeting, an FMC veteran leader, Even Sæther, warned that the FMC might "be completely ruined if strong measures are not taken to secure its future." He liked "the new company's business system and recommended a merger with it."[44]

A self-styled, lone-wolf reformer, who also opposed the status quo, called for "a more complete financial accounting." (Controversy had raged over high profit margins.)[45]

The defenders of the FMC admitted the need for better accounting and a full-time bookkeeper, which would cost money. One man "related some of his experiences in a consumers' cooperative in Norway," but his stories drew a complaint—"we are wasting time for no purpose."

Manager C. J. Moen, customers Olga Gronner and May Moen, and three clerks posed in the FMC's dry goods section around 1908–10. Groceries were stocked on the other side of the store and hardware in the back.

A critic responded that the FMC itself was time wasted. It "had done not a bit of good the whole time it had existed, neither for the town, nor the shareholders, nor the people as a whole." This sweeping statement drew two rebuttals. "After a great deal of talk backwards and forwards," the members agreed to hire "two competent bookkeepers" to check "the company's books before the next annual meeting." Then the consensus ended, and "a general chaos ensued in which many spoke at the same time until the meeting adjourned and most departed at once."

As voluntary polities, cooperatives had to accept members' right of secession so they had to try to secure consensus to forestall any defection. The FMC could not keep disgruntled members from switching to the RRL. Successful for nearly twenty-seven years, it was still vulnerable. It had become a closed, cautious group of longtime shareholders seeking their own economic interests — credit sales and long-term growth in share values. It paid no patronage dividends that might attract new members, and a majority wanted it that way. Few of the present members would benefit from the cooperative's growth so it stagnated. In contrast, the RRL was built on merchants' fears more than cooperative ideals, giving it a stronger motive to expand. It offered both a 6 percent patronage dividend and a stock dividend to shareholders and a 3 percent patronage refund to nonshareholders.[46] In July 1909 the front page of the *Fergus Globe* featured a list of RRL shareholders with the amount of patronage and stock dividends paid to each one.[47] Forced to respond, the FMC paid a year-end cash dividend, apparently its first — previous dividends only resulted in added share values.[48]

Right Relationship League Stores in Operation in Otter Tail County

By combining several stores into one countywide company, the RRL cut its costs through economies of scale, savings on administrative expenses, and greater leverage with wholesalers. Administration was centralized in Fergus Falls. The estimated annual savings from having all the stores purchase jointly from wholesalers ranged from two to five thousand dollars.[49] If the RRL passed the savings on to customers as lower prices or higher patronage dividends, the FMC would find it hard to compete. The FMC had a well-deserved reputation for selling at high profit margins to accumulate a large reserve. To make matters worse, the RRL had the support of former Populist Congressman and present *Globe* editor and

publisher Haldor E. Boen, who gave it favorable publicity in his newspaper. The FMC was one of those "few local, isolated, co-operative stores"
that the RRL saw as relics of a bygone era in cooperation, not suited to a
Progressive era of consolidation.[50]

Otter Tail County's merchants and editors were also worried about
the RRL invasion. At the first Underwood RRL meeting, merchants from
several towns came to investigate the RRL and to consider turning their
stores over to it.[51] The *Globe* editor predicted "there will be one branch of
the Cooperative Company at every trading station in the county." It was
the move of the RRL into Fergus Falls, the county seat, that provoked an
anti-RRL backlash.[52] Rumors circulated that the RRL company in Polk
County, Wisconsin, did not succeed because a countywide system incurred high expenses and, thus, would flounder in Otter Tail County,
too. To counter these reports, the *Globe* printed a letter from the RRL's
traveling auditor to the OTCCC's manager explaining the Polk failure
and reassuring him that "conditions in your company are the direct opposite in every way."[53] To dissuade middle-class shoppers from patronizing the OTCCC store in Fergus Falls, opponents "sneeringly referred to [it]
as 'The Farmer's Store,'" the *Globe* charged, although it had the same
manager as when it had been the fashionable "Chicago Store."[54]

The *Independent* of Parkers Prairie published warnings about cooperative stores that quit "with a large balance on the wrong side of the
ledger" and, setting up a straw man, attacked a garbled version of the RRL
operating system.[55] Elmer Adams of the *Fergus Falls Weekly Journal*
printed a letter allegedly written by a businessman who had visited Fergus Falls but decided against locating there: "Co-operative stores may be
all right but I don't want to get tied down in a community where no one
is willing that any one else should succeed to do any business, and the
producer to consumer [spirit] prevails. It is all right for a country village
but you can never make a town—a good prosperous town—on those
lines." The *Globe* pointed to the success of the Golden Rule department
store and another department store's move to Fergus Falls as proof the
RRL was not wrecking the business climate.[56]

Not since Alliance days had merchants and editors sounded so anti-
cooperative. They could live with a few village farmers' stores that did
not expand to other towns or combine their purchasing and management. The RRL was not linked to third-party politics, despite the support
from former Populists like Boen, but its countywide plans seemed as

great a threat to county-seat merchants and county editors as the Grange and Alliance had been.

As it turned out, no one needed to be so concerned. The OTCCC stores soon displayed weaknesses of their own. After only one year, the Underwood Department faced dissension over manager Loseth, whose personality offended some customers. He submitted his resignation early in 1909, but the executive committee refused to accept it, waiting until the store's membership voted to do so.[57] The Department was nearly as dependent on him as the FMC had been on Sivertson. As part of a regional RRL better able to recruit managers, however, it could more easily find a replacement.[58]

Lack of capital was a more serious problem. The RRL plan set the share price—one hundred dollars—higher than many farmers could afford. By August 1909, only nineteen of eighty-one shareholders had paid for their shares.[59] With RRL stores, once "the organizational stock was sold to buy out a store it was found impossible to sell additional stock to provide capital for expansion."[60] In Underwood, it is doubtful that there were enough receipts from share sales to buy out the Loseths completely. Credit sales contributed to a shortage of working capital. Although RRL principles called for cash sales only, they were ignored in this case. For June-August 1909, almost 33 percent of the store's sales were credit sales.[61] At the same time, the OTCCC paid out cash for stock and patronage dividends.[62] Accepting notes in payment of shares and allowing credit sales but paying dividends in cash were contradictory policies. Paper was coming in and cash going out.

The OTCCC store in Fergus Falls was sold by a "credit bureau" in early February 1917. The Underwood branch may have been closed out a year earlier. Certainly it was gone by January 1918.[63] In 1915 the regional RRL collapsed, depriving local stores of its organizational base. Shareholders' support for RRL stores seems always to have been relatively weak and overly dependent on the next cash dividend.[64] In contrast, the FMC survived World War I, the Great Depression, World War II, and postwar inflation and did not go out of business until 1967.[65] For

C. J. Moen's longevity—thirty-five years as manager and fifty-three years on the board—revealed both the FMC's strength (a tradition of stability) and weakness (control by a small in-group).

all its weaknesses, it had strong local roots, a long tradition, and a small, loyal group of shareholders—sufficient resources to outlast the aggressive RRL's chain-store system of consumers' cooperation.

A fate worse than competition from the RRL befell many small cooperative stores. Telephones, cars, and Rural Free Delivery made "long-distance marketing" feasible. Consumers traveled farther to larger trade centers to do their shopping and bypassed the crossroads community and its farmers' store. Also consumers purchased more specialized services and luxury goods: dental and medical services, fancy clothing and furniture. These the crossroads farmers' store could not provide.[66] Such trends showed the weakness in rural consumers' cooperation; it worked with groceries and dry goods but not with higher-priced services or goods. Cooperation was slow to adapt to the shifting demands of consumers and the changing consequences of new technologies while entrepreneurs were quick to anticipate both.

When the distance routinely traveled to trade centers increased from four to fifteen miles, the average number of farms in each trade center's territory grew from two hundred to more than twenty-eight hundred.[67] The lesser number could be organized for cooperation, but the greater number was much more difficult. Many farms were within fifteen miles of several trade centers. A cooperative organized at town A might see its members switch to shop at town B. Or members living at one end of its large territory might form a faction against other members. A University of Minnesota rural sociologist noted, "The extensive trading centers tend[ed] to break down the cohesion between members of the family and between families in the same area."[68] They strained cohesion within cooperatives. It was harder to recruit a polity sharing the common interest of a common trade center. A cooperative was less likely to have a local monopoly.

The FMC and HLHF were well established before the automobile, Rural Free Delivery, and the telephone brought change. Common Norwegian-American ethnicity and a common interest in a farmers' store preserved them once change came. Dependent on personal trust and face-to-face dealings, this Scandinavian-American consumers' cooperation was resilient, but it could not be expanded to a chain-store system by non-Scandinavian outsiders at the RRL's Minneapolis headquarters. Cooperators could not match mass retailers in the changing retail markets of the early twentieth century.

Terminal Market:
Equity Cooperative Exchange versus Chamber of Commerce

Farmers who cooperated in marketing their grain also found it difficult to match entrepreneurs. The local success of farmers' elevators tempted farmers to expand by creating a cooperative "line" with its own terminal elevator. That had been the Alliance plan, but too few farmers' elevators existed in the early 1890s to make the scheme practicable. By 1904 there were enough to make it seem realistic. Local farmers' elevators were "not the most important step," noted one Minneapolis grain merchant. "The next step the farmers should take is to operate a terminal house at each market." They were "very little better off by handling their own grain at their country station as long as the terminal houses can fix the price paid on the Exchanges."[69] When they tried the "next step," however, their dependence on commission firms limited them.

In 1904 farmers in the farmers' elevator movement organized the Minnesota Farmers' Exchange. Despite the name, it included many North Dakotans. The founders hoped to market "grain at terminal markets" through their own terminal elevator "so as to do away entirely with the middle-men who are now oppressing" farmers.[70] Like its predecessors, it sought membership on the Minneapolis Chamber of Commerce, but like them it failed.[71] It was plagued by dissension between Minnesota and North Dakota delegates over its name and representation on key committees.[72] Factionalism was lethal for a cooperative trying to enter terminal grain markets. By May 1908 the organization was dead.[73]

The next attempt, the Equity Cooperative Exchange (ECE), was not burdened with interstate jealousy. It was an outgrowth of a national farmers' organization, the American Society of Equity, begun in Indianapolis in 1902 by James A. Everitt, the publisher of a farm journal.[74] Everitt advocated withholding crops from market until prices rose and saw Equity as "a gigantic holding movement," according to one historian. In the northwestern states, Equity organized unsuccessful wheat-withholding campaigns in 1903 and 1907. In 1908 Equity leaders set up the ECE to control the grain marketing it could not stop. It would "receive grain shipped on consignment or, better still, ... be 'fed' by a chain of local cooperatives with ample storage facilities." Farmers would "retain control of their grain from the time it left the farm until it was sold on the terminal market."[75]

The ECE, like its predecessors, met one main obstacle, the Minneapolis Chamber of Commerce. It failed either to market wheat independently of the Chamber or to secure membership in the Chamber, but it would not be denied. The 1912 appointment as ECE sales manager of George S. Loftus, "an aggressive and uncompromising foe of the organized grain trade," sparked a sharp war between Chamber and Exchange. It was a lawyers' war of hearings and pleadings: a pro-Chamber inquiry by the state Senate, a pro-Exchange probe by the state House, congressional hearings sponsored by U.S. Representative James Manahan, an ECE friend, and lawsuits begun "in the hope of crushing the Exchange."[76] This war spilled over from hearing rooms and courtrooms to the convention halls of the farmers' elevator movement.

At the South Dakota Farmers' Grain Dealers' Association (FGDA) convention in December 1913, Loftus and Chamber secretary John G. McHugh "collided"; "invective, threats of physical violence, and defamatory statements were hurled at one another indiscriminately."[77] When the Tri-State Grain Growers' Association, an Equity "subsidiary," tried to meet in Fargo's Civic Auditorium on January 23, 1914, officials "blocked" them from the building and "serious violence was threatened."[78]

The atmosphere was tense when the Minnesota FGDA opened its convention in Minneapolis on February 5, 1914. Its president, H. R. Meisch of Argyle, was determined to keep order; "I didn't want to see the disgraceful scenes enacted at other conventions re-enacted here."[79] He allowed Chamber spokesmen and commission grain dealers to address the convention but refused Equity leaders equal time.[80] First McHugh explained the Chamber's workings. Then Magnus Johnson, Minnesota Equity president, asked the chair to allow an Iowa Equity leader to speak. Meisch refused; "if Mr. Johnson said any more he would call on the policeman who had been stationed at the door to arrest him."[81] Very revealing was Meisch's directive that "every speaker will be compelled to confine his talk to matters concerning the Farmers' Elevator movement." Meisch was not alone in his views; he was reelected president.[82] For many, local cooperative action was sufficient, and "the movement," almost by definition, did not include the ECE's idea of cooperation in terminal markets.

Equity men skipped the banquet given by the Minneapolis commission firms. Governor Adolph O. Eberhart, no friend of Progressives, was the speaker, and he praised Chamber members and commission merchants. Equity supporters decided to hold a separate meeting to form a

Farmers' Co-operative Elevator Association to rival the Minnesota FGDA, but they had trouble getting a room to meet in.[83] When Equity's Elias Steenerson tried to speak from "the hotel balcony," Loftus recalled, "The [hotel] phonograph . . . began to let loose just as Mr. Steenerson began to talk."[84] (Loftus wanted Equity to be seen as persecuted; privately he called Equity's protest a "splendid success . . . as you will note by the newspaper clippings.")[85]

Later in the year, the ECE moved its headquarters to St. Paul at the invitation of St. Paul business leaders, who saw it as "an opportunity to get for St. Paul a good share of the grain trade."[86] Using military terms oddly appropriate to the Chamber versus Equity battle (and the Minneapolis-St. Paul rivalry), the Chamber's supporters sarcastically reported the move:

Moving rapidly by the right flank to University Avenue and the Midway District, the Equity Co-Operative Exchange abandoned its Corn Exchange position at II a.m. today and evacuated Minneapolis. . . . The cavalry pushing rapidly forward . . . the TWO horses, closely followed by an armored supply train of ONE wagon, bearing the DESK, TYPE-WRITER and INK STANDS of the exchange. The St. Paul frontier line . . . was . . . crossed without opposition . . . the news reached Minneapolis that the Equity is directing its march upon the Pioneer Building, St. Paul.[87]

At its new location, the ECE faced the same old problem: the Chamber virtually controlled grain marketing in the Twin Cities. To switch cities was not to bypass the Minneapolis Chamber of Commerce.

The battle moved to local farmers' elevator associations, which had to choose between the two terminal marketing systems. The result was a series of rancorous divisions. On May 2, 1914, the Farmers' Elevator Company of Eden Valley met to hear spokesmen "debate the merits of the two grain buying systems."[88] Only Loftus showed up, not McHugh. He criticized three local company leaders who had urged reduced shipments to the ECE and increased use of the Chamber's commission firms. The resulting controversy illustrated the clash between businessmen who dominated farmers' elevators and Equity spokesmen with their ideological, class-based appeal.[89]

The three local leaders were the company secretary (a bank cashier), a local Catholic priest, and the company's grain buyer. All three believed that Loftus's ECE "was not obtaining good prices for the Elevators' grain." When marketing through ECE, their elevator paid two sales commissions since Loftus had to make the final sale through one of the Chamber's commission firms. Loftus charged that the three were tools of the grain trust and Chamber agents. Present at the meeting, the priest, Father Jeremiah O'Callaghan, retorted that Loftus was "attempt[ing] to spread suspicion amongst the farmers of the community against the bankers and merchants of the village." Responding to Loftus, he objected to paying two commissions and ridiculed Loftus and the ECE for lacking sales facilities, buyers, and terminal elevators: "He is forced to carry on many of his sales by telephone.... He cannot compete with the Chamber of Commerce."[90] The local newspaper editor defended the local leaders and attacked the outsider, Loftus.[91] The company was split between at least one pro-Equity director and several anti-Equity leaders. Loftus's speech energized the Eden Valley Equity unit, which "declared a boycott on Minneapolis mills and endorsed" the ECE's move to St. Paul.[92]

Similar struggles occurred within other farmers' elevator companies. Various ECE leaders charged that some managers received rebates from the Chamber's commission firms for shipping grain through them and that farmers' elevators borrowing from them were forced to market grain through the Chamber.[93] Directors or shareholders had to pressure managers to get them to sell through the ECE.[94] At its 1916 annual meeting, for instance, shareholders of the Farmers' Elevator Company of Roseau told the manager "to make some shipments of grain to the Equity Exchange of St. Paul to give that concern a try out."[95]

Professional managers had close ties to commission firms' traveling salesmen, who offered professional services, such as daily market reports, market letters, instruction in billing procedures, help in dealing with railroads, and "technical knowledge of the grain business."[96] They were not eager to sever this useful relationship to pursue a visionary terminal marketing plan. Administrative, hierarchical coordination had (de facto) largely replaced democratic coordination. The hierarchy descended from the commission merchant on the Chamber floor to his firm's traveling salesman to the elevator manager. Members' and directors' democratic role was thereby marginalized. Thus the ECE was undercut at both ends of the system. The Chamber excluded it from a seat at the nation's most important grain exchange and from a role at the FGDA state convention. Locally commission firms had such strong ties with farmers' elevators that many refused to ship grain through the ECE. The only recourse for the ECE was to set up its own farmers' elevators in order to obtain grain.[97]

By 1900 a strongly organized private grain trade dominated terminal markets, and farmers could not dislodge or bypass it over the next two decades. Unlike the Grange or Alliance warehouses, most of the new-style farmers' elevators succeeded, but the late timing of their success meant that they were relegated to a limited local role that posed no threat to the private grain trade. Once their Minnesota FGDA was co-opted by the Chamber and its commission members, they became mere "bargaining cooperatives" that failed to bypass middlemen. Learning one lesson from Granger and Alliance failures—the danger of linking third-party political action to cooperative wheat marketing—only helped them accept their marginal role. In the process, they contributed to that depoliticization of cooperation that the university's experts later encouraged.

Merchants Control Farmers' Elevators:
Northfield Farmers' Elevator

Even in marginal local roles, their success brought problems. The help of commission firms and local merchants had its price. The Northfield Farmers' Mercantile and Elevator Company was one that merchants controlled and ran as a quasi-private grain elevator. From a farmers' cooperative perspective, such success was failure.

It began as many others did—with several meetings of area farmers beginning in March 1896. By January 1897, farmers signed up for fifteen hundred dollars in stock, and, the *Northfield News* noted, "several business men have favored the plan by offering to assist financially." Construction of the elevator began shortly thereafter.[98] The company was an immediate success, with a profit of more than three hundred dollars its first year.[99] After the elevator burned in 1901, the company rebuilt and earned a profit of almost nineteen hundred dollars for 1902. Perhaps implying more than was stated, the *News* commented that "President [John] Miller and the officers in charge have made an exceptional record for themselves."[100]

After a 1909 profit of three thousand dollars, the *News* was more explicit: "This is certainly a remarkable showing," which raised the question whether it was "really serving the purpose" of a farmers' elevator, "namely that of affording farmers an opportunity to co-operate for self-protection." Less concerned about the purity of cooperative principles than about the loss of trade to nearby towns, the *News* could not refrain from editorializing in its front-page article reporting the 1909 profit that "the price paid for grain at Northfield has at times been less than at competing points—as at Dennison or Stanton." That situation apparently led farmers to stop "com[ing] to town to do their trading."[101] Once again, the strongest regulator of local grain prices was local merchants' need to maintain retail traffic. (However, merchants owning numerous shares in the farmers' elevator likely stood to make more money from a high-profit, high-dividend strategy than from a lower-profit, greater-retail traffic strategy.)

Merchants and farmers owning many shares favored large profits and large dividends. The company violated Rochdale principles in not limiting the number of shares one individual could own and in allowing one vote per share instead of one per member. Farmers did not complain loudly until the stormy January 1917 annual meeting. By then the company had accumulated more than twenty-two thousand dollars in undistributed profits, which many thought excessive. Some wanted to reduce this embarrassing surplus by declaring a huge 50 or 60 percent dividend on stock. The vice-president noted that was not a democratic or cooperative solution. The "dividend would be voted only to stockholders," and "the number of persons benefiting would not be increased" by augmenting the dividend percentage. With the help of proxies, the party favoring the status quo passed a motion to declare a 20 percent dividend instead.

This vote "aroused a storm of protest against the use of proxies"— legalized the previous May. Arguing from a farmer's perspective, one member "declared that it was wrong to pay big dividends to city stockholders, that the farmers who raise the grain should get the profits." With proxies, "one or two men [could] control a meeting." Many farmers, he said, were "opposed to the declaring of big dividends."[102]

From an investor's perspective, the vice-president argued it had not been "smooth sailing at the start . . . and the men who put their money in are now entitled to make something." From the firm's point of view, the secretary noted "that the surplus is a handy little interest-drawer." (Net interest income was more than $660 in 1916.) Buying and selling grain was risky, and a surplus covered the risks. Two directors agreed "that a surplus is needed for doing business, for selling feed, flour, etc., on credit."[103] But farming was risky, too. Farmers might need some of that surplus in order to pay for that feed or flour. After twenty years of operation, this "farmers'" elevator had become an investment opportunity, a firm whose interests had higher priority than farmers' interest in high grain prices. Institutional inertia was strong. The same directors and officers were reelected at this annual meeting, though shareholders voted to eliminate proxy voting and to buy back shares of a nonresident shareholder (nonresidency had been the reason given for instituting proxy voting).[104]

The debate continued in the *Northfield News*. Cooperative leader William F. Schilling had seen "a neighbor of mine living within three miles of Northfield unloading his wheat" at Shieldsville thirteen miles away where he got "twenty cents per bushel more than he could get at Northfield." He told of a "big dividend and surplus" elevator at Litchfield, where loss of retail traffic caused merchants to join farmers in starting a real farmers' elevator. He urged the Northfield "Commercial club or Ad club" to join in making the farmers' elevator a "co-operative and not a corporation to pile up a big surplus."[105]

The elevator manager responded by accusing Schilling of a "misleading statement" on prices and a serious error in "common school arithmetic." He asserted the elevator "is managed and conducted for the welfare of the public and not for the personal gain of a few individuals."[106]

Using University of Minnesota agricultural economist L. D. H. Weld's *Farmers' Elevators in Minnesota* as its authority, the *Northfield News* editorialized the next week. Tactfully the editorial, entitled "When Are Elevators Co-operative?" did not name the Northfield elevator, but the question mark was definitely placed next to its cooperative credentials. Citing Weld, the *News* implied it was not a true cooperative; it did not pay patronage dividends or limit the number of shares one person could own. The *News* quoted Weld's bulletin regarding the average gross profit margins earned by farmers' elevators. The Northfield elevator's margin per bushel was significantly higher for all grains.[107]

Despite the criticism, the Northfield elevator made no significant changes in the next three years. Once a farmers' elevator was controlled by a few large shareholders, internal revolt was unlikely. More outside pressure was needed. In November 1920 a local Farm Bureau unit held a meeting about changing grain marketing in Northfield. One speaker gave a brief history of the Northfield elevator, showing the consequences of farmers' loss of control.[108] Aided by its county agent, the Farm Bureau committee met with the company's board in that same month to talk about "putting the elevator on a co-operative basis." In January 1921 shareholders agreed to sell the elevator to a new cooperative company.[109]

The new company's organizational meeting showed the state's increasing influence on cooperation. County Agent Archibald A. McPheeters opened it. Hugh J. Hughes, the director of markets of the state Department of Agriculture, outlined some reasons why cooperatives failed and read the articles of incorporation that his department saw as "ideal for co-operative elevators" and that reflected Rochdale principles. They were "adopted with a few minor changes." To stress its co-operative nature, they named the new company the Co-operative Elevator Association of Northfield.[110]

The old company had been too successful for investors and too forgetful of farmers' interests as producers. (Yet farmers owned shares, and large stock dividends appealed to their interests as investors.) Farmers' successes with their own country elevators enticed them to expand into terminal markets with the ECE, but it was too late and markets were too well organized. Similarly the success of farmers' stores helped to inspire the RRL's scheme of cooperative county "chain stores," but democratic consensus could not be easily extended across community boundaries. The OTCCC's short life showed farmers lacked financial resources and, more importantly, the wealth-accumulating motive for such expansion. Consumers' cooperation cut costs and achieved small savings, but Rochdale rules kept it from becoming a wealth-creating engine, such as the Northfield farmers' elevator temporarily became. The success of cooperative creameries attracted a new competitor, the centralizer, that used a new technology, the hand-powered separator, which could be made to appear more democratic than the cooperative. An oversupply of butter partly caused by cooperatives' success threatened the local creameries—because it was difficult for a democratic polity to reduce its members' milk production.

In all these cases, success created problems because a cooperative was both an economic firm and a democratic polity, with each function carrying different and partly conflicting definitions of success. Profitability could endanger the democratic values of a fair and equal treatment of all members, an openness to recruit new members, and a willingness to transfer the benefits of technology from the firm to the individual farmer. Yet adherence to these democratic values—and to their definition of success—could imperil the survival or expansion of the cooperative as an economic entity. An entrepreneur had to balance many of the same economic factors as did a cooperative manager or director—cash and credit sales, long- and short-term goals, accounts receivable and payable, distributing or reinvesting profits, rapid or slow expansion—but not economic and democratic definitions of success. That last balancing act was peculiar to the cooperative and arose out of the very definition of one.

11

Telephone Companies

*"Merchants and farmers can hello back and forth
as much as they wish to"*

ON NOVEMBER 15, 1899, the *Willmar Tribune* reported that "A company of farmers have organized a telephone company in the western part of Mamre [Township]." The editor noted, "There is no reason why a farmhouse should not possess the convenience of telephone connection with the neighbors and with the local marketplace." Phone cooperatives "have proven very successful in the eastern states." He hoped Kandiyohi County would "be covered by a network of co-operative telephone systems, thus giving our farmers . . . rapid transmission of intelligence."[1]

To promote a rural phone company, an Atwater editor reprinted an article on the "incalculable benefit" of rapid transmission by phone:

> For a nominal rental per month a farmer is in direct communication, sitting in his own home, with the county seat and can call up at any time night or day, the central office, or any store or business place in town . . . getting the wheat market, ordering goods sent out by the neighbors, inquiring for mail at the post office, ordering machinery repairs in the fall when one trip to town might cost the rental of the telephone for several months . . . every farmer's wife and daughter will be able to . . . have a social chat with her neighbors or get the latest news from the outside world.[2]

The phone had many uses for rural people. Also it made possible a new form of cooperation, the livestock shipping association, which scheduled livestock deliveries by phone and did not need a holding facility.

Rapid transmission by phone was slow to reach rural Minnesota, unlike instantaneous communication by telegraph, which arrived in 1860. In conjunction with the railroads, the telegraph helped build an economy of swift ordering and shipping, of the speedy transmission of business intelligence. Yet its wires hugged rail lines; its one office in town was in the depot or nearby; it had few social uses; and its "greatest value . . . lay in long-distance rather than in local communication." It would never link farm to town or farm to farm.[3]

Alexander Graham Bell first sent an oral message over his invention on March 10, 1876. A sort of people's telegraph, this new technology could transmit a conversation or a performance instead of just business information, and it could link homes to homes. Like 1990s decisions about where to lay fiber-optic cables to provide access to an information superhighway, 1890s decisions over access to phone systems were key battles for power between entrepreneurs and cooperators and between rural and urban areas.[4]

Minnesotans' first uses of the phone were for performances.[5] In 1878, S. E. Ware planned to relay a concert from the courthouse in Mantorville to the Odd Fellows Hall in Kasson by telephone, but faulty equipment delayed it.[6] After the novelty wore off and access to phones became easier, Minnesotans used the telephone as a short-distance tool for businessmen to complement the long-distance telegraph. In 1877 or 1878, Duluth insurance agent Walter Van Brunt set up a phone line between his office and a local grain elevator to receive reports of daily grain receipts quickly so that he could adjust insurance coverage without leaving his office.[7] Other men availed themselves of the new technology to connect office to factory.[8] Unlike most families, businesses could afford the high fees for phone service and had obvious practical applications for it. Mere social use was not yet acceptable.[9]

Stillwater was one of the first towns outside the Twin Cities to obtain phone service. In the summer of 1879, direct-line phones were installed to link offices, stores, lumber mills, and the St. Croix boom site.[10] In small cities, the Northwestern Telephone Company, Minnesota's Bell licensee, owned almost all of the early phone lines and exchanges. (Bell company patents on telephone technology did not expire until 1893–94.)[11] After 1894 cities had other choices: allowing a citywide monopoly or granting more than one company the right to erect poles and string wires. Since state government did not regulate phone companies until 1915, these issues were left to city councils, city commercial clubs, and urban phone users to decide.[12] For Progressive-era urban leaders who favored home rule and municipal ownership of utilities, these questions were central to their politics and led to bitter battles, such as the one in Willmar from 1899 to 1912.

The Nature of the Telephone, of Cooperation, and of Rural Life

The question that few took seriously was how to extend phone service to farmers. Industry leaders showed antirural prejudice in refusing to see rural residents as potential phone subscribers. Sociologist Claude S. Fischer has noted that Bell and independent companies "hardly notified American farmers" of the new technology, "much less made any effort to sell telephones to them (mocking anecdotes of rustic incredulity over the talking machine were common in industry journals)." Independent companies later turned to the rural areas that Bell had neglected.[13] In 1901 one British observer claimed, "telephonic communication is not desired by the rural mind."[14]

The exact opposite was true. By 1920 about 33 percent of urban families had a phone, but 39 percent of farm families had one. In the Plains region over 80 percent of farms had phone service. Here, Fischer pointed out, were "people seeking out a technology, independent of or even in opposition to its corporate sponsors, and adapting the technology to their own needs." He posited several explanations: the business uses for a farm phone, its value in overcoming rural isolation, its usefulness in emergencies, and its special role in helping farm women to create social networks.[15]

Other explanations arise from the nature of the telephone. Broadcasting pulls individuals away from local concerns to focus on translocal events; a form of narrowcasting, the phone enables them to communicate local concerns to neighbors.[16] It was an expansion of the neighborhood news column in the weekly paper. Anyone could tell what news or opinions he or she wished to a select audience. In 1899 rural people were constrained by distance, location, and "geographical space." Phones tended to "mak[e] geographical space ... *fungible*," which "mean[t] that every point in that space would for all practical purposes be equivalent to any other point" and rural points would not be more isolated than urban ones.[17] Thus phones were sure to be popular with rural people. Rural construction costs were higher, but once poles were up and wire strung, the operating costs of rural phone service were lower because rural companies had fewer subscribers than urban ones.[18]

Cooperative telephone companies, or "farmer lines," brought these benefits to rural Minnesota, when private companies' neglect of the rural market left the field open for them. Corporate administrators failed to see a rural market. Stringing hundreds of miles of wire into sparsely populated areas was costly and unlikely to generate profits. Yet cooperating farmers who desperately wanted the service and were willing to donate labor, accept lower-quality service, and forgo profits could obtain and maintain telephone service.

Such phone companies were not producer cooperatives, although producers used phones to communicate with local or terminal markets. Telegraph and telephone "permitted ultimate buyers and sellers in many industries to make contact without the intervention of costly middlemen."[19] In fact better communications may have eliminated more middlemen than did cooperatives. Phone cooperatives were consumer cooperatives of sorts, but they rarely competed with private firms. Availability, not lower costs, was the main goal. They were "technology diffusion" cooperatives like the later rural electric cooperatives.

Unlike cars or radios, for instance, phones were well suited to cooperation. A farm family received benefits from owning a car or a radio even if none of their neighbors had one, but that was not true if their phone was the only one in their area. The value of a phone grew as the number of local phone subscribers increased.[20] The first family to join a phone cooperative had a strong incentive to persuade their neighbors to join, too. Phones required a local transmission network, and the United States had no tradition of government ownership of utility transmission lines (telegraph lines were privately owned). Private or cooperative companies had to construct and operate the lines. As with other types of cooperatives, the timing of cooperators' entry into this new field was important. Cooperative creameries' early use of the new centrifugal separators gave them great advantages, whereas Granger flour mills failed to enter before new technologies arrived and then could not afford them. The problems of late entry plagued phone cooperatives, formed long after American Bell Telephone Company became dominant. Cooperation would be limited to the industry's rural margins, and the rural phone cooperatives would find it impossible to form even a regional or statewide cooperative system.

A November 15, 1899, *Willmar Tribune* article cited a rural telephone cooperative in Genesee County, New York, as a model. Once again, Minnesotans imitated eastern models. Genesee's cooperative was begun by Grangers engaged in joint purchasing for which a phone "becomes a seeming necessity" because it was more efficient than a committee meeting.[21] As in cities, the new technology was first used for farm business.

Main Street proprietors encouraged phone cooperatives in order to forge links with their rural customers before entrepreneurs in rival towns could do so. Atwater merchants joined with farmers in nearby townships to organize the Union Telephone Company in May 1901.[22] Concerned about loss of control or inferior service, merchants wanted a township line to connect to Atwater but "the local system for the village to be an organization by itself." The "farmers objected, and the business men finally yielded to their wishes."[23] Town and township shared power and leadership in the new company, which was to be "run on a cooperative basis" since good low-cost service, not dividends, was "the object sought."[24]

Union Telephone sought connections with the towns of Spicer and Willmar. It would not expand into additional townships, according to the *Tribune* but "invites the organization of similar companies with whom it will" connect "and thus mutually extend the usefulness of all the phones of the system."[25] At this point, cooperation and technology parted ways. Telephone service invited, even demanded, networks and an interconnected interdependence; rural cooperators insisted on local control, independence, and more than one cooperative company.

Victor E. Lawson, a Progressive and copublisher of the *Tribune*, hated monopoly and supported local control. He had fought the 1899 decision of the local Minnesota Central Telephone Company (MCTC) to let Northwestern Telephone Company acquire a financial interest in the MCTC.[26] He favored municipal ownership of Willmar's phone system and cooperative ownership of rural systems. Believing the Bell monopoly gouged customers, he argued that a cooperative, furnishing "connections to the shareholders at cost," could set up a system with much lower charges. Atwater's new Union cooperative fit his vision, and he promised to keep "readers fully informed as to the progress made."[27] With his encouragement, Kandiyohi farmers formed many phone cooperatives from 1901 to 1904. Kandiyohi became one of Minnesota's best-organized counties in terms of telephone cooperation.[28]

Even in Kandiyohi County, farmers were years behind private firms, which were closely interconnected. Union Telephone faced immediate, organized opposition from them. Willmar Telephone Company owned the Willmar exchange and was linked to MCTC urban exchanges in west-central Minnesota. The MCTC was financially tied to Northwestern Telephone, which ran long-distance lines to the Twin Cities.[29] Willmar banker and MCTC manager David N. Tallman had set up and linked some twenty-five exchanges with hundreds of miles of wire.[30] Tallman was not interested in serving townships. He had looked into it, he said, "but found

In the midst of a bitter newspaper battle over expiration of a ten-year-old telephone franchise in Willmar, cartoonist Eben Lawson caricatured the Bell trust and favored his father's proposal for municipal ownership of the telephone exchange; "Say, Mister Bell'opoly, I guess you'd better get off."

that I could not get sufficient rental to maintain good lines and give efficient service and pay a reasonable dividend on the investment, so [I] gave up the idea."[31] He turned the townships over to a fourth company, the quasi-cooperative Kandiyohi County Telephone Company (KCTC), which hoped to provide phone service for all Kandiyohi townships.[32] All four companies agreed not to connect to, or contract with, any firm that was competing against any one of them.[33]

The Union company ran headlong into this tidy agreement to divide the county phone market. Its proposed line from Atwater to Spicer to Willmar would bring it into competition with all of them except the purely local Willmar company, so they refused to connect to the proposed Union line (no state or federal law required them to do so). The KCTC offered the Union some surrender terms: a marginal role with only farm-to-farm lines in townships around Atwater or the dissolution of the Union in exchange for minimal Atwater ownership of KCTC stock. The KCTC's trump card was its power (through its allies) to deny the Union connections both to Willmar (the county seat) and to all long-distance service. KCTC spokesmen warned that then the Union would be "a company that begins and ends nowhere and offers" its customers "only connection with their neighbors."[34]

The Union refused to surrender. Atwater's leaders feared having "an outside corporation . . . come in and build the Atwater local system." To maintain local control, they proceeded "regardless of connections."[35] Here was a territorial battle and a fight between cooperators and entrepreneurs. Located at the county's eastern end, Atwater needed telephone service to connect its farm area to its merchants and would not entrust its phone service to an outside firm like KCTC that was tied to Willmar businessmen and their interests.

The KCTC and its allies sent "attorneys and other emissaries" around to talk to farmers and townspeople "to convince them of the folly? of their undertaking."[36] The allies charged that the Union's manager was advertising ridicu-

Gilded Age entrepreneur and Lawson foe David N. Tallman promoted for-profit telephony in western Minnesota and later boosted townsites in North Dakota. For years he served on the Willmar city council that regulated his Minnesota Central Telephone Company.

lously low phone rental rates while secretly planning to meet operating expenses by periodic assessments against shareholders. Attempting to divide the town from the townships, they claimed that "nearly all of the business men of Atwater" supported the KCTC plan "as they want long distance connection with their exchange."[37]

Still the Union proceeded to construct its lines, which were operating by December 1901. The KCTC offered "to divide the territory in the county...with the main line of the railroad as dividing line." Presumably the KCTC would take the area south of the Great Northern's east-west track, and the Union, the area north. This offer displayed a monopolistic rather than cooperative spirit, for it was based on the assumption that rural service beyond Atwater could be decided without consulting residents of those townships. The Union rejected this offer.[38]

The allies had to bow to the solidarity shown by Union members. Unable to sign up enough subscribers in the Union's territory to operate profitably, the KCTC could only compete there by operating at a loss, which it would not do. Admitting defeat, the allies granted connections to the Union at stated switching and per-message rates.[39]

This tug-of-war showed how late entry led to serious problems. Established companies had clout due to the connective necessities of telephony. They could threaten to deny connections—to destroy farmer lines or to raise the price of connection privileges. If Atwater's leaders had waited five more years to organize, they might have failed. The KCTC would have had time to sell its one-hundred-dollar shares to more well-to-do farmers and to string phone lines in more prosperous areas, a practice known as "skimming the cream." The Union would have been left with poorer areas and customers.[40]

The Union's victory showed that cooperation was well suited to rural phone service. Cooperatives could best keep cost-only service and recruit with neighbor-to-neighbor solicitation and promises of low-cost service and local control. They dealt with farmers' proverbial penny-pinching attitudes better than did for-profit firms. One entrepreneur parodied the farmer who "wants free exchange with Afghanistan ... and other foreign countries. [He] did not agree to pay anybody any toll—the phone doesn't work anyway—think we'll go over on the other line—can get Ottumwa for a nickel there and you are a robber anyhow."[41] By joining a cooperative, he got working phones and Ottumwa for a nickel.

Organizing and Operating a Rural Telephone Cooperative

Timing helped to determine the size, location, and character of rural phone cooperatives. Most began during the heyday (1890–1920) of the crossroads community, so they tended to have small territories and few subscribers. The Union was split into four smaller crossroads companies after winning its fight. Attempts at countywide cooperation led to farmers battling Main Street for control or to the formation of companies like the KCTC, countywide but cooperative in name only.[42] In Freeborn County, many crossroads communities created by the creamery movement held meetings in the winter of 1903–04 to form rural phone companies.[43] Farmers would not assent to the organization of a countywide company, any more than a countywide creamery, in Albert Lea. Technology allowed one phone company to serve a whole county. Yet phone cooperatives were grass-roots efforts; farmers would not voluntarily and spontaneously organize a centralized, county-seat cooperative.

In strong dairy counties like Freeborn, creameries played an indirect role; creamery officers might assist in organizing a phone company.[44] In some areas, farmers' clubs did the organizing.[45] In Center City, Chisago's county seat, the county auditor helped to organize the Chisago County Mutual Telephone Company (not a true countywide company).[46] Elsewhere merchants aided the organizing efforts with the goal of linking customers to their stores. A local correspondent hailed the new phone line from Irving to Atwater and declared, "the merchants and farmers can hello back and forth as much as they wish to."[47]

The nature of the group that organized a cooperative affected its character. Norwegian-American farmers of Manchester organized an unincorporated company that relied on ethnic solidarity, minimized cash payments, and assessed members pro rata for actual costs rather than charging fixed rates. Each member bought "his or her own telephone, poles, wires and apparatus."[48] The creamery and farmers' mutual in Manchester were run along similar lines. In marked contrast, Chisago Mutual, started by county-seat politicos and villagers, was an incorporated company that bought its poles and equipment and paid cash for services—even those of its members and directors.[49]

All rural phone cooperatives shared some similarities. They held annual meetings and elected boards, though in some the board met only once or twice a year (boards faced few major decisions).[50] As small, non-profit, customer-owned companies, they were not attractive investment opportunities. They usually followed Rochdale rules of one vote per person, a limit on the number of shares one person could own, and a ceiling on stock dividends (often there were no dividends). They kept share prices relatively low, ranging from twenty to thirty dollars per share.[51] An attempt by one company to depart from these rules illustrates how firmly farmers believed in them and how hard it was to unite county-seat merchants and farmers in a countywide cooperative.

To raise capital in order to pay debts and to finance construction of more phone lines, the Redwood County Rural Telephone Company (RCRTC) board called a special shareholders meeting in June 1905. It proposed to make the RCRTC a good investment opportunity by issuing preferred stock that earned guaranteed interest, giving each share one vote, and doubling phone rentals to one dollar per month, thus departing from the low-cost, low-fee principle. Reporters colorfully depicted the resulting storm of disapproval. Farmers "turn[ed] out in force from all parts of the county" for a premeeting caucus at the courthouse.[52]

Apparently held in a courtroom, the actual meeting began in the afternoon. The company manager, "the particular object" of attack, "played the other side of the railing for safety." The appropriately named W. H. Gold, a banker and the RCRTC president, defended the proposed one vote per share, saying that "he would not run a bank on any other plan." A farmers' spokesman defended "the mutual plan—one vote to each man" and was "vigorously applauded." An urban-rural split seemed imminent when farmer A. D. Stewart offered a compromise resolution. It gave the board the right to issue preferred stock (with no voting rights) and guaranteed 7 percent interest to all shareholders (both common and preferred). It kept the one-vote-per-person rule and the low-cost rural rate of fifty cents per month.

This debate appears to be an exception. In other rural phone cooperatives, these principles regarding votes and shares were never questioned, despite the omnipresent problem of insufficient capital.

Financial Problems of Rural Telephone Cooperatives

Selling shares at twenty to thirty dollars might not raise enough funds to construct lines, much less supply working capital. In December 1906, Chisago Mutual's general manager halted construction after proceeds from sales of stock had been spent. The company borrowed three thousand dollars to finish construction.[53] (Companies whose members donated labor, tools, and materials did not need to borrow in order to pay construction costs.) To obtain working capital and to guarantee a monthly cash flow, Chisago charged monthly phone rental fees of seventy-five cents for members and one dollar for nonmembers. Yet an elected board was reluctant to raise the members' fee by twenty-five cents even when rental income did not cover operating expenses plus depreciation. Despite a consensus that the increase was needed, the directors cautiously deferred it to the next annual meeting. A large turnout of seventy shareholders listened to "a lengthy discussion of how to increase the revenue" but only agreed "that this question be laid over to the next annual meeting of stockholders." A customer-controlled company had trouble raising fees (it finally did).[54]

A monthly fee had advantages besides providing a regular cash flow. It was clearly a charge for services rendered. Customers could not complain about its fairness unless service was poor. More problematic were assessments. When payable in one lump sum, they did not provide a reliable cash flow through the year and were harder to collect. The member saw them as his or her share of the company's expenses, not as a fee for services rendered. If he or she disagreed with the board's spending practices, payment might be withheld on grounds they were unfair or unwise. (In township mutuals, assessments had more legitimacy because they were levied to pay for specific fire losses.)

One of Union Telephone's four successors, the Eastern Union Telephone Company, used the assessment system.[55] It had an unpredictable cash flow. At year's end, its treasurer or secretary sometimes had to pay the bills himself and wait for his "loan" to be repaid from a special assessment.[56] In May 1912 it faced a $150 deficit, almost 20 percent of its annual budget, so Secretary D. F. Seneschal loaned it that amount. Though it levied two assessments "to pay the outstanding debts" and "for Telephone service," it used proceeds from both to pay delinquent accounts payable, not to reimburse Seneschal. At the next annual meeting, the members renewed Seneschal's loan. He was finally repaid in May 1914, two years after the company had borrowed the money.[57]

Collecting assessments could be difficult. In 1912 a five-dollar lump-sum assessment was not pocket change to cash-poor farmers, who might question its fairness, wisdom, or legality.[58] The Erhards Grove phone company (Otter Tail County) levied a three-dollar assessment to hire "2 girls to look after" the switchboard. They could not collect from Carl Swenson: "We asked him to pay the three dollars which was necessary for the switching expenses, but in Carl Swenson's opinion it was not necessary."[59] Assessments strained members' loyalty and led them to complain anew about service. In 1910 Eastern Union's secretary reported that the delinquents' "refusal to pay was principally on the grounds that they got poor service, the wire being in poor shape." Often, at the annual meeting, members had to appoint a collections committee for each phone line.[60] Or the board had to threaten to cut off service in order to force delinquent members to settle up.[61]

Phone cooperatives were voluntary associations performing quasi-governmental functions. Members voted on rules for phone use that the officers then tried to enforce. They asked farmers to buy shares but had to deny service to those who refused. They could not allow free riders who received service without assuming the costs and duties of membership. Chisago Mutual's shareholders (who had already financed construction) insisted that nonshareholders along already-constructed lines be denied the right to buy shares.[62] They could not join after capital costs were met but must pay the higher nonshareholder rental fee forever. Assessment-based companies did not offer service to nonmembers and tried to ensure that they did not obtain free use of neighbors' phones. Eastern Union voted that nonmembers "pay the usual fee of 15 [cents] for 3 minute talk, the owner of the Phone so used shall be held responcible [sic] for the pay."[63] Chisago Mutual also fined members for allowing nonmembers to make calls using their telephones.[64]

The question facing these companies was whether such rules could be enforced. Eavesdropping on party lines and members' loyalty made phone cooperatives better able to enforce such rules than private firms. Yet enforcement of rules dealing with members' behavior in their homes would be difficult. No data showing members being fined for noncompliance was found in any company's records, but no evidence of payment of message fees by nonmembers was discovered either.

Shareholders also tried to protect their financial interests by requiring that the cost of new lines be covered by sales of stock to residents of new service areas. Few phone cooperatives showed an entrepreneurial spirit by extending service into new areas in hopes that service charges would pay for the new line.[65] Such practices contributed to the multiplication of small phone cooperatives. Residents of new areas preferred to start a new company rather than submit to the old one's penny-pinching members.

A major cost of expansion was operating a "central," or switchboard, in each place where two phone lines intersected (the "switch" was frequently in a farmhouse) and in all villages (it was often in a store).[66] No member could complain that a central was not a necessity. Eastern Union paid for switching at five places—Atwater, Crow River, Irving, Grove City, and Paynesville—all within a radius of seven miles of the crossroads community of Irving, its center of operations. At some places, it shared the costs with other companies.[67] The first operator of its Irving switchboard was a storekeeper and its treasurer, who could easily collect assessments and other charges. By 1912 it contracted with Mille Anderson and Amanda Anderson to operate the Irving central for $250 per year. Three cooperatives shared this switchboard and jointly hired the Andersons.[68]

Storekeeper-operators were usually males whose service was often less than satisfactory.[69] Rural phone companies, like urban ones, gradually dropped male operators and hired females. One urban phone official summarized the benefits of hiring females: "They are steadier, do not drink beer and are always on hand."[70] They were cheaper. And, for farmhouse switchboards, women were more often indoors to answer calls because, in most ethnic groups, the sexual division of labor assigned most field work to males.[71]

Switching costs caused some cooperatives to adopt the governmental role of ruling some phone calls socially useful and some not. In its contract with the Andersons, Eastern Union decreed, "Calls for doctors at any time shall be given free to all patrons."[72] The Stacy Telephone Company members voted "that the weather report be sent out on the lines every week day," and fire alarms rated the same service.[73] Gossip calls were not deemed socially useful and thus could be "taxed." One director called for fees "large enough to kill kid and gossip talk.... We have had in the last ten days twenty-one calls from one family[;] these calls were all gossip." Gossip calls were "not a paying proposition at any price & cheap talk keeps us from our work."[74]

Customers whose access to the party line was limited by gossipers' long calls were more than willing to tax them. One Kandiyohi company's shareholders left "the matter... of the Crescent Beach line" to the board "with instructions to see that the promiscuous talkers over the line to Willmar were made to pay more for the privilege than has previously been required."[75] As little democracies voicing local consensus, cooperatives could better act against gossip calls than could private firms lacking their direct means of ascertaining and adopting public opinion.

Phone Principalities Negotiate: Connections and Misconnections

Neighboring phone cooperatives negotiated issues of common concern, which were many, given telephony's connective character. The companies tended to be quite small, serving one or several townships. Like hundreds of tiny German principalities sprinkled across Minnesota, they dealt with each other as sovereign entities. Starting, operating, and ending exchanges or centrals; charging for calls across company boundaries; connecting the lines of different companies; allocating switching costs—these issues were not decided in the market but by one cooperative's committee consulting another's committee.

On March 1, 1905, the Eastern Union board chose a three-man committee to "meet with representatives of the Western Union and North Star Tel. Co. [to] decid[e] on an exchange at Irving." On March 16, the three delegations agreed to purchase jointly a switchboard and pay the operating expenses. They negotiated switchboard hours, set a charge for night calls, and chose an operator.[76] None could decide unilaterally to eliminate a switchboard. It had to consult the others.[77]

Cooperatives had to agree to connect their lines or to serve customers living on the borders between them.[78] Chisago Mutual's shareholders authorized a committee to "confer with adjoining telephone companies in regard to free telephone connection between" their subscribers "living close to each other." Its board denied a Washington County cooperative's request for free connections with Chisago.[79] No law or regulation forced these sovereign entities to make free connections or any connections at all. If they failed to connect, customers living on the border of two companies' service areas could not phone neighbors. At Simpson (Olmsted County), farmers lived at the edges of three uncommunicative phone systems. One local resident wrote, "we now have ... no established service from any one line ... this makes it necessary for Farmers to have two to three fones [sic] in order to have service with [their] neighbors."[80] Not surprisingly, these farmers wished to start their own company.

Usually a farmer had one phone, and his cooperative had a local monopoly. Another type of cooperative used a local monopoly to achieve
greater efficiency and lower per-unit costs. But phone cooperatives were
too small and telephony too dependent on extensive linkages for them to
achieve efficiency. They internalized transactions, but with so few members there was little business to be internalized. An enormous number of
transactions were still external to each company, and these were not decided by the market but by negotiations. Each company had to haggle
with the others about prices and services—issues that market mechanisms could have handled much more efficiently.[81]

Enforcement of agreements among these sovereign powers was sometimes impossible. Witness the dilemma facing A. E. Wilcox, manager of
a phone cooperative in Bricelyn village (Faribault County). Six farm
lines connected to Bricelyn. These tiny cooperatives agreed to pay switching fees to the Bricelyn company, which ran the switchboard there. But
farmhouse centrals were needed where two rural phone lines intersected. At one such point ("A.") northwest of town, a farmer from Blaine
Telephone Company refused to pay the Bricelyn switching fee. Wilcox
complained, "A. refuses to pay Bricelyn . . . on the claim that he is a 'Central' the same as we are, and inasmuch as we do not pay him for switching, he will not pay us." Wilcox admitted that Bricelyn used "A."'s switch
"three or four times per month."[82]

Farmer "A." with his home switchboard insisted that he, too, was a
phone principality with sovereignty. Though "A." was its member, Blaine
refused to make him pay his share of the fee the Blaine company owed to
Bricelyn. When Wilcox tried to collect "A."'s share from the Blaine company's treasurer, the latter replied, "A will settle with you personally."[83]
The market solution was for Wilcox to cut off access to Bricelyn for "A."
and those farmers who used "A."'s switch to call Bricelyn. Then the relative value of their access to Bricelyn versus Bricelyn's access to them
would be decided in the market. Yet this matter could not be so decided,
for it had been decided by the two cooperatives' agreement. But Blaine
would not enforce the terms on "A." It was so small, informal, and democratic that it would forgo its power over "A." rather than risk internal
conflict. Wilcox was frustrated; "the great trouble," he concluded, was to
make the Blaine people "understand that they are a company, rather
than a lot of individuals."

The matter could not be resolved democratically at an annual meeting. Bricelyn and Blaine were separate sovereign entities. Wilcox had no standing at Blaine's annual meeting. Disconnection was an unsatisfactory resolution. Interconnected phone principalities hated to "disorganize the service by disconnecting the line, which makes bad blood all around."[84] Used to negotiation and cooperation, they hated to settle disputes in the market or to go to court to enforce terms.[85]

They faced market mechanisms when dealing with private village exchanges. Entrepreneurs were not shy about using market power against them; cooperatives were used to internal democratic votes or external talks between equals. In both, they expected fairness. Market power did not seem fair. The Balaton-Russell cooperative complained when both Balaton and Russell exchanges charged a switching fee for all its phones. Such double-charging, complained the cooperative's secretary, was unfair, since "patrons tributary to, say[,] Balaton . . . would very seldom call Russell Central & patrons living near Russell very seldom call Balaton." Each exchange should halve its fee to reflect that fact.[86]

Yet a private owner could not make concessions that seemed fair but were feasible only if customers did not take advantage of him. In Wadena County, some members of one rural cooperative were closer to Hewitt and some closer to Verndale. The owner of the Verndale exchange offered a market solution: the members could pay five cents per call for measured service or three dollars per year for unlimited switching service at Verndale. He faced the free rider problem, the " 'smuggling' of calls." Members with unlimited service allowed their measured-service neighbors to use their phones to call Verndale.[87] He could not enforce rules or count on customer loyalty to stop this practice.

Conflict arose between entrepreneurs maximizing profit and cooperatives stressing low-cost service and fairness. One private company tried to coerce farmers into selling their rural line by charging them prohibitively high switching rates.[88] In another case, Grant County farmers who arose early had their own idea of reasonable service hours. They griped about a village exchange that did not open before 7:00 A.M.[89]

Township and village phone systems faced strong local pressures to settle their disputes. Farmers needed phone links to buyers and suppliers in the village. They could threaten to set up their own village exchange, but that was unlikely to succeed without the village council's approval.[90]

Merchants desired phone links with rural customers and could prevail upon a village exchange to be reasonable or to become a cooperative.[91] The *Willmar Tribune's* summary of conditions in one town could be applied to many other locales. The newspaper noted that "trade has never been better in the history of New London," since it "organized a co-operative exchange and offered free connections to all farmer lines that would build into" town. There were "no less than eleven firms that sell groceries and all seem to be doing well." Charging farmers for phone connections or for calls into town was as counterproductive as putting "toll gates on the roads leading into town."[92]

Farmer Lines versus Regional and Long-Distance Telephone Lines

Local pressure for compromise was less effective against regional firms or long-distance toll companies. Farmers' and merchants' buying power counted for little against the MCTC, Northwestern Telephone, or the independent Tri-State Telephone & Telegraph. This lack of clout showed phone cooperatives' marginal role in the industry. Several west-central towns experienced sharp disputes in 1907–08 between cooperatives and the MCTC, which owned urban exchanges but focused on its long-distance business as Northwestern's subsidiary. The MCTC used its control of urban exchanges "as a club" to dissuade rural lines from connecting to rival Tri-State for long-distance service.[93] In Pope County, rural companies threatened to set up a second exchange in Glenwood, the county seat. The Glenwood Commercial Club mediated to prevent that occurrence, which would force Glenwood citizens to buy two phones.[94] In Chippewa County, a "declared war" raged. MCTC "disconnected with the farmer lines," and Clara City residents threatened to drop MCTC service "unless connection was made with the rural lines."[95] After a six-month stalemate, the rural lines bought the Clara City exchange.[96]

Switching fees, toll charges, and long-distance service were also bones of contention between rural companies and the two long-distance companies. The president of People's Co-operative Telephone Company of Williams (Lake of the Woods County) complained, "we receive no percentage for handling the business they get off our line." Were farmer lines "compelled to donate the use of their line to the long distance [line] and the public free of charge[?] What must a Telephone Co do to get to the crib?"[97] Long-distance companies had market clout. The access they provided to thousands of phones in cities like St. Cloud or the Twin Cities was more in demand than the access to twenty or a hundred households provided by farmer lines. The former brought a fee; the latter came free. Here the market ruled and negotiating was futile.

What rural residents could control was service in their locality. Long-distance companies could not dictate who would provide local service. In Chisago County, Tri-State began to assemble equipment in Center City to build rural lines and persuaded some farmers to sign contracts.[98] However, local residents met "to discuss...establishing a rural telephone system with local headquarters."[99] Once a cooperative was begun with local support, Tri-State had to agree to its terms.[100]

Forcing long-distance companies to compete against each other was the cooperatives' best strategy for increasing their market power. In May 1909, Stacy's board told its secretary "to write to the Northwestern Tel. Co. and Tri State Tel. Co. for arrangements for better Telephone service." (It was then using Northwestern.) Terms from the two companies were discussed at a board meeting, then at the annual meeting in January 1910, to which "Mr. McDurmott" from Tri-State and "Mr. Whitney" from Northwestern came and competed head-to-head. By a margin of twenty-six to seventeen, members voted to connect with Tri-State.[101] This strategy could succeed as long as independents like Tri-State competed against Bell licensees such as Northwestern. In December 1913, however, Bell's landmark Kingsbury Commitment ended strong competition. A single, Bell-managed national phone network was created, with the independents safely in control of their areas while Bell companies consolidated service in their regions.[102] Appeal to state regulators now became the only recourse for cooperatives.

State and Federal Regulation of the Telephone Industry

The public dialogue over state regulation revealed how marginal rural phone cooperatives were in Minnesota. They were apparently not mentioned during this 1911–15 debate, although many of the state's five hundred phone companies were rural cooperatives, and the majority of citizens lived in rural areas and small towns.[103] The national debate shaped the state one. The alternatives were free competition, nationalization, municipal ownership, or a continued American Telephone and Telegraph (AT&T) (as Bell had become) monopoly. AT&T argued that the phone industry was a "natural monopoly." Having more than one company in a service area made no sense (as some farmers saw with several phone principalities in one area). According to AT&T's spokesman, the telephone linked people, but "two or more competing telephone plants ... separate people, and thus operate antagonistically to the purpose for which the telephone was established." AT&T offered a compromise, a "commission-regulated network manager system": one national network with long-distance lines managed by AT&T under state and federal regulation but with independents free to run local and regional systems.[104] That plan won out.

Minnesota followed with state regulation. After a 1911 bill for regulation by the state tax commission failed, Representative Frank E. Minette of Sauk Centre introduced a bill in the 1913 legislative session to give regulatory authority to the Railroad and Warehouse Commission. Advocates of municipal ownership, such as Victor Lawson's *Willmar Tribune*, attacked it.[105] It passed in both the Senate and House but was vetoed by Governor Eberhart, who wanted a public utility commission (which would likely be appointed by and controlled by him), not a Railroad and Warehouse Commission (elected and independent of him) with one more duty tacked on to its existing functions.[106] To the grudging approbation of the *Willmar Tribune* and *St. Paul Pioneer Press*, Minette's resubmitted bill passed in 1915 and was signed into law by Governor Winfield S. Hammond.[107]

Neither editors nor legislators nor governors discussed the bill's impact on rural phone cooperatives. To small-town and urban Progressive leaders, rural cooperatives were a constant in the equation. They would continue to extend phone service into townships no matter what laws were enacted. Legislators may have been afraid to admit that the law would have a pronounced impact on them for fear a storm of rural protest would overwhelm the bill.

The Minette law stirred up a hornets' nest anyway. The Railroad and Warehouse Commission was to obtain rate-fixing and regulatory authority on July 1, 1915. Before that date, private phone companies hiked rates, which produced "an awful uproar all over the county about this Minnette [*sic*] Law."[108] The attorney general ruled that cooperatives were included under the law and were subject to its antidiscrimination provision: "They are public utilities and they cannot refuse to install a telephone and furnish services to one applying for the same on the sole grounds that he is not a stockholder in the company."[109] (In 1913 the Minnesota Supreme Court had ruled that an assessment-funded rural cooperative did not have to serve a nonshareholder.)[110] The attorney general also ruled that they could not have different rates for shareholders and nonshareholders, nor a rental fee for nonshareholders and assessments for shareholders.[111] Both of these practices became discriminatory trade practices.

This seemingly wise, Solomonic decision did not reflect reality: purchasers of shares in phone cooperatives were not investing in a business but paying construction costs for their phone lines, costs normally paid by stock sales and not by per-phone charges. In order to encourage stock ownership and membership, phone cooperatives had to discriminate between those who helped pay these costs and those who refused to pay. Also the commission would decide if their rate increases were reasonable and if their negotiated agreements with each other violated the antidiscrimination clause. A Kenyon man complained that rural exchanges had given each other free connections, but the new law made that illegal, so "it now costs me 10 [cents] to talk to my nearest neighbors." The law ended the cooperative's right to set up a competing exchange in a village but not private companies' right to run competing lines into rural areas.[112]

The cooperatives brought phone service to farmers who surprised the industry by demanding it, but they entered the field too late to play other than a marginal role—filling in the edges of the phone system. There were too many of them.[113] The inefficiencies of negotiating connections and switching in nearly every rural township were considerable. They failed to unite to protect their interests. As marginal entities, they were at a disadvantage when negotiating with long-distance companies and even with the village exchanges. They were ignored during the Progressive-era debate over ownership and regulation of the phone industry. They strengthened crossroads cooperation and local democracy, but most were formed from 1900 to 1914 during the heyday of the crossroads community, before automobility and the integration of rural life into a centralized economy eroded the social and economic functions of the crossroads town. The tiny phone principalities were the last hurrah for local grass-roots cooperation shaped by amateurs, not experts.

12

County Agents as Cooperators

*"The farmer now pays a handsome salary
to this army of undesired instructors"*

WHEN THE STATE GOVERNMENT began regulating phone cooperatives, it broke sharply with its former avoidance of any significant role in
cooperatives' affairs. The Minette law was unlike the statute on cooperative associations, little changed since 1870. The tradition of governmental
regulation of utilities made the difference in the case of phone cooperatives. Laissez-faire notions of government's role in the economy limited
the state's involvement with other types of cooperatives to licensing
and inspection duties. Also, state officials could point to the U.S. Department of Agriculture (USDA) as the logical agency to handle any other
necessary government interaction with rural cooperatives. As patronage
appointees, these officials did not need to help cooperatives in order to
add to their list of clients and justify their state agencies' continued existence. Agrarian protest would later cause Republican politicians to advocate state assistance to cooperatives, but agrarian radicalism was at low
ebb in 1900–1916.

Matters were quite different with the University of Minnesota—and
the university would become a catalyst for state aid to cooperatives and a
major ally in that effort. The Morrill Act mandated that the university
aid agriculture, which could be construed as a rationale for aiding farm
cooperatives. Few traditions limited the role of innovative university
extension and research programs. The university needed clients to expand such programs; in the 1890s, its dairy school had shown how cooperatives could help it do so. A Progressive-era stress on experts enabled
the university to increase its role beyond what Theophilus Haecker had

done in the early 1890s. In the process, university experts redefined and reshaped rural cooperation.

Wary Partners:
University and Farmer Learn to Cooperate

Since the 1870s, farmers had suspected the university would fail to fulfill its responsibilities, as specified in the Morrill Act, to aid agriculture.[1] Land-grant monies "helped to save the university," but it continued to offer only a classical education. Farmers' sons took Greek and attended the university to escape farming, not to study it.[2] Farmers wanted to learn more about agriculture but not from the university.[3] They could not easily travel to the campus. When it offered a one-hundred-day short course in agriculture and a lecture series, no one enrolled in the course, and the lectures were attended mainly by Twin Cities residents.[4] From 1887 to 1907, Oren Gregg's Minnesota Farmers' Institutes were its attempt to deliver agricultural education in the way farmers wanted. Although a university employee, Gregg had much independence in running the institutes, which held week-long sessions of lectures and demonstrations in towns throughout the state. A practical farmer, he "generally opposed the use of men professionally trained in agriculture" and relied on practical farmers so the institutes did not promote the university's expertise, which was still under construction.[5]

Gregg was what historian Alan I. Marcus termed a "systematic" farmer, not a "scientific" farmer or agricultural scientist. Systematic farmers made farming a business-minded system: crop rotation, diversification, manuring. Keeping good records, they designed systems that worked in their area and wrote articles to inform other farmers. Scientific farmers experimented to discover the laws of agriculture. Agricultural scientists insisted that only trained specialists could use the scientific method. Others must follow their advice.[6] The three groups fought over the role of late nineteenth-century agricultural colleges and experiment stations.

Other states ran these "agricultural science touring road shows," or institutes, but there the systematic farmers did not achieve Gregg's dominance.[7] By 1900 the growing corps of experts at the university's farm campus chafed under his policy of excluding them. In August 1901 the Farmers' Institutes board discussed a "policy of exchanging our [university] workers for speakers from other states," but backed Gregg's opposite policy.[8] Yet Gregg's position became untenable as the experts' prestige grew, and they played on home-state pride by urging local (university) speakers, not "speakers from other states." In August 1907, Gregg resigned. University expert Archie D. Wilson replaced him and pledged "to incorporate into the Institute work more local talent."[9]

The University Incorporates Cooperation into Its Program

Wilson incorporated a cautious promotion of cooperation—farmers' clubs, contests for rural school children, "school house" institutes, and other

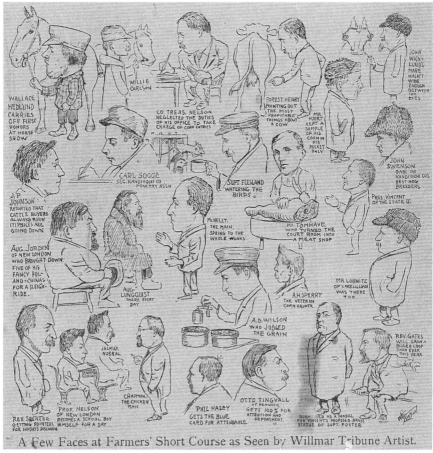

A Few Faces at Farmers' Short Course as Seen by Willmar Tribune Artist.

Under Archie D. Wilson's management, the university's week-long Farmers' Short Course in Willmar in January 1912 used university experts like Forest Henry, President Vincent, and Wilson himself. Eben Lawson gently caricatured the experts and their clients.

projects. These "constituted extension work in everything but name," used university staff, and "reflected the growing desire of the scientists to assume the entire burden of off-campus teaching."[10] The *Minnesota Farmers' Institute Annual* for 1907 contained much of Wilson's program: articles on boys' and girls' clubs, the good roads movement, a farmers' club in Wrenshall (Carlton County), and an article on cooperation by Sidney M. Owen, editor of *Farm, Stock and Home*. Owen's article did not describe a cooperative; instead he discussed farmers cooperating to grow one specialized crop. The Wrenshall club did not displace a private business but had social and educational purposes. Wilson urged farmers to form more clubs: "Such an organization offers a basis for more effective Farmers' Institute work." Instead of communicating with farmers individually, the institutes could interact with thirty farmers in a club. Some farmers' clubs engaged in joint purchasing, a step to further cooperation.[11]

Rural cooperatives made other university experts' tasks easier, too. Specialists in animal husbandry could give advice to livestock shipping associations, not individually to thousands of farmers; horticultural specialists, to fruit-growers' associations.

Wilson expanded the "Co-operation Department" in the 1908 *Annual*, which urged farmers to stay loyal to their creameries and not ship cream to centralizers.[12] He included a noncontroversial article on township mutuals and a brief question-and-answer section on cooperatives in the 1909 *Annual*.[13] In 1910 the institutes' lecturer on cooperation wrote innocuous articles on "Co-operation in Production" and "Closer Relations between Our Rural Districts and Towns." An article on joint marketing of garden produce highlighted harmonious relations between farmers' clubs and the Commercial Club of Duluth.[14] The 1911 *Annual* promoted livestock shipping associations, more controversial because they displaced private shippers.[15]

With the start of the Agricultural Extension Division in 1909, university experts moved beyond the institutes' format. In 1912 they introduced the key university-farmer linkage, the county-agent system, which used one-on-one instruction and talks before groups. Since creameries, township mutuals, farmers' stores, rural phone companies, and farmers' elevators existed, they could not ignore cooperation, but they promoted it cautiously. Its popularity might transfer to them, but so might its history of controversy. The potential advantages to them seemed to outweigh the risks, however. Farmers might take their advice when that was passed along by cooperatives, which vouched for their credibility.

Experts, Cooperation, and Three Progressive-era "Languages"

Agricultural extension work, the county agent, and the growing role of the university expert were all closely linked to the Progressive-era Country Life Movement (1900–20). During these two decades, historian David B. Danbom noted, "the interest of urban people in agriculture was probably more intense than ever before or since." They were seeking to make farmers more efficient in order to lower urban food costs, increase U.S. exports, and raise industrial productivity. When they focused on rural life, they often assumed its inferiority and prescribed more institutions, more consolidated schools, and more expert advice. They advocated more cooperatives, but more to "help standardize and improve food products, and . . . lower the cost of food for urban consumers." Cooperatives meant organization, and Country Life experts felt that would help correct the deficiencies of rural life.[16]

Cooperation fit Progressive-era values. Historian Daniel T. Rodgers argued that Progressives used "three distinct social languages": (1) "antimonopolism," (2) "an emphasis on social bonds and the social nature of human beings," rather than rugged individualism, and (3) "the language of social efficiency." All three attacked "arbitrary, unregulated individual power" but for different reasons and with different alternatives in mind.[17] Experts preferred the last two.

University experts almost never used antimonopolism to promote cooperation. That term was associated with Populism, and they shunned it. It applied especially to terminal markets, and, at first, they avoided terminal-market cooperation. They often used the language of social bonds. The 1913 *Minnesota Farmers' Institute Annual* featured cooperation and criticized "the old individualistic regime" in which investors "received an undue share of the earnings."[18] In 1914 the Douglas County agent attacked the old belief "that we as farmers were independent." Now farmers knew that "We have certain problems that belong to the community and all must co-operate if we are to succeed."[19]

The experts saw rural America as deficient in social bonds. Isolated farmsteads encouraged rugged individualism and discouraged social interaction—unlike in Europe's villages.[20] In promoting farmers' clubs, Archie Wilson claimed that "People are . . . not usually happy when isolated" and are unable to "develop properly except in groups." Farming "tends to keep people too much to themselves." Farmers' clubs brought "people to-

gether monthly or semi-monthly... a very desirable change from the ordinary routine of farm life." This led to economic gains. "A farmers' club
is the logical forerunner of coöperation," Wilson argued. "It gets the people
of a community acquainted and increases the confidence of each in the
other."[21]

Going beyond the concept of social bonds, university experts used the
language of social efficiency, "the new bureaucratic language of budgets,
human costs, and system," which "translat[ed] social sins into the new-
fangled language of social waste." Preferred by scientists who disliked
the "embarrassing pieties" of the language of social bonds, it combined
"the prestige of science with the prestige of the well-organized business
firm and factory."[22] In a 1916 speech to the Farmers' Grain Dealers' Association, University of Minnesota President George E. Vincent remarked,
"You cannot make any address in these days without using the word
efficient."[23]

The university stressed efficiency as the main reason for rural cooperation. Where it criticized private stores or elevators, it was for inefficiency,
not monopoly. College of Agriculture Dean Albert F. Woods defined cooperation's benefits in mathematical terms devoid of embarrassing pieties:
"Through... proper use of these methods of co-operation, the overhead
cost of production may be distributed over the maximum number of
acres."[24] The mission of the university's new Bureau of Research in Agricultural Economics was to discover "actual causes of waste and loss" in
marketing farm products and to compare the efficiency of "different
agencies performing middlemen functions."[25] As Danbom noted, "efficiency" had two meanings: "economic efficiency (increased income relative to expenditures)" and "productive efficiency (increased production
per acre and/or per man)." Country Lifers and university experts often
preferred the second; cooperatives usually sought the first.[26]

University Experts Alter the Meaning of "Cooperation"

As university experts used Progressive-era languages to justify cooperation, they subtly redefined it by removing old connotations and adding
new ones. It could mean almost anything an advocate wanted it to mean.
As Vincent said, "I can think of no word with which people juggle more
unsuccessfully than the word co-operation. How easily and smoothly it
can be used."[27] Redefining the word was not necessarily deceitful but

was very possibly intentional since the redefinition so exactly suited the experts' purposes—although no letters or memos exist to prove intent.

Removing old connotations came first. University experts and their allies in the farm press first stripped Minnesota's cooperative movement of its more controversial history from 1870 to 1900. They occasionally used the inspiring story of the Rochdale pioneers but dropped stories about Grangers and Alliancemen cooperating. Few were the references to pre-1900 cooperatives, except for the mostly nonpolitical cooperative creameries. And these few were strangely de-politicized. Professor Carl W. Thompson referred to cooperation's "era of speculative activity" in "the eighties and the nineties" but failed to mention the Alliance.[28] The university's policy statement noted, "Strong movements have been organized among the farmers to 'fight the interest[s]'" but did not name them. "When agriculture is efficiently organized for business and social purposes . . . the clashing will cease."[29]

Efficiency was an abstract term that connoted a world without opponents where waste was the sole enemy. When Dean Woods analyzed rural retailing, he saw inefficiency and waste, not attempts by retailers and middlemen to profit at farmers' expense. He blamed the surplus of rural retail outlets on the "unreasonable demands, buying inefficiency and laziness of the consumers." Though he faintly praised cooperative stores, he recommended "some method of district consolidation of middlemen agencies under municipal control, as public service corporations." Middlemen, not consumers, should cooperate.[30] Efficiency, not democracy, was the goal.

Having eradicated cooperation's history and its opponents, experts then argued that cooperation was in its beginning stages when caution and academic study were needed. At a 1912 conference, Thompson advocated "small beginnings in co-operation rather than the attempting of too elaborate plans." His remarks sparked "general criticism" from Equity members, who realized cooperation had a longer history than he gave it.[31] A university ally, The Farmer, ridiculed this caution "after almost twenty-five years of successful co-operation among the farmers of this state, originated and developed largely by themselves." It scoffed at advice that farmers go slow lest they "make a mistake."[32] Provoked by the experts' paternalism, The Farmer nevertheless approved their focus on local cooperation.

Experts and their allies promoted "simple local organizations" to avoid the political battles that accompanied terminal-level ones. Going slow was best; rapid growth might arouse merchant-farmer tensions and prove to be "suicidal" to their extension programs. These programs, not cooperatives, were in the crucial early stage and needed town-country alliances. It was their programs that lacked a history and needed cautious handling.

The farmer became less a citizen fighting political battles and more a client listening to expert advice. The experts stressed the need for careful studies, which could best be done by themselves. A 1913 committee on cooperative marketing reported that now "the principal work should be investigational and educational, rather than propagandist," and the university should do all three. It would conduct "the statistical study of the whole field." It had teachers, so it would carry out the educational work. The "propagandist work" could be done through its extension department and bulletins. Only a listening role was left to farmers and cooperatives.[33]

"Cooperation" lost its specific meaning in the experts' redefinition. President Vincent urged people "to distinguish between co-operation in the technical sense of the term and co-operation in its larger sense." The larger and vaguer sense won out. Wilson cited the family as the "best example" of cooperation, in which "we find all individuals working for the common good."[34] C. R. Barns, who edited an agricultural bulletin for the university, cited municipal services such as libraries, utilities, hospitals, streets, parks, and sidewalks as examples of how "in the city the principle of co-operation has found a larger development" than in the country. That was not true. Barns admitted urbanites cooperated "involuntarily" through taxation and mere residence. Yet Rochdale cooperation was not an involuntary regime imposed on rural residents by majority vote but a tradition of active, purposeful voluntarism.[35] Another writer argued that consolidated schools were "one of the most important phases" of cooperation—although experts often forced it on unwilling farmers.[36] Cooperatives, as voluntary associations, were not like largely involuntary government programs. When experts sold rural school consolidation to farmers as "co-operation," they showed an ability to make it a testimonial for almost any proposal.

They used it to mean farmers' and merchants' mutual support of their programs, when it had signified farmers' attempts to bypass merchants. The 1913 *Annual* stated that cooperation was based on "a union of the forces of a community for greater efficiency; not a union of one class

of people to fight another class." Yet class battles were a frequent occurrence in the history of rural cooperation.[37]

The Capstone of the Extension System:
The County Agent

The university needed unity between town and country in order to develop
the county-agent system, the capstone in its agricultural research and
extension work. A few bulletins, Farmers' Institutes, and an educational
train could not convert all farmers into its clients. "Many miles intervene
between St. Anthony Park and a farmer in Nobles or Kittson County."[38]
At a 1911 conference, Dean Woods explained that "the men most in need
of help do not read farm papers or bulletins to any great extent." Even if
they did, they could not understand them. The university had "to get in
personal touch with them on their own farms."[39] Farmers' clubs helped,
yet they met only periodically.[40] Experts could hardly take the word to all
of them. The university needed reliable local representatives.

The university first sent a representative to individual farms in 1902
when Professor Andrew Boss began a farm management survey in rural
Northfield. He assigned a graduate of the university's agricultural school
to travel a daily route and collect crop production data from about a
dozen farms. Boss discovered that "we could very profitably make [the
graduate] a sort of social leader and he became the organizer of farmers'
clubs, and lyceums . . . which offered us an opportunity to reach the farmers of the country."[41] Boss added routes near Marshall and Halstad. This
method could not reach all the state's farmers, but it taught the experts
the value of having an agent visiting farms.

The USDA was developing a county-agent system in the South. Started
in 1904 in Texas and Louisiana, it soon had seven hundred agents throughout the South giving on-site instruction in farming techniques. It received funding from John D. Rockefeller.[42] While a USDA plant pathologist,
Dean Woods had worked with this program, and he praised it highly.[43]

In 1910, with funding from the Minnesota Federation of Commercial
Clubs, the university set up farm demonstration tracts. A farmer agreed
to follow its experts' advice, and they used his farm to show farmers the
benefits of their techniques. Tracts were to be located near towns with
"an active commercial club" to guarantee "necessary local interest" (and
funding).[44] This step decentralized the university's work but did not
bring experts to each farm.

The university lacked the financial resources to expand the program. Twin Cities business leaders brought the county agent to the Upper Midwest, starting with North Dakota. "Implement manufacturers, lumber men, grain buyers, and bankers" formed the Better Farming Association of North Dakota, with a Minneapolis lumber dealer as its head. They secured financial backing from James Hill, his Great Northern, the other railroads serving North Dakota, and the North Dakota Bankers' Association. In January 1912 they sent out their first county agents to teach farmers better farming methods.[45] Other businessmen followed suit. In May 1912, Julius Rosenwald, president of Sears, Roebuck, "offered to contribute $1,000 to any county which wanted to employ a county agent and which agreed to raise" local funds. The Council of North American Grain Exchanges joined him on this offer.[46]

Heeding North Dakota's example, Minnesota businessmen entered into an agreement with the new West Central School of Agriculture at Morris (a branch of the university's School of Agriculture) to form the West Central Minnesota Development Association (WCMDA) in 1912. Concerned about the many tenant farms and their poor management, West Central School superintendent E. C. Higbie helped start the WCMDA to "get in more owner-settlers and help those already there." The object was to fund a county agent in each of the fifteen counties in its area. Toward that end, it secured a one-thousand-dollar Rosenwald grant, nearly seven thousand dollars from the USDA, and about eighteen hundred dollars from the Farmers' Institute, plus a "liberal local subscription by bankers and business men as well as farmers."[47] Each county was to contribute about fifteen hundred dollars.[48]

The first county agent, Frank F. Marshall, arrived in Traverse County in mid-September 1912.[49] Several weeks earlier, the WCMDA issued a press release in the local paper to prepare farmers for the new system: "Within a few weeks, a man" would be coming to "improv[e] and promot[e] agricultural development." He would "try to unite town and country interests in every possible way."[50] There was no word if he would help to organize cooperatives. When WCMDA Executive Secretary B. F. Woodard came to Wheaton (the Traverse County seat) to set up his headquarters, he left no doubt of WCMDA's commercial club origins. He stated that he was in "the business of knocking 'knockers,'" and he would "boost for West Central Minnesota at all times and in all places."[51] Marshall and other county agents were the university's men, supervised by Frank E. Balmer of the West Central School (Balmer was later stationed at St.

Paul). By June 1913, the WCMDA had six county agents in the field. It received favorable publicity in *The Farmer* and praise from Wilson, recently named director of the Agricultural Extension Division.[52]

With good reports from the South, from North Dakota, and from west-central Minnesota, the federal and state governments moved to expand the county-agent system. Aided by Woods and the university staff, the WCMDA's Frank W. Murphy drew up a bill—subsequently passed by the 1913 legislature—appropriating up to twenty-five thousand dollars in matching funds for county agents (one thousand dollars to the first twenty-five counties that raised a matching one thousand dollars). A county had to form a committee to work with the agent before state monies would be granted. (In most counties a Farm Bureau unit was the committee).[53] In May 1914, Congress passed the Smith-Lever Agricultural Extension Act that set federal rules and gave ten thousand dollars to each state for hiring county agents.[54] With this aid, the system spread across Minnesota. By the end of 1914, twenty-seven counties each had an agent.[55]

The agents had several constituencies: the university, Main Street merchants, county government, and farmers, but the university was

In April 1914, Eben Lawson depicted the WCMDA, the Farm Bureau, county agent C. A. McNelly, university experts, Superintendent Higbie, and Governor Adolph Eberhart—all leading the charge against hog cholera.

their main one. Woods had to approve the applicants for positions as agents. Normally these were agricultural college graduates. Once hired, each was supervised by Balmer as each carried out the university's program. As alumni, they were probably inclined to support it anyway. They were to combat hog cholera (there had been an outbreak in 1913), support rural school consolidation, hand out university and USDA bulletins, urge farmers to diversify, and introduce new crops like alfalfa. Because the university fostered livestock-shipping and cow-testing associations and Wilson promoted farmers' clubs, they were to help farmers form these organizations.[56] The experts emphasized efficiency so they were to estimate the dollars saved by these cooperatives. Pope County's agent figured that livestock marketing costs declined from 1.25 cents per pound with private buyers to .4 cents with the cooperative shipping associations he helped organize.[57]

The university was the agent's boss, but he had to remember that businessmen started the system and were its major financial backers. He was responsible to a local group, usually a Farm Bureau, in which local commercial clubs had considerable influence. In Norman County, 90 percent of the Farm Bureau leadership was urban while farmers were "indifferent." Bankers and merchants supplied 80 percent of its funds, which helped pay the agent's salary. In Jackson County, "the bankers of the county with the assistance of a cow-tester organized the work to secure a County Agent and secured the signatures of 500 farmers."[58] The county government was another constituency, but its board reflected the separate interests of merchants and farmers.

In their reports to Balmer, some agents expressed concern that promoting cooperatives might anger their Main Street financial backers. Clay County agent P. E. Clement tried "to promote a better mutual understanding between the farmers and the rural business men." It had "not seemed wise to work for any community shipping or buying this year," for these activities "when engaged in merely to be independent of the local merchants" were "a detriment to the community in the long run." He advised farmers that cooperation was helpful only when "great profit" could be made "or when desiring something not handled by local concerns." He reported that some Moorhead businessmen "endeavor[ed] to use the Agent to interest farmers in trading in Moorhead." This put him "in a rather delicate position."[59] Commercial clubs tried to get their money's worth by using agents to persuade farmers to shop locally.

Farmers were a constituency, albeit an often reluctant one. An editorial in *The Farmer* blamed a 1914–15 campaign (see below) against county agents on small-town opposition to agents' work in starting cooperatives, but the editor probably was seeking to deflect attention from the real cause—farmers' opposition to the agents.[60] For the university and its allies, the embarrassing reality was that the farmers who were to be the agent's clients were suspicious of him. One extension worker recalled that in Minnesota "the county agent was a sort of 'illegitimate child,' fathered by unhallowed business and left on the farmer's doorstep, certainly not wanted by many farmers of west central Minnesota."[61] That feeling threatened the perceived legitimacy of the cooperatives that the county agent helped to bring into the world.

Farmers in Some Counties Oppose the County-Agent System

Farmers, who financed state and county governments through the property tax, objected to what appeared to them to be a large expenditure for a county agent, who seemed superfluous, given the sums already spent on bulletins and institutes.[62] They also thought the agent's salary too high. He had "one of the best paying offices in the county," better than a rural mail carrier's job.[63] Some resented this college graduate living "from subscription or direct taxation" rather than making "his own living... if he knows so much more about farming than we do...why doesn't he get a farm and start in farming under the same conditions that we do[?]"[64] One farmer thought agents "would be of far more use to the public if the men appointed would go over public roads, picking up stones and fixing high places."[65] One newspaper charged that the university sought jobs "at attractive salaries for its graduates ... so they can get a soft job telling others how to farm."[66]

Farmers were offended at the notion that they needed to be instructed by nonfarmers:

> It is amusing to note how well most of them, the banker down to the candy girl back of the counter, are posted on farming. We farmers who have spent our entire lives tilling the soil and raising stock have nothing on them when it comes to farming—they know it all from A to Z, and the only one who knows nothing about this ancient profession is the farmer, who ... has been able to feed these wiseacres and now pays a handsome salary to this army of undesired instructors.[67]

To soothe hurt feelings, experts equated agriculture with other industries needing expert advice, which was not "a slur at the local farmers," Wilson argued. No one could master all phases of farming. As a
"large business corporation" needed attorneys and "competent bookkeepers and specialists, . . . so an agricultural community needs the advice
and assistance of the very best trained minds."[68] He ignored the tradition
of the self-employed farmer as independent citizen. Even a corporation
was often a client, but it was a major change to make the American
farmer one.[69]

In the debate in Douglas County, opponents of the county-agent system spoke as independent farmer-citizens while supporters stressed the
benefits of client status. Citing common reasons (high salaries, public
employees' lobbying, Twin Cities' control), Douglas County farmers,

*University of Minnesota Professor George Nesom spoke to farmers at the Alfalfa
Visiting Day at Coon Creek in Anoka County on June 7, 1928. The photograph was
taken by Kemper A. Kirkpatrick, the Hennepin County agent, who documented the
event with his photographs.*

who opposed the system, called for a vote on it at the March 1914 township elections.[70] They acted as citizens who assumed the issue should be decided democratically (by straw ballot—this was not a binding referendum). They saw the issue in political terms, wanting to know who was behind the county-agent plan, if it was a conspiracy, and what it might portend for local control and democratic freedom. The *Park Region Echo* (Alexandria), edited by Carl A. Wold, backed them. Voters rejected the county-agent idea by a 505-to-28-vote margin.[71]

The *Alexandria Citizen* and *Alexandria Post News*, whose publishers favored the agent, did not report the vote totals. Their editors argued that the agent should be retained despite the vote. Editors at the *Post News* and the *Citizen* recalled past merchant-farmer alliances "to build creameries and potato warehouses" and an independent wheat warehouse.[72] Hiring an outside expert was not a breach of this trust and mutuality. The client-farmer would benefit from the agent's services.[73]

Opponents were outraged that the agent stayed regardless of the straw ballot. How could the *Post News* claim his "services are in constant demand . . . after the farmers have almost unanimously by ballot declared, they don't want" him?[74] The agent was an issue in the next legislative campaign, with Wold the antiagent candidate.[75]

Alarmed, university leaders mounted a drive to win farmers' support. Theodore A. Erickson had been Douglas County superintendent of schools until the university extension hired him to work with rural schools as a specialist in agricultural extension.[76] Using his many local contacts, he came to Douglas County in July, visited more than one hundred farmers, induced them to sign a statement supporting the agent, and met with the Commercial Club to negotiate a transfer of funds and power to the farmers. He saw that the university had "to re-organize the county agricultural bureau [Farm Bureau] so that it shall be entirely in the hands of the farmers."[77] Farmers did not press him for this transfer. As citizens, they had voted against the agent. As clients of his organizational services, they were handed control of both the bureau and the agent—by the university experts—whether or not they wanted either one.

Erickson and Wilson called an organizational meeting for July 25, 1914, at the Commercial Club rooms in Alexandria to reorganize the bureau. Before the meeting, they met with Wold and won his support for a farmer-controlled, farmer-financed agent. Erickson presided over the meeting, which was attended by thirty farmers and a few businessmen. Though Wilson and he had prearranged the outcome, they opened the meeting for comments from the floor. Naturally those who came tended to favor the agent and spoke as his clients, many of whom he had helped with the hog cholera problem. A few spoke as citizens about the county paying for him and the issue being raised in a legislative campaign. One argued that farmers' clubs, not ad-hoc meetings, should act on the agent question. Wilson, a friend of farmers' clubs, smoothed this wrinkle: the meeting was a formality until the new bureau was turned over to farmers' clubs. No one objected to an outsider giving them this transitional role. Erickson was made temporary chairman, the new body was formed, and the chair urged the Commercial Club to hand the county-agent work over to the new group.[78]

The organizers called it the Douglas County Farmers' Union. Both Wilson and Woods came to Alexandria for its next meeting on December 5, 1914, which was held in the high school. Organized in part by the superintendent and high school faculty, the meeting was held *for*, not *by*, Douglas County farmers. It spotlighted them as satisfied clients of the high school (they had just been fed a dinner prepared by the school's domestic science department), the university, and its county agent. The latter even thought up a new feature: "Each person who came in was tagged—a slip of paper giving the name and township from which the person came was pinned to each coat. In that way no one needed an introduction to his neighbor in the next seat. The plan worked well." Name tags proved to be the ideal innovation to develop "social bonds." Farmers could not even meet and greet each other without the experts' help.[79]

Using the language of social bonds, Wilson spoke for more than an hour on farmers' clubs as places for socializing and for joint economic action. He distinguished between cooperatives "organized for co-operation" and those formed "for antagonism." Older cooperatives he placed in the latter group; university-sponsored livestock-shipping associations, in the former. At the afternoon session, Woods experienced a difficulty in the expert's relationship to the clients. A "question arose as to how long [hog cholera] serum could be kept." They asked him for an answer, despite his plan to talk on another (presumably, more interesting) topic. As an expert, and in this setting, he had little choice but to comply.

Unmindful of farmers' organizing efforts since the 1870s, experts now thought farmers needed the help of salaried professionals—teachers, superintendents, county agents, university experts. Farmers still knew how to protest, however. Wold criticized corporations and boards of trade that backed county agents "as the greatest hindrances to the farmer in securing an open and free market for his products." Farmers who favored Equity, not the agent, scheduled a meeting for the end of December.[80] Similar battles erupted in Grant, Otter Tail, Pope, Wilkin, and Kandiyohi Counties. Antiagent forces won straw votes in almost all cases, but the agents stayed.[81]

The continuation of the county-agent system despite being rejected at the polls called into question its democratic nature and the grass-roots legitimacy of the cooperatives organized by the agents. The university's orchestration in Douglas County showed a weakening of rural democracy. Clients had only a limited veto power over experts' proposals, not the initiating, organizing power that Granges and suballiances had. Stripped of its antimonopolism and its history, cooperation was losing its tradition of local control, too. The agent's cooperative was a representative, not a direct, democracy. Its board listened to experts. Members had only the referendum (the annual meeting) at which to overrule the experts.

Was this democratic coordination of transactions? Experts added features of administrative, hierarchical coordination used by corporations that Progressives admired as efficient. They advised local cooperatives to form regional and state associations. With experts at the top and managers of state, regional, and local associations following in descending order, hierarchy replaced democracy. Expertise meant power. Before, oratorical and political skills and friends were paramount. Now, university education and expertise gave the cooperatives' managerial class greater control than the old, untrained managers had ever had. A partial separation of ownership and control resulted. Ownership stayed with farmers; control passed to a managerial class advised by experts.[82]

Criticism of the University's Promotion of Cooperatives

As the university consolidated its expert-to-client ties to farmers, critics on both the right and the left attacked its policy on promoting cooperatives. On the left, Equity members criticized the university for not going far enough. They probably led opposition to agents in Douglas and other counties. Earlier, they had locked horns with university leaders at cooperative conferences in 1912 and 1913, when cooperators (many of them

Equity members) tried to form "an interstate co-operative league to deal with the problem of marketing farm produce." Equity favored the idea. University experts and their allies cautioned against it (ten years later they would support the idea).[83]

Several issues separated the two sides. First, Equity members accused experts of working "primarily to increase the crop production" when farmers felt "the question of marketing is as much in need of attention as that of production."[84] Here was a conflict between productive efficiency and economic efficiency. Equity members implied that experts wanted to keep them from the latter as too politically divisive. That was not the case. With its expertise in agronomy, animal husbandry, and dairying, the university seemed to be equipped to research production, not marketing, but it was willing to learn the latter. Experts' language of social efficiency gave a rationale for eliminating "waste" in marketing, but consumers, not farmers, might get the savings in the form of lower food prices. In 1911 the University of Minnesota Board of Regents created a Bureau of Research in Agricultural Economics to study the efficiency of "different agencies performing middlemen functions."[85] A bill was introduced in the Minnesota legislature directing the bureau to gather statistics on and give advice to rural cooperatives.[86] Passed in 1913, the law required university experts to study and promote cooperatives. They responded by writing a series of agricultural extension bulletins on cooperation that won "national attention."[87]

Secondly, Equity members and university officials differed over what type of cooperative was most needed. University bulletins stressed local cooperatives. Equity members favored cooperation in both local and terminal markets. They accused experts and the farm press of a suspicious silence on terminal-market cooperation. At a farmers' club meeting in Douglas County, an Equity organizer criticized county agents and their corporate sponsors:

> Apparently they want to organize us locally in order to keep us disorganized at the terminals.
>
> They tell us it is "dangerous to disturb the established avenues of trade" ... our "helpers" and our "old line" farm papers, published in the twin cities, seem to be afraid even to mention the terminal organizations and selling agencies now being established. . . .
>
> We have for years had certain local farmer's business enterprises, such as co-operative creameries, farmers' elevators ... they have had

to struggle desperately against the fight to drive them out of business.... So long as these associations have no central association they
are not in a position to co-operate and help one another.... Neither have
these local associations been strong enough to materially effect the situation at the terminal marketing points.[88]

The organizer provided a summary of forty years of cooperative history.
Local cooperatives could never be more than marginal.

The speaker's charge was correct. Neither the university nor its allies
endorsed terminal-market cooperation except in dairying where it lacked
radical political connotations. They knew it had been linked to agrarian
protests. They knew of the current Chamber-ECE fight and the verbal
battles between John McHugh and George Loftus. A writer in *The Farmer*
criticized Equity's "bitter denunciations of present conditions," its attempts "to revolutionize these conditions by comprehensive and statewide organizations."[89] Experts and editors preferred to contrast cooperation with individualism, not local with terminal cooperation.[90]

Partly they justified a focus on local cooperation by claiming the movement was young. Farmers must "learn the first steps in co-operation."[91]
That statement flew in the face of forty years of history, angered Equity
members, and seemed to instruct farmers, "Little children, don't play out
of your own back yard; you may get hurt." Using the language of republicanism that stressed the citizen, an Equity organizer asked, "Could
anything be more insulting to the manhood and intelligence of American farmers than that?"[92] What about democratic control? Did the farm
press "want to make us believe that the 'farmers' club' movement promoted by the extension division workers, farm papers, railroad companies,
farm machinery trusts, bankers' associations, etc, is more of a real farmers' movement than an organization [Equity] promoted, officered, and
controlled by the farmers themselves?"[93]

Experts also hesitated on terminal-market cooperation because they
felt a need for more study. Equity leader and future elected official Magnus
Johnson replied, "The professors at the agricultural colleges are always
investigating and advising delay."[94] In this case, both sides were right. After
forty years, farmers had enough experience in organizing cooperatives
in terminal markets. Yet the experience had not been observed and analyzed scientifically so experts could not generalize from it.

Finally, Equity members objected when the university accepted corporate donations for its extension programs. During the debate over a

county agent, Wold doubted if the Chicago Board of Trade and Minneapolis Chamber of Commerce were friendly to farmers' interests, despite their financing of county agents.[95] Rural legislators (some of them Equity leaders) raised this issue when they attacked the university in the 1915 session. At two hearings into the university's activities, a House committee called Vincent, Wilson, and Woods for "a severe cross examination" on corporate sponsorship, alleged misuse of funds, and alleged procorporate bias of university economists and county agents. The trio admitted that Rosenwald of Sears, Roebuck helped finance "the introduction of agricultural agents in Minnesota and North Dakota."[96] State Representative Magnus Johnson accused agents of favoring chambers of commerce. "Why don't they teach us better marketing, so we can dispose of our crops?"[97] Johnson did not spare the agents' expert supervisors but chastised L. D. H. Weld, who led university research on the economics of cooperation. Weld had entered the ECE-Chamber battle: "Secretary McHugh of the Chamber of Commerce let him see the [Chamber's] books because he knew Prof. Weld would be favorable to the Chamber." Weld had testified favorably on grain futures trading, too. Later that year, Weld headed for safety at Yale.[98]

By a vote of sixty-eight to fifty-seven, the House amended—and gutted—a bill to form a special committee to investigate the university.[99] The hearings, the close vote, and the near fisticuffs showed the depth of rural members' suspicions about the university: that its president was paid for his speeches and was linked to the Rockefeller Foundation, that it used its staff and alumni to lobby the legislature, and that its professors were bought by corporate donations to its programs.[100]

Along with a 1918 tussle over the allegedly procorporate bias of Weld's successor, E. Dana Durand, this episode contrasted Equity leaders' political style and university experts' professional style.[101] Equity leaders made broad, unsubstantiated charges often based on guilt by association with corporate interests. They then demanded a public investigation to ascertain the truth. They did not feel obliged to investigate before making charges. Guilt or innocence would be determined in public debate.

If Equity leaders had too broad an idea of improper associations and conflicts of interest, then university experts had too narrow a one. They objected to Equity's notion "that the members of the faculty are quasi-political appointees of the Board of Regents" who must hold politically correct views. A faculty member "owed a high obligation to his profession" and was only obliged to "deal with his subject in a scientific spirit." Faculty objected to unsubstantiated charges being publicized. They were not candidates whose merits were up for public debate.[102] They expected to be judged by their profession and by their university.

University leaders showed naïveté and lack of historical memory. Given years of rural suspicion of Rockefellers, railroads, and merchants, it was disingenuous to take large donations from them and then be surprised at rural attacks on corporate-sponsored extension work. With its staff of writers, it conducted extensive publicity campaigns for inherently political causes, such as the good roads movement and rural school consolidation.[103] Its claims to be outside the political arena sounded hollow.

Liberal critics did not understand that the university had to walk a narrow line between the champions of cooperation and the Main Street or corporate foes of cooperation. It needed close ties with business to gain the financing for its extension work. Seeing no need for these programs, Equity members underestimated financial need and overestimated political friendship as the motive for the university's search for corporate support.

The university also needed corporate support to deflect conservative criticism of its promotion of cooperatives. Its agricultural economists' research and "the promotion of cooperative organization by other divisions of the College of Agriculture created problems for the University in the small towns of Minnesota," according to one history of the agricultural economics department.[104] Evidence of such conservative criticism is scant, apparently because such critics contacted regents and experts privately, rather than use public forums.[105] By the summer of 1915, they were pressuring the university on the issue. Responding, the regents and Vincent implored Dean Woods to set "principles to guide our Agricultural Agents and Extension men in their field work" where that dealt with cooperation.[106] Woods sought counsel among his staff. On July 1, 1915, admitting a lack of "entire agreement" on one issue, he sent Vincent a list of principles that "represents the consensus of opinion."

Not a set of scientific generalizations, this was a political document that phrased cooperative principles so as to disarm small-town merchants' criticisms. It equated farmers' clubs with "civic, commercial and women's clubs in the cities." Farmers' groups were "as necessary" as those "for merchants, bankers or any other class of business men." It backed away from endorsing cooperative stores but reassured merchants that these could educate rural people to realize that retailing "requires special skill and hard work, and that the margins of profit, as a rule, are narrow and the risk is great." It promised that university staff would advise farmers to shop locally. It reminded merchants that the university offered "short courses" on how to reach "greatest efficiency" in retailing.[107] It used the least controversial language of social efficiency.

Vincent circulated copies of this proposed statement to individual regents.[108] Regent M. M. Williams criticized the (quite mild) section on cooperative stores: "My suggestion would be to say NO at No. 3" ("Do You Encourage the Organization of Cooperative Stores?").[109] Still no major changes were made. Approved by the regents' Agricultural Committee, it was printed as a circular, reprinted in the farm press, and sent to all county agents.[110]

County Agents Organize a Terminal-level Marketing Cooperative

Within months of its adoption, this policy was put to a test when county agents began to organize Twin Cities area dairy farmers who supplied whole milk to dealers in that urban market. These farmers faced unique marketing problems due to their highly perishable product, which was not made into less-perishable butter or cheese and had to be sold immediately in a local and terminal market. The circular neither prohibited nor recommended the organizing of milk producers by county agents. Once done, the action tended to disprove Woods's rule that "when agriculture is as efficiently organized . . . as other forms of business, the clashing will cease."[111]

Dairy farmers within a radius of forty miles of the Twin Cities—the approximate area of the milkshed—complained that the private dairies paid widely varying prices for milk, from farm to farm and from season to season, and unfairly docked them for sour milk that the dairies neglected to sell quickly. The underlying problem was that the dairies handled the marketing of milk, charged farmers for costs resulting from seasonal surpluses and the risks of perishability, and had little incentive to develop a more efficient system as long as they received their profit margin. In some localities, such as Northfield, farmers started cooperative creameries to provide a competing buyer and an outlet for their surplus milk, but that was only a local, partial solution. These farmers were geographically divided because they lived north, south, east, and west of the Twin Cities. They could not easily organize all dairy farmers in the milkshed to bargain with the private dairies or jointly to solve the marketing problem.[112]

Working together under the supervision of Balmer and using the model of the cooperative creameries, county agents in the Twin Cities milkshed began an organizational drive that could be justified by referring to the university circular that emphasized efficiency. Starting in Bloomington in February 1916, Hennepin County agent Kemper A. Kirkpatrick formed local milk producers' associations in the townships as part of the program of the new Hennepin County Farm Bureau Association. A county agent who met frequently with farmers was ideally suited for this task. At a meeting of the two sides on March 1, 1916, the dairies refused to negotiate with Hennepin County's newly organized farmers. Balmer and other university experts expanded the organizing drive. First the Ramsey and Dakota County agents, then agents from six other counties, joined in to mobilize farmers in the entire milkshed. Dean Woods, Balmer, Director Wilson, Haecker, other experts, and the county agents planned a milk producers' conference to be held in St. Paul during the 1916 Minnesota State Fair.[113]

At this conference, 150 farmer-delegates from the local associations voted to form the Twin City Milk Producers Association (TCMPA). Despite the democratic formalities, the delegates were clients of the experts more than active shapers of the TCMPA. Kirkpatrick described the conference in his diary: "Had hard work 'steering' but plans went thru pretty much as planned by 'us.' Washington Co. bunch—bullheaded miserable beings to handle." Balmer praised the TCMPA as "another demonstration of the 'worth-while-ness' of the county agent and farm bureau movement." The TCMPA and the Farm Bureau were closely linked. As agents recruited new TCMPA members, they invited farmers to pay joint membership dues to the TCMPA and the Farm Bureau. "Possibly this connection should not exist," Balmer admitted.[114]

To join the TCMPA, dairy farmers signed a one-year contract to deliver milk to the TCMPA and bought a one-dollar share of stock for every four cows they owned. As the county agents induced new members to sign the contract, the TCMPA leaders negotiated with Twin Cities dairies to sell its members' milk at one fixed price. On March 31, 1917, the TCMPA signed marketing agreements with eight or nine dairies.[115]

It looked as if the university experts and county agents had succeeded in showing dairy farmers their "worth-while-ness" by organizing a

Big Rally

FOR MILK PRODUCERS, AT NEW BRIGHTON TOWN HALL, THURSDAY, MAY 18, 8 p.m.

All milk producers in the surrounding territory of Ramsey, Hennepin and Anoka counties are invited to attend this big milk men's rally. The live issues connected with producing and marketing milk will be discussed. Features of the proposed Minneapolis ordinance that affect dairymen in territory tributary to the Twin Cities will be explained. The formation of a local milk producers' association will be considered.

GOOD SPEAKERS. DON'T MISS THIS MEETING. TELL YOUR NEIGHBORS.

Ramsey Co. Farm Bureau, Hennepin Co. Farm Bureau, U. of M. Ag. Ex. Div. and U. S. Dept. of Agriculture co-operating.

This flyer for a rally in 1916 was sent to dairy farmers in and near Fridley and New Brighton. The TCMPA and its local units could not have been organized without the help of the sponsoring agencies printed on the bottom.

terminal-level marketing cooperative. And they had done so without succumbing to radical agrarian protest. Formed under the aegis of the conservative Farm Bureau units, among dairy farmers who traditionally lacked radical views, and in one limited urban market, the TCMPA appeared able to raise farmers' incomes without angering conservatives.

American entry into World War I only days after the signing of the agreements altered the picture. Socialists, union activists, and urban political leaders in the Twin Cities attacked the TCMPA as a price-fixing monopoly after the agreements and wartime inflation hiked the retail price of milk from eight cents to twelve cents a quart by fall 1917. The Minnesota Commission of Public Safety (MCPS) investigated the increase as part of its attempt to control the urban cost of living. The MCPS ordered the price cut to eleven cents and the farmers' share to $3.10 per hundredweight. TCMPA leaders protested that the TCMPA was "merely a cooperative marketing Association" that did not fix prices; its members decided the appropriate price for their milk. That was a disingenuous answer—members signed a one-year contract to market through the TCMPA and could be fined five dollars per cow for violating the contract— but the MCPS refused to break up an association that it found useful in enforcing its orders on farmers.[116]

Minneapolis officials sought to dissolve the TCMPA. In late December 1917, Hennepin County Attorney John M. Rees convinced the grand jury to indict five TCMPA officers for "conspiring to fix milk prices and limit competition." The court case was delayed. Assistant county attorney Floyd B. Olson, later governor of Minnesota, was working on the case in March 1919 when the legislature passed a retroactive law exempting farmers' cooperatives from the state's antitrust laws. That ended the case and enabled later marketing cooperatives to function outside the antitrust restrictions.[117]

The formation of the TCMPA illustrated how cooperative organizing by county agents could have unexpected consequences. The acts of fairly conservative experts and dairy farmers were perceived as radical by urban consumers. Labor leaders could be anti-cooperative. University experts could support terminal-level cooperation. Their policy circular and its stress on economic efficiency could radically antagonize urban consumers rather than build rural-urban harmony. However, the TCMPA was an exception to the rule that university experts de-radicalized cooperation as their county agents took over the role of organizing rural cooperatives, and this wartime controversy was temporary.

University Experts and the Politics of Rural Cooperation

Normally conservatives objected to the county agents' organizing efforts. In January 1917, Fergus Falls editor, banker, and politician Elmer E. Adams complained to Regent Albert E. Rice about Professor E. Dana Durand's promotion of cooperative credit associations. Adams wondered why banks were taxed to support the university so it could "send out a corp of men to organize competition." That was no "more a part of the University's work than it is to organize [livestock] shipping associations which ship in and ship out in competition with business men who carry on that line of business."[118] Alarmed, Regents Rice and Fred B. Snyder asked Vincent, "Are we too active. What has Dean Woods to say?"[119]

Woods passed the buck to federal and state statutes. The 1913 state law required him to gather data on cooperatives. The Smith-Lever Act mandated that farmers be "urged to organize to do their work efficiently"—and many forms of cooperation seemed most efficient to him. His trump card was the support he received from "the largest and most influential business men's organizations in Minnesota."[120] Adams could not claim that the WCMDA was antibusiness. What Woods did not say was that university experts had so de-radicalized cooperation that it posed little threat to conservatives like Adams.

Progressive-era experts disdained the "reactionary" views of old-line conservatives, yet shared their fear of agrarian protest. President Vincent abhorred "Mr. Elmer Adams' attitude . . . he is utterly reactionary" and "influenced by prejudice and class interest." Trying "to keep the farmers in ignorance and prevent them from organizing, and to exploit them economically" would cause "just the sort of thing that is now sweeping North Dakota and is likely to have a great deal of influence in Minnesota."[121] Yet his fear of the Nonpartisan League showed his own class interest as a professional whose influence with farmers would be undermined by agrarian radicals' political style. To imply farmers were ignorant until the university enlightened them—and would not organize if it failed to assist them—was to deny forty years of rural cooperation.

To mollify Adams, the regents changed the policy on cooperative purchasing to discourage it more explicitly. But county agents, extension staff, and economists still promoted cooperation and dominated it by the 1920s. Their bulletins on cooperation went far beyond the technical capabilities or resources of the Alliance press or the Equity editors. Their influence was greater than any Alliance lecturer's. Across the rural United

States, this network of experts, strengthened by its role in World War I mobilization, took the lead in organizing cooperatives. From 1919 to 1924, county agents helped to form some 52 percent of all the cooperatives that existed between the Civil War and World War II.[122]

By 1920, Republican J. A. O. Preus could sell cooperation as an alternative to socialism. Cooperatives could turn away from politics to technical matters: accounting techniques, managers' training, Rochdale principles, and the Sapiro plan. The farmer was told that rural cooperation was a technical matter, on which he had to seek expert advice. Cooperation became a quasi-democratic, quasi-administrative coordination of transactions that adapted to the administered and managed American economy of the 1920s. Experts sought to federate local cooperatives into statewide associations that operated in terminal markets and used the methods of Big Business for farmers' benefit but lacked any hint of radical politics.

13

Republican Cooperation

"Farmers by the tens of thousands
were ballyhooed into the ranks of
'cooperative marketing associations' "

WITH THE 1920s, the focus shifted decisively from the local cooperative to state, regional, and national efforts in cooperation. It was no coincidence that in the 1920s the state or regional cooperatives with which many Minnesotans are so familiar were organized: Land O' Lakes, Midland, CENEX, and GTA. Several nationwide developments during that decade combined to cause a move by state and national leaders toward large-scale federations of cooperatives. These factors can be quickly summarized: transportation by truck and auto that threatened crossroads cooperatives, a chain-store movement in American business, a sharp drop in crop prices from July to December 1920 that triggered a decade-long farm recession, a national cooperative-marketing fad starting that year, and the maturation of those institutions offering expert advice and leadership to farmers. Minnesota Republicans' need to counter Nonpartisan League and Farmer-Labor appeals to farmers provided an added motivation for many to embrace large-scale cooperation.

Another fundamental factor in large-scale cooperation was already in place in Minnesota by 1919—an impressive number of successful local cooperatives. According to the U.S. Census taken in 1919, Minnesota farmers sold 44 percent of their output through cooperatives. The next highest ranking was South Dakota's 27 percent; other nearby states— Wisconsin, North Dakota, and Iowa—registered only 23, 22, and 20 percent respectively. Minnesota had more cooperatives than any other state— 390 grain elevators, 711 creameries, more than 400 livestock shipping associations, 110 stores, 900 rural telephone companies, and 150 fire in-

surance mutuals, as well as miscellaneous others.[1] These local cooperatives provided the state with a heritage of cooperative action and furnished any federation with a necessary list of potential members. A nas-
cent federation also required leaders who could transcend local interests
and articulate a set of goals, suited to the region, that would unify local
cooperatives. The requisite network of university experts, county agents,
Farm Bureau units, the farm press, and the state government's agricultural officials had been set up in the 1910s and was completed by 1920.
Created by the Minnesota legislature in 1919, the Minnesota Department
of Agriculture (MDA) began its operations that summer and fall. The
MDA made state government an effective player in Minnesota agriculture by coordinating and initiating state policies in that field. The law
empowered it to "assist farmers, producers and consumers in the organization and management of co-operative enterprises and the co-operative
marketing of farm products." Its first, and long-time (1919–31), commissioner was Nels J. Holmberg, a Renville County farmer, state legislator,
and University of Minnesota School of Agriculture graduate.[2] The second completing link was the Minnesota Farm Bureau Federation (MFBF),
formed by the county units in March 1920.[3] The MFBF could do what individual county Farm Bureaus could not readily do: sponsor statewide
federations of local cooperatives.

This completed alliance of like-minded groups moved quickly in
1919–21 to initiate and promote terminal-level cooperative marketing
by state federations. A mere eight years earlier, the university's experts
had cautioned against such tactics, but much had changed in the inter-
val. The experts had completed their initial research into various types
of local cooperation and published the results in a series of agricultural
extension bulletins. The U.S. Department of Agriculture (USDA) had created
its own Office of Markets in 1913 and increased its research in agricultural economics — moving toward but not yet reaching the promotion of
farmer-controlled cooperatives. In 1917 it published its first bulletin, giving statistical data on cooperatives.[4] County agents also had eight years of
experience in forming and assisting local cooperatives and one terminal-
level federation, the Twin City Milk Producers' Association (TCMPA), albeit
in a local terminal market. The agents and the state had two intensive
war years of organizing Liberty Loan, American Red Cross, and farm-
labor drives that taught them how to mobilize rural people on a statewide
basis.[5] This network of institutions and experts had matured and was
ready to undertake statewide federation.

Moreover politics had changed since 1911. The Nonpartisan League took control of North Dakota's state government in 1916 and attempted the same feat in Minnesota in 1918. Republican Party regulars used wartime accusations of disloyalty to defeat the NPL in the June 1918 primary, but the NPL was a highly organized machine of dues-paying farmers that posed a serious threat to Republicans' looser alliance of state employees, small-town merchants, and the more prosperous farmers. In the face of the NPL's farm-versus-Main-Street tactics and rhetoric, the county Farm Bureau became all the more important to the alliance by uniting farmers and businessmen in one group.[6] But these cooperatives and expert leaders did not instantly metamorphize into state federations—even with political rewards as a catalyst. Farmers and their local cooperatives had to have compelling economic reasons to federate. The war years of 1914–18 were prosperous ones for American agriculture, and the 1919 crop year continued that trend. It was a problem crop, potatoes, that first gave the institutional experts a chance to try statewide cooperative marketing.

The university proudly mapped its statewide network of agricultural institutions at the Minnesota State Fair in 1926.

The Origins and Trials of the Minnesota Potato Exchange

The growth of the Twin Cities created an urban market for many kinds of produce, potatoes being one such crop. Farmers north of the cities in Anoka, Chisago, and Isanti Counties grew potatoes to meet that demand. To diversify away from wheat, farmers in the Red River Valley also grew potatoes in large quantities—by 1919 more than fifty thousand acres were seeded to potatoes in Clay, Norman, and Polk Counties combined.[7]

However, as noted in *The Farmer*, "The potato crop admittedly offers more difficulties as to marketing than any other single crop."[8] It was a semiperishable crop, unlike wheat, and it was harvested and sold on the market at one season—September and October—unlike dairy products, which were made and marketed year-round. Potatoes showed greater variations in quality than did the small grains. Farmers could not adjust processing to compensate for poor growth in the field, since potatoes sold for table use were not processed. So potatoes of mixed quality were dumped on an uncertain market each fall, and farmers received one-half to one-fifth of the store price.[9]

The first task the Minnesota Department of Agriculture undertook was that of organizing the Minnesota Potato Exchange (MPE), modeled after a similar state federation in Michigan, which the USDA's Bureau of Markets had helped to form. Seizing on prior work by local potato-growers' cooperatives and county Farm Bureaus, as well as on publicity in *The Farmer*, Commissioner Holmberg and Hugh J. Hughes, MDA's director of markets, began a campaign in August 1919 to convince potato growers and their local associations to form a central marketing agency that would bypass local buyers and sell directly to terminal-market dealers. County agents, university experts, and the USDA Bureau of Markets were all enlisted to convince farmers to accept the idea. At a January 1920 meeting in Little Falls, the MPE was launched. Ludvig Mosbæk of Askov, president of the Pine County Farm Bureau, served as president and chief field organizer.[10]

A sixty-four-year-old Danish-American nurseryman and cooperative enthusiast, Mosbæk had the look and a good deal of the strong-mindedness of a white-bearded Old Testament prophet. He had been a local leader in Denmark's cooperative revolution of the 1880s before emigrating in 1891. The university experts and farm journals held Denmark's cooperatives in high regard. Mosbæk recalled the experts saying "we must adopt the Danish system of cooperation," and his ethnic background probably led them to respect his advice and to choose him for a leadership role. As he traveled around the state in 1920 promoting the MPE, he cited Danish cooperation as a model. (Ironically the one area in which the Danes failed was cooperative potato marketing; their association, begun in 1919, ceased its operation in 1920.)[11]

One distinguishing feature of Danish rural cooperation was the members' contractual obligation to market their crops through the cooperative. State and university experts sought to build statewide marketing cooperatives on this feature, but that proved to be difficult to transplant from Denmark, with its heritage of communal decision making in farming, to America, with its tradition of proud individualism in farming. S. B. Cleland, a supervisor of county agents, warned of the idea some farmers held that "it is optional with the grower whether he pledges all his crop or not," for that "would be fatal to the success of the Exchange." Mosbæk also insisted on an ironclad contract binding the potato grower to market all his crop through the Exchange "so as to secure the volume of business necessary" to minimize per-unit selling costs.[12]

The ironclad contract was not written into the MPE's bylaws, however, but was a policy decision of its board—one that many local potato marketing associations could not enforce because it was not in their bylaws either. Community pressure or ethnic solidarity might motivate their members to market only through the locals, but such inducements did not work for a statewide cooperative. The Exchange was organized, not from the grass roots, but from the top down by MDA and university experts, so it lacked any grass-roots consensus for its ironclad contract, which was not enforceable in court. Thus the MPE did not have a guaranteed, predictable volume of potatoes to market. By 1923 it had clearly failed.[13]

In some ways the MPE was a premature attempt at statewide cooperative marketing. Several events that occurred in the summer of 1920 as Mosbæk toured the state aided later organizing drives: a price drop starting in July, a growing Minnesota Farm Bureau Federation, and a national enthusiasm for the Sapiro or California plan of cooperative marketing—all played a part in the final event, the 1920 political campaign.

Republican J. A. O. Preus Uses Cooperation as a Campaign Issue

In no other Minnesota political campaign has rural cooperation been such a prominent issue as it was in 1920. Republican regulars had used charges of wartime disloyalty to defeat the NPL in 1918, but that issue lost much of its steam following the armistice in November 1918. Recalling his tactic of seizing some of the Populists' points in 1892–94, Knute Nelson urged Republicans to work for reform of agribusiness, as the NPL farmers demanded. The 1919 Republican-led legislature had created the MDA "with broad powers to investigate marketing practices and with specific orders to assist in co-operative organization," noted Hughes. It had also passed a cooperative-marketing law. But it was in 1920 that Republicans became totally and publicly committed to cooperative marketing.[14]

In a replay of 1892, they nominated a Nelson protégé, Jacob Aal Ottesen Preus, the young state auditor from a family prominent in the Norwegian-American Lutheran church, as the regulars' candidate for governor. Using its tactic of running its candidates in the major parties' primaries, the NPL countered with a Norwegian-American moderate, dentist Henrik Shipstead of Glenwood, in the June Republican primary. Two disgruntled Republicans also ran. Conservatives feared disaster. Preus hurled charges of socialism at the NPL like "fire and brimstone" and narrowly escaped with an eight-thousand-vote plurality. For the fall campaign, the NPL changed tactics and ran Shipstead as a pro-NPL Independent. That gave Preus reason to be more optimistic and positive.[15]

Under some pressure to be constructive and to "give the farmers of this State some substantial, necessary and desired relief," Preus decided "to push cooperation as contrasted with state socialism" in the fall.[16] The long-term success of local cooperatives—without disrupting normal channels of trade—made this idea less controversial among GOP conservatives in 1920 than it would have been for Nelson in 1892. Recent events also induced Preus to stress this issue. That summer the interests of state and national Republican candidates, the Farm Bureau, the MDA, university agricultural experts, farm journals, and Republican editors coalesced around a drive for cooperative marketing.

The newly organized American Farm Bureau Federation (AFBF—formed November 1919) and MFBF (March 1920) were looking for a conspicuous service they could perform for farmers in order to recruit members. The AFBF sponsored an agricultural marketing conference in Chicago, July 23–24, at which Aaron Sapiro, a young California attorney, gave an electrifying speech about cooperative marketing by the California Fruit Growers Exchange. The AFBF decided to push for nationwide use of this method—signing a large percentage of the growers of each

commodity to an ironclad contract, thus enabling each commodity marketing cooperative to control enough of the supply to dictate higher crop
prices. The July drop in crop prices made this plan timely for farmers
anxious for relief as well as for an AFBF seeking members.[17]

The fall in crop prices, "the most crushing that American agriculture had yet experienced" according to one historian, threatened to undo
Preus's optimism. "The [Nonpartisan] League is trying to make capital
out of it," warned one state legislator. Cooperative marketing became a
timely, attractive solution for Republicans. Without demanding government aid or price-fixing that was opposed by conservatives, Sapiro-
style cooperatives would force higher prices by controlling crop supplies and marketing these in an "orderly" manner. With Iowa farm editor
Henry C. Wallace as his farm-policy adviser, GOP presidential candidate
Warren G. Harding praised cooperative marketing in a speech at the
Minnesota State Fair.[18]

During the fair, the reliably Republican *Minneapolis Journal* ran a
series of front-page articles on the new MFBF, which was conducting a
membership drive. Shaped by Preus's main farm adviser, former MFBF
president S. L. Allen, the articles adroitly gave the impression that that
infant group deserved credit for the accomplishments of the county
agents and the state's fifty-year-old cooperative movement. Like the
Grange and the Alliance, the MFBF used cooperation to recruit members.
Two *Journal* editorials made the political message explicit: the MFBF,
not the NPL, was "the way out" of the farm crisis. The *Journal* reassured
middlemen that cooperative marketing would not end their "legitimate
functions."[19]

Catching the AFBF's Sapiro fever, *The Farmer*, edited by Henry's brother
Daniel A. Wallace, ran a long series of laudatory articles from late September until late November about California's marketing cooperatives.
Other farmers looked to California's growers, who were relatively unhurt
by the price crisis, for solutions to their dilemma.[20]

Republican editors and candidates, GOP appointees at MDA, and Republicans in the MFBF were united on this issue as Preus opened the fall
campaign with a speech at Red Lake Falls, praising Farm Bureau cooperative marketing over the NPL's state-owned elevators and mills in North
Dakota. (This was a politician's false choice; one could have both, since
state-owned terminal elevators were meant to assist local farmers' elevators in their cooperative marketing.) At Battle Lake the former insur-

ance commissioner hailed township mutuals. At Hanska he "cited the success of the California Fruit Growers Association." Everywhere he stressed cooperative marketing.[21]

Preus's speeches and his earlier fact-finding visit to the Equity Cooperative Exchange in St. Paul provoked surprise and consternation in the enemy camp. The NPL in the *Minnesota Leader* sarcastically noted, "Cooperation has suddenly gained a lot of strange friends." Equity's state president accused Preus of receiving Chamber of Commerce support while he praised the Chamber's late adversary, George Loftus. The NPL attacked the GOP's conversion to cooperation and insisted that farmer-cooperators also supported government action, but the election was less than a month away, the young Preus had no prior record as a foe of cooperation, and the NPL had been caught campaigning mainly for a tax on iron ore in the midst of a farm crisis.[22]

The Equity president told Preus, "You are entering the cooperative movement rather late, my dear sir, to expect it to follow you after a week's time."[23] Yet the chief result of Preus's stress on cooperation was not so much to give him the victory—he would have won anyway—but to commit him and his incoming administration to lead a cooperative marketing drive. The cooperative movement had little choice but to follow. The Farm Bureau and its GOP allies had seized the initiative.[24]

The Formation of Land O' Lakes Creameries

The state's dairy farmers and cooperative creameries had not at first been hard hit by the general fall in the prices for agricultural commodities in July 1920. They were more concerned about long-term trends in marketing dairy products. Here, too, university experts, the Farm Bureau, the farm press, and the MDA led the way and held up the California Fruit Growers Exchange as a model. Roles became confused. The university's extension expert on dairying, Arthur J. McGuire, was also *The Farmer's* dairy editor. Commissioner Holmberg was a founding father of a cooperative that his department was supposed to regulate and audit. Director Hughes could write to Preus, "I've tried [the idea of statewide cooperative marketing] out, again and again, on N[on] P[artisan] and socialistic crowds, and they like it."[25] They were all part of one interconnected network of agencies and experts.

An Irish-American prohibitionist and progressive from Swift County, McGuire had been Haecker's student at the university, and he carried on

Haecker's work among cooperative creameries.[26] As early as 1918, he became concerned about poor-quality butter resulting from cooperatives competing against each other (and against the centralizers' cream stations) and, thus, accepting inferior farm-separated cream. He lobbied for the creation of county associations of creameries, which could end competition among cooperatives, improve the quality of farm-separated cream, and cut freight costs by combining their butter shipments into carload lots. This agenda was similar to the one that Freeborn County's association had pursued in the 1890s. With the help of Hughes and county agents, dairy farmers formed several county associations—increasingly, these were seen as steps to a state federation.[27]

McGuire, Hughes, and others realized that the problems threatening the future of Minnesota dairying arose not only from changes in local production caused by the hand separator but also from shifting conditions in the national butter market. From the start in 1890, Minnesota's cooperative creameries had marketed high-quality butter through job-

Irrepressible Arthur J. McGuire (left in derby hat) posed with his University of Minnesota dairy class around 1910. He later traveled the state promoting better dairying and marketing practices and served as the first manager at Land O' Lakes.

bers and dealers in New York and Philadelphia. Retailers then packaged and sold it under various brand names, which did not indicate its origins, so consumers had no loyalty to Minnesota butter. Very little cooperative-made butter was sold in the Twin Cities market, which centralizers had captured with well-advertised, cheaper brands.[28]

The centralizers had adapted to the increased volumes and speeds of butter sales—caused partly by the growth of chain grocery stores like Atlantic & Pacific—by shipping uniform, but lower quality, butter in large quantities in carload lots. Minnesota cooperative creameries had not adapted. Their higher-quality butter was not uniform, but varied in color, taste, and salt content, so it could not be shipped in carload lots but had to be sold by the tub. Nor could it really be sold to jobbers under the state's Minnesota brand, for that did not guarantee uniformity, and the buyer still had to evaluate each tub. This "individualistic scheme of marketing" resulted from the local independence of each creamery and its buttermaker.

Because much of the cooperative creamery butter was of high quality, New York's discriminating dealers still bought it, despite the inconveniences. After World War I, however, the high exchange value of the dollar made it profitable for Danish cooperatives to export their uniform, high-quality Lur-brand butter to the United States. Because it was "famed for its uniformity of quality," buyers would purchase "an entire shipload of Danish butter" in one lot for one per-unit price, thus speeding up handling. Danish butter threatened Minnesota butter by appealing to the same consumers—ones with discriminating tastes and higher incomes.[29]

The Danish method—having the government enforce rules for a mandatory butter brand—was less attractive to a Republican administration than having a private federation administer a voluntary brand. Soon after the MDA was formed, Holmberg called a meeting of state dairy leaders, including McGuire and Archie Wilson from the university, to discuss the need for a federation of cooperative creameries. Holmberg recalled, "Our Department felt strongly that it should be a big, powerful federation rather than a number of weak local organizations that would inevitably get to quarreling among themselves." McGuire and Wilson agreed, but opposition to the MDA's ideas formed quickly.[30]

Holmberg's big federation might be good for the state's dairy industry, but it was not clearly in the interests of any single cooperative creamery. The one making the highest-quality butter already earned a good price and might receive less for standardized butter. The smaller one making poorer-quality butter might cease to exist as the federation mandated creamery consolidation. All creameries would suffer a loss of local control when the federation enforced rules for accepting cream, making butter, and shipping butter tubs. These factors had relegated the Minnesota Co-operative Dairies Association to a marginal role. Buttermakers and creamery managers had close ties to the creamery supply salesmen and commission merchants with whom they dealt and who opposed a federation that would help creameries cut costs and bypass middlemen. These dairymen's *Dairy Record* opposed the MDA's plans, partly because it depended on advertising from these private firms.[31]

To counter the NPL's appeal to farmers, Governor Preus needed a successful statewide cooperative marketing federation for which he could take credit. With Preus's strong backing, Holmberg, the governor's appointee, could boldly push for a state creamery federation over the objections of private industry. He and his deputy, Hughes, orchestrated

Still resting on 1890s laurels, creameries created this nostalgic 1918 display featuring Theophilus Haecker (right), a cooperative creamery, and old-fashioned butter tubs. The national market was no longer impressed by these accomplishments.

a series of meetings in the spring of 1921, culminating in an organizational meeting on June 7 in the House chamber at the Capitol. Hughes wrote to the county agents and Holmberg to the creameries, warning them of opposition and urging them to send pro-federation delegates to the gathering, which Holmberg chaired. Preus gave the state's pledge of support for the new Minnesota Cooperative Creameries Association (MCCA). The next day, in Hughes's office, its board met for the first time.[32]

Aiding Holmberg and Hughes's campaign was a drop in the wholesale price of high-quality butter in the dominant New York market from seventy cents a pound in April 1920 to a little more than thirty cents in May 1921. Alarmed creamery boards were more receptive to strong measures than were earlier complacent ones. By coincidence, the June 7 meeting came during a low point in butter prices, which rebounded to nearly fifty cents by October.[33]

Still only the state could have pushed through a plan of federation. The cooperative creameries were too divided on the issue and too local in their outlook. Some were receiving more than the average New York price and some less. The better creameries in Freeborn County, the lead dairying area, did not support the plan. *The Farmer* ran a series of articles on the marketing of Minnesota butter, but the farm press could only try to persuade reluctant creameries. The university lacked the political will or strength to oppose private industry on its own. The MFBF loaned MCCA its initial operating capital of one thousand dollars and helped with its organization, but the MCCA was a federation of creameries, not farmers, and it did not exactly follow the Sapiro plan the Farm Bureau favored. A USDA expert who had studied butter marketing encouraged Minnesota creameries to form the MCCA, but he went beyond USDA official policy in doing so, and private dealers could have pressured the agency into making him back down from his stand.[34] Unlike the state's potato farmers, dairy farmers had been organized into local associations for thirty years, and the inertia of institutional tradition made the MCCA harder to create than the Minnesota Potato Exchange had been.

The MCCA was formed before the year (1923) when enthusiasm for the Sapiro-type of centralized cooperative marketing organization hit its peak, and the new organization reflected Minnesota's dairying history as much as the recent interest in California's cooperative marketing successes. Hughes and others studied the contract that the California Fruit

Growers Exchange made with its district exchanges, but they did not fully adopt its rules. The local creameries were not eliminated; the MCCA was owned by and dealt directly with them, not by or with individual farmers. Member creameries were not legally obligated to ship all their butter through the MCCA, though they did have to pay a one-quarter-cent fee on all butter shipped, whether through the MCCA or not. That measure guaranteed the MCCA some income with which to pay its administrative costs even if it handled no butter at all. But that contract was for only two years. The lack of an ironclad, lengthy contract and the adoption of a modest fee fit Minnesota tradition, for local cooperative creameries had succeeded "without the general use of contracts between creameries and patrons."[35]

The MCCA was the capstone to Minnesota's system of dairying dominated by cooperative creameries, but only state government could have lifted the capstone into place in 1921. Even at that, the organizers left it uncertain at the start whether the MCCA would itself market butter and thus displace private buyers.[36] At first, the MCCA only offered services to member creameries—helping them to ship in carload lots, giving them market advice, and encouraging them to standardize their butter. It did not purchase their butter for resale under one brand. The MDA was supportive, agreeing to hire an MCCA employee as state butter inspector at its plant and twisting arms to get creameries to sign the MCCA contract. Holmberg even warned another state agency, the Dairy and Food Commission, to cease its opposition after one of its employees attacked the federation at its first annual meeting.[37] That the MDA played an indispensable role is further shown by the fact that Haecker and others led a similar campaign for a federation of cooperative creameries in 1907, before the MDA existed, with little appreciable success.[38]

The MCCA represented an attempt to handle within one statewide federation economic transactions that previously were taken care of through market mechanisms. To minimize initial opposition, the MCCA did not internalize the final, national market transaction in which a private dealer in New York purchased the butter from a Minnesota creamery. Instead, it eliminated a local market for cream—where cooperative creameries bid against each other for farmers' low-quality cream—by subjecting cream purchases to an internal policy for grading, inspecting, and possibly rejecting cream. One reason for state government's close ties to the MCCA was that it also performed quasi-governmental duties, such as educating farmers on better cream-handling methods and inspecting cream. McGuire stated that without the USDA, the MDA, the university, and the county agents the MCCA "would not have gotten across the first trench."[39] But they helped it partly because they might otherwise have had to attack that first trench—with less support from farmers than a cooperative could command.

1923—A Sapiro Commodity Cooperative Drive in Minnesota

The MDA and the university were not as prominent in the 1923 drive to organize Minnesota farmers around the idea of commodity marketing cooperatives that Sapiro had introduced at the July 1920 conference. The years 1921–25 were the heyday of farmers' cooperatives in America, and the Farm Bureau took the lead. In 1923 the AFBF orchestrated a nationwide drive to organize large-scale marketing cooperatives by commodity. It hired Walton Peteet of Texas to head its new cooperative marketing department and Sapiro to serve as legal counsel.[40]

The Farm Bureau and its editorial allies brought Sapiro and Peteet to Minnesota in early March 1923 to jump start the drive in the Upper Midwest. "It was believed in Minnesota particularly the greatest results could be obtained," explained editor Dan Wallace of *The Farmer.*[41] The success of local cooperatives in Minnesota made it a likely takeoff point for larger-scale cooperation. Sapiro spoke to three hundred people at a cooperative marketing conference at St. Paul's Ryan Hotel, to two hundred businessmen at the Minneapolis Club, and to a joint session of the legislature with Governor Preus present. Conference participants watched movies on the California raisin growers and their marketing association.[42]

While commending the California model of separate cooperatives to market separate commodities, Sapiro both praised and condemned Minnesota's history of cooperative action. "Minnesota was a pioneer in the co-operative movement," Sapiro said. "You have had a wonderful cooperative spirit here, but you've blundered by being headed wrong— toward local organization instead of commodity organization." One local cooperative competed against another in marketing crops. Such blundering, according to Sapiro, resulted from basing cooperation on "the Rochdale plan for consumers and not on the Danish plan for producers. Minnesota has been organizing cooperatives for 60 years without ever having made a dent in any market." Sapiro criticized Minnesota and

North Dakota as uniquely prone to agrarian radicalism, due to this marketing failure of their cooperatives, not to their history of rural cooperation. His answer was the grading, pooling, and selling of commodities by regional or national cooperatives under the ironclad contract—"merchandising farm crops as Ford cars are merchandised." Unlike agrarian protest, this "co-operative marketing is not against anything," he assured the business leaders.[43]

It was ironic, but true, that Minnesota farmers had not used Scandinavian models but had followed the cooperative methods of the New England states, Iowa, Michigan, and New York, and these were largely based on the Rochdale plan. But the key to the Scandinavian-cum-Sapiro model—the ironclad contract—proved to be hard to enforce beyond the local level, even in strongly Scandinavian-American Minnesota.

Sapiro returned for a ten-day tour to promote the new Minnesota Potato Growers Exchange (MPGE), starting at Farm Bureau Day (September 6) at the Minnesota State Fair and continuing with speeches to capacity crowds in Crookston, Moorhead, Brainerd, Detroit Lakes, Sauk Centre, and Princeton. Accompanying him was a contingent representing the Bureau-state-university-editors' network: Dan Wallace of *The Farmer*, Frank W. Peck and Walter C. Coffey from the university, the MDA's Hughes, and the MFBF's president and secretary. For farmers and their wives, Sapiro brought home his message that chain-store-type marketing could lift them out of the poverty of the farm crisis into urban-style prosperity. At Crookston, the *Minneapolis Journal* reported, a toil-worn couple sat toward the front and, as Sapiro neared the end of his speech, "a hush that had fallen on the audience was broken by a husky cough from this man, while his wife brushed aside a tear."[44]

Sapiro's tour set off an intense organizing drive for the new MPGE (Sapiro served as its counsel). The MPGE stressed its businesslike methods. At a planning meeting, Dan Wallace commented, "One of the great troubles with cooperatives is that they have been wet-nursed to death by the agricultural colleges, farm bureaus, etc." So the MPGE sought businessmen to serve on its organizing committee (the Farm Bureau and university were still active). The MPGE was to be a trial run for large-scale cooperative marketing in the Upper Midwest. Disillusioned, Hughes later recalled, "Bankers whose farm loans were 'frozen,' overstocked merchants and dealers in farm machinery, land speculators, economists with a desire to be of genuine service...were appealed to....The war-

Daniel A. Wallace, the Minnesota representative of Iowa's famous Wallaces, moved to Minnesota, farmed near Mora, lost his left arm in a hunting accident, and edited The Farmer *from 1905 to 1934. He enjoyed influence in Washington, D.C., when brother Henry and nephew Henry A. each served as secretary of agriculture.*

days' methods of the Liberty Loan drives were adopted and farmers by the tens of thousands were ballyhooed into the ranks of 'cooperative marketing associations.' "[45]

In the potato-growing district of the Red River Valley, the Farmer-Labor *Country Press* of Moorhead led the opposition to the MPGE drive. The Farmer-Labor Party was at the pinnacle of its 1920s success, having won two U.S. Senate seats for Shipstead and Magnus Johnson and two U.S. House seats in the past year. Congressman Knud Wefald, a Farmer-Laborite from nearby Hawley, was a strong supporter of the *Press*, which blasted the "co-operation howl" as "a clever camouflage scheme by the crowd of fat boys on the other side of the fence." The GOP fat boys would never attack the railroads' "robber freight rates," which the editor of the *Press* felt caused the farmers' current plight. About one thousand people attended a debate in Moorhead between the MPGE's chief organizer and a local attorney.[46]

The organizer signed fourteen thousand growers to the ironclad contract, but within three years this potato exchange was as dead as the first one. The special problems of marketing potatoes made it a questionable industry to pick for a trial run. The MPGE used the same top-down organizing "with propaganda from Bankers, Professors, and business men" as the old MPE, Mosbæk noted. He concluded that, "They are building a big institution (House) from the top and theoretically propose to put in the foundation afterwards." (He did not help with the MPGE drive.) The foundation had to have a sense of loyalty to the local cooperative, which MCCA's member creameries possessed. Then a guaranteed volume could be secured by binding the local cooperative to ship through the federation, as the MCCA was gradually doing. But it was hard for a distant, new federation to bind local farmers directly to an ironclad contract. The MPGE contracts guaranteed that it would handle twenty-two thousand cars of potatoes, but only ten thousand carloads were shipped through it.[47]

Given the American farmers' traditional independence, it was counterproductive for a state or regional cooperative like MPGE to take the non-complying member-farmer to court. If it secured a judgment against him, the MPGE's manager observed, that would create "a sore spot in his community that grows."[48] Local opinion would turn against the cooperative. The Sapiro-type cooperative thus had no effective answer to the free-rider problem. If the MPGE had succeeded in raising potato prices, nonmembers would have grown more potatoes to benefit from the high price, and members would have still sold to a private dealer proffering a slightly higher price than the one the MPGE offered.[49]

Success and Failure at Commodity Marketing:
Butter and Wheat

For statewide cooperatives with a foundation, however, the Sapiro movement of the early 1920s did serve to hasten and help the construction process. The Minnesota Cooperative Creameries Association was built on thirty years of successful operation of local creameries, and it had spent two years aiding creameries to ship in carload lots and to improve butter quality. The Twin City Milk Producers Association had shown how orderly marketing could succeed with whole milk, and the TCMPA was a strong supporter of—and member of—MCCA.[50] Cooperative creameries were not as susceptible to the free-rider problem. Specialized dairy farming required a sizable investment and a change in farming habits, so higher milk prices would not quickly bring many additional farmers into dairying. Creamery members could not ship a highly perishable product to any distant buyer who tempted them with a higher price. The MCCA further reduced competition for members' cream by persuading cooperatives to stop bidding against each other for it and to make sweet cream butter that the centralizers, who relied on cream that was shipped some distance and as a result had lost its sweetness, could not make. Finally because dairy farmers had integrated forward into manufacturing and selling butter, they were closer to Sapiro's goal of chain-store, Ford-style, brand-name marketing.[51]

As he traveled in the state in March and September 1923, Sapiro advocated centralized cooperative marketing of butter under one brand name. He also served as counsel to the AFBF's Committee of Nine, which was working to organize a national sales agency for dairy products. The MCCA's annual meeting in March 1923 endorsed this national plan, which would have Minnesota butter still being identified and sold as such. John Brandt, the new president of MCCA, used the cover provided by this AFBF plan and the wave of enthusiasm for Sapiro's ideas to convince the MCCA's board and member creameries to approve the long-awaited, but controversial, transformation of MCCA into a sales agency that would directly sell butter instead of a service agency aiding creameries to sell it themselves. Private dealers retaliated by threatening not to handle the butter of individual creameries if they signed a marketing agreement with MCCA. At a series of meetings in the fall of 1923, Brandt convinced nervous local boards to stick with MCCA and to sign the new agreement. By Christmas Day 1923, 292 creameries had signed. Disputes eventually derailed the national plan, but it had already served Brandt's purposes.[52]

Labelling MCCA's sweet-cream butter with a brand name in order to win consumers' loyalty was essential to the MCCA's marketing plan—and to Sapiro's emphasis on chain-store marketing methods. In February 1924, MCCA launched a well-advertised contest with a prize of "$500 in gold for a name for Minnesota's finest quality butter." More than one hundred thousand entries were examined by the judges, who included Preus and Dean Coffey of the university's College of Agriculture. Coffey picked out the name Land O' Lakes, which was submitted by two Twin Citians. This name and a scene of an Indian maiden by a lake were placed only on the MCCA's highest quality butter—along with a "Government Inspected" stamp.[53]

At first, MCCA sold Land O' Lakes butter through the commission firms, but by handling large volumes of uniform quality brand-name butter, it acquired more bargaining clout with these firms than the individual creameries had ever had. It began selling directly to retailers in the Twin Cities in 1924 and then slowly expanded to sell to other markets. The retailers tended to be chain stores, for MCCA's large-volume production matched their high-volume sales. This final move bypassed commission firms and completed dairy farmers' long process of integrating forward toward the consumer. Now, through their cooperative, they were making the butter under a brand name, packaging it in one-pound boxes, and selling it directly to the retail store—thereby capturing many of the profits of distributors and merchandisers. They had internalized transactions previously handled in the market. Private dealers turned to politics to oppose this move. They backed the Republican mayor of Minneapolis, George Leach, for governor in 1926, but former Governor Preus's policy of supporting MCCA—renamed Land O' Lakes—was continued by his successor, Theodore Christianson, who won reelection that year.[54]

Minnesota's wheat farmers found it harder to integrate forward—even to take the small step of selling grain in terminal markets—than had dairy farmers. They had lost their chance to mill their own wheat in the 1870s. They had built a foundation, an impressive 390 farmers' elevators by 1920, but these were more dependent on private grain dealers than creameries were on butter dealers. Grain was a fungible, nonperishable commodity that could be transported long distances, so Minnesota wheat farmers had been part of a national market since railroads arrived after the Civil War. They could hardly use a brand name to capture the loyalty of consumers in that market when they did not even process the wheat into flour. Dairy farmers competed in a national market, too, but a market in a finished product, not in raw materials. They could succeed with a brand name. Finally an intangible aura of failure rested on the idea of terminal-level cooperative grain marketing as a result of the lack of success of the Grange, the Alliance, and Equity in this field.

Nevertheless two new groups—the MDA and the MFBF—tentatively developed in the early summer of 1920 a plan "for a state grain marketing association." Then prices collapsed in July 1920, hitting wheat hard. The price fell from more than three dollars a bushel in May to two dollars by November 1920 to less than one dollar by July 1923. This economic crisis provided wheat farmers with a strong incentive to market cooperatively, and their attention turned to the new U.S. Grain Growers, Inc. (USGG), formed in 1921 as a result of the American Farm Bureau's leadership. The MDA and MFBF plans were quietly shelved.[55]

A veritable alphabet soup of associations attempted to market wheat cooperatively at terminal markets in the 1920s. The Equity Cooperative Exchange continued to market wheat from its string of Equity country elevators until the mid-1920s. The Farm Bureau's USGG sputtered along as an uneasy union of the Sapiro idea of pooling vast quantities of wheat to control the supply and raise prices with the more cautious idea of using farmers' elevators to reduce marketing inefficiencies. Farmers' elevators and wheat growers were slow to join the USGG, which failed miserably by 1923. In Minnesota, the USGG was also hurt by confusion over whether it was to replace the ECE or the ECE was to serve as its regional agent. Farmers' elevators dependent on loans from commission firms were reluctant to support the USGG, which those firms vigorously opposed.[56]

After the USGG's failure, advocates of pooling set up their system. In the spring of 1923, farmers and businessmen in northwestern Minnesota formed the Minnesota Wheat Growers Cooperative Marketing Association (MWGCMA), which was affiliated with the American Wheat Growers Associated (AWGA). The MWGCMA was a marketing pool with no capital stock, but it signed its members to a five-year contract requiring them to market all their wheat through the MWGCMA. In two years it spent thirty-three thousand dollars taking noncomplying members to court. The MDA's deputy commissioner, who served on its board, finally pressured it to cut back on this practice. Like other pools, the MWGCMA faced opposition from farmers' elevators, lacked sufficient volume to meet expenses, and could not enforce the ironclad contract. In 1923 only 3.4 percent of the wheat crop was marketed through pools—and that was the peak year.[57]

That percentage indicated the failure of Sapiro-type cooperative marketing of wheat, historian James H. Shideler noted, "since so small a fraction of the supply was woefully short of the amount considered necessary to stabilize prices."[58] The tactic of building terminal-level cooperative grain marketing on a foundation of local farmers' elevators had also failed in Minnesota and the Dakotas. The ECE was placed in receivership in March 1923.[59]

A Non-Sapiro Federation:
Minnesota Co-op Oil Company (Midland)

The Sapiro-type centralized cooperative that bound its producer-members to an ironclad contract and marketed their crops often failed, while the older-style federation of local cooperatives, whether consumer or producer ones, sometimes succeeded. The MCCA (Land O' Lakes) was itself a federation—its members were creameries, not individual farmers. The federation, by definition, was built on a foundation of successful local cooperatives.[60] Contrary to Sapiro's opinion, these could be Rochdale-style consumer cooperatives.

Changes in agriculture and transportation led to the development of a new type of consumers' cooperation—the cooperative oil company. In 1920 American farmers were at the start of a power revolution as tractors run by gasoline-powered, internal-combustion engines gradually replaced horse- and steam-powered farm machinery. By 1920, 30 percent of American farmers owned an automobile that also demanded gasoline. The number of gallons of gasoline shipped into Minnesota increased from 8 million in 1909 to 117 million in 1920.[61] A few corporations dominated the business of refining and selling gasoline and oil, and their profit margins were as high as 25 to 35 percent. With the price collapse of

July 1920, farmers sought ways to lower their cash outlays. These high margins on gas and oil offered one possibility for savings.[62]

At a Farm Bureau meeting in Cottonwood (Lyon County) in February 1921, local farmers discussed how to obtain gasoline at prices lower than the prevailing twenty-four to twenty-eight cents a gallon. In June they formed the Cottonwood Cooperative Oil Company (CCOC), the first such cooperative in the United States. The company rented six filling stations in town, began selling gas by mid-July, and placed front-page ads in the *Cottonwood Current* asking consumers to support this locally owned business and not the Standard Oil station. It did not appeal to cooperative loyalty, although it did follow Rochdale rules. Standard Oil started a price war to drive it out of business, but such was the margin that it could survive a 33 percent price cut. News of this success spread, and by October 1926 thirty-nine such cooperatives were in business, mostly in southern Minnesota where higher-acreage farms led to earlier use of tractors and greater gasoline consumption.[63]

Several factors contributed to farmers' success with this new type of cooperation. The obvious one was that they had had extensive experience with local cooperation by 1921; two members of the CCOC's first board had been officers in the local farmers' elevator. The wide margins virtually guaranteed that the oil cooperatives could quickly and consistently pay patronage dividends to their members (they charged the market price and distributed the profits through the patronage dividend). The business of selling this standardized product without added consumer services was simple and required little capital. Large-volume purchases of petroleum due to the prevalence of the tractor meant that small per-gallon savings through cooperation would add up to sizable savings per farm. Farmers bought gasoline from tank wagons in bulk, not just at the gas pump in small quantities. Following the price drop of July 1920, lower crop prices gave farmers an incentive to cooperate and save. Finally the average town had many filling stations, each inefficiently selling a small volume and vulnerable to a high-volume cooperative like the CCOC with its six stations. In several areas, one cooperative served the whole county to achieve even higher volumes and economies of scale.[64]

In many ways, the cooperative oil company of the 1920s was a replay of the cooperative country store of the 1870s, an attempt to rationalize a new, expanding retail field with too many retail outlets and excessively high margins by replacing many private firms with one cooperative and giving farmers the savings. The key difference was in the product sold.

Edwin Galion Cort, Freeborn county agent and founder of that county's cooperative oil company, led a drive to federate local cooperatives and form a state cooperative that would be their bulk supplier. He was partly inspired by the success of Land O' Lakes. In September 1926, the Minnesota Co-op Oil Company was launched with Cort as its manager, no capital, no storage facilities, and a rented office on East Hennepin Avenue in Minneapolis. It "shipped directly from the refinery to the locals which had bulk storage facilities," thus seeking to bypass the private wholesalers. So rudimentary was the business and so wide the profit margins, that it flourished despite that shaky start, a long price war in 1927–28, a bid by a private oil distributer to replace it, and the lack of any contract binding its member locals to purchase gas or oil from their cooperative wholesaler. MDA's deputy commissioner aided the federation and its member locals, and a state and federal investigation helped end the price war.[65]

By 1930 it had a new name, Midland Cooperative Oil Association (after several Wisconsin locals joined), and sixty-two member associations. Midland's mission evolved. Local cooperatives used profits from petroleum sales to expand into other lines, such as farm or automotive supplies and consumer goods. Cort came to believe that Midland should also become a broadly based consumers' cooperative rather than just a federation of oil cooperatives. That new mission would fit with the 1930s, the heyday of consumer cooperation.[66]

The University Answers Sapiro's Attack on Minnesota Cooperation

In April 1924 the university's agricultural experiment station issued a bulletin on cooperative central marketing organization. Authors John D. Black and H. Bruce Price soberly analyzed the claims made for Sapiro-style cooperative marketing and defended Minnesota's system of local cooperatives against Sapiro's criticisms. These economists acknowledged that local cooperatives could not adequately handle many marketing problems: quality control, standardizing and stabilizing production, orderly marketing according to consumer demand, and collective bargaining.[67] Still, they argued, the Sapiro centralized commodity-marketing cooperative was being oversold. It could address all those problems except collective bargaining, but that was the main one its promoters promised to solve. MCCA's chief hope of raising butter prices, they wrote, was "in improving quality, standardizing its product and establishing brands, and advertising these brands," not in controlling the butter supply as a Sapiro-type cooperative was supposed to do.[68]

Black and Price distinguished between a Sapiro-type centralized organization and a Minnesota-style federation of local cooperatives by citing several factors (see Table 6). In general, the centralized cooperative dispensed with local cooperatives and dealt directly with individual farmers who were bound to market their crops through it and to accept its grading, packing, and selling policies. The federation was an association of local cooperatives, each of which retained its right to negotiate directly with its farmer-members and to keep control of its members' crops as they went to market. Of course, any one marketing cooperative could combine the centralized and federated features in its own way. As Black and Price noted, the MCCA was moving toward centralization as it enforced stricter quality-control measures and directly sold butter, but it retained local creameries as members.[69]

Clearly the federated model was the one that Minnesota farmers used most and that fit best with their tradition of local cooperation. Black and Price argued that it was the model most frequently used in Denmark also—contrary to the impression left by Sapiro's speeches.[70] They stated that the nature of the commodity would determine which model worked best, but they showed a sensitivity to Sapiro's critique of Minnesota-style cooperation as too local, too voluntary, and too short term. Probably quoting an MCCA leader, they wrote, "We have been thirty years building up our system of local co-operatives.... If we were to allow them to lose their identity in a large marketing scheme, and it should fail, our work of thirty years would be largely wiped out." They feared that farmers would not remain loyal to a distant, centralized cooperative that lacked locals whose managers provided face-to-face contact and whose annual meet-

TABLE 6
Centralized Cooperative and Federation of Cooperatives

Factor	Centralized	Federated
Control of supply	Vital to success	Not vital to success
Price policy	Dictate price	Accept market price
Time of sale	Dictate time	Let locals pick time
Own product sold?	Own product sold	Agent, not owner
Quality control	Set/enforce grades	Educate locals only
Status of local	Abolish locals	Retain locals
Length of contract	More than 3 years	Usually 1 year

ings furnished access to democratic processes. They criticized Sapiro-type centralized cooperatives built on a high-pressure "whirlwind campaign of misinformation and exaggeration" regarding the benefits of ironclad, long-term contracts and the chances of dictating price by controlling the supply of farm crops.[71]

Black and Price were partly correct. The two potato exchanges organized in ballyhooing campaigns had both failed. The MWGCMA had not created or maintained any appreciable loyalty among wheat farmers, for it lacked locals with a tradition of success and so it failed to have personal contact with its members. The federated model best fit Minnesota's cooperative history, and the MCCA and Midland were both examples of that approach. Yet the two authors were overly critical of Sapiro's movement and ignored its ability to generate an enthusiasm for large-scale cooperation that helped even a federation like Land O' Lakes, which did not exactly fit its rules, to persuade farmers and their creameries to support a risky new marketing effort. Sapiro's ideas also cemented the Republicans' commitment to cooperative marketing, which was crucial to organizing Land O' Lakes and other cooperative federations.

Those cooperatives that traditionally had been linked to agrarian protest kept their distance from Sapiro and his GOP allies. Whether Minnesota's new Farmer-Labor Party could assist them as the Republicans had aided Land O' Lakes was soon to be determined. What was certain was that the Farmer-Laborites would have to deal with the existence of more conservative and more centralized cooperative federations that had not existed before the county agent movement, the start of the Minnesota Department of Agriculture, the formation of the Minnesota Farm Bureau Federation, the 1920 Preus campaign, and the Sapiro cooperative marketing fever of 1923–35. It would face a greatly altered cooperative landscape.

14

Farmer-Labor Cooperation

"The cooperative commonwealth
is Minnesota's American solution
to a predatory, ruthless capitalism"

On Saturday, July 4, 1936, three thousand picnickers met in the Glenwood city park by Lake Minnewaska to celebrate both Independence Day and International Co-operators Day. They listened to a speech by Dr. James Peter Warbasse, president of the Cooperative League of the United States of America, which was holding its national convention in Glenwood through that weekend. The Fremad Association still ran its store there, and a Wollan was the mayor, but the Norwegian-American farmers who started Fremad in 1873–74 would surely have been startled at the size and scope of this gathering of cooperators from many states and foreign countries. Midland Cooperative Wholesale dominated the proceedings, which included a parade of 24 oil trucks and 130 other vehicles and "dramatic re-enactments" of the founding of the Cottonwood oil cooperative and of the origins of the rainbow-colored international cooperative flag. The *New York Times* and *Time* magazine sent reporters. A newsreel cameraman took pictures.[1]

The exceedingly hot summer of 1936 was a good time to meet by Lake Minnewaska. More importantly, Minnesota was a good place because, as the *Times* reporter noted, it was "the nation's most cooperative state," and its Farmer-Labor Party (FLP) was pro-cooperative. In the 1930s interest in consumers' cooperation peaked in the United States, spurring President Franklin D. Roosevelt to send a commission to Europe to study it. It was the depth of the interest that explained the media's presence. Noticeably absent from the festivities were the FLP's leaders, who controlled state government and were campaigning in rural areas that election year. Midland's leaders were Farmer-Laborites, but none of the FLP candidates spoke at the Glenwood convention.[2]

This most cooperative-minded state had the most powerful third party, one whose stated goal was the cooperative commonwealth—a society in which cooperatives were to be the defining type of economic organization. Was this coincidence or cause and effect? Did cooperatives' strength partly contribute to the FLP's success?

Some evidence points to cooperation as a major reason why the FLP, as political scientist Richard M. Valelly noted, "is the most successful case of a radical, state-level third party that American politics has seen."[3] The FLP was critical of capitalism yet not committed to socialism so cooperation was its congenial third option or "middle way," one that was voluntary, democratic, locally controlled, not revolutionary or utopian, but practical and quickly beneficial. Cooperatives functioned in Minnesota, and many—Farmers' Union, Midland, and Finnish-American cooperatives especially—were allied with the FLP. The Grange and Farmers' Alliance provided ample precedent whereby a political movement used cooperatives to build its membership base. Finally, New Deal funding for a new type of cooperative—rural electrification associations—meant the FLP might be able to use federal dollars to recruit farmer-members for both the electric cooperatives and itself.

Other evidence points away from a link between cooperative strength and FLP success. The FLP's absence from Glenwood implied that relations between the party and the cooperatives were not as close as Farmer-Laborites claimed. Equity cooperatives, such as the Equity Cooperative Exchange, had made up only one strand in the party's original coalition, which was initially and most basically united by opposition to the World War I policies of the Minnesota Commission of Public Safety (MCPS). The FLP began as an anti-MCPS coalition that included conservative German-American farmers, urban workers, the Nonpartisan League, Scandinavian Americans opposed to U.S. involvement in the war, and iron range miners.[4] The FLP and the wartime home-front conflict that produced it were products of the increased regional diversity and heightened dissension created since 1885 by Finnish immigration, the formation of a mining region on the Mesabi Range, the growth of a Twin Cities metropolis, and the creation of a conservative dairying area in southern and central Minnesota. By 1929 the University of Minnesota had identified seven distinct agricultural regions in the state.[5] Regionalization within the state—more than rural cooperation—made third-party politics possible, but it meant that the FLP's internal differences were greater than those in North Dakota's Nonpartisan League or Saskatchewan's Cooperative Commonwealth Federation (CCF).

Roosevelt's New Deal nationalized American politics in ways that undercut a state third party, Valelly concluded. Canada's more decentralized federalism gave a provincial radical party like Saskatchewan's CCF a freedom of action and "a degree of stability in [its] political environment" that the centralizing, innovating New Deal took away from the FLP.[6] That is true—and the rural electrification program was a prime example—but Valelly ignored the major role of wheat-growers' cooperatives in the origins of the CCF. Here the CCF had another advantage; it flourished in a homogeneous political economy. Seymour Lipset noted that Saskatchewan was nearly "an economically undifferentiated society... for almost every farmer is dependent on wheat for his basic source of income." Right-wingers and left-wingers fought in its cooperatives, but they were all wheat growers.[7]

Minnesota's cooperative movement was quite diverse—by type of cooperative as well as by ideology—and not all of its elements supported the third party. The FLP could not count on help from the creameries, Land O' Lakes, or the Farm Bureau, but it did rely on several elements in the movement.

Liberal-leaning Cooperatives Friendly to Farmer-Laborism

Many members of the Finnish-American cooperative stores of northern Minnesota were part of the anti-MCPS coalition. These cooperatives developed out of the unique circumstances of the Finnish Americans there, and many remained more radical than the Norwegian-American co-ops in Hanska or Underwood. Generalizations are hazardous, for many Finnish Americans were conservative, church-going folk, but Finns tended to be more radical than other groups. Their later arrival in Minnesota at the turn of the century rather than in the late nineteenth century had radicalizing consequences. Too late to take good homestead land, they had to find work in the mines and lumber camps, where many became socialists if they had not been so when they emigrated. Their prominent role in the 1907 Mesabi Iron Range strike led to many being blacklisted and forced into farming cutover lands of St. Louis and adjoining counties. Here by 1917 they had formed some twenty-seven cooperative stores belonging to the wholesale Cooperative Central Exchange (CCE) of Superior, Wisconsin. Cooperative and socialist ideology combined with the language barrier to isolate many Finnish Americans in a radical enclave that confirmed and intensified their radicalism. Others' stereotyping of Finns as radicals added to this isolation.[8]

In the 1920s the CCE's network of stores in Minnesota, Wisconsin, and Michigan aided the Communists more than the Farmer-Laborites. (The FLP excluded Communists from membership in their party from 1925 to 1935.) But in 1929–30, the CCE split with the Communists after they demanded a loan from it and the firing of one CCE leader who refused their demand. The CCE turned to "'pure and simple' cooperativism," changed its name to Central Cooperative Wholesale (CCW) and its trade label from the Red Star to the twin pines, and welcomed non-Finns into its ranks. Communists formed their own wholesaler, the Workers' and Farmers' Cooperative Unity Alliance (CUA). By 1934, the CCW, with thirty-three stores in Minnesota, had far outpaced the CUA, which had five stores in the state. The CCW and Franklin Cooperative Creamery of Minneapolis dominated the Northern States Cooperative League, which promoted cooperation in the entire region. Free of Communist influence, the CCW drew closer to the FLP. But the political neutrality of "pure and simple" cooperation, the CCW's distance from St. Paul, and its multistate nature limited its clout in the FLP.[9]

More closely aligned with the FLP was Midland, a wholesaler of petroleum products and automotive supplies to cooperative oil associations. Midland enjoyed steady growth in the 1930s, from 62 member cooperatives in 1930 to 201 in 1938. It grew beyond its home base in southern and southwestern Minnesota to central and northern areas and into Wisconsin. By the early 1930s, argued sociologist Joel S. Torstenson, Midland had switched from its early "ideology of thrift" stressing cooperative savings to an anticapitalist ideology promoting a socially redeeming consumers' cooperation. Its manager, E. G. Cort, converted to that view partly through contact with the Northern States Cooperative League and its Finnish-American leaders. From the League, Cort hired two of his chief aides, George W. Jacobson and Joseph Gilbert, both staunch Farmer-Laborites who developed close ties to the FLP administration of

Governor Floyd B. Olson (1931–36). By 1935 Gilbert chaired the FLP's fifth ward club in Minneapolis, and Jacobson was active in the drive for a national third party.[10]

Midland's expansionary policies gave the FLP a strong ally in the cooperative movement. Midland's goal was also a cooperative commonwealth. Its "small staff of devoted field men, organizers, and promoters" preached cooperation as if engaged in "a religious crusade." Wherever they traveled, they often approached Farmer-Laborites as the people likely to help start local cooperatives. Under Cort's leadership, Midland wanted to move beyond the farm supply business into selling groceries through urban cooperative stores.[11]

That was more than a business decision; it took Midland from producer cooperation to a broader consumers' cooperation that tried to enlist all citizens and to change society radically—a concept suited to a third party like the FLP. Midland joined the 1930s drive for consumers' cooperation that generated few lasting cooperatives but some influential books, including Horace M. Kallen's *The Decline and Rise of the Consumer* and Warbasse's *Cooperative Democracy* and FDR's delegation to Europe. This enthusiasm differed from the 1920s fad of cooperative marketing associations. The 1930s movement scorned producers' cooperation as an inferior type that could hardly be considered cooperation at all. Farmers' cooperatives looked for higher profits for one class in society and did not challenge the profit system. Consumers' cooperatives sought to replace the production-for-profit with a production-for-use system in which supply would equal demand. Consumers' needs, not producers' hopes of profits, would dictate the amount of goods produced. The boom-and-bust business cycle would be a thing of the past, an attractive idea in the Great Depression.[12] "Production for use" and the "cooperative commonwealth" were some of Governor Olson's favorite phrases. In a February 1935 article contrasting Farmer-Laborism and Communism, his chief aide, Vince Day, wrote, "The program of the Farmer-Labor party is the Cooperative Commonwealth," which he defined as:

> a state wherein public utilities and natural resources are state owned or cooperatively owned and other enterprises are cooperatively owned with the state aiding cooperative business exactly as it aids private business today....The Cooperative Commonwealth is Minnesota's American solution to the American problems brought on by a predatory, ruthless capitalism.

Cooperation allowed the FLP to have it both ways; it was, Day claimed, "the highest type of private ownership"—thus was in accord with American values—and "the purest type of public ownership"—thus was opposed to capitalism. Olson claimed he had not read Karl Marx, but he had picked up his idea of "production for use . . . by watching the operations of the cooperatives, of which he proudly says that there are 'more in Minnesota than in all the rest of the States put together.' "[13]

A third FLP ally was the Farmers' Union and its cooperatives headquartered in St. Paul: the Farmers Union Grain Terminal Association (GTA) and Farmers Union Central Exchange (CENEX). Myron W. Thatcher was the main leader of GTA (which went through several name changes before settling on that title). A bookkeeper and auditor, Thatcher worked for the ECE from 1914 until it was placed in receivership in 1923 when he became its acting secretary. Through a herculean effort, he persuaded all who had claims on the ECE's assets to accept ten cents on the dollar plus stock in the new Farmers Cooperative Terminal Association, which was organized in 1926 and became the GTA in 1937. Thatcher served as a lobbyist in Washington, D.C., from March 1932 to the summer of 1937 so he was absent from the state for much of the Farmer-Labor period. The GTA received most of its grain and its members from North Dakota and Montana, not Minnesota; in 1930 it had six thousand members in Minnesota, thirty thousand in North Dakota, and ten thousand in Montana. Its ties to the Farmers' Union and its headquarters in St. Paul gave it some influence at the Capitol, however.[14]

CENEX grew out of joint purchasing of supplies by buying clubs of Farmers' Union members, who purchased goods—mainly binder twine— from the Farmers Union Exchange, a wholesale branch of GTA. In 1928 the Farmers' Union began to form oil cooperatives in western Minnesota, North Dakota, and Montana. Almost all of these did not compete directly against Midland's members, located mainly in southern Minnesota and Wisconsin. In January 1931, local cooperatives decided to separate the Exchange from GTA and to incorporate it as the Farmers Union Central Exchange. By 1936, CENEX sold petroleum products and farm supplies to 36 oil cooperatives in Minnesota and 160 in North Dakota and Montana. It, too, served mainly the northwestern grain-growing area of Minnesota, but it carried some clout in the state's complex politics of rival regional farm groups.[15]

Because they served different regions, Midland, CCW, and CENEX tended not to compete against each other as cooperative wholesalers. All were partners in National Cooperatives, Inc., a manufacturer jointly owned by several cooperative wholesalers. CCW purchased Midland's petroleum products. Neither CENEX nor CCW could hope to outsell Midland in oil and gasoline; Midland's affiliated cooperatives sold nearly five times the volume that CENEX's stations sold, and eight times CCW's volume.[16] Midland's member cooperatives sold nearly twenty-four times as much gas and oil as did the Farm Bureau's.[17] Given the liberal or even radical bent of the Farmers' Union, the GTA and CENEX were bound to side with the FLP and its allies. The economic interests of these liberal-minded cooperatives did not clash so as to interfere with their mutual support for the FLP. But the FLP had to cultivate the support, which was not automatic, of these economically powerful allies.

Conservative cooperatives, such as the Farm Bureau ones, creameries, Land O' Lakes, and TCMPA, did not directly aid the Farmer-Labor Party. But they increased the significance of cooperation in Minnesota, and that made third-party politics and the FLP's "middle way" more plausible alternatives to the procapitalist Republicans and Democrats. Indirectly the success of any cooperative added to the plausibility of the Farmer-Labor critique of the American political economy.

In a practical way, a local cooperative provided an alternative rung on the leadership ladder whereby a farmer or a farmer's son or daughter could climb to responsible posts in the town, county, or state without adopting the procapitalist, chamber-of-commerce views of county-seat or metropolitan elites. It was hard to step directly from farming to a leadership role, as Alliancemen like Christian Ahlness of Lake Hanska had discovered. Even the prototypical dirt-farmer politician, Magnus Johnson, first gained experience and entered politics by participating in the ECE, where he was discovered by George Loftus.[18] Minnesota's cooperatives offered managerial positions that trained rural people and prepared them to lead a third-party movement.

The Depression made cooperators' anticapitalist critique more credible than it would later appear to Americans living in prosperous times. Cooperators could explain why profit-driven capitalism had failed and thus disprove the procapitalist views of the chambers of commerce. The Depression aided both the cooperatives and the FLP, bonding them together. It remained for the FLP's leaders to take the initiative to make an FLP-cooperative alliance an actuality.

The Farmer-Labor Party and Cooperatives, 1931–34

The leaders were slow to do so. Day saved the memorandums that he wrote to inform Olson about the mind-boggling rush of issues, complaints, factional politics, gossip, and jobseekers pouring into the governor's office. For the years 1931–33, Day recorded few cooperative issues or leaders vying for Olson's attention. In 1932 Day proposed using the 1923 Sapiro-inspired Cooperative Marketing Act as legal authorization for combining all farm groups in "a single cooperative marketing association" that could enforce a farm holiday or strike *"in a peaceful and legal way."* That step was never taken. On the opposite, miniscule scale, Day reported that oil cooperatives pressed state departments to buy oil and gas from them and that A. J. McGuire was disappointed over not being appointed to the University of Minnesota Board of Regents.[19]

Olson faced serious issues and a crisis situation before New Deal programs began operating in late 1933. Farm foreclosures, bank failures, high unemployment, desperate jobhunters seeking state jobs, a threatened farm strike, the frantic efforts to persuade the legislature to pass the governor's program, and the daily challenges of administering state government in turbulent times all preoccupied Olson and his aides.[20]

Cooperatives did not emerge from the wings and onto center stage until the spring and summer of 1934. In his March 27 speech to the 1934 Farmer-Labor state convention, Olson stated that the FLP's "ultimate" goal was "a co-operative commonwealth wherein the government will stifle as much as possible the greed and avarice of the private profit system." As a good orator seeking to electrify the audience before him, Olson ad-libbed, "Now, I am frank to say that I am not a liberal.... I am what I want to be—I am a radical." The delegates responded with more than applause. After Olson hurried to Washington to lobby for Land O' Lakes president John Brandt's farm recovery plan, they adopted a radical platform calling for "immediate steps... to abolish capitalism in a peaceful and lawful manner" and for the "complete re-organization of the present social structure into a co-operative commonwealth" in which "all the natural resources, machinery of production, transportation and communication shall be owned by the government" and operated according to democratic principles.[21] This was a dangerous indiscretion—akin to printing verbatim in the newspaper one's remarks after consuming a few beers. Republicans gleefully seized on this election-year admission of ultimate goals. A month after the convention, Day reported to Olson that "a feeling of panic" had hit some FLP members and state officeholders. Olson's biographer, George H. Mayer, exaggerated only slightly when he concluded, "The situation became so critical during the first two weeks of May that survival of the party seemed in retrospect to be nothing less than miraculous."[22]

Party leaders clutched at the ambiguities of cooperation to rescue them from this crisis. On May 1, Day met with three FLP leaders, includ-

Floyd B. Olson, governor from 1931 to 1936, performed one of a governor's duties—promoting the state. Here he joined a 4-H member in advertising potatoes from the Arrowhead Region.

ing Hjalmar Petersen, the candidate for lieutenant-governor, for five hours to develop an "analysis" of the platform, which could replace the actual platform in public debate. They turned to cooperation as a non-radical idea that fit with and yet moderated the platform's anticapitalist rhetoric. The Scandinavian nations were model cooperative common-wealths, and, they asserted, "The cooperative movement has nowhere in America made greater strides than it has made in Minnesota." State government, via the 1919 law establishing the MDA, had legal authority to aid cooperatives. They portrayed this controversial platform as having two steps, and they focused on the first, least-controversial one, the vol-untary step of forming cooperatives, which could be done immediately. They safely placed the second step of public ownership somewhere in the unlikely future, dependent on constitutional changes and a popular referendum.[23]

Explaining their work to Olson, Day emphasized that confiscation of private property for public use was not the FLP's position, despite what the platform indicated and socialism demanded. Unequal distribution and "wrong uses of private property" were the evils of capitalism that the FLP opposed, and both ills could be solved, he implied, through coop-eration. "Our movement is a cooperative and not a socialistic move-ment," for "cooperation favors the ownership of private property." Mem-bers invested their property (money) in the cooperative, but they could withdraw it at any time. It was not confiscated as it was under a socialist system.[24]

The effort to use cooperation as a cover to downplay an unpopular platform continued. In July 1934, Day asked Jacobson to write one or two campaign speeches on the cooperative movement in Minnesota. Jacobson assigned the task to Gilbert, editor of the *Midland Cooperator*, and prom-ised to meet with Day to discuss Gilbert's rough draft.[25] An FLP campaign tract included a cartoon showing a hysterical Republican shouting, "The Reds are coming—co-operative creameries are only the start." It high-lighted what it said were contradictory GOP claims that "the cooperative commonwealth idea [was] communism" and that Republicans were "the defenders of co-operatives in Minnesota." But it, too, was inconsistent in its portrayal of the political diversity of the state's cooperatives: conser-vative ones like creameries proved the idea was not communism; GOP opposition to liberal cooperative leaders like Loftus and Manahan dis-proved GOP claims to be the friend of cooperatives.[26] The political tint of cooperation was in the eye of the beholder, and it could change from one sentence to the next. There were enough cooperatives of all colors to affirm whatever claims either party wished to make.

It is impossible to ascertain what effect the calming rhetoric about cooperation had on the election results. The FLP retained the statewide offices it had won in 1932 and Shipstead's U.S. Senate seat but lost control of the state's officially nonpartisan House of Representatives. Olson's vote declined from 49.6 percent in 1932 to 44.0 percent in 1934. He won the three-man race because of his seventy-three thousand vote margin in Hennepin, Ramsey, and St. Louis Counties. He lost support in the eighty-four rural counties—losing an average of nearly 12 percent of his 1932 votes in the rural counties where he had been strongest two years earlier.[27] Probably, taking shelter in cooperation kept the FLP from suffering even higher losses in rural areas and a defeat in the gubernatorial race.

Liberal cooperative leaders were emboldened by Olson's request for their campaign help. Together with cooperative-minded Farmer-Laborites employed at the MDA, they formed an ad hoc committee in August 1934 to promote and coordinate cooperation statewide and to pressure Olson to force the MDA to do more of both tasks. Neither Commissioner Rollef A. Trovatten nor James H. Hay, deputy commissioner and chief MDA liaison to cooperatives, was on the committee, which became a watchdog critically assessing their performance. Midland's Jacobson and Gilbert, and others, thought the MDA was not carrying out its 1919 legal mandate to organize cooperatives, by which they meant liberal consumers' cooperatives.[28]

The committee became embroiled in the patronage and ideological battles of Olson's administration.[29] Trovatten, a farmer, had been elected to the House as a Farmer-Laborite in 1922; after his one term, he had left farming to organize cooperatives. Ambitious to use his contacts with farmers and his Norwegian ancestry to win statewide elective office, Trovatten was "a conservative Farmer-Labor voice" who straddled the divide between Midland and the Farm Bureau and resisted FLP attempts to force him to hire only loyal Farmer-Laborites at the MDA. A graduate and former employee of the university's School of Agriculture and a former NPL member, he tried to bridge that gulf, too. Hay, a former school superintendent and a Republican holdover, also tried to work with both the Minnesota Farm Bureau Federation (MFBF) and liberal cooperatives.[30] An underlying issue was Midland's desire to emphasize consumers' cooperatives and to move beyond the farmers' cooperatives with which both men were identified. Trovatten and Hay's work was thus criticized from several angles—patronage, political, and cooperative—and by divers persons with several motives that seemed to merge within this committee. From a managerial standpoint, it was odd to have the two bosses' work assessed by those of their subordinates with enough clout in the FLP to be immune to dismissal by them. On the committee sat Charles Ommodt, assistant MDA commissioner, who may have been angling for Trovatten's job. Meeting like a jury with the defendant out of the room, the committee on December 6, 1934, heard arguments on whether Trovatten should remain at MDA. It voted to support him "provided he would pledge to carry out the" mandate of the 1919 law. He was called into the room and informed of the decision. He gave the pledge.[31]

The committee had other goals besides that of holding Trovatten's feet to the fire. The members discussed Jacobson's "plan for coordinating cooperatives in Minnesota" that evolved into a demand that Olson secure a fifty-thousand-dollar appropriation from the legislature and hire five or six field directors "to help coordinate existing cooperatives and to systematically build new ones." County agents performed both tasks, but in ways too conservative to suit this committee, which thus sought a state-funded alternative. Committee members asked farm groups to pressure Olson to agree to their plan and discussed how the MFBF's monopoly of county-agent work could be ended or circumvented.[32] Their activity culminated on January 17, 1935, when four committee members (Gilbert, John Bosch, V. S. Alanne, and W. E. Boie) met with the governor, after cooling their heels waiting for three hours. This was possibly the only meeting cooperative leaders had with Olson regarding his relations with the cooperative movement. Olson perceived (or pretended to perceive) a patronage-motivated committee demanding that present MDA jobholders be replaced by new ones. The four men denied this, but the reelected governor used his skills of evasion to avoid making any commitments. He may have been too beleaguered by jobseekers to recognize the visitors' cooperative idealism or too politically vulnerable to antagonize the Farm Bureau by adopting their ideas or by firing Trovatten. Controversy was sure to result from sending state-paid fieldmen to start liberal-leaning cooperatives that would compete with existing businesses or conservative-leaning ones. The committee had not secured the support of a broad spectrum of cooperative leaders but represented just one wing of the movement. The 1919 law authorized the MDA to aid consumers' cooperatives, but it required the MDA to rely on the county agents' services. It did not empower the MDA to do what the committee wanted done—to form aggressive consumers' cooperatives in rural areas to create a new social order.[33]

Despite Olson's use of cooperation to save his 1934 campaign from charges of socialism, liberal cooperative leaders could not secure his commitment to use his office to advance consumers' cooperation. The cooperative idea was not copyrighted, and he acknowledged no debt to them for his use of it. Nor did he seem to fear them. The Rochdale rule of political neutrality and the lack of a tradition of aggressive politicking by cooperatives meant that Olson did not expect to lose votes by annoying them. Voters had not looked to economic leaders to tell them how to vote in political elections.

Meanwhile, the MDA was sponsoring a project, a federally funded statewide survey of all types of cooperatives, which was a step toward what the committee wanted. The project had "its headquarters in a vacant room in" Midland's Minneapolis plant. The work began in late March 1934 under the supervision of Russell K. Lewis, a recent field worker for Midland and a doctoral candidate in agricultural economics at the university. Ostensibly under the MDA's control, the survey's public purpose was to write reports on each type of cooperative, the first of which was ready by April 1935; however, Midland influenced the project more than the MDA did and accomplished some private goals. Survey workers wrote articles for the *Midland Cooperator,* mailed Midland literature, designed a special questionnaire for use by oil cooperatives, used that data to write cost analyses and a co-op oil manual for Midland, and inquired in rural areas about opportunities to expand Midland-style consumers' cooperation. Lewis asked the rural survey workers to gather data on the "organization, activity . . . membership and interest" of the Farm Bureau, Farmers' Union, and Grange. To Lewis and Midland, these were not "private purposes," for by definition true cooperatives "are not private enterprises."[34]

The reports reflected Midland's ideology of a society-transforming consumers' cooperation. The report on producers' cooperation treated it as a means to the end of consumers' cooperation and devoted much space to the latter to compensate for the "undue prominence" given to the former. The report on consumers' cooperation criticized Farm Bureau cooperatives for their ties to county agents and for other deficiencies, farmers' stores for not attempting "the establishment of a new social system," and independent stores not affiliated with Midland or ccw for merely "effecting a small saving to the consumer at the retail end" instead of pursuing "production for use, and a changed economic and social order." It praised Finnish Americans and the ccw for seeking a new order, a goal that "never entered [the] minds" of other farmers.[35]

Jacobson and Gilbert seemed to credit this project to the New Deal that funded it, not to the Farmer-Labor state agency that officially sponsored it. They responded to Olson's evasions with a harsh editorial, "Cooperatives and the Farmer-Labor Party," written by Gilbert with advice from Jacobson.

The Farmer-Labor Party and Cooperatives, 1935–36: The REA

Five months after the committee met with Olson, a new opportunity "to systematically build new" cooperatives arose. It sparked a battle between liberal and conservative leaders over who would build them and benefit from them. It demonstrated Valelly's point that the New Deal "radically changed the political environment" of the FLP.[36]

On May 11, 1935, President Roosevelt by executive order created a temporary Rural Electrification Administration (REA), to disburse one hundred million dollars appropriated for constructing electric lines in rural areas. Exactly one year later, Congress passed the Norris-Rayburn Act making REA permanent and giving it an additional 420 million dollars over ten years.[37] Rural electrification became entangled in the long-standing feud between Progressives and the utility industry. The REA head, Morris Cooke, a mechanical engineer and Progressive, had served Progressive Governors Roosevelt (New York) and Gifford Pinchot (Pennsylvania) as an adviser on rural electrification. In both states, Cooke had battled the utility companies, and though he claimed to be willing to see REA funds go to them, his suspicion of their methods left the field open to rural electric cooperatives.[38]

Cooke and other Progressives suspected that the utility companies were not interested in extending service beyond the most profitable farm customers to provide "area coverage" to all farmers in a given region. They had built lines to only 10 percent of U.S. farms and 12 percent of Minnesota's farms by July 1935. They typically charged farmers five hundred to one thousand dollars as an initial fee to help pay the more expensive costs of constructing rural lines. Few farmers could afford those sums or their high rural rates—nine to ten cents per kilowatt hour when urban rates were four to five cents. A Catch-22 blocked progress: "recipients of service used little power because of high rates, and the utilities charged such rates because of low usage."[39]

Utility firms expected farmers to solve this problem by buying more appliances and increasing their usage so that the companies could lower the rates. Farmers wanted the utilities to lower the rates so that they could afford to buy appliances and increase their usage.[40] A similar problem had delayed rural telephone service in 1900, and here, too, cooperation offered a solution. If farmers owned the utility, the debate over who should act first would end. Both could act without fearing the other would take advantage.

Such cooperation began well before the New Deal. In 1914 farmers in Stony Run Township (Yellow Medicine County) had formed Stony Run Light & Power Company, probably the nation's first rural electric cooperative. John J. Mooney, organizer of neighboring Lisbon Township's suballiance in 1890, played a leading role in starting Stony Run Light & Power. It purchased electricity from the municipal power plant in Granite Falls and charged each farmer $200 for construction, plus $150 for the equipment connecting each farm to the line. Although successful, Stony Run was not a prototype for national rural electrification. It served only fifty families by 1921, and it had the advantage of access to a municipal plant.[41]

In the 1920s the Farm Bureau-university-county agent network worked with private utilities through state Committees on the Relation of Electricity to Agriculture to develop a prototype. In a major pilot program, Northern States Power Company built a six-mile line to serve nineteen dairy farms near Red Wing. E. A. Stewart, professor of agricultural engineering, directed this study, which achieved higher electric usage and a modest reduction in rates. The Red Wing project was publicized in many bulletins, but it was an experiment in a small area where farms were atypical in their "high use of machinery, close proximity to an existing power line and regular income from dairy production."[42] Electricity was more costly to provide and involved more technical problems than phone service. The farm recession of the 1920s made that decade a poor time to electrify rural America.

The creation of the REA in 1935 was the right time. The Farm Bureau had dropped its support for the private utilities' committees and now sought government involvement.[43] New Dealers were willing to spend millions on rural electrification, partly to give work to the unemployed. Cooke, the nation's foremost expert on the issue, had both the agency and the budget to begin the task. He knew that the most rapid electrification would occur if REA loaned funds to utility companies or municipal plants to construct rural power lines since they were equipped to do so. From July to December 1935, the program drifted: the REA lacked technical data; Cooke was suspicious of the utilities, and they were hostile to the New Deal; municipalities were indifferent to farmers' needs.

Cooke turned to the idea of creating rural electric cooperatives that would serve as the REA's local agents. This decision was made slowly, for some REA staffers doubted farmers' ability to run rural power systems while others favored the use of cooperatives. Boyd Fisher, head of REA's Development Section, "steadily prodded Cooke" to choose cooperatives, but Fisher "insisted that REA not engage in the propagandizing of co-ops" and that REA loan money only to cooperatives started on local initiative and "in a solid business-like manner." Cooke increasingly saw cooperatives as a middle way between the extremes (to him) of ownership of rural power systems by either private utilities or the government.[44] While the REA made its decision, liberal and conservative cooperative leaders in Minnesota prepared to organize cooperatives that could qualify for REA loans. The REA's one hundred million dollars at 3 percent interest represented the largest government aid ever offered to organize new cooperatives. By the 1930s access to electric power was the greatest need and hope of rural people. The farm group that organized rural electric cooperatives and brought electricity to the farm would earn the gratitude of thousands of Minnesota farmers—a huge reward that sparked a bitter battle over who would earn it.[45]

The June 1935 annual meeting authorized Midland to sponsor and organize rural electric cooperatives in Minnesota and Wisconsin on behalf of the liberal wholesalers (Midland, CENEX, and CCW). In September 1935 Midland's district meetings approved this plan, and Midland's assistant manager, Alwin N. Howalt, was named as its fieldman on rural electrification. On January 25, 1936, his initial efforts culminated in the formation of Federated Electric Cooperative (FEC), a statewide federation to provide organizing, promotional, and engineering services to local cooperatives, who would be its shareholding owners. Midland loaned FEC five thousand dollars to pay start-up costs and gave it office space. Howalt became its manager. In the March 1936 issue of the *Midland Cooperator*, Howalt linked the REA to Midland's view of a society-transforming consumers' cooperation. By starting REA, he asserted, the Roosevelt administration "has placed its stamp of approval on the only American, democratic and fair method of doing business, namely, Consumers' Cooperation." He said nothing about farmer-producers choosing electrification to improve business operations.[46]

The Minnesota Farm Bureau Federation's more cautious, behind-the-scenes approach was to encourage its county units to start rural electric cooperatives. The MFBF's main hope was that the Meeker County Farm Bureau would play a pioneering role as it had done in 1921 by forming the first county unit of the Minnesota Cooperative Creameries Association. By early July 1935, Meeker's farmers had already sent in a well-prepared application for loan funds to REA.[47] A successful Meeker project could serve as a model for other Farm Bureau–sponsored projects, which would build MFBF's membership in all counties. New Deal agricultural programs operated through a county-agent system linked to the MFBF, which could recruit and retain members by using that connection.[48] A similar tie to the REA would bring the MFBF a comparable advantage.

Also trying to win political credit for electrification, the Farmer-Labor administration had its state planning board issue a "vast rural electric plan" in July 1935 that called for "a state power authority, a vast network of public-owned" power plants, "and possibly a state-wide farmers cooperative system." But the 1935 legislature had refused to create a state power authority, and the REA undercut such agencies when Cooke announced, "we are not going to have state or regional authorities." Localities had to deal directly with REA.[49]

Yet the REA could not take away MDA's mandate to aid farmers in organizing cooperatives. Hay became the MDA's point man on rural electrification, setting up meetings with interested farmers and supplying information to them. The FLP's *Minnesota Leader* trumpeted the "Farmer-Labor" MDA's efforts and Olson's trips to Washington to promote local REA applications as FLP accomplishments, but Hay and Olson helped Bureau-sponsored cooperatives as much as FEC ones. In July 1935 liberal leaders tried to get Olson and Hay to call an electrification conference excluding the Farm Bureau and Land O' Lakes. Hay backed out when he learned of the exclusion. At Cooke's request, Olson called a September 3 meeting of all groups, but a polarized cooperative movement could not unite on rural electrification with so much at stake.[50]

The battle intensified in 1936. The FEC and Midland could pressure the Farmer-Labor administration in St. Paul, but given Cooke's dictum excluding a mediating role for states, the Farm Bureau's close ties to the REA in Washington proved to be a stronger asset. And the MDA's dependence on help from county agents closely tied it to the Farm Bureau. In early January 1936 the MFBF took a more conservative turn by ousting its eight-year president, Andrew J. Olson, who had worked with Floyd Olson in the fight for a state income tax. In a narrow, surprise upset, State Representative Frank W. White beat Andrew Olson, who was suspected of not being fully supportive of the Agricultural Adjustment Act program, which the Farm Bureau used to recruit new members.[51]

To defeat REA staffers skeptical of cooperatives, Boyd Fisher kept at arm's length cooperatives perceived as radical, unreliable, or controversial. He preferred safe, cautious, reliable ones. He wrote to Trovatten, "I have felt that the Midland stepped out too soon, too confidently, and too ambitiously." He objected to Midland starting "a statewide service cooperative" before "the formation of locals" and then loaning it money, which it would repay with service fees charged to locals and paid by them out of REA funds—all of these plans made without consulting the REA.[52] As his ally in the contest with the private utilities, Cooke preferred the AFBF, a national farm group that had helped in the fight to start REA, over Midland, a merely regional farm cooperative. A new agency needing to prove itself quickly, the REA, one REA executive wrote, should not choose cooperatives "for vague social purposes" but to gain "successful projects." Midland's leaders were committed to the "vague social purposes."[53]

The Farm Bureau was ready in August 1936 to play its trump card—a visit by Cooke, AFBF President Edward O'Neal, Hay, and other dignitaries to Litchfield to celebrate the start of construction on Meeker County's electric lines, the first REA project in the Upper Midwest to reach that stage. The MFBF carefully planned the event as a springboard for creating a statewide rural electric group to rival the FEC. It invited representatives from many rural electric cooperatives, who would want to meet and greet Cooke, the REA chief who would soon be approving or rejecting their loan applications. In Litchfield on August 7 these men selected a committee "to investigate the possibility of forming" a statewide group.[54]

By birthing this group at an event attended by leaders of the REA, the MDA, and the university, the MFBF created the impression that the new statewide group had the support of all those agencies. That was not exactly the case. Cooke attended the meeting, and the REA wanted a state group formed, but Cooke and Fisher intended that it unite pro-FEC and anti-FEC cooperatives and not be Bureau-run.[55] Hay "was a bit surprised at" the Litchfield meeting. He, too, desired "harmony," not a battle between rival groups.[56] The university's specialist in rural electrification, Louis P. Zimmerman, was chosen secretary of the investigating committee, but Frank Peck, director of Agricultural Extension, claimed the university took "a neutral attitude" on the FEC–Farm Bureau controversy. He noted that Zimmerman was not a university employee on August 7.[57]

Despite these caveats, all three public bodies had been enlisted de facto in the MFBF effort, which met with some obstacles. Midland was not about to concede their support to the Farm Bureau. Howalt suggested that the three agencies favored the FEC, and Farmer-Labor liberals could pressure them to aid Howalt. Hay and Frank Peck spoke at the FEC's annual meeting in June 1936. However, the REA was the key agency, and Farmer-Laborites at Midland lacked any political leverage there. The desire of the REA, the MDA, and neutral cooperatives for a compromise led to the selection of a six-man arbitration committee—three from the FEC and three from the Farm Bureau. After three all-day sessions, they remained deadlocked. The Bureau men objected both to Midland's dominance of the FEC and to an unpaid loan (now thirteen thousand dollars) to the FEC, which locals had to repay in the form of FEC's fees. The FEC men felt the MFBF was creating a duplicating, competing state group, which was a breach of cooperative principles.[58]

The showdown came on November 16, 1936, when delegates from forty local electric cooperatives met in St. Paul's Lowry Hotel to hear the report of the six-man committee. It gave two reports, one pro-FEC and one pro-MFBF. After the delegates voted twenty-nine-to-eleven for the pro-FEC one, the pro-Bureau chair, Meeker's Irving J. Clinton, quickly announced, "this meeting is adjourned in the interest of harmony," and the Bureau men walked out and over to the St. Francis Hotel, where they established the Minnesota Rural Electric Association (MREA). The majority continued the meeting and passed a resolution in support of the FEC. The very opposite of harmony resulted.

Through the *Minnesota Farm Bureau News*, the MFBF launched a public relations drive on behalf of the MREA and against the FEC. It turned

the tables on Midland by attacking the FEC for not adhering to cooperative principles: the FEC was organized "from the top down" by "a group of
Minneapolis promoters" (Midland's urban leaders) with "money gained
from farmer patrons" of oil cooperatives in order to profit by selling
equipment to local cooperatives. It called FEC a "middleman," a pejorative
term among cooperators. By contrast, it claimed, the MREA received
spontaneous support from local cooperatives meeting in rural Litchfield.
Unlike Midland, the MFBF "made no effort to capitalize on the REA movement in Minnesota."[59] None of this was totally correct. The FEC was a
genuinely cooperative state federation. Midland had organized the FEC,
but so had the MFBF taken the initiative in forming the MREA—not for
monetary profit but to recruit members by showing its usefulness to
farmers. This battle between liberal and conservative cooperators was an
unequal one, for the loan-granting REA was critical of the FEC—a point
Farm Bureau men were not slow to publicize.[60] Organized by FLP sym-
pathizers, the FEC secured the support of Farmer-Labor governors Hjalmar Petersen and Elmer A. Benson. While Trovatten and Hay led the
MDA, it took a neutral stance. Given its close ties to the university and the
county agents, both linked to the MFBF, in practice neutrality meant
greater aid to MREA cooperatives.[61]

By November 1937, thirteen of Minnesota's rural electric cooperatives had joined the MREA while twenty had affiliated with the FEC and
nineteen were independent. This statistic was misleading, for these cooperatives existed only on paper until they secured an REA loan. By that
November, the REA had loaned nearly four times as much money to
twelve MREA cooperatives as it had to the six FEC groups that had received
funds. Only one MREA group had not been funded; fourteen of twenty
FEC groups had not. The amount loaned per approved project was nearly
twice as much for MREA cooperatives as for FEC ones.[62] The FEC's Howalt
complained to Farmer-Labor state officials about MDA's "biased attitude
in favor of the Farm Bureau and county agent activities in the sponsoring of R.E.A. projects."[63] But with loaning authority in REA's Washington
office and REA's bias against FEC, he exaggerated MDA's responsibility.

Competition between the FEC and MREA did speed the organizing of
rural electric cooperatives. By 1941 Minnesota ranked in the top four
states in all categories of REA activity. But the FEC lost the contest and
during 1938 ceased to exist.[64]

The FEC and its Farmer-Labor supporters encountered the results of
Minnesota's history of cooperation, which produced a network of con-

servative cooperatives, farm experts, and leaders who had public funding and the prestige accruing to public institutions. Five years of FLP control of state government had not greatly diminished that network's clout.

The Farmer-Labor Party and Cooperatives, 1937:
House File 1017

For liberal cooperative leaders, the answer to this problem seemed obvious: end the Bureau's ties to publicly funded institutions and fire Hay and Trovatten. They had pressured Olson to fire Trovatten, whose 1931 appointment reflected Olson's early, moderate "All-Party" strategy. By 1937 a coalition of state employees, left-wing Farmer-Laborites, and advocates of a national third party had seized control of the FLP and had elected Elmer A. Benson governor.[65] (Olson died in office on August 22, 1936; Lieutenant-governor Petersen completed the final four months of Olson's term.) In Benson, liberal cooperative leaders gained a governor who agreed to both their funding and their personnel changes.

In his inaugural address, Benson called for legislative action to deprive the Farm Bureau of the benefits it received from the public funding of county-agent work. According to USDA and university rules, county agents were not to provide the Bureau with services such as leading membership drives, receiving dues, or editing Bureau publications. These rules were not enforced, and the agents' work constituted an indirect public subsidy of the Bureau. To make matters more objectionable to other farm groups, by 1937 the MFBF paid only .14 percent of the county agents' salaries and expenses, compared to 30.2 percent in 1921.[66]

Benson's proposal was introduced as House File 1017, with sixty state representatives as coauthors. Apparently they believed there was safety in numbers, for they were sure to be attacked at home by the MFBF. H.F. 1017 replaced the county Farm Bureau as sponsor of the county agent with a county agricultural and education association open to all farmers without payment of dues.[67] The MFBF, one coauthor noted, was soon "shrieking to high heaven." H.F. 1017 was, one Bureau editor wrote, a "legislative monstrosity" that would "destroy" extension work. Far from being subsidized through extension funds, he added, "the Farm Bureau contributes liberally in cash" to that work, which would be politicized once it was run by the FLP-controlled departments of agriculture and education. Clearly alarmed at H.F. 1017, he suggested that liberals' attack on the Bureau was really labor unions' assault on New Deal farm programs that the Bureau had supported.[68]

It was not true that the Bureau's .14 percent share added up to a liberal contribution.[69] Given the politicization of state employees under Farmer-Labor administrations, however, the *Minneapolis Journal*'s charge that H.F. 1017 would bring county agents "under political control" had more merit. Not that the Bureau was apolitical, as liberal farm leaders were quick to point out. Aided by seventy-one government-paid fieldmen, it organized GOP-leaning cooperatives to compete against ones sympathetic to the FLP. Yet Benson's failure to champion civil service reform and liberal leaders' desire to control county-agent work gave scant hope that their farmer-elected, MDA-run extension service would be politically neutral.[70]

By calling for change in the county-agent system, Benson alienated the Bureau without receiving a comparable political benefit. Under pressure at home, eight state representatives asked to be removed from the list of coauthors. On March 15, after "a sharp debate over alleged political activities of the Farm Bureau," representatives failed to give H.F. 1017 the two-thirds majority needed to guarantee a final up-or-down vote. The main author stripped it of offending references to the FLP-dominated MDA and education department, but it died in the House. All the bill accomplished was to aggravate tensions between liberal and conservative cooperative leaders.[71]

This attempt was especially futile because the bill had even less chance of passing the more conservative Senate, and the Bureau also received indirect aid from its participation in New Deal farm programs, which H.F. 1017 would not end. As Valelly pointed out, the New Deal's centralization of farm policy in Washington gave a national farm group like the AFBF major advantages over the Farmers' Union, Midland, and CCW, which were only regional. Liberal leaders like Howalt tried to pressure the USDA into setting up farmers' county committees that were not linked to the AFBF to run its programs, but to no avail.[72]

Valelly overestimated the role that the New Deal's aid to the Bureau played in weakening the FLP. As one Farmer-Labor and Farmers' Union leader noted, "We have a few friends who vote our ticket among the Farm Bureau membership." Skillful political leadership could add more friends; Olson allied with the Bureau to gain passage of a state income tax law in 1933 and refused to antagonize it by adopting the voluntary committee's ideas.[73] The MFBF and opposing groups had common features—commitment to cooperatives, German and Scandinavian ethnicity, support for Olson's mortgage moratorium—which a good politician would stress instead of what divided them. Benson was not an effective politician.

The Farmer-Labor Party and Cooperatives, 1937:
Hay and Trovatten

Three weeks after the regular 1937 legislative session ended, Benson granted the liberal cooperative leaders' second demand—personnel changes at MDA. He fired Trovatten and appointed Charles Ommodt MDA commissioner. By mid-August 1937, he had removed Hay and named Sam L. Hauge deputy commissioner. Ommodt and Hauge had been district fieldmen for Land O' Lakes.[74] By appointing Farmer-Labor men from the conservative creamery movement, Benson tried to strike a balance, but the Farm Bureau charged that he was playing politics with MDA by siding with Farmer-Laborites who had long sought control of the agency. The MFBF journal speculated "that Mr. Hay was too loyal to the farm cooperative movement for his own good," for as "lines are being drawn between producer and consumer co-ops," the latter "regarded Mr. Hay as an obstacle to their plans" to dominate the movement. Ommodt represented the views of the old voluntary committee. One of his first acts was to expand MDA's work in cooperation, "particularly in the organizational field." In a July 21 letter to Ommodt that could have been written by the 1934 voluntary committee, Benson called on his administration "to assist the cooperatives in any way that they may desire."[75]

Benson's shakeup of the MDA aided Hjalmar Petersen, who was bitter at the FLP's rejection of him as Olson's successor and who planned to run against Benson in 1938. By siding with the Farmers' Union and Midland so openly, Benson gave Petersen the Farm Bureau's eager support. By contrast, Olson had tried hard not to alienate the Bureau. To be fair, in 1937–38, Roosevelt's USDA also increasingly antagonized the Bureau by allying with the Farmers' Union against the AFBF, which then edged rightward; however, Bureau opposition posed a greater risk to Benson's state party than to FDR's national one.[76]

Petersen spoke to at least three county MFBF picnics in 1937—one speech got front-page praise in the *Minnesota Farm Bureau News*. In August 1937, Petersen's chief strategist wrote to inform him, "The firing of . . . J. H. Hay, Trovatten and many others is going to inspire a good many friends of these men to a fierce determination to get retribution." By January 1938, Trovatten, Hay, and Petersen were hobnobbing with MFBF leaders. Trovatten chaired Petersen's volunteer committee and gave speeches for him in the 1938 FLP primary race. H.F. 1017 and the MDA firings added a key element to his coalition.[77]

The Farmer-Labor Party and Cooperatives, 1938: Land O' Lakes

Before the campaign began, a bitter strike at Land O' Lakes handed the anti-Benson forces an even more polarizing issue. Almost by definition, there was nothing more dangerous for a farmer-labor party than an issue that pitted organized labor against organized farmers, in this case, a union strike against a producers' cooperative. Individual workers griped about farmers in general (high food costs) and individual farmers, about workers (high urban wage rates), but these opposing complaints did not directly clash so as to force the FLP to decide between them. The party could support both the workers' battle against employers for higher wages and the farmers' fight against middlemen for a larger share of re-tail food prices. Each part of its coalition dealt with a separate enemy, not with each other. Farmers did not employ urban workers nor did they sell bread to them. But a cooperative plant in the city was an employer subject to unionization. A cooperative battling a union hurt the FLP far worse than did individual griping because both organizations had a strongly moral, democratic ethos. Each side deeply grieved the other when it struck at the other's democratic mobilization.[78]

The clash came between dairying cooperatives with plants in the Twin Cities and truck drivers, confident after their 1934 strike victory in Minneapolis. Local No. 471, the Milk Drivers and Dairy Employees Union, had a twenty-five-year history of success in Minneapolis, where it formed Franklin Cooperative Creamery Association and added creamery plant employees to its membership.[79] In 1935 Local 471 began to organize work-ers and drivers at Land O' Lakes and TCMPA plants in and around the Twin Cities. In September 1935, Vince Day negotiated an agreement be-tween Land O' Lakes and Local 471 that averted a threatened strike. The union demanded higher wages and a closed shop, but Day convinced or pressured it to accept the Land O' Lakes offer (not a contract) of collective bargaining rights for employees who chose to join the union.[80]

In 1936–37 Local 471 concentrated on unionizing both the drivers who hauled milk for TCMPA's farmer-members and the workers at TCMPA plants in Minneapolis and Farmington. The TCMPA's board tried to reason its way out of unionization: individual farmers paid the haulers so the TCMPA had no power to set milk-hauling rates, and TCMPA plants were really rural cooperative creameries, which were not unionized in Minnesota. At an informational meeting attended by several hundred dairy farmers at Farmington, a union leader "stressed the importance of men organizing and presenting their grievances in a body instead of as an individual," but TCMPA members supported the board's policy of not dealing with employees in a body. In April 1937 the TCMPA complained that keeping to its policy was "made more difficult because of the attitude of those in authority toward strikes"—a reference to the Benson and Roosevelt administrations' prolabor stance. After a one-day strike, the TCMPA finally agreed in late May to a contract with Local 471 for workers at its Minneapolis plant only.[81]

Local 471 faced a different rhetorical, moral situation when confronting farmer-owned cooperatives from when it battled corporate employers. No dairy farmers were becoming wealthy from the low wages of cooperatives' employees. The TCMPA cited the inadequate return farmers received for milk compared to dairy employees' wages. Even the more prolabor Farmers' Union asserted that unions dealing with cooperatives "should recognize that the ordinary relationship between boss and worker does not apply."[82] Local 471 feared that if it made an exception for cooperatives, then "other employers would point to Land O' Lakes as an excuse for refusing such a union agreement." By April 1938 Land O' Lakes was the only open-shop dairy plant in Minneapolis, and its wage rates were significantly lower as well. On April 1 the old open-shop agreement expired, and Local 471 demanded a closed shop and a wage increase of more than 30 percent.[83]

The Benson administration saw the political dangers a strike posed, and it persuaded the local to hold off so Benson and Ommodt could negotiate a settlement. They failed, and an eighteen-day strike began on the morning of April 13. Local 471 claimed, "Our strike is solely against

[Land O' Lakes president] John Brandt and the Directors" and not against "the farmers who are affiliated with Land O' Lakes." But in the preceding months, Brandt had secured what he termed "an almost unanimous mandate against [the] closed shop," and the directors who backed him were elected by the farmer-members so farmers could not be easily divorced from directors' decisions.[84] Local 471 also had the democratic consensus of 150 employees, 90 percent of whom were farmers' sons and daughters, the children of TCMPA members. One economic democracy confronted another, and organized farmers confronted their organized sons and daughters.[85]

The democratic nature of the collision intensified the rhetoric on both sides, but it also meant that the conflict could spread to small towns where farmers had cooperated and workers might unionize. Benson faced a more difficult task in localizing and limiting a strike against a state federation of cooperatives than one against a private employer. Brandt, the directors, and many farmers feared that union workers at the Minneapolis plant would help to unionize rural creameries by refusing to handle butter made by nonunion creameries. The directors held meetings throughout the state to rally support for the anti-closed-shop stand.

Local 471 struck this TCMPA plant in Farmington on June 20, 1936. Claiming this plant was equivalent to a rural cooperative creamery, the TCMPA won its farmer-members' backing against the union.

On April 22, for example, eighty-eight directors of nineteen Freeborn County creameries met in Albert Lea and passed a resolution of support. Creamery boards sent letters to Benson, who before the strike had mailed Land O' Lakes butter and cheese samples to dozens of elected officials around the nation. Republican small-town editors capitalized on this conflict by charging that labor received the main benefits from the Farmer-Labor coalition.[86]

Benson's efforts to mediate culminated in an all-day negotiating session on Saturday, April 30, that produced a tentative agreement, finalized the next day. He claimed the deal "embraced compromises on both sides," but he had pressured Local 471 to drop its demand for a closed shop and to accept wage increases of only $2.50 to $3.00 per week. As with H.F. 1017, Benson's labor allies had gained little in exchange for handing the GOP a campaign issue that threatened the FLP coalition. A more skillful political leader would have told Local 471 before the strike, as Day had done in 1935, that they could not gain a closed shop.[87]

From left to right, employees demonstrated the process of wrapping and packaging Land O' Lakes butter. "An inspiring feature of the [1938] strike," Local 471 boasted, "was the militancy and loyalty of women strikers."

Role of Cooperative and Farm Issues in Benson's 1938 Defeat

Some Farmer-Laborites and many Minnesota leaders and voters perceived Benson as having aligned himself with liberal cooperative and labor forces against conservative farm groups. That perception gave an anti-Benson candidate a chance to gain rural support. The first one was Petersen, who might not have run and certainly would not have done so well against Benson in the June 1938 primary if it had not been for Trovatten's removal. State Senator J. Lawrence McLeod of Grand Rapids and Trovatten were Petersen's main advisers. After an October 1937 meeting with them, he decided to run and to form a volunteer committee with Trovatten as chair. Trovatten loaned Petersen six hundred dollars for the campaign and was one of its paid staff workers. His former assistant attorney general at MDA, Phil Scherer, was the Hennepin County campaign manager.[88]

At least one Benson adviser believed that TCMPA leaders were using antiunion rhetoric in early 1938 "for the purpose of developing senti-ment" for Petersen and against Benson.[89] There is no evidence that this occurred. Farm Bureau and TCMPA leaders undoubtedly preferred Peter-sen over Benson, but they took no open steps to help the former. Petersen was a Farmer-Laborite, and both groups tended to favor the GOP.

Benson won the Farmer-Labor primary with a narrow 16,000-vote margin (out of 420,000 cast). Farm Bureau and TCMPA leaders turned openly to support the winner of the Republican primary, Harold E. Stassen, the young county attorney for Dakota County. Stassen's rise to political prominence in Dakota County and to the status of a serious contender in the 1938 primary were partly due to support from TCMPA leaders. In October 1932 he had helped turn Twin Cities-area Farm Holi-day members away from a potentially violent milk strike and toward the TCMPA's orderly milk-marketing efforts. In 1935 he served as attorney for TCMPA members seeking a distribution of that cooperative's large re-serves. These acts gained him the valuable support of longtime TCMPA leader William Schilling of Northfield and Edward J. Thye, TCMPA direc-tor and Dakota County Farm Bureau president.[90] Conservative farm leaders expected Governor Stassen to aid them in dealing with aggres-sive unions. More importantly, Stassen discovered that aiding a coopera-tive also won a Republican popularity among thousands of farmer-members, just as much as it would a Farmer-Labor candidate.

Thye and his fellow Dakota County TCMPA and MFBF members gave crucial assistance to Stassen from October 1937 to March 1938 when the thirty-one-year-old attorney had to overcome skepticism about his youth and inexperience. At the Hastings kick-off, "Thye almost stole the show" with a resounding two-minute speech. Thye introduced Stassen at many subsequent events, gave speeches supporting him, and worked full time on his 1938 campaign. After the primary, TCMPA president William S. Moscrip openly supported Stassen, introducing him at a July 24 picnic in Delano as "the man of the hour in Minnesota."[91]

Schilling spoke at a Stassen dinner in Rochester on January 27, but his main contribution to the anti-Benson drive was to organize the Associated Farmers of Minnesota (AFM), starting in late May 1938 after the Land O' Lakes strike. The AFM, which was opposed to the Congress of Industrial Organizations (CIO), was patterned after the Associated Farmers of California, which fought striking farm workers. In Minnesota, few farmers were large-scale employers subject to unionization. Instead Schilling's AFM protested unionization and strikes at Land O' Lakes, TCMPA, and local creameries. His recruiting success came mainly in TCMPA territory, especially Chisago, Rice, Dakota, and Washington Counties. The AFM functioned as an unofficial arm of the Stassen campaign in keeping alive until the November election the anti-Benson, anti-FLP feelings stirred up by the Land O' Lakes strike.[92]

Numerous factors led to Stassen's landslide victory: anti-Semitic slurs, charges of Communists in state government, anger over the FLP patronage machine, Benson's temper, Stassen's political skills, the split within the FLP, and a conservative trend nationwide in 1938.[93] Yet one cause was Benson's alignment with liberal cooperative leaders against conservative ones. With unintended help from Local 471, Republican politicians portrayed this as Benson aligning with labor against farmers, and many voters believed this version. In 1938 cooperation was not a weapon in the FLP arsenal, as it had been in 1934, but a wedge used by the GOP. As small democracies, cooperatives posed risks for the FLP; a slight to a cooperative angered more farmers than did a law adversely affecting a few farmers. Republicans could persuade farmers that H.F. 1017, the removal of longtime cooperative leaders such as Hay and Trovatten, and the Land O' Lakes strike were insults to their democratic organizations. The fact that Republicans had helped form the MDA, Land O' Lakes, TCMPA, and other cooperatives gave their arguments more weight.

Cooperation was an ambiguous idea whose ideological coloring lay in the eye of the beholder. Farmer-Laborites had used that ambiguity to escape disaster in 1934. It was given a conservative coloring and used against them in 1938. Republican Ed Thye of the TCMPA and Farm Bureau turned out to be the rural cooperator with a future as governor (1943–47) and U.S. Senator (1947–59). The New Deal's AAA and REA programs strengthened the Farm Bureau and, by so doing, weakened the FLP-aligned Farmers' Union and Midland. But the explanation for the FLP's failure to form a strong alliance with the cooperative movement lay further back in Minnesota's history of rural cooperation—in the Granger, Alliance, and Progressive periods. Midland's Jacobson analyzed the producers' cooperatives formed then "around the urgent needs of the hour" as "hit and miss" affairs suited to a frontier era, not to a mature economy. Distribution, not production, was the 1930s problem, and consumers' cooperatives could solve it.[94] Yet a state third party could not wait for allies to be born. The American political economy had allowed cooperatives to thrive only at the rural margins where investors saw too great a risk and too small profits. The FLP had to make do with those allies. Instead, by adopting Jacobson's vision, it lost the support of the strong producer cooperatives, and its liberal allies were unable to create a strong network of leftist cooperatives. A key blow was losing the rural electrification battle. A liberal-radical movement that had been unable to form a strong network of left-leaning cooperatives could not expect to be greatly helped by the politically mixed assortment that developed. Minnesota's rural cooperatives prospered after 1939 while the Farmer-Labor Party collapsed.

Epilogue

IN THE PAST FIFTEEN YEARS, rural historians have debated at length the "agricultural transition" from a semi-subsistence farming supplying the family's needs to a commercial agriculture growing a surplus to sell in the market.[1] The debate has centered on when this transition occurred and what its causes and effects might have been. An accompanying assumption is that once farmers crossed this watershed they moved inexorably to embrace small-town, middle-class values until many of them left the land altogether. Or, that they did so after one final, doomed charge on behalf of agrarian values in the Populists' 1892 and 1896 presidential campaigns. In their acclaimed study of the Midwest, Andrew Cayton and Peter Onuf focused on "an urban and village bourgeoisie" as the historical actors who reshaped the region after farmers opted for the market. In this reading, once Jeffersonian agrarians decided to grow wheat for the market, it was only a matter of time before George Babbitt defined midwestern values.[2]

This study of rural cooperation in one state demonstrates that such an interpretation is seriously flawed. Opting for the market did not mean bowing to merchants' control of local markets nor did it mean joining the small-town institutions that merchants organized. Cooperatives gave the farmer an alternative mode—a distinctly rural mode—of experiencing the market and of achieving the self-discipline needed to compete in the market. In this mode, goods would be sold at very low profit margins, services provided at cost, insurance charges assessed only after a fire, and the number of salaried managers and employees kept to a minimum. The structure, rules, and prices of both local and terminal markets were vigorously contested over the period of this study. The cooperative, Grange, farmers' club, suballiance, and Farm Bureau or Farmers' Union provided the farmer with institutions in which to discuss farming methods and marketing, to purchase or sell jointly, to lobby for legislation or to nominate candidates for office, and to acquire leadership skills. Farmers did not need to choose between stubbornly growing only enough to feed their families and meekly attending commercial club or Masonic functions in order to learn market etiquette.

This exaggerated dichotomy reveals an anti-rural bias—the underlying assumption being that farmers could not have defined their own market rules and formed their own definition of commercial agriculture. That false premise leads to the conclusion that farmers entered the market and then, when the post-1860s fall in crop prices dashed their hopes, they reacted with agrarian protest and the start of cooperatives. But rural cooperation was not primarily a reaction to the rise of corporate capitalism. Starting with the Union stores of the 1840s and 1850s and the township mutuals of the 1870s, it was an innovative attempt to internalize market transactions, achieve economies of scale, eliminate inefficiencies in retailing and overcharging in rural fire insurance, and to create discount, cash-only, high-volume stores. Thereafter, the "technology diffusion" cooperatives—creameries, telephone companies, and rural electric associations—brought the centrifuge, telephone, and electricity to the countryside. Farmers' stores were often creative ways to complete a partial and inadequate rural retailing network rather than reactions to private stores' policies. And they came well before chain stores had an appreciable impact on rural areas (but not before the mail-order houses did). The store and the creamery built a crossroads community that was more amenable to farmers' influence than was the county seat. Farmers' elevators and cooperative gas stations reduced profit margins on grain storage and on gas and oil sales. The fact that forward-looking university experts and county agents endorsed these forms of cooperation showed that the latter were not products of farmers' nostalgia for the good old Jeffersonian days.

It is true that in Minnesota the success of many nineteenth-century cooperatives partly or mainly rested on their location in ethnic enclaves, and these ethnic groups conservatively attempted to defeat or delay powerful Americanizing forces in an individualistic, market-oriented society. But Minnesota's Scandinavian immigrants did not use Scandinavian models for their cooperatives. And the cooperative brought new technologies or retailing techniques even if its business was transacted in a foreign language. In 1890, "centrifuge" meant change—even in Danish or German. In the late nineteenth century, ethnicity facilitated cooperation, but the gradual assimilation of the second and third generations did not bring a cooperative crisis after World War I.

It is true that Minnesota's cooperative movement—in the opinion of outside experts like Aaron Sapiro—was so localistic that it remained marginal in a regional and national economy. That characteristic could be charged to farmers' parochialism. Yet the democratic methods inherent in cooperation were harder to expand across geographical space than were the unilateral decisions or the buying power of an entrepreneur. Sapiro's expertise, the California fruit growers' example, the USDA's support, and the Farm Bureau's organizational network could not create viable, national cooperative marketing associations in the 1920s. And Minnesota's much-criticized farmers transcended localism by marketing their creameries' butter in eastern markets under the single Land O' Lakes label. Minnesota's network of rural cooperatives far outlived the 1920s national fad for cooperative marketing. Minnesota's localistic cooperation proved to be more resilient than did the fad.

In the 1930s Midland's leaders charged that Minnesota farmers lacked the vision needed to use rural cooperation to create a new economic and social order and that producers' cooperation inherently lacked such a vision. Yet early farmers' elevators and the Equity Cooperative Exchange envisioned more radical change than did consumers' cooperatives like the Hanska-Linden store or the Farmers' Store in Underwood. Midland's leaders sounded embarrassed at the fact that farmers had formed hundreds of cooperatives while urban consumers had created very few. But that truth did not demonstrate a comparative lack of vision on the farmers' part. The postrailroad, national, centralizing economy provided few niches in which cooperation could survive. Minnesota farmers took what that system gave them—the crossroads creamery and store, rural fire insurance, rural phone and electric service, livestock shipping, and the country elevator, plus assorted farm-improvement cooperatives such as cow-testing associations. They had not staked everything on a futile attempt to break into the grain exchanges or to nationalize the railroads or to boycott Sears, Roebuck. They generally acted in pragmatic, not radical or reactionary, ways.

Changing realities shape the pragmatist, and they altered rural cooperation over the decades. The Minneapolis millers' breakthrough in the technology of milling spring wheat foreclosed any chance for wheat farmers to capture significant processing profits by operating cooperative flour mills. Wheat farmers had to be content with using cooperative grain storage to lower the local storage costs; however, the railroads' need to capture freight traffic in grain-growing areas, their preference for line elevators, and the line elevators' ability to wage price wars meant that farmers' elevators had to fight to survive and needed financial aid from commission firms. Southern Minnesota farmers' specialization in dairying and their cooperative creameries' success ensured that the politics of wheat was not as salient in twentieth-century Minnesota as it was in North Dakota or as it had been in the Granger era. Yet the resulting competition from centralizers forced the cooperatives to accept the hand separator that tended to lower the quality of their cream. Competition from Danish butter and the chain stores' need for uniform-quality butter that was attractively packaged and distributed in large quantities compelled the localistic creameries to surrender some of their autonomy to Land O' Lakes. The automobility of the 1910s and 1920s and the marketing of luxury goods in those decades undercut the crossroads farmers' stores and forced many of them out of business. Consumers' cooperation was better suited to selling necessities. The Right Relationship League's attempt at establishing cooperative chain stores failed. The nationalization of politics during the New Deal robbed the Farmer-Labor Party of an excellent opportunity to use rural electrification to expand its political base. America's changing political economy and rapidly developing technology set limits on what cooperators could accomplish.

The hundreds of rural cooperatives that Minnesota farmers had voted into existence, had financed with their purchases of shares, and had supported with their patronage represented a significant achievement that made rural Minnesota "the cooperative commonwealth"; however, the strength of corporate capitalism and consumerism—even in the depths of the Great Depression—meant that the reality fell short of the phrase's original utopian dimensions. Depending on the observer's perspective, the glass was either half empty—a commonwealth of farmers with no bonds of union except buying cheap and selling dear—or half full—an island of cooperators in a national sea of corporate business. From either perspective, the existence of this commonwealth makes it inaccurate to write the history of Minnesota or of rural America from 1859 to 1939 without factoring in the rural cooperative. Whether it was a store or a creamery, an elevator or a phone company, it was also a church preaching a utopian vision of brotherhood, a school instructing farmers in bookkeeping and pricing and better farming methods, a party working for favorable legislation, a local government deciding which phone calls were socially useful or what types of cattle feed were acceptable, a club encouraging farmers and farm wives to socialize and to help each other, and an ethnic society preserving Old World languages and ethnic social ties. It shaped rural life in Minnesota—and in much of the United States—for decades. It changed the economic geography of Minnesota. Perhaps those were sufficient accomplishments even if they did not add up to the new form of human society hoped for by promoters of the "cooperative commonwealth."

Appendix

TABLE A
Towns with Grange Store or Purchasing Agent

Town	Store or Agent	County Seat?
Red Wing	Store	Yes
Owatonna	Store	Yes
Medford	Store	No
Fairmont	Store	Yes
Faribault	Store	Yes
Benson	Store	Yes
St. Charles	Agent	No
Dover	Agent	No
Windom	Agent	Yes
Albert Lea	Agent	Yes
Goodhue Center	Agent	No

Sources:
Glenwood Eagle, 28 February 1874, p. 2; *Martin County before 1880,* p. 77; *Farmers' Union,* 15 December 1872 and 14 June 1873, both p. 4, and *Farmers' Union,* 29 March 1873, p. 6; *Owatonna Journal,* 14 August and 16 October 1873 and 26 November 1874, all p. 3; *Waseca News,* 20 November 1872, p. 2; *Record and Union,* 28 April 1876, p. 3; *Farmers' Union,* 25 July 1872, p. 5, and 26 July 1873, p. 6.

TABLE B
Comparison of Centrifugal Separator (CS) & Gathered Cream (GC) Systems:
Price Received for Butter

		Average Price Received	% of New York Price
Luck (GC)	1st Year 1886	20.4 cents/pound	76%
	2nd Year July–Sept 1887	20.2 cents/pound	76%
Clarks Grove (CS)	1st Year 1890	18.2 cents/pound	77%
	2nd Year 1891	21.5 cents/pound	82%
	3rd Year 1892	22.9 cents/pound	87%
Clover Valley (CS)	1st Year 1891	20.4 cents/pound	78%

TABLE C
Comparison of Centrifugal Separator (CS)
& Gathered Cream (GC) Systems: Other Data

	Luck (GC)	Clarks Gr (CS)	Cl. Valley (CS)
Buttermaking Efficiency	3.93 (1886)*	4.32 (1890)	4.2 (1891)
(lbs. butter/cwt. milk)	3.82 (1887)*	4.35 (1891)	
		4.29 (1892)	
Operating Expenses Per	$.08 (1886)	$0.18 (1890)	$.03 (1891)
Pound of Butter Made		.015 (1891)	
		.015 (1892)	
Payment to Farmers Per	$.41 (1886)*	$.66 (1890)	$.675 (1891)
100 lbs. Milk Delivered		.84 (1891)	
		.86 (1892)	
Volume of Production	9920 (1886)	84,097 (1890)	70,533 (1891)
in Pounds of Butter		218,992 (1891)	
		226,874 (1892)	

Note:

* denotes an estimate. Clover Valley had both a "sinking fund" and a "separator fund." The latter represented depreciation on the separator. I have added the two. The buttermaking statistics of the Luck Creamery Company are reported in terms of pounds of butter made and "inches" of cream gathered. An "inch" was defined as the amount of cream needed to make one pound of butter; however, the Luck creamery actually made 1.11 pounds per "inch." To convert lbs./inch to lbs./cwt., I have taken dairy expert J.H. Monrad's estimate that the separator was 10% more efficient in separating cream from skim milk; therefore, if Clarks Grove creamery's centrifugal separator system produced 4.32 lbs./cwt, then Luck's gathered cream system would produce 3.93 lbs./cwt. Similarly, Luck's payment to farmers per "inch" is thus translated into payment per hundredweight of milk, with 1 "inch" equaling 28.24 lbs. of milk. See J.H. Monrad, *A.B.C. in Butter Making for Young Creamery Butter-makers, Creamery Managers and Private Dairyman* (Winnetka, Ill., 1899), p. 34.

TABLE D
Freeborn County's Cooperative Creameries, 1890–1900

Name of CA	Date Started	Diffusion Cause	Village/ Township	Members' Ethnicity	Years to Pay Debt
Clarks Grove	1/1890	(Iowa example)	T	Danish	3 years
Riceland	3/1890	1 Distance (&3)	T	Norwegian	?
Clover Valley	3/1890	(Iowa example)	T	German & OS	6 years
Armstrong	4/1890	2 Site Split	T+	German & OS	7 years
North Star	8/1890	4 Merchants	V	Scandinavian	5–6 years
Glenville	10/1890	6 Buttermaker	V	?	4 years
Bancroft	12/1890	1 Distance	T	Norwegian	4 years
Hartland	12/1890	4 Merchants*	V	Irish/Norwegian	8 years#
Manchester	1/1891	3 Johnsrud	T+	Norwegian	4 years#
Geneva (T)	1/1891	?	T	OS American	Dissolve
Hayward	1/1891	7 Separators	V	Norwegian	3 years
Mansfield	1/1891	2 Site Split	T	German	7 years
Carlston	3/1891	?	T	?	Dissolve
Moscow	Fall/1891	?	T	?	?
Albert Lea	12/1891	4 Merchants	CS	Varied	4 years
Poplar Grove	1/1892	1 Distance	T	Irish/Norwegian	4 years
Twin Lakes	8/1892	4 Merchants	V	Irish/Norwegian	6 years
Freeborn	10/1892	6 Buttermaker	T	OS American	5 years
State Line	2/1893	(Iowa example?)	T	Norwegian	2 years
Sumner Valley	6/1893	1 Distance	T	Norwegian	?
Oakland	9/1893	5 Davis & Rankin	T	?	?
Geneva (V)	2/1894	4 Merchants	V	Dane/OS American	?
Newry	1894	?	T	OS American	?
London	1894	7 Separators	T	OS American	?
Trenton	3/1895	?	T	OS American	?
Banner	2/1898	1 Distance	T	OS American	?
Freeman	9/1899	1 Distance (?)	T	Scandinavian	?

Notes:

Date Started: Usually, the date organizational meetings began, not necessarily the date the creamery began operating, though that is sometimes the date shown

Years to Pay Debt: Years needed to repay the initial debt incurred in order to build the creamery

+ a railroad station and store, but no village status

a creamery fire delayed the debt repayment

* Hartland Farmers' Alliance also helped start it

CA Creamery Association

CS County Seat

OS Old Stock American

TABLE E
Comparison of Milk Prices Paid — October 1893

Name of CA	Price/cwt. milk	Name of CA	Price/lb. butterfat
Armstrong	$ .97	Twin Lakes	$.22
Bancroft	1.02	Albert Lea	.235
Clover Valley	1.03	Glenville	.24
Emmons	1.04	Hayward	.243
Hartland	1.04	North Star	.26
Clarks Grove	1.05		
Manchester	1.05		
Riceland	1.09		
State Line	1.09		
Poplar Grove	1.09		

Note:
Some creameries used a butterfat test and paid by butterfat content.

TABLE F
Blooming Grove Wheat Marketing Committees, 1886–87

Date	Appointed/Elected	Members
5/29/86	Appointed	K. Swift, A. Remund, Geo. Hand
9/3/86	Appointed	K. Swift, L.C. Remund, A. Schuette
10/16/86	Elected	K. Swift, Fred McKune, N. Stearns, J.F. Schuette, Christian Sutter
2/19/87	Appointed*	K. Swift, A. Schuette, John Hecht
3/5/87	Appointed**	K. Swift, John Knause, John Hecht, A. Remund, C. Remund
4/5/87	Elected#	K. Swift, J.C. Knause, John Hecht
11/5/87	Elected	K. Swift, D.R. Davis, A. Remund

Notes:
* appointed to choose a site for a wheat warehouse
** appointed to estimate costs of a wheat warehouse
\# elected to "buy or build"

TABLE G
Comparative Financial Data:
Farmers' Elevators (FE)

Elevator (Year)	Volume (bu.)	Margin* (per bu.)	Costs/Bu. (cents)	Labor Cost (% expenses)	Surplus (% gross)
Zumbrota (1895)	148,429	1.2 cts.	2.4 cents	37.0%	8.3%
Northfield (1898)	107,931	(1.8) cts.	1.3 cents	60.5%	29.3%
Redwood Falls (1904–05)	144,488	0.2 ct.	1.7 cents	47.5%	23.9%
Alpha (1906–07)**	308,147	.1 ct.	1.3 cents	?	34.2%
Hardwick (1907–08)**	83,723	1.3 cts.	2.0 cents	59.7%	12.1%
Lakefield (1906–07)**	177,224	5.1 cts.	2.1 cents	28.8%	29.9%
Lakefield (1907–08)	164,747	7.3 cts.	2.3 cents	?	13.7%

Notes:
* Gross profit margin on sales of wheat
** These elevators handled little wheat—mostly oats. Volume is number of bushels *handled*, not capacity.

List of Abbreviations

BG	Burnside Grange
BGL	Blooming Grove Lyceum
C&NW	Chicago and Northwestern Railway
CCMTC	Chisago County Mutual Telephone Company
CGCF	Clarks Grove Creamerie Forening (Clarks Grove creamery)
CM&SP	Chicago, Milwaukee, and St. Paul Railway
CVCA	Clover Valley Creamery Association
ECE	Equity Cooperative Exchange
EUTC	Eastern Union Telephone Company
FCCPH	Freeborn County Council of the Patrons of Husbandry
FMC	Farmers Mercantile Corporation
GN	Great Northern Railway
HLHF	Hanska-Linden Handelsforening (Hanska-Linden Store)
LCC	Luck Creamery Company
LHFA	Lake Hanska Farmers' Alliance
LTFA	Lisbon Township Farmers' Alliance
M&SL	Minneapolis and St. Louis Railway
MDBT	Minnesota Dairy Board of Trade
MGGA	Minnesota Grain Growers Association
MHS	Minnesota Historical Society, St. Paul
NFMEC	Northfield Farmers' Mercantile and Elevator Company
NP	Northern Pacific Railway
NPL	Nonpartisan League
RWC	Railroad and Warehouse Commission
SOO LINE	Minneapolis, St. Paul and Sault Ste. Marie Railroad
SSMIC	Sverdrup Scandinavian Mutual Insurance Company
STC	Stacy Telephone Company
TCMPA	Twin City Milk Producers Association
TD, RWC/DPS	Telephone Division, Railroad and Warehouse Commission/ Department of Public Service
UM Archives	University of Minnesota Archives, Minneapolis
W&SP	Winona and St. Peter Railroad
WCMDA	West Central Minnesota Development Association
WFA	Washington Farmers' Alliance

Reference Notes

Notes to Introduction

1. Anker M. Simonsen, *Builders with Purpose* (Askov, Minn.: Printed by American Publishing Co., 1963), 42.

2. Alexis de Tocqueville, *Democracy in America*, ed. J. P. Mayer and Max Lerner, trans. George Lawrence (New York: Harper & Row, 1966), 485–88.

3. See Russell L. Hanson, *The Democratic Imagination in America: Conversations with Our Past* (Princeton: Princeton University Press, 1985), especially Chapters 6–8.

4. Richard B. Heflebower, *Cooperatives and Mutuals in the Market System* (Madison: University of Wisconsin Press, 1980), 9.

5. Alfred D. Chandler Jr., *The Visible Hand: The Managerial Revolution in American Business* (Cambridge: Harvard University Press, Belknap Press, 1977), 6, 8.

6. For a brief discussion of this point, see my review of *Out on the Wind: Poles and Danes in Lincoln County, Minnesota, 1880–1905* by John Radzilowski in *Annals of Iowa* 53 (Spring 1994): 177–78.

7. Tocqueville, *Democracy in America*, 489.

Notes to Chapter 1

1. Gerald Carson, *The Old Country Store* (New York: Oxford University Press, 1954), ix, 3. See also Merrill E. Jarchow, *The Earth Brought Forth: A History of Minnesota Agriculture to 1885* (St. Paul: Minnesota Historical Society, 1949), 107.

2. Daniel J. Boorstin, *The Democratic Experience*, vol. 3 of *The Americans* (New York: Random House, 1973), 131.

3. John Mack Faragher, *Sugar Creek: Life on the Illinois Prairie* (New Haven: Yale University Press, 1986), 133–35.

4. Carson, *Old Country Store*, 21–24; William Cronon, *Nature's Metropolis: Chicago and the Great West* (New York: W. W. Norton and Co., 1991), 104–5, 318–20 (quote p. 105); Charles Russell Hoffer, "Services of Rural Trade Centers in Distribution of Farm Supplies" (Ph.D. diss., University of Minnesota, 1925), 7; Gustav P. Warber, *Social and Economic Survey of a Community in Northeastern Minnesota*, University of Minnesota Bulletin No. 5 (Minneapolis: University of Minnesota, March 1915), 47; Henrietta M. Larson, *The Wheat Market and the Farmer in Minnesota, 1858–1900* (New York: Columbia University, 1926), 19–20. An "all-purpose businessman" buying and selling many commodities and goods through face-to-face relationships, the storekeeper retained the modus operandi of the colonial "general merchant." See Chandler, *Visible Hand*, 17–19.

5. Carson, *Old Country Store*, 24; Christian Ahlness, "Recollections of an Emigrant, As Told by Himself," 1916, copy of typescript, 214–15, Brown County Historical Society (hereafter BCHS), New Ulm.

6. Jarchow, *Earth Brought Forth*, 208–9; Louis D. H. Weld, *Social and Economic Survey of a Community in the Red River Valley* (Minneapolis: University of Minnesota, 1915), 43–44, 46–47.

7. For the prerailroad merchant as retailer of store goods and marketer of farm produce, see Cronon, *Nature's Metropolis*, 104–6, and 318–20.

8. Cronon, *Nature's Metropolis*, 318–24 (quote p. 324).

9. Ahlness, "Recollections," p. 213–14.

10. Warber, *Social and Economic Survey*, 47; Hoffer, "Services of Rural Trade Centers," 42–45.

11. Quoted in Carson, *Old Country Store*, 28. For an interesting account of the lack of trust between buyer and seller at the country store, see "Trading in a Country Store," *Canby News*, 24 September 1886, p. 3.

12. *Minnesota Monthly* (St. Paul), December 1869, p. 423.

13. *Farmers' Union* (Minneapolis), 26 July 1873, p. 238.

14. Chandler, *Visible Hand*, 6–7.

15. Chandler, *Visible Hand*, 6–7. Chandler argued from the perspective of the firm: "administrative coordination permitted greater productivity, lower costs, and higher profits than coordination by market mechanisms." Increased volume forced firms to opt for administrative coordination. *Consumers had already chosen democratic coordination*, not to maximize profit but to lower retail prices. The NEPU often had more than one store per town, with consequences that typically were negative. See Edwin Charles Rozwenc, *Cooperatives Come to America: The History of the Protective Union Store Movement, 1845–1867* (Mount Vernon, Iowa: Hawkeye-Record Press, 1941), 62, 93.

16. *The Standard* (Northfield), 24 February 1870, p. 2. See also *St. Peter Tribune*, 9 February 1870, p. 3; *The Standard*, 17 March 1870, p. 2.

17. Joseph G. Knapp, *The Rise of American Cooperative Enterprise: 1620–1920* (Danville, Ill.: Interstate Printers and Publishers, 1969), 21–23; James Ford, *Co-operation in New England: Urban and Rural* (New York: Survey Associates, 1913), 13–15; Horace M. Kallen, *The Decline and Rise of the Consumer: A Philosophy of Consumer Cooperation* (New York: D. Appleton-Century Co., 1936), 233.

18. Knapp, *American Cooperative Enterprise*, 22; Ford, *Co-operation in New England*, 15; Kallen, *Decline and Rise*, 233.

19. For more on this concept, see Heflebower, *Cooperatives and Mutuals*, 9.

20. Rozwenc, *Cooperatives Come to America*, 60–61, 80.

21. Charles Sellers, *The Market Revolution: Jacksonian America, 1815–1846* (New York: Oxford University Press, 1991), 391–92; Chandler, *Visible Hand*, 82–83, 86, 96–97, quotation on p. 97. Rozwenc does not mention the connection between the NEPU and railroad development. I have inferred it.

22. Rozwenc, *Cooperatives Come to America*, 80–83, 86, 87, 88–89. The mass retailer's efficiencies are summarized in Chandler, *Visible Hand*, 223, 225, 227, 229, 235, 236. He emphasizes high inventory turnover and barely mentions the move to "cash and carry" as a factor in mass retailers' lower per-unit costs. Boorstin makes clear that the mass retailers' ability to avoid vexing, time-consuming problems of extending credit enabled them to benefit from economies of scale and speed without worsening their credit and collection problems; Boorstin, *Democratic Experience*, 109–10, 114–15, 122. For the railroads' impact in reducing capital requirements, see Cronon, *Nature's Metropolis*, 325–26.

23. Rozwenc, *Cooperatives Come to America*, 97–99, 101, 104. One Minnesotan pointed to the dispute over the agent's commission as an argument against the movement: "No advantage could possibly accrue to any one but the agents"; *Red Wing Sentinel*, 26 February 1859, p. 2. Some stores likely did not buy through the Central Agency because they lacked railroad links to Boston, site of the agency.

24. Knapp, *American Cooperative Enterprise*, 25; Ford, *Co-operation in New England*, 16.

25. These factors were noted by one opponent of the Northfield Union Store, who claimed never to have heard "of one such store being a success when supported mainly by a farming community"; *The Standard*, 17 March 1870, p. 2. Though the NEPU started in urban areas, it later spread to small towns and enlisted the support of farmers; see Rozwenc, *Cooperatives Come to America*, 61.

26. Warber, *Social and Economic Survey*, 52–53.

27. Madeline Angell, *Red Wing, Minnesota: Saga of a River Town* (Minneapolis: Dillon Press, 1977), 59–63; *Red Wing Sentinel*, 19 February 1859, p. 3. For a definition of Old Stock Americans, see John G. Rice, "The Old-Stock Americans," in *They Chose Minnesota: A Survey of the State's Ethnic Groups*, ed. June Drenning Holmquist (St. Paul: Minnesota Historical Society Press, 1981), 55.

28. *Red Wing Sentinel*, 19 February 1859, p. 3.

29. *Red Wing Republican*, 18 February 1859, p. 2; *Red Wing Sentinel*, 26 February 1859, p. 2. In his history of Red Wing, C. A. Rasmussen reported this "first attempt" at cooperation, in which a Union store was "established" and "prospered for a time" but "was abandoned because of internal dissensions." Just what he meant by "established" and "prospered" and for how long a time is unclear. C. A. Rasmussen, *A History of the City of Red Wing, Minnesota* ([Red Wing?]: Privately published, 1933), 64.

30. Charles H. Hession and Hyman Sardy, *Ascent to Affluence: A History of American Economic Development* (Boston: Allyn and Bacon, 1969), 364, 367–68, 444–52.

31. *The Standard*, 10 March 1870, p. 2; *Nordisk Folkeblad* (Minneapolis), 12 January 1870, p. 2.

32. There is only a newspaper notice on the Marine store ("We predict a 'fizzle' in less than one year") and the incorporation papers filed with the secretary of state (one vote per shareholder and a price of twenty dollars per share). James Taylor Dunn, *Marine Mills: Lumber Village, 1838–1888* (Marine on St. Croix: The Author, 1963), 33; Minnesota, Secretary of State, Corporation Division, Record of Incorporations (Articles of Incorporation), 1858–1946, Vol. B, 202–4, Minnesota State Archives, Minnesota Historical Society, St. Paul (hereafter MHS).

33. *Goodhue County Republican* (Red Wing), 4 and 11 December 1868, both p. 3.

34. John G. Rice, "The Swedes," in *They Chose Minnesota*, ed. Holmquist, 252; Trued Granville Pearson, *En skånsk banbrytare i Amerika: Trued Granville Pearsons självbiografi*, ed. Arvid Bjerking (Oskarshamn, Swed.: A.-B., A. Melchiors Bokhandel, 1937), excerpts translated from Swedish into English by unidentified translator, typescript, Trued G. Pearson File, Goodhue County Historical Society, Red Wing (hereafter GCHS); W. H. Mitchell, *Geographical and Statistical Sketch of the Past and Present of Goodhue County* (Minneapolis: O. S. King, 1869), 130. The STC articles of incorporation are in Minnesota, Secretary of State, Corporation Division, Record of Incorporations, Vol. B, 148–50. See the *Goodhue County Republican*, 15 March 1867, p. 3, for a report by Pearson on the agricultural development among the Swedish-American farmers in Vasa Township, 1859–66, as statistically demonstrated in the assessors' returns. By 1866 the average farmer in Vasa was producing about six hundred bushels of wheat annually, and wheat acreage was 60 percent of total cultivated acreage.

35. Pearson, *Skånsk banbrytare*, excerpts, Pearson File, GCHS.

36. Heflebower notes that one factor in the success or failure of a cooperative is the ability (or lack thereof) of private companies to compete against it; Heflebower, *Cooperatives and Mutuals*, 10–11.

37. *Goodhue County Republican*, 4 December 1868, p. 3; *Daily Republican Eagle* (Red Wing), 25 November 1967, p. 1.

38. Mitchell, *Sketch of Goodhue County*, 130; *Goodhue County Republican*, 4 December 1868, p. 3; *Daily Republican Eagle*, 25 November 1967, p. 1, 3.

39. *Goodhue County Republican*, 11 February 1869, p. 3; Mitchell, *Sketch of Goodhue County*, 130; *Cannon Falls Beacon*, 17 February 1983, p. 24. Called "The Farmer's Commercial Union," this second Swedish-American store may not have been as fully cooperative as the first, for it was "a joint stock concern, in which eight to ten of the farmers of that neighborhood are the stockowners"; *Goodhue County Republican*, 11 February 1869, p. 3.

40. *Nordisk Folkeblad*, 12 January 1870, p. 2.

41. *Red Wing Argus*, 25 November 1869, p. 4.

42. *Nordisk Folkeblad*, 12 January 1870, p. 2.

43. *St. Peter Tribune*, 15 December 1869, p. 3.

44. *St. Peter Tribune*, 1 December 1869, p. 3. The *Tribune* reported similar merchants' meetings elsewhere in the state; *St. Peter Tribune*, 1 and 22 December 1869, both p. 3.

45. Rice, "The Swedes," in *They Chose Minnesota*, ed. Holmquist, 253; Howard M. Nelson, "The Transition of the Traverse des Sioux and St. Peter Areas from Indian to Pioneer Community" (master's thesis, Mankato State Teachers College, 1956), 76, 78–81, 83, 85–95.

46. *Nordisk Folkeblad*, 12 January 1870, p. 2.

47. *Nordisk Folkeblad*, 12 January 1870, p. 2.

48. *Nordisk Folkeblad*, 17 March 1869, p. 2, and 31 March 1869, p. 3.

49. It is unclear whether a "union store" actually functioned in New Sweden and Lake Prairie Townships or whether this Scandinavian-American antimerchant protest was subsumed within the Union-store movement outlined below. *Nordisk Folkeblad 's* correspondent in Nicollet County, Swen Swenson, joined the cooperative association formed in St. Peter; *St. Peter Tribune,* 23 March 1870, p. 2.

50. For St. Peter's railroad hopes, see *St. Peter Tribune,* 1 December 1869 (p. 3), 2 February (p. 3), 22 June (p. 3), 9 February (p. 2, 3), 9 March (p. 2, 3), 6 April (p. 3), 22 June (p. 3), and 29 June (p. 3), all 1870, and 25 October 1871, p. 3. The first train did not cross the Minnesota River until May 6, 1871; *St. Peter Tribune,* 10 May 1871, p. 2, 3.

51. *St. Peter Tribune,* 19 January and 2 February 1870, both p. 3.

52. *St. Peter Tribune,* 2 February 1870, p. 3, and 9 February 1870, p. 2. The editor repeated his call for home manufacturing after the first organizational meeting; *St. Peter Tribune,* 2 March 1870, p. 3.

53. Here and below, see *St. Peter Tribune,* 9 February 1870, p. 3. One report from the *New York Tribune* on an eastern cooperative store was reprinted in the *St. Peter Tribune,* 23 February 1870, p. 2. For biographical information on Bryant and Schoenbeck, see Warren Upham and Rose B. Dunlap, comps., *Minnesota Biographies, 1655–1912* (St. Paul: Minnesota Historical Society, 1912), 87, 679.

54. *St. Peter Tribune,* 9 March 1870, p. 2. The constitution and bylaws of the Minnesota Co-operative Union did not, for example, state a place of business, adopt the one man-one vote principle, or provide for the accumulation of a sinking fund equal to 30 percent of the capital stock. All these provisions were required by the law passed by the legislature on March 4, 1870. See Minnesota, *The Statutes at Large of the State of Minnesota,* comp. A. H. Bissell, 2 Vols. (Chicago: Callaghan and Co., 1873), 1:468–70.

55. *St. Peter Tribune,* 23 March 1870, p. 2. They apparently used a constitution from a Massachusetts association.

56. *St. Peter Tribune,* 9 March 1870, p. 2. Since it was started by urban workers, the NEPU had no plans to construct farm produce warehouses, though it hoped to set up

cooperative workshops. See Knapp, *American Cooperative Enterprise,* 22–23.

57. *St. Peter Tribune,* 9 March 1870, p. 3, and 23 March 1870, p. 2; Upham and Dunlap, comps., *Minnesota Biographies,* 131, 464, 601.

58. *St. Peter Tribune,* 23 March 1870, p. 2.

59. *St. Peter Tribune,* 23 March 1870, p. 2. For Alfred Wallin's occupational status as a lawyer, see *St. Peter Tribune,* 9 February 1870, p. 2. They knew that NEPU divisions, as unincorporated voluntary associations, lacked a clear legal status before Massachusetts's 1866 cooperative statute. Rozwenc, *Cooperatives Come to America,* 92, 97.

60. *St. Peter Tribune,* 6 April 1870, p. 3.

61. *St. Peter Tribune,* 22 June (p. 3) and 27 July (p. 2), both 1870, and 2 August (p. 3), 25 October (p. 3), and 8 November (p. 1), all 1871. In late December 1871, the Workingmen's Co-operative Association announced its annual meeting for January 3, 1872, at Charles Bryant's office, but I have been unable to locate any news of that in the *Tribune.* See *St. Peter Tribune,* 27 December 1871, p. 3.

62. In an article on the Finnish-American consumers' cooperative movement, Leonard C. Kercher argued that urban consumers displayed less "group solidarity" than did rural consumers, due to greater "occupational and other class differences," "more secondary and impersonal" contacts among individuals, greater heterogeneity of population and culture, and a greater degree of individualism; Leonard C. Kercher, "Some Sociological Aspects of Consumers' Cooperation," *Rural Sociology* 6 (December 1941): 317.

63. Upham and Dunlap, comps., *Minnesota Biographies,* 120; *St. Paul Daily Press,* 5 January 1870, p. 1; *Dakota County Union* (Hastings), 27 October 1869, p. 2. For the Massachusetts statute, see Massachusetts, *The General Statutes of the Commonwealth of Massachusetts: Supplement . . . , 1860–1866,* ed. William A. Richardson and George P. Sanger (Boston: The Commonwealth, 1867), chap. 290. For Minnesota's law, see Minnesota, *Statutes at Large,* 1:468–70.

64. *St. Paul Daily Pioneer,* 10 February 1870, p. 1.

65. *St. Paul Daily Pioneer,* 10 February 1870, p. 1. Other Twin Cities newspapers made no mention of this bill other than to

report its introduction and, a month later, its passage.

66. Apparently the legislature amended Chewning's bill to exclude the Massachusetts provision of protection for shareholders against liability for the association's debts. (I have not located the copy of Chewning's original bill to verify this assumption.) The St. Peter organizers may have had an unamended copy of the bill, for they mistakenly believed that "when all the stock is paid up the members, individually, will not be responsible for any debts contracted by the Society." They set the capital stock at only one thousand dollars so it would be soon "paid up" and the protective clause activated; see *St. Peter Tribune*, 23 March 1870, p. 2.

67. *St. Peter Tribune*, 23 March 1870, p. 2; Minnesota, *Statutes at Large*, 1:468–69.

68. Rozwenc, *Cooperatives Come to America*, 92.

69. In December 1869, the *Northfield Enterprise* called on the legislature to pass a "stay law" to protect farmers' assets from repossession and to give them more time to repay. Placing the blame safely beyond its Main Street advertisers, it criticized "eastern capitalists" for lack of sympathy for farmers suffering from low wheat prices; see *Northfield Enterprise*, 10 December 1869, p. 2.

70. Lynn Carlin, ed., *Continuum: Threads in the Community Fabric of Northfield, Minnesota* (Northfield: The City, 1976), 47; *Northfield Enterprise*, 3 March 1870, p. 3. For a biographical sketch of Barton, see Upham and Dunlap, comps., *Minnesota Biographies*, 37.

71. *The Standard*, 17 February 1870, p. 2. There is no clear evidence that the Grange initiated the Union store movement here. "Merchant" did not charge the Grange with doing so; the local Grange was only one or two months old when the movement began; and there was no suggestion of limiting membership to Grangers or to farmers. Grange sponsorship is possible though.

72. "Farmer"'s letter is in *The Standard*, 24 February 1870, p. 2; "Abraham Quipps"'s letter is in the *Northfield Enterprise*, 24 February 1870, p. 3.

73. *The Standard*, 3 March 1870, p. 2. Advocates of consumers' cooperation often exaggerated the importance of small savings on retail prices. See Clarke A. Chambers's analysis of consumers' cooperation in Chambers, "The Cooperative League of the United States of America, 1916–1961: A Study of Social Theory and Social Action," *Agricultural History* 36 (April 1962): 60, 68, 70, 74, 80.

74. "Quipps" admitted rural villages' lack of jobs kept St. Paulites from moving there. He turned "Merchant"'s argument on its head by arguing the cost of living was generally lower in St. Paul; *Northfield Enterprise*, 10 March 1870, p. 3.

75. *The Standard*, 10 March 1870, p. 2.

76. *The Standard*, 17 March 1870, p. 2.

77. *Northfield Enterprise*, 31 March 1870, p. 2. The issues of *The Standard* for January and February 1871 contain no notice of a second annual meeting.

78. Richard Hartshorne, "Morphology of the State Area: Significance for the State," in *Essays in Political Geography*, ed. Charles A. Fisher (London: Methuen & Co., 1968), 27–32.

Notes to Chapter 2

1. "Annual Message of Governor Austin," p. 10, *Executive Documents of the State of Minnesota, for the Year 1872*, vol. 1.

2. *Minnesota Monthly*, August 1869, p. 253.

3. *St. Charles Herald*, 5 November 1869, p. 3; *Rochester Post*, 13 and 27 November 1869, both p. 3, and 9 July 1870, p. 2, 3.

4. *Rochester Post*, 9 July 1870, p. 2, 3. The Halfway group was also concerned about railroad freight rates. For the higher rates at Rochester, see Larson, *Wheat Market*, 75–76.

5. *St. Charles Herald*, 19 November 1869, p. 2, 3, and 4 March 1870, p. 1; *Rochester Post*, 20 and 27 November 1869, both p. 3; *Minnesota Monthly*, August 1869, p. 254.

6. Thomas A. Woods, *Knights of the Plow: Oliver H. Kelley and the Origins of the Grange in Republican Ideology* (Ames: Iowa State University Press, 1991), 22–23, 27, 48, 51–52, 54, 82–84, 90. The two clergymen who helped Kelley found the Grange were not meddling moralists, but government employees; William D. Barns, "Oliver Hudson Kelley and the Genesis of the Grange: A Reappraisal," *Agricultural History* 41 (July 1967): 233, 234. Kelley rejected the idea that

the Patrons "adopt a temperance clause" and "insisted on prohibiting any discussion of . . . denominational religious subjects during meetings"; Woods, *Knights of the Plow*, 96–97.

7. Woods, *Knights of the Plow*, 22, 88–90; Barns, "Genesis of the Grange," 229–42 (quote on p. 240).

8. *Sauk Rapids Sentinel*, 2 October 1868, p. 2; Woods, *Knights of the Plow*, 29, 41. For contrasts between Yankees' commercialized farming and Southerners' semisubsistence farming, see Jeremy Atack and Fred Bateman, "Yankee Farming and Settlement in the Old Northwest: A Comparative Analysis," in *Essays on the Economy of the Old Northwest*, ed. David C. Klingaman and Richard K. Vedder (Athens: Ohio University Press, 1987), 78, 85–86, 94. For a different view, see John C. Hudson, *Making the Corn Belt: A Geographical History of Middle-Western Agriculture* (Bloomington: Indiana University Press, 1994). Dennis Sven Nordin argued that educational "uplift" "overshadowed every other aspect of grangerism," but he failed to prove this point. He examined primarily "the Second Granger Movement" from 1880 to 1900, not the First Granger Movement of the 1870s; Nordin, "A Revisionist Interpretation of the Patrons of Husbandry, 1867–1900," *The Historian* 32 (August 1970): 630–43, especially 630–32.

9. In *Knights of the Plow*, Woods stressed agrarian and "liberal" republicanism as the ideology motivating Kelley to found the Grange—and farmers to join it. This is too narrow an interpretation. Given the spread of commercialized farming, the 1870s seems too late to employ the republican paradigm without adding significant reservations. Also republicanism fails to explain: (1) the secret, ritualistic nature of the Grange, (2) Grange rules against partisan politics in Grange meetings, and (3) the Grange's relative failure to recruit immigrant farmers. However, Grange activities were publicized in local newspapers and nonfarmers often were allowed to join so that Grange secrecy and exclusiveness were watered down in practice. Also county councils and the State Grange became quite involved in local and state politics regardless of the rules covering subordinate Grange meetings. See my

review of *Knights of the Plow* in *Minnesota History* 52 (Fall 1991): 290–91. For overuse of "republicanism" as an explanatory concept, see Daniel T. Rodgers, "Republicanism: The Career of a Concept," *Journal of American History* 79 (June 1992): 11–38.

10. Woods, *Knights of the Plow*, 95, 110, 118; Rice, "Old-Stock Americans," in *They Chose Minnesota*, ed. Holmquist, 55–72; Barns, "Genesis of the Grange," 240. Led by Walter A. Nimocks's *Farmers' Union* and John H. Stevens, the farmers' clubs were trying to organize a state farmers' club, but they failed, "probably because the Grange began to fulfill the organizational role envisioned for the state club"; Woods, *Knights of the Plow*, 132–33.

11. Woods, *Knights of the Plow*, 155–57; Theodore C. Blegen, *Minnesota: A History of the State* (Minneapolis: University of Minnesota Press, 1975), 291–93; Martin Ridge, "Ignatius Donnelly and the Granger Movement in Minnesota," *Mississippi Valley Historical Review* 42 (March 1956): 693–709. Several historians argued that the Grange began to decline in 1874–75. I use 1878 instead because signs of continued vitality (such as publication of the *Grange Advance*) were present until 1878. Also Kelley resigned as national secretary of the Grange in November 1878, and North Star Grange No. 1 disbanded in September 1878. See Woods, *Knights of the Plow*, 162–64; Jarchow, *Earth Brought Forth*, 118; D[ennis] Sven Nordin, *Rich Harvest: A History of the Grange, 1867–1900* (Jackson: University Press of Mississippi, 1974), 37, 39.

12. *Federal Union* (Rochester), 13 June 1873, p. 2. Grange success in uniting Old Stock Americans of the North and South, plus the success of the Second Granger Movement (1880–1900) among overwhelmingly Old Stock farmers in New England, New York, Pennsylvania, and Ohio show its "ethnic" appeal. For the Second Granger Movement, see Nordin, "Revisionist Interpretation," 631–32. For definitions of ethnicity, see William Petersen, "Concepts of Ethnicity," in Petersen, Michael Novak, and Philip Gleason, *Concepts of Ethnicity* (Cambridge: Harvard University Press, Belknap Press, 1982), 1–26. In Petersen's terms, the Grange exemplified ethnogenesis—union

of Yankee and Southerner, promotion of farmers as a distinct group, and schism between farmers and nonfarmers. Because it was unable to unite farmers permanently, it is failed ethnogenesis. If ethnicity seems too strong a term, see Michael Novak on the nonterritorial, voluntary, associational nature of ethnicity in America; Novak, "Pluralism in Humanistic Perspective," 39–40. Woods aptly described Grange ritual as civil religion; Woods, *Knights of the Plow*, 172.

13. Nordin, *Rich Harvest*, 9. See also, Woods, *Knights of the Plow*, 94–95; and Solon J. Buck, *The Granger Movement: A Study of Agricultural Organization and Its Political, Economic, and Social Manifestations, 1870–1880* (Cambridge: Harvard University Press, 1933), 40–41, 280–81. The first Grange circular stressed the first three features; Oliver H. Kelley, *Origin and Progress of the Order of the Patrons of Husbandry in the United States: A History from 1866 to 1873* (Philadelphia: J. A. Wagenseller, 1875), 68–69.

14. Donald B. Marti argued that the Grange was "virtually forced" to address the "woman question" because "it grew up among aspiring, middle-class Protestant folk [Old Stock Americans] in the years just after the Civil War"; Marti, "Sisters of the Grange: Rural Feminism in the Late Nineteenth Century," *Agricultural History* 58 (July 1984): 247–61, especially, p. 247–48 and 250–51.

15. *St. Paul Daily Pioneer*, 8 July 1874, p. 2.

16. Quoted in Woods, *Knights of the Plow*, 76.

17. *Record and Union* (Rochester), 28 April 1876, p. 3.

18. *Farmers' Union*, 7 March 1874, p. 69.

19. The above-mentioned case of women buying shares in a warehouse company is the only one found for any cooperatives researched for this study. Marti argued that in Texas and New England "women stayed away from discussions of cooperatives," although they discussed "poultry and dairying, which came within women's sphere, apparently, as other agricultural matters did not"; Marti, "Sisters of the Grange," 253–54. For evidence that economic action was sometimes discussed at township Grange meetings, see Record, Burnside Grange No. 148, GCHS.

20. Woods, *Knights of the Plow*, 15–21, 75–80.

21. Geographer Robert C. Ostergren reported that Swedish and German immigrant farmers stayed loyal to wheat after American-born farmers abandoned it for more remunerative crops. "For the American farmer, the desire to maximize return was quite likely much more strongly ingrained," while "the transplanted peasant may well have been happy with limited returns." Historian Jon Gjerde's study of Norwegian-American farmers in Norway Grove, Wisconsin, showed that, once accustomed to growing wheat for the market, Norwegian-American farmers "remained more enamored with wheat production than their New England-born neighbors." Robert C. Ostergren, *A Community Transplanted: The Trans-Atlantic Experience of a Swedish Immigrant Settlement in the Upper Middle West, 1835–1915* (Madison: University of Wisconsin Press, 1988), 197–200; Jon Gjerde, *From Peasants to Farmers: The Migration from Balestrand, Norway, to the Upper Middle West* (Cambridge: Cambridge University Press, 1985), 173, 181.

22. *Freeborn County Standard* (Albert Lea), 24 July and 27 November 1873 and 15 January 1874, all p. 3. See also the list of delegates to a county Patron's Convention in Albert Lea in the *Standard*, 24 July 1873, p. 3. Of the forty delegates, only four had surnames that are possibly Scandinavian or German.

23. "Subordinate Granges in Minnesota" copy of typescript, Minnesota State Grange Records, MHS.

24. *Glenwood Eagle*, 13 December 1873, p. 3.

25. Minutes of 15 and 22 April 1873 meetings, Record, Burnside Grange No. 148, GCHS. Grange officers in Bancroft and Manchester (Freeborn County) were almost exclusively Old Stock; *Freeborn County Standard*, 27 November 1873, p. 3, and 15 January 1874, p. 3. In Dakota Territory, most Grange members were "settlers of native American stock," and in one Swedish-American area "the Grange was never even introduced." Herbert S. Schell, "The Grange and the Credit Problem in Dakota Territory," *Agricultural History* 10 (April 1936): 59–83 (quotes p. 75). Gerald Prescott noted that Old Stock Amer-

icans "dominated Wisconsin farm organizations during the Gilded Age" while Germans and Scandinavians rarely joined them. Gerald Prescott, "Wisconsin Farm Leaders in the Gilded Age," *Agricultural History* 44 (April 1970): 183–99 (quote p. 188).

26. Nordin, *Rich Harvest*, 22–25; O. Fritiof Ander, "The Immigrant Church and the Patrons of Husbandry," *Agricultural History* 8 (October 1934): 155–68. For Catholic opposition to the Grange, see Fergus Macdonald, *The Catholic Church and the Secret Societies in the United States* (New York: United States Catholic Historical Society, 1946), 77–79.

27. Grangers "called upon pagan deities . . . for knowledge and guidance in much the same way the Romans had called upon Father Jupiter and Mother Earth and the lesser agricultural gods centuries earlier"; Woods, *Knights of the Plow*, 172. Church opposition to secret societies did not doom them. The Sons of Norway, condemned by the Lutheran church, became "by far the largest secular organization" among Norwegian-Americans. Odd S. Lovoll, *The Promise of America: A History of the Norwegian-American People* (Minneapolis: University of Minnesota Press and Norwegian-American Historical Assn., 1984), 187–89.

28. Ander, "Immigrant Church," 162–64. For the Catholic church's response to the Grange and the efforts of Catholic farmers to form separate agricultural societies, see Macdonald, *Catholic Church and the Secret Societies*, 73–74, 77–79; *Minneapolis Daily Tribune*, 23 July 1875, p. 2; *Farmers' Union*, 28 February 1874, p. 60; *Farmington Press*, 29 July 1875, p. 3, and 8 July 1875, p. 2; *Minnesota Record* (Rochester), 30 August 1873, p. 3.

29. For the Vasa debate, see *Luthersk Kyrkotidning* (Red Wing), vol. 2, no. 4 (April 1873): 66–69, and vol. 2, no. 8 (June 1873): 129; Emeroy Johnson, *Eric Norelius: Pioneer Midwest Pastor and Churchman* (Rock Island, Ill.: Augustana Book Concern, 1954); *Red Wing Argus*, 8 May (p. 1), 15 and 22 May (both p. 4), and 24 July (p. 4), all 1873.

30. *Nordisk Folkeblad*, 3 September 1873, p. 1. *Nordisk Folkeblad* was a strongly Republican paper; the anger expressed may have been a pose designed to persuade Norwegian Americans to support the Republican ticket. For a brief description of *Nordisk Folkeblad*, see Lovoll, *Promise of America*,

121. For favorable reports about the Grange, see *Nordisk Folkeblad*, 21 May 1873, p. 1, and 30 July 1873, p. 2. In the July 30 editorial, the editor admitted that many would hesitate to join the Grange due to its secrecy rule, which was "rather superfluous," but the rule "will likely soon end."

31. *Budstikken* (Minneapolis), 20 October 1874, p. 1.

32. Woods, *Knights of the Plow*, 76.

33. *Nordisk Folkeblad*, 25 June 1873, p. 1.

34. Granger appeals to class interest did elicit some support among immigrants. For one favorable Norwegian-American response to Grangers' rhetoric, see *Nordisk Folkeblad*, 21 January 1874, p. 1.

35. In Wisconsin, many immigrants "postponed participation" in groups like the Grange "until they were better conditioned to their new surroundings." On average, an immigrant was not elected to an office in a farm organization until he had been in Wisconsin for twenty years; see Prescott, "Wisconsin Farm Leaders," 188–89.

36. For the Norwegian-American commitment to farming, see Carlton C. Qualey and Jon A. Gjerde, "The Norwegians," in *They Chose Minnesota*, ed. Holmquist, 230.

37. John G. Wells, *The Grange Illustrated: Or, Patron's Hand-book: In the Interests of the Order of Patrons of Husbandry* (New York: Grange Publishing Co., 1874), pt. 1, p. 73. Minnesota's first permanent Grange was North Star Grange of St. Paul. It was "the heart of the Order in 1869"; Woods, *Knights of the Plow*, 112, 118.

38. *Minnesota Monthly*, April 1869, p. 120. Kelley "formed a Grange in Manhattan" with his brother-in-law as Master. He "always believed that the Grange should be open to anyone. . . . It didn't matter to him whether they lived in the city or the country"; Woods, *Knights of the Plow*, 192–93.

39. *Farmers' Union*, 19 April 1873, p. 122. For a debate between the editors of the *St. Paul Daily Pioneer* and the *St. Paul Daily Press* on this subject, see *St. Paul Daily Pioneer*, 26 February 1874, p. 2.

40. *Waseca Weekly News*, 30 April 1873, p. 2; *Farmers' Union*, 28 June 1873, p. 205.

41. Child claimed to be "the first farmer, now living, that settled in Waseca county" and he "still own[ed] the 'old homestead.'" (He owned the farm but was not farming it

himself.) *Farmers' Union*, 28 June 1873, p. 205; *Waseca News*, 18 May 1870, p. 3; *Waseca Weekly News*, 7 May, p. 3, and 21 May, p. 2, both 1873; Gladys A. Harshman, "The History of the Settlement of Waseca County, 1854–1880" (master's thesis, University of Minnesota, 1931), 168; *Waseca Weekly News*, 16 July 1873, p. 2. During the debate, one Granger charged, "The worst enemies in and out of the Grange are these county seat editors—nine out of every ten are run by county seat rings, and will stoop to the dirtiest work to strengthen the ring, and build up the county seat"; *Waseca Weekly News*, 18 June 1873, p. 2.

42. *Minnesota Radical* (Waseca), 24 November 1875, p. 5.

43. *Fillmore County Republican* (Preston), 6 June (p. 3), 4 July (p. 3), 11 July (p. 2, 3), 10 October (p. 3), all 1873. Eight delegates from Preston Grange were at one council meeting (most Granges sent three).

44. *Freeborn County Standard*, 19 February 1874, p. 3. For an amusing account of Grange life written by a snobbish Iowa townswoman whose husband joined the Grange—"the army of the great unwashed ... and became Worthy Master, as about the only person ... competent to fill the place," see *Freeborn County Standard*, 22 January 1874, p. 4.

45. G. W. Schatzel, "Among the Wheat-Fields of Minnesota," *Harper's New Monthly Magazine* 36 (January 1868): 190–201 (quotes on p. 197, 199).

46. Woods, *Knights of the Plow*, 122–23.

47. *Minnesota Monthly*, April 1869, p. 134–35. For the difficulty Grange agents had in dealing with one farm implement manufacturer, see Arthur H. Hirsch, "Efforts of the Grange in the Middle West to Control the Price of Farm Machinery, 1870–1880," *Mississippi Valley Historical Review* 15 (March 1929): 473–96. Hirsch's account is based on the McCormick company papers and is biased in favor of the company.

48. *Farmers' Union*, 12 April 1873, p. 115.

49. *Farmers' Union*, 11 October 1873, p. 325, and 1 November 1873, p. 348.

50. *Farmers' Union*, 25 October 1873, p. 341, and 1 November 1873, p. 348. See also the letter by "No. 231" and the action of the Hennepin County Council reported by "Justice" in the November 1 issue.

51. *Farmers' Union*, 11 October 1873, p. 325.

52. The need for county Granges had apparently first been recognized by Lincoln Grange No. 46 in October 1870; Woods, *Knights of the Plow*, 143–44, 160. In February 1873, the State Grange passed a resolution "that Subordinate Granges be recommended to form District or County Councils"; *Farmers' Union*, 15 March 1873, p. 83.

53. *Farmers' Union*, 19 April 1873, p. 122–23.

54. See the constitution and bylaws of the Goodhue, Fillmore, and Northfield Councils in *Farmers' Union*, 8 March 1873, p. 76–77; *Farmers' Union*, 19 April 1873, p. 122–23; *Northfield Standard*, 5 April 1873, p. 4; *Fillmore County Republican*, 28 March 1873, p. 2. For state authorization of district councils, see *Farmers' Union*, 19 April 1873, p. 122–23. Spring Valley-area Granges also sent delegates to the Fillmore County Council.

55. For an example of nineteenth-century limits on government's economic activities, see the governor's veto of a bill authorizing Kasson village to issue bonds to build a grist mill; *Federal Union*, 1 March 1873, p. 2. For evidence that the Goodhue County Council, at least, did not always meet at Red Wing, the county seat, see Burnside Grange No. 148 Record.

56. Freeborn County Council of the Patrons of Husbandry, Record Book, 1874–82 (hereafter FCCPH), p. 24–25, 26–27, 83–84, Freeborn County Historical Society, Albert Lea (hereafter FCHS). The council first approved, then withdrew, "a call to the several towns for a county convention of the anti-Monopoly party."

57. H. E. Mayhew, a Grange leader, was the manager of the Grange warehouse in Delavan and the main leader in the county-seat-removal movement. See *Blue Earth City Post*, 5 December 1874 (p. 2), 12 December 1874 (p. 3), and 23 October 1875 (p. 3).

58. Woods, *Knights of the Plow*, 153–56 (quote p. 155).

59. *Owatonna Journal*, 26 June 1873, p. 2; *Fillmore County Republican*, 9 May 1873, p. 2. Similarly the editor of the *Freeborn County Standard* advised "our Granges" to "not fritter away their strength upon local issues of minor importance"; *Freeborn County Standard*, 7 August 1873, p. 3.

60. *Waseca Weekly News*, 18 June 1873, p. 2.

61. *Freeborn County Standard*, 25 December 1873, p. 3; FCCPH, Record Book, p. 21, 23, 24–27, 34, 47–48, 74–75, 94–95.

62. Later, two more agents were elected— one for Rushford and one for Spring Valley. Each agent would buy from each town's merchants on behalf of farmers in each town's hinterland. *Fillmore County Republican*, 6 June and 10 October 1873, both p. 3, and 9 January and 13 February 1874, both p. 2.

63. *Faribault Republican*, 9 April 1873, p. 3.

64. *Fillmore County Republican*, 9 January 1874, p. 3; FCCPH, Record Book, p. 34.

65. The Freeborn County Council chose local Grange secretaries "to Solicit order[s] for the Workman seeder." Orders for thirteen seeders were received. E. K. Pickett placed a bulk order for the seeders with the Wisconsin state Grange agent. The price was $36.25 per seeder, plus a total freight charge of $84.34 and $1.51 for telegrams and postage. FCCPH, Record Book, p. 47–48, 57, 305–7, 310. Pickett was probably not the agent because the council had just refused to elect one. For information on Wisconsin agent L. G. Kniffen, see Nordin, *Rich Harvest*, 144.

66. *Farmers' Union*, 26 July 1873, p. 238, and 8 March 1873, p. 77. For other reports of savings, see Woods, *Knights of the Plow*, 161; Nordin, *Rich Harvest*, 133–35; and George Cerny, "Cooperation in the Midwest in the Granger Era, 1869–1875," *Agricultural History* 37 (October 1963): 187–205, especially p. 192–93 for the Minnesota examples. Burnside Grange dealt directly with a Red Wing merchant; see minutes, 8 April 1873, Burnside Grange No. 148 Record.

67. *Record and Union*, 28 April 1876, p. 3.

68. For the role of the railroad in reducing merchants' capital requirements, see Cronon, *Nature's Metropolis*, 325–26.

69. For McCormick's decision to build its own sales organization, see Chandler, *Visible Hand*, 302–3, 305–6; Cronon, *Nature's Metropolis*, 313–15.

70. *Fillmore County Republican*, 18 April 1873, p. 2.

71. McCormick's private letter was printed in *Fillmore County Republican*, 18 April 1873, p. 2. It was later reprinted in a Springfield, Illinois, newspaper, and Cyrus McCormick was forced to issue a clarification in the *Chicago Daily Tribune*, 14 May 1873; see Hirsch, "Efforts of the Grange," 480–81.

72. *Fillmore County Republican*, 18 April 1873, p. 2. For another editorial comment, see *Federal Union*, 3 May 1873, p. 3.

73. Hirsch, "Efforts of the Grange," 480–81; *Chatfield Democrat*, 12 April 1873, p. 2.

74. Nordin, *Rich Harvest*, 144, 146.

75. FCCPH, Record Book, p. 26, 36, 40; Nordin, *Rich Harvest*, 146.

76. Minutes, 17 February 1874, Burnside Grange No. 148 Record.

77. " 'Church records' contain historical find: first farmers' co-op here started in 1874," clipping from Granite Falls paper, (1991?), in author's possession.

78. Cronon, *Nature's Metropolis*, 333–39.

79. FCCPH, Record Book, p. 23. The words "Grange store" could mean a cooperative or a merchant-owned store with which the Grange had an agreement. In this case, each Grange was instructed to give the committee a list of patrons who would support any deals the committee might make with merchants; therefore, it appears that the latter meaning applied here.

80. Forty-three Grangers gave personal notes to purchase stock. In November 1877, a "discussion on the prospects of a co-operative store" led to a motion "to return to the members the notes given last year for a co-operative store—carried unanimously"; FCCPH, Record Book, p. 59–60, 61, 64–65, 94, 95.

81. FCCPH, Record Book, p. 98–99. These small stores may have been deals with individual merchants. Since each was operated by one Grange, they were probably not incorporated.

82. *Freeborn County Standard*, 24 July 1873 and 15 January 1874, both p. 3; *Farmers' Union*, 2 August 1873, p. 243. For ethnic and geographical information, see *Map of Freeborn County, Minnesota: Drawn from Actual Surveys and the County Records* (Red Wing and Philadelphia: Warner & Foote, 1878); *Plat Book of Freeborn County, Minnesota: Drawn from Actual Surveys and County Records* (Philadelphia: Union Publishing Co., 1895); and the Minnesota 1885 and 1895 manuscript census schedules, Bancroft and Bath Townships, Freeborn County, microfilm, MHS. Two officers lived across the line, in Bath Township, yet all lived within two miles of the schoolhouse.

83. Fremad Association, Protokol [minute book], p. 36–37, Pope County Historical So-

ciety, Glenwood; *Glenwood Herald*, 1 January 1897, p. 11. It is not clear whether these Fremad members were Grangers.

84. *Glenwood Eagle*, 7 and 14 February 1874, both p. 3, and 7 March 1874, p. 2.

85. In New Ulm, they made arrangements with one merchant in each specialty: dry goods, hardware, groceries and drugs, and footwear; *St. Peter Tribune*, 31 December 1873, p. 3.

86. *Farmers' Union*, 17 May 1873, p. 156.

87. Dropping "propositions to merchants," that is, proposed deals offered to merchants, Windom Grangers jointly ordered groceries and other items from Chicago; *Farmers' Union*, 26 July 1873, p. 238.

88. See Table A in Appendix. Apart from Medford, all towns having stores were larger, "county seat" towns; apart from Albert Lea (a county seat), all towns with an agent were smaller towns (though a county seat, Windom was not yet a large town in the early 1870s).

89. Schell described the large-volume operation of a merchant who operated the "Wigwam," a Grange store in Dakota Territory, and also a warehouse "where goods were sold to [Grange] members in exchange for grain"; Schell, "Grange in Dakota Territory," 72–73.

90. *Glenwood Eagle*, 28 February 1874, p. 2; *Farmers' Union*, 12 December 1872, p. 5, and 14 June 1873, p. 188, and 29 March 1873, p. 102; *Owatonna Journal*, 14 August and 16 October 1873, and 26 November 1874, all p. 3; *Waseca Weekly News*, 20 November 1872, p. 2. There may have been Granger stores in Red Wing and Fairmont; William H. Budd, *Martin County before 1880* (Trimont: Walter Carlson, 1974), 77. For railroads through Owatonna, Medford, and Faribault, see Edward V. Robinson, *Early Economic Conditions and the Development of Agriculture in Minnesota* (Minneapolis: University of Minnesota, 1915), 37; for Benson, see Ralph W. Hidy, Muriel E. Hidy, Roy V. Scott, and Don L. Hofsommer, *The Great Northern Railway: A History* (Boston: Harvard Business School Press, 1988), 20.

91. The difference was that Grangers buying from Wards bypassed local retailers, while the Grange store was a special kind of local retailer. For the early history of Montgomery Ward and Co., see Chandler, *Visible*

Hand, 230; Boorstin, *Democratic Experience*, 121–24; and Cronon, *Nature's Metropolis*, 334–38.

92. *Owatonna Journal*, 26 June, 21 August, 11 September, 16 October—all 1873, 12 and 19 February and 26 November—all 1874, and 7 January 1875, all p. 3. The *St. Paul Weekly Pioneer* reported on 13 February 1874 (p. 6) that Cansdell's store had "failed." That false report shows the danger of relying on daily newspapers and state farm journals and of neglecting local sources. The store was still operating almost a year later; *Owatonna Journal*, 7 January 1875, p. 3.

93. Wells, *Grange Illustrated*, pt. 1, p. 165.

94. *Farmers' Union*, 29 March, p. 102, and 26 July, p. 238, both 1873. For a tongue-in-cheek letter, ostensibly written by a miller urging Grangers not to start "a union store" (but confirming Grangers' often negative views of merchants and millers), see *Faribault Republican*, 9 April 1873, p. 3. For an attack on Grange-owned cooperatives, see *Federal Union*, 5 April 1873, p. 2.

95. Victor N. Valgren, *Farmers' Mutual Fire Insurance in the United States* (Chicago: University of Chicago Press, 1924), 5–8, 11–14.

96. *Minneapolis Journal*, 3 December 1927, p. 1; *Farmers' Union*, August 1867, p. 3. For the MFMFIAM page, see *Farmers' Union*, October 1867 and March 1868, both p. 8.

97. Nothing in the idea itself dictated the size of a mutual's territory. In New England, the territory was commonly limited to one or more towns. In the South, statewide companies were organized first; in North Carolina, some county companies developed. Valgren, *Farmers' Mutual Fire Insurance*, 11–13, 18–20, 38–39.

98. Treasurer Richard J. Mendenhall was president of the State National Bank of Minneapolis and a Grange Master; President H. H. Smith of Brooklyn Township was "one of the best and most influential farmers" in Hennepin County. *Farmers' Union*, August 1867, p. 3, 5, and August 1868, p. 4. The August 1867 issue, p. 5, lists the directors, almost all of whom have Old Stock surnames.

99. John A. C. Hetherington, *Mutual and Cooperative Enterprises: An Analysis of Customer-owned Firms in the United States* (Charlottesville: University Press of Virginia, 1991), 20–21. Hetherington was referring to

life insurance mutuals, but the same principle applies to a statewide farmers' mutual like the MFMFIAM.

100. For every one hundred dollars of property insured, policyholders had to deposit two dollars in Mendenhall's bank; *Farmers' Union*, August 1867, p. 5.

101. Charter of the Minnesota Farmers' Mutual Fire Insurance Association of Minneapolis, Minnesota, Secretary of State, Corporation Division, Record of Incorporations, Vol. B, p. 388–91; *Farmers' Union*, August 1867, p. 5, and November 1867, p. 8. The deposit of two dollars per each hundred dollars of property insured belonged to the member, who earned 7 percent interest on it. The company withdrew interest or principal from each member's deposit—on a pro rata basis—to pay fire losses.

102. "First Annual Report of the Insurance Commissioner, of the State of Minnesota," 605–6, *Executive Documents of the State of Minnesota, for the Year 1872*, vol. 1.

103. "Second Annual Report of the Insurance Commissioner, of the State of Minnesota," p. 28, 33, 89–90, 115–17, *Executive Documents of the State of Minnesota, for the Year 1873*, vol. 1.

104. For the Old Stock American population in Olmsted County, see Rice, "Old-Stock Americans," in *They Chose Minnesota*, ed. Holmquist, 61–62.

105. *Federal Union*, 8 February 1873, p. 3.

106. Minnesota, Legislature, House of Representatives, *Journal* (hereafter *House Journal*), 1873, p. 73; *Minnesota Record*, 8 February 1873, p. 2.

107. *Federal Union*, 15 February 1873, p. 3.

108. *Minnesota Record*, 8 February 1873, p. 2.

109. *House Journal*, 1873, p. 158, 268–69, 348; Minnesota, Legislature, Senate, *Journal* (hereafter *Senate Journal*), 1873, p. 393; *Federal Union*, 1 March 1873, p. 3. Passage came after the Grange's February 1873 state convention urged local Granges "to organize their own insurance companies." The amendments were added by a special committee consisting of the four state senators from Houston and Goodhue Counties; *Senate Journal*, 1873, p. 346, 355. For charges of insurance industry lobbying, see *Minnesota Record*, 10 May 1873, p. 3.

110. *Rochester Post*, 26 April 1873, p. 2.

111. *Minnesota Record*, 29 March 1873, p. 3.

112. *Rochester Post*, 26 April 1873, p. 2. Viola Grangers were aware that there was some problem concerning the law. One week before "Uncle Henry"'s letter appeared, a Viola correspondent reported, "There is some doubt as to whether the Governor signed the bill permitting the farmers to form town insurance companies"; *Federal Union*, 19 April 1873, p. 3.

113. M. C. Fuller to Horace Austin, 16 April 1873, in miscellaneous correspondence, April–May 1873, Minnesota, Governor (1870–1874: Austin), Records, Minnesota State Archives, MHS. The governor's notes are written on the back of the letter.

114. *Federal Union*, 10 May 1873, p. 3; *Minnesota Record*, 10 May 1873, p. 3.

115. *Rochester Post*, 26 April 1873, p. 2. At a mid-May meeting of the Viola Grange, there was no further talk of a township mutual insurance company; *Federal Union*, 24 May 1873, p. 3.

116. "Annual Message of Governor Austin," p. 21, Minnesota, *Executive Documents of the State of Minnesota, for the Year 1871*, vol. 1.

117. "Third Annual Report of the Insurance Commissioner, of the State of Minnesota," p. 52, *Executive Documents of the State of Minnesota, for the Year 1874*, vol. 2.

118. A similar charge surfaced in 1886 when McGill ran for governor (supported by the insurance industry). In the 1886 session a bill that the industry opposed disappeared after Senate passage. McGill was charged with conniving with the "insurance gang"; *St. Paul Dispatch*, 3 September 1886, p. 2 (quoting *Freeborn County Standard*, 1 September 1886, p. 4). See also a defense of McGill by "Truth," *St. Paul Daily Pioneer Press*, 6 September 1886, p. 8.

119. *Farmers' Union*, 12 April 1873, p. 115, 17 May 1873, p. 156, 10 January 1874, p. 429, and 31 January 1874, p. 28.

120. *St. Paul Daily Pioneer*, 3 March 1874, p. 2. See also *Farmers' Union*, 7 March 1874, p. 68.

121. *St. Paul Daily Pioneer*, 3 March 1874, p. 2; *St. Paul Daily Press*, 26 February 1874, p. 4; *Farmers' Union*, 7 February 1874, p. 37.

122. *St. Paul Daily Pioneer*, 3 March 1874, p. 2; *St. Paul Daily Press*, 26 February 1874, p. 4;

Minneapolis Daily Tribune, 3 March 1874, p. 2.

123. *St. Paul Daily Press*, 26 February 1874, p. 4; *St. Paul Daily Pioneer*, 3 March 1874, p. 2. Burbank wrote to one legislator to make "some hits at the Farmers' Mutual"; *Farmers' Union*, 7 March 1874, p. 68.

124. *Minneapolis Daily Tribune*, 27 February and 1 March 1874, both p. 2.

125. *St. Paul Daily Pioneer*, 3 March 1874, p. 2.

126. The report noted minor inconsistencies in MFMFIAM's charter and bylaws and a supposed link between the MFMFIAM and its former treasurer, the principal in a much-publicized bankruptcy case; *St. Paul Daily Press*, 26 February 1874, p. 4; *Minneapolis Daily Tribune*, 26 and 27 February 1874, both p. 4.

127. *St. Paul Daily Press*, 26 February 1874, p. 4.

128. See, for example, "First Annual Report of the Insurance Commissioner," 605–6, *Executive Documents . . . 1872*, vol. 1.

129. *St. Paul Daily Pioneer*, 3 March 1874, p. 2. For McGill's appointment as commissioner and the financing of his salary, see *St. Peter Tribune*, 31 December 1873, p. 3.

130. *Farmers' Union*, 21 February, p. 52, 7 March, p. 68, 21 March, p. 84, and 28 March, p. 92—all 1874. For a Norwegian-American newspaper's defense of the MFMFIAM, see *Budstikken*, 16 March 1875, p. 1. The report and the officers' defense were printed in many small-town newspapers. See *Mankato Record*, 7 March 1874, p. 1, and *Western Progress* (Spring Valley), 25 March 1874, p. 1. Sherwood was called "a played out politician from Filmore [sic] county"; *Farmers' Union*, 28 February, p. 60, and 7 March, p. 68, both 1874. He was hurt by his eagerness to have himself and two others appointed as a committee to lobby the legislature, despite a recent Grange convention's decision that no such committee was needed.

131. *Minneapolis Daily Tribune*, 3 March 1874, p. 2.

132. *St. Paul Daily Pioneer*, 3 March 1874, p. 2.

133. "Fifteenth Annual Report of the Insurance Commissioner of the State of Minnesota," p. 7, 246, *Executive Documents of the State of Minnesota, for the Year 1885*, vol. 1.

134. *Farmers' Union*, 28 February 1874, p. 60.

135. Old Stock farmers failed to form any lasting township mutuals in the new law's first four years. "Eighth Annual Report of the Insurance Commissioner of the State of Minnesota," p. xliv–xlv, *Executive Documents of the State of Minnesota, for the Year 1878*, vol. 3.

136. Chambers, "Cooperative League of the United States," 60, 68, 70, 74, 80; Heflebower, *Cooperatives and Mutuals*, 130–31.

Notes to Chapter 3

1. *Rice County Journal*, 10 and 31 May, 5 and 19 and 26 July 1877, all p. 3; George D. Rogers, "History of Flour Manufacture in Minnesota," *Minnesota Historical Collections* 10, pt. 1 (1905): 40–41. Due to the controversy, the lawyers struck off all prospective jurors from Northfield and all farmers. The jury consisted of townsmen from Faribault and Warsaw. For the Yankee character of early Northfield, see Stewart H. Holbrook, *The Yankee Exodus: An Account of Migration From New England* (New York: Macmillan Co., 1950), 167–70. Norwegian Americans lived in the area, but their strong influence in the region came later.

2. *Rice County Journal*, 19 July 1877, p. 3.

3. Here and below, *Rice County Journal*, 26 July 1877, p. 3

4. *Rice County Journal*, 19 October 1882, p. 3. The case was back in court in 1882, for the Grangers had not directly complied with the ruling but had relied on a natural settling of the dam to lower it. See Jesse Ames & Sons v. Cannon River Manufacturing Co., File No. 60, Minnesota District Court, Rice County, Case Files and Miscellaneous Court Papers, 1856–ca. 1896, State Archives, and 27 *Minnesota Supreme Court Reports*, 245–50 (1880).

5. Lance E. Davis and Douglass C. North, *Institutional Change and American Economic Growth* (Cambridge: Cambridge University Press, 1971), 94; Jarchow, *Earth Brought Forth*, 117–18. Wayne G. Broehl, Jr., attributed the Grange's radicalization to the Panic of 1873 and the ensuing depression, but the radical resolution he cited was passed in July 1873, two months before the September 1873 Panic; Wayne G. Broehl, Jr., *Cargill: Trad-*

ing the World's Grain (Hanover, N.H.: University Press of New England, 1992), 28, 35.

6. Hession and Sardy, *Ascent to Affluence*, 453, 456; Woods, *Knights of the Plow*, 151; Robinson, *Early Economic Conditions*, 59, 75.

7. Jarchow, *Earth Brought Forth*, 165–66, 169, 175, 185; Woods, *Knights of the Plow*, 77–78; Robinson, *Early Economic Conditions*, 60–61; George S. Biscoe to "Ellen," 21 August 1862, 18 May 1866, George S. Biscoe and Family Papers, MHS. The first large wheat harvests came in 1859 and 1860.

8. Robinson, *Early Economic Conditions*, 57–59. Robinson (p. 57) stated that wheat raising increased greatly due to "the upward course of wheat prices during the later fifties and early sixties" although wartime inflation reduced the real price increase, and inflated prices for farm machinery and other goods cut profits.

9. Morton Rothstein, "The American West and Foreign Markets, 1850–1900," in *The Frontier in American Development: Essays in Honor of Paul Wallace Gates*, ed. David H. Ellis (Ithaca: Cornell University Press, 1969), 381–406.

10. Jarchow, *Earth Brought Forth*, 131–47.

11. Jarchow, *Earth Brought Forth*, 167; Larson, *Wheat Market*, 23–24, 39–40, 58, 62–63; L[ars] J[ørgensen] [Hauge], "Fra Freeborn County," in *Nordisk Folkeblad*, 26 May 1869, p. 2.

12. Larson, *Wheat Market*, 17–54, 55–73, 81–91, 94. Price data for the years 1859–67 are given on page 53.

13. Robinson, *Early Economic Conditions*, 107; Robert M. Frame III, *Millers to the World: Minnesota's Nineteenth Century Water Power Flour Mills* (St. Paul: Minnesota Historical Society, Division of Field Services, Historic Sites, and Archaeology, 1977), 21–22; Charles Byron Kuhlmann, *The Development of the Flour-Milling Industry in the United States, with Special Reference to the Industry in Minneapolis* (Boston: Houghton Mifflin Co., 1929), 106–8. Kuhlmann's figure of 507 mills in 1870 seems certainly mistaken, according to Robinson and Frame. For Goodhue County's mills, see *Grange Advance* (Red Wing), 24 January 1877, p. 4.

14. Larson, *Wheat Market*, 76–78, 81–82, 94.

15. *Freeborn County Standard*, 1 December 1870, p. 2. See also a letter from "X" in the *Standard*, 29 December 1870, p. 1. Complaints like "X"'s led to the start of a farmer-owned wheat warehouse in Albert Lea in December 1870; *Freeborn County Standard*, 15 December 1870, p. 2, and 29 December 1870, p. 3.

16. *Freeborn County Standard*, 24 July, 7 August, 18 September, and 2 October, all 1873, all p. 3, and 12 February 1874, p. 3. For W. W. Cargill's operations in Albert Lea, which was his headquarters from 1871 to 1875, see Broehl, *Cargill*, 22–39.

17. For the impact of railroads on the grain trade, see Cronon, *Nature's Metropolis*, 104–32, 143–46 (quote on p. 144).

18. Margaret Snyder, *The Chosen Valley: The Story of a Pioneer Town* (New York: W. W. Norton Co., 1948), 301–11 (quote on p. 303); "Testimony Taken by the Senate Investigating Committee on the Southern Minnesota Railroad," *Senate Journal*, 1874, p. 556–58; Larson, *Wheat Market*, 84–90, 93; Broehl, *Cargill*, 21–22, 26–28. According to Broehl, the SMRR owned the warehouses and contracted with Easton, who operated them and bought and sold wheat, aided by very preferential treatment from the railroad.

19. Snyder, *Chosen Valley*, 306–7; Douglass C. North, Terry L. Anderson, and Peter J. Hill, *Growth and Welfare in the American Past: A New Economic History*, 3d ed. (Englewood Cliffs, N.J.: Prentice-Hall, 1983), 127–31.

20. Anne Mayhew argued that farmers were dissatisfied with features of commercial farming: the need to buy farm implements and supplies (possibly at inflated prices), increase their borrowing, grow a cash crop to meet interest and principal payments, and deal in an impersonal marketplace, where agents and dealers "did not respond, as the country store owner had earlier, to tales of a bad year, family illness, or other such problems." No longer praised for making a subsistence living, the farmer faced "a new test by which ... to judge himself—the test of business success." More than the prices, the farmer protested being "locked into a system where his success or failure now depended on prices." Anne Mayhew, "A Reappraisal of the Causes of Farm Protest in the United States, 1870–1900," *Journal of Eco-*

nomic History 32 (June 1972): 464–75, especially p. 473–75. There is much truth to her argument, but by forming wheat-marketing cooperatives and joint-purchasing agencies, Grangers tried to improve the terms of commercial farming, not to escape it. They may have formed Grange stores to escape credit problems and Granges to lift farming's status.

21. Heflebower, *Cooperatives and Mutuals*, 9 (emphasis added).

22. Larson, *Wheat Market*, 45, 158.

23. *Wright County Eagle* (Delano), 10 January 1873, p. 2 (emphasis added).

24. Minutes of 15 and 22 April 1873, 7 July 1874, and 2 March 1875 meetings, Burnside Grange No. 148 Record. For the farmer's tendency not to "regard himself as being in competition with other producers" and how that affected cooperatives, see Hetherington, *Mutual and Cooperative Enterprises*, 131. Farmers started cooperatives "once these organizing costs had been undertaken" in forming Granges; Davis and North, *Institutional Change*, 94.

25. Larson, *Wheat Market*, 35, 97; *Record and Union*, 17 March 1876, p. 3; FCCPH, Record Book, p. 119. For one wheat buyer's response to the charge of "exorbitant" storage fees, see *Rochester Post*, 1 April 1876, p. 4.

26. Larson, *Wheat Market*, 75–76. Farmers at Meriden, only ten miles west of Owatonna, received ten cents less for their wheat than did farmers selling at Owatonna; *Owatonna Journal*, 30 October 1873, p. 2, and 6 November 1873, p. 3; Larson, *Wheat Market*, 84–86. For an explanation of how railroads set rates to encourage long-haul, or "through," traffic in order to lower their per-unit costs, see Cronon, *Nature's Metropolis*, 83–86.

27. Broehl, *Cargill*, 47. For Easton's near-monopoly on the SMRR, see Broehl, *Cargill*, 26–28.

28. Davis and North saw cooperation as one form of "arrangemental innovation": "as a result of changing relative economic position, farmers may abruptly revise their view of benefits to be expected from arrangemental innovation." They viewed changes in "economic position" over time, from prosperity to depression, and interpreted the Grange's growth as a result of "hard times in the 1870s." Table I indicates that "relative

economic position" changed from place to place as well. Farmers near noncompeting points revised upward "their view of benefits" from cooperation. Davis and North, *Institutional Change*, 94.

29. Woods, *Knights of the Plow*, 137, 162; Nordin, *Rich Harvest*, 153–63.

30. *Mower County Transcript* (Austin), 10 July 1873, p. 3; *Farmers' Union*, 2 August 1873, p. 243. A resolution before the State Grange convention in February 1873 encouraged Granges "to bring about a reduction of 5 per cent. in the production of wheat." That would have been an unenforceable rule encouraging non-Grange wheat farmers to increase their production; *Farmers' Union*, 19 April 1873, p. 123.

31. Robinson, *Early Economic Conditions*, 37; Richard S. Prosser, *Rails to the North Star* (Minneapolis: Dillon Press, 1966), 20–21, 142–43, 187–88.

32. Larson, *Wheat Market*, 145.

33. For the failures of the National Grange in the area of cooperative leadership, see Woods, *Knights of the Plow*, 162–64.

34. *Farmers' Union*, 14 February 1874, p. 45; *Fairmont Chain*, 3 December 1873, p. 4.

35. For the greater importance farmers often attach to a producers' marketing cooperative than to a consumers' purchasing cooperative, see Hetherington, *Mutual and Cooperative Enterprises*, 124–25; Heflebower, *Cooperatives and Mutuals*, 72–73.

36. *Mower County Transcript*, 5 March 1874, p. 2.

37. *Austin Register*, 12 March 1874, p. 2. That same year, State Grange Master George I. Parsons also stressed the advantages of Grangers' control of wheat stored in their own warehouse; George I. Parsons, Speech to Grange annual meeting at Mankato, 1874, p. 11, George Ithmar Parsons and Family Speeches and Biographic Data, microfilm, MHS.

38. *Mower County Transcript*, 19 March 1874, p. 2 (emphasis in the original); Broehl, *Cargill*, 53–55.

39. *Austin Register*, 26 March 1874, p. 2. Of course, farmers might still have to sell in the fall to pay pressing debts.

40. *Faribault Republican*, 9 April 1873 and 22 November 1876, both p. 3. For other editorial support of flour mill construction, see *Goodhue County Republican*, 25 Febru-

ary 1869, p. 2; *Northfield Standard*, 7 May 1874, p. 3; *Grange Advance*, 24 January 1877, p. 4.

41. *Northfield Standard*, 8 March and 8 November 1873, both p. 3. On 5 March 1874 (p. 3), the *Standard* added, "There is plenty of wheat to feed them all."

42. See the account of how Northfield Grangers decided to build their mill; "A Word from the Grangers," *Rice County Journal*, 19 July 1877, p. 3. They were tired of having "to sell their wheat at low frontier prices, and pay Eastern rates for flour."

43. Larson, *Wheat Market*, 76.

44. *Faribault Republican*, 9 April 1873, p. 3. Grangers near Red Wing cooperated with wheat buyers and merchants in forming joint-stock milling companies; *Goodhue County Republican*, 17 April 1873, p. 1, 4. See also comments by Rice County Council secretary, O. F. Brand, in favor of buying from home merchants and manufacturers in *Farmers' Union*, 30 August 1873, p. 276.

45. *Faribault Republican*, 9 and 23 April 1873, both p. 3; *Farmers' Union*, 15 March 1873, p. 84.

46. Kuhlmann, *Flour-Milling Industry*, 107–8; Larson, *Wheat Market*, 129; James Gray, *Business Without Boundary: The Story of General Mills* (Minneapolis: University of Minnesota Press, 1954), 18. Eight flour mills were operating in Rice County at the time of the U.S. 1870 census.

47. Robinson, *Early Economic Conditions*, 107.

48. *Farmers' Union*, 17 May 1873, p. 158.

49. In 1873–74, two joint-stock companies with possible ties to the Grange built small, wind-powered mills in Elliota (Fillmore County) and Claremont (Dodge County), costing eight to ten thousand dollars each. The Claremont mill was not financially successful, and neither one had much impact on wheat prices. *Fillmore County Republican*, 28 March 1873, p. 3; Jessie M. Bowen, ed., *A Chronicle of Claremont Township and Village* (Claremont: [Ladies Aid of the Presbyterian Church?], 1937), 44; "Claremont Wind Mill" information, Dodge County file, Robert M. Frame III, Flour Milling Research Files, MHS; *Owatonna Journal*, 29 January 1874, p. 3.

50. *St. Peter Tribune*, 23 March 1870, p. 2.

51. *Rice County Journal*, 21 July 1875, p. 4.

52. *Northfield Standard*, 5 March 1874, p. 3; "Grange Mill" information, Dakota County file, Frame Flour Milling Research Files; *A Waterford History, 1852–1970*, p. 13, 15; United States, 1880 manuscript Manufacturing Census for Waterford, Dakota County, Minnesota, microfilm, roll 11, frame 433, MHS.

53. For the importance of grist mills to a semisubsistence farming area, see Faragher, *Sugar Creek*, 67–69; Merle Curti, *The Making of an American Community: A Case Study of Democracy in a Frontier County* (Stanford: Stanford University Press, 1959), 237–38, 240.

54. *Rice County Journal*, 19 and 26 July 1877, both p. 3; *Northfield Standard*, 8 March 1873, p. 3. The county council and a local newspaper implied that the Grange mill offered gristing services while the Ames mill refused to do so. In the *Journal* (26 July), Ames charged that the opposite was true.

55. U.S., 1880 Manufacturing Census for Waterford, roll 11, frame 433.

56. For the company's later history, see *Rice County Journal*, 12 January 1882, and 19 July 1883, both p. 3; *Northfield News*, 30 May 1896, p. 3; "Grange Mill" information, Frame, Flour Milling Research Files.

57. Kuhlmann, *Flour-Milling Industry*, 128–30.

58. Chandler, *Visible Hand*, 250–53.

59. *History of Rice County, including Explorers and Pioneers of Minnesota, and Outline History of the State of Minnesota*, by Rev. Edward D. Neill; also *Sioux Massacre of 1862 and State Education*, by Charles S. Bryant (Minneapolis: Minnesota Historical Co., 1882), 332–34.

60. *Northwestern Miller*, February 1875, n.p., and 17 November 1876, p. 178, clippings in Rice County Grange Mill Co., Faribault, Minn., file, Donald N. Gregg Flour Milling Collection, MHS.

61. *Faribault Republican*, 8 and 15 November and 13 December, all 1876, all p. 3; *Northwestern Miller*, 17 November 1876, p. 178; *Faribault Democrat*, 17 November 1876, p. 3. Several weeks later the privately owned Bean Brothers and Tennant mill also burned.

62. For a discussion of how "proprietary firms" tend to "place the risk of overproduction squarely on the grower" while growers try to shift that risk on to their cooperative,

see Hetherington, *Mutual and Cooperative Enterprises*, 196–97.

63. For changes in flour milling, see Kuhlmann, *Flour-Milling Industry*, 106–8, 113–23, 126–30; Chandler, *Visible Hand*, 250–53.

64. "The warehouses are low buildings especially adapted for handling grain in sacks, while the elevator is a high building especially adapted for handling grain in bulk"; Joseph B. Kenkel, *The Cooperative Elevator Movement: A Study in Grain Marketing at Country Points in the North Central States* (Washington, D.C.: Catholic University of America, 1922), 3n10.

65. *History of the Delavan Community, 1856–1977*, vol. 1, *General History* (Delavan: Delavan Community Centennial Committee, 1977), 129–31.

66. *History of the Delavan Community*, 1:131; *Delavan Bee*, 15 and 29 June 1872, both p. 3, and 20 July and 10 August 1872, both p. 2.

67. *Blue Earth City Post*, 20 June 1874, p. 3. William N. Plymat, the secretary of the county council, issued the public notice of the mass meeting.

68. *Blue Earth City Post*, 20 June 1874, p. 3. In the sources, there is no further mention of this proposed arrangement.

69. Minnesota Secretary of State, Corporation Division, Record of Incorporations, Vol. C, p. 121–22.

70. *Blue Earth City Post*, 21 November 1874 (p. 3), 5 December 1874 (p. 2, 3), and 9 January 1875 (p. 3).

71. *Blue Earth City Post*, 29 May 1875, p. 3; *History of the Delavan Community*, 1:131.

72. *History of the Delavan Community*, 1:131–32; *Blue Earth City Post*, 23 October 1875, p. 3, and 18 September 1875, p. 2. The county seat was Blue Earth.

73. Jarchow, *Earth Brought Forth*, 186; Robinson, *Early Economic Conditions*, 79. *Blue Earth City Post*, 1 June and 7 December 1878, both p. 3, and 18 January and 22 February 1879, both p. 3. Several townships near Delavan were 25 to 50 percent Norwegian American; Qualey and Gjerde, "Norwegians," in *They Chose Minnesota*, ed. Holmquist, 226.

74. *Farmers' Union*, 14 February 1874, p. 45, and 7 March 1874, p. 69.

75. Heflebower, *Cooperatives and Mutuals*, 16, 190–93.

76. *Farmers' Union*, 14 February 1874, p. 45; *Freeborn County Standard*, 23 and 30 October, 13 and 27 November (all 1873), 10 June 1875, and 8 June 1876, all p. 3; *History of the Delavan Community*, 1:129–32; *Blue Earth City Post*, 9 January 1875, 30 June 1877, and 1 June 1878, all p. 3; *Lake City Leader*, 23 April 1874 (p. 4), 10 June 1875, 27 May 1876, 26 May 1877 (all p. 5), and 8 June 1878, p. 3; *Rice County Journal*, 9 August 1877, p. 2; *Austin Register*, 26 February and 26 March 1874, both p. 3; *Spring Valley Centennial, 1855–1955* (Spring Valley, [1955]), 10; (Spring Valley) *Western Progress*, 7 July 1875 and 4 July 1877, both p. 3; *Spring Valley Vidette*, 28 June 1878, p. 4; *Minnesota Radical*, 4 August and 22 September and 24 November 1875, all p. 5; *Lake City Leader*, 7 May 1874, p. 7. Only the building dimensions of the Grange elevator at Dover are reported in the local newspaper; *Eyota Advertiser*, 1 November 1875, and 1 April 1876, both p. 1.

77. *Austin Register*, 22 January, 26 February, and 26 March, all 1874, all p. 3.

78. *Freeborn County Standard*, 16 October 1873, p. 3; *Blue Earth City Post*, 20 June 1874, p. 3; *Lake City Leader*, 16 April 1874, p. 5; Harshman, "History of the Settlement of Waseca County," 173. The "Spring Valley Council" had been created in 1873, and it is likely that this council facilitated the organizing of the Spring Valley Grange Union the following year. See *Fillmore County Republican*, 28 March 1873, p. 2.

79. *Freeborn County Standard*, 16, 23, and 30 October 1873, all p. 3; Minnesota, Secretary of State, Corporation Division, Record of Incorporations, Vol. C, p. 104–6. Some incorporators had Scandinavian names, including Mons Grinager, a Norwegian-American politician. There is some confusion regarding the "Farmers' Association." An entity by that name was formed in December 1870, before the Grange came to Freeborn County. Yet a "Farmers' Warehouse" company was formed in the fall of 1873—with a warehouse built after October 1874 when the county council again called for "the erection of an elevator, by grangers." These may have been two separate companies, or they may have merged at some point. *Freeborn County Standard*, 29 December 1870, 13 November 1873, and 22 October

1874, all p. 3. The non-Grangers may have referred to the 1870 association, which was not Grange sponsored.

80. *Freeborn County Standard*, 11 December 1873, p. 3 (probably referring to the Farmers' Warehouse Association facility). For other editors' praise of Grange warehouses and elevators, see *Blue Earth City Post*, 5 December 1874 and 29 May 1875, both p. 3; *Minnesota Radical*, 4 August 1875, p. 5; *Western Progress*, 7 July 1875, p. 3; *Austin Register*, 26 March 1874, p. 3.

81. Waseca's Grangers were praised for being content to "run a warehouse without loss." Their profits for the first eight months were only $26.85; *Minnesota Radical*, 4 August 1875, p. 5.

82. *Freeborn County Standard*, 10 June 1875, p. 3; *Blue Earth City Post*, 9 January 1875, p. 3; *Lake City Leader*, 10 June 1875, p. 5; *Western Progress*, 7 July 1875, p. 3.

83. At Delavan, "red hot" competition among wheat buyers came in 1878–79, just when the Grange warehouse failed; *Blue Earth City Post*, 7 December 1878, p. 2, and 18 January and 22 February 1879, both p. 3. In the spring of 1874, the Alden warehouse competed against four buyers; it apparently failed in 1874 or 1875. Two new wheat buyers arrived in Lake City during the 1877 harvest season, after the Grange warehouse had failed, and probably because that failure opened up new opportunities for them. *Austin Register*, 9 April 1874, p. 2; *Lake City Leader*, 25 August and 15 September 1877, both p. 3; *Rice County Journal*, 9 August 1877, p. 2.

84. *Minnesota Radical*, 4 August, 22 September and 24 November 1875, and 19 January 1876, all p. 5.

85. Larson, *Wheat Market*, 105. For some warehouses, the only evidence of failure was that a notice of the annual meeting failed to appear in the newspaper the next year; *Spring Valley Vidette*, 11 July 1879; *Blue Earth City Post*, June 1879.

86. Buck, *Granger Movement*, 274–76; Larson, *Wheat Market*, 104–5; Nordin, *Rich Harvest*, 149, 151; Kenkel, *Cooperative Elevator Movement*, 13–15; Cronon, *Nature's Metropolis*, 361–64. Among other causes of failure, Woods stressed the lack of a "clear strategy" on the part of national Grange leaders "to develop a strong cooperative

system"; Woods, *Knights of the Plow*, 162–63.

87. Hetherington, *Mutual and Cooperative Enterprises*, 113, 171–72. Heflebower also noted that cooperatives' "difficulty in obtaining member-supplied capital" was a "common thread" characterizing most cooperatives; Heflebower, *Cooperatives and Mutuals*, 177–78.

88. *Pioneer Press* (St. Paul and Minneapolis), 7 February 1878, p. 1.

89. Heflebower, *Cooperatives and Mutuals*, 198–99.

90. Hetherington, *Mutual and Cooperative Enterprises*, 127.

91. Robinson, *Early Economic Conditions*, 114; Jarchow, *Earth Brought Forth*, 178. Because they operated gradually and did not catch the eye of the local editor, long-term causes often cannot be documented from contemporary sources; however, neither do these sources clearly support the argument that internal weaknesses doomed Granger cooperatives.

92. Chandler, *Visible Hand*, 250–51; Larson, *Wheat Market*, 129–30, 139–48. For an account of the creation of one such entrepreneurial empire, see Broehl, *Cargill*, 3–65.

93. Broehl, *Cargill*, 26, 29.

94. The general characteristics of administrative coordination are taken from Chandler, *Visible Hand*, 6–11.

95. *Rice County Journal*, 26 July 1877, p. 3; Cronon, *Nature's Metropolis*, 125, 257, 259. See also Steven J. Keillor, *This Rebellious House: American History and the Truth of Christianity* (Downers Grove, Ill.: InterVarsity Press, 1996), especially Chapter 7 (much of which draws on Cronon's analysis).

Notes to Chapter 4

1. "The terms 'mutual' and 'cooperative' insurance have been used as interchangeable not only in most of the literature on insurance but also by the mutual and cooperative societies themselves"; P. K. Ray, *Agricultural Insurance: Theory and Practice and Application to Developing Countries*, 2d ed. (New York: Pergamon Press, 1981), 73.

2. *Grange Advance*, 11 April 1877, p. 4.

3. For the history of fire insurance in the United States, see Valgren, *Farmers' Mutual Fire Insurance*, 3–10.

4. *Nordisk Folkeblad*, 7 July 1869, p. 4.

For similar praise four years later, see *Nordisk Folkeblad*, 21 January 1874, p. 4.

5. *Grange Advance*, 11 April 1877, p. 4; Jarchow, *Earth Brought Forth*, 23, 266–67n36; *Nordisk Folkeblad*, 17 March 1869, p. 2, and 31 March 1869, p. 3; Minnesota, Secretary of State, Corporation Division, Records of Incorporations, Vol. B, 289–90. The Leon mutual's articles stated that only Scandinavians could join. Swedish-American farmers near Carver formed "a fire insurance company" on the assessment plan in the late 1860s; *Minneapolis Tribune*, 2 March 1869, p. 2. By the early 1870s, Minnesota's Scandinavian Americans could buy insurance from a regional Scandinavian company, Hekla Fire Insurance Company of Madison, Wis.; *Budstikken*, 23 February 1875, p. 2.

6. *Skandinaven* (Chicago), 23 April 1868, p. 3; *Nordisk Folkeblad*, 17 March 1869, p. 2, and 31 March 1869, p. 3. Lake Prairie Township was 25 to 50 percent Norwegian American and 10 to 25 percent Swedish American according to the U.S. 1880 census; Rice, "The Swedes," and Qualey and Gjerde, "The Norwegians," in *They Chose Minnesota*, ed. Holmquist, 226, 257.

7. *Nordisk Folkeblad*, 17 March 1869, p. 2, 31 March 1869, p. 3, and 12 January 1870, p. 2; *St. Peter Tribune*, 12 January 1870, p. 3, and 23 March 1870, p. 2.

8. *Nordisk Folkeblad*, 17 March 1869, p. 2, and 31 March 1869, p. 3.

9. See, for example, Lake Hanska Lutheran Church, Protokol, Book 1, p. 107, BCHS. The 1885 annual meeting of Lake Hanska Lutheran Church elected a six-man committee to make the assessment (*ligning*) according to its best judgment. The solidarity arising from homogeneity and cooperative traditions must not be exaggerated. Norwegian-American farmers near Holden Township disagreed over premiums versus assessments in their proposed farmers' mutual. A supporter of the former policy warned that members might withdraw after assessments were levied, but this may have been a debater's point; *Budstikken*, 26 January 1875, p. 3.

10. Jarchow, *Earth Brought Forth*, 23.

11. *Grange Advance*, 11 April 1877, 4. Old Stock Americans formed the Monongalia County Mutual Insurance Company in April 1867, but I have been unable to find additional information on it; Minnesota, Secretary of State, Corporation Division, Records of Incorporations, Vol. B, 54–56.

12. When McGill attacked "Unauthorized Insurance" in that report, he meant sales of insurance by stock companies not complying with Minnesota law; "Third Annual Report of the Insurance Commissioner," p. 44-45, 52-55, *Executive Documents . . . 1874*, vol. 2.

13. A schoolteacher, Ottun served as Wanamingo town clerk and justice of the peace before his election in 1873 (the peak Granger year) to the House. A resident of Holden, Finseth had also served in local offices, notably county commissioner, before entering the Senate; *Budstikken*, 5 January, p. 1, and 12 January, p. 2, both 1895. Farmers in Holden talked of starting a township mutual in early January 1875, prior to Finseth introducing his bill; *Budstikken*, 26 January 1875, p. 3. As of December 31, 1878, three of the nine township mutuals in the state were located in Wanamingo and Holden Townships; "Eighth Annual Report of the Insurance Commissioner," p. xlv, *Executive Documents . . . 1878*, vol 3.

14. *House Journal*, 1874, p. 123, 441; *Senate Journal*, 1874, p. 428. A similar township mutual bill, H.F. 59, was introduced in the House on January 22 by Representative Henry Hill. It passed the House on February 20 on a vote of sixty-three to twenty-two but also lay in the Senate judiciary committee as the session ended; *House Journal*, 1874, p. 76, 212, 331; *Senate Journal*, 1874, p. 360, 413, 439. Hill represented the area that had been Monongalia County until 1870 so it is possible that he acted to legalize local mutuals at the request of the Monongalia County mutual (see note 11, above). For Monongalia County, see Warren Upham, *Minnesota Geographic Names: Their Origin and Historic Significance* (1920; St. Paul: Minnesota Historical Society, 1969), 268.

15. *Farmers' Union*, 28 February 1874, p. 4.

16. "Third Annual Report of the Insurance Commissioner," p. 52-55, *Executive Documents . . . 1874*, vol. 2.

17. Hetherington, *Mutual and Cooperative Enterprises*, 13–14, 17–18.

18. *Budstikken*, 26 January 1875, p. 1, 3; *Senate Journal*, 1875, p. 30, 38, 63, 89–90.

19. *Nordisk Folkeblad*, 24 February 1875, p. 1.

20. *Budstikken*, 23 February 1875, p. 2. A search of the *Minneapolis Tribune* and *St. Paul Pioneer* failed to uncover discussion of S.F. 18, just mention of its title and the House or Senate action taken.

21. "Fourth Annual Report of the Insurance Commissioner," p. 63, *Executive Documents of the State of Minnesota, for the Year 1875*, vol. 1; *House Journal*, 1875, p. 389, 401, 533.

22. The Featherstone mutual was not included in later lists of functioning companies; "Seventh Annual Report of the Insurance Commissioner," p. 44, *Executive Documents of the State of Minnesota, for the Year 1878*, vol. 2; "Eighth Annual Report of the Insurance Commissioner," p. xliv, *Executive Documents . . . 1878*, vol. 3.

23. These long-lived mutuals proved McGill wrong when he predicted "that this class of companies must, from the very nature of things, prove failures"; "Fourth Annual Report of the Insurance Commissioner," p. 63, *Executive Documents . . . 1875*, vol. 1.

24. "Second Annual Report of the Insurance Commissioner," p. 28–29, *Executive Documents . . . 1873*, vol. 1. By "private" I mean all the joint-stock companies offering fire and inland insurance.

25. "Annual Message of Governor Austin," p. 21–22, *Executive Documents of the State of Minnesota, for the Year 1871*, vol. 1. Only St. Paul Fire and Marine Insurance Company and MFMFIAM were Minnesota companies; "Second Annual Report of the Insurance Commissioner," p. 4–5, *Executive Documents . . . 1873*, vol. 1. For an editorial criticizing the eastward drain of capital, see *Budstikken*, 23 February 1875, p. 2.

26. "First Annual Report of the Insurance Commissioner," p. 596, 599, 604, 606, *Executive Documents . . . 1872*, vol. 1.

27. "Second Annual Report of the Insurance Commissioner," p. 38, *Executive Documents . . . 1873*, vol. 1.

28. Jarchow, *Earth Brought Forth*, 266n36.

29. "Second Annual Report of the Insurance Commissioner," p. 31–32, *Executive Documents . . . 1873*, vol. 1.

30. *Farmers' Union*, November 1867, p. 8.

31. "Fourth Annual Report of the Insurance Commissioner," p. 49, *Executive Documents . . . 1875*, vol. 1.

32. Valgren, *Farmers' Mutual Fire Insurance*, 8. For an account of mutual fire insurance in Iowa that stressed "farmers' desires to preserve local control" as the original motive more than cost savings, see Jack Lufkin, "Property Insurance for Iowa Farmers: The Rise of the Mutuals," *Annals of Iowa*, 3d ser., 54 (Winter 1995): 25–45.

33. Hetherington, *Mutual and Cooperative Enterprises*, 24–25; Heflebower, *Cooperatives and Mutuals*, 166–67.

34. Valgren, *Farmers' Mutual Fire Insurance*, 3–10; Hetherington, *Mutual and Cooperative Enterprises*, 33–34. A farmers' mutual was one type of "class mutual"—a company that insured one type of property (e.g., lumberyards) and was owned by one specialized group of policyholders (e.g., lumber dealers).

35. For the general characteristics of mutual insurance companies, see Ray, *Agricultural Insurance*, 73–79.

36. For mutual policyholders' conflicting interests, see Hetherington, *Mutual and Cooperative Enterprises*, 31–32.

37. Hetherington, *Mutual and Cooperative Enterprises*, 116–17.

38. "Second Annual Report of the Insurance Commissioner," p. 4 ("peculiar mode"), *Executive Documents . . . 1873*, vol. 1; "First Annual Report," p. 605 ("difficult to classify"), *Executive Documents . . . 1872*, vol. 1.

39. "Third Annual Report of the Insurance Commissioner," p. 54, *Executive Documents . . . 1874*, vol. 2.

40. "Third Annual Report of the Insurance Commissioner," p. 52–55, *Executive Documents . . . 1874*, vol. 2; "Fourth Annual Report of the Insurance Commissioner," 63–64, *Executive Documents . . . 1875*, vol. 1.

41. Farmers' Mutual Insurance Company Record (hereafter in this chapter, Record), 1–2, minute book, Farmers' Mutual Insurance Company, Manchester. The early minutes are written in Norwegian. For the constitution and bylaws see, for example, insurance policy number 1624 issued to Anders O. Horpedal, 20 February 1892, copy in Record.

42. Record, 1–3; *Freeborn County Standard*, 27 July 1876, p. 3; *Albert Lea Enterprise*, 28 December 1876, p. 5.

43. Record, 2; "Eighth Annual Report of the Insurance Commissioner," p. xlv, *Executive Documents . . . 1878*, vol. 3. From the start this mutual violated Article 3 of its Articles of Incorporation, which stated that "no person shall be eligible to membership in said corporation except residents of said town (of Manchester), and also persons who own property therein"; *Farmers Mutual Insurance Company—Manchester Minnesota: 100 Years of Service, 1876–1976* (1976), 9, pamphlet, copy in company office.

44. For the addition of Shell Rock Township in southern Freeborn County, see Record, 40. For the provisions of the law as of 1881, see Minnesota, *The General Statutes of the State of Minnesota, 1878–83*, chap. 34, sec. 338–54.

45. "Fourth Annual Report of the Insurance Commissioner," p. 63–64, *Executive Documents . . . 1875*, vol. 1.

46. See constitution, Horpedal policy, Record. One secretary was paid $17.50 for receiving thirty-one applications in 1899; Record, 257.

47. When an agent suffered a fire loss, two of his neighbors were chosen to appraise the damages; Record, 48, 60, and constitution, article 7, Horpedal policy.

48. In one township near Northfield in 1912, 57 percent of farm owners belonged to the mutual, while only 35, 31, and 10 percent belonged to the cooperative creamery, grain elevator association, and rural telephone company, respectively; Carl W. Thompson and Gustav P. Warber, *Social and Economic Survey of a Rural Township in Southern Minnesota*, University of Minnesota Studies in Economics no. 1 (Minneapolis: University of Minnesota, 1913), 28–29. These percentages reflect the situation in the 1880s, too.

49. Record, 5–7, 8–11, 13–16, 17–19, 20–23, 25–27, 31–33, 35–36, 39, 43, 45, 48–50, 53–56, 58–59, 64–65, 72–73, 83–85, 101–2, 117–19, 123, 130, 141, 146, 160, 169–70, 185–86.

50. This mutual's annual meetings were frequently reported in the local Norwegian-American press; see, for example, *Albert Lea Posten*, 10 January 1884, p. 4. The *Freeborn County Standard* also reported on the annual meeting; *Freeborn County Standard*, 16 January 1890, p. 4. For a debate on Norwegian-American cultural life in Manches-

ter, see *Albert Lea Posten*, 13 January and 10 February 1885, both p. 4.

51. For the two-dollar fee, see bylaws, Horpedal policy, Record. With 102 members and $135,172 of property insured on December 31, 1877, the average insurance per member was $1,325. Thus, the two-dollar fee equaled fifteen cents per one hundred dollars of property insured; Record, 5–7.

52. Record, 5–7.

53. Record, 8–10, 13; *Albert Lea Enterprise*, 6 July 1876, p. 1. In 1885 Gulbrandson [Guldbrandsen] was acting as an agent for the Hekla insurance company; *Albert Lea Posten*, 27 January 1885, p. 4.

54. Record, 12, 18–19, 21.

55. Record, 8–11, 13–16, 20–23, 35–36, 39.

56. Record, 26–27.

57. Record, 12–13, 15.

58. *St. Paul Daily Press*, 26 February 1874, p. 4.

59. For this characteristic of a mutual, see Ray, *Agricultural Insurance*, 74.

60. Hetherington discussed conflicts between "prior" and "present and future members" of a cooperative over its accumulated surplus. A mutual's current policyholders would "attempt to minimize their contributions to surplus because it may ultimately accrue to the benefit of future policyholders" and would "have an interest in having insurance sold to themselves at or below cost, thus effecting a gradual distribution of the surplus to themselves in the form of reduced premiums"; Hetherington, *Mutual and Cooperative Enterprises*, 31, 113.

61. Record, 34, 35, 37–38. They also decided not to assess for less than two mills; a smaller assessment was not worth the time and expense of having the secretary calculate it and write up and mail notices to members.

62. For the advantages of the prepayment system over the assessment plan, see Hetherington, *Mutual and Cooperative Enterprises*, 13–14.

63. In the 1890s the board's policy was to assess two mills almost every year (eight out ten years) to accumulate a cash reserve: on 12/31/96 the company had 15.3 cents/$100 in reserve; on 12/31/97 the company had 8.1 cents/$100 in reserve; on 12/31/98 the company had 10.6 cents/$100 in reserve; on

12/31/99 the company had 12.1 cents/$100 in reserve. See Record, 185, 207, 231, 251.

64. For a list of the officers, see _Farmers Mutual Insurance Company_, 25.

65. Record, 10.

66. Hetherington, _Mutual and Cooperative Enterprises_, 126.

67. See, for example, Record, 29–31, 35, 37–38, 58, 60.

68. Ray, _Agricultural Insurance_, 74.

69. Record, 5–7, 8–11, 13–16, 17–19, 20–23, 25–27, 31–33, 35–36, 39, 43, 45. The St. Paul Fire and Marine figures are taken from the annual reports of the insurance commissioner for 1872, 1873, 1878, and 1885.

70. For payments to the mutual's officers and directors, see, for example, Record, 185–86, 207, 210, 231, 234, 251, 256–57.

71. Record, 5–7, 53–56; "Second Annual Report of the Insurance Commissioner," p. 89–90, 115–16, _Executive Documents . . . 1873_, vol. I.

72. Record, 5–7, 8–11, 13–16, 17–19, 20–23, 25–27, 31–33, 35–36, 39, 43, 45. The St. Paul Fire and Marine and MFMFIAM figures are taken from the annual reports of the insurance commissioner.

73. Record, 85, 103, 144, 301.

74. Record, 146, 191.

75. Record, 29–31, 33, 34, 36. The Rodahl loss, larger than any the company had suffered, raised an issue of fairness: should policyholders who signed up after Rodahl's fire be assessed for his loss? They were charged only one-half the regular assessment.

76. Record, 62. After a "spirited discussion" about this and other hay-loss cases at the 1889 annual meeting, members left the final decision to the board of directors; Record, 65.

77. Record, 71.

78. Ray noted that in mutuals "the insured's personal position, his character and the opinion of his fellow members on these matters, play an important part in the evaluation of risk as well as of the damage to be compensated"; Ray, _Agricultural Insurance_, 75.

79. Hetherington argued, "It is generally in the interest of each policyholder that the insured be generous in evaluating his own claims and ungenerous in dealing with the claims of third parties, and other policy-

holders"; _Mutual and Cooperative Enterprises_, 32.

80. Record, 78–81, 86, 88, 119, 123, 131, 132.

81. Record, 86, 119, 123, 131, 132. The case came up again at the 1892 annual meeting, but the minutes do not clearly distinguish the claimants' arguments from the members' decision—if any.

82. In Denmark, by contrast, a cooperative's members had no right to sue the cooperative in court. Chris L. Christensen, _Agricultural Cooperation in Denmark_, Bulletin no. 1266 (Washington, D.C.: U.S. Department of Agriculture, 1924), 30–31.

83. Record, 55–56.

84. Record, 17–19, 55–56.

85. Record, 133, 135, 141.

86. Victor E. Lawson, ed., _Illustrated History and Descriptive and Biographical Review of Kandiyohi County, Minnesota_ (Willmar, 1905), 184.

87. Quoted in _Fergus Globe_, 10 September 1891, p. 3.

88. The Sverdrup mutual was formed at an April 1883 meeting of the Sverdrup Farmers' Club; its constitution and bylaws were modeled after those of a Norwegian-American farmers' mutual in Winneshiek County, Iowa. See Protokol (hereafter SSMIC Protokol), 5, 124–29, Sverdrup Mutual Insurance Company, Underwood.

89. Christopher F. Case, _History and Description of Lyon County, Minnesota_ (Marshall: Messenger Printing House, 1884), 55–56; _The Cottonwood Community, My Home Town: 1963 Diamond Jubilee_ ([Cottonwood: W. E. Anderson, 1963]).

90. SSMIC Protokol, 23, 40, 45.

91. The question may also have arisen due to the start of a Norwegian-American Unitarian congregation in Underwood in 1889. Unitarians may have wished to be less linguistically and ethnically exclusive than Lutherans. See Nina Draxten, _Kristofer Janson in America_ (Boston: Published for the Norwegian-American Historical Association by Twayne Publishers, 1976), 224–25; Referat-Protokol, vol. 4, p. 35–38, Unitarian Church of Underwood, Records, microfilm, Northwest Minnesota Historical Center, Moorhead State University, Moorhead. When the anti-exclusive resolution was voted down at the January 1890 annual

meeting, several Alliance and Unitarian leaders voted in favor and several Lutheran leaders voted against it; SSMIC Protokol, 45.

92. The Old Stock Americans were being held up as the victims here, but Bjørnaas (wrongly) stated it "can hardly be the Scandinavians—in my opinion—who got such a law passed. The smart Americans can just as well get themselves out of this knot by getting the law amended"; *Fergus Falls Ugeblad*, 22 January 1890, p. 4.

93. SSMIC Protokol, 52, 96, 104.

94. "Eighth Annual Report of the Insurance Commissioner," p. xliv–xlv, *Executive Documents . . . 1878*, vol. 3; "Nineteenth Annual Report of the Insurance Commissioner of the State of Minnesota," p. 698–99, *Executive Documents of the State of Minnesota, for the Year 1889*, vol. 2; "Twenty-seventh Annual Report of the Insurance Commissioner of the State of Minnesota," p. 408–11, *Executive Documents of the State of Minnesota, for the Year 1897*, vol. 1.

95. "Twenty-seventh Annual Report of the Insurance Commissioner," p. 366, 390–92, *Executive Documents . . . 1897*, vol. 1.

96. *Fergus Falls Ugeblad*, 16 January 1889, p. 5.

Notes to Chapter 5

1. In the 1880s, rural parts of thirteen southeastern counties of Minnesota lost population as farmers migrated to new wheat-growing areas of the state; Robinson, *Early Economic Conditions*, 76, 113–14; Jarchow, *Earth Brought Forth*, 185–87; Eric E. Lampard, *The Rise of the Dairy Industry in Wisconsin: A Study in Agricultural Change, 1820–1920* (Madison: State Historical Society of Wisconsin, 1963), 23–26, 40–42, 45–48. For the earlier but similar problems of wheat farmers in Iowa and Illinois, see Allan G. Bogue, *From Prairie to Corn Belt: Farming on the Illinois and Iowa Prairies in the Nineteenth Century* (Chicago: University of Chicago Press, 1963; Ames: Iowa State University Press, 1994), 125–27.

2. Atack and Bateman, "Yankee Farming," 93; Sally McMurry, *Transforming Rural Life: Dairying Families and Agricultural Change, 1820–1885* (Baltimore: Johns Hopkins University Press, 1995), 17; Bogue, *Prairie to Corn Belt*, 127–28.

3. Hudson, *Making the Corn Belt*, 151–55; Atack and Bateman, "Yankee Farming," 92; Bogue, *Prairie to Corn Belt*, 235–38; Rice, "Old-Stock Americans," in *They Chose Minnesota*, ed. Holmquist, 57–58, 60, 66. Bogue noted that cultural factors could be exaggerated. For other specialties, see Blegen, *Minnesota*, 392–93, 395–96, 400–404; Robinson, *Early Economic Conditions*, 19–20, 138, 176–77; Jarchow, *Earth Brought Forth*, 192–206, 232–36, 240–44.

4. Jarchow used the term "diversification" (*Earth Brought Forth*, 22, 185) without explaining that it often meant specializing in a crop besides wheat. On March 2, 1875, Burnside Grange held "an experience meeting" to discuss the "diversified plan," by which they meant raising several crops in addition to wheat; Burnside Grange No. 148 Record.

5. *Canby News*, 24 September 1886, p. 3; *Freeborn County Standard*, 10 February 1886, p. 4. The leading dairy specialist was William Dempster Hoard, publisher of *Hoard's Dairyman* and owner of Hoard's Dairyman Farm. Hoard contemptuously asked of dual-purpose farmers, "are they half and half dairymen, standing with one short leg and one long leg?" See Loren H. Osman, *W. D. Hoard: A Man for His Time* (Fort Atkinson, Wis.: W. D. Hoard & Sons Co., 1985), 297–98.

6. *Canby News*, 24 September 1886, p. 3. For a prerailroad economy, railroads, and specialization, see Cronon, *Nature's Metropolis*, 104–13, 222–24, 318–33.

7. For the towns losing county-seat status, see Upham, *Minnesota Geographic Names*, 105, 108, 268, 270, 302, 308, 339, 394, 455, 458, 514, 551, 566, 575, 597. New London lost county-seat status when the county of Monongalia was abolished in 1870.

8. *Blue Earth City Post*, 26 June (p. 3), 3 July (p. 3), 18 September (p. 2), and 23 October (p. 3), all 1875. In 1879, only seven of some fifty counties having railroad service in southern and central Minnesota had a county seat lacking such service. See Robinson, *Early Economic Conditions*, 37. Preston, Caledonia, Mantorville, Blue Earth, Le Sueur Center, Beaver Falls, and Center City lacked rail service.

9. Jarchow, *Earth Brought Forth*, 213.

10. Minnesota Butter, Cheese, and Dairy Stock Association, *Annual Convention . . .*

Proceedings ([Minnesota: The Association], 1886), 17.

11. Weld, *Social and Economic Survey*, 43–44. See also Jarchow, *Earth Brought Forth*, 207–9; Edward Wiest, *The Butter Industry in the United States: An Economic Study of Butter and Oleomargarine* (New York: Columbia University Press, 1916), 13–17; Theophilus L. Haecker, "There is no state in the union," untitled, undated manuscript (ca. 1900?), Theophilus Levi Haecker Papers, MHS; W. A. Ellis, "Co-operative Butter Making," *Pope County Press*, 1 February 1884, p. 1.

12. W[illiam] F. Schilling, "First Minnesota Creamery Co-op 50 Years Old Today," *Minneapolis Journal*, Home ed., 7 June 1939, p. 15.

13. *Freeborn County Standard*, 18 September 1873, p. 3.

14. Patrick Nunnally, "From Churns to 'Butter Factories': The Industrialization of Iowa's Dairying, 1860–1900," *Annals of Iowa*, 3d series, 49 (Winter 1989): 556–58, 560, 562. See also Virginia E. McCormick, "Butter and Egg Business: Implications from the Records of a Nineteenth-Century Farm Wife," *Ohio History* 100 (Winter–Spring 1991): 57–67.

15. *Pope County Press*, 1 February 1884, p. 1. See also *Canby News*, 24 September 1886, p. 3; Nunnally, "From Churns to 'Butter Factories,'" 556; McMurry, *Transforming Rural Life*, 125, 139–43, 201, 207–10. The elimination of women's buttermaking role was part of what Jon Gjerde described as the observation of "bourgeois customs" among Norwegian-American farmers; Gjerde, *From Peasants to Farmers*, 196–201.

16. H. E. Erdman, "The 'Associated Dairies' of New York as Precursors of American Agricultural Cooperatives," *Agricultural History* 36 (April 1962): 82–90; Lampard, *Dairy Industry in Wisconsin*, 91–94; Wiest, *Butter Industry*, 20.

17. Lampard, *Dairy Industry in Wisconsin*, 94.

18. McMurry, *Transforming Rural Life*, 125, 129, 135–37, 139–43. Nunnally also argued that there is only "unclear" evidence "about whether farmers actually profited economically from the sale of milk as opposed to butter." As shown in this chapter and the next, the economies of scale and

skill involved in separating cream in a centrifugal separator and making butter at a central factory were dramatic. Nunnally correctly noted that the move to factory production involved "the devaluation of women's traditional work"; Nunnally, "From Churns to 'Butter Factories,'" 556–58, 560, 562.

19. Here and below, see Erdman, "'Associated Dairies' of New York," 83–89. Erdman asserted that the importance of these New York developments was that these "associated dairies" were "the American farmers' first significant experience in operating joint off-the-farm ventures to serve their respective farm businesses."

20. *Minnesota Monthly*, July 1869, p. 233; Jarchow, *Earth Brought Forth*, 211, 213; *Farmers' Union*, 15 August 1872, p. 10; *Blue Earth City Post*, 26 June and 3 July 1875 and 28 March 1879, all p. 3.

21. *Pope County Press*, 1 February 1884, p. 1.

22. Lampard, *Dairy Industry in Wisconsin*, 98–100; McMurry, *Transforming Rural Life*, 169, 188, 215. The term "socialized farming" is mine, not Lampard's.

23. *Blue Earth City Post*, 3 July 1875 and 28 March 1879, both p. 3; Jarchow, *Earth Brought Forth*, 213–14.

24. Lampard, *Dairy Industry in Wisconsin*, 64–84. On p. 82–83 Lampard mentioned local markets: immigrants awaiting a first crop, lumber companies feeding lumbermen, and residents of an urban area—Milwaukee. Similar markets probably existed in Minnesota.

25. Lampard, *Dairy Industry in Wisconsin*, 94, 95, 110–11, 122–23; Wiest, *Butter Industry*, 39–40; Jarchow, *Earth Brought Forth*, 213; Nunnally, "From Churns to 'Butter Factories,'" 558; Roy Ashmen, "Price Determination in the Butter Market: The Elgin Board of Trade, 1872–1917," *Agricultural History* 36 (July 1962): 156–62.

26. Lampard, *Dairy Industry in Wisconsin*, 197–98, 204–6; Wiest, *Butter Industry*, 21–22. For an assessment of the U.S. dairy industry to the 1880s, see J. D. Frederiksen, *Mejerivæsenet i Nord-Amerika* (Copenhagen: P. G. Philipsens forlag, 1888). For an argument for the factory system, see *Pope County Press*, 1 February 1884, p. 1.

27. Jarchow, *Earth Brought Forth*, 216.

28. Haecker, "There is no state in the union," Haecker Papers.

29. Ironically in an 1884 newspaper, an argument for the gathered-cream system faced a notice in the next column for the De Laval cream separator; *Pope County Press*, 1 February 1884, p. 1.

30. Wiest, *Butter Industry*, 23–25; Lampard, *Dairy Industry in Wisconsin*, 207–10.

31. Freeborn is the county that has best preserved the records of its creameries, and its Clarks Grove creamery was the model creamery in the state—although not the first cooperative one. For the debate over which was the first one, see, for example, *Fergus Globe*, 18 June 1909, p. 2; *Minneapolis Journal*, 5 June 1939, p. 15. For an account of dairying in another county, see Marilyn Brinkman, *Bringing Home the Cows: Family Dairy Farming in Stearns County, 1853–1986* (St. Cloud: Stearns County Historical Society, 1988).

32. U.S., 1880, Manufacturing Census for Freeborn County, 1880; "Statistics of Minnesota for 1879," *Executive Documents of the State of Minnesota, for the Year 1879*, 430–31.

33. *Freeborn County Times* (Albert Lea), Creamery ed., 9 February 1900, p. 8.

34. *Freeborn County Standard*, 3 February 1886, p. 4, and 24 February, 3 and 24 March, and 14 April 1886, all p. 8, and 9 June 1886, p. 1; *Freeborn County Times*, Creamery ed., 9 February 1900, p. 9–10.

35. The creameries were at Hartland, Glenville, Emmons, Albert Lea, Alden, Hayward, and Gordonsville; the cheese factories at Turtle Creek, London, and Oakland. *Freeborn County Times*, Creamery ed., 9 February 1900, p. 8, 9, 12, 13, 16; *Freeborn County Standard*, 21 April 1886, p. 8; *History of Freeborn County* (Minneapolis: Minnesota Historical Co., 1882), 368–69; Franklyn Curtiss-Wedge, comp., *History of Freeborn County, Minnesota* (Chicago: H. C. Cooper, Jr. & Co., [1911]), 455–59, 472–73, 475.

36. *History of Freeborn County* (1882), 368–69. A partnership ran the Glenville creamery, while individuals owned those at Emmons, Hartland, and Hayward. *Freeborn County Times*, Creamery ed., 9 February 1900, p. 9, 10, 13, 16; *Freeborn County Standard*, 5 May 1886, p. 4. For Iowa's first gathered-cream plants, begun in 1877, see *A Century*

of Farming in Iowa, 1846–1946 (Ames: Iowa State College Press, 1946), 219.

37. "Statistics of Minnesota for 1879," *Executive Documents . . . 1879*, 430–31, and "Twenty-third Annual Report of the Commissioner of Statistics of the State of Minnesota, for the Year 1891," *Executive Documents of the State of Minnesota for the Fiscal Year Ending July 31, 1891*, 233.

38. *Freeborn County Times*, Creamery ed., 9 February 1900, p. 1, 10, 13. The Hayward creamery also failed. The Emmons creamery seems to have been financially successful until a farmer-owned cooperative began to compete with it.

39. *Freeborn County Standard*, 15 October (quote), 5 and 19 November, all 1884, all p. 5.

40. *Freeborn County Standard*, 10 February 1886, p. 4. See also the letter from "A Member," p. 1.

41. *Freeborn County Times*, Creamery ed., 9 February 1900, p. 12.

42. *Freeborn County Times*, Creamery ed., 9 February 1900, p. 16; *Freeborn County Standard*, 30 January 1890, p. 5, and 6 February 1890, p. 5, 8. A gathered-cream plant at Emmons "organized on a combined cooperative and stock company plan" and by providing one vote per patron, rather than one vote per share, succeeded for more than two years; however, this was a village creamery, and the merchants played a key role in supporting this enterprise; *Freeborn County Times*, Creamery ed., 9 February 1900, p. 10. Alden farmers began meeting in January 1890 and were probably not influenced by the Clarks Grove meetings that began that month. This Alden cooperative was a different entity from the gathered-cream plant mentioned in note 36, above; Curtiss-Wedge, comp., *History of Freeborn County*, 466.

43. *Freeborn County Times*, Creamery ed., 9 February 1900, p. 3; Curtiss-Wedge, comp., *History of Freeborn County*, 460. Nelson later took a leading role in organizing a cooperative creamery in Meeker County; see *Album of History and Biography of Meeker County, Minnesota* (Chicago: Alden Ogle and Co., 1888), p. 431–32. There are numerous accounts of the founding of the Clarks Grove creamery. Many are derived, sometimes word-for-word, from the *Freeborn County Times*, Creamery ed., 9 February

1900, p. 1–16, which is the best source. See also Anders Bobjerg, "Andelsmejerier i Amerika," *Andelsbladet* (Copenhagen), 1910, p. 849; A. W. Warren, comp., *A Brief Historical Sketch of the First Danish Baptist Church, Clarks Grove, Minnesota, 1863–1923* (Clarks Grove: The Church, 1923), 42; Ann Regan, "The Danes," in *They Chose Minnesota*, ed. Holmquist, 278, 281; Floyd Sorenson, "The Development of a Co-operative Community—Clarks Grove," *Evening Tribune* (Albert Lea), 6 July (p. 7), 7 July (p. 6), 9 July (p. 10), 10 July (p. 12), 11 July (p. 12)—all 1934; Anthon C. Sørensen, "Danske i amerikansk landbrug og mejeri," in *Danske i Amerika* (Minneapolis: C. Rasmussen, 1908), 1, pt. 2, 271–72; Thomas P. Christensen, "De Danske Baptister i Clarks Grove, Freeborn County, Minn.," in *Danske i Amerika* (Minneapolis: C. Rasmussen, 1916), 2:280–81.

44. The quoted historians are Theodore C. Blegen ("direct line"), *Minnesota*, 397; Ann Regan ("imported from Denmark"), "The Danes," in *They Chose Minnesota*, ed. Holmquist, 281; D. Jerome Tweton ("successful operations"), "The Business of Agriculture," in *Minnesota in a Century of Change: The State and Its People Since 1900*, ed. Clifford E. Clark, Jr. (St. Paul: Minnesota Historical Society Press, 1989), 272. The best account of the early Danish cooperative creameries is Claus Bjørn, "Andelsmejeriernes gennembrud," in Bjørn et al., *Mejeribrug gennem 200 aar, 1882–2000* (Odense, Denmark, 1982). For a history of Clarks Grove, see Kathy Jensen, *Clarks Grove: "A Place We Call Home"* ([Clarks Grove, 1990]).

45. Lampard, *Dairy Industry in Wisconsin*, 376n65. Lampard criticized the resulting misconceptions:

Another popular notion is that co-operative farming generally, and dairying in particular, represent "immigrant contributions" to American agriculture. In fact, the "associated factory system" arose from specific economic and technical conditions; the early business leadership was supplied by Americans, chiefly residents of New York and Ohio. . . . the majority of farmers, native-born and immigrant alike, did little by way of "innovation." They waited to be shown.

Though Lampard too strongly disparages farmers' inventiveness, he is correct that the factory system was developed before dairy cooperation and that Minnesota farmers first received both ideas from New York State or Iowa and not from Scandinavia or Germany.

46. Nels Sørensen Lawdahl, "Danske Baptister i Amerika," in *Danske i Amerika*, 1, pt. 2, p. 186–89; Sørensen, "Danske i amerikansk landbrug og mejeri," 272; Bobjerg, "Andelsmejerier," 722–23, 849–50. It is clear from reading Bobjerg's article that his source for Hauge's role was Hauge.

47. Nels Sørensen Lawdahl, *De danske Baptisters Historie i Amerika* (Morgan Park, Ill.: Forfatterens forlag, 1909), 152–54; Minutes, First Danish Baptist Church, Book 1, p. 5, Baptist Church, Clarks Grove; Lawdahl, "Danske Baptister i Amerika," 186–91. See also L[ars] Jørgensen [Hauge], *Amerika og de danskes liv herovre: kortelig fremstillet til slægtninges, venners og landsmænds gavn og oplysning* (Copenhagen: H. Hagerups boghandel, 1865), 3–5. N. P. Jensen replied cautiously when asked to confirm Hauge's good character: "I have known Mr. Hauge for a number of years. Religiously I differ from him very radically and would not be entrusted to his care, but I think him perfectly honest" in financial matters; Jensen to G. A. Wood, 18 September 1885, letter book, N. P. Jensen Collection, Det danske Baptistsamfunds Arkiv (Danish Baptist Union Archives), Tølløse, Denmark.

48. In May 1890 a brief notice appeared in the Clarks Grove news of a missionary returned from work among the Indians: "L. Jorgenson [sic], an old settler of this vicinity, was around greeting friends the 24st inst." That item implied that Hauge was an infrequent visitor with no official role or strong influence by 1890; *Freeborn County Standard*, 29 May 1890, p. 8. An 1895 plat map of Bath Township shows an Adventist church in northwestern Bath where Hauge may have preached; however, the Clarks Grove creamery grew out of the Baptist congregation, not the Adventist one; *Plat Book of Freeborn County*, 19.

49. H. Hansen and P. Olsen, *De danske baptisters historie* (Copenhagen: Den danske Baptist-Litteratur-Komite, 1896), 188. The story of Hauge's "butter sermons" as "a contributing cause for the growth of the coop-

erative creamery idea in America" is repeated in an otherwise excellent 1989 history of Danish Baptists. See Bent Hylleberg et al., *Et kirkesamfund bliver til: danske baptisters historie gennem 150 År* (Denmark: Føltveds forlag, 1989), 77.

50. A letter in the Baptist Union archives in Denmark confirms H. P. Jensen's visit; Inger Maria to N.O.S., 22 July 1884, N. P. Jensen Collection. Yet his visit and return are not noted in newspapers in his home region in Denmark or in the *Freeborn County Standard* or *Albert Lea Posten*, a Scandinavian-language paper. I searched the 1884 issues of *Holbæk posten* and *Holbæk amts avis* at the University of Copenhagen and the 1884 issues of the *Freeborn County Standard* and *Albert Lea Posten*. For a recent account that stresses Danish creameries as models for Danish-American ones without giving specific evidence of this, see Henrik Bredmose Simonsen, *Kampen om danskheden: tro og nationalitet i de danske kirkesamfund i Amerika* (Århus: Århus universitetsforlag, 1990), 104–5.

51. Hylleberg et al., *Kirkesamfund*, 146–47, 149; *De danske baptistmenigheders Forenings-Konferents holdt i Vandløse menighed den 6te og 7de juni 1884* (N.p., n.d.), 21; *Oliebladet* (Chicago), 1 August, 1 and 15 September 1884. The last two sources are in Det danske Baptistsamfunds Arkiv.

52. August Broholm, *Guds fodspor paa min vej* (Copenhagen: Forlaget fraternitas, 1977), 72, 78, 94–97; August Broholm to Jensen, 12 November 1889, N. P. Jensen Collection.

53. Warren, comp., *Brief Historical Sketch*, 40. For the poverty and minority status of Danish Baptists and the aid from American Baptists, see Hylleberg et al., *Kirkesamfund*. For one decision to send money "to the needy in the church at Frederikshavn, Denmark," see Minutes, First Danish Baptist Church, 1 March 1884, Book 1, p. 110. Probably H. P. Jensen's visit concerned these donations; Niels Hansen to N. Olsen, 3 December 1884, N. P. Jensen Collection.

54. Sørensen, "Danske i Amerikansk Landbrug og Mejeri," 272. According to one account, H. P. Jensen was surprised in 1884 to see a prospering Denmark; *Minneapolis Tribune*, 18 July 1915, 1st sec., p. 8.

55. T. Christensen, "Danske Baptister i

Clarks Grove," 275–79. This essay was not published until 1916, but I believe that it fairly represents a tendency already evident in the early 1890s. Pietist Lutheran (Inner Mission) Danish Americans were known for the same traits in contrast to the Grundtvigian Lutheran Danes. For the split between these two groups, see Simonsen, *Kampen om danskheden*.

56. Record, Clarks Grove Creamerie Forening (Clarks Grove creamery; hereafter CGCF Record), p. 11, Freeborn County Historical Society, Albert Lea. The minutes for 1890–93 are in Danish.

57. *Freeborn County Times*, Creamery ed., 9 February 1900, p. 3–4.

58. CGCF Record, p. 11; *Freeborn County Times*, Creamery ed., 9 February 1900, p. 3 (the "Freemott" referred to here is apparently Fremont Township); Helen Moeller, ed., *Out of the Midwest: A Portrait: An Informal History of Fayette County, Iowa, Prepared in Commemoration of America's Bicentennial* (Marceline, Mo.: Walsworth Pub. Co., 1976), 366; *Plat Book of Fayette County, Iowa* (Philadelphia: Union Pub. Co., 1896), 23; *Plat Book of Bremer County, Iowa* (Philadelphia: Union Pub. Co., 1894), 22. J. P. Larson and Peder Lawson's return from the Iowa trip was noted in the *Freeborn County Standard*, 13 February 1890, p. 8. An article about a cooperative creamery organized in Olmsted County in May 1889 also influenced Clarks Grove farmers; *Farm, Stock and Home* (Minneapolis), 15 January 1890, p. 76.

59. CGCF Record, p. 11; *Freeborn County Times*, Creamery ed., 9 February 1900, p. 3.

60. CGCF Record, p. 12–13, 14–15. Some of the changes were: in the name, "Company" was changed to "Forening," the time to deliver milk was set at 9:00 A.M. in the summer and 10:00 A.M. the rest of the year, rules for resigning membership in the association were set, and a rule was adopted "that no one is permitted to start any store near the creamery unless he is a member of the same." None of the changes (except the first—and that merely one of language) would seem to be based on Danish practices.

61. *Freeborn County Standard*, 15 May 1890, p. 8.

62. Ostergren, *Community Transplanted*, 192–93, 202–3, 207, 240–41.

63. A search of the collections of the Danske udvandrerarkiv (Danish Emigration Archives) in Alborg, Denmark, turned up only six nineteenth-century references to cooperative creameries' success in Denmark or the need for them in America—in periodicals or letters sent to Danish Americans or in letters they sent to Denmark. These six references are brief, even cryptic ones. See *Kors og stjærne* (Copenhagen), vol. 1, no. 2 (1 April 1889): 10–11 (quote), vol. 3, no. 4 (May 1891): 29, and vol. 3, no. 6 (September 1891): 46; Laurits Sorensen (?) to Ole J. Stevns, 25 March 1898, and Niels ? to Dorothea and Ole Stevns, 27 March [1898], both in Ole J. Stevns Papers; and Ida Jensen to Karen [Briel], 12 October 1889 (quote), Ida Jensen Papers. *Kors og stjærne* was published by the Danish branch of Dansk Folkesamfund (a Grundtvigian Danish-American colonization society) for Danes interested in news from their countrymen in America. Simonsen stated that Danish-American farmers rapidly received news of Danish cooperative dairying from letters and newspapers, but he cited no letters or articles and only one secondary source—a 1950s work on Danish revivals, P. G. Lindhardt, "Vækkelse og kirkelige retninger"; Simonsen, *Kampen om danskheden*, 105, 238, 248.

64. Simonsen, *Kampen om danskheden*, 52–53, 105–6. For A. Boysen's role as land agent, see p. 42–45, 50–53. Simonsen used the Danish term *fællesmejeri*, which was understood by 1886 (the friend wrote in 1887) to mean a privately owned creamery; Bjørn, "Andelsmejeriernes gennembrud," 55, 63, 65.

65. Simonsen, *Kampen om danskheden*, 40–41, 43–44, 105–6.

66. West Denmark had a folk school, young people's society, lectures, Danish festivals, and a strong Lutheran congregation. Anders Bobjerg, *En dansk nybygd i Wisconsin. 40 aar i storskoven (1869–1909)* (Copenhagen: I Kommission hos G. E. C. Gad, 1909), 33–35, 63–67; Luck Creamery Company, Minutes (hereafter LCC Minutes), p. 3–5, 133, photocopy at Luck Public Library, Luck, Wis., original owned by the State Historical Society of Wisconsin and housed at the University of Wisconsin–River Falls Area Research Center. The minutes do not

mention American models, but some evidence points to non-Danish influence. At the organizational meeting, one had to pay one dollar before being allowed to vote. In Denmark organizational meetings were usually open to all farmers in the village; Bjørn, "Andelsmejeriernes gennembrud," 72–73, 109–12.

67. LCC Minutes, p. 28, 55, 59–61, 92, 103, 114. It is an error to assume that "for the most part, creameries provided milk and butter to a restricted local market" until the formation of "a large cooperative that could bring Minnesota's dairy products to a broader—perhaps regional, even national—market"; Tweton, "Business of Agriculture," in *Minnesota in a Century of Change*, ed. Clark, 272. That is true of milk but not of butter. Minnesota's cooperative creameries marketed their butter in New York and Chicago in the early 1890s while they were still lone crossroads creameries.

68. LCC Minutes, p. 145. Simonsen cited the Luck creamery as one based on Danish models, but he did not recognize that it was a failure as a cooperative; Simonsen, *Kampen om danskheden*, 104–5.

69. For a discussion of the gathered-cream system, see below, p. 117–19. For another pre-1890 Danish-American cooperative creamery that failed—in Nysted, Nebraska—see Peter Ebbesen, "Historisk Omrids af Danske Kolonier i Howard County, Nebr.," *Danske i Amerika*, 2: 88–89. Danish Americans were not always willing or successful cooperators. A Danish American with a large farm wrote, "We had a cooperative creamery here for many years (also 2 Danish buttermakers). . . . But in the end each farmer got his own centrifuge, and now we ship the cream in cans to the [centralizer] on the train, and ours as well as most of the cooperative creameries died a natural death"; letter to Anders Bobjerg, n.d. (ca. 1905–15), p. 11–12, Anders Bobjerg Papers, Danske udvandrerarkiv.

70. The many nationally known Danish-American experts included: Mads and Hans Søndergaard; Hans Peter Olsen, manager of the *Dairy Record* (St. Paul); James Sorenson; and Christian Larsen. *Mælkeritidende* (Copenhagen) 17, no. 1 (1904): 14; Marie Grand Berg, "Hans Peter Olsen. En

dansk mejerist holder 25 aars jubilæum som amerikansk forlægger," typescript, Hans Peter Olsen Papers, Danske udvandrerarkiv; Christian Larsen and George L. McKay, *Principles and Practice of Butter-making*, 3d ed. (New York: John Wiley and Sons, 1922).

71. *Mælkeritidende*, 14. See also *Den danske Amerikaner* (Copenhagen), 25 March 1897, p. 90; Georg Standvold, "Danes Who Have Helped Build America" (specifically the article on C. Julius Moldenhower), typescript, Georg Strandvold Papers, Danske udvandrerarkiv; Sorensen, "Danske i Amerikansk Landbrug og Mejeri," 265–326. For an analysis of the broker's role played by Danish Americans in linking the Danish and American dairying industries, see Steven J. Keillor, "Agricultural Change and Crosscultural Exchange: Danes, Americans and Dairying, 1880–1930," *Agricultural History* 67 (Fall 1993): 58–79.

72. *Freeborn County Standard*, 11 February 1891, p. 1. For an account that stressed butter prices as a key to the success of Clarks Grove, see Bobjerg, "Andelsmejerier," 849.

73. LCC Minutes, p. 75, 112, 114, 120; "Opgjör til Dec. 1, 1890" (p. 166), "Aarlige Rapport af Sekretaren" (p. 176), and "Aarlige Report af Sekretaren til Clarks Grove Cry Forening den 2nd Jan 1893" (p. 184), CGCF Record. New York prices are taken from United States, Bureau of the Census, *Historical Statistics of the United States: Colonial Times to 1957* (Washington, D.C.: Dept. of Commerce, Bureau of the Census, 1960), 293. The first fiscal year for Clarks Grove ended 1 December 1890.

74. *Freeborn County Times*, Creamery ed., 9 February 1900, p. 1; LCC Minutes, p. 61. There were also some shipments to Chicago and other places. The Clover Valley creamery was located in the now-vanished village of Clover in the southern part of section 33 in Pickerel Lake Township, directly north of Nunda Township; *Historiography/Freeborn County Historical Society* (Albert Lea), 3, no. 3 (July 1984): 3, and issue no. 14 (October 1985): 2. The second fiscal year for Clover Valley began on 1 November 1890. See Clover Valley Creamery Association Minutes (hereafter CVCA Minutes), p. 51, 80–81, 83–84, FCHS.

75. For an explanation of how these figures were calculated, see notes to Table C in the Appendix. For more on the greater efficiency of the centrifugal separator, see Otto F. Hunziker, *The Butter Industry* (La Grange, Ill., 1920), 115–17.

76. Hunziker, *Butter Industry*, 88.

77. J. H. Monrad, *A.B.C. in Butter Making for Young Creamery Butter-makers, Creamery Managers and Private Dairymen* (Winnetka, Ill., 1899), 35. Early tests showed .09 percent butterfat content of skim milk separated by the centrifugal method as compared to .29 percent for skim milk separated by the old gravity method. Later tests by Hunziker showed different results "under most favorable conditions": .02 percent with a hand separator and .17 percent with the deep-setting method; Hunziker, *Butter Industry*, 115.

78. In their first years, Clarks Grove made 4.32 pounds per hundredweight of milk, Clover Valley made 4.2 pounds, and Luck made only 3.93 pounds. See Table C in the Appendix.

79. Heflebower, *Cooperatives and Mutuals*, 29.

80. CGCF Record, p. 160, 165, 177. To be sure, dairying profits were larger during the winter because of the reduced supply of butter; however, the full-year average for 1891 was an impressive eighty-four cents per hundredweight.

81. For example, the directors had to co-sign notes for the Geneva Village and Clover Valley creameries; *Freeborn County Times*, Creamery ed., 9 February 1900, p. 9, 10.

82. For the list of Clarks Grove charter members, see CGCF Record, p. 8–9. The land holdings of these members have been located on the 1895 plat map of Bath, Bancroft, Riceland, and Geneva Townships; *Plat Book of Freeborn County*, 14, 15, 18, 19. The only non-Scandinavian name on the list is that of Clark H. Dills, an Old Stock American from New York State.

83. *Clarks Grove: The Story of a Co-operative Community* ([St. Paul?]: Minnesota, Dept. of Education, Home Study Program, S.E.R.A. Project, [1936?]), 8; Bobjerg, "Andelsmejerier," 849.

84. Letter to Anders Bobjerg, n.d. (ca. 1905–15), p. 11–12, Bobjerg Papers. With evident relief, this unidentified farmer noted,

"Ours as well as most of the cooperative creameries died a natural death."
85. T. Christensen, "Danske Baptister i Clarks Grove," 275–77; McMurry, *Transforming Rural Life*, 188.
86. Warren, comp., *Brief Historical Sketch*, 27, 40–42, 54; CGCF Record, p. 11, 12–13, 14–15; Sorenson, "Development of a Co-operative Community," *Evening Tribune*, July 1934.
87. Warren, comp., *Brief Historical Sketch*, 38–39. Clarks Grove Baptists also formed daughter churches through missionary work, as well as through migration.
88. *Map of Freeborn County* (1878), sections 13–14, 22–27, and 34–36 in Bath Township and sections 15–22 and 28–30 in Bancroft Township. Only those parcels with a dwelling on them were counted as farms. Thomas Christensen noted this same pattern of small farms of forty to eighty acres in 1915–16; "Danske Baptister i Clarks Grove," 280.
89. *Freeborn County Standard*, 21 January 1891, p. 8.

Notes to Chapter 6

1. *Freeborn County Standard*, 10 April 1890, p. 8. For ethnic and geographical information, see *Map of Freeborn County* (1878); *Plat Book of Freeborn County* (1895); and Minnesota, 1885 and 1895 census schedules for Bath Township, Freeborn County.
2. *Map of Freeborn County* (1878); K. Jensen, *Clarks Grove*, 83; "Twenty-third Annual Report of the Commissioner of Statistics," p. 296, Minnesota, *Executive Documents . . . 1891*. There was a Bath post office in section 36 of Bath Township. Manchester became a town later.
3. CGCF Record, p. 15–17. For the four-to-five mile limit, see T. L. Haecker, *Organizing Co-operative Creameries*, University of Minnesota, Agricultural Experiment Station Press Bulletin 2 (March 1, 1894), 1–2; Haecker, *Co-operative Creameries*, University of Minnesota, Agricultural Experiment Station Bulletin 35 (October 1894), 93.
4. Harold Severson, *Blooming Prairie Update* (Blooming Prairie: First National Bank, 1980), 285.
5. CGCF Record, p. 15.
6. *Freeborn County Standard*, 15 May 1890, p. 8.

7. CGCF Record, p. 8–9.
8. K. Jensen, *Clarks Grove*, 20, 22; *Freeborn County Standard*, 2 August 1893, p. 8.
9. K. Jensen, *Clarks Grove*, 20, 33, 42, 46–47, 51; *Plat Book of Freeborn County* (1895); Minnesota, 1895 census schedule for Bath Township, Freeborn County.
10. "Fourth Biennial Report of the Minnesota State Dairy and Food Commissioner," in Minnesota, *Executive Documents of the State of Minnesota for the Fiscal Year Ending July 31, 1892*, 2:485–88; E. Fred Koller to George S. Hage, 2 March 1944, George S. Hage Papers, Watonwan County Historical Society, Madelia.
11. "Fourth Biennial Report of the Dairy and Food Commissioner," in *Executive Documents . . . 1892*, 2:485–88, 492–95. I have eliminated from the statistics the small collection stations owned by the Crescent Creamery Co., Minnesota Creamery Co., and Rochester Separator Co. The patron totals came only from creameries inspected by the state from January 1891 to July 1892. Ten were in Freeborn County, and twenty-three were in other parts of the state.
12. "The farmers of Nunda are organizing a creamery association and will build a creamery on Mr. [William P.] Pickle's farm this season"; *Freeborn County Standard*, 3 April 1890, p. 5, 8. See also *Freeborn County Times*, Creamery ed., 9 February 1900, p. 1, 10.
13. Two months after the organizational meetings, there was dissatisfaction with the Alden gathered-cream cooperative; *Freeborn County Standard*, 20 and 27 March 1890, both p. 8. For a description of the Riceland creamery that stressed the wonders of "the centrifugal process" compared to the gathered-cream process and did not mention cooperation, see *Freeborn County Standard*, 6 August 1890, p. 8.
14. *Freeborn County Standard*, 25 June 1890, p. 8.
15. U.S., Bureau of the Census, *Historical Statistics*, 293. The Gordonsville plant was destroyed by fire; the Alden and North Star plants were converted to separator creameries; the Hayward plant was abandoned and a separator creamery built in the spring of 1891; *Freeborn County Times*, Creamery ed., 9 February 1900, p. 10, 12, 13–14, 16. The price fluctuations were as follows:

	N.Y. Price		N.Y. Price
Year	per pound	Year	per pound
1888	27.5 cents	1891	26.2 cents
1889	24.4 cents	1892	26.3 cents
1890	23.7 cents	1893	27.1 cents

16. CGCF Record, p. 8–9, 17–18.

17. See, for example, the comments of Danish dairy expert Bernhard Bøggild in his *Nogle iagttagelser fra en rejse i Amerika* (Odense, Denmark, 1910), 40–45. For the Danish use of delivery contracts, see Christensen, *Agricultural Cooperation in Denmark*, 10–11, 16, 18.

18. CGCF Record, p. 153, 167–69, 176–77; Bobjerg, "Andelsmejerier," 849.

19. For an interesting early account of the history of Freeborn County's cooperative creameries by N. T. Sandberg of Bancroft, see *Freeborn County Standard*, 9 March 1898, p. 1.

20. *Albert Lea Enterprise*, 16 October and 27 November 1890, both p. 4, and 25 December 1890, p. 3.

21. *Freeborn County Standard*, 21 January 1891, p. 8.

22. *Freeborn County Standard*, 25 February and 11 and 18 March, all 1891, all p. 8.

23. *Freeborn County Standard*, 4 February 1891, p. 8.

24. *Freeborn County Standard*, 11 February 1891, p. 1. Assuming this writer correctly estimated an output of one pound of butter per thirty pounds of milk and an average price of 9.5 cents per pound of farm butter, the gross earnings would be 31.67 cents per hundredweight.

25. In this respect, Minnesota resembled the western counties of Wisconsin where "the proliferation of small creameries marked the first substantial gain for industrial dairying" and "leadership in dairy enterprise fell to farmer-co-operative organizations established by relatively recent converts to livestock husbandry"; Lampard, *Dairy Industry in Wisconsin*, 271–72. For the role of dairy specialists in Wisconsin, see p. 104–9.

26. Curtiss-Wedge, ed., *History of Freeborn County*, 461. This group used the Clarks Grove constitution and bylaws.

27. *Freeborn County Times*, Creamery ed., 9 February 1900, p. 9, 14. A similar reason lay behind the establishment of the Banner creamery in Oakland Township in 1898.

28. *Freeborn County Times*, Creamery ed., 9 February 1900, p. 5, 10. Northern Pickerel farmers' preference for making cheese ("several ... had come from the cheese districts of New York or Wisconsin") may have contributed to the split. After farmers of eastern Hartland and western Bath Townships met to decide on a site, Bath farmers pulled out and tried to form a creamery near the Irish Catholic church (they would not join Clarks Grove); see *Hartland Vidette*, 4 and 25 December 1890. The Poplar Grove creamery later stood near the Irish church. The *Hartland Vidette* had its own masthead and editor but was published as page 8 of the *North Star* (New Richland).

29. *Freeborn County Times*, Creamery ed., 9 February 1900, p. 14; *Freeborn County Standard*, 11 February 1891, p. 5, and 4 and 11 March 1891, both p. 8.

30. CGCF Record, p. 12; Curtiss-Wedge, ed., *History of Freeborn County*, 461; *Freeborn County Times*, Creamery ed., 9 February 1900, p. 12. See also Manchester Creamery Association Record, p. 5–7, FCHS.

31. There are numerous references in Freeborn County newspapers to the Johnsruds' political role, especially in the Farmers' Alliance; see *Freeborn County Standard*, 26 May 1886, p. 4, and 25 March 1891, p. 5. For their role in a previous farmers' club, see *Albert Lea Posten*, 13 March, 10 and 24 April 1884, 12 June 1884, all p. 4.

32. *Albert Lea Enterprise*, 4 October and 1 November 1894, both p. 1; *Freeborn County Standard*, 31 October 1894, p. 4; Minnesota State Dairymen's Association, *Proceedings of the 16th Annual Convention ... Held at Waseca, Minnesota, Dec. 12, 13, and 14, 1893* (Minneapolis, 1894), 42–52; *Anoka County Union* (Anoka), 27 July 1892, p. 8. For Lawson's and Gibbs's careers, see T. Christensen, "Danske Baptister i Clarks Grove," 280, and Christensen, "De Danske i og omkring Geneva og Ellendale, Minnesota," in *Danske i Amerika*, 2: 289–90. For an amusing attack on a campaign to elect Speaker Gibbs governor "just because the editor saw him milking a cow and with old clothes on," see *Canby News*, 3 September 1886, p. 3.

33. *Hartland Vidette*, 11 February 1891.

34. *Freeborn County Standard*, 7, 14 and 28 January 1891, all p. 8; *Hartland Vidette*, 15

January 1891. The best account of the Alliance is Robert C. McMath, Jr., *American Populism: A Social History, 1877–1898* (New York: Hill and Wang, 1993).

35. *Freeborn County Standard*, 21 January and 4 March, both 1891, both p. 8; *Hartland Vidette*, 26 February and 9 April and 11 June, all 1891. The call for the first meeting contained language surely applauded by the merchants: "Let us . . . establish our headquarters at the village of Hartland and have branch creameries all over this part of the county"; *Freeborn County Standard*, 17 December 1890, p. 8.

36. *Hartland Vidette*, 23 April, 21 May, 4 and 18 and 25 June, all 1891.

37. *Albert Lea Enterprise*, 11 October 1894, p. 2, and 23 January 1896, p. 4; *Freeborn County Standard*, 18 October 1893, p. 1, and 12 February 1896, p. 5.

38. Haecker argued, "Where a cash dividend is declared every month," at the creamery, "farmers are enabled to promptly pay their store bills and all lines of trade benefited, and in a short time all business will be conducted upon a cash basis"; Haecker, *Organizing Co-operative Creameries*, 3.

39. *Freeborn County Standard*, 30 June 1897, p. 1. The preceding year, 1896, was a depression year of low butter prices. The average New York price of butter fell from a peak of 27.1 cents in 1893 to 23 cents in 1894 to 21.2 cents in 1895. For 1896 it was only 18.5 cents per pound—lower than it had been since 1851 and lower than it would ever drop again, even in the 1930s Depression; see U.S., Bureau of the Census, *Historical Statistics*, 293.

40. *Freeborn County Times*, Creamery ed., 9 February 1900, p. 10. In Albert Lea, Emmons, Geneva, and Hayward, merchants helped organize and finance creamery associations. For Hayward, Geneva, and Albert Lea, see Creamery ed., p. 9, 13, 15. See also Charles Nelson, *History of Hayward: 1849–1949, Centennial Edition* ([Hayward], 1949), 11–13.

41. *Freeborn County Standard*, 28 January 1891, p. 8. Geneva did have a cheese factory before it acquired a cooperative separator creamery, but the factory was losing farmer-patrons to the Clarks Grove creamery. *Freeborn County Standard*, 20 March 1890, p. 8; *Albert Lea Enterprise*, 16 October 1890, p. 4.

42. *Freeborn County Standard*, 6 January 1892, p. 5. "A Denial" by two officers of the Geneva Township creamery is so emphatic and the rumors so specific as to warrent the inference that some attempt at persuasion was made, although not supported by these two officers.

43. *Freeborn County Times*, Creamery ed., 9 February 1900, p. 9.

44. See, for instance, Manchester Creamery Association Record, p. 8. An interesting description of one bidding process is given in the article on the Albert Lea Dairy Association in *Freeborn County Times*, Creamery ed., 9 February 1900, p. 15.

45. *Freeborn County Times*, Creamery ed., 9 February 1900, p. 7.

46. *Albert Lea Enterprise*, 21 September and 12 October 1893, both p. 4.

47. Travel notes, 11 July 1892, Haecker Papers.

48. Haecker reported that a Pipestone creamery cost seven thousand dollars; Freeborn's creameries often cost less than five thousand dollars; undated (late 1920s?) manuscript titled "Wis Dairy course," Haecker Papers; O[ren] C. Gregg, "Address," in Minnesota State Dairymen's Assn., *Proceedings . . . 1893*, 16–18. Haecker's speech notes on his 1892 trip are worth quoting: "Creamery Promoters[—]Large plants, Over Capitalized[,] Overstocked with Inferior machines[—]Located where there were few cows[—]$80,000 Rec'd by one Chicago Co for plants practically worthless"; Haecker Papers. In his farm bulletins, Haecker warned against creamery promoters; see Haecker, *Organizing Co-operative Creameries*, 2–3, and *Co-operative Creameries*, 94.

49. *Freeborn County Standard*, 18 February 1891, 12 and 19 October 1892, 4 January and 14 June 1893, all p. 8; *Freeborn County Times*, Creamery ed., 9 February 1900, p. 7, 8. For some unknown reason Richards ceased to be the Glenville buttermaker.

50. Raymond Breton, "Institutional Completeness of Ethnic Communities and the Personal Relations of Immigrants," *American Journal of Sociology* 70 (September 1964): 193–205.

51. That may have been why Bath's Irish-American farmers pulled out of negotiations with farmers in eastern Hartland Township and ultimately formed their own

Poplar Grove creamery; *Hartland Vidette*, 4 and 25 December 1890.

52. "Fourth Biennial Report of the Dairy and Food Commissioner," in *Executive Documents . . . 1892*, 2:485–88, 492–95.

53. Untitled, undated manuscript beginning "I owned a farm in Cottage Grove" and travel notes, 2 and 3 August 1892, Haecker Papers.

54. Andrew Boss, *The Early History and Background of the School of Agriculture at University Farm, St. Paul* ([St. Paul?]: University of Minnesota, 1941), 31–32; Blegen, *Minnesota*, 393–94; Roy V. Scott, *The Reluctant Farmer: The Rise of Agricultural Extension to 1914* (Urbana: University of Illinois Press, 1970), 82–83; Roy V. Scott, "Early Agricultural Education in Minnesota: The Institute Phase," *Agricultural History* 37 (January 1963): 23–24; Roy V. Scott, "Pioneering in Agricultural Education: Oren C. Gregg and Farmers' Institutes," *Minnesota History* 37 (March 1960): 21–25. The institutes merged the dairymen's desire to promote diversification with the university's goal of teaching farmers and thereby deflecting Alliance criticisms. The Northwestern Dairymen's Association began the institutes in Minnesota in 1884–86.

55. Scott, "Early Agricultural Education," 25, 29, 30, 31; Minutes, Board of Administration for the Minnesota Farmers' Institutes, 5 May 1899, Institute of Agriculture, Director's Office Papers, University of Minnesota Archives (hereafter UM Archives), Minneapolis. In the winter of 1898–99, no institutes were held in the Red River Valley or other grain-growing areas.

56. *Great West* (St. Paul), 14 February 1890, p. 8.

57. Untitled, undated manuscript beginning "Retrospect of events," and Willet M. Hays to Haecker, 27 January 1891, Haecker Papers; John A. Vye, "History of the School of Agriculture," typescript, 6 July 1939, John A. Vye Papers, UM Archives.

58. *Hoard's Dairyman*, 10 July 1927, p. 708. Haecker's Grange membership card, dated 22 March 1875, is in volume 2, Haecker Papers.

59. For another version of Haecker's role in the founding of the dairy school, see Vye, "History of the School of Agriculture," 4–6.

60. See Haecker's notes on his trip, volume 3, and "Retrospect of events," Haecker Papers.

61. Haecker, "I owned a farm in Cottage Grove," and travel notes, 3 August 1892, Haecker Papers.

62. Travel diary, 1892, Haecker Papers. Haecker mentioned this prior connection to cooperatives: "I knew about these because I belonged to one in Wisconsin"; see "I owned a farm in Cottage Grove," Haecker Papers.

63. Frank E. Balmer, "The Cooperative Movement in the Minnesota Dairy Industry," manuscript for a speech to be delivered 14 June 1930 at Clarks Grove, Haecker Papers; "The Farmers' School . . . Questions Answered by T. L. Haecker," *Minnesota Farmers Institute Annual*, no. 6 (1893), p. 36. I have not found any evidence to substantiate Haecker's account of opposition. When a university instructor used the story of Haecker's role to convince an Equity-dominated convention that the university supported cooperatives, his account "brought a storm of protesting testimony." It is not clear if farmers objected to the story's accuracy or to its relevance to the issues being debated then. See *St. Paul Pioneer Press*, 8 March 1912, p. 7. Vye disputed the exaggerated claim that Haecker started the cooperative creamery system in Minnesota; Haecker never made that claim, however, and Vye verified the important supportive role that he did play; see Vye, "History of the School of Agriculture," 5.

64. Haecker to Knute Nelson, 20 December 1892, C. H. Higgs to Nelson, 1 December 1892, H. C. Howard to Nelson, 28 December 1892, all in Minnesota, Governor (1893–1895: Nelson) Records, State Archives; Minnesota, Secretary of State, *Legislative Manual*, 1891, p. 454, and 1893, p. 330. Berndt Anderson, editor of *Skaffaren* (St. Paul and Minneapolis), was the new commissioner; *Legislative Manual*, 1897, p. 584.

65. Minutes, Board of Regents, University of Minnesota, 31 May, 17 June, 27 December 1893 meetings, UM Archives. Haecker's rival was Clinton D. Smith; see Vye, "History of the School of Agriculture," 4–6. Governor Nelson was on the board of regents *ex officio*.

66. Haecker, *Organizing Co-operative Creameries*, 1–3.

67. Typescript beginning "The University of Minnesota did not inaugurate a short

course," undated [1903?], William M. Liggett folder, University of Minnesota, Institute of Agriculture, Director's Office Papers, UM Archives; Blegen, *Minnesota*, 398. It is difficult, of course, to tell which creameries were truly cooperative.

68. For Nelson's relationship with patronage jobholders, see Millard L. Gieske and Steven J. Keillor, *Norwegian Yankee: Knute Nelson and the Failure of American Politics, 1860–1923* (Northfield: Norwegian-American Historical Association, 1995), 144–46, 167–70.

69. Ahlness, "Recollections," 272–74. Ahlness may be exaggerating for humorous effect and overstressing his personal role.

70. Lake Hanska Farmers' Alliance, Journal (hereafter LHFA Journal), p. 7–18 (quotes p. 15, 17, 18), BCHS; *Sleepy Eye Herald*, 13 February 1891, p. 1. In its first ten months, the Lake Hanska suballiance met at four different sites.

71. *Sleepy Eye Herald*, 10 and 30 January and 20 March, all 1891, all p. 1.

72. Vance Chambard, historical notes on Hanska, undated typescript, Hanska file, BCHS; *Madelia Times*, 18 March 1892, p. 1. Nora leaders Anton O. Ouren, Johannes Moe, and Ole Jorgensen also led the creamery organizational effort. For the Nora church, see Nora Free Christian Church, *Seventy-fifth Anniversary, 1881–1956* (Hanska, 1956), 3–7; Nora Free Church, *1881–1906: Nora Fri-kristne Menighed (Norsk Unitarisk)* (Hanska, 1906), 21–22, 31; and Nina Draxten, *Kristofer Janson in America* (Boston: Published for the Norwegian-American Historical Association by Twayne Publishers, 1976), 56–57, 67–69, 71–72, 96–100, 138–39.

73. "Dairying in Minnesota: Second Report," *Northwest Illustrated Monthly Magazine* (St. Paul), February 1897, p. 27. See also Robinson, *Early Economic Conditions*, 76, 112, 137–38, 141.

74. John L. Gibbs, "Co-operative Dairying," in Minnesota Farmers' Institute, *Annual* (1893), 286–87.

75. The sources for the ethnicity and operating characteristics of individual creameries are *Freeborn County Times*, Creamery ed., 9 February 1900, p. 1–16; *Freeborn County Standard*, 25 March 1891, p. 8; Minnesota, 1885 and 1895 census schedules for Bancroft,

Bath, Manchester, Nunda, and Pickerel Lake Townships, Freeborn County.

76. CGCF Record, p. 8–9; *Plat Book of Freeborn County* (1895); Minnesota, 1885 and 1895 census schedules for Bancroft and Bath Townships, Freeborn County. The Clarks Grove "milkshed" extended into Bancroft Township in a wedge that included only Danish Americans (and one Old Stock American).

77. Manchester Creamery Association Record, p. 3–4, 7–8; *Plat Book of Freeborn County* (1895); Minnesota, 1885 and 1895 census schedules for Manchester Township, Freeborn County.

78. CVCA Minutes, p. 58; *Plat Book of Freeborn County* (1895); Minnesota, 1885 and 1895 census schedules for Nunda and Pickerel Lake Townships, Freeborn County. Most of the ten Scandinavian-American farmers lived closer to the Twin Lakes creamery, however.

79. Common ethnic ties linking farmers in different townships were another factor in the diffusion of separator creameries. In the case of the Danes and Norwegians, there were links among creamery formations in Clarks Grove, Riceland, Bancroft, Manchester, and Deer Creek (State Line). See *Freeborn County Times*, Creamery ed., 9 February 1900, for information on these creamery associations.

80. The Old Stock creamery in Geneva Township dissolved in 1894 with four thousand dollars still owing to one individual; *Freeborn County Times*, Creamery ed., 9 February 1900, p. 7.

81. CVCA Minutes, p. 2, 68–69, 99; *Freeborn County Times*, Creamery ed., 9 February 1900, p. 10–11; *Freeborn County Standard*, 6 January 1892, p. 5, and 4 March 1891, p. 8.

82. However, a serious site selection dispute in Bancroft Township, apparently between members of west and east Bancroft congregations of the Norwegian Lutheran church, hampered that association at first; *Albert Lea Enterprise*, 25 December 1890, p. 4; *Freeborn County Times*, Creamery ed., 9 February 1900, p. 13.

83. *Freeborn County Times*, Creamery ed., 9 February 1900, p. 13.

84. Manchester Creamery Association Record, p. 7–8; *Hartland Vidette*, 26 February

1891. Manchester had Norwegian-American clubs, including a reading society and a Manchester Debating Library, which likely added to a sense of solidarity among creamery members; *Hartland Vidette*, 19 February 1891; *Freeborn County Standard*, 11 and 18 February, and 4 and 11 March, all 1891, all p. 8.

85. In its first year, Clover Valley paid $1,277.54 for "Hauling milk." CVCA Minutes, p. 83; CGCF Record, p. 159–84; Bobjerg, "Andelsmejerier," 849.

86. Manchester Creamery Association Record, p. 28, 30–31.

87. Manchester Creamery Association Record, p. 14. For the Old Stock creamery that paid the secretary and manager "to do the hauling of butter and tubs" and paid patrons "to haul the coal," see *Freeborn County Times*, Creamery ed., 9 February 1900, p. 7.

88. The Clarks Grove, Manchester, State Line, and Hayward creameries hired buttermakers without regard to ethnicity; see *Freeborn County Times*, Creamery ed., 9 February 1900, p. 5–6, 12, 13; *Freeborn County Standard*, 15 May 1890, p. 8. For Scandinavian rural decision making, see, for example, Joan Rockwell, "The Danish Peasant Village," *Journal of Peasant Studies* 1 (July 1974): 409–61.

89. In its weekly "Farm, Stock and Creamery" column, the *Albert Lea Enterprise* often published milk prices and other financial reports of creamery associations; see *Enterprise*, 11 January 1899, p. 2. The *Freeborn County Standard* frequently did the same; see *Standard*, 3 August 1892, p. 1.

90. *Freeborn County Times*, Creamery ed., 9 February 1900, p. 5.

91. *Freeborn County Standard*, 25 January 1893, p. 8; *Freeborn County Times*, Creamery ed., 9 February 1900, p. 16.

92. *Freeborn County Times*, Creamery ed., 9 February 1900, p. 5, 10–11, 12.

93. *Albert Lea Enterprise*, 26 October 1893, p. 5.

94. *Albert Lea Enterprise*, 12 October 1893, p. 8. Halvorsen was also known as Halvorson. Many so-called commission firms bought butter outright from creameries based on the Elgin or New York price. Selling butter on commission became outdated. For a firm's request to market Freeborn

creamery butter, see G. M. Wattles and Son to Armstrong creamery association, 23 September 1903, Pickerel Lake Township (Armstrong) Creamery Association Records, FCHS. For the shift from commission to contract-price marketing, see Wiest, *Butter Industry*, 149–51.

95. *Freeborn County Standard*, 27 July and 3 August 1892, both p. 1.

96. *Freeborn County Standard*, 20 September 1893, p. 8.

97. *Albert Lea Enterprise*, 12 October 1893, p. 8; *Freeborn County Standard*, 18 October 1893, p. 1.

98. *Albert Lea Enterprise*, 12 October 1893, p. 8. Of course, Halvorsen, as a New York agent, was not unbiased.

99. *Freeborn County Standard*, 18 October 1893, p. 1. Day and Halvorsen disagreed on politics so their agreement here is evidence that this view was widely held in Freeborn County.

100. Gibbs, "Home or Co-operative Dairying," in Minnesota State Dairymen's Association, *Proceedings* (1893), 49.

101. *Freeborn County Standard*, 7 June 1893, p. 5.

102. Lawrence Goodwyn, *Democratic Promise: The Populist Moment in America* (New York: Oxford University Press, 1976), 110–11.

103. *Albert Lea Enterprise*, 7 September 1893, p. 8; *Freeborn County Standard*, 6 September 1893, p. 4; Gieske and Keillor, *Norwegian Yankee*, 155, 359n64.

104. Quoted in *Freeborn County Standard*, 13 September 1893, p. 4; *Pioneer Press* (St. Paul), 9 September 1893, p. 5. Assistant Commissioner Edwin J. Graham was appointed by Nelson in 1893; Bertram was a holdover from the previous administration; see *Legislative Manual*, 1893, p. 330, and 1891, p. 454.

105. *Redwood Gazette* (Redwood Falls), 28 September 1893, p. 1.

106. Quoted in *Evening Post* (New York), 6 (?) August 1894. See also *Warren Sheaf*, 16 and 30 August 1894, both p. 4; and *Marshall County Banner* (Argyle), 2 and 9 August 1894, both p. 1.

107. *Freeborn County Standard*, 26 September 1894, p. 1, 5; *Albert Lea Enterprise*, 27 September 1894, p. 5; Gieske and Keillor, *Norwegian Yankee*, 187–207.

Notes to Chapter 7

1. *Alliance Advocate* (Henning), 9 July 1891, p. 7. This incident is described in Lowell J. Soike, *Norwegian Americans and the Politics of Dissent, 1880–1924* (Northfield: Norwegian-American Historical Association, 1991), 98. The chapter title is a shortened version of a resolution passed by the Granite Falls suballiance; *Granite Falls Tribune*, 17 June 1890, p. 1.

2. *Fergus Falls Weekly Journal*, 9 July 1891, p. 5. Members of the Grand Army of the Republic post in Battle Lake later condemned the attempt to mix politics with celebrating the Fourth; *Alliance Advocate*, 6 August 1891, p. 1, and *Battle Lake Review*, 9 July 1891, p. 1.

3. *Alliance Advocate*, 6 August 1891, p. 6.

4. The *Journal* editor, Elmer E. Adams, apparently investigated secretly to determine who was supporting the *Advocate*; *Alliance Advocate*, 6 August 1891, p. 6. He sarcastically referred to Editor Frank Hoskins of the *Advocate* as "Prof. Hoskins, the well known political economist"; *Fergus Falls Weekly Journal*, 6 August 1891, p. 4. For the private discussions preceding the start of the *Advocate*, see letters to Charles W. Brandborg from John B. Hompe?, 27 January 1891, Frank Hoskins, 17 December 1890, and Hans Nelson, 22 August 1890, all in Charles W. Brandborg and Family Papers, MHS.

5. *Fergus Falls Weekly Journal*, 6 August 1891, p. 4.

6. *Fergus Falls Weekly Journal*, 9 July 1891, p. 5, and 16 July 1891, p. 6.

7. *Alliance Advocate*, 9 July 1891, p. 7, and 6 August 1891, p. 6; *Fergus Falls Weekly Journal*, 9 July 1891, p. 5.

8. *Battle Lake Review*, 30 July 1891, p. 4.

9. *Alliance Advocate*, 6 August 1891, p. 6; *Fergus Falls Weekly Journal*, 6 August 1891, p. 4.

10. *Alliance Advocate*, 26 November 1891, p. 1. For another account of the July 4 incident and the trial, see "Story of the trial of C. W. Brandborg as recalled by Jennie Brandborg Sacrider," typed manuscript, n.d. [1972?], Brandborg Papers.

11. Quote from McMath, *American Populism*, 44.

12. "Fourth Biennial Report of the Minnesota State Dairy and Food Commissioner,"

in Minnesota, *Executive Documents ... 1892*, 2:487, 489, 494.

13. Lawrence Goodwyn, *The Populist Moment: A Short History of the Agrarian Revolt in America* (New York: Oxford University Press, 1978), 66.

14. Goodwyn, *Democratic Promise*, 110–11. For critical responses, see Stanley B. Parsons, Karen Toombs Parsons, Walter Killilae, and Beverly Borgers, "The Role of Cooperatives in the Development of the Movement Culture of Populism," *Journal of American History* 69 (March 1983): 866–85; Robert W. Cherny, "Lawrence Goodwyn and Nebraska Populism: A Review Essay," *Great Plains Quarterly* 1 (Summer 1981): 181–94; and James Turner, "Understanding the Populists," *Journal of American History* 67 (September 1980): 354–73. For a good summary of the debate over Populism, see McMath, *American Populism*, 9–16.

15. Goodwyn, *Democratic Promise*, 47–49.

16. Parsons et al., "The Role of Cooperatives," 870, 882–83. This article used the records of R. G. Dun and Company, a credit agency, to determine the number of cooperatives. It mentioned joint purchasing in only one Kansas suballiance. Parsons discussed joint marketing and purchasing and hostile Main Street reaction to them in *The Populist Context: Rural versus Urban Power on a Great Plains Frontier* (Westport, Conn.: Greenwood Press, 1973).

17. McMath, *American Populism*, 4–5, 66; John D. Hicks, *The Populist Revolt: A History of the Farmers' Alliance and the People's Party* (Minneapolis: University of Minnesota Press, 1931), 98. The Blooming Grove suballiance used the Cook County constitution as its model; see Blooming Grove Lyceum (Farmers' Alliance) (hereafter BGL), Minutes, p. 9, Waseca County Historical Society, Waseca.

18. Hicks, *Populist Revolt*, 100.

19. This is not a representative sample. There is no suballiance from Otter Tail County and only one from the Red River Valley. Yet it is sufficiently varied to depict the Alliance in different agricultural regions with different ethnic populations. The Moorhead Alliance #148 conducted no joint or cooperative activities and is included for comparative purposes only. The local news-

papers of the other four counties were examined to complete the account of Alliance economic activities hinted at in the suballiance minutes. The statewide Alliance paper, the *Great West*, was also consulted.

20. *Worthington Advance*, 21 September 1882, p. 3 and 28 September 1882, p. 2; Washington Farmers' Alliance, Minute Book (hereafter WFA Minute Book), title page, Nobles County Historical Society, Worthington. The statement on the title page indicates that the suballiance was formed "under the auspices of G[orge] W. Sprague of Good Thunder." Sprague, president of the Minnesota Alliance, probably accompanied the congressional candidate, Jacob A. Latimer, to Nobles County.

21. Lisbon Township Farmers' Alliance, Yellow Medicine County, Minutes (hereafter LTFA Minutes), 28 February 1890, Southwest Minnesota Historical Center, Southwest State University, Marshall; Arthur P. Rose, *An Illustrated History of Yellow Medicine County, Minnesota* (Marshall: Northern History Publishing Co., 1914), 150, 152; *Reform-Advocate* (Clarkfield), 29 October 1896, p. 4. "A vote of thanks was tendered Mr. Mooney for his services during the meeting in aiding to organize our alliance"; LTFA Minutes, 28 February 1890. By April 8, Mooney had been appointed the county's Alliance lecturer and charged with organizing suballiances in each township; *Granite Falls Tribune*, 8 April 1890, p. 1.

22. BGL Minutes, p. 9; James E. Child, *Child's History of Waseca County, Minnesota* (Owatonna: Whiting & Luers, 1905), 363, 683. In Waseca, lawyer Lewis Brownell led attacks on local wheat buyers. Two weeks later, "Some farmers ... met at Mr. Brownell's office ... for the purpose of organizing a farmers' alliance"; *Waseca County Herald* (Waseca), 12 March 1886, p. 2, and 19 March 1886, p. 3; Child, *Child's History of Waseca*, 225; *History of Steele and Waseca Counties, Minnesota* (Chicago: Union Publishing Co., 1887), 510.

23. For examples of the reports sent back from the field by organizing lecturers, see *Great West*, 18 April, 23 May, 20 June, and 11 July, all 1890, all p. 8.

24. *Great West*, 20 June 1890, p. 8.

25. *Great West*, 11 April 1890, p. 1.

26. No identifiably female names appear on the lists of members of the five suballiances included in this study. Women may have played some role not revealed in the suballiance's minutes. For women's role in the Alliance elsewhere, see McMath, *American Populism*, 123–27. He concluded that "the role of women actually diminished" when the Alliance moved to third-party political action.

27. *Waseca County Herald*, 26 February 1886, p. 4, and 5 March and 12 March 1886, both p. 2; *Waseca Radical*, 17 March 1886, p. 5, and 7 April 1886, p. 1.

28. United States, 1880 manuscript Agricultural Census for Minnesota, Waseca County, microfilm, roll 9, MHS; BGL Minutes, p. 2, 10, 12, 18, 20, 22, 24, 30, 27, 31–35, 39, 41–42, 52. I counted only farmers who joined the suballiance during its first year, that is, by April 5, 1887. Members also had more total acreage under cultivation—an average of 123.35 acres compared to 107.7 acres for nonmembers. For the other suballiances, the 1880 Agricultural Census was not a useful measure. Some were formed in 1890, long after the census was taken. One—Dewald—was a very small suballiance, drawing members from so many townships as to make such comparisons unreliable. The Blooming Grove results confirm John Dibbern's conclusion regarding Alliance membership in Dakota Territory: "The Alliance appealed somewhat more to men of median wealth ... the Alliance held little appeal to men of little property.... Populism was not a class movement of the 'have-nots' "; John Dibbern, "Who Were the Populists?: A Study of Grass-Roots Alliancemen in Dakota," *Agricultural History* 56 (October 1982): 677–91 (quotes p. 682).

29. BGL Minutes, p. 9–10, 17; Child, *Child's History of Waseca*, 363; *Morristown Rustler*, 26 February 1889, p. 2 and 3, 21 May 1889, p. 3, and 11 June 1889, p. 3; *History of Steele and Waseca Counties*, 580. Three Remunds and George Soule were four of five Blooming Grove delegates to the county Alliance convention in May 1886. Editor James E. Child visited Blooming Grove in 1870 and reported, "This township contains more wealthy farmers than any other in the county"; *Waseca News*, 6 July 1870, p. 3. Soule was

also a town clerk, a hardware dealer, and the owner of a custom steam thresher. The Remunds sold horse breeding services. Albert Remund was a Blooming Grove town clerk, a justice of the peace, and a school director.

30. Author's computation based on U.S., 1880, Census schedule for Blooming Grove Township, Waseca County; and BGL Minutes, p. 130–31.

31. Norwegian-American settlers lived in the west and southwest part of the township; the suballiance met in the north-central part. Distance and ethnicity are factors difficult to separate. Most charter members lived within two-and-a-half miles of the meeting place. However, many Norwegian Americans lived the same distance from the site as did some of the German-speaking members. *Standard Atlas of Waseca County, Minnesota* (Geo. A. Ogle & Co., 1896), 9.

32. Donna M. Fostveit, comp., *Waseca County, Minnesota: Landowners of Record, 1879* (Waseca: Waseca County Historical Society, 1982), 12; *Plat Book of Rice County, Minnesota* ([Philadelphia]: North West Publishing Co., 1900), 9. A history of the Blooming Grove Methodist Church names the Wilkowske, Saufferer, and Reinhardt families as ones who belonged to the suballiance; Mrs. W. B. Schmidtke et al., *100 Years in Morristown, 1855–1955* (Morristown, [1956]), 56–57. For the area's Norwegian Lutheran churches, see North Waseca Evangelical Lutheran Church, *Seventy-Fifth Anniversary 1858–1933* ([Waseca?, 1933?]), 4–9. In the early 1890s, Norwegian Lutherans built their creamery a half mile from their church on the township's western border; German-speaking farmers built theirs midway between their Methodist and Evangelical churches in its northern end; *Standard Atlas of Waseca County*, 9.

33. Blooming Grove members C. Bloomer, William Hobein, R. A. Wolf, John Gibson, F. J. Mariska, and N. M. Stierns lived in Morristown Township, Rice County; see *Plat Book of Rice County*, 9.

34. *Plat Book of Yellow Medicine County, Minnesota* ([Philadelphia?]: North West Publishing Co., 1900), 28–29. There were also members in Hazel Run and Friendship Townships; *Plat Book*, 20, 21. The Lake

Hanska suballiance included many farmers from neighboring Linden Township; M. B. Haynes, *Map of 1886 Plat Book of Brown County, Minn.* (Mankato: The Author, 1886); LHFA Journal, p. 2–3.

35. John Hicks quoted a "prominent Allianceman" who listed four functions: " 'first, social; second, educational; third, financial; fourth, political' "; Hicks, *Populist Revolt*, 128.

36. *Waseca News*, 25 May and 22 June 1870, both p. 2. For these newspaper references, I am indebted to Harshman, "History of the Settlement of Waseca County," 162.

37. *Waseca News*, 6 July 1870, p. 3.

38. *Waseca News*, 25 May and 22 June 1870, both p. 2, and 12 July 1870, p. 3. For example, Albert Remund was a delegate to the Waseca County Council (1873) and to a county convention (1886); *Farmers' Union*, 28 June 1873, p. 204–5; *Waseca County Herald*, 17 September 1886, p. 3. For more on the Remund family, see L. E. Swanberg, ed., *Then and Now: A History of Rice County, Faribault and Communities* ([Faribault?]: Rice County Bi-Centennial Commission, 1976), 193–94.

39. McMath, *American Populism*, 50, 54–64, 66; Goodwyn, *Democratic Promise*, 44–46; Woods, *Knights of the Plow*, xvii–xviii. McMath brilliantly analyzed the "cultures of protest" in northern Texas but thereby overemphasized the Texas Alliance, as Goodwyn also did; see McMath, 66–72.

40. BGL Minutes, p. 9, 78, 79; LTFA Records; *Plat Book of Yellow Medicine County* (N.p.: Northwest Publishing Co., 1900), 28–29; LHFA Journal, p. 7–18; *Map of Brown County* (1886).

41. WFA Minute Book, 3 March 1883 and 24 September 1887.

42. Wayne E. Fuller, *The Old Country School: The Story of Rural Education in the Middle West* (Chicago: University of Chicago Press, 1982), 45, 74–75, 87; Yellow Medicine County, school district treasurer's reports, 1880–1897, p. 18, J. J. Heimark Papers, Norwegian-American Historical Assn., Northfield; LTFA Minutes, 28 February and 8 March 1890.

43. *Freeborn County Standard*, 20 March 1890, p. 8.

44. Parsons et al., "The Role of Cooperatives," 884.

45. *Granite Falls Journal*, 4 June 1891, p. 1. For a description of how school boards let the annual contract for firewood, see Fuller, *Old Country School*, 48–49. For a contract awarded by Windom's suballiance, see *Great West*, 7 February 1890, p. 7.

46. McMath, *American Populism*, 123–25; *Great West*, 11 April 1890, p. 2.

47. WFA Minute Book, 20 August and 5 November 1887. At a meeting regarding joint purchasing of twine, the Blooming Grove suballiance asked nonmembers to leave. "The Stearns Bros. not liking the Idea of having any secrets going on," applied for membership and were accepted. In September 1886, president Soule "asked the privilege of scolding a little . . . he thought we ought to be more careful about keeping our business to ourselves etc"; BGL Minutes, p. 25, 28. Here and below, see also Goodwyn, *Democratic Promise*, 51.

48. *Worthington Globe*, 23 April 1891, p. 4; *The Citizen* (Adrian), 7 July and 29 September 1892, both p. 1.

49. *Worthington Globe*, 2 and 23 April 1891, both p. 1; *Adrian Guardian*, 3 April 1891, p. 4. The *Guardian* was strongly anti-Alliance; see *Adrian Guardian*, 3 October 1890, p. 1.

50. *Great West*, 28 February 1890, p. 6, 28 March 1890, p. 2, and 10 October 1890, p. 4.

51. Rose, *History of Yellow Medicine County*, 135–36, 139, 207–9. Earlier, in 1878–79, voters in Yellow Medicine County approved a proposal to create the new county of Canby out of western Yellow Medicine, southwestern Lac qui Parle, and northern Lincoln Counties; Upham, *Minnesota Geographic Names*, 593.

52. *Reform Advocate*, 22 April 1897, p. 1; *Granite Falls Journal*, 18 June 1891, p. 1. The Reform Publishing Association began the Alliance paper, the *Reform Advocate*, in spring 1892.

53. *Sleepy Eye Herald*, 20 September and 4 October 1890, p. 1. See also *New Ulm Weekly Review*, 3 December 1890, p. 5.

54. LHFA Journal, p. 11, 22; *Sleepy Eye Herald*, 29 November and 6 and 13 December 1890, all p. 4, and 15 November and 13 December 1890, both p. 1. The *Herald* consistently supported the Farmers' Alliance after it was organized in Brown County in 1890; see, for example, *Sleepy Eye Herald*, 21 June 1890, p. 1.

55. Parsons described rural resentment over county-seat "cliques" who dominated Nebraska politics; *Populist Context*, 57–59.

56. James Turner suggested that "geographic isolation from towns and villages" was an important factor in some farmers becoming Populists: "isolation breeds a political culture at odds with the mainstream of political habits and attitudes"; Turner, "Understanding the Populists," 358, 372.

57. McMath, *American Populism*, 84–86, 94–95.

58. Goodwyn, *Democratic Promise*, 259–60.

59. *Great West*, 18 October 1889, p. 5, 15 November 1889, p. 4, and 10 January 1890, p. 4. Far from being blind to the economic advantages of Alliance organizing, Donnelly stressed the importance of the price savings achieved by the Dakota company.

60. *Great West*, 18 October 1889, p. 5, 15 November 1889, p. 4, 10 January 1890, p. 4, and 21 March 1890, p. 8.

61. *Great West*, 14 February and 2 May 1890, both p. 4. The writer of the appeal to westerners used the term "Grangers" to describe Alliance members; granger was also a general word for a farmer.

62. *Great West*, 2 May 1890, p. 4, 8.

63. *Great West*, 30 May 1890, p. 1.

64. *Great West*, 2 May and 6 June 1890, both p. 8.

65. *Great West*, 19 December 1890 and 16 January 1891, both p. 4. As in the Grange with J. S. Denman, so in the Alliance with Henry Loucks—the purchasing agent was roundly criticized, but the *Great West* strongly defended him; *Great West*, 31 October 1890 and 16 January 1891, both p. 4.

66. After the governor's investigating committee returned from the East and recommended against the idea, Alliance leaders appointed their own committee, which recommended in favor. Governor William R. Merriam then sent another committee (including two Alliance leaders) east, and that committee returned with a favorable report. *Great West*, 14 March 1890, p. 8, 30 May 1890, p. 1, and 13 June 1890, p. 5; *Madelia Times*, 5 August 1892, p. 1.

67. *Great West*, 13 June 1890, p. 5.

68. See, for example, *Waseca County Herald*, 31 December 1886, p. 2.

69. BGL Minutes, p. 18, 21–23, 28–30, 32, 33, 43, 45. On pages 140–41 of the Minutes is a list of members with an amount opposite each name. This is a list "of those that have Rec'd there amt. of Alliance Profits to Jan. 1, 1887." It is uncertain just what is meant here by "Alliance Profits," although the date would indicate some connection to the joint wheat-marketing deal. Warsaw was located three miles northeast of Morristown; apparently Bean Brothers, whose central office was in Faribault, had warehouses in both towns. *Plat Book of Rice County* (N.p.: Northwest Publishing Co., 1900), 9–10.

70. BGL Minutes, p. 59, 63, 64, 65.

71. On April 5, 1887, the committee was authorized to bring the list to the wheat buyer in town and to "make a Settlement," but the chairman reported "that the Wheat [buyer] wanted every member to come and Settle for Himself'"; BGL Minutes, p. 54, 56.

72. When the Washington suballiance let buyers pay individual farmers, buyers "lent themselves ... as tools to Bankers & others for forcing collections on farmers" by deducting debt payments from grain sales proceeds; WFA Minute Book, 5 November 1887.

73. BGL Minutes, p. 46–47, 49, 50–51, 52, 53–55. From April 1888 to June 1891, it chose no wheat committees, due either to that project being under way or dissatisfaction with committees or both; Minutes, p. 72–91.

74. *Great West*, 31 January 1890, p. 8.

75. The Lisbon suballiance negotiated with private flour mills but also voted to discuss "joining in with other alliances" and "purchasing [the] Farmer warehouse of the Clarkfield Produce company at that place and make it into an alliance warehouse"; LTFA Minutes, 7 February 1891. While organizing a stock company to build a warehouse, the Washington suballiance set up a temporary three-man grain marketing committee; WFA Minute Book, 13 and 20 August, 3, 17, and 24 September, 1 and 22 October, all 1887.

76. BGL Minutes, p. 17, 19, 23, 55, 73, 74–75, 77, 78, 89. At its first official meeting in July 1890, the Lake Hanska suballiance selected two men "for the specific purpose of bar-gaining with Dealers in Twine to supply members of this Alliance"; LHFA Journal, p. 8.

77. WFA Minute Book, 27 April 1889; LHFA Journal, p. 9.

78. BGL Minutes, p. 69.

79. LTFA Minutes, 3 May and 14 June 1890.

80. LHFA Journal, p. 9, 10.

81. WFA Minute Book, 30 March and 13 and 27 April 1889.

82. *Waseca Radical*, 30 June 1886, p. 1; *Waseca County Herald*, 2 July 1886, p. 3; BGL Minutes, p. 23, 24.

83. *New Ulm Weekly Review*, 9 July 1890, p. 5; *Madelia Times*, 11 July 1890, p. 1.

84. LHFA Journal, p. 10. The Austin dealer's price was for twine "on board cars at Chicago." See also BGL Minutes, 8 July 1887; LTFA Minutes, 20 June 1891.

85. LHFA Journal, p. 10.

86. For a suballiance's resolution on forming a cooperative store, see *Great West*, 27 June 1890, p. 8.

87. *Great West*, 31 January 1890, p. 8.

88. *Sleepy Eye Herald*, 6 February 1891, p. 4.

89. LTFA Minutes, 8 and 29 March 1890.

90. *Granite Falls Tribune*, 15 April 1890, p. 1; *Canby News*, 25 April 1890, p. 1. The *Tribune* editor titled Tredway's letter, "Good Advice." Earlier, in its 11 January 1890 issue, the *Springfield Advance* made the same argument. See also *Sleepy Eye Herald*, 25 January 1890, p. 4.

91. *Granite Falls Tribune*, 3 and 17 June 1890, both p. 1. For another Alliance-merchant conflict over this collection agency, see *Great West*, 7 March 1890, p. 1.

92. *Canby News*, 13 June 1890, p. 1.

93. *Great West*, 23 May 1890, p. 4.

94. *Canby News*, 2 May 1890, p. 1.

95. *Granite Falls Tribune*, 10 March 1891, p. 1.

96. LTFA Minutes, 7 February 1891.

97. WFA Minute Book, 2 February 1889; Moorhead Farmers' Alliance No. 148, Minutes, p. 4, 6, 14, Clay County Historical Society, Moorhead.

98. *Granite Falls Tribune*, 17 June 1890, p. 1.

99. LTFA Minutes, 14 June, 5 July, and 13 December 1890.

100. *Great West*, 18 October 1889, p. 5.

101. LHFA Journal, p. 15–19; Forhandlings-Protokol (hereafter Protokol) for Hanska-

Linden Handelsforening (hereafter HLHF), p. 1–5, in Hanska-Linden Handeslforening Records (hereafter HLHF Records), BCHS.

102. Turner, "Understanding the Populists," 358, 372.

Notes to Chapter 8

1. *Battle Lake Review*, 5, 12, and 19 December 1889, all p. 1; *Fergus Falls Weekly Journal*, 12 December 1889, p. 4. The Minneapolis firm was the Farmers' Grocery Company.

2. John W. Mason, ed., *History of Otter Tail County, Minnesota* (Indianapolis: B. F. Bowen, 1916), 1:239. For merchants in pre- and postrailroad eras, see Cronon, *Nature's Metropolis*, 318–33.

3. *Battle Lake Review*, 5 and 19 December 1889, both p. 1. The editorial quoted was from the *Perham Bulletin*.

4. *Fergus Falls Ugeblad*, 11 December 1889, p. 5. The editor sounded cautious about editorializing on this controversial subject, and his editorial opened the floodgates for a stream of letters to the editor. For his position on the Alliance, see Soike, *Politics of Dissent*, 102–4, 107, 109. In the mid-1890s, Alliancemen began to discuss founding an Alliance newspaper, and Henning's *Alliance Advocate* started in March 1891. Hans Nelson to Brandborg, 22 August 1890, Frank Hoskins to Brandborg, 17 December 1890, John B. Hompe? to Brandborg, 27 January 1891, all in Brandborg Papers; *Alliance Advocate*, 12 March 1891, p. 1; Mason, ed., *History of Otter Tail County*, 1:342. For the Ugeblad's history, see Mason, 1:333.

5. *Fergus Falls Ugeblad*, 18 December 1889, 8 and 22 January 1890, all p. 4.

6. *Fergus Falls Ugeblad*, 18 December 1889, p. 4.

7. Cronon, *Nature's Metropolis*, 83–90, 92; Chandler, *Visible Hand*, 125–26, 134, 215–24; Paul Kleppner et al., *The Evolution of American Electoral Systems* (Westport, Conn.: Greenwood Press, 1981), 152–53.

8. *Fergus Falls Ugeblad*, 29 January 1890, p. 5.

9. *Fergus Falls Ugeblad*, 11 December 1889, and 8 January 1890, both p. 5, and 5 and 12 February 1890, both p. 4.

10. *Fergus Falls Ugeblad*, 29 January 1890, p. 5. The reference to cancelled subscriptions came in a letter from "S. B." of Stony Brook Township printed in *Fergus Falls Ugeblad*, 19 February 1890, p. 4. The debate was not noticeably bitter, except for several anti-Semitic notes. "S. B." used the term "Jew-price" ("Jødepris"), and G. T. Hagen wrote, "it must be the most depraved Jew who now demands the kind of prices which our merchants demanded in pioneer days"; see *Fergus Falls Ugeblad*, 5 and 19 February 1890, both p. 4.

11. *Canby News*, 24 September 1886, p. 3.

12. Boorstin, *Democratic Experience*, 108.

13. *Fergus Falls Ugeblad*, 8 January 1890, p. 5, 8. Not all farmers took this view. One writer ("H") from Tordenskjold (south of Underwood) agreed that ordering goods from the Twin Cities was unwise, for only local merchants took farmers' produce. See *Fergus Falls Ugeblad*, 25 December 1889, p. 4.

14. Minute Book, 1891–1908, September 1891 meeting, Farmers Mercantile Corporation Collection (hereafter FMC Collection), Otter Tail County Historical Society (OTCHS), Fergus Falls. Bjørge served in the legislature in 1885–87 and in 1891–93. For the Alliance in Otter Tail County, see Soike, *Politics of Dissent*, 84–115. For an account of Bjørge's career, see *Fergus Falls Ugeblad*, 30 September 1908, p. 1. For Bjørge and Pederson's role in the Alliance, see *Fergus Falls Ugeblad*, 5 February 1890, p. 5. In this issue, the editor remarked: "We noticed with amazement that by far the greatest number present were Scandinavians. There were only a few Americans and, as far as we could see, no Germans." Another evidence of an Alliance link is the FMC board's decision to order twine from the Minnesota State Prison and "to receive orders from Alliances and individuals" for twine; Minute Book, 1891–1908, 3 April 1894 meeting, FMC Collection. Bjørge and Pederson were directors of the Sverdrup mutual; see SSMIC Protokol, p. 5, and *Fergus Falls Ugeblad*, 22 January 1890, p. 4.

15. Also in 1891, men at an Alliance meeting talked of "a Farmer Store" in nearby Dalton and called an organizational meeting; *Fergus Falls Ugeblad*, 11 March 1891, p. 5. Local suballiances' minutes have not been preserved. No newspaper accounts link them directly to the Farmers' Store—only conjecture and circumstantial evidence.

16. *Alliance Advocate*, 23 July 1891, p. 5. Bjørge played no role in the FMC. For the name "Farmer's Store" and for some excellent photos of the FMC, see Underwood History Book Committee, *Underwood Centennial, 1881–1981* (Battle Lake: Battle Lake Review, 1981), 24, 26. The Bjørge and Sjordal store was the local Alliance agent for binding twine.

17. Other Unitarians were Peder Jensen (president of Tordenskjold suballiance), Otto Nilsby (first FMC vice-president), and John O. Kolstad (Sverdrup suballiance treasurer). For the members of the Unitarian church, see Referat-Protokol, vol. 4, p. 3, Unitarian Church of Underwood Records. For Alliance and FMC posts held by them, see *Fergus Falls Ugeblad*, 26 February 1890, p. 4; and Minute Book, 1891–1908, September 1891 and 16 January 1892 meetings, FMC Collection. For Kristofer Janson's role, see Draxten, *Janson in America*, 224–25.

18. For the Lutheran activities of Bjørnaas and Pederson, see Mason, ed., *History of Otter Tail County*, 1:398; *Underwood Centennial*, 16–18.

19. *Fergus Falls Ugeblad*, 1 October 1890, p. 5. Janson also spoke at the Otter Tail County courthouse on behalf of the Alliance during the 1890 campaign; *Fergus Falls Ugeblad*, 5 November 1890, p. 5.

20. In his speech, Janson referred to the Lutheran pastor as "Brother Haugan." Pastor Haugan responded with a letter to the *Ugeblad* denying any kinship, but the editor refused to print it for fear that "it will give occasion for more scribbling on that issue and we don't want any such thing"; *Fergus Falls Ugeblad*, 8 October 1890, p. 5.

21. For example, Unitarian Otto Nilsby took the initiative in organizing a society of common-school teachers in Otter Tail County in 1889; *Fergus Falls Ugeblad*, 4 December 1889, p. 4.

22. Chr. Sørgaard of Tordenskjold described Unitarianism as "the devilish doctrine," which had, "according to what we understand, captured more unstable souls than people think." Responding to the start of Underwood's Unitarian church, Pastor Fosmark gave a series of lectures in Tordenskjold and around Otter Tail County on Christ's divinity; see *Fergus Falls Ugeblad*, 8 January 1890, p. 8, and 15 January 1890, p. 2.

23. Minute Book, 1891–1908, 17 and 26 October 1891 meetings, FMC Collection; *Underwood Centennial*, 24.

24. Minnesota, *General Statutes*, 1894, chapter 34, sections 2903–12. The law on cooperative associations was one section of chapter 34 (Corporations).

25. C[harles] R[ussell] Hoffer. "Co-operation as a Culture Pattern within a Community," *Rural Sociology* 3 (June 1938): 153–58 (quote p. 157).

26. For the debates, see *Sleepy Eye Herald*, 25 January 1890 and 6 February 1891, both p. 4. For joint purchasing by the Lake Hanska suballiance, see LHFA Journal, p. 8, 9, 10, 13, 15, 16, 17; and *Sleepy Eye Herald*, 13 March 1891, p. 1. For early life in Linden, see *Nordisk Folkeblad*, 26 May 1869, p. 2.

27. LHFA Journal, p. 15, 16, 17, 18, 19; *Sleepy Eye Herald*, 13 February 1891, p. 1. During the winter of 1890–91, the Linden suballiance also "investigate[d] the feasibility of building and starting a creamery," but these talks failed, too; see "Linden" column in *Sleepy Eye Herald*, 10 January, 30 January, and 20 March 1891, all p. 1.

28. Ahlness, "Recollections," 236–37; Lake Hanska Lutheran Church, Protokol, Book 1, p. 74–77, 80, 81.

29. Chambard, notes on Hanska; *Madelia Times*, 18 March 1892, p. 1. According to Chambard, Nora leaders Anton Ouren and Johannes Moe were prominent in forming the creamery, and Ole Jorgensen was present at some organizational meetings. See also Nora Free Christian Church, *Seventy-fifth Anniversary*, 3–7; *1881–1906, Nora Frikristne Menighed*, 21–22, 31; Draxten, *Janson in America*, 56–57, 67–69, 71–72, 96–100, 138–39.

30. According to one unconfirmed report, Anton Ouren "guaranteed" all the store's "bills the first four years of its existence, and they from the beginning discounted all bills"; see L. A. Fritsche, ed., *History of Brown County, Minnesota* (Indianapolis: B. F. Bowen & Co., 1916), 2:486.

31. *Madelia Times*, 14 April 1892, p. 1.

32. Ahlness, "Recollections," 285–88. Ahlness exaggerated his role in both the creamery and the store. He claimed to have presided at the store's first organizational meeting, but the minutes show that Johannes Moe presided. See Protokol, p. 1, 3, HLHF Records.

33. In nearby Albin Township (Brown County), farmers rejected a company's offer to build a store at their creamery site, the future crossroads community of Godahl in Watonwan County. Instead in 1894 they started the Nelson and Albin Cooperative Mercantile Association Store, which in 1999 was the state's oldest continuously operating cooperative store. See *Sleepy Eye Herald*, 3 April 1891, p. 1; *History of Watonwan County, Minnesota* (Dallas: Curtis Media, 1995), 80–81.

34. Protokol, p. 1, HLHF Records.

35. *Madelia Times*, 27 January 1893, p. 4.

36. Ole Synsteby, *Interesting Tales of Pioneer Days in Lake Hanska and Vicinity* ([Lake Hanska?, 1942?]), 30–31.

37. Hetherington, *Mutual and Cooperative Enterprises*, 124–25.

38. *Underwood Centennial*, 24 (quote).

39. *Articles of Incorporation and Bylaws of the Farmers Mercantile Corporation* (4 February 1892), p. 4, booklet in FMC Collection.

40. Journal No. 2 (7 March 1893–28 November 1894), p. 51, 327, FMC Collection.

41. Protokol, p. 1, 3, and Record of Proceedings of the Board of Directors (Minute Book B, 1900–1917; hereafter Proceedings), p. 3–13, both HLHF Records; *Articles of Incorporation*, p. 1–5, Constitution for Underwood Handelsforening, manuscript (originally in Minute Book, 1891–1908), and Minute Book, 1891–1908, 17 October 1891 meeting—all in FMC Collection.

42. Proceedings, p. 8, HLHF Records. In another section, grain *(kornvarer)* was excluded, but vegetables *(grønvarer)* were not.

43. Proceedings, p. 7, HLHF Records.

44. Constitution, Article 4, FMC Collection.

45. Minute Book, 1891–1908, 3 October 1904 board meeting, 19 May 1906 special shareholders meeting, 14 January 1907 annual meeting, and 13 January 1908 annual meeting—all in FMC Collection. For a list of incorporators of the Underwood Co-operative Creamery Company, which included many FMC shareholders, see *Fergus Falls Daily Journal*, 29 April 1908, p. 2.

46. A cooperative "carries out functions delegated by its members," the main one being "to augment members' gains in the primary activity from which their patronage comes." Farmers' stores increased members' savings "in the primary activity" (consump-

tion) but performed other delegated functions; Heflebower, *Cooperatives and Mutuals*, 15.

47. The HLHF limited the outstanding balance to the amount of capital that the customer-member had invested in the store. Protokol, p. 1, and Proceedings, p. 8, HLHF Records.

48. Constitution, paragraph 9, and *Articles of Incorporation*, bylaw 17, FMC Collection.

49. Minute Book, 1891–1908, 14 January 1901, 2 December 1901, 4 October 1902, October 1903, 2 October 1905, and 2 October 1906 board meetings, FMC Collection.

50. Minute Book, 1891–1908, 1 October 1892, 4 October 1902, October 1903, 27 October 1904, and 2 October 1906 board meetings and 13 January 1902 annual meeting, FMC Collection.

51. Minute Book, 1891–1908, 2 May and 2 July 1892 board meetings, FMC Collection.

52. Minute Book, 1891–1908, 1 October 1892 board meeting, 9 January 1893, 14 January 1895, and 13 January 1896 annual meetings, FMC Collection.

53. Minute Book, 1891–1908, 9 January 1899 annual meeting, FMC Collection.

54. In April 1901 they attempted to forestall summer borrowing by ordering a renewed debt collection effort; Minute Book, 1891–1908, 3 July 1893, 11 June 1898, 3 April and 3 July 1899, and 8 April 1901 board meetings, FMC Collection. The cash-flow problem often lasted into October. The 2 October 1906 board minutes stated, "Book accounts were larger than at any time before." They had to collect money "to meet current expenses" so they sent out statements "with a strong request to come and pay as soon as possible."

55. Minute Book, 1891–1908, 27 July 1904 board meeting, FMC Collection.

56. Record of Proceedings, p. 27, 28, 36, 39, 50–51, 53, 63, 68, 70, 77, HLHF Records.

57. Overdue accounts were still a problem in December 1912 according to an otherwise laudatory report in *The Farmer*. In spite of delaying payment of dividends, "the store has to borrow several thousand dollars in order to carry a large amount of book accounts, somewhere about $13,000"; *The Farmer* (St. Paul), 14 December 1912, p. 1507.

58. A consumers' cooperative in Two Harbors (Lake County) also had a problem with

overdue accounts. Unlike farmers' stores, the Scandinavian Cooperative Mercantile Company's credit problems were not seasonal but were linked to members' (railroad workers) periodic unemployment. In 1896–97, layoffs "made it necessary to extend an unusual amount of credit." At another point, the auditor called the board's "attention to the excessive credit business carried on by the company"; see Scandinavian Cooperative Mercantile Company, Minute Book A (16 December 1896 to 20 November 1901), p. 17–18, 88, Lake County Historical Society, Two Harbors.

59. Stock Ledger, 1891–1919, p. 2, FMC Collection. See also, for example, p. 38, 64.

60. Minute Book, 1891–1908, 11 January 1904 annual meeting, FMC Collection.

61. Minute Book, 1891–1908, 8 January 1906 annual meeting, FMC Collection. The annual "surplus" was not inconsiderable, ranging from a low of $152.43 in 1900 to a high of $1,846.21 in 1903; see list in Minute Book.

62. For an alphabetical list of FMC shareholders, see Stock Ledger, 1891–1919, p. 108–10, FMC Collection.

63. Protokol, p. 9, 15, 21, 22, 40–46, 150–60, HLHF Records. Forgone dividends were quite high during the years 1899–1907, from 11 percent (1905) to 24 percent (1899). For a list of shareholders showing frequent change of share ownership, see p. 40–46; for net profits and dividends, p. 21, 45, 150–60.

64. Protokol, p. 5, 25, HLHF Records; Ahlness, "Recollections," 287–88.

65. Ahlness, "Recollections," 288–91, 294–95. Taken in June 1895, the state census confirms Ahlness's story, for it listed Brubaker and four young men (including the two Hanska-Linden store clerks) as boarding at Hans Blessum's place (the creamery and store lots had been purchased from Blessum and were located on his farm). See Minnesota, 1895 census schedule for Lake Hanska Township, Brown County.

66. Ahlness, "Recollections," 294–95. For the status of the two clerks, see Protokol, p. 14, 16, 17, 19, HLHF Records. The clerk-president was Ole Synsteby.

67. Protokol, p. 18, 19, HLHF Records. A notice appeared in March 1899 that "The Hanska & Linden store . . . does not invite loafing by furnishing free tobacco"; see *Madelia Times*, 10 March 1899, p. 5. The 15 March 1897 board meeting passed a resolution stating "that the company not permit free tobacco smoking, and that it be forbidden in the strongest terms to smoke in the Clothing Department."

68. See, for example, Protokol, p. 19, 21, 23, 27, 35–36, HLHF Records; Minute Book, 1891–1908, 6 April 1893, 3 April 1899, and 3 April 1900 board meetings, FMC Collection. The first FMC annual meeting resolved "that the hiring of help in the store be placed in the hands of the board of directors"; Minute Book, 1891–1908, 16 January 1892 meeting, FMC Collection.

69. Proceedings, p. 50–51, HLHF Records.

70. Christian Ahlness reported a faction within the Hanska-Linden creamery association that was opposed to having his son-in-law as buttermaker. They took control of the board at the 1905 annual meeting and fired him, but a pro-Ahlness faction regained control in 1906. Ahlness, "Recollections," 319–20; *Hanska Herald*, 6 January 1905, p. 4.

71. Protokol, p. 34–36, HLHF Records; Minute Book, 1891–1908, 3 April 1899 and 3 April 1900 board meetings, FMC Collection. In 1903, however, the HLHF board hired a male to replace Miss Ahlness (who had resigned), even though two women had applied for her position; Protokol, p. 51–52, HLHF Records.

72. The three were Ole Midtbruget, Ole Synsteby, and Ole Sundt. R. L. Polk & Co., *1901 Brown County Directory*, 195–97; *Madelia Times*, 29 September 1899, p. 4. Midtbruget and Sundt were teenagers when they worked at HLHF in 1895; see Minnesota, 1895 census schedule for Lake Hanska Township, Brown County.

73. Minute Book, 1891–1908, 10 October 1891 (held in Sivertson's store), 17 October 1891, 26 October 1891, 16 January 1892, 9 January 1893, 8 January 1894, 14 January 1895, 13 January 1896, 10 January 1898, and 9 January 1899 meetings, FMC Collection. The manager's monthly salary increased from fifteen dollars in 1891 to fifty dollars in 1900 (plus ten dollars in monthly rent); Minute Book, 1891–1908, 26 October 1891 board meeting and 14 January 1895, 13 January 1896,

and 8 January 1900 annual meetings, FMC Collection.

74. Minute Book, 1891–1908, 9 January 1899 annual meeting and board of directors' meeting, FMC Collection.

75. Minute Book, 1891–1908, 3 April 1899 board meeting, FMC Collection.

76. Minute Book, 1891–1908, 9 January 1899 and 8 January 1900 annual meetings, 7 February 1900 special shareholders meeting, and 12 February 1900 board meeting, FMC Collection.

77. Minute Book, 1891–1908, 14 February 1900 board meeting, FMC Collection.

78. Minute Book, 1891–1908, 14 January 1901 annual meeting and 14 and 16 January 1901 board meetings, FMC Collection; *Fergus Falls Ugeblad*, 24 January 1901, p. 4.

79. Minute Book, 1891–1908, 11 May 1901 special shareholders meeting, FMC Collection.

80. Minute Book, 1891–1908, 11 May 1901 special shareholders meeting, 20 May 1901 committee meeting, and 27 May 1901 board meeting, FMC Collection. Perhaps illness weakened the forty-five-year-old Sivertson's position by eliminating any credible threat that he could run the store himself to compete with them. For Sivertson's age, see U.S., 1900 manuscript census schedule, Sverdrup Township, Otter Tail County, Minnesota, microfilm, MHS. Sivertson financed thirteen hundred dollars of the purchase amount.

81. For cooperatives' difficulties in hiring and keeping highly skilled managers, see Hetherington, *Mutual and Cooperative Enterprises*, 125–26.

82. Minute Book, 1891–1908, 14 January 1901 annual meeting, FMC Collection; *Fergus Falls Ugeblad*, 24 January 1901, p. 4. Despite the disagreement, three of five board members were reelected. The two changes resulted from Sivertson's resignation and a director's death. See Minute Book, 1891–1908, and Stock Ledger, 1891–1919, for the surplus earned for the years 1891–1906. The earlier efforts were to decrease the cost of a share from twenty-five dollars to five dollars and to pay a patronage dividend. See Minute Book, 1891–1908, 10 January 1898, 9 January 1899, and 8 January 1900 annual meetings.

83. Minute Book, 1891–1908, 9 January 1899 annual meeting, FMC Collection. The FMC displayed a strong record of stability in its board of directors; the membership was remarkably constant from year to year.

84. The source for Table 4 is Protokol, p. 9, 18, 31, 43, HLHF Records. Yearly reelection of incumbents on unanimous ballots was not the pattern at the HLHF; its annual meetings always saw numerous candidates and a numerical count of ballots cast.

85. "On motion the President read off the amounts traded for during the year by each shareholder"; Protokol, p. 43, HLHF Records.

86. Minute Book, 1891–1908, 7 February 1900 special shareholders meeting, FMC Collection.

87. Minute Book, 1891–1908, 14 February 1903 special shareholders meeting, FMC Collection. The minutes do not state whether these trial ballots were taken by standing count or by written ballot, although the latter seems more likely.

88. For the role of railroads in creating the network of towns in North Dakota, see John C. Hudson, *Plains Country Towns* (Minneapolis: University of Minnesota Press, 1985).

89. Ahlness, "Recollections," 302–3.

90. *Madelia Times*, 27 January 1899, p. 5, and 3 February 1899, p. 1.

91. *St. James Journal*, 10 March 1899, p. 4, reprinting a report from the *Minneapolis Journal*, 6 March 1899, p. 6.

92. *Madelia Times*, 7 April 1899, p. 5.

93. *St. James Journal*, 21 April 1899, p. 4. For the complete story of the bidding war among St. James, Madelia, and other towns, see *New Ulm Review*, 8 February 1899, p. 1; *Madelia Times*, 10 March 1899, p. 5, and 17 March 1899, p. 1; *St. James Journal*, 10 and 31 March and 21 April 1899, all p. 4.

94. *Madelia Times*, 21 April 1899, p. 5, and 5 May 1899, p. 1 (a reprint of an article from the *New Ulm News*, 29 April 1899, p. 4).

95. Plat of Blessum, 7 June 1898, Brown County Recorder's Office, New Ulm. In October 1893, Blessum sold two small plots to the creamery and the store. The deeds specified that if the creamery stopped making butter or cheese or the store "discontinue[d] its business of selling general mer-

chandise at retail" then "the land hereby conveyed shall at once revert to the owner of the fee." Abstract of title, W ½ of NE ¼ of Section 24, Lake Hanska Township, Brown County Recorder's Office.

96. *New Ulm Review,* 2 August 1899, p. 1; plat of Hanska, 10 October 1899, Brown County Recorder's Office. The townsite was platted by Harry L. and Anna L. Jenkins, who were apparently associated with the M&SL.

97. *New Ulm Review,* 2 August 1899, p. 1; abstract of title, W ½ of NE ¼ of Section 24, Lake Hanska Township; *Madelia Times,* 11 August 1899, p. 5. The townsite company agent, H. A. Outcalt, said "the town site cost about $6,500" and that, by late December 1899, "they ha[d] already sold that many dollars' worth of lots." The company platted other townsites along the railroad route; *Madelia Times,* 29 December 1899, p. 8 (reprint of article from the *Brown County Journal;* obNew Ulm], 23 December 1899, p. 5).

98. *Madelia Times,* 11 and 18 August 1899, both p. 5.

99. Ahlness, "Recollections," 311–12.

100. *Madelia Times,* 17 November 1899, p. 5.

101. Protokol, p. 34–35, HLHF Records.

102. *Brown County Journal,* 3 February 1900, p. 8; *New Ulm Review,* 7 February 1900, p. 8.

103. *New Ulm Review,* 14 February 1900, p. 8.

104. The 1901 directory lists Martin B. Erickson as the postmaster; he had been employed by the Hanska-Linden Store as a clerk. See R. L. Polk & Co., *1901 Brown County Directory,* 195–96; Protokol, p. 21, 23, 27, HLHF Records.

105. *Madelia Times,* 29 September 1899, p. 4, 27 October 1899, p. 5, and 5 January 1900, p. 4.

106. *Madelia Times,* 5 January 1900, p. 4.

107. R. L. Polk & Co., *New Ulm City and Brown County Directory, 1911–12* (St. Paul, 1911), 202; *1901 Brown County Directory,* 198.

108. Stores were prohibited within three miles of Norwegian market towns until 1874 and one-and-a-half miles of many Danish ones til 1920. Flemming Just, *Brugsforen-*

ingsbevægelsen, 1866–1920: med udgangspunkt i Ribe amt (Esbjerg, Denmark: Sydjysk universitetsforlag, 1984), 12–13, 46; Inge Debes, *Forbruker kooperasjonens,* 2 vols. (Oslo: Norges kooperative landsforening, 1925, 1931), 1:254, 2:122, 153.

109. Debes, *Forbruker kooperasjonens,* 2:113.

110. Just, *Brugsforeningsbevægelsen,* 12–19, 46–47. Just did not specify lack of private capital as a reason merchants did not fill the need for new stores; however, he mentioned that this was a capital-hungry region (p. 15).

111. For an excellent discussion of crossroads communities, see Vernon E. Bergstrom and Marilyn McGriff, *Isanti County, Minnesota, 1985: An Illustrated History* (Braham, 1985), 77–96. I am much indebted to McGriff's emphasis on crossroads communities, an emphasis I first encountered here.

112. "If the market is growing, actual entry [of new stores, in this case] need not affect prices for, were entry to occur, the established sellers could then expand less or not at all"; Heflebower, *Cooperatives and Mutuals,* 29.

113. For the move to administrative coordination in retailing and wholesaling, see Chandler, *Visible Hand,* 209–39.

114. *Fergus Falls Ugeblad,* 11 and 25 December 1889, both p. 5.

115. *Fergus Falls Ugeblad,* 2 September 1891, p. 5. The Bee Hive had bought many items from the bankrupt Soule Brothers store.

Notes to Chapter 9

1. *Cottonwood County Citizen* (Windom), 9 December 1899, p. 1.

2. The relationships between elevators and railroads are analyzed in depth in Hudson, *Plains Country Towns,* 54–69. "Vesta railway village was platted in 1899"; Upham, *Minnesota Geographic Names,* 452.

3. Hudson, *Plains Country Towns,* 60, 62, 64; Thomas W. Harvey, "The Making of Railroad Towns in Minnesota's Red River Valley" (master's thesis, Pennsylvania State University, 1982), 172.

4. Larson, *Wheat Market,* 148–51, 157.

5. Larson, *Wheat Market,* 140–44, 174, 235–37; Cronon, *Nature's Metropolis,* 116–26; Broehl, *Cargill,* 39, 59–60, 75, 96–97. Larson

(p. 139) defined a "line" as "a group of country elevators ... under one central management." For a description of the Millers' Association pool and its profit margins, see *Moorhead Weekly News,* 16 September 1886, p. 5.

6. Kenkel, *Cooperative Elevator Movement,* 3.

7. *Minneapolis Journal,* 17 April 1888, p. 1; Larson, *Wheat Market,* 216.

8. *Great West,* 25 October 1889, p. 5. For analyses of farmers' attitudes toward and attempts to organize terminal markets, see Theodore Saloutos, "The Spring-Wheat Farmer in a Maturing Economy, 1870–1920," *Journal of Economic History* 6 (November 1946): 184–89; Saloutos, "The Rise of the Equity Cooperative Exchange," *Mississippi Valley Historical Review* 32 (June 1945): 31–40; Saloutos, "The Decline of the Equity Cooperative Exchange," *Mississippi Valley Historical Review* 34 (December 1947): 405–26; Theodore Saloutos and John D. Hicks, *Twentieth-Century Populism: Agricultural Discontent in the Middle West, 1900–1939* (Lincoln: University of Nebraska Press, 1951), 132–34.

9. See *Fergus Falls Ugeblad,* 14 October 1891, p. 4, for Eric Olson's accusation that Charles A. Pillsbury traveled to England to "break up" a deal between the syndicate and English millers.

10. *Great West,* 2 May 1890, p. 8.

11. *Great West,* 25 October 1889, p. 5.

12. *Great West,* 16 May 1890, p. 1; Larson, *Wheat Market,* 216–17.

13. Larson, *Wheat Market,* 218.

14. *Great West,* 25 October 1889, p. 5, and 12 September 1890, p. 7.

15. *Fergus Falls Ugeblad,* 23 September 1891, p. 5, and 14 October 1891, p. 4; Larson, *Wheat Market,* 217.

16. Larson, *Wheat Market,* 217–18; *Fergus Falls Ugeblad,* 23 September 1891, p. 5, and 14 October 1891, p. 4; R. J. Hall to Brandborg, 26 August 1891, Charles Canning to Brandborg, 7 January 1892, Brandborg Papers. The reputations of MGGA's founders and Eric Olson's letter (*Ugeblad,* 14 October 1891) indicate that Larson was incorrect in describing the MGGA as the more "conservative" of the two—unless she meant that it proceeded more slowly in building up its business.

17. *Fergus Falls Ugeblad,* 14 October 1891, p. 4. According to Larson, terminal cooperatives lacked capital, faced private traders' "hostility," and had an inadequate supply of grain because there were too few farmers' elevators before 1900; Larson, *Wheat Market,* 218.

18. At St. James (Watonwan County), farmers organized a farmers' warehouse after a rousing speech by Dr. Everett W. Fish, the editor of the *Great West.* In Grant County, directors of the Herman farmers' elevator were elected at the county Alliance meeting. State Alliance leader Theodore H. Barrett was one director. *St. James Journal,* 3 and 17 May 1890, both p. 1; *Grant County Herald* (Elbow Lake), 31 October 1889, p. 3, and 29 May 1890, p. 4.

19. *Sleepy Eye Herald,* 19 February 1892, p. 4.

20. *Sleepy Eye Herald,* 19 February 1892, p. 4.

21. *Waseca County Herald,* 2 and 23 September 1887, both p. 2.

22. *Waseca County Herald,* 2 September 1887, p. 2; *Minneapolis Directory, 1887–88,* 1022, *1888–89,* 1414.

23. *Waseca County Herald,* 26 August and 2 September, both 1887, both p. 2; *Waseca Radical,* 31 August 1887, p. 1.

24. *Waseca Radical,* 31 August 1887, p. 1.

25. *Waseca County Herald,* 16 September 1887, p. 3; "Annual Report of the Railroad and Warehouse Commission of Minnesota," pt. 1, p. 85–86, in Minnesota, *Executive Documents of the State of Minnesota for 1887,* vol. 1.

26. See, for example, *Cokato Observer,* 5 and 12 September 1889, both p. 4; *American Co-operative Journal* (Chicago), January 1908, p. 173, February 1908, p. 217. For the problems of evaluating farmers' complaints, see *Willmar Tribune,* 9 and 30 October, both p. 4, and 16 October, p. 1, all 1907. For a good account of how an editor led a drive to start a farmers' elevator in Chokio in 1897, see Mary Logue, *Halfway Home: A Granddaughter's Biography* (St. Paul: Minnesota Historical Society Press, Midwest Reflections, 1996), 42–44.

27. *McIntosh Times,* 16 February 1892, p. 8, and 21 June 1892, p. 1; *The News* (McIntosh), 3 and 17 February and 25 May, all 1892, all p. 1. The *Times* editor apparently led an

earlier effort to build a farmers' warehouse. The *News* editor disparaged his efforts; see *The News*, 17 February 1892, p. 1. Attorney M. A. Brattland of McIntosh served as secretary of the new farmers' elevator company.

28. Broehl, *Cargill*, 126–27. This controversy occurred in January 1908.

29. *Cottonwood County Citizen*, 19 and 26 August 1905, both p. 1; *The Centennial History of Cottonwood County, Minnesota* ([Windom]: Cottonwood County Historical Society, 1970), 559–61. For other examples of merchant-farmer cooperation, see *American Co-operative Journal*, January 1908, p. 173; *Grant County Herald*, 31 October 1889, p. 1; *American Co-operative Journal*, August 1908, p. 299.

30. *Glenwood Herald*, 6 October 1905, p. 8.

31. The commissioner asserted, "Railway companies should have no identity of interests with the elevators," but they did; see "Annual Report of the Railroad and Warehouse Commission of Minnesota," 35, in Minnesota, *Executive Documents of the State of Minnesota for the Year 1882*, vol. 3. See also Larson, *Wheat Market*, 88–89.

32. Henry Feig, a warehouse inspector for the state, made this very point: "All other commodities are handled by railroads directly from the shipper. Only in grain is there a complete departure from this rule"; *American Co-operative Journal*, June 1908, p. 211.

33. A. B. Robbins to James J. Hill, 31 October 1893, Hill to Robbins, 1 November 1893, file 2321, Subject Files, President's Office, Great Northern Railway Company Records, MHS; A. D. Thomson to John J. Toomey, 9 and 12 October 1909, Toomey to Thomson, 11 October 1909, all in General Correspondence, James Jerome Hill Papers, James J. Hill Group (formerly the James H. Hill Reference Library), St. Paul.

34. *American Co-operative Journal*, January 1907, p. 25.

35. Telegram, Merriam to Brandborg, 11 October 1889, Brandborg Papers. For other cases of railroads allegedly denying cars to independents or cooperatives, see *Fergus Falls Ugeblad*, 16 November 1887, p. 5; "Annual Report of the Railroad and Warehouse Commission of Minnesota," p. 548, in Minnesota, *Executive Documents of the State of*

Minnesota for the Year 1884, vol. 2; "Complaint of S. L. Chapin," 3 October 1905, in Correspondence, Supervising Inspector of County Elevators, 1902–1907, Miscellaneous correspondence and reports, 1888–1915, Railroad and Warehouse Commission Records, Minnesota State Archives.

36. *Grant County Herald*, 31 October 1889, p. 1. See also *Grant County Herald*, 22 May 1890, p. 1.

37. *Grant County Herald*, 31 October 1889, p. 1.

38. *Grant County Herald*, 31 October 1889, p. 1. Larson reported that the GN and M&SL refused cooperatives sites or leases from 1890 to 1897. In 1906, Wylie Farmers' Elevator Company had to file suit against the GN to secure a site. Larson, *Wheat Market*, 218; *American Co-operative Journal*, June 1906, p. 23, December 1906, p. 23; *Red Lake Falls Gazette*, 31 May and 7 June 1906, both p. 1. Oscar Refsell suggested that railroads gave farmers' elevators sites only at competing points to capture freight from competing roads, but this seems to apply to Iowa and Illinois, not Minnesota; see Oscar N. Refsell, "The Farmers' Elevator Movement," *Journal of Political Economy* 22, pt. 1 (November 1914): 889–90. Of ten farmers' elevators in Minnesota in 1887, three were at competing points; "Annual Report of the Railroad and Warehouse Commission," pt. 2, p. 274–75, 300, 448–49, 497–501, in Minnesota, *Executive Documents . . . 1887*. At times, railroads set a minimum elevator capacity—thirty thousand bushels—that discriminated against farmers' elevators whose capacities were often less than twenty thousand bushels; "Annual Report of the Railroad and Warehouse Commission," p. 546–47, in Minnesota, *Executive Documents . . . 1884*, vol. 2; Larson, *Wheat Market*, 145–46, 194–95. That rule may have still applied along the GN in 1905; see *American Co-operative Journal*, October 1905, p. 14.

39. *Grant County Herald*, 31 October 1889, p. 1. Months later, farmers in Wendell and Barrett appealed to Governor Merriam, who apparently persuaded Underwood to allow them to build warehouses on the Soo Line; see *Grant County Herald*, 15 May 1890, p. 1. The GN denied a similar request by Erdahl farmers; see *Grant County Herald*, 22 May 1890, p. 4.

40. "Annual Report of the Railroad and Warehouse Commission," p. 36, in Minnesota, *Executive Documents . . . 1882*, vol. 3.

41. "Annual Report of the Railroad and Warehouse Commission," p. 546, in Minnesota, *Executive Documents . . . 1884*, vol. 2. Refsell pointed out that "frequently" there were managerial and financial interconnections between line companies and railroad companies; Refsell, "Farmers' Elevator Movement," 876–77. His analysis, however, is biased in favor of the farmers' elevator movement.

42. H. Roger Grant, *Self-Help in the 1890s Depression* (Ames: Iowa State University Press, 1983), 75–76, 78–81, 83–88, 89–95. Ironically the FG&S succeeded partly by avoiding the status of a common carrier, which would have forced it to accept all freight and to stay in operation during the winter.

43. Minnesota, *General Statutes*, 1881, chap. 124, sec. 8–9; Larson, *Wheat Market*, 145. According to Larson, private parties were reluctant to file suit against the railroads to ensure enforcement of this 1874 law.

44. Larson, *Wheat Market*, 173–76, 181–84. The two cases are (1) State of Minnesota v. Chicago, Milwaukee & St. Paul Railway Company (1887) and (2) Farwell Farmers' Warehouse Ass'n v. Minneapolis, St. Paul & Sault Ste. Marie Railway Co. (1893). See 36 *Minnesota Supreme Court Reports*, 402–5, and 55 *Minnesota Reports*, 8–13. In the first, the court left standing a rule that railroads had to run a sidetrack to elevators built off its right-of-way.

45. *St. Paul Pioneer Press*, 20 February 1891, p. 1, and 19 April 1891, p. 2; *Great West*, 24 April 1891, p. 6. The House reported to the Senate that it had passed Hompe's bill, S.F. 76, as amended, and then the Senate passed the amended bill, but Merriam refused to sign it on the grounds that the corrected *House Journal* indicated the bill had not passed that body. See *House Journal*, 1891, p. 1198–99, 1227; *Senate Journal*, 1891, p. 1051, 1052; *Minneapolis Tribune*, 24 April 1891, p. 1.

46. *Minneapolis Tribune*, 31 January 1893, p. 3.

47. *Minneapolis Tribune*, 17 February 1893, p. 2.

48. *Minneapolis Tribune*, 31 January 1893, p. 4.

49. For an early expression of that view, see Randolph M. Probstfield to Solomon G. Comstock, 5 February 1887, typescript copy, Randolph M. Probstfield Correspondence, MHS. The Alliance also opposed the bill because its passage might help Nelson win reelection; see Gieske and Keillor, *Norwegian Yankee*, 178–80.

50. *St. Paul Pioneer Press*, 1 March 1893, p. 6.

51. *St. Paul Pioneer Press*, 24 March 1893, p. 3.

52. *Minneapolis Tribune*, 9 February 1893, p. 3; *St. Paul Pioneer Press*, 9 February 1893, p. 2.

53. Republican grain inspectors allegedly eased grading standards prior to the 1898 election so that higher prices would lead farmers to vote Republican; *Minneapolis Journal*, 17 April 1899, p. 1, 2.

54. Larson, *Wheat Market*, 244–45.

55. For Cargill's unsuccessful challenge to the 1893 law and its 1895 successor, see Broehl, *Cargill*, 93–94.

56. *Glenwood Gopher-Press*, 30 November 1905, p. 2; *Glenwood Herald*, 6 October 1905, p. 8.

57. *Glenwood Gopher-Press*, 31 August and 7 September 1905, both p. 6, and 30 November 1905, p. 1–2.

58. *Glenwood Gopher-Press*, 21 September and 30 November 1905, both p. 2.

59. *Glenwood Herald*, 29 September 1905, p. 4, and 6 October 1905, p. 4, 8.

60. *Glenwood Herald*, 29 September 1905, p. 4, and 6 October 1905, p. 8.

61. *Glenwood Herald*, 25 November 1905, p. 1.

62. *Glenwood Gopher-Press*, 9 November 1905, p. 2.

63. *Glenwood Gopher-Press*, 16 November 1905, p. 1.

64. *Glenwood Herald*, 25 November 1905, p. 8; *Glenwood Gopher-Press*, 14 December 1905, p. 6. For the editorial stance of the two Glenwood papers, see *Glenwood Gopher-Press*, 12 October 1905, p. 6, and *Glenwood Herald*, 25 November 1905, p. 1.

65. *Glenwood Gopher-Press*, 30 November 1905, p. 1.

66. *Glenwood Gopher-Press*, 30 November 1905, p. 1–2; *Glenwood Herald*, 1 December

1905, p. 2; *American Co-operative Journal,*
December 1905, p. 12, January 1906, p. 18.
  67. Carl H. Chrislock, *The Progressive
Era in Minnesota, 1899–1918* (St. Paul: Minnesota Historical Society, 1971), 22–25.
  68. *Glenwood Gopher-Press,* 30 November 1905, p. 2. Young claimed, "This is not
the first time that elevator companies have
threatened to install or actually have installed 'elevator stores,' for the purpose of
intimidating local merchants who encourage the establishment of independent farmers' elevators." I know of no other examples,
though.
  69. Chrislock, *Progressive Era,* 19. See
also Winifred G. Helmes, *John A. Johnson,
the People's Governor: A Political Biography*
(Minneapolis: University of Minnesota Press,
1949).
  70. Quoted in *Glenwood Herald,* 15 December 1905, p. 1.
  71. *Glenwood Herald,* 8 December 1905,
p. 5; *Glenwood Gopher-Press,* 14 December
1905, p. 6.
  72. See, for example, *American Co-operative Journal,* September 1906, p. 20, December 1907, p. 137; Larson, *Wheat Market,*
211; Kenkel, *Cooperative Elevator Movement,*
20–21; *Northfield News,* 17 November 1900,
p. 4; Refsell, "Farmers' Elevator Movement,"
886, 889, 890.
  73. *Detroit Record,* 4 October 1907, p. 3.
Also quoted in *American Co-operative Journal,* October 1907, p. 65. For Frank Peavey's
line of elevators—435 of them by 1900—see
Tweton, "Business of Agriculture," in *Minnesota in a Century of Change,* ed. Clark,
267–68.
  74. When the line elevator at Campbell
(Wilkin County) hiked its price one penny
above the farmers' elevator's price, the latter told its buyers "to pay two or three cents
more than the grain is worth and then let
the load pass on to the line houses at a cent
higher." It tried to push the line's losses up to
unacceptable levels. *Kerkhoven Banner,* 1
November 1907, p. 1.
  75. *Redwood Gazette,* 28 June 1905, p. 8,
25 October 1905, p. 1; *Redwood Reveille*
(Redwood Falls), 30 June 1905, p. 6.
  76. *Redwood Gazette,* 28 June 1905, p. 8;
American Co-operative Journal, August 1906,
p. 8–9. It did not sell grain at a loss in 1904–

05. A $765 gain on grain sales just did not
offset fixed operating expenses. The 1905–
06 gain on grain sales of $2,517 was nearly
enough to cover operating expenses (it sold
coal and other commodities as well).
  77. For an analysis of the penalty clause
and the story of how the farmers of Rockwell, Iowa, originated it in 1890, see Refsell,
"Farmers' Elevator Movement," pt. 2 (December 1914): 890–93, 974–75; Philip J. Nelson, "The Rockwell Co-operative Society
and the Iowa Farmers' Elevator Movement,
1870–1920," *Annals of Iowa,* 3d ser., 54 (Winter 1995): 1–24.
  78. *Redwood Reveille,* 30 June 1905, p. 6.
A. D. Stewart introduced this resolution "to
provoke discussion"; *Redwood Gazette,* 28
June 1905, p. 8. In the event of "a surplus,"
the monies would be paid back to farmers
pro rata.
  79. *Redwood Reveille,* 30 June 1905, p. 6;
Redwood Gazette, 28 June 1905, p. 8. Farmers
would be reimbursed "based on the amount
of grain so marketed" by each farmer to another company.
  80. Nelson, "Rockwell Co-operative Society," 7–10, 21–22; Refsell, "Farmers' Elevator Movement," 973–75. By 1914 an Iowa
Supreme Court decision, *Reeves v. Decorah
Farmers' Co-operative Society,* had weakened
the legality of the penalty clause by pre-
venting a livestock association from enforcing it; Refsell, "Farmers' Elevator Movement," 983. For the bitterness of the "Farmers'
Elevators vs. Grain Trust" fight in Iowa and
Illinois, see *American Co-operative Journal,*
March 1907, p. 10–14, April 1907, p. 11–13.
  81. In 1915 only 19 percent of reporting
farmers' elevators had a penalty clause in
their bylaws; L. D. H. Weld, *Farmers' Elevators in Minnesota,* University of Minnesota,
Agricultural Experiment Station Bulletin
152 (St. Paul, August 1915), 8. For an example
of such a clause, see the Kerkhoven Farmers' Elevator Company bylaws in *Kerkhoven
Banner,* 11 October 1907, p. 8.
  82. Weld, *Farmers' Elevators,* 6.
  83. E. Dana Durand and J. P. Jensen, *Farmers' Elevators in Minnesota, 1914–1915,* University of Minnesota, Agricultural Experiment Station Bulletin 164 (St. Paul, October
1916), 15. This report found their volumes to
be double those of private ones.

84. Refsell, "Farmers' Elevator Movement," 893–95, 969–73.

85. *American Co-operative Journal*, December 1907, p. 145–46. At this first Minnesota convention, three speakers from Illinois and Iowa told of the battles between farmers' and line elevators in those states.

86. *American Co-operative Journal*, December 1907, p. 147.

87. Heflebower, *Cooperatives and Mutuals*, 10, 33.

88. *American Co-operative Journal*, June 1908, p. 209–10. Feig, a Republican congressional candidate in the 1890s, gave a Progressive speech stressing "a 'community of interests' between the farmer and local business man." "We are living in an age of combinations—'good ones and bad ones,' as President Roosevelt has so aptly stated."

89. Benjamin B. Drake, "Just at this season of the year," undated typescript, Equity Cooperative Exchange Papers, MHS; Weld, *Farmers' Elevators*, 11–12.

90. See, for example, "The Co-operation of the Commission Merchants and the Farmers' Elevator Company," *American Co-operative Journal*, February 1914, p. 446. Some local banks loaned to farmers' elevators. For the advantages to a country bank, see *American Co-operative Journal*, October 1910, p. 99.

91. Weld, *Farmers' Elevators*, 11–12.

92. Drake, "Just at this season of the year," Equity Cooperative Exchange Papers.

93. *Farm, Stock and Home*, 15 April 1908, p. 245. Philip Nelson described the valuable aid some commission firms gave to the Iowa farmers' elevator movement, but he ignored the conditions attached to such assistance; "Rockwell Co-operative Society," 14–16.

94. For the example of the Farmers' Elevator Company of Ivanhoe, see *American Co-operative Journal*, July 1906, p. 24.

95. *American Co-operative Journal*, October 1910, p. 93. For examples of relationships between farmers' elevators and commission firms, see Minute Book, p. 9, Farmers' Elevator Company of Foxhome, Papers, Wilkin County Historical Society, Breckenridge; and Record, p. 5, 7, Farmers Grain Company of Storden Papers, Cottonwood County Historical Society, Windom.

96. *Cokato Observer*, 5 and 12 September 1889, both p. 4; Minutes, p. 185, Cokato Elevator Company, Corporate Records, MHS. Initially, more than 64 percent of the shares were owned by three individuals.

97. Minutes, p. 44, Cokato Elevator Company Records.

98. Minutes, p. 44–45, and A. M. Woodward to Frank Swanson, 25 September 1902, Cokato Elevator Company Records.

99. By 1915 "many of the so-called farmers' elevators are not owned by farmers at all"; Weld, *Farmers' Elevators*, 6.

100. Weld, *Farmers' Elevators*, 6–7. Weld defined a farmers' elevator as one where farmers had majority control. He stressed three Rochdale principles: one person-one vote, a limit on the shares one individual could own, and payment of patronage dividends. By other, less-strict, definitions, there were even more farmers' elevators.

101. Durand and Jensen, *Farmers' Elevators*, 8, 15.

102. Durand and Jensen, *Farmers' Elevators*, 8, 15. Another pocket of strength was in Goodhue and Dodge Counties.

103. Durand and Jensen, *Farmers' Elevators*, 14.

104. Larson, *Wheat Market*, 218.

105. Here and below, see Cronon, *Nature's Metropolis*, 111, 116, 120, 126–27, 257, 259. The quotes on capital's logic and places losing particularity come in Cronon's treatment of meat packing, but they are equally applicable to grain marketing.

Notes to Chapter 10

1. Hetherington, *Mutual and Cooperative Enterprises*, 168, 179. The chapter title is a quote from the *Northfield News*, 12 January 1901, p. 1.

2. *Freeborn County Standard*, 29 April 1896, p. 8.

3. *Albert Lea Enterprise*, 30 April and 7 May 1896, both p. 1; U.S., Bureau of the Census, *Historical Statistics*, 293.

4. Rothstein, "American West and Foreign Markets," in *Frontier in American Development*, ed. Ellis, 400.

5. Hetherington, *Mutual and Cooperative Enterprises*, 168–70, 179–80, 243.

6. *Albert Lea Enterprise*, 30 April and 28 May 1896, both p. 1.

7. *Albert Lea Enterprise*, 24 September 1896, p. 4.

8. *Albert Lea Enterprise*, 31 December 1896, and 21 January, 3 November and 15 December 1897, all p. 1, and 25 August 1897, p. 4.

9. *Albert Lea Enterprise*, 8 October 1896, p. 1.

10. *Freeborn County Standard*, 29 January 1896, p. 5, and 12 February 1896, p. 1; *Albert Lea Enterprise*, 13 February 1896, p. 1. The excluded buttermakers warned that if it sought "to combine to reduce their wages, all the best buttermakers will leave the county"; *Freeborn County Standard*, 12 February 1896, p. 1, and 11 March 1896, p. 4.

11. *Freeborn County Standard*, 29 January 1896, p. 1, 5, and 12 February 1896, p. 1, and 26 January 1898, p. 4; *Albert Lea Enterprise*, 13 February 1896 and 4 March 1897, both p. 1, and 2 June 1897, p. 3.

12. *Albert Lea Enterprise*, 4 March 1897, p. 1, and 6 October 1897, p. 8.

13. *Albert Lea Enterprise*, 8 October 1896, p. 3, and 22 and 29 October 1896, both p. 1.

14. *Freeborn County Standard*, 7 October 1896, p. 4. The other issue important to Lawson was county option on liquor sales.

15. *Albert Lea Enterprise*, 13 February 1896, p. 1.

16. One sign of maturation and of a recognition of the cooperative separator creamery as an institution was a paper read "to the association on the history of co-operative dairying in Freeborn county" by N. T. Sandberg; *Freeborn County Standard*, 9 March 1898, p. 1. This was undoubtedly the first attempt to collect historical information on this topic.

17. *Albert Lea Enterprise*, 2 June 1897, p. 3. Three years later, competition remained so they suggested grading milk; *Freeborn County Times*, 26 January 1900, p. 1.

18. *Freeborn County Standard*, 28 December 1898, p. 1.

19. *Albert Lea Enterprise*, 8, 15 and 21 April 1897, all p. 1; *Freeborn County Standard*, 5 May 1897, p. 1; Joseph H. Beek (MDBT secretary) to Editor, *Freeborn County Standard*, 14 May 1897, Beek to Benjamin D. White (Freeborn County buttermaker and MDBT vice-president), 12 June 1897 and many other dates, Beek to M. M. McKillop, 23 and 26 April 1897—all in Minnesota Dairy Board of Trade, Letterpress Book, April–July 1897, MHS. The MDBT was modeled after the Elgin (Illinois) Board of Trade. For the producer-dominated Elgin board's efforts to raise butter prices, see Wiest, *Butter Industry*, 148–49, 181–92; Ashmen, "Price Determination in the Butter Market," 156–62; Lampard, *Dairy Industry in Wisconsin*, 311–13, 321.

20. Lampard, *Dairy Industry in Wisconsin*, 311–13. For a critique of boards of trade, see J. H. Monrad, "Stray Thoughts and Jottings," in *Hoard's Dairyman*, 9 April 1897, p. 143. The Freeborn County dairy association stopped discussing the MDBT after May 1897, and the MDBT Letterpress Book begins and ends with 1897, so I assume the MDBT ceased to exist then.

21. Rothstein, "American West and Foreign Markets," in *Frontier in American Development*, ed. Ellis, 400. He argued, "Dairy farmers refused to accept reforms of market standards for their butter and cheese and were served by a highly decentralized processing industry" (p. 401–2). Buttermaking was decentralized, but the Freeborn dairy specialists were willing to alter their product to suit foreign tastes.

22. *Albert Lea Enterprise*, 3 December 1896, p. 1, and 1 September 1897, p. 4.

23. Beek to White, 19 June 1897, MDBT, Letterpress Book.

24. *Albert Lea Enterprise*, 6 October 1897, p. 8. The U.S. Department of Agriculture had sent an "experimental shipment of butter to London," and Minnesota creamery butter was included; *Hoard's Dairyman*, 24 September 1897, p. 636.

25. *Albert Lea Enterprise*, 30 June 1897, p. 1. Other creamery officers "expressed favorable views concerning" hand separators.

26. Kenneth D. Ruble, *Men to Remember: How 100,000 Neighbors Made History* ([Chicago?], 1947), 19–20, 26.

27. Lampard, *Dairy Industry in Wisconsin*, 209; John Michels, *Creamery Butter-Making* (Farmingdale, N.Y., 1914), 59; Wiest, *Butter Industry*, 28–30; Ruble, *Men to Remember*, 19. The " 'Alpha Baby' N2" hand separator cost $125 in 1899; Minnesota farmers new to dairying were unwilling to make that large an investment in the early 1890s; Monrad, *A.B.C. in Butter Making*, 31. Freeborn's creameries were listed in *Freeborn County Times*, Creamery ed., 9 February 1900, p. 2.

28. *Todd County Independent* (Clarissa),

14 February 1908, p. 1, quoted in *Long Prairie Leader*, 21 February 1908, p. 4.

29. Ruble, *Men to Remember*, 20.

30. One newspaper called centralizers "trust creameries," echoing the era of trust-busting, but cooperatives also sought and needed monopoly; *Willmar Tribune*, 3 July 1907, p. 4. For a Danish dairy expert's assessment of Minnesota cooperative creameries, see Bøggild, *Nogle iagttagelser*, 40–46.

31. Thompson and Warber, *Social and Economic Survey of a Rural Township in Southern Minnesota*, 30–33.

32. *Farm, Stock and Home*, 15 March (p. 209), 15 April (p. 285), 1 July (p. 395), and 1 December (p. 632), all 1907. See also *Willmar Tribune*, 3 July 1907, p. 4.

33. *The Farmer*, 10 April 1920, p. 1081; Ruble, *Men to Remember*, 54–55, 57–58, 60–65.

34. *The Farmer*, 10 January 1914, p. 46. *The Farmer* opposed the law as "retaliatory or prohibitive legislation" that would encourage centralizers to build local "branch plants."

35. *St. Paul Pioneer Press*, 25 March 1913, p. 5.

36. *Fergus Globe*, 17 July 1908, p. 4.

37. *Fergus Falls Ugeblad*, 22 July 1908, p. 1.

38. *Fergus Falls Ugeblad*, 22 April 1908, p. 2; *Fergus Falls Free Press*, 22 April 1908, p. 1; *Co-operation* (Minneapolis), May 1909, p. 9; *Fergus Globe*, 31 July 1908, and 4 June 1909, both p. 4. *Co-operation* was the monthly journal of the Right Relationship League.

39. Knapp, *American Cooperative Enterprise*, 397–98; Interstate Right Relationship League Co-operative Conference, *Proceedings of Second Annual Meeting, January 14–17, 1908* (Minneapolis, 1908), 37.

40. Interstate Right Relationship League, *Proceedings of Second Annual Meeting*, 18–20, 26–27; Knapp, *American Cooperative Enterprise*, 398–99. For a description of a successful RRL store in Lakefield in Jackson County, see *The Farmer*, 10 May 1913, p. 771–72.

41. The quote is from Bernard Bailyn et al., *The Great Republic: A History of the American People*, 2 vols., 4th ed. (Lexington, Mass.: D. C. Heath and Co., 1992), 2:185.

42. For a description of the terms on which a merchant in Good Thunder in

Blue Earth County sold out to the RRL company, which later went bankrupt, see the 1918 case of A. J. Whitman & Company v. H. C. Mielke, 139 *Minnesota Supreme Court Reports*, 231–33.

43. *Fergus Falls Ugeblad*, 15 July 1908, p. 4.

44. Here and below, Minute Book, 1891–1908, 25 July 1908 meeting, FMC Collection. Sæther had been present in September 1891 at the first meeting to consider forming the cooperative.

45. For the earlier controversies, see Minute Book, 1891–1908, 12 January 1903, 11 January 1904, and 8 January 1906 annual meetings, FMC Collection.

46. *Fergus Globe*, 4 and 25 June 1909, both p. 2; *Co-operation*, June 1909, p. 12.

47. *Fergus Globe*, 16 July 1909, p. 1. The lists for the Wall Lake, Weggeland, and Phelps stores appeared on the same page. The *Globe*'s message was clear: "Members, as well as others, should study these tables as they prove beyond cavil that Co-operation ... pays for the Co-operators."

48. *Fergus Falls Ugeblad*, 13 January 1909, p. 1. This account of the 1909 annual meeting is the first clear evidence of a cash distribution of part of the FMC's year-end profits.

49. *Co-operation*, June 1910, p. 29.

50. Interstate Right Relationship League, *Proceedings of Second Annual Meeting*, 19. O. F. Loseth, Odin Loseth's father and co-owner of their store, had apparently been a Populist as well. See his letter to the editor in *Fergus Falls Ugeblad*, 15 October 1890, p. 1.

51. *Fergus Globe*, 17 July 1908, p. 4.

52. *Fergus Globe*, 31 July 1908 (p. 4), 14 May 1909 (p. 2), and 4 June 1909 (p. 2, 4). For the Phelps branch, see Rosanne Bergantine, *Phelps: A Peek into Its Past* (N.p.: Privately published, 1970), 13.

53. *Fergus Globe*, 14 May 1909, p. 2.

54. *Fergus Globe*, 4 June 1909, p. 2.

55. *The Independent* (Parkers Prairie), 3 June 1909, p. 1, quoted in full in *Fergus Globe*, 11 June 1909, p. 2. The *Independent* editor cited a plan as supposedly described to a Parkers Prairie merchant by an RRL agent. Boen responded by defending the RRL system and correcting the mistaken points in the *Independent*'s article; *Globe*, 11 June 1909, p. 2.

56. *Fergus Falls Weekly Journal*, 17 June 1909, p. 3. Boen reprinted the letter in his

Fergus Globe, 18 June 1909, p. 2, and suggested that "the Journal gang" had written it themselves to attack the OTCCC stores and a new cooperative elevator under construction in Fergus Falls.

57. *Fergus Globe*, 18 June 1909, p. 2; *Co-operation*, June 1909, p. 12, July 1909, p. 14–15.

58. J. P. Harrang of Stanley, Wis., was hired in December 1909; *Co-operation*, January 1910, p. 27.

59. *Fergus Globe*, 11 June 1909, p. 2; *Co-operation*, December 1909, p. 26.

60. Knapp, *American Cooperative Enterprise*, 400.

61. *Co-operation*, December 1909, p. 26.

62. *Co-operation*, June 1909, p. 12.

63. *Fergus Falls Free Press*, 7 February 1917, p. 5; *Fergus Falls Ugeblad*, 14 February, p. 2, and 21 February, p. 4, both 1917; *Fergus Falls Weekly Journal*, 18 January 1917 and 24 January 1918, both p. 3. The Underwood Department was not on the January 1918 personal property tax list, but it was on the January 1917 list. Its tax was only $73.96; the FMC tax was $145.27, showing that the FMC was in better financial condition. The Phelps store went out of business in 1916; Bergantine, *Phelps*, 16. The Underwood RRL store held a "gigantic clearance sale" in January 1916, which may or may not have been a going-out-of-business sale; *Fergus Falls Ugeblad*, 12 January 1916, p. 2.

64. Knapp, *American Cooperative Enterprise*, 400. There were no notices in the Fergus Falls newspapers announcing a March 1916 annual meeting of the OTCCC.

65. The second FMC Minute Book, written in English, covers the years 1922 to (May 15) 1967, when the store was sold.

66. Carle C. Zimmerman, *Farm Trade Centers in Minnesota, 1905–29: A Study in Rural Social Organization*, University of Minnesota, Agricultural Experiment Station Bulletin 269 (St. Paul, September 1930), 7–9, 14–16, 18–19, 22–23, 30–32. The term "long-distance marketing" is taken from "Relations of the Country Store to the Farm," *The Farmer*, 4 December 1915, p. 1529.

67. Zimmerman, *Farm Trade Centers*, 37.

68. Zimmerman, *Farm Trade Centers*, 38.

69. *American Co-operative Journal*, October 1910, p. 98.

70. *American Co-operative Journal*, February 1906, p. 27, June 1906, p. 25. Theodore Saloutos appears to be incorrect in stating that the Minnesota Farmers' Exchange was "established in 1902"; "Rise of the Equity Cooperative Exchange," 40. The Exchange's printed appeal to farmers states that it was formed in 1904; *American Co-operative Journal*, June 1906, p. 25.

71. *American Co-operative Journal*, March 1906, p. 13. In March 1906, the Exchange's committee went to the Chamber and "was most courteously received." Chamber officials "assured the committee that they would treat them like any one else." They had to investigate the Exchange, however. The final answer was negative. According to Saloutos, "Chamber representatives claimed that membership was denied" to the Farmers' Exchange "on grounds of insolvency, the truth of which charge the Minnesota Exchange leaders denied"; Saloutos, "Rise of the Equity Cooperative Exchange," 41.

72. *American Co-operative Journal*, March 1906, p. 9, March 1907, p. 46.

73. Saloutos, "Rise of the Equity Cooperative Exchange," 41.

74. Saloutos and Hicks, *Twentieth-Century Populism*, 113.

75. Saloutos and Hicks, *Twentieth-Century Populism*, 114–15, 135–36; Saloutos, "Rise of the Equity Cooperative Exchange," 42–45.

76. Saloutos, "Rise of the Equity Cooperative Exchange," 48–58.

77. Saloutos, "Rise of the Equity Cooperative Exchange," 57.

78. Chrislock, *Progressive Era*, 106; Thomas W. Howard, ed., *The North Dakota Political Tradition* (Ames: Iowa State University Press, 1981), 69, 72–73. This event helped lead to the formation of the Nonpartisan League in North Dakota.

79. *Minneapolis Morning Tribune*, 7 February 1914, p. 15; *Marshall County Banner*, 5 February 1914, p. 1, 4, 5.

80. *Minneapolis Morning Tribune*, 7 February 1914, p. 15. A spokesman for the commission firms, B. F. Benson, asserted that the firms and the farmers' elevators depended on one another; *American Co-operative Journal*, February 1914, p. 446.

81. *American Co-operative Journal*, February 1914, p. 445–47; *Commercial West*, 14

February 1914, p. 47. The program of the convention was given in detail in the February 1914 issue of the *American Co-operative Journal*, p. 442–49.

82. *American Co-operative Journal*, February 1914, p. 442, 443; *Minneapolis Morning Tribune*, 7 February 1914, p. 15; *Minneapolis Journal*, Home ed., 7 February 1914, p. 2.

83. *American Co-operative Journal*, February 1914, p. 449; *Minneapolis Journal*, 5 February 1914, p. 20; *Minneapolis Morning Tribune*, 7 February 1914, p. 15, and 6 February 1914, p. 1; *Commercial West*, 14 February 1914, p. 47.

84. *Minneapolis Journal*, 5 February 1914, p. 20.

85. George S. Loftus to Benjamin B. Drake, 28 January 1914, in Drake, Exchange Papers.

86. *Dassel Anchor*, 14 May 1914, p. 6. This article in the *Anchor* was a press release put out by the Equity movement.

87. *The Chamber of Commerce of Minneapolis:...History of the Equity Co-operative Exchange since Its Removal to St. Paul, Minn.*, reprinted from *The Co-operative Manager and Farmer* (Minneapolis), 1914?, p. 38. This periodical was subsidized by the Chamber of Commerce.

88. *Eden Valley Journal*, 30 April 1914, p. 1.

89. *Eden Valley Journal*, 7 May, p. 5, and 14 May, p. 1, 1914.

90. *Eden Valley Journal*, 7 May, p. 5, and 14 May, p. 1, 1914. Father O'Callaghan's response was printed in the *Co-operative Manager and Farmer*, June 1914, p. 38–39.

91. *Eden Valley Journal*, 7 May 1914, p. 5. The editor's comments could be read to infer that the bank had a great deal of power over the elevator company.

92. *Eden Valley Journal*, 7 May 1914, p. 5; *Dassel Anchor*, 14 May 1914, p. 1.

93. Undated typescripts beginning "The Chamber of Commerce people and their agents...," (probably 1914), and "Just at this season of the year...," both in Drake, Exchange Papers.

94. "Record of Testimony before Senate Committee, February 18, 1913, to April 1, 1913. Grain Investigation," 2: 793–97, 1028–43, typescript, in Minnesota, Legislature, Records of Special Investigating Committees, 1858–1942, 1913 Senate Grain Inquiry Committee: Testimony, Minnesota State Archives. The

manager of the Voltaire (North Dakota) farmers' elevator also testified that "the directors of our Company" requested that he use the Exchange: "I was to ship it, and see how good a business we could do with them."

95. Corporation Record, p. 32–33, Farmers' Elevator Company of Roseau, Papers, Roseau County Historical Society, Roseau.

96. *American Co-operative Journal*, October 1905, p. 12. For a description of the traveling salesmen, written by an elevator manager, see *American Co-operative Journal*, September 1910, p. 31.

97. For reports on local Equity elevators, see the *Farmers Equity News* (Alexandria), 1917–18.

98. *Northfield News*, 14 March 1896, p. 10, 9 January 1897, p. 5, 23 January 1897, p. 8, and 6 February 1897, p. 5; Minute Book, 1897–1917, 16 January 1897 meeting, Northfield Farmers' Mercantile and Elevator Company (hereafter NFMEC), Papers, Rice County Historical Society, Faribault.

99. *Northfield News*, 15 January 1898, p. 1.

100. *Northfield News*, 13 January 1900, p. 1, 24 August 1901, p. 4, 12 January 1901, p. 1.

101. *Northfield News*, 22 January 1910, p. 1. This company was becoming a board oligarchy. At the 1910 annual meeting, "some one sought to stampede the meeting with a motion to re-elect the entire old board by acclamation." The effort failed, but only one incumbent was defeated; *Northfield Independent*, 13 January 1910, p. 1.

102. *Northfield News*, 12 January 1917, p. 1. Directors and officers had secured proxies in advance to counter a rumored move to unseat some directors and to vote large dividends.

103. *Northfield News*, 12 January 1917, p. 1.

104. *Northfield News*, 12 January 1917, p. 1, 10.

105. *Northfield News*, 19 January 1917, p. 4. Schilling had helped to organize the Twin City Milk Producers Association, a farmers' milk-marketing cooperative (see Chapter 12).

106. *Northfield Independent*, 25 January 1917, p. 3.

107. *Northfield News*, 19 and 26 January 1917, both p. 4. In his January 19 letter, Schilling had made a serious mistake in long division to arrive at a gross margin of twenty-five cents on wheat.

108. *Northfield News*, 26 November 1920, p. 1, 6.

109. *Northfield News*, 3 December 1920, and 14 January 1921, both p. 1; Minute Book, 1918–21, 11 January 1921 annual meeting, NFMEC Papers. At the last annual meeting in January 1921, shareholders voted a 100 percent stock dividend.

110. *Northfield News*, 18 March 1921, p. 1; *Rice County Directory, 1921*, 112, 137. The final sale was approved June 6, 1921, by the old company's board; Minute Book, 1918–21, 27 May and 6 June 1921 meetings, NFMEC Papers.

Notes to Chapter 11

1. *Willmar Tribune*, 15 November 1899, p. 4.

2. *Republican Press* (Atwater), 5 May 1901, p. 1.

3. Blegen, *Minnesota: A History*, 254; Chandler, *Visible Hand*, 77, 195, 197–200. In his study of North Dakota, John Hudson took the telegraph for granted as part of a railroad network, but merchants and grain elevators could hardly survive without it; see Hudson, *Plains Country Towns*, 105, 111–14.

4. Sidney H. Aronson, "Bell's Electrical Toy: What's the Use? The Sociology of Early Telephone Usage," in *The Social Impact of the Telephone*, ed. Ithiel de Sola Pool (Cambridge: MIT Press, 1977), 15, 19–20; Robert W. Garnet, *The Telephone Enterprise: The Evolution of the Bell System's Horizontal Structure, 1876–1909* (Baltimore: Johns Hopkins University Press, 1985), 1.

5. *Minneapolis Tribune*, 29 October 1877, p. 4. By June 1877, Richard L. Hankinson had a private line in his Minneapolis home, which may have been the first phone in Minnesota, although James C. Rippey reported that "a druggist in Little Falls" may "have set up [a line] between his home and his clerk's house in 1876"; James C. Rippey, *Goodbye, Central—Hello, World: A Centennial History of Northwestern Bell: The Diary of a Dream* (N.p.: Telephone Pioneers of America, 1975), 10.

6. *Mantorville Express*, 12 July 1878, p. 3. For other examples of performances, see Aronson, "Bell's Electrical Toy," in *Social Impact*, ed. de Sola Pool, 20–21.

7. Rippey, *Goodbye, Central*, 9–10.

8. *Minneapolis Tribune*, 29 October 1877, p. 4.

9. Garnet, *Telephone Enterprise*, 20, 22; Aronson, "Bell's Electrical Toy," in *Social Impact*, ed. de Sola Pool, 27.

10. *Stillwater Messenger*, 12 July 1879, p. 4. For many early references to the telephone industry in the state, I am indebted to the "Annals of Minnesota," a large group of typed transcripts of articles copied from Minnesota newspapers and dating chiefly from 1849 to 1887. For examples, see *Stillwater Gazette*, 11 June 1879 (frame 1486), and 25 June 1879 (frame 1488), in microfilm M529, roll 123 ("Transportation—Communications—Telephone"), "Annals of Minnesota": Subject Files, 1849–1942, Works Projects Administration, Minnesota, Papers, MHS.

11. Garnet, *Telephone Enterprise*, 15, 90.

12. For local phone companies, see *Lake City Graphic*, 13 May 1937, p. 1, 10; *Hutchinson Leader*, 26 March 1943, p. 3; and *Mankato Free Press*, 5 April 1937, Pioneer Mankato sec., p. 12. For a "telephone war" between the Faribault city council and Northwestern Telephone Co., see *Faribault Republican*, 8 and 15 August 1883, both p. 3, and 29 August 1883, p. 2. For Progressive-era regulation, see Alan Stone, *Public Service Liberalism: Telecommunications and Transitions in Public Policy* (Princeton: Princeton University Press, 1991).

13. Claude S. Fischer, "The Revolution in Rural Telephony, 1900–1920," *Journal of Social History* 21 (Fall 1987): 7, 10. See also Garnet, *Telephone Enterprise*, 124.

14. Charles R. Perry, "The British Experience, 1876–1912: The Impact of the Telephone during the Years of Delay," in *Social Impact*, ed. de Sola Pool, 76.

15. Fischer, "Rural Telephony," 5, 8, 13–15. For a more complete version of Fischer's analysis, see Claude S. Fischer, *America Calling: A Social History of the Telephone to 1940* (Berkeley: University of California Press, 1992), especially p. 92–107, which cover rural telephony.

16. John R. Pierce, "The Telephone and Society in the Past 100 Years," in *Social Impact*, ed. de Sola Pool, 173.

17. Jean Gottmann, "Megalopolis and Antipolis: The Telephone and the Struc-

ture of the City," in *Social Impact*, ed. de Sola Pool, 306.

18. "Until fully automated switching" arrived (and it was not used much until 1919), "the company's cost of serving each subscriber was greater the larger the number of other subscribers"; Ithiel de Sola Pool et al., "Foresight and Hindsight: The Case of the Telephone," in *Social Impact*, ed. de Sola Pool, 130. For the move to automatic switching and its impact on female work roles, see Kenneth Lipartito, "When Women Were Switches: Technology, Work, and Gender in the Telephone Industry, 1890–1920," *American Historical Review* 99 (October 1994): 1074–1111.

19. Stone, *Public Service Liberalism*, 40.

20. De Sola Pool et al., "Foresight and Hindsight," in *Social Impact*, ed. de Sola Pool, 131.

21. *Willmar Tribune*, 15 November 1899 and 6 November 1901, both p. 4.

22. *Willmar Tribune*, 22 May 1901, p. 4. Harrison, Dovre, Green Lake, and Gennessee were the townships. Earlier that year, David N. Tallman tried to start a phone system in Atwater—backed by the city council and the *Republican Press*; see *Republican Press*, 18 January 1901, p. 6.

23. *Republican Press*, 17 May 1901, p. 5.

24. *Republican Press*, 24 May 1901, p. 5; *Willmar Tribune*, 22 May 1901, p. 1, 4.

25. *Republican Press*, 5 May 1901, p. 5; *Willmar Tribune*, 22 May 1901, p. 1, 4. A preliminary committee was instructed "to make a thorough investigation as to the matter of connections with other lines."

26. See, for example, *Willmar Tribune*, 18 October, p. 4, and 8 November, p. 8, both 1899.

27. *Willmar Tribune*, 22 May 1901, p. 4.

28. For cooperative phone companies in Kandiyohi County, see the chapters on individual townships in Lawson, ed., *Illustrated History...of Kandiyohi County, Minnesota*.

29. *Republican Press*, 10 May 1901, p. 5; *Willmar Tribune*, 19 June 1901, p. 4, and 4 February 1903, p. 8.

30. "Stockholders Profit," *Willmar Tribune*, 10 February 1904, p. 1. Tallman was soon to become a major town promoter and branch banker in North Dakota; see Hud-

son, *Plains Country Towns*, 84–85, 100–101, 133, 134, 141, 144–45.

31. *Republican Gazette* (Willmar), 13 June 1901, p. 5.

32. Lawson charged that the KCTC was "organized for the purpose of paying dividends to its stockholders." The price of KCTC stock at one hundred dollars per share was much higher than normal for a rural phone cooperative—evidence that the KCTC was quasi cooperative. See *Willmar Tribune*, 19 June 1901, p. 4; *Republican Gazette*, 13 June 1901, p. 4.

33. *Republican Gazette*, 13 June 1901, p. 4, 5; *Republican Press*, 10 May 1901, p. 5.

34. *Republican Gazette*, 13 June 1901, p. 4; *Republican Press*, 10 May and 7 June, 1901, both p. 5.

35. *Republican Press*, 24 May 1901, p. 5.

36. *Willmar Tribune*, 19 June 1901, p. 4.

37. *Republican Gazette*, 13 June 1901, p. 4.

38. *Willmar Tribune*, 4 December 1901, p. 1.

39. *Willmar Tribune*, 4 December 1901, p. 1.

40. *Willmar Tribune*, 4 December 1901, p. 1. Despite the Union's successful stand, the *Tribune* worried that the agreed-upon switching rates and message fees were too high.

41. Quoted in Fischer, "Rural Telephony," 11.

42. *Willmar Tribune*, 29 January 1902, p. 3; *Republican Press*, 17 and 24 January 1902, both p. 5.

43. *Freeborn County Times*, 8 January 1904, p. 10, and 22 and 29 January 1904, both p. 7, and 5 February 1904, p. 3; *Freeborn County Standard*, 13 January 1904, p. 8, and 20 January 1904, p. 5, and 27 January 1904, p. 4.

44. One main organizer in Bath was the vice-president of the Poplar Grove creamery association; see *Freeborn County Times*, 15 January 1904, p. 8.

45. See, for example, Albert Emerson to Railroad and Warehouse Commission (hereafter RWC), 17 December 1915, file 62, John Y. O'Neil to RWC, 12 October 1915, file 67, and Archie D. Wilson to RWC, 9 December 1915, file 64, all in Correspondence with consumers ("N" files), 1915–60, Telephone Division, Railroad and Warehouse Commission/Department of Public Service Records (hereafter TD, RWC/DPS Records), Minnesota State Archives. (All duties of the Railroad

and Warehouse Commission were transferred to the Department of Public Service
when it was established in 1967.)

46. *Chisago County Press* (Lindstrom), 26
July and 9 August 1906, both p. 1.

47. *Republican Press*, 6 September 1901,
p. 4.

48. *Freeborn County Times*, 29 January
1904, p. 7.

49. See, for example, Corporate Record
Book (hereafter Book), p. 3, 80, Chisago
County Mutual Telephone Company Cor-
porate Records (hereafter CCMTC Records),
MHS.

50. Minute Book A, 1901–4, 1909–13, p.
27–29, 30–32, 36–38, 43, 49, 53, Minute Book
B, 1905–8, Eastern Union Telephone Company Records (hereafter EUTC Records),
Kandiyohi County Historical Society, Willmar. During most of these years, Eastern
Union's board met only once or twice a year.

51. See, for example, Book, p. 3, 5, 22, 27,
28, 281–84, CCMTC Records; Minute Book A,
p. 2–5, EUTC Records.

52. Here and below, see *Redwood Reveille*,
16 June 1905, p. 1, 4; *Redwood Gazette*, 14
June 1905, p. 1, 8.

53. Book, p. 39–41, 45–46, 71, CCMTC
Records.

54. Book, p. 36, 53–56, Minutes of Direc-
tors' Meetings, 1909–44, p. 8, Minutes of
Stockholders' Meetings, p. 4, 9, CCMTC
Records.

55. Minute Book A, p. 2, 6, 25, 29, 43, 47,
49, 52, 55, 59, Minute Book B, minutes of
1906–9 annual meetings, EUTC Records.

56. Treasurer Jonas Jacobson "covered" a
$175 deficit with his own funds on 28 May
1910, and was repaid two months later from
the proceeds of a five-dollar assessment
voted at the 4 June 1910 annual meeting; see
Minute Book A, p. 38–39, 43, Accounts of
1904 (day book), 28 May and 1 August 1910,
EUTC Records.

57. Minute Book A, p. 49, 50, 52, and Accounts of 1904, 4 March 1912 and 21 May
1914, EUTC Records. For collection and dis-
bursement of the assessment monies, see
Accounts of 1904 for 1912–13. Earlier it took
almost five years to repay a five-hundred-
dollar bank loan; Accounts of 1904, 9 April
1904, 22 April 1907, 21 January 1908, 28 January 1909. Eastern Union was woefully late
in paying switchboard operators, too.

58. In February 1904 Eastern Union
sought legal advice about "Whether or not
the Company had legal authority to make
and collect assessments." Presumably, some
shareholder(s) had demanded to know; see
Minute Book B, 27 February 1904 special
shareholders meeting, EUTC Records.

59. *Fergus Falls Ugeblad*, 25 February
1914, p. 1, and 11 March 1914, p. 2.

60. Minute Book A, p. 40, Minute Book
B, 7 February 1906 annual meeting, EUTC
Records.

61. See, for example, Minute Book B, 1
July 1909 board of directors meeting, EUTC
Records; Corporation Record, p. 49–50, Stacy
Telephone Company Records (hereafter STC
Records), 1909–60, MHS.

62. Book, p. 36, 106, CCMTC Records.

63. Minute Book A, p. 51, EUTC Records.
The Stacy Telephone Company's board made
a similar rule; see Corporation Record, p.
49, STC Records. For another example, see
Clara City Herald, 31 May 1907, p. 8.

64. Book, p. 36, CCMTC Records. See also
Minute Book A, p. 6, EUTC Records.

65. Minute Book B, 21 December 1906
board of directors meeting and 5 February
1908 annual meeting, EUTC Records; Book,
p. 51, CCMTC Records. For other examples of
the same policy, see Minute Book A, p. 28,
53, 55, 58, Minute Book B, 1 March 1905
board of directors meeting, EUTC Records.
For a signed agreement between Eastern
Union and new shareholders on a proposed
new line, see "To Whom it May Concern,"
agreement, 7 February 1905, EUTC Records.

66. For the development of switchboards,
see Garnet, *Telephone Enterprise*, 20–24;
Stone, *Public Service Liberalism*, 74–76; Kenneth Lipartito, *The Bell System and Regional
Business: The Telephone in the South, 1877–
1920* (Baltimore: Johns Hopkins University
Press, 1989), 15–17.

67. Exhibit A, attached to 30 June 1911
contract, and Accounts of 1904, 1912–13 en-
tries, EUTC Records.

68. See 13 July 1912 agreement, and Accounts of 1904, 2 August 1905 and 30 January 1907, EUTC Records; Lawson, ed., *Illustrated History of Kandiyohi County*, 243. For
a description of Irving, see "A Trip Through
the County: By the Editor: I. In Irving Township," *Willmar Tribune*, 5 August 1903, p. 3.

69. D. C. Lent in Stacy barely won a share-

holders vote "on the question if to leave the Central at D. C. Lents [sic] store"; Corporation Record, p. 27, 29, 30, 50, STC Records.

70. Quoted in Rippey, *Goodbye, Central*, 30. For evidence of difficulties with female operators, see Book, p. 92, CCMTC Records. For advantages of hiring females in an urban setting, see Lipartito, "When Women Were Switches," 1088.

71. Like other rural cooperatives, phone companies found it hard to supervise employees, including operators; see, for example, Directors' Minutes, p. 33, and Book, p. 92, CCMTC Records.

72. 13 July 1912 agreement, EUTC Records.

73. Corporation Record, p. 30–31, STC Records.

74. George B. Wynn to RWC, 21 January 1917, and RWC to Wynn, 27 January 1917, both in file 25, Correspondence with telephone companies ("O" files), 1915–60, TD, RWC/DPS Records. Wynn was a director of the Wing River Telephone Line (Otter Tail County).

75. *Willmar Tribune*, 19 June 1907, p. 3, and 17 January 1903, p. 8.

76. Minute Book B, 1 and 16 March 1905 meetings and 13 July 1912 note, EUTC Records.

77. Minute Book B, 3 February 1909 annual meeting, Minute Book A, p. 36, EUTC Records. Consultation was also sometimes required when one company thought of building an added line. The Stacy company appointed a committee "to meet with the Chisago City Telephone Co. about the construction of a line between Stacy and Chisago City"; Corporation Record, p. 29, 59, STC Records.

78. Minnesota did not regulate telephone companies, including the cooperatives, until 1915 (see below, note 90, 107).

79. Stockholders' Minutes, p. 12, 15, CCMTC Records. Its board approved a connection with the Osceola Telephone Company subscribers; see Book, p. 46.

80. O'Neil to RWC, 12 October 1915, and Archie D. Wilson to RWC, 24 November 1915, file 67, "N" files, TD, RWC/DPS Records. The three systems were Rochester, Pleasant Grove, and Stewartville.

81. For a discussion of the internalizing of market transactions, see Chandler, *Visible Hand*, 6–7.

82. A. E. Wilcox to RWC, 2 March 1916, file 97, "O" files, TD, RWC/DPS Records.

83. Wilcox to RWC, 11 March 1916, file 97, "O" files, TD, RWC/DPS Records.

84. Wilcox to RWC, 11 March 1916, file 97, "O" files, TD, RWC/DPS Records.

85. RWC to Wilcox, 14 March 1916, file 97, "O" files, TD, RWC/DPS Records. See also RWC to Wilcox, 4 March 1916, file 97, "O" files, TD, RWC/DPS Records. The Bricelyn dispute apparently began when there was no state agency to which to appeal. When Wilcox wrote to the RWC, it had regulatory authority, but it "prefer[ed] to leave the manner of procedure as to collection of this kind to your own judgment."

86. Similarly, Wilcox felt that "A." should pay Bricelyn because "Bricelyn is his main trading point and his most used 'Central.'" G. H. Riddell to RWC, 20 December 1915, file 36, Wilcox to RWC, 2 March 1916, File 97, "O" files, TD, RWC/DPS Records.

87. C. F. Kampa to RWC, 31 July 1915, Kampa to RWC, 11 August 1915, and contract between Kampa and Aldrich and Verndale Telephone Co. dated 26 June 1915, file 22, E. W. Erickson to RWC, 21 July 1915, RWC to Erickson, 27 July 1915, file 3, all in "O" files, TD, RWC/DPS Records; *Verndale Sun*, 10 June 1915, p. 1.

88. Charles N. Crandall to RWC, 25 August 1915, and RWC to Crandall, 3 September 1915, file 19, "N" files, TD, RWC/DPS Records.

89. George J. Reuss to RWC, 10 September 1915, file 48, "N" files, TD, RWC/DPS Records. The Leslie Rural Telephone Company complained about the Osakis village exchange's 67 percent increase in switching fees; C. L. Osman to RWC, 24 August 1915, James Kirk to RWC, 14 September 1915, both in file 20, "O" files, TD, RWC/DPS Records.

90. After state regulation began in 1915, it was illegal to have two exchanges in one village without state approval. For two exchanges in Rollingstone (Winona County) and Murdock (Swift County), see Rep. Henry Steen to O. P. B. Jacobson, 23 August 1915, and Jacobson to Steen, 26 August 1915, both in file 18, and Swan C. Hillman to RWC, 8 June and 8 July 1915, both in file 12, all in "N" files, TD, RWC/DPS Records.

91. Riddell to RWC, 20 December 1915, file 36, "O" files, TD, RWC/DPS Records.

92. *Willmar Tribune*, 11 September 1907, p. 1.

93. *Willmar Tribune*, 29 May, p. 6, and 5

June, p. 4, 5, and 26 June, p. 1—all 1907, and 1 April 1908, p. 4.

94. *Glenwood Herald,* 31 May 1907, p. 1; *Glenwood Gopher-Press,* 30 May 1907, p. 4. For use of the *Gopher-Press* article in the Willmar and Clara City battles, see *Clara City Herald,* 14 June 1907, p. 1, and *Willmar Tribune,* 5 June 1907, p. 4.

95. *Clara City Herald,* 12 April 1907, p. 5.

96. *Clara City Herald,* 19 April, 3 May, and 28 June, all 1907, all p. 5; *Willmar Tribune,* 9 October 1907, p. 4. For other indications of MCTC's struggles with local phone companies, see *Renville Star-Farmer,* 13 March 1908, p. 1; *Willmar Tribune,* 11 March 1908, p. 1; *Clara City Herald,* 27 March 1908, p. 5, and 12 July 1907, p. 4. For a contract between MCTC and a rural phone cooperative, see 30 June 1911 contract, EUTC Records.

97. James Clark to RWC, 2 December 1915, file 45, "O" files, TD, RWC/DPS Records. Some rural companies received payment from the long-distance company. Tri-State paid Eastern Union 25 percent of all long-distance fees that Eastern Union collected; see 9 September 1904 contract, EUTC Records. For the bargaining that led to such agreements, see Minute Book A, p. 41, 46, EUTC Records.

98. *Chisago County Press,* 9 August 1906, p. 3, and 6 September 1906, p. 1. Also Northwestern and MCTC had failed to compel the Union company near Atwater to surrender the field to the KCTC.

99. *Chisago County Press,* 12 July 1906, p. 6.

100. *Chisago County Press,* 9 August 1906, p. 3, and 6 September 1906, p. 1; Book, p. 34, CCMTC Records.

101. Corporation Record, p. 25, 51, STC Records. For another attempt to play long-distance lines off against each other, see Book, p. 34, 38, 47, 52, Directors' Minutes, p. 6, 7, CCMTC Records.

102. Garnet, *Telephone Enterprise,* 152–54; Stone, *Public Service Liberalism,* 186–95; Lipartito, *Bell System and Regional Business,* 164–66, 175–76.

103. For a listing of the state's telephone companies in 1911, see *Legislative Manual,* 1911, p. 550–59.

104. Stone, *Public Service Liberalism,* 130, 132, 141, 143–51, 165, 195–98, 204.

105. *Willmar Tribune,* 9 April 1913, p. 6, and 5 April 1911, p. 2. For the demise of the

1911 bill, see *St. Paul Pioneer Press,* 19 April 1911, p. 10. Minette's name was sometimes misspelled as "Minnette," including in the *House Journal* and the 1913 legislative manual.

106. *St. Paul Pioneer Press,* 16 and 23 April 1913, both p. 1; *Willmar Tribune,* 23 April 1913, p. 4.

107. *Willmar Tribune,* 10 March 1915, p. 4; *St. Paul Pioneer Press,* 12 January 1915, p. 10, and 16 April 1915, p. 6. For the text of the Minette law, see Minnesota, *Session Laws of the State of Minnesota, 1915,* chap. 152, p. 208–15.

108. John Peshon to RWC, 19 July 1915, file 9, "N" files, TD, RWC/DPS Records.

109. "Thirty-second Annual Report of the Railroad and Warehouse Commission of the State of Minnesota," p. 71–72, in Minnesota, *Executive Documents of the State of Minnesota, for 1915–1916,* vol. 2.

110. *Olivia Times,* 6 February 1913, p. 1; 139 *Northwestern Reporter* 711–12.

111. "Thirty-second Annual Report of the Railroad and Warehouse Commission," p. 70–71, in Minnesota, *Executive Documents . . . 1915–1916,* vol. 2.

112. Minnesota, *Session Laws, 1915,* chap. 152, p. 208–15; Carl Erlandson to RWC, 12 July 1915, and John R. Stensrud to RWC, 30 July 1915, file 11, "N" files, J. H. Craft to RWC, 22 November 1915, C. B. Randall to RWC, 9 December 1915, and RWC to J. H. Craft, 14 December 1915, file 52, "O" files, J. H. Bradley to RWC, 7 July 1915, RWC to Bradley, 16 July 1915, file 2, "N" files, all in TD, RWC/DPS Records.

113. In 1992, Minnesota had ninety-four local phone companies and ranked third in the nation; see *Star Tribune* (Minneapolis), Minneapolis ed., 20 December 1992, p. 1A, 16A, 18A.

Notes to Chapter 12

1. This is not an obsolete issue. See Wendell Berry, *The Unsettling of America: Culture and Agriculture* (San Francisco: Sierra Club Books, 1977) for a modern agrarian criticism of universities for not properly fulfilling their duties under the Morrill Act.

2. James Gray, *The University of Minnesota, 1851–1951* (Minneapolis: University of Minnesota Press, 1951), 55–59; Boss, *School of Agriculture,* 18–19, 20–21, 23–25. In 1873 President William Watts Folwell reported

that "not a single young man has come to the University desirous to learn the science of farming" (Boss, 22).

3. The Grange wanted its "degree work" to be "a sort of quasi-college course on agriculture" conducted at a Grange hall by farmers. Woods, *Knights of the Plow*, 99. Nordin's *Rich Harvest* stressed the post-1870s educational role of the Grange.

4. Gray, *University of Minnesota*, 58, 60–61; Boss, *School of Agriculture*, 30–31.

5. Scott, "Early Agricultural Education," 28. For the view that university extension work would create "a middle class of well-informed men and women" who could mediate between the "professional class" and the uneducated farmers and thus reduce political strife, see *Budstikken*, 20 April 1892, p. 4.

6. Alan I. Marcus, *Agricultural Science and the Quest for Legitimacy: Farmers, Agricultural Colleges, and Experiment Stations, 1870–1890* (Ames: Iowa State University Press, 1985), 13–27.

7. Marcus, *Agricultural Science*, 39–40.

8. Minutes, 23 August 1901, Board of Administration for Minnesota Farmers' Institutes, University of Minnesota, Institute of Agriculture, Director's Office Papers, UM Archives. The minutes do not reveal both sides' arguments. Agricultural scientists generally objected to "the erroneous and loose statements and unsound views which are promulgated by speakers and debaters" at institutes; Marcus, *Agricultural Science*, 40. Gregg felt the scientists "lacked the necessary enthusiasm and the ability to make themselves intelligible to average farmers"; Scott, "Early Agricultural Education," 28.

9. Minutes, 8 August 1907, Board of Administration; *The Farmer*, 1 September 1907, p. 556; *Farm, Stock and Home*, 1 September 1907, p. 455. Wilson had a B.S. in agriculture from the university's College of Agriculture; Archie D. Wilson personnel file, Box 9, Director's Office Papers.

10. Scott, "Early Agricultural Education," 32–33.

11. Sidney M. Owen, "Co-operating to Specialize in Farm Production," 280–83; F. B. McLeran, "A Successful Co-operative Movement," 284–86—both in *Minnesota Farmers'*

Institute Annual 20 (1907); C. L. McNelly, *The County Agent Story: The Impact of Extension Work on Farming and Country Life [in] Minnesota* (Berryville, Ark.: Braswell Printing Co., 1960), 21–22.

12. *Minnesota Farmers' Institute Annual* 21 (1908): 99, 121–51.

13. *Minnesota Farmers' Institute Annual* 22 (1909): 338, 366.

14. William W. P. McConnell, "Co-operation in Production," 207–10, "Closer Relations between Our Rural Districts and Towns," 214–17, A. B. Hostetter, "Co-operative Marketing at Duluth," 217–21—all in *Minnesota Farmers' Institute Annual* 23 (1910); see also p. 211–13, 221–25, 233–37, 346.

15. *Minnesota Farmers' Institute Annual* 24 (1911): 26–42.

16. David B. Danbom, *The Resisted Revolution: Urban America and the Industrialization of Agriculture, 1900–1930* (Ames: Iowa State University Press, 1979), 23, 29–30, 36, 41–43, 47–49, 51–54.

17. Daniel T. Rodgers, "In Search of Progressivism," *Reviews in American History* 10 (December 1982): 123.

18. *Minnesota Farmers' Institute Annual* 26 (1913): 22.

19. *Alexandria Citizen*, 30 April 1914, p. 1.

20. *University Farm Press News* (broadside; University of Minnesota, Department of Agriculture, Extension Division), 15 February 1912; Danbom, *Resisted Revolution*, 29–30. For a nineteenth-century example of this argument, see Marcus, *Agricultural Science*, 9.

21. Archie D. Wilson, *Farmers' Clubs*, Minnesota Farmers' Library, vol. 4, no. 10 (Extension Bulletin no. 46)([St. Paul?]: University of Minnesota, Department of Agriculture, October 1913), 2, 4.

22. Rodgers, "In Search of Progressivism," 126.

23. *American Co-operative Journal*, March 1916, p. 707.

24. *The Farmer*, 12 April 1913, p. 636. For a similar statement by Woods, see *University Farm Press News*, 1 May 1913.

25. News Release, 3 March 1913, Carl William Thompson Papers, UM Archives; Willard W. Cochrane, *Agricultural Economics at the University of Minnesota, 1886–1979* (St. Paul: Department of Agricultural and

Applied Economics, University of Minnesota, 1983), 11.

26. Danbom, *Resisted Revolution*, 94.

27. *American Co-operative Journal*, March 1916, p. 707.

28. *American Co-operative Journal*, November 1912, p. 186. See the report of a committee on cooperative marketing and agricultural credits in *Minneapolis Journal*, 11 December 1913, Home ed., p. 1, 12. Danbom noted this same reticence about "Populism or its predecessors," in *Resisted Revolution*, 28.

29. *Agricultural Organization and Cooperation* (St. Paul: Department of Agriculture, University of Minnesota, 1915), 7–8 (copy in UM Archives). James J. Hill described the revolution in Danish farming and French Canadians' successful dairying at Gentilly, Minnesota—without noting that cooperation was a major cause of both. Conference of the Committees on Agricultural Development and Education of the State Bankers' Associations, *Annual Conference* (1912), 264–65, 267, 270; Virgil Benoit, "Gentilly: A French-Canadian Community in the Minnesota Red River Valley," *Minnesota History* 44 (Winter 1975): 278–89.

30. *The Farmer*, 12 April 1913, p. 641.

31. *The Farmer*, 16 March 1912, p. 414.

32. *The Farmer*, 27 December 1913, p. 1634.

33. *The Farmer*, 15 February 1913, p. 270; *Minneapolis Journal*, 11 December 1913, Home ed., p. 12.

34. *University Farm Press News*, 1 December 1911.

35. *University Farm Press News*, 1 November 1911.

36. *The Farmer*, 29 June 1912, p. 854.

37. *The Farmer*, 28 June 1913, p. 940; McConnell, "Closer Relations between Our Rural Districts and Towns," 214–17; *Minnesota Farmers' Institute Annual* 26 (1913): 21.

38. *Fergus Falls Weekly Journal*, 12 March 1914, p. 5. Frank W. Murphy, president of West Central Minnesota Development Assn., made client status quite explicit. The county agent was "the people's counsellor, adviser, doctor, teacher, leader."

39. Conference . . . State Bankers' Associations, *Annual Conference* (1911), 76, 77.

40. Conference . . . State Bankers' Associations, *Annual Conference* (1911), 88.

41. Conference . . . State Bankers' Associations, *Annual Conference* (1911), 15–16.

42. Scott, *Reluctant Farmer*, 212–26.

43. Conference . . . State Bankers' Associations, *Annual Conference* (1911), 77; Albert F. Woods personnel file, University of Minnesota, Institute of Agriculture, Director's Office Papers; *University Farm Press News*, 15 December 1912.

44. Conference . . . State Bankers' Associations, *Annual Conference* (1911), 77–78; *Willmar Tribune*, 26 January 1910, p. 4; McNelly, *County Agent Story*, 35–36. To lead the new program, the Minnesota Bankers Association pressed the university regents to name Woods dean of the university's department of agriculture; *Minneapolis Journal*, 20 November 1913, Home ed., p. 1, 4. McNelly erroneously gave 1913 as the year for the start of the demonstration farms.

45. Conference . . . State Bankers' Associations, *Annual Conference* (1912), 12–18; Scott, *Reluctant Farmer*, 265–66.

46. Scott, *Reluctant Farmer*, 267; *The Farmer*, 14 September 1912, p. 1094.

47. *The Farmer*, 12 October 1912, p. 1211–12; Scott, *Reluctant Farmer*, 266; "Extension in Minnesota—General History" file, Director's Office Papers, and Minutes, 23 August 1912, Board of Administration for Minnesota Farmers' Institutes; Boss, *School of Agriculture*, 82–83; *The Farmer*, 14 September 1912, p. 1094; *Morris Sun*, 26 September 1912, p. 7; McNelly, *County Agent Story*, 19–20, 26.

48. *Wheaton Gazette-Reporter*, 23 August 1912, p. 1.

49. *Wheaton Gazette-Reporter*, 6 September 1912, p. 2.

50. *Wheaton Gazette-Reporter*, 23 August 1912, p. 1.

51. *Wheaton Gazette-Reporter*, 20 September 1912, p. 1.

52. *The Farmer*, 12 October 1912, p. 1211–12, 28 June 1913, p. 939–40, 942, 943; *Morris Tribune*, 27 September 1912, p. 1; Frank E. Balmer, "Annual Report, State Leader of County Agent Work in Minnesota," 1914, p. 1, in United States, Federal Extension Service, Annual Reports of Extension Service Field Representatives: Minnesota, 1914–44, microfilm M474, roll 1, MHS (hereafter U.S. Extension Service, Annual Reports).

53. Balmer, "Annual Report," 1914, p. 1–2, U.S. Extension Service, Annual Reports; *Minneapolis Journal*, 7 February 1913, Home ed., p. 8; *The Farmer*, 3 May 1913, p. 742; *Park Region Echo* (Alexandria), 25 March 1915, p. 1.

54. Scott, *Reluctant Farmer*, 309–11.

55. Balmer, "Annual Report," 1914, p. 1, U.S. Extension Service, Annual Reports. McNelly cited a total of twenty-six agents by the end of 1914; *County Agent Story*, 43.

56. For agents' work, see *Alexandria Citizen*, 30 April 1914, p. 1; *Breckenridge Telegram*, 16 April 1914 (p. 1), 24 December 1914 (p. 7), and 14 January 1915 (p. 1); *The Farmer*, 20 September 1913, p. 1199–1200, 1204, and 30 August 1913, p. 1115–16, 1119, and 21 November 1914, p. 1415; *Farm, Stock and Home*, 1 January 1914, p. 6; McNelly, *County Agent Story*, 31–32, 78–84. Balmer expressed satisfaction that by December 31, 1914, county agents had formed "many needful cooperative associations"; Balmer, "Annual Report," 1914, p. 16, U.S. Extension Service, Annual Reports.

57. Pope County report, p. 4, and Supplement, p. 3, both 1914, U.S. Extension Service, Annual Reports. William A. McKerrow, a member of the university's Extension staff, was also secretary of a Minnesota livestock shippers' association; *University Farm Press News*, 1 November 1914.

58. Norman County report, p. 4, and Jackson County report, p. 4, both 1914, U.S. Extension Service, Annual Reports.

59. Clay County report, p. 1, and Supplement, p. 1, 3, both 1914, U.S. Extension Service, Annual Reports.

60. *The Farmer*, 4 April 1914, p. 538, and 17 April 1915, p. 640.

61. McNelly, *County Agent Story*, 40. For the university's and the county agents' perspective on farmers' opposition to the county agent system, see *County Agent Story*, 38–43.

62. *Fergus Falls Weekly Journal*, 19 March 1914, p. 5; *Grant County Herald*, 26 February 1914, p. 1; *Glenwood Herald*, 4 March 1915, p. 6; *Park Region Echo*, 2 April 1914, p. 4; *Fergus Falls Ugeblad*, 4 March 1914, p. 3.

63. *Grant County Herald*, 26 February 1914, p. 1.

64. *Park Region Echo*, 2 April 1914, p. 4; *Fergus Falls Weekly Journal*, 19 March 1914, p. 5.

65. *Park Region Echo*, 23 July 1914, p. 5. This was a quote taken from the *Farmers' Dispatch* (St. Paul), 14 July 1914, p. 2, and sent to the *Park Region Echo* by a Douglas County farmer, who presumably agreed with the sentiments expressed.

66. Quoted from the *Buffalo Journal*, 13 August 1914, p. 4, in the *Park Region Echo*, 20 August 1914, p. 1.

67. *Park Region Echo*, 6 August 1914, p. 5. See also *Grant County Herald*, 26 February 1914, p. 1; *Glenwood Herald*, 4 March 1915, p. 6.

68. *Morris Tribune*, 27 September 1912, p. 1.

69. For the discussion of the transformation of citizens into clients, I am indebted to Christopher Lasch, *The True and Only Heaven: Progress and Its Critics* (New York: W. W. Norton, 1991).

70. *Park Region Echo*, 12 February 1914, p. 1, and 5 March 1914, p. 4.

71. *Park Region Echo*, 5 March 1914, p. 4, and 12 March 1914, p. 1.

72. *Alexandria Post News*, 9 April 1914, p. 4; *Alexandria Citizen*, 2 and 9 April 1914, both p. 1; *Park Region Echo*, 13 August 1914, p. 4.

73. *Alexandria Citizen*, 2, 9, and 23 April 1914, all p. 1. For an appeal to the farmer as client, see *Alexandria Post News*, 26 March 1914, p. 4.

74. *Park Region Echo*, 2 April 1914, p. 4. See also the article "Agent Will Stay Regardless of Vote," on p. 1 of this issue.

75. *Park Region Echo*, 2 April 1914, p. 1, and 16 April 1914, p. 4; *Alexandria Post News*, 9 April 1914, p. 4.

76. Theodore A. Erickson personnel file, Institute of Agriculture, Director's Office Papers, and Theodore A. Erickson Papers, both in UM Archives. Erickson became famous as the founder of Minnesota's 4-H club movement.

77. *Park Region Echo*, 30 July 1914, p. 1; *Alexandria Post News*, 30 July 1914, p. 1.

78. *Park Region Echo*, 30 July 1914, p. 1; *Alexandria Post News*, 30 July 1914, p. 1.

79. Here and below, see *Alexandria Post News*, 10 December 1914, p. 1; *Park Region Echo*, 10 December 1914, p. 10.

80. *Park Region Echo*, 17 December 1914, p. 4, and 24 December 1914, p. 1.

81. *Glenwood Herald*, 4 March 1915, p. 6, and 11 March 1915, p. 1; *Wheelock's Weekly* (Fergus Falls), 5 March 1914, p. 1, and 19

March 1914, p. 4; *Fergus Falls Weekly Journal*, 12 and 19 March 1914, both p. 5; *Fergus Falls Ugeblad*, 4 March 1914, p. 3, and 18 March 1914, p. 1, 2; *Grant County Herald*, 19 and 26 February 1914, both p. 1; *Grant County Review* (Herman), 12 March 1914, p. 1, 8; *Ashby Post*, 27 February 1914, p. 1; *Willmar Tribune*, 30 June, p. 6, and 7 July, p. 4, and 14 July, p. 4—all 1915; Wilkin County report, Supervisor's Comments, 1914, U.S. Extension Service, Annual Reports.

82. For the separation of ownership and control, see Chandler, *Visible Hand*, 9–10.

83. *The Farmer*, 15 February 1913, p. 270, 16 March 1912, p. 414.

84. Washington County report, Supervisor's Comments, 1914, U.S. Extension Service, Annual Reports; *Park Region Echo*, 1 April 1915, p. 1; *The Farmer*, 23 March 1912, p. 456.

85. Cochrane, *Agricultural Economics*, 11.

86. *Minneapolis Journal*, 5 February 1913, Home ed., p. 11.

87. Cochrane, *Agricultural Economics*, 12, 13. The bill was introduced by Senator Fremont J. Thoe (Dodge County), president of a farmers' elevator. See *American Co-operative Journal*, April 1914, p. 637. The bulletins were: L. D. H. Weld, *Statistics of Cooperation among Farmers in Minnesota*, Bulletin 146 (December 1914); L. D. H. Weld, *Farmers' Elevators in Minnesota*, Bulletin 152 (August 1915); E. Dana Durand, *Cooperative Livestock Shipping Associations in Minnesota*, Bulletin 156 (February 1916); Durand and Frank Robotka, *Cooperative Creameries and Cheese Factories in Minnesota, 1914*, Bulletin 166 (March 1917); Durand and H. Bruce Price, *Cooperative Buying by Farmers' Clubs in Minnesota*, Bulletin 167 (June 1917); Durand and Robotka, *Cooperative Stores in Minnesota, 1914*, Bulletin 171 (October 1917).

88. Quoted from a speech by Thomas Raleigh, Equity organizer, in *Park Region Echo*, 1 April 1915, p. 5. See also, *St. Paul Pioneer Press*, 7 March 1912, p. 10.

89. *The Farmer*, 15 February 1913, p. 270. For a similar report on the 1912 convention, see *The Farmer*, 16 March 1912, p. 414.

90. In one report on the 1912 conference, a writer connected to the Minnesota Farmers' Institutes did not see the Equity versus university debate as a debate on terminal versus local cooperatives. *The Farmer*, 23 March 1912, p. 452, 456. The university's 1915 policy statement ignored terminal level cooperation; Cochrane, *Agricultural Economics*, 13–15.

91. *The Farmer*, 15 February 1913, p. 270, 16 March 1912, p. 414.

92. *Park Region Echo*, 1 April 1915, p. 5.

93. *Park Region Echo*, 1 April 1914, p. 5.

94. *St. Paul Pioneer Press*, 7 March 1912, p. 10; *The Farmer*, 23 March 1912, p. 456.

95. *Park Region Echo*, 17 December 1914, p. 4.

96. *Park Region Echo*, 18 March 1915, p. 1, and 25 March 1915, p. 1, 4.

97. *Park Region Echo*, 18 March 1915, p. 1; *St. Paul Pioneer Press*, 13 March 1915, p. 7. Representatives Wold, Pascal H. Frye (Kandiyohi), A. F. Teigan (Chippewa), and Ole A. Pickop (Grant) also criticized the county agents. Former Governor and former University of Minnesota Regent John Lind tried to deflect the broad ideological criticisms by changing the subject to that of the qualifications of individual agents.

98. Cochrane, *Agricultural Economics*, 12, 13; *Park Region Echo*, 25 March 1915, p. 5; *St. Paul Pioneer Press*, 13 March 1915, p. 7; *Minneapolis Journal*, 13 March 1915, Home ed., p. 9.

99. *Minnesota Daily* (Minneapolis), 17 March 1915, p. 1.

100. *St. Paul Pioneer Press*, 13 March 1913, p. 7; *Park Region Echo*, 18 and 25 March and 1 April 1915, all p. 4. A month before the 1915 session, the regents discussed lobbying activities of staff and alumni and decided to ask both "not to approach individual members of the Legislature in the interests of University appropriations." The appropriations for extension work were threatened in the 1915 session. See Circular Letter to Faculty and Alumni of the University of Minnesota, signed by Fred B. Snyder, Benjamin F. Nelson, and George E. Vincent, 19 January 1915, in Legislature: Lobbying, 1915–1931 file, University of Minnesota, President's Office Papers; *Park Region Echo*, 1 April 1915, p. 4.

101. In January–February 1918, the NPL and the St. Paul Trades and Labor Assembly accused Durand of bias in favor of large meat-packing companies. He was exonerated after an investigation by the regents;

Durand Investigation 1918 file, President's Office Papers; *Minnesota Leader* (St. Paul), 16 February (p. 3), 16 March (p. 2), and 30 March (p. 7), all 1918.

102. "In re petition for the dismissal of Professor Durand by the Board of Regents," presented 5 March 1918, in Durand Investigation 1918 file, President's Office Papers.

103. Because of his success as country-life editor of the *Minneapolis Journal*, William P. Kirkwood joined the university's department of agriculture as "bulletin editor and publicity man" in August 1914; Kirkwood, "The Memoirs of Homo Sap, Alias W. P. Kirkwood: With Some Hitherto Unwritten History of the University of Minnesota," manuscript, 1957, MHS. For an example of Kirkwood's *Journal* articles covering the agricultural work of the university and other subjects relating to farming and farm life in the region, see *Minneapolis Journal*, 20 November 1913, Home ed., p. 1.

104. Cochrane, *Agricultural Economics*, 13. Cochrane, however, cited no direct evidence of these "problems" other than the 1915 policy statement, which was issued in response to the criticism from conservatives.

105. See, for example, Elmer E. Adams to Albert E. Rice, 4 January 1917, in Durand Investigation 1917 file, President's Office Papers. I have not found any newspaper articles or letters attacking the university's pro-cooperative policy. The only evidence of private contact by conservatives critical of the university that I have found is this letter from Adams to Regent Rice.

106. Vincent to Woods, 29 June 1915, Department of Agriculture file, President's Office Papers. The initial discussion apparently came at a regents' meeting on June 9, 1915. Other colleges were under similar pressure. Agricultural economist O. B. Jesness failed to get a post at Iowa State College in Ames. He later wrote that "Ames was getting some heat from private grain elevators because county agents were providing services to farmers' elevators," and the college's president "decided that I was 'Too radical'"; Jesness to Joseph G. Knapp, 9 July 1975, O. B. Jesness Papers, UM Archives. In 1916 Secretary of Agriculture David F. Houston issued a policy statement on the national level; Frank E. Balmer, "Annual Report,"

1916, p. 30, U.S. Extension Service, Annual Reports.

107. *Agricultural Organization and Cooperation*, 3, 5–6, 7. Woods added, "I would not say that certain individuals might not have more extreme ideas in regard to some phases of agricultural organization and cooperation."

108. Vincent to Board of Regents, 30 July 1915, Vincent to Woods, 4 August 1915, both in Department of Agriculture file, President's Office Papers.

109. Handwritten note appended to Vincent to Board of Regents, 30 July 1915, President's Office Papers.

110. Woods to Vincent, 1 November 1915, Vincent to Woods, 11 November 1915, both in Department of Agriculture file, President's Office Papers, and Minutes, November 1915, Board of Regents, UM Archives; *Agricultural Organization and Cooperation*; Cochrane, *Agricultural Economics*, 13–15; *The Farmer*, 4 December 1915, p. 1533.

111. *Agricultural Organization and Cooperation*, 8.

112. William F. Schilling, *Lest We Forget; or, Eternal Vigilance Is the Price of Economic Liberty: A History of the Twin City Milk Producers' Association* (Northfield: Mohn Printing Co., 1942), 7–11, 13–14, 24–25; *Northfield News*, 11 August 1916, p. 1; *Twin City Milk Producers Bulletin* (St. Paul), May 1922, p. 3; Saloutos and Hicks, *Twentieth-Century Populism*, 311–12.

113. Work diaries, 2 February, 23 June, 7 July, 11 and 28 August, all 1916, Kemper A. Kirkpatrick files, Hennepin County Extension Service Records, Minnesota State Archives; Frank E. Balmer, "A Worth While Piece of Work in County Agent Effort in Minnesota in 1916: The Organization of the Twin Cities' Milk Producers Association," manuscript, Kirkpatrick files; *Minneapolis Tribune*, 12 December 1915, sec. 3, p. 1, and 2 March 1916, p. 2. For a typical organizational meeting at the local level, see *Northfield News*, 11 August 1916, p. 1. Kirkpatrick held twenty-two local meetings from June 1916 to January 1917; Work diaries, 8 June 1916, and 26 January 1917, Kirkpatrick files. For biographical information on Kirkpatrick, a horticulturist with a degree from Iowa State College, see Kemper Austin Kirk-

patrick personnel file, University of Minnesota, Institute of Agriculture, Director's Office Papers, and Kemper A. Kirkpatrick Papers, University Archives, Special Collections Department, Library, Iowa State University, Ames.

114. *St. Paul Pioneer Press*, 2 September 1916, p. 10; *Minneapolis Tribune*, 2 September 1916, p. 7; Work diaries, 1 September 1916, and Balmer, "Organization of the Twin Cities' Milk Producers Association," both in Kirkpatrick files. A quarter century later, longtime TCMPA president William Schilling praised the agents' work but stated that "their 'bosses' at the university" hesitated to organize the farmers "as we were somewhat on the Bolshevik order in their eyes"; *Lest We Forget*, 21. That memory is suspect. Bolshevism was not an issue in September 1916, nor could the bosses then foresee the future controversy with the Minnesota Commission of Public Safety.

115. TCMPA contract forms and Work diaries, 31 October 1916, 9 November 1916, and 9 January 1917, and "Report of County Agent to Farm Bureau Executive Committee," 28 March 1917, all in Kirkpatrick files; Schilling, *Lest We Forget*, 16–17; contracts and agreements, April 1–September 30, 1917, Twin City Milk Producers Association Records, MHS.

116. "Order Number Thirteen" (pamphlet) and John B. Irwin et al. to Minnesota Public Safety Commission, 20 November 1917, both in Investigation of TCMPA file (F137), Main Files, Minnesota Commission of Public Safety Papers (hereafter MCPS), Minnesota State Archives; *Minneapolis Journal*, 28 December 1917, Home ed., p. 1; Carl H. Chrislock, *Watchdog of Loyalty: The Minnesota Commission of Public Safety during World War I* (St. Paul: Minnesota Historical Society Press, 1991), 206, 208; contract forms, Kirkpatrick files.

117. *Minneapolis Journal*, Home ed., 28 December 1917 (p. 1), and 4 February 1919 (p. 1, 2); *Minneapolis Tribune*, 28 December 1917, p. 1; *St. Paul Pioneer Press*, 6 March 1919, p. 5; William M. Nash to Henry W. Libby, 13 May 1919, Investigation of TCMPA file, MCPS Papers; Schilling, *Lest We Forget*, 18–19; *Twin City Milk Producers Bulletin*, February 1919, p. 1, 7.

118. Adams to Rice, 4 January 1917, and attached *St. Paul Pioneer Press* clipping, 26 October 1916—both in Durand Investigation 1917 file, President's Office Papers.

119. Rice to Snyder, 5 January 1917, and Snyder's handwritten note on letter, Durand Investigation 1917 file.

120. Woods to Vincent, 13 January 1917, Durand Investigation 1917 file.

121. Vincent to Snyder, 20 January 1917, Durand Investigation 1917 file.

122. R. H. Elsworth and Grace Wanstall, *Farmers' Marketing and Purchasing Cooperatives, 1863–1939* (Washington, D.C.: Farm Credit Administration, U.S. Department of Agriculture, August 1941), 5.

Notes to Chapter 13

1. J. A. O. Preus, *Cooperative Marketing in Minnesota, Address . . . June 15, 1922* (St. Paul, 1922); *Minneapolis Journal*, 3 September 1920, p. 1. The percentages are rounded off to the nearest whole number. The chapter title is a quote from Hugh J. Hughes, *Cooperation Here and Abroad: A Brief Survey of Cooperative Achievement* (Minneapolis: Northern States Cooperative League, 1933), 9.

2. *Session Laws of Minnesota for 1919*, 525; *St. Paul Pioneer Press*, 14 June 1951, p. 1. The bill (H.F. 803) creating the MDA was introduced by the House Committee on Markets and Marketing and passed both the House and Senate unanimously; see *House Journal*, 1919, and *Senate Journal*, 1919.

3. *Minneapolis Journal*, 9 September 1920, p. 1 (one of a series of articles on the MFBF running from 2 September to 9 September in the *Journal*, all p. 1).

4. James H. Shideler, *Farm Crisis, 1919–1923* (Berkeley: University of California Press, 1957), 7, 131–35; David E. Hamilton, *From New Day to New Deal: American Farm Policy from Hoover to Roosevelt, 1928–1933* (Chapel Hill: University of North Carolina Press, 1991), 17–19; Donald L. Winters, *Henry Cantwell Wallace as Secretary of Agriculture, 1921–1924* (Urbana: University of Illinois Press, 1970), 123–26; Wayne D. Rasmussen, *Farmers, Cooperatives, and USDA: A History of Agricultural Cooperative Service*, USDA Agricultural Information Bulletin no. 621 (Washington, D.C.: U.S. Department of Agriculture, 1991), 51–53.

5. For an excellent account of the wartime drives, see Chrislock, *Watchdog of Loyalty,* especially chapters 5, 10, and 11.

6. For the organizational characteristics of the NPL and the Republican regulars, see Gieske and Keillor, *Norwegian Yankee,* 304–6, 316, 317.

7. Tweton, "Business of Agriculture," in *Minnesota in a Century of Change,* ed. Clark, 283–84.

8. *The Farmer,* 2 May 1925, p. 670 (p. 8 of that issue).

9. *Potato Grower* (St. Paul), 5 and 20 September 1923, both p. 2; Ludvig Mosbæk, "The Marketing Problem Between Producer and Consumer," p. 1–2, undated manuscript [1919], Danske Udvandrerarkiv, Aalborg.

10. *The Farmer,* 21 June (p. 1311), 26 July (p. 1502), 9 August (p. 1584), 30 August (p. 1703), and 22 November (p. 2379–80), all 1919, and 7 February (p. 388) and 1 May (p. 1262), both 1920; *Askov American,* 19 June 1919, p. 1; *Moorhead Weekly News,* 6 November, p. 1, and 13 November, p. 2, both 1919; *Little Falls Daily Transcript,* 26 January (p. 1), 27 January (p. 1, 8), and 30 January (p. 1), all 1920; *Minneapolis Journal,* 6 September 1920, p. 1, 11.

11. Else Mogensen, *Askov: En by i Minnesota* (Copenhagen: Nyt Nordisk Forlag Arnold Busck, 1984), 31, 69; Ludvig Mosbæk, "Erindringer fra min tidligst Barndom," undated typescript copy in author's possession; Ludvig Mosbæk to John W. Lewis, 29 January 1924, Ludvig Mosbæk Arkiv, Udvandrerarkivet, Aalborg; *Warren Register,* 10 June 1920; C. Christensen, *Agricultural Cooperation,* 12. For other accounts of Mosbæk's potato-marketing talks around the state, see *Sherburne County Star News* (Elk River), 1 July 1920, p. 1; *Thief River Falls Times,* 17 June 1920, p. 9; and "Minnesota Potato Exchange Column," *Askov American,* 17 and 24 June, 1, 8, and 15 July, all 1920, all p. 6. *The Farmer* (8 May 1920) called him "one of the staunchest friends of true co-operation to be found in the Northwest."

12. C. Christensen, *Agricultural Cooperation,* 11, 13; Keillor, "Agricultural Change," 78–79; *The Farmer,* 1 May 1920, p. 1262 (Cleland quote), and 24 July 1920, p. 1808; *Askov American,* 15 July 1920, p. 6 (Mosbæk quote). For the importance of the ironclad contract

to the Sapiro Plan of commodity marketing and for farmers' individualistic revolt against it, see Hamilton, *New Day to New Deal,* 15–17; Shideler, *Farm Crisis,* 92, 102, 104.

13. *The Farmer,* 24 July 1920, p. 1808, and 24 March 1923, p. 438; Mosbæk to Lewis, 29 January 1924, Mosbæk Arkiv.

14. Chrislock, *Watchdog of Loyalty,* 292–313; Millard L. Gieske, *Minnesota Farmer-Laborism: The Third-Party Alternative* (Minneapolis: University of Minnesota Press, 1979), 24–31, 48–50, 53; Hugh J. Hughes to My Dear Governor [Preus], J. A. O. Preus and Family Papers, MHS; *Minneapolis Journal,* 8 September, 1920, p. 1.

15. Gieske, *Farmer-Laborism,* 54–62.

16. P. A. Gandrud to Preus, 10 May 1920, Frank L. Cliff to Preus, 28 July 1920, V. E. Anderson to Preus, 10 August 1920 (quoted), Preus to H. W. Haislet, 28 September 1920 (quoted), all in Preus Papers. The Republican platform of May 8 had praised cooperation, so Preus's decision was simply a change of emphasis, not a new theme; "Republican State Platform," 8 May 1920, typescript, Preus Papers.

17. *The Farmer,* 31 July 1920, p. 1842, and 31 March 1923, p. 468; *Minneapolis Journal,* 2 and 9 September 1920, both p. 1; Shideler, *Farm Crisis,* 43–44, 46, 99–101; Hamilton, *New Day to New Deal,* 15–17.

18. Shideler, *Farm Crisis,* 46 (quoted); C. R. Adams to J. A. O. Preus, 7 October 1920, Preus Papers; *Minneapolis Journal,* 8 September 1920, p. 1.

19. *Minneapolis Journal,* 2 September (p. 1, 21), 3 September (p. 1, 2, 14, quote p. 14), 5 September (p. 1 of Editorial sec.), 6 September (p. 1, 11), 8 September (p. 1, 20), and 9 September (p. 1, 14, 25, quote p. 14), all 1920; A. A. D. R. to W. A. Durst, 14 September 1920, Preus to V. E. Anderson, 17 August 1920, and S. L. Allen to Preus, 29 July 1920, all in Preus Papers. Anderson, the MFBF treasurer, also advised Preus. Allen "was asked to resign as president" due to his Republican campaigning (and did resign) but became chief organizer of the fall MFBF membership drive; Allen to Preus, 19 July, and A. A. D. R. to Durst, 14 September, both 1920, Preus Papers.

20. *The Farmer,* 25 September 1920, p. 2187, and 31 March 1923, p. 468.

21. *Red Lake Falls Gazette,* 7 October 1920, p. 1, 8; *Battle Lake Review,* 14 October 1920, p. 1; *Hanska Herald,* 22 October 1920, p. 1. Later Preus recalled that he was "very tyrannical" in insisting that Republican speakers stick to this issue; Preus to R. A. Nestos, 17 September 1921, Preus Papers.

22. *Minnesota Leader,* 9 October (p. 3, quote), 16 October (p. 1, 3), 23 October (p. 1, 4), and 30 October (p. 4), all 1920; R. L. Harmon to Preus, 5 October 1920, A. C. Welch to Preus, 7 October 1920, Preus Papers. For a running debate over cooperation between the Republican *Crookston Daily Times* and the NPL *Polk County Leader*—sparked by Preus's speech at Crookston—see *Crookston Daily Times,* 5, 8, and 16 October, all 1920, all p. 1; *Polk County Leader* (Crookston), 8 October (p. 1), 15 October (p. 4), and 22 October, all 1920, all p. 1. Two of the Chamber's grain merchants supported Preus; J. H. Riheldaffer to Preus, and E. F. Carlson to Preus, both 10 May 1920, Preus Papers.

23. A. C. Welch to Preus, 7 October 1920, Preus Papers. Clearly written for publication, this letter was printed in the *Minnesota Leader,* 23 October 1920, p. 4.

24. The *Polk County Leader,* for example, could only insist before the vote that the NPL was not opposed to the AFBF's plans; *Polk County Leader,* 22 October 1920, p. 1.

25. Hugh J. Hughes to Preus, 23 October 1921, Preus Papers.

26. For McGuire's political views, see A. J. McGuire to Geo. F. Wells, 21 April 1919, [A. J. McGuire], typescript, 19 January 1919, [McGuire], "Saturday Lunch Club April 17—[19]20," notes, Associate Professor of Agriculture [McGuire] to Pres. [Woodrow] Wilson, 31 May 1920, all in Arthur J. and Marie McGuire Papers, MHS. For his early education and career, see *The Farmer,* 16 May 1925, p. 731.

27. McGuire to Dear Sir, 31 July 1918, McGuire, "Cooperation Between Cooperative Creameries," typescript, December 1918, W. W. Clark to Frank E. Balmer, 10 July 1919, all in McGuire Papers; McGuire, Dairy 1920 report in Specialists Annual Reports, University of Minnesota, Agricultural Extension Service Papers, UM Archives; *The Farmer,* 1 May, p. 1258, and 29 May, p. 1472, both 1920.

28. Here and below, *The Farmer,* 27 March 1920 (p. 949, 970), 10 April 1920 (p. 1081, 1100), 12 February 1921 (p. 285, 298–300), 21 May 1921 (p. 871, 880), and 16 April 1927 (p. 5); Minnesota Cooperative Creameries Association, *Land O' Lakes Creameries, Incorporated: Its Organization, Nature and History* (Minneapolis: Land O' Lakes Creameries, 1934); Roy C. Potts, *Marketing Practices of Wisconsin and Minnesota Creameries,* USDA Bulletin no. 690 (Washington D.C.: U.S. Department of Agriculture, 1918), 10, 15; Chandler, *Visible Hand,* 233–39.

29. *The Farmer,* 27 March 1920 (p. 949, 970), 10 April 1920 (p. 1081, 1100), 1 May 1920, and 12 February 1921 (p. 285). In 1920 the Danish *krone* hit a low value of only 15.63 cents—in 1918 it had been worth 30 cents; C. Christensen, *Agricultural Cooperation,* table facing p. 1.

30. C. Christensen, *Agricultural Cooperation,* 22–23; N. J. Holmberg to J. A. Drake, 16 July 1924, Minnesota Department of Agriculture, Records Re: Minnesota Cooperative Creameries Association (MCCA), Minnesota State Archives.

31. Holmberg to Drake, 16 July 1924, MDA Records Re: MCCA; *The Farmer,* 10 April 1920 (p. 1081), 17 April 1920 (p. 1156), 4 June 1921 (p. 926); Kenneth D. Ruble, *Men to Remember: How 100,000 Neighbors Made History* (Chicago: R. R. Donnelly & Sons, 1947), 60–62.

32. Holmberg to Drake, 16 July 1924, Minnesota Cooperative Creameries Association, Minutes, 7 June 1921, and Board of Directors' Minutes, 8 June 1921, all in MDA Records Re: MCCA; *The Farmer,* 30 April, p. 760, and 18 June, p. 987, both 1921; *St. Paul Pioneer Press,* 24 April, sec. 1, p. 8, and 8 June, p. 1, both 1921; *Minneapolis Journal,* 7 June, p. 9, and 8 June, p. 1, 12, both 1921; Ruble, *Men to Remember,* 60–62; Hugh J. Hughes to "All Presidents and Secretaries of Minnesota Creameries," 1 June 1921, McGuire Papers.

33. United States, Department of Agriculture, *Yearbook, 1922* (Washington, D.C.: GPO, 1923), 372.

34. *The Farmer,* 27 March (p. 949, 970), 3 April (p. 1018, 1039), 10 April (p. 1081, 1100), 17 April (p. 1147, 1162,), 24 April (p. 1202, 1220), 1 May (p. 1260, 1268), all 1920; *Land O'*

Lakes Creameries: Its Organization, Nature and History; A. J. McGuire to County Agents, 6 July 1921, McGuire Papers; MCCA, Articles of Incorporation, p. 21, MDA Records Re: MCCA; Ruble, *Men to Remember*, 58, 64. Roy C. Potts was a USDA expert and the author of *Marketing Practices of Wisconsin and Minnesota Creameries*.

35. Ruble, *Men to Remember*, 58, 67, 77; "Agreement Between California Fruit Growers Exchange and its District Exchanges," undated typescript, and "Articles of Incorporation," both in MDA Records Re: MCCA; John D. Black and H. Bruce Price, *Cooperative Central Marketing Organization*, University of Minnesota Agricultural Experiment Station Bulletin no. 211 (April 1924), 21.

36. American Institute of Cooperation, *American Cooperation* 2 (1925): 38; *The Farmer*, 18 June 1921, p. 987; *Minneapolis Journal*, 8 June 1921, p. 12. Hughes stated that the MCCA would help creameries sell butter "through closer co-operation with present distributing agencies and wholesale market receivers"; *Minneapolis Journal*, 7 June 1921, p. 9. But the prospect of MCCA displacing these agencies and receivers was hinted at in the *Journal* the next day (p. 12).

37. *The Farmer*, 18 June 1921 (p. 987, 997), 7 October 1922 (p. 1148, 1168–69, 1174), and 16 May 1925 (p. 733, 747); H. F. Meyer to Holmberg, 5 February 1924, McGuire to J. H. Hay, 2 September 1925, Hay to McGuire, 18 September 1925, Holmberg to Chris Heen, 17 April 1922, all in MDA Records Re: MCCA; "Gustafson Accepts Position in the West," undated typescript [1926–33], McGuire Papers; TCMPA *Bulletin*, March 1922. Holmberg advised MCCA manager McGuire on the design of the Land O' Lakes label; N. J. Holmberg to A. J. McGuire, 25 July 1924, MDA Records Re: MCCA.

38. *Farm, Stock and Home*, 15 April (p. 285), 1 July (p. 395), and 1 December (p. 632), all 1907; *Willmar Tribune*, 3 July 1907, p. 4.

39. McGuire, "Development of the Cooperative Creamery in Minnesota," *American Cooperation* 2 (1925): 37–38.

40. Shideler, *Farm Crisis*, 43–44, 101, 250–51.

41. *Minneapolis Tribune*, 3 March 1923, p. 1; Minute Book (1923–24), 24 March 1923, p. 8, General State Organization Committee, Minnesota Potato Growers Exchange (MPGE), MPGE Papers, MHS.

42. *Minneapolis Tribune*, 3 March 1923, p. 1, 36; *St. Paul Pioneer Press*, 3 March 1923, p. 3. The legislature was considering a bill on cooperative marketing.

43. *St. Paul Pioneer Press*, 3 March 1923, p. 3 (quote); *Minneapolis Tribune*, 3 March 1923, p. 1 (quote), 16–17, 36; *The Farmer*, 17 March 1923, p. 404 (quote).

44. *Potato Grower*, 5 and 20 September 1923, p. 1–4; *Polk County Leader*, 7 and 14 September 1923, both p. 1; *Crookston Daily Times*, 11 September 1923, p. 1; *Detroit Record*, 14 September 1923, p. 4; *Brainerd Dispatch*, 14 September 1923, p. 1 (quoting *Minneapolis Journal*), and 21 September 1923, p. 4; *Princeton Union*, 20 September 1923, p. 1, 2; *Moorhead Weekly News*, 13 and 20 September 1923, both p. 2; *Moorhead District Herald*, 20 September 1923, p. 1.

45. *Potato Grower*, 5 and 20 September 1923, p. 2; Minutes, 24 March 1923, p. 5, 6, 12, 14, MPGE Organizing Committee, MPGE Papers; Hughes, *Cooperation Here and Abroad*, 9. With the "approval" of the MDA, university, and Farm Bureau, no representatives of those groups were placed on the organizing committee; Minutes, p. 5, MPGE Organizing Committee, MPGE Papers. For a confirmation of Hughes's characterization, see Hamilton, *New Day to New Deal*, 16; *Polk County Leader*, 23 [21] September 1923, p. 1.

46. Gieske, *Farmer-Laborism*, 75–79; *Country Press* (Moorhead), 14 September and 2 November 1923, both p. 1 (quotes), and 12 October 1923, p. 1; *Moorhead Weekly News*, 18 October 1923, p. 1. See also *Country Press*, 12 October and 2 November, both 1923, both p. 4.

47. S. G. Rubinow, "The Minnesota Potato Growers' Exchange," *American Cooperation* 2 (1925): 478, 479, 483; *The Farmer*, 20 February 1926, p. 298; Mosbæk to John W. Lewis, 29 January 1924, Udvandrerarkivet, Aalborg; Hughes, *Cooperation Here and Abroad*, 9–10.

48. Rubinow, "Minnesota Potato Growers' Exchange," 479.

49. Hamilton, *New Day to New Deal*, 15, 17; Hughes, *Cooperation Here and Abroad*, 10; Shideler, *Farm Crisis*, 92, 104.

50. TCMPA *Bulletin*, vol. 6, no. 3 (March 1922).

51. For the MCCA's early (1921–23) operations, see Ruble, *Men to Remember*, 72–110; *The Farmer*, 7 October 1922, p. 1148, 1168–69, 1174; *Land O' Lakes Creameries: Its Organization, Nature and History*; Hugh J. Hughes to K. Ulmanis, 23 January 1923, MDA Records Re: MCCA.

52. *The Farmer*, 17 March, p. 386, 399, 404, and 21 April, p. 593, 601, both 1923; *Daily Journal-Press* (St. Cloud), 15 September 1923, p. 1; *Potato Grower*, 5 and 20 September 1923, both p. 2; Ruble, *Men to Remember*, 113–14, 126–30, 133; Shideler, *Farm Crisis*, 253; Black and Price, *Cooperative Central Marketing Organization*, 21. For an account of one meeting where Brandt argued for the sales plan and quoted a threatening letter, see *Askov American*, 1 November 1923, p. 1. Schilling reported that, at first, McGuire opposed direct sales by MCCA for fear the commission firms would fight the MCCA; Schilling, *Lest We Forget*, 29.

53. Ruble, *Men to Remember*, 134–35, 138–42; N. J. Holmberg to A. G. McGuire, 25 July 1924, MDA Records Re: MCCA; *The Farmer*, 16 May 1925, p. 733, 747, and 16 April 1927, p. 5, 19.

54. Ruble, *Men to Remember*, 131, 140, 148–50, 189–90; *The Farmer*, 7 May 1927, p. 758, and 15 August 1931, p. 896; Holmberg to John Brandt, 22 June 1926, attached letter, Brandt to Holmberg, 17 June 1926, and copy of George E. Leach to Gentlemen [n.d.], MDA Records Re: MCCA. For a Danish account of the success of Land O' Lakes, see S. Sørensen, "Minnesotas store Andels-Smørsalgsforening," *Andelsbladet* (Copenhagen), 1926, p. 1107–12.

55. *The Farmer*, 31 July 1920, p. 1842; Shideler, *Farm Crisis*, 44, 51, 104–7, 254; Saloutos and Hicks, *Twentieth-Century Populism*, 295.

56. Shideler, *Farm Crisis*, 106–11; Saloutos and Hicks, *Twentieth-Century Populism*, 277–79, 295–300; Philip D. Jordan, "Equity, Justice, and Politics: A History of the Farmers Union Grain Terminal Association," 74–80, undated typescript, Myron W. Thatcher Papers, MHS; Thomas E. Cashman to J. A. O. Preus, 17 October 1921, and attached copy of Cashman to Harry N. Owen, same date, both in Preus Papers. Cashman expressed the MFBF's opposition to ECE serving as exclusive sales agent for USGG, for the MFBF was using "the great hope" offered by USGG to recruit members.

57. Saloutos and Hicks, *Twentieth-Century Populism*, 291–94; *Thief River Falls Tribune*, 6 and 20 June 1923, both p. 1; "Official Proceedings of Minnesota Wheat Growers Cooperative Marketing Association," p. 10–11, 13, 14–17, 50–51, 73, 92, 96, 101, 196, 198, 203a, typescript, MWGCMA Minutes and Related Records, 1923–1926, MHS; Shideler, *Farm Crisis*, 251; *The Farmer*, 3 September 1927, p. 1196, and 1 October 1927, p. 1324; Black and Price, *Cooperative Central Marketing Organization*, 24–25.

58. Shideler, *Farm Crisis*, 251.

59. Jordan, "Equity, Justice, and Politics," 81, 83, 87. In Canada both the pooling approach and the farmers' elevator approach worked side by side, and by 1926 the Canadian Wheat Pool was handling 53 percent of that nation's wheat crop; *The Farmer*, 1 October (p. 1321, 1332), 8 October (p. 1357, 1368–69), and 15 October (p. 1389, 1398–99), all 1927.

60. For the distinction between a federation and a centralized cooperative organization and for an argument that the former could work just as well as the latter, see Black and Price, *Cooperative Central Marketing Organization*, 30–32, 80–91.

61. R. Douglas Hurt, *American Agriculture: A Brief History* (Ames: Iowa State University Press, 1994), 242–48; David B. Danbom, *Born in the Country: A History of Rural America* (Baltimore: Johns Hopkins University Press, 1995), 165; Rudolph Froker, "Organization and Management Problems of Cooperative Oil Companies in Minnesota" (master's thesis, University of Minnesota, 1927), 5–6.

62. Norman Eugene Taylor, "The Midland Cooperative Wholesale, Inc.: Its History and Analysis" (Ph.D. diss., University of Minnesota, 1955), 17–18.

63. Taylor, "Midland Cooperative Wholesale," 17–18, 22; Richard Lynne, "Cottonwood Cooperative Oil Company," in *Cottonwood Community*; Joel S. Torstenson, "The Development of an Institution: A Case History of Midland Cooperatives Incorporated" (Ph.D. diss., University of Minnesota, 1958), 28–29; *Cottonwood Current*, 3 June (p. 5), 1 July (p. 4), 8 July (p. 5), 15 July (p. 1), 12 August (p. 1), and 19 August (p. 5), all 1921; Froker,

"Organization and Management Problems," 6, 8, 9.

64. Taylor, "Midland Cooperative Wholesale," 18–20; Froker, "Organization and Management Problems," 6, 8–9, 11–12; Minnesota Co-op Oil Co., *The Co-operative Oil Movement in the Northwest* (1928), 2, pamphlet in Midland Cooperative Records, 1917–1982, MHS.

65. Torstenson, "Development of an Institution," 33–34; Taylor, "Midland Cooperative Wholesale," 20–25; Froker, "Organization and Management Problems," 53–54C; *Co-operative Oil Movement*, 7, 13–14.

66. Taylor, "Midland Cooperative Wholesale," 26, 32–33; Torstenson, "Development of an Institution," 14, 39–41.

67. See Black and Price, *Cooperative Central Marketing Organization*, 6–15, for an analysis of "sixteen problems which local co-operatives acting alone" could not solve.

68. Black and Price, *Cooperative Central Marketing Organization*, 13–14.

69. Table 6 is based on Black and Price, *Cooperative Central Marketing Organization*, 27–35.

70. Black and Price, *Cooperative Central Marketing Organization*, 36–38.

71. Black and Price, *Cooperative Central Marketing Organization*, 12–14, 27–28, 80–83 (quote p. 81), 91, 110–111 (quotes).

Notes to Chapter 14

1. *Glenwood Herald*, 9 July 1936, p. 1; *Pope County Tribune* (Glenwood), 9 July 1936, p. 1. A *New York Times* reporter estimated the attendance at five thousand; M. Lowell Gunzberg, "The 'Co-op' Idea Takes Root: In Minnesota a Scheme of Economic Reform, New to America but Old in Europe, Is Tried Out by Large Consumer Groups," *New York Times Magazine*, 13 September 1936, p. 10. The chapter title is a shortened quote from the *Minnesota Leader*, 16 February 1935, p. 2. Glenwood's mayor, Arnold O. ("Cornie") Wollan, had given a welcoming address to convention visitors the previous evening.

2. *New York Times Magazine*, 13 September 1936, p. 10, 21. For FLP candidates' July 4 speaking schedules, see *Minnesota Leader*, 4 July 1936, p. 1. The *Leader* merely printed press releases on the Glenwood

convention and did not send its own representative; *Minnesota Leader*, 13 June (p. 2), 27 June (p. 7), 4 July (p. 7), all 1936.

3. Richard M. Valelly, *Radicalism in the States: The Minnesota Farmer-Labor Party and the American Political Economy* (Chicago: University of Chicago Press, 1989), xiii.

4. Gieske, *Minnesota Farmer-Laborism*, 15–31; Chrislock, *Watchdog of Loyalty*, 332–33; Valelly, *Radicalism in the States*, 23–27. By focusing on political economy, Valelly underestimated the ethnic side of the FLP — hence, of the role of German-American voters in this anti-MCPS coalition. The *New York Times* reporter had clearly been briefed at Midland's Minneapolis office before driving out to Glenwood and Morris, but he wrote nothing about the FLP's views on cooperatives; *New York Times Magazine*, 13 September 1936, p. 10, 21.

5. L. F. Garey, *Types of Farming in Minnesota*, University of Minnesota, Agricultural Experiment Station Bulletin no. 257 (August 1929), 32; L. F. Garey and F. F. Elliott, *Systems of Farming in Eastern and Southern Minnesota*, University of Minnesota, Agricultural Experiment Station Bulletin no. 276 (January 1931), 40. The regional classification is identical in each of these bulletins.

6. Valelly, *Radicalism in the States*, 158–65 (quote on 163).

7. Seymour Martin Lipset, *Agrarian Socialism: The Cooperative Commonwealth Federation in Saskatchewan. A Study in Political Sociology* (New York: Doubleday, Anchor Books, 1968), 44, 54, 60–68, 73, 83, 84–90, 93, 101–5, 111–14, 212 (quote), 213–14. Lipset (214) explicitly compared the CCF's success to that of the NPL in North Dakota, also "a one-crop wheat economy."

8. Timo Riippa, "The Finns and Swede-Finns," in *They Chose Minnesota*, ed. Holmquist, 296–322, especially 298 (quote), 303–5, and 308–11; Arnold Alanen, "The Development and Distribution of Finnish Consumers' Cooperatives in Michigan, Minnesota and Wisconsin, 1903–1973," in *The Finnish Experience in the Western Great Lakes Region: New Perspectives*, ed. Michael G. Karni et al. (Turku, Finland: Institute for Migration, 1975), 110–13; Karni, "Struggle on the Cooperative Front: The Separation of

Central Cooperative Wholesale from Communism, 1929–30," in *Finnish Experience*, 190–92; Peter Kivisto, *Immigrant Socialists in the United States: The Case of Finns and the Left* (Cranbury, N.J.: Associated University Presses, 1984), 70, 73, 101–3, 121; Neil Betten, "The Origins of Ethnic Radicalism in Northern Minnesota, 1900–1920," *International Migration Review* 4 (Spring 1970): 44–55; Reino Kero, "The Roots of Finnish-American Left-Wing Radicalism," *Publication No. 5* (Turku: University of Turku), 45, 46, 142–44, 156, 169–72; Michael G. Karni, *The Founding of the Finnish Socialist Federation and the Minnesota Strike of 1907* (Superior: Tyomies Society, 1977), 67–70, 73–79, 82.

9. Gieske, *Minnesota Farmer-Laborism*, 95, 97–98; Leonard C. Kercher et al., *Consumers' Cooperatives in the North Central States* (Minneapolis: University of Minnesota Press, 1941), 80, 377–79; Karni, "Struggle on the Cooperative Front," in *Finnish Experience*, 191, 194–97, 199 (quote), 200; Kivisto, *Immigrant Socialists*, 169–72; Russell K. Lewis and Mauritz Seashore, *Consumers' Cooperation in Minnesota* ([St. Paul]: Minnesota Department of Agriculture, Dairy and Foods, April 1937), Appendix B-2.

10. Torstenson, "Development of an Institution," 40, 41, 45, 76–77 (quote), 78–79, 83, 86–88, 97; Davis Douthit, *Nobody Owns Us: The Story of Joe Gilbert, Midwestern Rebel* (Chicago: Cooperative League of the U.S.A., 1948), 201–3, 206–15; George W. Jacobson to Thomas Amlie, 13 June 1935, and letterhead, Howard Y. Williams to Executive Committee, League for Independent Political Action, 17 May 1934, both in George W. Jacobson files, Personal, LIPA, FLPF, ACPF, 1933–1935 folder, Russell K. Lewis and George W. Jacobson Papers, 1925–1966, MHS.

11. Torstenson, "Development of an Institution," 45, 47, 83 (quote), 85, 122.

12. Kercher et al., *Consumers' Cooperatives*, 7–8, 178–93; Torstenson, "Development of an Institution," 94, 97–98, 109; Lewis and Seashore, *Consumers' Cooperation in Minnesota*, 10, 30–31, 58–59; Sam B. Morison, "Producer Cooperation in Minnesota," 40–41, 43, typescript, Cooperative Survey Studies, 1935, Cooperatives Division, Minnesota Department of Agricul-

ture, Dairy, and Food, Records (MDA), State Archives. Morison examined consumers' cooperation at length in his study of producers' cooperation, and he assumed that the latter's role was temporary until "consumers' organizations take over the production of all raw materials" (p. 43). In 1936 Warbasse published a third, "completely rewritten" edition of his *Cooperative Democracy* (New York: Harper & Brothers), first issued in 1923.

13. Gieske, *Minnesota Farmer-Laborism*, 187; George H. Mayer, *The Political Career of Floyd B. Olson* (1951; St. Paul: Minnesota Historical Society Press, Borealis Books, 1987), 170–71; *Minnesota Leader*, 16 February 1935, p. 1, 2 (quote), 6; *New York Times*, 19 May 1935, sec. 7, p. 5 (quote). Day undoubtedly cleared his article with Olson, who likely was a coauthor, but cautiously ran it under his name alone.

14. Philip D. Jordan, "Equity, Justice, and Politics," 64–66, 74–79, 83, 87, 91–93, 95, 97, 149–50, 172–73; *Farmers Union Herald*, May 1932, p. 1, 5; *St. Paul Pioneer Press*, 29 January 1930, p. 1.

15. "Farmers Union Central Exchange," undated typescript, box 9, Farmers Union Central Exchange Records, MHS; Leo N. Rickertsen, *To Gather Together: cenex, The First Fifty Years* (Minneapolis: CENEX, 1980), 36, 57–58, 63; Farmers Union Central Exchange, *Set-Up, History, Growth and Development* (St. Paul, 1937), 9–10, 12–15; Kercher et al., *Consumers' Cooperatives*, 406–7; *Farmers Union Herald*, 9 February 1931, p. 1. A 1935 study of cooperatives gave conflicting reports on CENEX's number of retail customers in the state. One table lists only nine oil cooperatives buying petroleum products from CENEX—seven of these being in northwestern Minnesota; "Total Listing of Oil Cooperatives Operating," in Frank C. Eustis, "The Cooperative Store Movement (with special reference to Minnesota)," typescript (April 1935), Cooperative Survey Studies, MDA Records. In another text, CENEX is credited with twenty-three local cooperative customers in the state; Lewis and Seashore, *Consumers' Cooperation in Minnesota*, 52.

16. Kercher et al., *Consumers' Cooperatives*, 375–76, 386, 411; Lewis and Seashore, *Consumers' Cooperation in Minnesota*, 18–19,

44–45. The exact percentages of light petroleum products (gas and oil) sold in Minnesota in 1936 are: Standard Oil—17.48; all cooperatives—9.25; Midland—4.53; independent cooperatives—3.06; Farmers Union—93; CCW—.54; and Farm Bureau Service Company—.19 percent; Lewis and Seashore, 44–45.

17. Lewis and Seashore, *Consumers' Cooperation in Minnesota*, 44–45.

18. See Johnson's obituary in *Minnesota Leader*, 19 September 1936, p. 1, 2; Gieske, *Minnesota Farmer-Laborism*, 21, 80.

19. Memorandum for Governor, 26 August 1932, Notes for Governor, 20 February 1933 and 10 May 1933, all typescripts, box 2, Vince A. Day Papers, MHS. Not all of the memos have been preserved so these may not have been the only cooperative issues raised.

20. See, for example, Mayer, *Floyd B. Olson*, chapters 4–7, and Gieske, *Minnesota Farmer-Laborism*, 142–50, 172–78.

21. Mayer, *Floyd B. Olson*, 170–72; Gieske, *Minnesota Farmer-Laborism*, 187–89; Steven J. Keillor, *Hjalmar Petersen of Minnesota: The Politics of Provincial Independence* (St. Paul: Minnesota Historical Society Press, 1987), 103–5; *Minneapolis Journal*, 28 March 1934, p. 10–11; *Analysis of the Farmer-Labor Platform* and *Farmer-Labor Platform of Minnesota 1934*, pamphlets in box 1, Farmer-Labor Association of Minnesota Records, 1918–1948 (hereafter FLA Records), MHS.

22. Gieske, *Minnesota Farmer-Laborism*, 191–92; Keillor, *Hjalmar Petersen*, 105–7; Mayer, *Floyd B. Olson*, 173–81 (quote p. 178); Memorandum for Governor: Farmer-Labor Platform, 2 May 1934, Day Papers. See also Charles B. Cheney, "Minnesota Politics" column, *Minneapolis Journal*, 1 May 1934.

23. Memorandum for Governor, 2 May 1934, Day Papers; Analysis of the Farmer-Labor Platform, 2–3, 14–15, FLA Records; Keillor, *Hjalmar Petersen*, 106–7.

24. Memorandum for Governor, 2 May 1934, Day Papers. In this memo, Day admitted that "the Preamble advocates, at least in one portion, complete socialization of all private and public property."

25. George W. Jacobson to Vince Day, 19 July 1934, in George W. Jacobson files, Farmer-Labor Party & Assn, 1934–1935 folder, box 17, Lewis Papers.

26. *Bread or Straw: The Issues of the Campaign*, pamphlet [1934], p. 4, Jacobson files, box 17, Lewis Papers.

27. Gieske, *Minnesota Farmer-Laborism*, 171, 200; Arthur Naftalin, "A History of the Farmer-Labor Party of Minnesota" (Ph.D. diss., University of Minnesota, 1948), 271; Valelly, *Radicalism in the States*, 117–18.

28. Minutes of Voluntary Committee, 29 August, 24 September, 12 November, and 6 December, all 1934, and George W. Jacobson to Joseph Gilbert, 31 January 1935, all in Jacobson files, box 17, Lewis Papers. The original members of the committee were: Jacobson, W. E. Boie of Land O' Lakes, Gideon Edberg of Minneapolis, and MDA employees John Bosch (also a Farm Holiday leader), Charles Ommodt, Hemming Nelson, Harold Peterson, Emil F. Mattson, and Paul Peterson. Added later were Gilbert and V. S. Alanne of the Northern States Cooperative League.

29. For the Farmer-Labor Party's use of patronage to build its "infrastructure of political clubs" and its coalition—and the costs of this strategy, see Valelly, *Radicalism in the States*, 60–68.

30. Gieske, *Minnesota Farmer-Laborism*, 145 (quote); Minnesota, *Legislative Manual*, 1939, p. 504; *Minneapolis Journal*, 13 February 1939, p. 9; *Clarkfield Advocate*, 12 October 1922, p. 1, 4; Notes for Governor, 10 December 1932, p. 1–2, and "Memorandum for Governor," 28 September 1933, p. 2, 20 October 1933, p. 2, and 22 November 1934, Day Papers; Rollef A. Trovatten to Carl G. O. Hansen, 13 December 1935, Commissioner's Letters, MDA Records; Irwin Herness Interview, 20 January 1977, transcript, p. 2, 3, 5, 11, 12, 20th Century Radicalism in Minnesota Oral History Project, MHS. For a biographical sketch of Hay, see *St. Paul Dispatch*, 16 March 1950, p. 33, and *Minneapolis Journal*, 17 March 1950, p. 27.

31. Minutes of the Voluntary Committee, 12 November and 6 December 1934, Jacobson files, box 17, Lewis Papers; *National Farm Holiday News*, 21 May 1937, p. 3. The committee did not discuss personnel changes at MDA until November 12, after the 1934 election. Ommodt was appointed as Trovatten's successor in May 1937. Trovatten was accused by other sources of mismanage-

ment and of tolerating "corruption" and "conflict between Jews and Norwegians" at MDA; Memorandum for Governor, 25 August (quote), 28 September (quote), and 20 October, all 1933, Day Papers. Some MDA employees leaked these charges and others to the *St. Paul Daily News*; see *St. Paul Daily News*, 21 September (p. 1), 24 September (first sec., p. 4), 25 September (p. 1), and 27 September (p. 6), all 1933.

32. Minutes of the Voluntary Committee, 24 September, 12 November, and 6 December 1934, and Jacobson to Gilbert, 31 January 1935, all in Jacobson files, Lewis Papers.

33. Joseph Gilbert to George W. Jacobson, 18 January 1935, and Jacobson to Gilbert, 31 January 1935, both in Jacobson files, Lewis Papers; Minnesota, *Session Laws*, 1919, chap. 444, p. 525. For unknown reasons, Olson had requested that Alanne be added to the committee. This analysis of the meeting is based on Gilbert's account, the only available source. For Olson's evasive response to many petitioners, see Mayer, *Floyd B. Olson*, 236–37.

34. "Co-operative Survey by Russell Lewis," undated typescript, 3–4, box 18, Lewis Papers; Frank C. Eustis, "The Cooperative Store Movement (With Special Reference to Minnesota)," typescript, April 1935, Cooperative Survey Studies, MDA Records. For the internal workings of the survey, see Lewis to Trovatten, 16 February 1934, [Lewis] "To Interviewers" [March 1934] (quote) and to "Dear Investigator," [November 1934?], "Work Done for Midland Co-op Oil Co. by the Co-op Survey," typescript [January 1935?], H. J. Friedl to Lewis, 13 December 1934, and John D. Prestidge to Lewis [December 1934]—all in box 107.K.8.8(F), MDA Records; printed and edited versions of some reports, dated 1937, are at MHS. It is not clear how many copies were printed or how these were distributed. *Midland Cooperator*, May 1934 (p. 2), August and September 1934 (both p. 1), and April 1935 (p. 1). By December 1935, the project had moved to the Sexton Building in Minneapolis; Lewis to J. H. Hay, 14 December 1935, box 107.K.8.8(F). One evidence of MDA's limited role is that Hay did not even review the format of the questionnaires before they were sent out; Hay to W. A. Gordon, 6 April 1934, box 107.K.8.8(F).

35. Morison, "Producer Cooperation in Minnesota," 1 (quote), 25–41, 43, 58, MDA Records; Lewis and Seashore, *Consumers' Cooperation in Minnesota*, 10 (quote), 30–31 (quote), 55. Lewis and Seashore (p. 58) did not think that farm supply cooperatives were true consumers' cooperatives since the purchased goods, such as seeds, feeds, oil, were used in production.

36. Valelly, *Radicalism in the States*, 83.

37. D. Clayton Brown, *Electricity for Rural America: The Fight for the REA* (Westport, Conn.: Greenwood Press, 1980), 45, 65–66.

38. Brown, *Electricity for Rural America*, 22–34; Kenneth E. Trombley, *The Life and Times of a Happy Liberal: A Biography of Morris Llewellyn Cooke* (New York: Harper & Bros., 1954), 102–11, 149. Those who take the REA and Cooke's side stress that Cooke was willing to lend to private utilities but that their plans were inadequate. Despite his bias in favor of the private utilities, Forrest McDonald makes a convincing case that Cooke's willingness was more apparent than real; Forrest McDonald, *Let There Be Light: The Electric Utility Industry in Wisconsin, 1881–1955* (Madison, Wis.: American History Research Center, 1957), 359–68.

39. Brown, *Electricity for Rural America*, 5 (quote), 6, 45, 50; *Minnesota Leader*, 20 July 1935, p. 1.

40. Brown, *Electricity for Rural America*, 5–6.

41. *Granite Falls Tribune*, 10 March (p. 4), 7 April (p. 4), 14 April (p. 5), and 21 April (p. 8), all 1914, and 20 April 1944, p. 5; Brown, *Electricity for Rural America*, 13.

42. Brown, *Electricity for Rural America*, 6–7 (quote p. 7); Harry Slattery, *Rural America Lights Up* (Washington, D.C.: National Home Library Foundation, 1940), 15–19; E. A. Stewart, J. M. Larson, J. Romness, *The Red Wing Project on Utilization of Electricity in Agriculture* (St. Paul: University of Minnesota, Agricultural Experiment Station, [1928?]); Minnesota Committee on the Relation of Electricity to Agriculture, *Presentation of Purpose of the Red Wing Experimental Rural Electric Line* ([Minneapolis, 1925?]).

43. Brown, *Electricity for Rural America*, 33–34; Slattery, *Rural America Lights Up*, 21.

44. Brown, *Electricity for Rural America*, 48–55 (quote p. 54); Trombley, *Happy Lib-*

eral, 148–56; McDonald, *Let There Be Light*, 360–68. In a parallel way, Cooke had preferred government regulation of existing electric systems to either government ownership or unregulated private ownership; *Happy Liberal*, 109

45. In August 1935, Vince Day was already informing Olson that the REA "has been advised that the various leaders of this State are engaged in warring upon one another" over the projected rural electrification program; Day, "Memorandum for Governor," 9 August 1935, p. 1, Day Papers.

46. Federated Electric Cooperative, *Minnesota Rural Electrification Activities!* (Minneapolis, 1936), 1–3; Alwin N. Howalt to Wisconsin Cooperatives, 17 December 1935, box 17, Lewis Papers; Howalt, "Federated Electric Cooperative—Manager's Report—1935–36," typescript, 10 June 1936, p. 2–3, Governor's Executive Letters, 1936 ("Has to Me"), Minnesota State Archives; *Minnesota Leader*, 15 February 1935, p. 1, 2. National Cooperatives, Inc., was the liberal wholesalers' group that first "urged" Midland to "sponsor the electrification program"; *Rural Electrification Activities!* 1. For one report of a Howalt-led meeting, see *Renville Star-Farmer*, 16 January 1936, p. 1. For Howalt on REA, see *Midland Cooperator*, March 1936, p. 6.

47. *Minnesota Leader*, 13 July 1935, p. 2; *The Farmer*, 23 April 1921, p. 725, 736–37; J. S. Jones to Henrik Shipstead, 13 July 1935, box 1, Henrik Shipstead Papers, 1913–1953, MHS.

48. Valelly emphasized how the Agricultural Adjustment Administration (AAA), by working through county agents, aided the Farm Bureau at the expense of the Farmers' Union; *Radicalism in the States*, 97–100.

49. *Minnesota Leader*, 20 July 1935, p. 1, 6; *St. Paul Dispatch*, 1 July 1935, p. 22. By contrast, Wisconsin's legislature created a "state office of Rural Electrification Co-ordinator," who worked to organize and promote rural electric cooperatives; McDonald, *Let There Be Light*, 370.

50. *Minnesota Leader*, 27 July (p. 1), 24 August (p. 1, 6), 14 September (p. 6), 21 September (p. 2), and 23 November (p. 7), all 1935; Hay to Shipstead, 17 July 1935, and Morris L. Cooke to Shipstead, 29 August 1935, both in box 1, Shipstead Papers; Vince

A. Day, "[Notes to] Gov:," undated typescript [July 1935?], Governor's Executive Letters, 1936 ("Has to Me"); *Rural Electrification Activities!* 1. Day's memo to Olson began, "John Bosch wants to know if you will issue a call for a meeting…"; according to this memo, the Farm Holiday Association, Midland, and national third-party advocate Howard Y. Williams requested the conference be held without "Land O' Lakes, the Farm Bureau and similar groups" being present. In a letter to Olson after he backed out, Hay tried to impress the governor with his wide-ranging activities in this field; Hay to Olson, 13 August 1935, Governor's Executive Letters, 1936 ("Has to Me").

51. *Minnesota Farm Bureau News*, South Central ed. (St. Peter), 1 February 1936, p. 1, 8–9; *St. Paul Pioneer Press*, 10 January 1936, p. 1, 3; *Minneapolis Journal*, 10 January 1936, p. 19; *Renville Star-Farmer*, 23 January 1936, p. 2; Christiana McFadyen Campbell, *The Farm Bureau and the New Deal: A Study of the Making of National Farm Policy, 1933–40* (Urbana: University of Illinois Press, 1962), 156–59, 169–71. For Andrew Olson's career, see *Renville Star-Farmer*, 7 October 1965, p. 1.

52. Boyd Fisher to Trovatten, 29 July 1936, and Fisher to Howalt, 27 August 1936, both in Agricultural Extension, Department of Agriculture files, University of Minnesota, President's Office Papers.

53. An REA executive (probably Boyd Fisher) quoted in Frederick William Muller, *Public Rural Electrification* (Washington, D.C.: American Council on Public Affairs, 1944), 51n33. For Midland's social philosophy, see Torstenson, "Development of an Institution," 93–110.

54. *Litchfield Independent*, 5 and 12 August 1936, both p. 1; *Meeker County News*, 13 August 1936, p. 1; *Minnesota Farm Bureau News*, Southwest ed., 1 August and 1 September 1936, both p. 1. See also, J. S. Jones to Trovatten, 24 July 1936, Trovatten to Jones, 27 July 1936, Jones to Trovatten, 28 July 1936, all in box 8, Commissioner's Correspondence, MDA Records. For the Meeker County project, see McNelly, *County Agent Story*, 126–27; *The Farmer*, 29 August 1936, p. 4, 11. Once a key part of the Farm Bureau-county-agent-university network, *The Farmer* had by 1936 dropped its crusading role and be-

come a much more bland, politically neutral farm journal trying to avoid offending subscribers.

55. Fisher to Howalt, 27 August 1936, and Frank Peck to Lotus D. Coffman, 12 October 1936, both Agricultural Extension file, President's Office Papers.

56. Hay to Irving J. Clinton, 11 August 1936, Governor's Executive Letters, 1936 ("Has to Me").

57. Coffman to Peck, 7 October 1936, and attached resolution dated 17 September 1936, Peck to Coffman, 12 October 1936, Coffman to Beauford Johnson, 15 October 1936, all Agricultural Extension file, President's Office Papers. Zimmerman reported that Peck "decided to discontinue" his work from 1 August to 1 October 1936, the period when the investigating committee did most of its work; Zimmerman to Coffman, 25 November 1936, Agricultural Extension file. Papers in Zimmerman's personnel file, University of Minnesota, Institute of Agriculture, Director's Office Papers, confirm the August 1 date but provide no reason for the layoff. He returned to work the first six months of 1937 for the university. On 6 October he resigned as the committee's secretary; *Minnesota Farm Bureau News*, Southwest ed., 1 November 1936, p. 1.

58. Here and below, *Midland Cooperator*, July, p 5, November, p. 4, December, p. 1, 4 — all 1936; *Minnesota Farm Bureau News*, Southwest ed., 1 November 1936, p. 1, and 1 December 1936, p. 2; *Minnesota Leader*, 28 November 1936, p. 3; Henry T. Johnson, Paul Ferguson, and Beauford Johnson to Officers of Minnesota Rural Electric Associations, 10 November 1936, and "Farm Bureau Men Bolt Electric Meeting," typescript, 17 November 1936, both in Governor's Executive Letters, 1936 ("Has to Me"); *Rural Electrification Activities!* 7–8.

59. *Minnesota Farm Bureau News*, Southwest ed., 1 July (p. 1), 1 September (p. 1, 7), and 1 December (p. 2), all 1936.

60. See Howalt, "General Criticisms of the R.E.A. and Factors which Indicate Gross Discrimination," typescript [1937?], in Governor's Executive Letters, 1937 ("M to Pe").

61. For correspondence between the FEC, the governor's office, and the MDA, see the Rural Electrification folders in Governor's

Executive Letters, 1936 and 1937, especially George W. Jacobson to Hjalmar Petersen, 1 October 1936, Petersen to Howalt, 5 November 1936, and Hay to Petersen, 27 November 1936.

62. "Rural Electrification in Minnesota," November 1, 1937," typescript, box 11, Commissioner's Correspondence, MDA Records. The exact figures were: $ 2,962,500 loaned to MREA cooperatives and $781,000 to FEC ones; $ 246,875 per MREA project and $ 130,333 per FEC project. For different figures on affiliation from a different date, see Lewis and Seashore, *Consumers' Cooperation in Minnesota*, 87.

63. Howalt to Trovatten, 16 March 1936 (quote), and Federated Electric Cooperative, Resolution, 10 June 1936, and Hay to Hjalmar Petersen, 27 November 1936, all in Governor's Executive Letters, 1936 ("Has to Me"); "Criticisms of the R.E.A. and Factors which Indicate Gross Discrimination," Governor's Executive Letters, 1937 ("M to Pe"); Boyd Fisher to Trovatten, 29 July 1936, and Fisher to Howalt, 27 August 1936, Agricultural Extension file, President's Office Papers.

64. Muller, *Public Rural Electrification*, 32. FEC's disappearance can be inferred from the absence of any reference to it in Midland's annual reports after 1937; Midland Cooperative Wholesale, "11th Annual Financial Statement, January 1, 1936—December 31, 1936," p. 10, "12th Annual Report and Financial Statement, January 1, 1937–December 31, 1937," p. 14, "13th Annual Report and Financial Statement, January 1, 1938—December 1938"; *Midland Cooperator*, July 1938, p. 3.

65. Gieske, *Minnesota Farmer-Laborism*, chapters 7 and 8.

66. Charles Ommodt to George F. Bryan, 31 March 1938, Commissioner's Correspondence, MDA Records; "The Development of Agricultural Extension Work in Minnesota," p. 5–7, typescript, and cover letter, Walter Coffey to Guy Stanton Ford, 13 December 1937, both in Agricultural Extension file, President's Office Papers; McNelly, *County Agent Story*, 59–60, 175, 176. In 1937 funds for county-agent work in Minnesota were derived from the following sources: 29.5 percent from the USDA, 25.77 percent from the state, 34.59 percent from the individual

counties, and .14 percent from the Farm Bureau; McNelly, *County Agent Story,* 176. McNelly's figures add up to only 90 percent. It is unclear where the other 10 percent came from.

67. For a good description of H.F. 1017 by one of the coauthors, Rep. Archie Whaley of Moorhead, see *Country Press,* 19 March 1937, p. 1, 8.

68. *Country Press,* 19 March 1937, p. 1 (quote); *Minnesota Farm Bureau News,* Southwest ed., 1 March 1937, p. 2 (quote). For the Bureau's position on H.F. 1017, see also *Minneapolis Journal,* 6 March 1937, p. 2, 4; *Country Press,* 12 March 1937, p. 2; *Minnesota Farm Bureau News,* Southwest ed., 1 May 1937, p. 1; *National Farm Holiday News,* 11 June 1937, p. 1.

69. McNelly, *County Agent Story,* 176. According to one letter to the editor, the Bureau's 1936 contribution was $536; *Minneapolis Journal,* 10 March 1937, p. 16.

70. *Minneapolis Journal,* 6 March 1937, p. 4. For the anti-Bureau position, see *Country Press,* 2 April, p. 5, and 19 March, p. 1, both 1937; *National Farm Holiday News,* 12 March, p. 1, 2, and 4 June, p. 8, both 1937; *Midland Cooperator,* March 1937 (p. 1), July 1937 (p. 8); *Minneapolis Journal,* 10 March 1937, p. 16; John H. Bosch to Oscar Christensen, 4 March 1937, and Archie Whaley to Christensen, 10 March 1937, both in Otto A. Christensen and Family Papers, MHS. For the liberal leaders' desires, see Minutes of the Voluntary Committee, 6 December 1934, box 17, Lewis Papers. For Benson and civil service reform, see Gieske, *Minnesota Farmer-Laborism,* 240.

71. *House Journal,* 1937, p. 603–4, 672, 839, 878, 960, 1021, 1373, 1974, 2073–74; *St. Paul Pioneer Press,* 16 March 1937, p. 4 (quote); *Minneapolis Journal,* 16 March 1937, p. 13.

72. Valelly, *Radicalism in the States,* 87–91, 98–99, 101; Howalt to Charlie Ommodt, 23 February, 1938, and attached resolution, Ommodt to Howalt, 1 March 1938, Howalt to Ommodt, 7 March 1938, and Ommodt to Howalt, 18 March 1938, all in Commissioner's Correspondence, MDA Records. For the MFBF's explicit use of its ties to the USDA's Agricultural Adjustment Administration, see *Minnesota Farm Bureau News,* Southwest ed., 1 March 1937, p. 2.

73. Valelly, *Radicalism in the States,* 99–101, 155; Charles D. Egley to Harold Peterson, 8 March 1938, copy in Commissioner's Correspondence, MDA Records; Keillor, *Hjalmar Petersen,* 90. As Valelly noted (p. 101), "The Minnesota Farm Bureau was not out-and-out hostile to the Minnesota Farmer-Labor party" (at least, not until 1938).

74. *Minnesota Farm Bureau News,* Southwest ed., 1 June and 1 September 1937, both p. 1; *National Farm Holiday News,* 21 May (p. 3), 11 June (p. 4), and 18 June (p. 4), all 1937. Farm Bureau leader Andrew Olson had defended Trovatten in October 1933; Day, "Memorandum for Governor," 20 October 1933, p. 2, Day Papers.

75. *Minnesota Farm Bureau News,* Southwest ed., 1 September 1937, p. 1, 2. The editorial ended with a quote from Hjalmar Petersen, an attack on the spoils system in state government. For Ommodt's plans, see *National Farm Holiday News,* 11 June 1937, p. 4; and Elmer A. Benson to Charles Ommodt, 21 July 1937, box 34, Governor's Executive Letters.

76. Campbell, *Farm Bureau and New Deal,* 156–59, 169–71.

77. Hjalmar Petersen to E. M. Nelson, 23 June 1937, Petersen to Mr. McNabb, 30 June 1937, Petersen to Ancher Nelsen, 13 July 1937, J. Lawrence McLeod to Petersen, 3 August 1937 (quote), A. J. Zoerb to Petersen, 16 May 1938, and Petersen to Zoerb, 18 May 1938, all in Hjalmar Petersen Papers, MHS; *Minnesota Farm Bureau News,* Southwest ed., 1 July 1937, p. 1; Howalt to Charles Ommodt, 24 January 1938, Commissioner's Correspondence, MDA Records; Gieske, *Minnesota Farmer-Laborism,* 263; *Minneapolis Journal,* 24 May 1938, p. 2.

78. For a general analysis of the problem, see [John Bosch], "Memorandum to the Governor on the Twin City milk shed situation and the general situation between Cooperatives, particularly dairy cooperatives, and Labor," typescript, 19 April 1938, box 8, Elmer A. Benson Papers, MHS.

79. Steven J. Keillor, "'A Remedy Invented by Labor': The Franklin Co-operative Creamery Association, 1919–1939," *Minnesota History* 51 (Fall 1989): 260, 265, 266. For the 1934 truckers' strike, see Peter Rachleff, "Turning Points in the Labor

Movement: Three Key Conflicts," in *Century of Change*, ed. Clark, 207–10. There were close ties between Local 471 and Local 544, the Teamsters local of truck drivers led by the Dunne brothers and William Brown; *Twin City Milk Producers Bulletin*, September 1936, p. 1.

80. Day, "Memorandum to Governor," 3 September 1935, Day Papers; *Land O' Lakes News*, September 1935, p. 15. For an employee's request that Olson send an organizer to unionize Land O' Lakes workers, see P. K. Eilertson to Olson, 15 October 1934, and Day to Eilertson, 18 October 1934, both in box 19, Central Labor Union of Minneapolis and Hennepin County Papers, MHS.

81. *Twin City Milk Producers Bulletin*, February (p. 3), March (p. 3), April (p. 2–3), May (p. 2), June (p. 3), July (p. 2), August (p. 3), all 1936, and April (p. 3, quote), May (p. 4), and June (p. 2–3), all 1937; *Dakota County Tribune* (Farmington), 17 July, p. 1, and 7 August, p. 1 (quote), both 1936; *The Farmer*, 5 December 1936, p. 14G.

82. *Twin City Milk Producers Bulletin*, April 1936, p. 2–3; *National Farm Holiday News*, 3 December 1937, p. 1 (quote). See also [Bosch], "Memorandum to the Governor on the Twin City milk shed situation," p. 2.

83. *Northwest Organizer* (Minneapolis), 7 and 14 April 1938, both p. 1; *Minneapolis Labor Review*, 15 April 1938, p. 1; *St. Paul Pioneer Press*, 29 April, p. 1, 7, and 2 May, p. 1, both 1938. The wage demands are outlined in an undated typescript in Land O' Lakes Strike folder, box 11, Commissioner's Correspondence, MDA Records.

84. *Northwest Organizer*, 14 April 1938, p. 1 (quote); *Land O' Lakes News*, April 1938, p. 1 (quote); [Bosch], "Memorandum to the Governor on the Twin City milk shed situation," p. 1.

85. Milk Drivers and Dairy Employees Union, "Press Release," 19 April 1938, Land O' Lakes Strike folder, box 11, Commissioner's Correspondence, MDA Records; *St. Paul Pioneer Press*, 29 April 1938, p. 7; *Minneapolis Labor Review*, 22 April 1938, p. 1.

86. *Dairy Record*, 20 April 1938, p. 8, and 4 May 1938, p. 14; *Albert Lea Evening Tribune*, 23 April 1938, p. 3, 4; *Watonwan County Plaindealer* (St. James), 21 April 1938, p. 1;

Minutes, 23 April 1938 meeting at Mankato, and numerous letters and telegrams, e.g., Eddy Cooperative Creamery, 25 April 1938, all in Land O' Lakes Creameries, Inc., folder, box 11, Commissioner's Correspondence, MDA Records; *Minneapolis Journal*, 26 April 1938, p. 1, 21; *Twin City Milk Producers Bulletin*, May 1938, p. 4. For editors' use of the strike, see, for example, *Cannon Falls Beacon*, 6 May 1938, p. 4, and the *Tribune* articles cited above.

87. *Minneapolis Journal*, 2 May 1938, p. 1; *St. Paul Pioneer Press*, 2 May 1938, p. 1, 2 (quote p. 1); Land O' Lakes Present Salaries..., typescript, Land O' Lakes Strike folder, box 11, Commissioner's Correspondence, MDA Records; *Northwest Organizer*, 5 May 1938, p. 1, 3; *Minnesota Leader*, 7 May 1938, p. 1; *Dairy Record*, 4 May 1938, p. 5. Benson sought the help of the Roosevelt administration; Henry G. Teigan to Benson, 2 May 1938, box 8, Benson Papers. The strike created a rift between John Bosch and Ommodt, both of whom claimed to represent Benson on farm issues; Paul H. Appleby to Benson, 21 April 1938, and Benson to Appleby, 27 April 1938, both in box 7, Benson Papers. Benson ought to have known about the Land O' Lakes stand against a closed shop, for he spoke at its March 1938 annual meeting; *Minnesota Leader*, 12 March 1938, p. 6.

88. Petersen to McLeod, 4 and 18 October 1937, receipts for November and December 1937, and Petersen to T. J. Perusse, 2 March 1938, all in Petersen Papers; Statements of Disbursements and Receipts by Candidate for Public Office," items from the Petersen campaign in Ray P. Chase Papers, MHS; *Barnum Herald*, 2 June 1938, p. 1; Day, "Memorandum for Governor," 7 January 1933, p. 1, Day Papers; *Winthrop News*, 25 April 1957, p. 1. Scherer was a nephew of former Governor John Lind.

89. [John Bosch], "Brief on the Immediate Twin Cities Milk Shed," typescript [19 April 1938?], box 8, Benson Papers. This memo is attached to "Memorandum to the Governor on the Twin City milk shed situation." Although it appears under Ommodt's letterhead, its call for a conference of union and cooperative leaders is the same as the call that Bosch suggested in a May 2 letter; Bosch to Roger Rutchick and attached memo,

both 2 May 1938, both in box 8, Benson Papers. Therefore, I consider it to be Bosch's memo.

90. Ivan Hinderaker, "Harold Stassen and Developments in the Republican Party in Minnesota, 1937–1943" (Ph.D. diss., University of Minnesota, 1949), 43, 49–51; *Dakota County Tribune*, 14, 21, and 28 October 1932, all p. 1; *Northfield Independent*, 21 and 28 November 1935, both p. 1; *Twin City Milk Producers Bulletin*, June 1936, p. 2, 3. These two Stassen actions were publicized in the 1938 campaign; "The New Leader Minnesota Needs: Harold E. Stassen for Governor," campaign leaflet, 1938, box 1, Harold E. Stassen Papers, MHS.

91. Hinderaker, "Harold Stassen," 79, 81, 83n5 (quote), 185; *St. Paul Pioneer Press*, 19 November, p. 2, and 25 November, p. 8, both 1937; *Delano Eagle*, 28 July 1938, p. 1; *New Ulm Daily Journal*, 6 May 1938, p. 1.

92. Hinderaker, "Harold Stassen," 89, 91n24; *Minneapolis Journal*, 27 May 1938, p. 15; Clarke A. Chambers, *California Farm Organizations: A Historical Study of the Grange, the Farm Bureau and the Associated Farmers, 1929–1941* (Berkeley: University of California Press, 1952), 39–52, 71–72, 76–81; *Appleton Press*, 12 August, p. 4, and 2 September, p. 2, both 1938; *Morris Tribune*, 2 September 1938, p. 1; *Associated Farmers of Minnesota* (Northfield), August–September 1938, p. 3, October–November 1938, p. 1, and December 1938–January 1939, p. 1. Pro-Benson hecklers disrupted an AFM meeting in Benson; *Swift County Monitor* (Benson), 2 September 1938, p. 1

93. See, for example, Gieske, *Minnesota Farmer-Laborism*, 268–74; and Keillor, *Hjalmar Petersen*, 163–69.

94. *Midland Cooperator*, October 1933, p. 4.

Notes to Epilogue

1. The literature devoted to this debate is voluminous. Some major works are: James A. Henretta, "Families and Farms: *Mentalite* in Pre-Industrial America," *William and Mary Quarterly* 35 (January 1978): 3–32; Winifred B. Rothenberg, "The Market and Massachusetts Farmers, 1750–1855," *Journal of Economic History* 41 (June 1981): 283–314; Donald H. Parkerson, *The Agricultural Transition in New York State: Markets and Migration in Mid-Nineteenth Century America* (Ames: Iowa State University Press, 1995); Jeremy Atack and Fred Bateman, *To Their Own Soil: Agriculture in the Antebellum North* (Ames: Iowa State University Press, 1987); and Stephen Hahn and Jonathan Prude, eds., *The Countryside in the Age of Capitalist Transformation: Essays in the Social History of Rural America* (Chapel Hill: University of North Carolina Press, 1985).

2. Andrew R. L. Cayton and Peter S. Onuf, *The Midwest and the Nation: Rethinking the History of an American Region* (Bloomington: Indiana University Press, 1990), 30–32, 35, 43–45 (quote), 116–20. Cayton and Onuf described the Grange as the defender of "the 'traditional' world of commercial agriculture" and "the republican vision of a world of independent agricultural capitalists" (p. 99); therefore, they must perceive traditional and nontraditional forms of commercial agriculture.

Bibliography

Primary Sources

MANUSCRIPTS

Ahlness, Christian. "Recollections of an Emigrant, As Told by Himself." 1916. Copy of typescript. Brown County Historical Society, New Ulm.

Blooming Grove Lyceum. Minutes. Waseca County Historical Society, Waseca.

Bobjerg, Anders. Papers. Danske udvandrerarkiv (Danish Emigration Archives), Alborg, Denmark.

Brandborg, Charles W., and Family Papers. MHS.

Burnside Grange No. 148. Record. Goodhue County Historical Society, Red Wing.

Chisago County Mutual Telephone Company. Corporate Records. MHS.

Clarks Grove Creamerie Forening. Record. Freeborn County Historical Society, Albert Lea.

Clover Valley Creamery Association. Minutes. Freeborn County Historical Society, Albert Lea.

Cokato Elevator Company. Corporate Records. MHS.

Drake, Benjamin B. Equity Cooperative Exchange Papers. MHS.

Eastern Union Telephone Company. Records. Kandiyohi County Historical Society, Willmar.

Erickson, Theodore A. Papers. University of Minnesota Archives, Minneapolis.

Farmers' Elevator Company of Foxhome. Papers. Wilkin County Historical Society, Breckenridge.

Farmers' Elevator Company of Roseau. Papers. Roseau County Historical Society, Roseau.

Farmers Grain Company of Storden. Papers. Cottonwood County Historical Society, Windom.

Farmers Mercantile Corporation Collection. Otter Tail County Historical Society, Fergus Falls.

Farmers' Mutual Insurance Company of Manchester. Record. Farmers Mutual Insurance Company, Manchester.

First Danish Baptist Church. Minutes. Baptist Church, Clarks Grove.

Frame, Robert M., III. Minnesota Flour Milling Research Files. MHS.

Freeborn County Council of the Patrons of Husbandry. Record. Freeborn County Historical Society, Albert Lea.

Fremad Association. Protokol. Pope County Historical Society, Glenwood.

Gregg, Donald N. Flour Milling Collection. MHS.

Haecker, Theophilus Levi. Papers. MHS.

Hanska-Linden Handelsforening. Records. Brown County Historical Society, New Ulm.

Heimark, J. J. Papers. Norwegian-American Historical Association, Northfield.

Jensen, Ida. Papers. Danske udvandrerarkiv, Alborg, Denmark.

Jensen, N. P. Collection. Det danske Baptistsamfunds Arkiv (Danish Baptist Union Archives), Tølløse, Denmark.

Jesness, O. B. Papers. University of Minnesota Archives, Minneapolis.

Lake Hanska Farmers' Alliance. Journal. Brown County Historical Society, New Ulm.

Lake Hanska Lutheran Church. Protokol. Brown County Historical Society, New Ulm.

431

Lisbon Township Farmers' Alliance, Yellow Medicine County. Records. Southwest Minnesota Historical Center, Southwest State University, Marshall.

Luck Creamery Company. Minutes. Photocopy at Luck Public Library, Luck, Wis. Original owned by the State Historical Society of Wisconsin and housed at the University of Wisconsin-River Falls Area Research Center.

Manchester Creamery Association. Record. Freeborn County Historical Society, Albert Lea.

Minnesota Dairy Board of Trade. Letterpress Book, April-July 1897. MHS.

Minnesota State Grange Records. MHS.

Moorhead Farmers' Alliance No. 148. Minutes. Clay County Historical Society, Moorhead.

Northfield Farmers' Mercantile and Elevator Company. Papers. Rice County Historical Society, Faribault.

Olsen, Hans Peter. Papers. Danske udvandrerarkiv, Aalborg, Denmark.

Pearson, Trued Granville. Excerpts from *En skånsk banbrytare i Amerika* translated from Swedish into English by unidentified translator. Typescript. Trued G. Pearson File. Goodhue County Historical Society, Red Wing.

Pickerel Lake Township (Armstrong) Creamery Association. Records. Freeborn County Historical Society, Albert Lea.

Probstfield, Randolph M. Correspondence. MHS.

Scandinavian Cooperative Mercantile Company. Minute Book A. Lake County Historical Society, Two Harbors.

Stacy Telephone Company. Records. MHS.

Stevns, Ole J. Papers. Danske udvandrerarkiv, Alborg, Denmark.

Strandvold, Georg. Papers. Danske udvandrerarkiv, Alborg, Denmark.

Sverdrup Scandinavian Mutual Insurance Company. Protokol. Sverdrup Mutual Insurance Company, Underwood.

Thompson, Carl William. Papers. University of Minnesota Archives, Minneapolis.

Unitarian Church or Underwood. Records. Microfilm. Northwest Minnesota Historical Center, Moorhead State University, Moorhead.

University of Minnesota. Board of Regents. Minutes. University of Minnesota Archives, Minneapolis.

———. Institute of Agriculture. Director's Office. Papers. University of Minnesota Archives, Minneapolis.

———. President's Office. Papers. University of Minnesota Archives, Minneapolis.

Vye, John A. "History of the School of Agriculture." Typescript. 6 July 1939. In John A. Vye Papers. University of Minnesota Archives, Minneapolis.

Washington Farmers' Alliance. Minute Book. Nobles County Historical Society, Worthington.

Works Projects Administration, Minnesota. Papers. Microfilm M529. MHS.

GOVERNMENT DOCUMENTS AND RECORDS

Brown County Recorder's office. Abstracts of title and plats. Brown County Courthouse, New Ulm.

Massachusetts. *The General Statutes of the Commonwealth of Massachusetts: Supplement... 1860-1866*, edited by William A. Richardson and George P. Sanger. Boston: The Commonwealth, 1867.

Minnesota. Census. 1885 and 1895 manuscript census schedules. Microfilms, MHS.

———. District Court (Rice County). Case Files and Miscellaneous Court Papers, 1856-ca. 1896. Minnesota State Archives, MHS.

———. *Executive Documents of the State of Minnesota.* 1872-1916.

———. *The General Statutes of the State of Minnesota.* 1878-94.

———. Governor (1870-1874: Austin). Records. Minnesota State Archives, MHS.

———. Laws, etc. *Session Laws of the State of Minnesota.* 1915. St. Paul: Pioneer Co., 1915.

———. ———. *The Statutes at Large of the State of Minnesota*, compiled by A. H. Bissell. 2 vols. Chicago: Callaghan & Co., 1873.

———. Legislature. House of Representatives. *Journal.*

———. ———. Records of Special Investigating Committees, 1858-1942. 1913 Senate Grain Inquiry Committee: Testimony. Minnesota State Archives, MHS.

——. ——. Senate. *Journal.*
——. Railroad and Warehouse Commission/ Department of Public Service Records. Telephone Division. Correspondence. Minnesota State Archives, MHS.
——. Railroad and Warehouse Commission Records. Miscellaneous correspondence and reports, 1888–1915. Minnesota State Archives, MHS.
——. Secretary of State. Corporation Division. Record of Incorporations (Articles of Incorporation), 1858–1946. Minnesota State Archives, MHS.
——. ——. *Legislative Manual.*
United States. Bureau of the Census. *Historical Statistics of the United States: Colonial Times to 1957.* Washington, DC.: U.S. Department of Commerce, The Bureau, 1960.
——. Census. 1880 and 1890 manuscript population censuses, 1880 manuscript Agricultural and Manufacturing censuses for Minnesota. Microfilms, MHS.
——. Federal Extension Service. Annual Reports of Extension Service Field Representatives: Minnesota, 1914–44. Microfilm M474, roll 1, MHS.

NEWSPAPERS AND PERIODICALS

Adrian Guardian
Albert Lea Enterprise
Albert Lea Posten
Alexandria Citizen
Alexandria Post News
Alliance Advocate (Henning)
American Co-operative Journal (Chicago) (at University of Minnesota Libraries)
Ashby Post
Austin Register
Battle Lake Review
Blue Earth City Post
Breckinridge Telegram
Brown County Journal (New Ulm)
Budstikken (Minneapolis)
Canby News
Cannon Falls Beacon
Chatfield Democrat
Chisago County Press (Lindstrom)
Citizen, The (Adrian)
Clara City Herald
Cokato Observer
Commercial West (Minneapolis)

Co-operation (Minneapolis)
Cottonwood County Citizen (Windom)
Country Press (Moorhead)
Daily Journal-Press (St. Cloud)
Daily Republican Eagle (Red Wing)
Dakota County Union (Hastings)
Dassel Anchor
Delavan Bee
Detroit Record (Detroit Lakes)
Eden Valley Journal
Evening Tribune (Albert Lea)
Eyota Advertiser
Fairmont Chain
Faribault Republican
Farm, Stock and Home (Minneapolis)
Farmer, The (St. Paul)
Farmers Equity News (Alexandria)
Farmers' Union (Minneapolis)
Farmington Press
Federal Union (Rochester)
Fergus Falls Daily Journal
Fergus Falls Free Press
Fergus Falls Ugeblad
Fergus Falls Weekly Journal
Fergus Globe (Fergus Falls)
Fillmore County Republican (Preston)
Freeborn County Standard (Albert Lea)
Freeborn County Times (Albert Lea)
Glenwood Eagle
Glenwood Gopher-Press
Glenwood Herald
Goodhue County Republican (Red Wing)
Grange Advance (Red Wing)
Granite Falls Journal
Granite Falls Tribune
Grant County Herald
Grant County Review (Herman)
Great West (St. Paul)
Hanska Herald
Hartland Vidette
Hoard's Dairyman (Fort Atkinson, Wis.)
Hutchinson Leader
Kerkhoven Banner
Lake City Graphic
Lake City Leader
Luthersk Kyrkotidning (Red Wing)
Madelia Times
Mankato Free Press
Mankato Record
Mantorville Express
McIntosh Times
Minneapolis Daily Tribune
Minneapolis Journal

Minneapolis Tribune
Minnesota Daily (Minneapolis)
Minnesota Monthly (St. Paul)
Minnesota Radical (Waseca)
Minnesota Record (Rochester)
Morris Sun
Morris Tribune
Morristown Rustler
Mower County Transcript (Austin)
New, The (McIntosh)
New Ulm Review
New Ulm Weekly Review
Nordisk Folkeblad (Minneapolis)
Northfield Enterprise
Northfield Independent
Northfield News
Northfield Standard
Olivia Times
Owatonna Journal
Park Region Echo (Alexandria)
Pioneer Press (St. Paul)
Pioneer Press (St. Paul and Minneapolis)
Pope County Press (Glenwood)
Record and Union (Rochester)
Red Lake Falls Gazette
Red Wing Argus
Red Wing Republican
Red Wing Sentinel
Redwood Gazette (Redwood Falls)
Redwood Reveille (Redwood Falls)
Reform Advocate (Clarkfield)
Renville Star-Farmer
Republican Gazette (Willmar)
Republican Press (Atwater)
Rice County Journal (Northfield) (issues in
  Northfield Public Library, Northfield)
Rochester Post
St. James Journal
St. Paul Daily Pioneer
St. Paul Daily Pioneer Press
St. Paul Daily Press
St. Paul Dispatch
St. Paul Pioneer Press
St. Paul Weekly Pioneer
St. Peter Tribune
Sauk Rapids Sentinel
Sleepy Eye Herald
Spring Valley Vidette
Standard, The (Northfield)
Stillwater Messenger
University Farm Press News (broadside, University of Minnesota, Department of Agriculture, Extension Division)

Verndale Sun
Waseca County Herald (Waseca)
Waseca News
Waseca Radical
Waseca Weekly News
Western Progress (Spring Valley)
Wheaton Gazette-Reporter
Wheelock's Weekly (Fergus Falls)
Willmar Tribune
Worthington Advance
Worthington Globe
Wright County Eagle (Delano)

PAMPHLETS AND
OTHER PRINTED MATERIALS

Conference of the Committees on Agricultural Development and Education of the State Bankers' Associations. *Annual Conference.* [Minneapolis, St. Paul, 1911, 1912?].

De danske baptistmenigheders Forenings-Konferents holdt i Vandløse menighed den 6te og 7de juni 1884. N.p., n.d.

Durand, E. Dana, and J. P. Jensen. *Farmers' Elevators in Minnesota, 1914–1915.* Bulletin, 164. University of Minnesota, Agricultural Experiment Station, October 1916.

Ford, James. *Co-operation in New England: Urban and Rural.* New York: Survey Associates, 1913.

Frederiksen, J. D. *Mejerivæsenet i Nord-Amerika.* Copenhagen: P. G. Philipsens forlag, 1888.

Haecker, T[heophilus] L[evi]. *Organizing Co-operative Creameries.* Press Bulletin, 2. University of Minnesota, Agricultural Experiment Station, March 1, 1894. Copy bound in "Investigation in Milk Production, University of Minnesota, 1891–1903," by Haecker, MHS.

[Hauge], L[ars] Jørgensen. *Amerika og de danskes liv herovre: kortelig fremstillet til slægtninges, venners og landsmænds gavn og oplysning.* Copenhagen: H. Hagerups boghandel, 1865.

Interstate Right Relationship League. *Co-operative Conference. Meeting. Proceedings of the First Annual Meeting* and *Proceedings of the Second Annual Meeting.* Minneapolis: The League, 1907, 1908.

Jørgensen, L[ars]. *See* [Hauge], L[ars] Jørgensen.

Kelley, Oliver H. *Origin and Progress of the Order of the Patrons of Husbandry in the United States: A History from 1866 to 1873.* Philadelphia: J. A. Wagenseller, 1875.

Minnesota Butter, Cheese, and Dairy Stock Association. *Annual Convention of the Minnesota Butter, Cheese and Dairy Stock Association Held at Red Wing, Minnesota, December 15, 16 and 17, 1885: Proceedings.* [Minnesota: The Association], 1886.

Minnesota Farmers' Institute Annual. 1893–1913. (St. Paul, etc.)

Minnesota State Dairymen's Association. *Proceedings of the Sixteenth Annual Convention . . . Held at Waseca, Minnesota, Dec. 12, 13 and 14, 1893.* Minneapolis, 1894.

Thompson, Carl W., and Gustav P. Warber. *Social and Economic Survey of a Rural Township in Southern Minnesota.* Studies in Economics, no. 1. Minneapolis: University of Minnesota, 1913.

University of Minnesota. Department of Agriculture. *Agricultural Organization and Cooperation.* St. Paul: The Department, 1915. Copy in UM Archives.

Warber, Gustav P. *Social and Economic Survey of a Community in Northeastern Minnesota.* Current Problems, no. 5. Minneapolis: University of Minnesota, 1915.

Weld, L. D. H. *Farmers' Elevators in Minnesota.* Bulletin, 152. University of Minnesota, Agricultural Experiment Station, August 1915.

———. *Social and Economic Survey of a Community in the Red River Valley.* Current Problems, no. 4. Minneapolis: University of Minnesota, 1915.

Wells, John G. *The Grange Illustrated: Or, Patron's Hand-book: In the Interests of the Order of Patrons of Husbandry.* New York: Grange Publishing Co., 1874.

Wilson, A[rchie] D. *Farmers' Clubs.* Minnesota Farmers' Library, vol. 4, no. 10: Extension Bulletin, no. 46. University of Minnesota, Department of Agriculture, Extension Division, October 1913.

Secondary Materials

BOOKS

Album of History and Biography of Meeker County, Minnesota. Chicago: Alden Ogle & Co., 1888.

Aronson, Sidney H. "Bell's Electrical Toy: What's the Use? The Sociology of Early Telephone Usage." In *The Social Impact of the Telephone,* edited by Ithiel de Sola Pool, 15–39. Cambridge: MIT Press, 1977.

Atack, Jeremy, and Fred Bateman. "Yankee Farming and Settlement in the Old Northwest: A Comparative Analysis." In *Essays on the Economy of the Old Northwest,* edited by David C. Klingaman and Richard K. Vedder, 77–102. Athens: Ohio University Press, 1987.

Bailyn, Bernard, et al. *The Great Republic: A History of the American People.* 2 vols. 4th ed. Lexington, Mass.: D. C. Heath and Co., 1992.

Bergantine, Rosanne. *Phelps: A Peek into Its Past.* N.p., [1970].

Bergstrom, Vernon E., and Marilyn McGriff. *Isanti County, Minnesota, 1985: An Illustrated History.* Braham: The Authors, 1985.

Berry, Wendell. *The Unsettling of America: Culture and Agriculture.* San Francisco: Sierra Club Books, 1977.

Bjørn, Claus, et al. *Mejeribrug gennem 200 aar, 1882–2000.* Odense, Denmark, 1982.

Blegen, Theodore C. *Minnesota: A History of the State.* Minneapolis: University of Minnesota Press, 1975.

Bobjerg, Anders. *En dansk nybygd i Wisconsin. 40 aar i storskoven (1869–1909).* Copenhagen: I Kommission hos G. E. C. Gad, 1909.

Bogue, Allan G. *From Prairie to Corn Belt: Farming on the Illinois and Iowa Prairies in the Nineteenth Century.* Chicago: University of Chicago Press, 1963. Reprint, Ames: Iowa State University Press, 1994.

Boorstin, Daniel J. *The Democratic Experience.* Vol. 3 of *The Americans.* New York: Random House, 1973.

Boss, Andrew. *The Early History and Background of the School of Agriculture at University Farm, St. Paul.* [St. Paul?]: University of Minnesota, 1941.

Bowen, Jessie March, ed. *Chronicle of Claremont Township and Village: A History of Claremont, Dodge County, Minnesota.* Claremont: [Ladies Aid of the Presbyterian Church?], 1937.

Broehl, Wayne G., Jr. *Cargill: Trading the World's Grain.* Hanover, N.H.: University Press of New England, 1992.

Broholm, August. *Guds fodspor paa min vej.* Copenhagen: Forlaget fraternitas, 1977.

Buck, Solon J. *The Granger Movement: A Study of Agricultural Organization and Its Political, Economic, and Social Manifestations, 1870–1880.* Harvard Historical Studies, vol. 19. Cambridge: Harvard University Press, 1933.

Carson, Gerald. *The Old Country Store.* New York: Oxford University Press, 1954.

Case, C. F. *History and Description of Lyon County, Minnesota.* Marshall: Messenger Printing House, 1884.

Chandler, Alfred D., Jr. *The Visible Hand: The Managerial Revolution in American Business.* Cambridge: Harvard University Press, Belknap Press, 1977.

Child, James E. *Child's History of Waseca County, Minnesota.* Owatonna: Press of the Owatonna Chronicle, 1905.

Chrislock, Carl H. *The Progressive Era in Minnesota, 1899–1918.* St. Paul: Minnesota Historical Society, 1971.

Christensen, Chris L. *Agricultural Cooperation in Denmark.* Bulletin no. 1266. Washington, D.C.: U.S. Department of Agriculture, 1924.

Christensen, Thomas P. "De danske baptister i Clarks Grove, Freeborn County, Minn." and "De danske i og omkring Geneva og Ellendale, Minnesota." In *Danske i Amerika,* 2:271–86 and 287–92. Minneapolis: C. Rasmussen, 1908, 1916.

Clark, Clifford E., Jr., ed. *Minnesota in a Century of Change: The State and Its People since 1900.* St. Paul: Minnesota Historical Society Press, 1989.

Clarks Grove: The Story of a Co-operative Community. [St. Paul]: Minnesota Department of Education, Home Study Program, S.E.R.A. Project, [1936?].

Cochrane, Willard W. *Agricultural Economics at the University of Minnesota: 1886–1979.* St. Paul: Department of Agricultural and Applied Economics, University of Minnesota, 1983.

Cottonwood County Historical Society. *The Centennial History of Cottonwood County, Minnesota.* [Windom?], 1970.

Cronon, William. *Nature's Metropolis: Chicago and the Great West.* New York: W. W. Norton and Co., 1991.

Curti, Merle. *The Making of an American Community: A Case Study of Democracy in a Frontier County.* Stanford: Stanford University Press, 1959.

Curtiss-Wedge, Franklyn, comp. *History of Freeborn County, Minnesota.* Chicago: H. C. Cooper, Jr. & Co., [1911].

Danbom, David B. *Born in the Country: A History of Rural America.* Revisiting Rural America Series. Baltimore: Johns Hopkins University Press, 1995.

——. *The Resisted Revolution: Urban America and the Industrialization of Agriculture, 1900–1930.* Ames: Iowa State University Press, 1979.

Davis, Lance E., and Douglass C. North. *Institutional Change and American Economic Growth.* Cambridge: Cambridge University Press, 1971.

Debes, Inge. *Forbruker kooperasjonen.* 2 vols. Oslo: Norges kooperative landsforening, 1925, 1931.

Draxten, Nina. *Kristofer Janson in America.* Authors Series, vol. 3. Boston: Published for the Norwegian-American Historical Association by Twayne Publishers, 1976.

Dunn, James Taylor. *Marine Mills: Lumber Village, 1838–1888.* Marine on St. Croix: The Author, 1963.

Ebbesen, Peter. "Historisk omrids af danske kolonier i Howard County, Nebr." In *Danske i Amerika* 2:78–100. Minneapolis: C. Rasmussen, 1908, 1916.

Faragher, John Mack. *Sugar Creek: Life on the Illinois Prairie.* New Haven: Yale University Press, 1986.

Fostveit, Donna M., comp. *Waseca County, Minnesota, Landowners of Record, 1879.* [Waseca]: Waseca County Historical Society, 1982.

Frame, Robert M., III. *Millers to the World: Minnesota's Nineteenth Century Water Power Flour Mills.* St. Paul: Minnesota Historical Society, Division of Field Services, Historic Sites, and Archaeology, 1977.

Fuller, Wayne E. *The Old Country School: The Story of Rural Education in the Middle West.* Chicago: University of Chicago Press, 1982.

Garnet, Robert W. *The Telephone Enterprise: The Evolution of the Bell System's Hori-*

zontal Structure, 1876–1909. The Johns Hopkins/AT&T Series in Telephone History. Baltimore: Johns Hopkins University Press, 1985.

Gieske, Millard L., and Steven J. Keillor. Norwegian Yankee: Knute Nelson and the Failure of American Politics, 1860–1923. Biographical Series, vol. 3. Northfield: Norwegian-American Historical Association, 1995.

Gjerde, Jon. From Peasants to Farmers: The Migration from Balestrand, Norway, to the Upper Middle West. Interdisciplinary Perspectives on Modern History Series. Cambridge: Cambridge University Press, 1985.

Goodwyn, Lawrence. Democratic Promise: The Populist Moment in America. New York: Oxford University Press, 1976.

——. The Populist Moment: A Short History of the Agrarian Revolt in America. Abridged ed. of Democratic Promise. New York: Oxford University Press, 1978.

Grant, H. Roger. Self-Help in the 1890s Depression. Ames: Iowa State University Press, 1983.

Gray, James. Business without Boundary: The Story of General Mills. Minneapolis: University of Minnesota Press, 1954.

——. The University of Minnesota, 1851–1951. Minneapolis: University of Minnesota Press, 1951.

Hansen, H., and P. Olsen. De danske baptisters historie. Copenhagen: Den danske Baptist-Litteratur-Komite, 1896.

Heflebower, Richard B. Cooperatives and Mutuals in the Market System. Madison: University of Wisconsin Press, 1980.

Helmes, Winifred G. John A. Johnson, the People's Governor: A Political Biography. Minneapolis: University of Minnesota Press, 1949.

Hession, Charles H., and Hyman Sardy. Ascent to Affluence: A History of American Economic Development. Boston: Allyn and Bacon, 1969.

Hetherington, John A. C. Mutual and Cooperative Enterprises: An Analysis of Customer-owned Firms in the United States. Charlottesville: University Press of Virginia, 1991.

Hicks, John D. The Populist Revolt: A History of the Farmers' Alliance and the People's Party. Minneapolis: University of Minnesota Press, 1931.

Hidy, Ralph W., et al. The Great Northern Railway: A History. Boston: Harvard Business School Press, 1988.

History of Freeborn County. Minneapolis: Minnesota Historical Co., 1882.

History of Rice County. Minneapolis: Minnesota Historical Co., 1882.

History of Steele and Waseca Counties, Minnesota. Chicago: Union Publishing Co., 1887.

History of the Delavan Community, 1856–1977. Vol. 1, General History. Delavan: Delavan Community Centennial Committee, 1977.

Holbrook, Stewart H. The Yankee Exodus: An Account of Migration from New England. New York: Macmillan Co., 1950.

Holmquist, June Drenning, ed. They Chose Minnesota: A Survey of the State's Ethnic Groups. St. Paul: Minnesota Historical Society Press, 1981.

Howard, Thomas W., ed. The North Dakota Political Tradition. North Dakota Centennial Heritage Series. Ames: Iowa State University Press, 1981.

Hudson, John C. Making the Corn Belt: A Geographical History of Middle-Western Agriculture. Bloomington: Indiana University Press, 1994.

——. Plains Country Towns. Minneapolis: University of Minnesota Press, 1985.

Hunziker, Otto E. The Butter Industry. La Grange, Ill.: The Author, 1920.

Hylleberg, Bent, et al. Et kirkesamfund bliver til: danske baptisters historie gennem 150 År. Denmark: Føltveds forlag, 1989.

Jarchow, Merrill E. The Earth Brought Forth: A History of Minnesota Agriculture to 1885. Minnesota Centennial Publications, no. 4. St. Paul: Minnesota Historical Society, 1949.

Jensen, Kathy. Clarks Grove: "A Place We Call Home." [Clarks Grove, 1990].

Johnson, Emeroy. Eric Norelius: Pioneer Midwest Pastor and Churchman. Rock Island, Ill.: Augustana Book Concern, 1954.

Just, Flemming. Brugsforeningsbevægelsen 1866–1920: med udgangspunkt i Ribe amt. Esbjerg, Denmark: Sydjysk Universitetsforlag, 1984.

Kallen, Horace M. *The Decline and Rise of the Consumer: A Philosophy of Consumer Cooperation.* New York: D. Appleton-Century Co., 1936.

Kenkel, Joseph B. *The Cooperative Elevator Movement: A Study in Grain Marketing at Country Points in the North Central States.* Washington, D.C.: Catholic University of America, 1922.

Kleppner, Paul, et al. *The Evolution of American Electoral Systems.* Contributions in American History, no. 95. Westport, Conn.: Greenwood Press, 1981.

Knapp, Joseph G. *The Rise of American Cooperative Enterprise: 1620–1920.* Danville, Ill.: Interstate Printers and Publishers, 1969.

Kuhlmann, Charles Byron. *The Development of the Flour-Milling Industry in the United States, with Special Reference to the Industry in Minneapolis.* Boston: Houghton Mifflin Co., 1929.

Lampard, Eric E. *The Rise of the Dairy Industry in Wisconsin: A Study in Agricultural Change, 1820–1920.* Madison: State Historical Society of Wisconsin, 1963.

Larsen, Christian, and George Lewis McKay. *Principles and Practice of Buttermaking.* 3d ed. New York: John Wiley & Sons, 1922.

Larson, Henrietta M. *The Wheat Market and the Farmer in Minnesota, 1858–1900.* Studies in History, Economics, and Public Law, no. 269. New York: Columbia University, 1926.

Lasch, Christopher. *The True and Only Heaven: Progress and Its Critics.* New York: W. W. Norton, 1991.

Lawdahl, Nels Sørensen. *De danske Baptisters Historie i Amerika.* Morgan Park, Ill.: Forfatterens forlag, 1909.

———. "Danske baptister i Amerika." In *Danske i Amerika* I: part 2, p. 181–200. Minneapolis: C. Rasmussen, 1908, 1916.

Lawson, Victor E., ed. *Illustrated History and Descriptive and Biographical Review of Kandiyohi County, Minnesota.* [Willmar: The Author and J. Emil Nelson], 1905.

Lipartito, Kenneth. *The Bell System and Regional Business: The Telephone in the South, 1877–1920.* The Johns Hopkins/AT&T Series in Telephone History. Baltimore: Johns Hopkins University Press, 1989.

Lovoll, Odd S. *The Promise of America: A History of the Norwegian-American People.* Minneapolis: University of Minnesota Press in cooperation with the Norwegian-American Historical Association, 1984.

Macdonald, Fergus. *The Catholic Church and the Secret Societies in the United States.* Monograph Series, 22. New York: United States Catholic Historical Society, 1946.

Marcus, Alan I. *Agricultural Science and the Quest for Legitimacy: Farmers, Agricultural Colleges, and Experiment Stations, 1870–1890.* The Henry A. Wallace Series on Agricultural History and Rural Studies. Ames: Iowa State University Press, 1985.

Mason, John W., ed. *History of Otter Tail County, Minnesota.* 2 vols. Indianapolis, Ind.: B. F. Bowen, 1916.

McMath, Robert C., Jr. *American Populism: A Social History, 1877–1898.* American Century Series. New York: Hill and Wang, 1993.

McMurry, Sally. *Transforming Rural Life: Dairying Families and Agricultural Change, 1820–1885.* Revisiting Rural America Series. Baltimore: Johns Hopkins University Press, 1995.

Michels, John. *Creamery Butter-making.* 8th ed., rev. Farmingdale, N.Y.: The Author, 1914.

Moeller, Helen, ed. *Out of the Midwest: A Portrait: An Informal History of Fayette County, Iowa, Prepared in Commemoration of America's Bicentennial.* Marceline, Mo.: Walsworth Publishing Co., 1976.

Monrad, J. H. *A.B.C. in Butter Making for Young Creamery Butter-makers, Creamery Managers and Private Dairymen.* Winnetka, Ill., 1899.

Nelson, Charles. *History of Hayward: 1849–1949, Centennial Edition.* [Hayward], 1949.

Nora Free Christian Church. *Seventy-Fifth Anniversary, 1881–1956.* Hanska: The Church, 1956.

Nordin, D[ennis] Sven. *Rich Harvest: A History of the Grange, 1867–1900.* Jackson: University Press of Mississippi, 1974.

North, Douglass C., Terry L. Anderson, and Peter J. Hill. *Growth and Welfare in the American Past: A New Economic History.* 3d ed. Englewood Cliffs, N.J.: Prentice-Hall, 1983.

North Waseca Evangelical Lutheran Church. *Seventy-fifth Anniversary, 1858–1933.* Waseca County: The Church, [1933?].

North West Publishing Company. *Plat Book of Rice County, Minnesota.* [Philadelphia]: The Company, 1900.

———. *Plat Book of Yellow Medicine County, Minnesota.* N.p.: The Company, 1900.

Osman, Loren H. *W. D. Hoard: A Man for His Time.* Fort Atkinson, Wis.: W.D. Hoard & Sons Co., 1985.

Ostergren, Robert C. *A Community Transplanted: The Trans-Atlantic Experience of a Swedish Immigrant Settlement in the Upper Middle West, 1835–1915.* Social Demography Series. Madison: University of Wisconsin Press, 1988.

Parsons, Stanley B. *The Populist Context: Rural versus Urban Power on a Great Plains Frontier.* Contributions in American History, no. 22. Westport, Conn.: Greenwood Press, 1973.

Pearson, Trued Granville. *En skånsk banbrytare i Amerika: Trued Granville Pearsons självbiografti,* edited by Arvid Bjerking. Oskarshamn, Swed.: A.-B., A. Melchiors bokhandel, 1937.

Perry, Charles R. "The British Experience, 1876–1912: The Impact of the Telephone during the Years of Delay." In *The Social Impact of the Telephone,* edited by Ithiel de Sola Pool, 69–96. Cambridge: MIT Press, 1977.

Petersen, William, Michael Novak, and Philip Gleason. *Concepts of Ethnicity.* Dimensions of Ethnicity Series. Cambridge: Harvard University Press, 1982.

Pierce, John R. "The Telephone and Society in the Past 100 Years." In *The Social Impact of the Telephone,* edited by Ithiel de Sola Pool, 159–95. Cambridge: MIT Press, 1977.

Pool, Ithiel de Sola, et al. "Foresight and Hindsight: The Case of the Telephone." In *The Social Impact of the Telephone,* edited by Ithiel de Sola Pool, 127–57. Cambridge: MIT Press, 1977.

Prosser, Richard S. *Rails to the North Star.* Minneapolis: Dillon Press, 1966.

Rasmussen, C. A. *A History of the City of Red Wing, Minnesota.* [Red Wing: Printed by the Red Wing Advertising Co.], 1933.

Ray, P. K. *Agricultural Insurance: Theory and Practice and Application to Developing Countries.* 2d ed. New York: Pergamon Press, 1981.

Rippey, James Crockett. *Goodbye, Central—Hello, World: A Centennial History of Northwestern Bell: The Diary of a Dream.* N.p.: Published for the Telephone Pioneers of America, 1975.

Robinson, Edward Van Dyke. *Early Economic Conditions and the Development of Agriculture in Minnesota.* Studies in the Social Sciences, no. 3. Minneapolis: University of Minnesota, 1915.

Rose, Arthur P. *An Illustrated History of Yellow Medicine County, Minnesota.* Marshall: Northern History Publishing Co., 1914.

Rothstein, Morton. "The American West and Foreign Markets, 1850–1900." In *The Frontier in American Development: Essays in Honor of Paul Wallace Gates,* edited by David M. Ellis, 381–406. Ithaca, N.Y.: Cornell University Press, 1969.

Rozwenc, Edwin Charles. *Cooperatives Come to America; The History of the Protective Union Store Movement, 1845–1867.* Mount Vernon, Iowa: Hawkeye-Record Press, 1941.

Ruble, Kenneth D. *Men to Remember: How 100,000 Neighbors Made History.* [Chicago?], 1947.

Saloutos, Theodore, and John D. Hicks. *Twentieth-Century Populism: Agricultural Discontent in the Middle West, 1900–1939.* Lincoln: University of Nebraska Press, Bison Books, 1951.

Scott, Roy V. *The Reluctant Farmer: The Rise of Agricultural Extension to 1914.* Urbana: University of Illinois Press, 1970.

Sellers, Charles. *The Market Revolution: Jacksonian America, 1815–1846.* New York: Oxford University Press, 1991.

Severson, Harold. *Blooming Prairie Update.* Blooming Prairie: First National Bank, 1980.

Simonsen, Henrik Bredmose. *Kampen om danskheden: tro og nationalitet i de danske kirkesamfund i Amerika.* Studier i indre missions og de religiøst-folkelige bevægelsers historie, 1. Århus: Aarhus universitetsforlag, 1990.

Snyder, Margaret. *The Chosen Valley: The Story of a Pioneer Town.* New York: W. W. Norton Co., 1948.

Soike, Lowell J. *Norwegian Americans and the Politics of Dissent, 1880–1924.* Northfield: Norwegian-American Historical Association, 1991.

Sørensen, Anthon C. "Danske i amerikansk landbrug og mejeri." In *Danske i Amerika,* 1: part 2, p. 263–326. Minneapolis: C. Rasmussen, 1908, 1916.

Spring Valley Centennial, 1855–1955. Spring Valley: Printed by Tribune, [1955].

Standard Atlas of Waseca County, Minnesota. Chicago: Geo. Ogle & Co., 1896.

Stone, Alan. *Public Service Liberalism: Telecommunications and Transitions in Public Policy.* Princeton: Princeton University Press, 1991.

Swanberg. L. E., ed. *Then and Now: A History of Rice County, Faribault and Communities.* [Faribault]: Rice County Bi-Centennial Commission, 1976.

Synsteby, Ole. *Interesting Tales of Pioneer Days in Lake Hanska and Vicinity.* [Lake Hanska?, 1942?].

Underwood History Book Committee. *Underwood Centennial, 1881–1981.* Battle Lake: Battle Lake Review, 1981.

Union Publishing Company. *Plat Book of Bremer County, Iowa.* Philadelphia: The Company, 1894.

——. *Plat Book of Fayette County, Iowa.* Philadelphia: The Company, 1896.

——. *Plat Book of Freeborn County, Minnesota.* Philadelphia: The Company, 1895.

Upham, Warren. *Minnesota Geographic Names: Their Origin and Historic Significance.* St. Paul: Minnesota Historical Society, 1920, reprint, 1969.

——, and Rose Barteau Dunlap, comps., *Minnesota Biographies, 1655–1912.* St. Paul: Minnesota Historical Society, 1912.

Valgren, Victor Nelson. *Farmers' Mutual Fire Insurance in the United States.* Chicago: University of Chicago Press, 1924.

Warren, A. W., comp. *A Brief Historical Sketch of the First Danish Baptist Church, Clarks Grove, Minnesota, 1863–1923.* Clarks Grove: The Church, 1923.

Wiest, Edward. *The Butter Industry in the United States: An Economic Study of Butter and Oleomargarine.* Studies in History, Economics and Public Law, vol. 69, no. 2; whole no. 165. New York: Columbia University Press, 1916.

Woods, Thomas A. *Knights of the Plow: Oliver H. Kelley and the Origins of the Grange in Republican Ideology.* The Henry A. Wallace Series on Agricultural History and Rural Studies. Ames: Iowa State University Press, 1991.

Zimmerman, Carle C. *Farm Trade Centers in Minnesota, 1905–29: A Study in Rural Social Organization.* Bulletin, 269. University of Minnesota, Agricultural Experiment Station, September 1930.

ARTICLES

Ander, O. Fritiof. "The Immigrant Church and the Patrons of Husbandry." *Agricultural History* 8 (October 1934): 155–68.

Ashmen, Roy. "Price Determination in the Butter Market: The Elgin Board of Trade, 1872–1917." *Agricultural History* 36 (July 1962): 156–62.

Barns, William D. "Oliver Hudson Kelley and the Genesis of the Grange: A Reappraisal." *Agricultural History* 41 (July 1967): 229–42.

Benoit, Virgil. "Gentilly: A French-Canadian Community in the Minnesota Red River Valley." *Minnesota History* 44 (Winter 1975): 278–89.

Cerny, George. "Cooperation in the Midwest in the Granger Era, 1869–1875." *Agricultural History* 37 (October 1963): 187–205.

Chambers, Clarke A. "The Cooperative League of the United States of America, 1916–1961: A Study of Social Theory and Social Action." *Agricultural History* 36 (April 1962): 59–81.

Cherny, Robert W. "Lawrence Goodwyn and Nebraska Populism: A Review Essay." *Great Plains Quarterly* 1 (Summer 1981): 181–94.

Dibbern, John. "Who Were the Populists?: A Study of Grass-Roots Alliancemen in Dakota." *Agricultural History* 56 (October 1982): 677–91.

Erdman, H. E. "The 'Associated Dairies' of New York as Precursors of American Agricultural Cooperatives." *Agricultural History* 36 (April 1962): 82–90.

Fischer, Claude S. "The Revolution in Rural Telephony, 1900–1920." *Journal of Social History* 21 (Fall 1987): 5–26.

Hirsch, Arthur H. "Efforts of the Grange in the Middle West to Control the Price of Farm Machinery, 1870–1880." *Mississippi Valley Historical Review* 15 (March 1929): 473–96.

Hoffer, C[harles] R[ussell]. "Co-operation as a Culture Pattern within a Community." *Rural Sociology* 3 (June 1938): 153–58.

Keillor, Steven J. "Agricultural Change and Crosscultural Exchange: Danes, Americans, and Dairying, 1880–1930." *Agricultural History* 67 (Fall 1993): 58–79.

———. " 'A Remedy Invented by Labor': Franklin Co-operative Creamery Association, 1919–1939." *Minnesota History* 51 (Fall 1989): 259–69.

Kercher, Leonard C. "Some Sociological Aspects of Consumers' Cooperation." *Rural Sociology* 6 (December 1941): 311–22.

Lipartito, Kenneth. "When Women Were Switches: Technology, Work, and Gender in the Telephone Industry, 1890–1920." *American Historical Review* 99 (October 1994): 1074–11.

Lufkin, Jack. "Property Insurance for Iowa Farmers: The Rise of the Mutuals." *Annals of Iowa*, 3d ser. 54 (Winter 1995): 25–45.

Marti, Donald B. "Sisters of the Grange: Rural Feminism in the Late Nineteenth Century." *Agricultural History* 58 (July 1984): 247–61.

Mayhew, Anne. "A Reappraisal of the Causes of Farm Protest in the United States, 1870–1900." *Journal of Economic History* 32 (June 1972): 464–75.

McCormick, Virginia E. "Butter and Egg Business: Implications from the Records of a Nineteenth-Century Farm Wife." *Ohio History* 100 (Winter–Spring 1991): 57–67.

Nelson, Philip J. "The Rockwell Co-operative Society and the Iowa Farmers' Elevator Movement, 1870–1920." *Annals of Iowa*, 3d ser. 54 (Winter 1995): 1–24.

Nordin, Dennis S[ven]. "A Revisionist Interpretation of the Patrons of Husbandry, 1867–1900." *The Historian* 32 (August 1970): 630–43.

Nunnally, Patrick. "From Churns to 'Butter Factories': The Industrialization of Iowa's Dairying, 1860–1900." *Annals of Iowa*, 3d ser. 49 (Winter 1989): 555–69.

Parsons, Stanley B., et al. "The Role of Cooperatives in the Development of the Movement Culture of Populism." *Journal of American History* 69 (March 1983): 866–85.

Prescott, Gerald. "Wisconsin Farm Leaders in the Gilded Age." *Agricultural History* 44 (April 1970): 183–99.

Refsell, Oscar N. "The Farmers' Elevator Movement." *Journal of Political Economy* 22 (November 1914): 872–94 (December 1914): 969–91.

Rodgers, Daniel T. "In Search of Progressivism." *Reviews in American History* 10 (December 1982): 113–32.

Saloutos, Theodore. "The Decline of the Equity Cooperative Exchange." *Mississippi Valley Historical Review* 34 (December 1947): 405–26.

———. "The Rise of the Equity Cooperative Exchange." *Mississippi Valley Historical Review* 32 (June 1945): 31–62.

Schatzel, G. W. "Among the Wheat-Fields of Minnesota." *Harper's New Monthly Magazine* 36 (January 1868): 190–201.

Schell, Herbert S. "The Grange and the Credit Problem in Dakota Territory." *Agricultural History* 10 (April 1936): 59–83.

Scott, Roy V. "Early Agricultural Education in Minnesota: The Institute Phase." *Agricultural History* 37 (January 1963): 21–34.

Turner, James. "Understanding the Populists." *Journal of American History* 67 (September 1980): 354–73.

UNPUBLISHED THESES

Harshman, Gladys Adeline. "The History of the Settlement of Waseca County, 1854–1880." Master's thesis, University of Minnesota, 1931.

Harvey, Thomas White. "The Making of Railroad Towns in Minnesota's Red River Valley." Master's thesis, Pennsylvania State University, 1982.

Index

Picture credits

Frontispiece—Private collection
Page 18, 22 (Map Collection), 43 (E. H.
James, photographer), 59, 70 (Andreas
Atlas), 121, 158, 269 (Hennepin County
Extension, Kemper A. Kirkpatrick
files), 279 (Hennepin County Extension,
Kirkpatrick files), 291, 293, 298, 316, 333,
334—Minnesota Historical Society
Page 20—Goodhue County Historical
Society
Page 23—Nicollet County Historical Society
Page 36—Olmsted County Historical
Society
Page 91, 97, 111, 118, 129, 131, 137, 141—Free-
born County Historical Society

Page 152, 175, 183, 188—Brown County
Historical Society
Page 171, 220, 222, 225—Otter Tail County
Historical Society
Page 199—Norwegian American Histori-
cal Association
Page 241 (*Willmar Tribune*, May 13, 1908,
p. 1), 242, 258 (*Willmar Tribune*, January
31, 1912, p. 1), 266 (*Willmar Tribune*, April
29, 1914, p. 3)—Kandiyohi County His-
torical Society
Page 285—University of Minnesota

Maps drawn by Patti Isaacs,
Parrot Graphics

Cooperative Commonwealth is set in the Wessex typeface family. Wessex was designed in 1993 by Matthew Butterick. Book design by Will Powers. Typesetting by Allan S. Johnson, Phoenix Type, Milan, Minnesota. Printed by Thomson-Shore, Inc, Ann Arbor, Michigan.